Literary Research Guide

A Guide to Reference Sources for the Study of Literatures in English and Related Topics

JAMES L. HARNER

Modern Language Association of America
New York 1989

Library of Congress Cataloging-in-Publication Data

Harner, James L.
Literary research guide: a guide to reference sources for the study of literatures in English and related topics / James L. Harner
p. cm.
Includes indexes.
ISBN 0-87352-182-X ISBN 0-87352-183-8 (pbk.)
1. Reference books—English literature—Bibliography. 2. Bibliography—English literature—Bibliography. 3. English literature—Research—Methodology. 4. English literature—Bibliography. I. Title.
Z2011.H34 1989
[PR83]
016.8209—dc20 89-12409

Published by The Modern Language Association of America
10 Astor Place, New York, NY 10003-6981

Contents

Acknowledgments

A work such as this depends on the assistance of a multitude of individuals who patiently answered requests for information, recommended works for inclusion, or offered advice and other assistance. In particular, I want to thank the following: Jessica Wade and Mary Jo Smith tended a recalcitrant printer as it cranked out draft after draft of the manuscript. The staffs of libraries at Bowling Green State University, the University of Michigan, Indiana University, the University of Toledo, the University of Illinois at Urbana-Champaign, the University of Texas at Austin, Texas A&M University, and the University of Toronto were invariably helpful. Kausalya Padmaraj and Catherine Sandy of the interlibrary loan office at Bowling Green were typically efficient in securing copies of elusive works. My former colleagues Lester Barber, Thomas Wymer, and Thomas Klein generously allocated a portion of their NEH grant to defray some of my travel costs. The Bowling Green State University Faculty Research Committee granted me an uninterrupted semester for editing the manuscript, and the English department at Texas A&M allowed me a course reduction so that I could make final revisions. Walter Achtert, a model editor, provided sound guidance on a host of problems, and Susan Joseph, my copyeditor, gave careful attention to my manuscript. Darinda and Lenée Harner, who have reconciled themselves to living with a bibliographer, made their usual valued contributions.

My greatest debt, however, is to those who read portions of the manuscript and generously responded with encouragement and valuable suggestions: Richard D. Altick, Carl T. Berkhout, Florence S. Boos, Jerome S. Dees, Donald C. Dickinson, John H. Fisher, Willard Fox, Hal W. Hall, Robert D. Hume, Nancy M. Ide, W. J. Keith, Paul J. Klemp, Raoul Kulberg, Alan Lawson, Virginia Leland, J. A. Leo Lemay, Michael Marcuse, Jack W. Marken, Harrison T. Meserole, Eric L. Montenyohl, David J. Nordloh, Robert M. Philmus, Frances Povsic, Fred C. Robinson, Harris Ross, Brownell Salomon, Patrick Scott, Jack Stillinger, G. Thomas Tanselle, Mary Helen Thuente, Marshall B. Tymn, Rosemary T. Van Arsdel, Ulrich Weisstein, and Joe Weixlmann. (Of these, both Harry Meserole and Skip Fox deserve a special note of thanks, for they read, in various stages, the entire manuscript.) That I benefited from the advice of my readers is an understatement, but they must not be held accountable, individually or collectively, for the selection or evaluation of works, or for any errors; the responsibility for these—especially the errors—is mine alone.

Introduction

Scope. This *Literary Research Guide* is a selective, annotated guide to reference sources essential to the study of British literature, literatures of the United States, other literatures in English, and related topics. In it I describe and, in most instances, evaluate important bibliographies, abstracts, surveys of research, indexes, data bases, catalogs, general histories and surveys, annals, chronologies, dictionaries, encyclopedias, and handbooks; I also list, but generally make no attempt to evaluate, major journals and background studies. When possible, I am rigorously selective, admitting only works that are reasonably thorough, accurate, effectively organized, and adequately indexed; in many instances I have had to include works that fail to meet one or more of these criteria because they are the only available resources in their fields. I have based decisions about what to include—as well as evaluations—on my own experience in using these works and on published surveys of research, authoritative reviews, the advice of scholars from a variety of fields, and existing guides to literary reference sources.

Limitations. Since this *Guide* is intended as a vademecum for researchers—from advanced undergraduates to experienced scholars—pursuing a topic at a more than superficial level, I have omitted elementary works (such as collections of plot synopses or excerpts from criticism and handbooks that consist of little more than brief critical commentary). Readers who lack basic library skills or require an orientation to using literary reference works should begin with Baker, *Research Guide for Undergraduate Students* (80). I have been especially selective in listing background studies, since the focus of this *Guide* is reference sources. Where a good survey of background works exists, I refer the reader to it in lieu of citing individual titles. I have omitted general critical studies as well as publications devoted to a single author or literary work, since such materials are readily identifiable in library catalogs and in the sources listed in various period sections.

Although a majority of the entries are for works published and available by February 1989, I have included some significant works in progress or in press when authors have provided detailed descriptions or extensive samples. In some few instances I have listed works announced for publication when it appears that they will be important reference sources. Users should watch for these unpublished works but regard my citations and annotations as provisional.

Organization. The *Guide* is organized in divisions for general literary reference works, national literatures, and topics or sources related to literature. Each division is variously subdivided, and each subdivision classified by type of reference work. The table of contents offers a detailed overview of the divisions and subdivisions, each of which begins with an outline of its organization. Where possible, I use the following organization:

Research Methods
Guides to Reference Works
Histories and Surveys
Literary Handbooks, Dictionaries, and Encyclopedias
Annals
Bibliographies of Bibliographies
Guides to Primary Works
- Guides to Collections
- Manuscripts
- Printed Works

Guides to Scholarship and Criticism
- Surveys of Research
- Serial Bibliographies
- Other Bibliographies
- Abstracts
- Dissertations and Theses
- Review Indexes
- Related Topics

Language
- Guides to Primary Works
- Guides to Scholarship
- Dictionaries
- Thesauruses
- Concordances
- Studies of Language

Biographical Dictionaries
Microform Collections
Periodicals
- Research Methods
- Histories and Surveys
- Guides to Primary Works
- Guides to Scholarship
- Scholarly Journals

Background Reading
Genres
- Fiction
  - (Research Methods, Guides to Reference Works, Histories and Surveys, etc.)
- Drama
- Poetry
- Prose

Under each heading, truly seminal works appear first, followed by important works that, while not seminal, are noteworthy for their accuracy and value as research tools, then the remainder in alphabetical order by author, editor, or title (for an anonymous work or an edited one better known by its title). (I make no attempt, however, to rank journals or background studies.) I use the letter-by-letter system to alphabetize entries.

Entry numbers. At a late stage of work on the manuscript, I numbered entries in increments of five and left two or three entry numbers open at the end of each section or division to accommodate insertions as well as to preclude complete renumbering in succeeding editions.

The entries. I describe a work fully under the most appropriate classification and provide cross-references in related ones. (Cross-references cite entry numbers; a number followed by *a* means that the work appears in the annotation rather than citation.) Thus users of this *Guide* must be certain to examine the *See also* references in each classification and consult appropriate headings in the subject index.

An entry consists of two parts: the citation and the annotation. Citations follow the form recommended in *The MLA Style Manual* (6400) but add the following: a commonly used acronym or short title, pagination for a single-volume work, and Library of Congress and Dewey Decimal Classification numbers. Journal acronyms are those used by the *MLA International Bibliography* (335); other acronyms and short titles are those in common use. For pagination, I cite the final printed arabic page number in a book. My sources for Library of Congress and Dewey numbers are Library of Congress Cataloging in Publication information or Library of Congress cataloging records in OCLC (225); in some few instances I have had to rely on less accurate sources. I omit classification numbers for microform publications because most libraries have individual systems of cataloging and storing works in this medium. Users should remember that these classification numbers are merely general guides, since libraries vary in their cataloging practices.

The citations. I cite the most recent edition or corrected reprint of a work, noting an earlier one only when it retains independent value. For unrevised works, I cite the earliest edition (making no attempt to list reprints). For works published independently in two or more countries, I give the publication information for the copy I consulted (although I do record a variant title). For multivolume works published over a number of years, place and publisher are those of the most recent volume. Rather than give the editor, edition, and year of works revised annually or biennially, I cite the title, place, and publisher of the most recent edition, the year of initial publication, and the frequency. I generally record separately published supplements or continuations in the citation; where appropriate, titles of individual volumes of a multivolume work appear in a list following the citation. In some instances, I include a parenthetical note on revisions or new editions in progress or announced for publication—some of which will be delayed or never appear. I give the current title of a journal and usually record up to two earlier titles; for those with numerous title changes, I simply note that the title varies. Because journals change place of publication or publisher so frequently, I give only the year of initial publication and frequency.

The annotations. The second part of an entry is the annotation, which does the following:

1. describes the type of work; its scope, major limitations (with particular attention to criteria governing selection), and basic organization (with details of significant changes in a multivolume work); parts of a typical entry; type and number of indexes; and aids to its use (such as detailed evaluations, historical studies, and separately published supplements, indexes, or lists of additions and corrections);

2. offers an evaluation (with particular attention to coverage, organization, or accuracy) combined, usually, with a description of the work's important uses in research;
3. lists significant reviews that more fully define the importance or uses of the work or its place in a scholarly tradition, detail its deficiencies or strengths, or provide significant additions and corrections;
4. notes related works, including supplementary, complementary, or superseded ones not accorded separate entries in the *Guide*.

Although I attempt to keep annotations to a reasonable size by emphasizing major points, important or particularly complex works receive lengthier treatment. The annotations—which will offer too much information for some users and too little for others—are meant to allow researchers to determine what works will best suit their needs (and at the same time alert them to major strengths and deficiencies), but the annotations cannot substitute for a careful perusal of the works themselves.

Indexes. The index of persons includes authors, editors, compilers, and others responsible for any of the works I include in citations or annotations. The title index cites all titles referred to in the entries. The subject index includes entries for kinds of reference works as well as other appropriate headings. Each index is alphabetized according to the letter-by-letter system. Most index entries cite entry numbers (an *a* following a number means that the person or title is referred to in the annotation rather than in the citation). In the few instances where I refer to a page, the abbreviation *p.* or *pp.* precedes the number.

Since this *Guide* is intended to replace (not revise) Margaret Patterson's *Literary Research Guide*, 2nd ed., 2nd rev. printing (New York: MLA, 1984), readers may benefit from a brief discussion of differences between the two. In some ways I have relied heavily on her work and retained many of its features, but I have also made numerous changes. The major ones include:

defining the scope as British literature, literatures of the United States, other literatures in English, and related topics (which was actually Patterson's effective scope);
narrowing the audience to researchers pursuing a topic at a more than elementary level, since Baker, *Research Guide for Undergraduate Students* (80) adequately addresses the needs of beginners;
deleting entries for superseded works; for sources that, in my judgment, were useful only to the beginning undergraduate preparing a basic term paper; for author newsletters (which are covered in Patterson, *Author Newsletters and Journals* [620]); and for series lists (since individual titles vary so much in quality and are handily identified in *NUC: Books: LC Series Index* [245] or *Bibliographic Index* [145]);
omitting the list of "Indexed in . . ." references at the end of annotations to journals, because all but a few of those included are covered by *MLA International Bibliography* (335) and *Annual Bibliography of English Language and Literature* (340), and because OCLC (225) cites full indexing information in journal records;
adding numerous works—recently published as well as older ones;
writing entirely new citations and annotations.

I trust that Patterson would have approved of these changes, since she was always cognizant of the need for evolution and improvement in guides to reference sources.

It is the fate of every bibliographer to produce a work that includes errors and is outdated before the last sheet of the final draft cranks out of the computer printer or typewriter. Even worse is the lot of one who prepares a selective critical bibliography, for he or she will inevitably omit important works, misjudge others, and fail to notice every new work or revised edition. I therefore append the bibliographer's infrequently heeded plea that those who use this *Guide* inform me of outright errors, suggest additions and deletions, and point out disagreements in matters of judgment.

A

Research Methods

General Guides

5 Altick, Richard D. *The Art of Literary Research*. 3rd ed. Rev. John J. Fenstermaker. New York: Norton, 1981. 318 pp. PR56.A68 807.2.

A guide to research techniques, emphasizing the traditional in both subject matter and method. The discussions of the vocation and spirit of scholarship, scholarly occupations (biography, textual study, source investigation, reception and influence study, and historical research), the tracking down of materials, major libraries, note taking, and the composing process are full of sound practical advice and leavened with instructive examples. Concludes with a selective bibliography and exercises keyed to the text. Indexed by persons, titles, and subjects. The discussion of computer applications is inadequate (see Sec. U: Literature-Related Topics and Sources/Computers and the Humanities); the survey of textual study is dated (see Sec. U: Literature-Related Topics and Sources/Bibliography and Textual Criticism); and—despite contrary claims—newer fields such as women's studies, black studies, film, and science fiction are glossed over. Nonetheless, this work remains the best general introduction to literary research. Review: William Kuppersmith, *Literary Research Newsletter* 8 (1983): 75–77.

For an entertaining and instructive account of the literary detective work behind some major scholarly discoveries, see Altick, *The Scholar Adventurers*, rpt. with a new preface (Columbus: Ohio State UP, 1987, 338 pp.).

10 Barzun, Jacques, and Henry F. Graff. *The Modern Researcher*. 4th ed. San Diego: Harcourt, 1985. 450 pp. D13.B334 001.4'32.

A multidisciplinary guide that emphasizes techniques important in historical research. Of most use to literature scholars are the discussions of note taking, the researcher's virtues (accuracy, love of order, logic, honesty, self-awareness, imagination), verification, the establishment of dates, kinds of evidence, and bias. Indexed by persons and subjects. Some chapters suffer from discursiveness and an attempt to address both the neophyte and the experienced scholar (e.g., the neophyte will benefit from the detailed explanation of the card catalog—even though the authors do not address the implications of AACR2 [see 35]—but will be mystified by the use of only an author's or editor's surname to refer to basic sources). This guide offers an instructive overview of research techniques, but literary scholars will find Altick, *Art of Literary Research* (5), more concise and immediately helpful.

Thomas Mann, *A Guide to Library Research Methods* (New York: Oxford UP, 1987, 199 pp.), is also addressed to a range of academic and research library users, but the discussions of encyclopedias, the card catalog, systematic browsing, subject and citation indexes, computer searches, and bibliographies are so superficial that only the novice will benefit. Although the title reads "methods," the emphasis is on reference sources rather than strategies and procedures.

15 Bateson, F. W. *The Scholar-Critic: An Introduction to Literary Research.* London: Routledge, 1972. 202 pp. PN73.B3 801'.95.

Intended as a guide for the graduate student, with chapters on reference works, literary theory, stylistic analysis, textual criticism (now outdated), literary history, and matters of scholarly style, as well as a highly selective bibliography. Detailed examples, primarily from English literature, illustrate points. *The Scholar-Critic* is more valuable for its demonstration of the necessity of combining scholarship and criticism than for explanations of techniques and procedures. Reviews: R. L. Brett, *Modern Language Review* 68 (1973): 136–38; Herman Servotte, *English Studies* 54 (1973): 305–06.

20 Beaurline, Lester A., ed. *A Mirror for Modern Scholars: Essays in Methods of Research in Literature.* New York: Odyssey, 1966. 395 pp. PN85.B34 801.95.

A collection of previously published essays and excerpts from books illustrating methods and problems in bibliography; textual criticism; historical interpretation; stylistic analysis; biography; authorship attribution; dating; source study; literary periodization; and analysis of history of ideas, literary forms, and conventions. The work also reprints McKerrow's classic "Form and Matter in the Publication of Research" (6375). Some selections have been superseded, but *Mirror for Modern Scholars* remains the best collection of its kind.

25 Gibaldi, Joseph, ed. *Introduction to Scholarship in Modern Languages and Literatures.* New York: MLA, 1981. 143 pp. PB35.I57 402.

Six essays on the aims and methods of literary and linguistic scholarship: Winfred P. Lehmann, "Linguistics"; G. Thomas Tanselle, "Textual Scholarship"; Barbara Kiefer Lewalski, "Historical Scholarship"; Lawrence Lipking, "Literary Criticism"; Paul Hernadi, "Literary Theory"; and Wayne C. Booth, "The Scholar in Society." Each essay concludes with a selective bibliography. Although directed to a student audience, the essays offer authoritative introductions for all nonspecialists.

Specialized Topics

30 Harner, James L. *On Compiling an Annotated Bibliography*. New York: MLA, 1985. 40 pp. Z1001.H33 010'.44.

A succinct guide to planning, organizing, researching, writing, editing, and indexing a comprehensive or selective bibliography on a literary subject or author. Although directed to those preparing an annotated bibliography for publication, the practical advice on planning research and identifying scholarly works is valuable for anyone compiling a preliminary bibliography for other scholarly or critical studies. Review: Robert Murray Davis, *Analytical and Enumerative Bibliography* ns 1 (1987): 24.

D. W. Krummel, *Bibliographies: Their Aims and Methods* (London: Mansell, 1984, 192 pp.), which ranges beyond literary bibliographies, also offers useful advice on compilation and organization.

35 Chervinko, James S. "Chaos in the Card Catalog." *Literary Research Newsletter* 5 (1980): 115–23.

Outlines the implications for literature scholars of the implementation in 1981 of the second edition of *Anglo-American Cataloguing Rules* (AACR2). Every library user—even those searching online catalogs—must be aware of the dislocations in card catalogs and shelving and the variation from library to library that may result from application of the new rules. For a basic explanation of AACR2 changes in the treatment of personal and corporate name headings, see Carol A. Johnson, "An Introduction to AACR2 Heading Changes in the Card Catalog," *Literary Research Newsletter* 7 (1982): 59–64.

40 Erdman, David V., and Ephim G. Fogel, eds. *Evidence for Authorship: Essays on Problems of Attribution*. Ithaca: Cornell UP, 1966. 559 pp. PR61.E7 809.

A collection of previously published essays and parts of books designed to illustrate the techniques, kinds of evidence, and pitfalls involved in attribution studies of English-language literary works. The essays are grouped in five divisions: internal evidence, English literature to 1660, English literature from 1660 to 1775, English and American literature since 1775, and detection of forgery. Readers interested in the principles and methods of authorship attribution should begin with the subject index, since a majority of the essays are concerned with the particulars of individual questions of authorship. The selective bibliography of studies published between c. 1940 and 1960 offers numerous annotations that are, effectively, summaries of the state of scholarship on the authorship of individual works. Contains two indexes: names and titles; subjects (i.e., types of evidence, methods, and assessment techniques). This work remains the best overall introduction to attribution study, but readers must dig out the principles and practices and supplement the collection with recent discussions of statistical methodology and the application of computers to authorship determination.

See also

Sec. U: Literature-Related Topics and Sources/Computers and the Humanities/General Introductions.
Hartman, *Women in Print* (6595).
Howard-Hill, *Literary Concordances* (5680).
Searing, *Introduction to Library Research in Women's Studies* (6580).
Thorpe, *Use of Manuscripts in Literary Research* (275).

Periodicals

45 *Literary Research: A Journal of Scholarly Method and Technique* (*LRN*). 1976– . Quarterly. Former title: *Literary Research Newsletter* (1976–85). PN73.L57 809.

Addressed to teachers of bibliography and research methods courses, *LRN* publishes surveys of research in various fields; articles on research methods, tools, and pedagogy; notes on new and revised reference works, library acquisitions, and work in progress; and reviews of bibliographies and reference books. Annual index; cumulative index: vols. 1–10, as 10.4 (1985): 78 pp.

B

Guides to Reference Books

General Guides

60 Sheehy, Eugene P., ed. *Guide to Reference Books* (Sheehy). 10th ed. Chicago: American Library Assn., 1986. 1,560 pp. Z1035.1.S43 011'.02.

A guide to general and specialized reference works published through 1984 (along with a few from 1985). Entries are organized alphabetically by author, editor, or title in five extensively classified sections: general works; humanities; social and behavioral sciences; history and area studies; and science, technology, and medicine. Although the descriptive annotations sometimes cite significant reviews, they seldom evaluate or compare works. Indexed by persons, titles, and subjects (although subject indexing is not as detailed or complete as it should be). Weak in covering data bases, including some works of dubious value, and offering too little evaluation, Sheehy is principally useful to literature scholars for its general coverage of reference works essential to research in areas related to literature. Along with "Selected Reference Books" in the January and July issues of *College and Research Libraries*, periodic supplements will update this edition. For a history of the work, see Donald C. Dickinson, "The Way It Was, the Way It Is: 85 Years of the *Guide to Reference Books*," *RQ* 27 (1987): 220–25. Review: *Reference Books Bulletin* [published in *Booklist*] 83 (1987): 988–89.

Complemented by Walford, *Walford's Guide to Reference Material* (65). Although now dated, Louise-Noëlle Malclès, *Les sources du travail bibliographique*, 3 vols. in 4 (Genève: Droz, 1950–58), is occasionally a useful supplement to Sheehy because of its extensive coverage of Continental publications and older works. More current but less thorough is Malclès, *Manuel de bibliographie*, 4th ed., rev. Andrée Lhéritier (Paris: PU de France, 1985, 448 pp.). For timely notices of new and revised reference books, see *American Reference Books Annual* (745) and *Choice* (750).

65 Walford, A. J., and L. J. Taylor, eds. *Walford's Guide to Reference Material* (Walford). 4th ed. 3 vols. London: Library Assn., 1980–87. Z1035.1.W33 011'.02.

Vol. 1: *Science and Technology*. 1980. 697 pp.
Vol. 2: *Social and Historical Sciences, Philosophy and Religion*. 1982. 812 pp.
Vol. 3: *Generalia, Language and Literature, the Arts*. 1987. 872 pp.

The British counterpart to Sheehy (60), but more international and comprehensive in coverage (with a British slant). Entries are organized by the Universal Decimal Classification system. Although annotations are frequently evaluative and helpfully identify related works, especially supplements or titles that have been superseded, the placement of works in annotations sometimes defies logic, and far too many evaluations and some descriptions are derived from reviews in library journals. Indexed by authors, compilers, editors, titles, and subjects in each volume; vol. 3 has two cumulative indexes: authors and titles; subjects. Vol. 3—the one of most interest to literary researchers—is poorly edited, marred by typographical errors, and generally short of the quality one could formerly expect from this work: it retains outdated descriptions, fails to note many new editions or excise superseded works, prints several duplicate entries, and relies far too heavily on reviews of dubious authority for evaluative judgments.

Walford and Sheehy are ultimately complementary works: Sheehy is more current and accurate, but Walford offers broader coverage (including reference works on individual authors) and more evaluation. Although this *Literary Research Guide* offers more current coverage of sources for the study of language and literature, both Sheehy and Walford are essential guides to reference sources necessary to research in related areas.

Specialized Guides

70 *Reader's Adviser: A Layman's Guide to Literature*. 13th ed. 6 vols. Series eds. Barbara A. Chernow and George A. Vallasi. New York: Bowker, 1986–88. Z1035.G73 016.028.

Vol. 1: *The Best in American and British Fiction, Poetry, Essays, Literary Biography, Bibliography, and Reference*. Ed. Fred Kaplan. 1986. 783 pp.
Vol. 2: *The Best in American and British Drama and World Literature in English Translation*. Ed. Maurice Charney. 1986. 898 pp.
Vol. 3: *The Best in General Reference Literature, the Social Sciences, History, and the Arts*. Ed. Paula T. Kaufman. 1986. 780 pp.
Vol. 4: *The Best in the Literature of Philosophy and World Religions*. Ed. William L. Reese. 1988.
Vol. 5: *The Best in the Literature of Science, Technology, and Medicine*. Ed. Paul T. Durbin. 1988.
Vol. 6: *Indexes*. 1988.

Ostensibly a guide to the best editions, studies, biographies, and reference books in print at the time of compilation; however, the lack of discrimination in the selection of works and the limitation to books in print render this work virtually useless as a *critical* guide, especially for the lay reader. In effect, *Reader's Adviser* is a repackaging of noncurrent information from *Books in Print* (4225). See

Bateson, *Guide to English and American Literature* (85), *Year's Work in English Studies* (330), and *American Literary Scholarship* (3265) instead.

75 Taylor, Archer. *General Subject-Indexes since 1548*. Publications of the A. S. W. Rosenbach Fellowship in Bibliography. Philadelphia: U of Pennsylvania P, 1966. 336 pp. Z695.T28 017.

A historical and critical account of important subject indexes in Latin and European vernacular languages published through the 1950s. Organized by century, the full descriptions, which illustrate uses in modern scholarship, offer helpful introductions to earlier reference works now little known but still essential to research in many periods.

See also

Searing, *Introduction to Library Research in Women's Studies* (6580).

Literature Guides

The following works cover two or more national literatures. Guides devoted to a single national literature or period appear in appropriate sections under the heading "Guides to Reference Books."

80 Baker, Nancy L. *A Research Guide for Undergraduate Students: English and American Literature*. 2nd ed. New York: MLA, 1985. 61 pp. PR56.B34 807.2.

An introduction for undergraduate students to the use of major bibliographies of bibliographies, bibliographies and indexes of criticism, book review indexes, biographical dictionaries, concordances and quotation indexes, dictionaries, and literary encyclopedias, as well as the card catalog. The thorough explanations are accompanied by reproductions of entries from the reference works. An appendix provides a highly selective, descriptively annotated bibliography of reference sources, including several not discussed in the text. The selection is generally sound and the advice clear and helpful, but there are a number of errors in the descriptions, as well as in the evaluations of definitiveness and comprehensiveness, of works.

85 Bateson, F. W., and Harrison T. Meserole. *A Guide to English and American Literature*. 3rd ed. London: Longman, 1976. 334 pp. Z2011.B32 [PR83] 016.82.

An evaluative survey of the best editions and criticism of important authors as well as the reference works, literary histories, anthologies, and special studies essential to the study of a period. In addition, there are chapters on general works, modern literary criticism, and research techniques, as well as "interchapters" offering historical perspectives on the medieval, Renaissance, Augustan, and Romantic periods. Readers will disagree with some of the frequently trenchant evaluations; many authors are treated more fully elsewhere; and all sections need updating; but no single work encompasses so much, so successfully, and so conveniently. Review: Rodney L. Smith, *Seventeenth-Century News* 36 (1978): 23–24.

For recent works see *Year's Work in English Studies* (330) and *American Liter-*

ary Scholarship (3265). *Reader's Adviser* (70) offers broader, but far less discriminating, coverage.

90 Marcuse, Michael J. *A Reference Guide for English Studies*. Berkeley: U of California P. Scheduled for 1989. PR56.M37 016.82'09.

A selective guide to reference works (through early 1987) important to the study of literatures in English. Entries are organized in 24 variously classified divisions for general reference works; libraries; retrospective and current national bibliographies; guides to serial publications; miscellaneous topics (including dissertations, microforms, reviews, indexes to anonymous and pseudonymous works, and films); historical sources; biography and biographical references; archives and manuscripts; language, linguistics, and philology; literary materials and contexts (including folklore, mythology, the Bible, proverbs, quotations, and symbols); literatures (a miscellany including sections for literary dictionaries, various foreign literatures, children's literature, and women and literature); English literature (with sections for general works as well as various new literatures in English); medieval literature; Renaissance and early seventeenth century; Restoration and eighteenth century; nineteenth century; twentieth century; American literature; poetry and versification; theater, drama, and film; prose and prose fiction; literary theory and criticism, rhetoric, and composition; bibliography; and the profession of English (including sections on research guides, scholarly writing and publishing, computers, and careers). Within a typical section, guides and reviews of research appear first, then bibliographies, and then other reference works; many sections also include unannotated lists of journals and frequently recommended studies. Reference sources are fully annotated, usually with descriptions of a work's history, purpose, scope, and organization; comments on uses; a judicious evaluation; and references to related works, many of which are not entered separately. Indexed by authors, titles, and subjects. Given the principles determining placement of a work and the sometimes confusing organization, the subject index offers the best access to contents. Thorough in annotations, usually judicious in selection and evaluation, and covering some non–English language works, *Reference Guide for English Studies* is a valuable complement to the present *Literary Research Guide* and a trustworthy companion for the novice as well as for the advanced scholar.

Marcuse and the present *Guide* supersede the following:

Altick, Richard D., and Andrew Wright. *Selective Bibliography for the Study of English and American Literature*. 6th ed. New York: Macmillan; London: Collier, 1979. 180 pp. For many years the standard guide. Its introduction "On the Use of Scholarly Tools" offers sound advice on evaluating a reference work.

Patterson, Margaret C. *Literary Research Guide*. 2nd ed., 2nd rev. printing. New York: MLA, 1984. 559 pp. Although the work is extensive in coverage and evaluative in annotations, neither the selection process nor the evaluations are trustworthy.

Schweik, Robert C., and Dieter Riesner. *Reference Sources in English and American Literature: An Annotated Bibliography*. New York: Norton, 1977. 258 pp. Although this work is occasionally worth consulting for its inclusion of German-language reference publications, its usefulness is marred by arbitrary organization, inadequate indexing (titles are excluded; subject headings are too broad or inexact), and insufficient bibliographical information in the citations for books and journals.

See also

Thompson, *Key Sources in Comparative and World Literature* (4850).
YWES (330): Some chapters survey reference works.

C

Literary Handbooks, Dictionaries, and Encyclopedias

This section is limited to works devoted to literary terminology or more than one national literature. For an evaluative overview of 20 handbooks, several of which are omitted from this *Guide*, see Thomas Clayton, "Literary Handbooks: A Critical Survey," *Literary Research Newsletter* 5 (1980): 67-87.

This *Guide* excludes collections of plot summaries; those needing to locate a synopsis of a specific work can consult Carol Koehmstedt Kolar, comp., *Plot Summary Index*, 2nd ed., rev. and enl. (Metuchen: Scarecrow, 1981, 526 pp.).

Literary Terminology

105 Holman, C. Hugh, and William Harmon. *A Handbook to Literature*. 5th ed. New York: Macmillan; London: Collier, 1986. 647 pp. PN41.H6 803.

A dictionary of places, groups, movements, -isms, critical terms, forms, genres, periods, character types, concepts, and other literary terms associated with English and American literature. Each entry provides a succinct, admirably clear definition, frequently accompanied by examples, liberal cross-references, and citations to important scholarship. Concludes with a chronology of English and American literary history (through 1984) and four appendixes: Nobel prizes in literature; Pulitzer prizes for fiction, poetry, and drama (through 1985). Indexed by persons. The most authoritative and clear of the numerous general handbooks to English and American literature, *Handbook to Literature* is the classic in its field and an essential desktop companion.

Also trustworthy is Northrop Frye, Sheridan Baker, and George Perkins, *The Harper Handbook to Literature* (New York: Harper, 1985, 563 pp.), but its entries are less full than those in Holman.

110 *Dictionnaire international des termes littéraires*. Ed. Robert Escarpit. Bern: Francke, 1979– . (Published in fascicles.) PN44.5.E8.

A dictionary of terms, genres, forms, concepts, and movements that encompasses a variety of literatures and periods. Organized alphabetically by the French form, the signed entries typically outline the etymology and semantics of a term; list equivalents in German, English, Arabic, Chinese, Spanish, French, Italian, Japanese, and Russian (with occasional notes on differing senses); provide a detailed historical commentary (sometimes in English); and conclude with a selected bibliography. Because there is no introduction, users without access to the unpublished "Rapport" (1964) are denied essential information about the scope (which is not as broad as the title suggests), criteria for selecting terms, and projected indexes. The fascicles are slow to appear (Cosmopolitisme–Dialectique was published in 1986), entries are very uneven in quality, and several bibliographies were already dated when they appeared, but the work offers some of the most thorough discussions of any terminological dictionary and is valuable for its international scope. Review: Ulrich Weisstein, *Canadian Review of Comparative Literature* 12 (1985): 469–71.

For a list of 2,604 equivalent literary terms in German, English, Dutch, French, Spanish, Italian, and Russian, see W. V. Ruttkowski, ed., *Nomenclator Litterarius* (Bern: Francke, 1980, 548 pp.).

See also

Lanham, *Handlist of Rhetorical Terms* (5560).

General Literary Guides

115 *The Oxford Classical Dictionary*. 2nd ed. Ed. N. G. L. Hammond and H. H. Scullard. Oxford: Clarendon, 1970. 1,176 pp. DE5.O9 913.38003.

A dictionary of classical civilization through the early Christian era (c. 337), with entries for authors and other important persons, places, peoples, mythological figures, deities, written works, forms, genres, historical events, and literary terms. The signed entries by established scholars range from a few lines to several pages, but even the brief ones are replete with information. Almost all conclude with references to important scholarship through 1967–68. Indexed by names and terms not accorded a separate entry. Authoritative and informative, the work is the best single-volume classical dictionary in English and an essential desktop reference for deciphering classical allusions in literary works. Review: M. L. Clarke, *Classical Review* ns 21 (1971): 124–25.

Also useful—but less authoritative and with briefer discussions—is *The Oxford Companion to Classical Literature*, comp. Paul Harvey, rpt. with corrections (Oxford: Oxford UP, 1984, 468 pp.). Fuller discussions of mythological figures are offered by Pierre Grimal, *The Dictionary of Classical Mythology*, trans. A. R. Maxwell-Hyslop, corrected rpt. (Oxford: Blackwell, 1987, 603 pp.), which prints a helpful set of genealogical tables.

120 *Benét's Reader's Encyclopedia*. 3rd ed. New York: Harper, 1987. 1,091 pp. PN41.B4 803.

A general dictionary of authors, works, terms, groups and organizations, movements, concepts, literary characters, and historical and mythological figures from all periods and a variety of literatures. Although limited in its treatment of modern literature and not always accurate, *Benét's* offers the broadest coverage of any single-volume literary dictionary in English.

125 *Cambridge Guide to Literature in English.* Ed. Ian Ousby. Cambridge: Cambridge UP, 1988. PR85.C29 820'.9.

A dictionary of American, British, Canadian, Irish, Australian, New Zealand, Indian, African, and Caribbean literatures in English. The approximately 4,500 signed contributions treat writers, major works, literary journals, genres, movements, critical terms, and literary concepts.

This replaces Michael Stapleton, *The Cambridge Guide to English Literature* (Cambridge: Cambridge UP; Feltham, Middlesex: Newnes, 1983, 992 pp.), an unbalanced, untrustworthy attempt to cover works, characters, and authors of literature of the English-speaking world.

130 *Kindlers Literatur Lexikon.* 7 vols. Zürich: Kindler, 1965–72. *Supplement.* 1974. 1,376 cols. PN41.K53.

A dictionary of literary works—along with some important philosophical, historical, and scholarly ones—from all literatures and eras. Listed alphabetically by original title. The signed entries provide a synopsis and lists of selected editions, translations, and studies. Vol. 7 prints general essays on national literatures. Contains four indexes: literary authors; titles of anonymous and collective works; titles in German, short titles, and variant titles; literary authors and anonymous works discussed in the essays on national literatures in vol. 7. The most international in scope and extensive in coverage of any dictionary of literary works, *Kindlers* is valuable for its succinct summaries of major and minor works.

A useful complement is *Dizionario letterario Bompiani delle opere e dei personaggi di tutti i tempi e di tutte le letterature*, 9 vols. (Milano: Bompiani, 1947–50); *Appendice*, 3 vols. (1964–79). The model for *Kindlers*, the *Dizionario* includes signed entries for literary and musical works before about 1900 from all literatures, entries for literary characters (in vol. 8), and brief (and generally superficial) essays (in vol. 1) on intellectual and artistic movements. Works are alphabetized by Italian titles, characters by the Italian form of the surname (e.g., Horatio Alger becomes Orazio Alger and is alphabetized in the *O* section). Three indexes in vol. 9: original titles; literary authors; illustrations.

See also

Enzyklopädie des Märchens (5830).

D

Bibliographies of Bibliographies

The following works are essential sources for identifying subject, title, genre, and author bibliographies. Those sources restricted to a single national literature appear under the heading "Bibliographies of Bibliographies" in appropriate sections of this *Guide*. For an evaluative survey of early works, see Archer Taylor, *A History of Bibliographies of Bibliographies* (New Brunswick: Scarecrow, 1955, 147 pp.).

General Bibliographies of Bibliographies

Serial Bibliographies

145 *Bibliographic Index: A Cumulative Bibliography of Bibliographies*. New York: Wilson, 1937– . 3/yr., inc. annual cumulation. Z1002.B595 016.016.

A subject index to bibliographies that are published separately, as parts of books, or in about 2,600 periodicals (currently). Concentrates on works in Germanic and Romance languages, and is now limited to bibliographies with at least 50 entries. Like other Wilson indexes, *Bibliographic Index* offers generous subdivisions and cross-references for easy location of entries. Listings since November 1984 can be searched through WILSONLINE (525). Especially valuable for its inclusion of parts of books, this reference work is the most current and thorough subject index to bibliographies. It must, however, be supplemented with *Bibliographische Berichte* (150), whose coverage of European publications is generally superior.

150 *Bibliographische Berichte/Bibliographical Bulletin*. Frankfurt am Main: Klostermann, 1959– . Annual. Z1007.B5815 011.

A bibliography of bibliographies (including books, essays in collections, and journal articles) published for the most part in German, English, Romance, and East European languages since 1956. Bibliographies are currently listed by author or title (for edited and anonymous works) in 18 divisions, most of them extensively classified: general; education; geography; history; information science, librarianship, and museums; the arts (including theater and film); agriculture; mathematics; medicine; natural sciences; language and literature; philosophy; psychology; law; religion; social sciences (including folklore); sport and games; and technology. The language and literature division is classified by language or geographical area. Entries, which provide basic bibliographical information, are based on acquisitions of a small number of German libraries or copied from national bibliographies. Indexed by subject in each volume through 13 (1971); cumulative indexes: vols. 1–5 (1965, 140 pp.); vols. 6–10 (1970, 176 pp.). Although the work is not comprehensive and is sometimes inaccurate, the extensive coverage of European publications makes this an important complement to *Bibliographic Index* (145).

Bibliographische Berichte supersedes the bibliography in *Zeitschrift für Bibliothekswesen und Bibliographie* 1–5 (1954–58).

See also

ABELL (340): Since the volume for 1973, the Bibliography section has a subdivision for Subject, Genre, and Period Bibliographies, Checklists, and Indexes, and in the volumes for 1973 through 1976, a subdivision for author bibliographies.

Bibliographie der Buch- und Bibliotheksgeschichte (5280).

Other Bibliographies

155 Besterman, Theodore. *A World Bibliography of Bibliographies, and of Bibliographical Catalogues, Calendars, Abstracts, Digests, Indexes, and the Like*. 4th ed. 5 vols. Lausanne: Societas Bibliographica, 1965–66. Z1002.B5685 016.01.

A World Bibliography of Bibliographies, 1964–1974. 2 vols. Comp. Alice F. Toomey. Totowa: Rowman, 1977. Z1002.T67 016.011.

A subject guide to 117,187 bibliographies (published through 1963) on all subjects. Ostensibly, only separately published bibliographies are admitted; however, issues of periodicals and offprints of journal articles haphazardly find their way into the listings. Booksellers' and auction catalogs, art lists, general library catalogs, and works printed in Oriental languages are excluded. Arranged chronologically under subject headings, entries record the number of items in a bibliography as well as the first and last, but usually not intervening, editions. Indexed in vol. 5 by persons, titles of anonymous bibliographies, and libraries. Although noteworthy for its broad coverage, Besterman must be supplemented with *Bibliographic Index* (145). For a detailed critique, see Roderick Cave, "Besterman and Bibliography: An Assessment," *Journal of Librarianship* 10 (1978): 149–61.

The supplement uncritically reproduces, sometimes illegibly, about 18,000 Library of Congress catalog cards in a subject list without an index. Of the various sections that have been extracted from Besterman and published by Rowman in the Besterman World Bibliographies series, the two of most interest to the literature scholar are *Literature: English and American: A Bibliography of Bibliographies* (1971, 457 pp.) and *Music and Drama: A Bibliography of Bibliographies* (1971, 365 pp.). Blackwell has published revisions of two sections by J. D. Pearson: *A World Bibliography of African Bibliographies* (1975, 241 cols.) and *A World Bibliography of Oriental Bibliographies* (1975, 727 cols.). Each more than doubles the number of entries in Besterman.

Because they include articles and parts of books, the following are occasionally useful supplements to Besterman:

Courtney, William P. *A Register of National Bibliography*. 3 vols. London: Constable, 1905–12.

Northup, Clark Sutherland. *A Register of Bibliographies of the English Language and Literature*. Cornell Studies in English. New Haven: Yale UP; London: Oxford UP, 1925. 507 pp.

Van Patten, Nathan. *An Index to Bibliographies and Bibliographical Contributions Relating to the Work of American and British Authors, 1923–1932*. Stanford: Stanford UP, 1934. 324 pp.

160 Arnim, Max. *Internationale Personalbibliographie, 1800–1943*. 2nd ed., expanded and rev. 2 vols. Stuttgart: Hiersemann, 1944–52. Gerhard Bock and Franz Hodes. Vol. 3: *1944–1959*. 1963. 659 pp. Hodes. 2nd ed. of vol. 3. 3 vols. 1978– . Z8001.A1.A723 016.012.

A bibliography of bibliographies of works by and about writers and scholars from 1800 through c. 1975. Although international in scope and covering all disciplines, the work emphasizes German authors. Under each writer is a list of bibliographies, including books, articles, and entries in a wide range of biographical dictionaries, handbooks, registers, and sections of other bibliographies of bibliographies published through the late 1970s. *Internationale Personalbibliographie, 1850–1935, in der preussischen Staatsbibliothek* (Leipzig: Hiersemann, 1936, 572 pp.) indexes a few works omitted in the second edition. Although it is not comprehensive, the scope and coverage of foreign publications and collective works make *Internationale Personalbibliographie* an important complement to the other bibliographies of bibliographies in this section. Because of the nature of many of the collective works indexed, it is also a useful source for locating biographies and obituaries.

165 Bewsey, Julia J. "Festschriften Bibliographies and Indexes." *Bulletin of Bibliography* 42 (1985): 193–202.

An annotated guide to 63 bibliographies and indexes (including journal articles but excluding serial bibliographies) of festschriften published worldwide. Bewsey is noteworthy because standard serial bibliographies frequently overlook such collections.

See also

Ballou, *Women: A Bibliography of Bibliographies* (6585).
Reynolds, *Guide to Theses and Dissertations* (455).
Wortman, *Guide to Serial Bibliographies* (325).

Indexes

170 Weiner, Alan R., and Spencer Means. *Literary Criticism Index*. Metuchen: Scarecrow, 1984. 685 pp. Z6511.W44 [PN523] 016.809.

An index to 86 period and genre bibliographies principally of literatures in English. After an initial section for anonymous works, entries are arranged by author, then by literary works, with page references cited for individual bibliographies. A time-saving source for determining which specialized bibliographies include sections on a work or an author.

National Bibliographies

Bibliographies

180 Domay, Friedrich. *Bibliographie der nationalen Bibliographien/Bibliographie mondiale des bibliographies nationales/A World Bibliography of National Bibliographies*. Hiersemanns Bibliographische Handbücher 6. Stuttgart: Hiersemann, 1987. 557 pp. Z1002.A1.D65.

A bibliography of approximately 3,000 retrospective and current national bibliographies (and related works) published by the end of 1980 (with coverage of some countries extending through mid-1982). Organized by continent, then region, countries variously and inconsistently include divisions for a variety of reference works (e.g., historical overviews, bibliographies of bibliographies, guides to reference books, lists of auction catalogs, biographical dictionaries, lists of dissertations) besides the national bibliographies and trade lists (listed by initial year of coverage). The annotations describe content, organization, and scope; cite cumulations or related works and scholarship; and occasionally offer an evaluative comment. Indexed by persons and titles (but with numerous errors and inconsistencies). Although admitting numerous works that are hardly national bibliographies, inexplicably omitting New Zealand, haphazardly organized within several countries, citing numerous superseded works, and less current than one should expect, *Bibliographie der nationalen Bibliographien* nonetheless offers the fullest guide to national bibliographies worldwide.

For more current and better organized—but generally less thorough—coverage, see:

Beaudiquez, Marcelle, ed. *Inventaire général des bibliographies nationales rétrospectives/Retrospective National Bibliographies: An International Bibliography*. IFLA Publications 35. München: Saur, 1986. 189 pp. An inventory of retrospective national bibliographies for all countries except European socialist ones, with French or English annotations that describe sources, scope, coverage, and organization. The quality of annotations varies with the contributor, much information is taken secondhand, and there are significant omissions, but this work defines national bibliography more narrowly than Domay and describes some works omitted by him.

Bell, Barbara L. *An Annotated Guide to Current National Bibliographies.* Government Documents Bibliographies. Alexandria: Chadwyck-Healey, 1986. 407 pp. A bibliography of national bibliographies that record current publications within a country. A typical annotation identifies scope, coverage, contents, cataloging rules and classification scheme, content of an entry, arrangement, indexing, predecessors, supplementary works, published guides, currency, and selected scholarship. Although the extensive but diffuse and loosely organized commentary would benefit from a good copyediting, the annotations are much fuller and the coverage more current than in Domay.

Background Reading

185 Linder, LeRoy Harold. *The Rise of Current Complete National Bibliography.* New York: Scarecrow, 1959. 290 pp. Z1001.3.L5 015.

A history of current national bibliographies published in England, France, Germany, and the United States from the sixteenth century through 1939. Limited to current complete national bibliographies (and thus excluding retrospective ones such as the *Short Title Catalogues* [1990, 1995, and 2230] and Evans, *American Bibliography* [4005]), Linder also covers some periodical indexes and lists of newspapers and dissertations. After an initial definition of national bibliographies and discussion of their importance, chapters proceed chronologically, surveying by country the content, organization, and development of individual works. Concludes with three appendixes (the most useful one being a chronological list of national bibliographies by country, with dates of coverage and symbols indicating scope and organization) and a selected bibliography. Indexed by titles and persons. The chronological organization means that the discussion of some works is split between two or more chapters; the focus is blurred by the admission of numerous works that hardly qualify as national bibliographies; there is little evaluation; and the work still reads like the dissertation it originally was. Nonetheless, it is the most complete history of current national bibliographies through 1939. Review: Archer Taylor, *Library Quarterly* 30 (1960): 150–52.

E

Libraries and Library Catalogs

Research Libraries

Although most public, national, and academic libraries in North America and Europe are open to qualified researchers, many require some kind of professional identification for admission and a few require advance application. Researchers planning to work in an unfamiliar library—especially in special collections or at a European institution—should inquire well in advance about admission procedures, restrictions on materials in special collections, and hours of operation.

Becoming familiar with a major research library can occupy the better part of a morning, but researchers can reduce this lost time by requesting in advance a copy of any locally produced guide (which usually prints maps and a stack guide) and consulting published descriptions of collections or catalogs. (For example, one can save considerable time in the Main Reading Room of the British Library by copying out shelf numbers in advance from the *British Library General Catalogue of Printed Books* [250]; many libraries sponsor journals that print articles on their holdings and news of acquisitions.) For valuable advice on preparing to visit an unfamiliar library, see Thorpe, *Use of Manuscripts in Literary Research* (275).

Major general research libraries in the United States, Canada, and Great Britain include the following:

Boston Public Library

British Library. *Directory of Rare Book and Special Collections* (210), pp. 106–55, offers the best overview of the collections. *The British Library Journal* (*BLJ*). 1975– . 2/yr. Preceded by *British Museum Quarterly*. 1926–73. See also *British Library General Catalogue of Printed Books* (250) and *Index of Manuscripts in the British Library* (300).

University of California, Berkeley

University of California, Los Angeles. *Dictionary Catalog of the William Andrews Clark Memorial Library, University of California, Los Angeles*. 15 vols. Boston: Hall, 1974.

Cambridge University. A. N. L. Munby, comp. *Cambridge College Libraries: Aids for Research Students*. 2nd ed., rev. and enl. Cambridge: Heffer, 1962. 56 pp. Although now outdated in its information on hours, the guide remains useful for its descriptions of important collections of manuscripts and printed books held by the college libraries, Fitzwilliam Museum, and University Archives. See also the section on Cambridge libraries in *Directory of Rare Book and Special Collections* (210), pp. 23–37.

Center for Research Libraries, Chicago

University of Chicago

Columbia University

Cornell University

Duke University

Harvard University. *The Printed Catalogue of the Houghton Library, Harvard University*. New York: Garland, 1987. Microfiche. *Widener Library Shelflist*. 60 vols. Cambridge: Harvard U Library, 1965–79. *Catalogue of Manuscripts in the Houghton Library, Harvard University*. 8 vols. Alexandria: Chadwyck-Healey, 1986–87. *Harvard Library Bulletin* (*HLB*). 1947– Quarterly.

University of Illinois. *Catalog of the Rare Book Room, University Library, University of Illinois, Urbana-Champaign*. 11 vols. Boston: Hall, 1972. *First Supplement*. 2 vols. 1978.

Indiana University

Library of Congress. Charles A. Goodrum and Helen W. Dalrymple. *The Library of Congress*. [Rev. ed.] Westview Library of Federal Departments, Agencies, and Systems. Boulder: Westview, 1982. 337 pp. A critical overview of the history, organization, acquisitions policies, services, and role of the library. Of particular interest to literary researchers are the chapters on using the research services (pp. 101–28) and on the library and the scholarly world (pp. 259–89). Annett Melville, comp. *Special Collections in the Library of Congress: A Selective Guide*. Washington: Library of Congress, 1980. 464 pp. Descriptions of 269 collections, excluding those within the scope of *National Union Catalog of Manuscript Collections* (295).

University of Michigan

University of Minnesota

National Library of Canada

National Library of Scotland. For an overview of collections, see *Directory of Rare Book and Special Collections* (210), pp. 549–58.

Newberry Library. Lawrence W. Towner. *An Uncommon Collection of Uncommon Collections: The Newberry Library*. 2nd ed. Chicago: Newberry Library, 1976. 47 pp.

New York Public Library. Sam P. Williams, comp. *Guide to the Research Collections of the New York Public Library*. Chicago: American Library Assn., 1975. 336 pp. Detailed description of collections, with notes on published and unpublished finding aids. *Dictionary Catalog of the Research Libraries of the New York Public Library, 1911–1971*. 800 vols. New York: New York Public Library, 1979. *Dictionary Catalog of the Henry W. and Albert A. Berg Collection of English and American Literature*. 5 vols. Boston: Hall, 1969. *First Supplement*. 1975. 757 pp. *Second Supplement*. 1983. 773 pp.

University of North Carolina

Ohio State University

Oxford University. Paul Morgan, comp. *Oxford Libraries Outside the Bodleian: A Guide*. 2nd ed. Oxford: Bodleian Library, 1980. 264 pp. Following a brief history of each college, hall, faculty, departmental, institute, or other library is a full description of its catalogs, collections of printed books and manuscripts, and archives. An appendix lists libraries not described. See also *Directory of Rare Book and Special Collections* (210), pp. 429–72. *The Bodleian Library Record* (*BLR*). 1938– . 2/yr. Preceded by *Bodleian Quarterly Record*, 1914–38.

University of Pennsylvania

Pennsylvania State University

Princeton University. *Princeton University Library Chronicle* (*PULC*). 1939– 3/yr.

Stanford University

University of Texas

University of Toronto

University of Washington

University of Wisconsin

Yale University. *Yale University Library Gazette* (*YULG*). 1926– . 2/yr.

Important specialized libraries include the following:

American Antiquarian Society. *The Collections and Programs of the American Antiquarian Society: A 175th-Anniversary Guide*. Worcester: American Antiquarian Soc., 1987. 183 pp.

Folger Shakespeare Library. *Catalog of Printed Books of the Folger Shakespeare Library, Washington, DC*. 28 vols. Boston: Hall, 1970. *First Supplement*. 3 vols. 1976. *Second Supplement*. 2 vols. 1981. *Catalog of Manuscripts of the Folger Shakespeare Library, Washington DC*. 3 vols. 1971. *First Supplement*. 1987. 524 pp.

Huntington Library. *Huntington Library Quarterly: Studies in English and American History and Literature* (*HLQ*). 1931– . Quarterly. Former title: *Huntington Library Bulletin* (1931–37).

Guides to Libraries

200 *World Guide to Libraries/Internationale Bibliotheks-Handbuch*. Handbook of International Documentation and Information/Handbuch der Interna-

tionalen Dokumentation und Information 8. München: Saur, 1966– . Biennial. Z721.I63 027'.0025.

A guide to research, national, governmental, public, and academic libraries with holdings of more than 30,000 volumes and special libraries with more than 5,000 volumes. The approximately 37,700 libraries from 167 countries are organized alphabetically by country, then type of library (national, general research, academic, professional school, government, ecclesiastical, corporate and business, special, and public), then place, and then name of library (with academic libraries listed by institution). A typical entry includes the name of the library, address, telephone and telex numbers, director or head, main departments (with descriptions of important holdings or special collections in a few instances), special divisions, statistics on holdings, data bases available, and indication of participation in interlibrary loan. Indexed by libraries (with academic libraries entered by institution). Since the material is based on questionnaires, the detail, accuracy, and currency of descriptions vary, but the *World Guide to Libraries* is the fullest international source for basic information on libraries worldwide.

More thorough guides to individual countries include the following:

American Library Directory. New York: Bowker, 1923– . Annual. Updated bimonthly by *American Library Directory Updating Service*. A guide to public, academic, government, and special libraries in the United States, Puerto Rico and other regions administered by the United States, and Canada. Within divisions for each of the three areas, libraries are listed alphabetically by state, region, or province, then city, then library or institution name. A typical entry includes name, address, telephone number, major administrative personnel and subject specialists, statistics on holdings, lists of special collections, automation information, and names of departmental libraries with addresses and information on holdings. Indexed by names. The directory, which can be searched through Dialog (520), is the most thorough general guide to United States and Canadian libraries.

Special libraries, divisions of academic libraries, archives, and research centers in the United States and Canada are more exhaustively covered in the most recent edition of *Directory of Special Libraries and Information Centers* (Detroit: Gale, 1963– , irregular; updated between editions by *New Special Libraries*). The best approach is through the subject index.

Aslib Directory of Information Sources in the United Kingdom. 5th ed. 2 vols. London: Aslib, 1982–84. A directory that ranges beyond libraries to include institutions, repositories, archives, groups, art galleries, charities, and other organizations. Vol. 1 covers science, technology, and commerce; vol. 2, the social sciences, medicine, and the humanities. Organized alphabetically by name of organization, entries typically include address, telephone, description of the organization, restrictions on admission, subject interests, special collections (citing name or giving a one-line description), and publications. Two indexes: abbreviations (acronyms); subjects. Unfortunately, the minimal space allocated to subject interests and special collections and the lack of sufficiently full subject indexing make the directory much less useful than it might be. Although less thorough in coverage, *Directory of Rare Book and Special Collections* (210) is superior as a guide to collections.

Guides to Collections

205 Ash, Lee, and William G. Miller, comps. *Subject Collections: A Guide to Special Book Collections and Subject Emphases as Reported by University, College, Public, and Special Libraries and Museums in the United States and Canada.* 6th ed., rev. and enl. 2 vols. New York: Bowker, 1985. Z731.A78 026'.00025'7.

A subject guide to specialized collections in North American libraries and other institutions. Most local history collections and those in separate departmental units of large academic libraries are excluded. Under subject headings, entries are listed alphabetically by state (with United States territories and Canadian provinces appearing after states), then city, and then library. A typical entry includes library address; person in charge of the collection; kinds of holdings and cataloging status; and notes on specific holdings, size of the collection, guides or catalogs, and restrictions on use. Because entries are based on questionnaires, the sophistication and specificity of the descriptions vary considerably. Although many subject headings are frustratingly broad, there are numerous headings for individual authors and literary topics. *Subject Collections* is the best guide to identifying specialized library collections, but it retains some unrevised entries from the preceding edition, omits or inadequately describes collections in several major research libraries, and includes disproportionately lengthy descriptions of holdings that hardly justify the appellation "collection."

Collections in some European libraries are described in Richard C. Lewanski, comp., *Subject Collections in European Libraries*, 2nd ed. (London: Bowker, 1978, 495 pp.). Organized alphabetically by broad Dewey Decimal classifications, then alphabetically by country, city, and then library, entries include address, information on cataloging status, and notes on the size and content of holdings, restrictions, and published finding aids. Indexed by subject headings. Although many important collections are omitted or incompletely described and subject headings are frequently too broad, this is a useful preliminary guide to subject collections in European libraries, especially those with no published descriptions of their collections.

210 *A Directory of Rare Book and Special Collections in the United Kingdom and the Republic of Ireland.* Ed. Moelwyn I. Williams. London: Library Assn., 1985. 664 pp. Z791.A1.D58 027'.0025'41.

A guide to collections in public, national, academic, church, and institutional libraries (along with a few private collections that are accessible to researchers). Manuscript holdings are noted only when closely related to rare book collections. Organized by country, roughly by county (in the case of England), city, and then institution, entries typically include address, telephone number, hours, requirements for admission, research facilities, and sometimes a brief history of the library. Each collection is then described separately, typically with a note on its origin and history, indication of size, summary of content and major holdings, and citations to finding aids. The thoroughness and quality of the descriptions vary considerably; the better ones cite specific works by referring to standard bibliographies such as the *Short-Title Catalogues* (1990 and 1995), note unrecorded works, and comment on provenance. Indexed by persons, places, and subjects; however, the indexing is insufficiently thorough. For some cities (notably London) and individual libraries (such as the British Library and the Bodleian), the entries offer the best available general descriptions of collections. Unfortunately, however, the numerous significant omissions, unevenness in descriptions, frequent typographical errors, and incomplete indexing leave this a seriously flawed work that must be used with caution. Reviews: R. C. Alston, *Book Collector* 34 (1985): 246–50; David J. Shaw, *Library* 6th ser. 8 (1986): 390–92.

See also

Field, *Special Collections in Children's Literature* (5460).
Schatz, *Directory of Afro-American Resources* (3730).

Interlibrary Loan

From time to time, researchers need to obtain books, dissertations, articles, or microforms through interlibrary loan. While each institution will have its own procedures and forms, most United States libraries subscribe to the National Interlibrary Loan Code of 1980, which requires that requests include full bibliographic information and be verified in a standard bibliography (such as the *National Union Catalogs* [235, 240, and 245], *MLA International Bibliography* [335], or *Annual Bibliography of English Language and Literature* [340]) or data base (such as OCLC [225] or RLIN [230], which are particularly good sources, since each includes an interlibrary loan subsystem).

Filling a request sometimes takes several weeks; however, the process can be expedited if researchers specify exactly the edition required or discriminate between journals with the same or similar titles. Some research libraries do not lend any of their holdings and most will not send rare, valuable, fragile, or unique books; manuscripts; or reference books. Most libraries, however, will photocopy or film manuscripts or rare items if their physical condition or restrictions on use permit reproduction. Although some libraries will lend dissertations, copies must usually be obtained through University Microfilms International or the British Library Document Supply Centre.

Library Catalogs

Published library catalogs are essential sources for locating copies, identifying unique items, building a preliminary bibliography, and (because of some special indexing systems) conducting subject searches.

Bibliographies and Guides

215 Downs, Robert B. *American Library Resources: A Bibliographical Guide.* Chicago: American Library Assn., 1951. 428 pp. *Supplement, 1950–1961.*

1962. 226 pp. *Supplement, 1961–70*. 1972. 244 pp. *Supplement, 1971–1980*. 1981. 209 pp. American Library Resources*: Cumulative Index, 1870–1970*. Comp. Clara D. Keller. 1981. 89 pp. Z1002.D6 016.016.

———. *British and Irish Library Resources: A Bibliographical Guide*. London: Mansell, 1981. 427 pp. Z791.A1.D68 016.0252'07.

The works list printed catalogs, guides to libraries, union lists, descriptions of collections, calendars, indexes, surveys of holdings, and exhibition catalogs, along with some library reports, miscellaneous bibliographies, and unpublished works. Users must remember that the *Library Resources* are guides to published materials and not to collections themselves. Entries are listed alphabetically by library or author within classified subject divisions, including ones for general works (with sections for general library catalogs, manuscripts, rare books, and printing history), social sciences (including folklore), linguistics, literature (organized by national literatures, with subsections in the American volume for general works, genres, and individual authors), and biography and genealogy. The British volume is more extensively and precisely classified and includes a division for individuals (predominantly literary authors), but it is far less thorough than the American volumes. Some entries are accompanied by a brief description of content. Indexed in each American volume and the *Cumulative Index* by persons, subjects, and libraries; the British volume has two indexes: authors, compilers, editors; subjects. Because of inadequate subject indexing, inconsistencies in classifying items, and a lack of cross-references, users must exercise considerable ingenuity to locate all works on a topic or library. Although incomplete in covering journal articles and general bibliographies that cite locations, the *Library Resources* are valuable for identifying works that provide important access to special collections and describe unique items. They are especially strong in covering local publications that usually are not listed in the standard bibliographies and indexes given in section G, in *American Book Publishing Record* (4110), or in *Books in Print* (4225). Review: (British) R. J. Roberts, *Notes and Queries* ns 31 (1984): 252–53.

220 Nelson, Bonnie R. *A Guide to Published Library Catalogs*. Metuchen: Scarecrow, 1982. 342 pp. Z710.N44 019.

A classified list of important general and specialized catalogs, the majority of which are multivolume works published since 1960 and representing the holdings of North American or Western European libraries. The approximately 429 entries are listed alphabetically by main entry in 33 divisions, with the following of most interest to literature researchers: general catalogs of major research libraries; manuscripts, rare books, and book arts; anthropology, American Indians, and folklore; American West; Continental languages and literatures; English and American literature; African and black studies; women's studies; performing arts; and education and children's books. A majority of the entries are accompanied by annotations that describe the organization of a catalog, its library classification and subject indexing system, and special features. Two indexes: subjects; libraries. Although Nelson omits some important catalogs published before 1960 and includes a few serial bibliographies that are not library catalogs, it is the best guide to published library catalogs.

See also

Sec. U, Literature-Related Topics and Sources/Bibliography and Textual Criticism/Guides to Scholarship/Serial Bibliographies.

ABELL (340): Bibliography/Book Production, Selling, Collecting, Librarianship, the Newspaper (with variations in the title) in the volumes for 1934 through 1972; and Bibliography/Booksellers', Exhibition, and Sale Catalogues in later volumes.

MLAIB (335): See the heading Collection Study in the index to post-1980 volumes.

Taylor, *Book Catalogues: Their Varieties and Uses* (5395).

Union Catalogs

Union catalogs are indispensable for identifying and locating copies of editions and translations of almost any book. Since entries reflect the cataloging practices of a variety of libraries, union catalogs generally include a number of ghosts and must be used with care for verification of dates, titles, publishers, editions, or series. Although OCLC (225) and RLIN (230) are more efficient, accessible, and (for recent books) comprehensive sources than the *National Union Catalogs* (235, 240, and 245), the following data bases and printed catalogs are complementary research tools.

DATA BASES

The following data bases are designed for cataloging, interlibrary loan, serials control, acquisitions, and production of online catalogs by libraries, but the widespread availability of public terminals offers researchers access to records of reported holdings of books, manuscripts, maps, audiovisual media, machine-readable data files, microforms, musical scores, serials, and sound recordings. The extensive coverage (which for works published after 1956 generally surpasses that of *NUC* [240] and *NUC: Books* [245]), variety of access points, continual updating of information, interlibrary loan subsystems, and general ease of use make OCLC and RLIN more efficient to search than the *NUC*s. Given the magnitude and versatility of the data bases, no researcher can afford to avoid an OCLC or RLIN terminal.

225 Online Computer Library Center (OCLC). 656 Frantz Rd., Dublin, OH 43017. (Formerly Ohio College Library Center.)

A data base whose several million unique records form the largest union catalog. Mastering OCLC search strategies requires less than an hour. Next to most public terminals will be copies of the *OCLC Searching Guide* or a chart that demonstrates how to locate a work by author, title, author and title, or corporate author, as well as International Standard Serial (ISSN), International Standard Book (ISBN), Library of Congress card, or OCLC number. Some records for works published after 1982 can be searched by subject through BRS (515). (Unlike RLIN [230], OCLC does not allow free text searches, extensive subject access, or the use of Boolean operators.) Keying in the correct information will produce on the screen a bibliographic record that includes LC and Dewey call numbers (which might vary according to the cataloging practices of individual libraries), author's name, title, edition, publication information, physical description (such as pagination, number of volumes, illustrations, size), LC subject headings, and listings of joint authors and illustrators. Records for journals cite former titles and provide the most complete and current list of indexing sources. When faced with a choice of several records for a work or an edition, searchers should first choose the one(s) ending with "DLC," which identifies cataloging prepared by the Library of Congress. DLC records are usually fuller and more accurate than those contributed by other sources.

Using the OCLC system, a researcher can quickly determine whether the home library owns a work, and—depending on the reported holdings of cooperating libraries—discover what libraries hold copies, expedite interlibrary loan service by providing an OCLC record number, and identify separately published works by an author as well as editions and translations of a particular book.

230 Research Libraries Information Network (RLIN). Research Libraries Group, Jordan Quadrangle, Stanford, CA 94305. 415-328-0920.

RLIN (the automated information retrieval system of the Research Libraries Group [RLG]) contains several million unique records representing the holdings of participating libraries or included in several special data bases. Although coverage overall is not as extensive as OCLC and its search strategies less easy to master, RLIN offers several advantages to the literary researcher. Both OCLC and RLIN (depending on reported holdings) allow a user to determine what libraries own a work, expedite interlibrary loan, and identify an author's separately published works as well as editions and translations of particular books; both can be searched by author, title, author and title, corporate author, and ISBN, ISSN, and Library of Congress card numbers. RLIN, however, is more flexible and offers more ways of accessing records, since it accepts key title words or phrases in any order, allows searches by series, permits users to expand, combine, or limit searches with Boolean operators (i.e., "and," "or," or "not"), provides more extensive subject access, and offers a variety of choices for the display of bibliographic records.

Three features unique to RLIN are of particular importance to literature scholars: the archive and manuscript file, RLG Conspectus On-line, and the *Eighteenth-Century Short Title Catalogue* data base (2230). Since 1984 RLIN has led in developing a machine-readable format for cataloging manuscripts and in establishing a national data base for these materials. (RLIN is exploring the feasibility of integrating entries from *National Union Catalog of Manuscript Collections* [295].) The RLG Conspectus On-line (a record of collection strengths of RLG member libraries in over three thousand fields) allows researchers to identify institutions with research- or comprehensive-level collections in a subject. In addition, the Modern Language Association and Research Libraries Group are planning a research-in-progress data base that will record work accepted for publication in selected journals and grants funded through the NEH Research Programs Division. This data base will be available through RLIN in 1989.

The greater usefulness of RLIN to the literary scholar can best be illustrated by an example. An RLIN terminal would allow someone interested in John Steinbeck to identify and locate books by and about him, films or recordings based on his novels, and manuscript material by and about him. The same person using an OCLC terminal would be limited to identifying books and manuscripts by Steinbeck, film adaptations, and recordings; the books or manuscripts about him could be located only if the author or exact title of each work was already known.

Although RLIN is a superior resource for the literature scholar, the two data bases are ultimately complementary, and fortunate researchers will have access to both. Unfortunately, few libraries subscribe to both; however, RLIN, unlike OCLC, does allow individuals to open search accounts.

PRINTED CATALOGS

235 *National Union Catalog, Pre-1956 Imprints* (*NUC, Pre-56*). 754 vols. London: Mansell, 1968–81. Microfiche ed. Chicago: American Library Assn., 1983. Z881.A1.U518 021.6'4.

An author catalog of reported holdings of the Library of Congress and about one thousand other North American libraries. The majority of the 11 million or so author entries are for printed works, although some manuscripts, theses, and dissertations are listed. Since entries reproduce catalog cards from many libraries, information ranges from detailed analytical descriptions to truncated records, but each entry identifies at least one library that owns an item. Users should keep the following points in mind:

1. A work can be located only by author, title for an anonymous publication, or (sometimes) editor for an anthology or collection; RLIN (230), *Library of Congress Shelflist* (260a), and *LC Subject Catalog* (260a) provide subject access to some entries, and RLIN, OCLC (225), *Cumulative Book Index* (375), and *Cumulative Title Index to the Library of Congress Shelflist* (260a) offer title access.
2. There are numerous errors and ghosts, particularly because a card that includes even a minor variation is frequently treated as representing an "edition."
3. Not all holdings of cooperating libraries are listed (e.g., works in non-Latin alphabets are included only if represented by a printed LC card).
4. Listings for prolific major authors are subclassified.
5. The supplement (vols. 686–754) corrects errors, provides the only adequate cross-references in the work, and records new titles, editions, and locations.
6. Additional locations are recorded in *National Union Catalog: Register of Additional Locations* (1963–).

For an account of the history and editing of the *NUC, Pre-56*, see David A. Smith, "*The National Union Catalog, Pre-1956 Imprints*," *Book Collector* 31 (1982): 445–62. Continued by *National Union Catalog* (240) and *NUC: Books* (245).

Libraries unable to afford the *NUC, Pre-56* will probably have one or more of the following:

Library of Congress and National Union Catalog Author Lists, 1942–1962: A Master Cumulation. 152 vols. Detroit: Gale, 1969–71. (This work incorporates the following catalogs.)

A Catalog of Books Represented by Library of Congress Printed Cards Issued to July 31, 1942. 167 vols. Ann Arbor: Edwards, 1942–46. *Supplement: Cards Issued August 1, 1942–December 31, 1947*. 42 vols. 1948.

Library of Congress Author Catalog: A Cumulative List of Works Represented by Library of Congress Printed Cards, 1948–52. 24 vols. Ann Arbor: Edwards, 1953.

The National Union Catalog . . . 1953–57. 28 vols. Ann Arbor: Edwards, 1958.

Important complements to the *NUC*s are the MARC and REMARC data bases, which are available through OCLC (225), RLIN (230), BRS (515), Dialog (520), and BLAISE-LINE (510). REMARC represents the cataloged Library of Congress collection from 1897 to 1980. MARC contains records for books in English cataloged since 1968; French since 1973; German, Spanish, and Portuguese since 1975; other European languages in the roman alphabet since 1976; and romanized Cyrillic and South Asian languages since 1979. The MARC data base is updated monthly, and both MARC and REMARC can be searched by author, title, series, and publication date (and other access points, including subject headings and title words, through BRS and Dialog).

For comprehensive searches involving several works or editions by an author, begin with *NUC, Pre-56* and supplement its listings with OCLC (225) and RLIN (230); for interlibrary loan requests or searches for a few specific works or editions, begin with the data bases.

240 *National Union Catalog: A Cumulative Author List Representing Library of Congress Printed Cards and Titles Reported by Other American Libraries (NUC)*. Washington: Library of Congress, 1958–83. 9/yr. with quarterly, annual, and quinquennial cumulations. Z881.A1.U372 018.1.

An author catalog that continues *NUC, Pre-56* (235) for works published after 1956. Since a work is not listed until a cooperating library prepares a catalog card, a book published outside the United States may not be entered until several years after its publication date. Additional locations are recorded in *National Union Catalog: Register of Additional Locations* (1963–). Continued by *NUC: Books* (245).

Cumulative Title Index to the Library of Congress Shelflist (260a), OCLC (225), RLIN (230), and *Cumulative Book Index* (375) offer title access to many works recorded in the *NUC*; and *LC Subject Catalog* (260a), RLIN, and *Library of Congress Shelflist* (260a) provide subject access to many listings. For author, title, or location searches, researchers will find OCLC or RLIN more efficient and generally more comprehensive than *NUC*. (See also the discussion of the MARC and REMARC data bases in entry 235.)

245 *NUC: Books*. Washington: Library of Congress, 1983– . Microfiche. Published in five parts: *Register*, monthly; *Name Index*, *Title Index*, *LC Series Index*, *LC Subject Index*, quarterly, with annual and larger cumulations. *NUC: U.S. Books* extracts records for books published in the United States.

A continuation of the *National Union Catalog* (240). The *Register*—to which the other four parts are keyed—lists books by *NUC* number and is the only part that records full cataloging information and locations. (For additional locations, see *National Union Catalog: Register of Additional Locations* [1963–].) The other parts are alphabetical indexes to the *Register*, and, except for the *Title Index*, print abbreviated entries. Although the four indexes remedy access problems that plague users of the earlier *NUC*s, they are time-consuming to search because of the necessity of locating full catalog information in the numerically arranged *Register*. Users would be better served if each index printed complete information and locations. Literary researchers will find OCLC (225) and RLIN (230) more efficient to use and generally more comprehensive than *NUC: Books*. (See also the discussion of the MARC data base in entry 235.)

See also

New Serial Titles (640).
Serials in the British Library (645).

Catalogs of National Libraries

Because of copyright deposit privileges and the magnitude and quality of their general collections, which transcend national boundaries, the major national libraries are among the great research centers. Their catalogs are essential complements to the union catalogs.

250 *The British Library General Catalogue of Printed Books to 1975* (*BLC*, *GK4*). 360 vols. London: Bingley; New York: Saur, 1979–87. *Supplement*. 6 vols. London: Saur, 1987– . *1976 to 1982*. 50 vols. 1983. *1982 to 1985*. 26 vols. 1986. *1976–1985*. London: British Library, 1986. Microfiche. *1986 to 1987*. 22 vols. London: Saur, 1988. Z921.L553.B74 018'.1.

The dictionary catalog of the unrivaled collection of the British Library's Department of Printed Books. The main *Catalogue* includes books published before 1971 and cataloged by the end of 1982; the *Supplement* records books published between 1971 and 1975 and cataloged by the end of 1982, and revises some entries in the *BLC*. Works are listed alphabetically by author, corporate author, or title (for anonymous works). Entries for prolific authors include subdivisions for complete works, collections, special categories (e.g., letters), individual works (including studies devoted to a work), selections and doubtful works, and (what is frequently overlooked by researchers) works about the individual. An internal index is provided for an author (such as Shakespeare or Dickens) who has a lengthy or complicated sequence of entries. There are also subject entries for some other persons. The two-page Explanation of Filing describes alphabetization rules and the order of entries within each heading but is otherwise inadequate to alert researchers to the complex British Library cataloging rules and fails to explain that a "D" preceding a shelfmark means that the copy was destroyed during World War II. The *1976 to 1982* and *1982 to 1985* continuations provide author and title entries (but no subject access) for works cataloged, not just published, during 1976–85. Books printed after 1971 and acquired since 1976 can be searched through BLAISE-LINE's DPB data base (510). By 1991 the *General Catalogue of Printed Books to 1975* is expected to be accessible online through BLAISE-LINE; a CD-ROM version is also in the planning stage. For an instructive account of the origin and evolution of the General Catalogue and its bewildering cataloging rules, see A. H. Chaplin, *GK: 150 Years of the General Catalogue of Printed Books in the British Museum* (Aldershot: Scolar, 1987, 177 pp.).

GK4 supersedes the British Museum *General Catalogue of Printed Books* (*GK3*), 263 vols. (London: British Museum, 1959–66) and its three supplements, which many libraries unable to afford *GK4* will retain.

Subject access is provided by R. A. Peddie, *Subject Index of Books Published up to and Including 1880*, 4 vols. (London: Grafton, 1933–48); and *The British Library General Subject Catalogue [1881–]* (London: British Library, 1902– ; in microfiche only since the 1975–85 cumulation; title varies: *Subject Index of the Modern Works Added to the Library of the British Museum*; *Subject Index of the*

Modern Books Acquired by the British Museum; *Subject Index of the Modern Works Added to the British Museum Library*; *Subject Index of Modern Books Acquired*).

Because of the British Library's extensive holdings, the *General Catalogue* is an invaluable source for identifying works by and—in many cases—about authors. Overseas visitors can save time by copying out shelf numbers before arriving at the Reading Room.

255 *Catalogue général des livres imprimés de la Bibliothèque Nationale: Auteurs*. 231 vols. Paris: Imprimerie Nationale, 1897–1981. (The corrected working copy of the Inventaire général of the Bibliothèque Nationale is available on microfiche as *Catalogue général des livres imprimés, 1879–1959, avec corrections et annotations* [Paris: Chadwyck-Healey France, 1986].) *Catalogue général des livres imprimés, 1879–1959: Supplément sur fiches*. Paris: Chadwyck-Healey France, 1986. Microfiche. *Catalogue général des livres imprimés: Auteurs, collectivités-auteurs, anonymes, 1960–1969*. Série 1: Caractères latins. 23 vols. Paris: Bibliothèque Nationale, 1973–76. *1970–1979*. 11 vols. 1983–85. Z927.P2 018.1.

The author catalogs of the Bibliothèque Nationale (BN), whose extensive collections of French publications (including translations of British and American works) along with important holdings in other national literatures rank it among the great research libraries. A thorough search requires the use of the three *Catalogue*s as well as the *Supplément sur fiches*. Through vol. 187 (This-Thomov) the *Catalogue général* (1897–1981) includes only books cataloged before the publication of an individual volume—e.g., the 16 pages of Dickens's works (vol. 40, 1910) lists nothing published after 1909. After vol. 187 only works cataloged through 1959 are included; books acquired between the date of publication of an earlier volume and 1959 are identifiable only through catalogs in the Catalog Room of the library or the *Supplément sur fiches*. Books cataloged (not just published) between 1960 and 1979 are listed in the continuations. Books cataloged since 1970 are being entered into a data base from which microfiche catalogs will eventually be published. Although the main printed catalog admits only books by an identifiable individual, the continuations include anonymous and collectively authored works. The Reader's Office at the Bibliothèque Nationale distributes an essential guide (available in English) to the use of the library's bound catalogs and card indexes; also useful is Annick Bernard, *Guide de l'utilisateur des catalogues des livres imprimés de la Bibliothèque Nationale* (Paris: Chadwyck-Healey France, 1986, 60 pp.).

Scholars planning to use the Bibliothèque Nationale, Bibliothèque de l'Arsenal, Bibliothèque Mazarine, or Bibliothèque Marguerite Durand can still benefit from the advice in Theodore Grieder and Josephine Grieder, "Selected Parisian Libraries and How to Use Them," *PMLA* 88 (1973): 550–56.

260 *Main Catalog of the Library of Congress: Titles Cataloged through December 1980*. München: Saur, 1984– . Microfiche.

A reproduction of the author, title, and subject cards for works cataloged by the Library of Congress between c. 1898 and 1980. Because of the superior coverage and indexing of titles in *Cumulative Title Index* (see below), of authors in the *National Union Catalog*s (235, 240, and 245), and of subjects in the *Library of Congress Catalogs: Subject Catalog* (see below), as well as the inclusion of Library of Congress holdings in OCLC (225) and RLIN (230) and the existence of the MARC and REMARC data bases (235a), the *Main Catalog* is only occasionally useful for the subject access it provides to works cataloged before 1950.

Related works that catalog portions of the Library of Congress collection include the following:

Library of Congress Shelflist (*LC Shelflist*). Ann Arbor: University Microfilms International, 1979. *Supplement, 1978–79*. 1980. Microfiche. Since the *Shelflist* reproduces Library of Congress catalog cards by LC classification number, it offers broad subject access to many works listed in *NUC, Pre-56* (235) and *National Union Catalog* (240). Users should be aware that some changes in the classification schedule have resulted in the separation or juxtaposition of subjects in the shelflist. Linda K. Hamilton, ed., *The Library of Congress Shelflist: A User's Guide to the Microfiche Edition*, 2 vols. (Ann Arbor: University Microfilms International, 1979), provides a basic introduction to the use of the shelflist.

Cumulative Title Index to the Library of Congress Shelflist: A Combined Listing of the MARC and REMARC Databases through 1981. 158 vols. Arlington: Carrollton, 1983. Also available on microfiche. A title list of works cataloged by the Library of Congress through 1981. Along with the title, an entry cites author, publication information, and LC call and card numbers. Valuable as a source for identifying an author when only a title is known.

Library of Congress Catalogs: Subject Catalog (*LC Subject Catalog*). Washington: Library of Congress, 1950–83. Quarterly with annual and quinquennial cumulations. Former title: *Library of Congress Catalog: Books: Subjects.* Classifies Library of Congress catalog cards prepared during 1950–82 according to the current edition of *Library of Congress Subject Headings* (Washington: Library of Congress, 1910– , irregular), and thus offers subject access to many works listed in *NUC, Pre-56* (235) and *National Union Catalog* (240). Continued by *NUC: Books: LC Subject Index* (245). RLIN (230), however, is a more efficient tool for subject searches.

F

Guides to Manuscripts and Archives

This section includes general works on manuscripts and archives, as well as guides, catalogs, and other finding aids that cover two or more national literatures. Works limited to a single national literature appear under the "Manuscripts" heading in appropriate sections in this *Guide*.

Research Methods

275 Thorpe, James. *The Use of Manuscripts in Literary Research: Problems of Access and Literary Property Rights*. 2nd ed. New York: MLA, 1979. 40 pp. Z692.M28.T47 026'.091.

An introduction to locating, gaining access to, and obtaining permission to publish manuscripts. Beginning with the essential but frequently unheeded dictum that "much work should precede any effort to use manuscript materials," Thorpe offers practical advice on locating manuscripts, corresponding with libraries, preparing to visit a collection, approaching a private collector, gaining admittance to a collection (with a survey of common regulations and courtesies), obtaining photocopies (with notes on typical and atypical restrictions), acquiring permission to publish, and understanding literary property rights (principally in the United States). Although it cites some outdated sources, the work is essential preliminary reading for anyone who needs to consult manuscripts in public or private hands.

Guides to Repositories and Archives

280 *Directory of Archives and Manuscript Repositories in the United States*. 2nd ed. Phoenix: Oryx, 1988. 853 pp. CD3020.D49 016.091'025'73.

A guide to archives and repositories that hold manuscripts (including microfilms of originals in foreign or private collections) written after c. 1450, photographs, sound recordings, films, drawings, and other materials. Organized alphabetically by state or territory, city, and then institution, the 4,225 entries include address and telephone number; restrictions on access; information on copying facilities; statistics on holdings; a brief general description of the collection; and references to catalogs, guides, or descriptions (including *National Union Catalog of Manuscript Collections* [295]). Contains two indexes: repositories and subjects. Since the *Directory* is a guide to repositories and archives, holdings are described in general terms; however, researchers will find the work an essential source for identifying institutions that might own manuscripts related to an author or a subject.

Philip M. Hamer, ed., *A Guide to Archives and Manuscripts in the United States* (New Haven: Yale UP, 1961, 775 pp.)—the original version of the *Directory*—remains useful for information about institutions that did not return a questionnaire for the first or second editions and for its fuller descriptions of holdings.

285 *Guide to the Contents of the Public Record Office.* 3 vols. London: HMSO, 1963–68. CD1043.A553.

A guide to the legal and governmental records held at the Public Record Office (PRO) as of the end of 1966. The papers, which date from the Norman Conquest, encompass legal and judicial records (described in vol. 1) and state papers and records of departments of government (vols. 2 and 3). Vol. 3 describes records transferred between 1 September 1960 and 31 December 1966, and prints additions and corrections to vols. 1 and 2. After an introductory discussion of the history, organization, and general nature of the records of an office, department, or other unit, each class of records is briefly described, and references to any published descriptions, transcripts, catalogs, indexes, or calendars are provided. (Unpublished finding aids are identified in the Card Index of Lists and Indexes at the PRO.) Vol. 1 concludes with a glossary of technical terms; vols. 1 and 2 have a key to regnal years, accompanied by a chronological list of statutes cited in the text (an essential feature, since many documents are dated by regnal year). There are two indexes in vols. 1 and 2 (persons and places; subjects); a single index in vol. 3. Because of the nature and organization of the various classes of records, the *Guide* is essential preliminary reading for anyone who plans to work at the PRO. The *Guide* is being updated, with drafts of some sections available at the PRO. Still useful for those new to the PRO is V. H. Galbraith, *An Introduction to the Use of the Public Records*, rpt. with corrections (London: Oxford UP, 1952, 112 pp.).

With its extensive holdings of governmental, political, civil, legal, and ecclesiastical records, the PRO is an essential and sometimes lengthy stop for many literary biographers. Researchers should be certain to take the following steps:

1. obtain a reader's ticket;
2. ascertain which location holds the records they need (most of the wills and older records—essentially those described in vol. 1—are at Chancery Lane [London WC2A 1LR], while those of modern governmental departments are at Kew [Rusking Avenue, Kew, Richmond, Surrey TW9 4DU]; a general checklist identifying locations is available to readers);
3. learn as much as possible, in advance, about the nature and organization of the classes of records they need to consult, and examine any published transcripts and finding aids; see Mullins, *Texts and Calendars* (1375) for a convenient annotated list;

4. search the Card Index of Lists and Indexes at the PRO to identify unpublished finding aids (and realize that many classes of documents remain uncataloged and even unsorted);
5. secure permission before publishing any records.

290 *Guide to the National Archives of the United States*. Washington: National Archives and Records Administration, 1974. 884 pp. CD3023.U54 027.573.

A descriptive guide to governmental and other records under the jurisdiction of the National Archives as of 30 June 1970. This excludes material held in presidential libraries. Organized by department or agency within divisions for general records, legislative branch, judicial branch, executive branch, records of other governments, and miscellaneous holdings, the brief entry for each group or class of records typically includes a descriptive title, inclusive dates, quantity, location, notes (on content, type or purpose of documents, completeness, or organization), and finding aids. Each agency or department is prefaced by a description of its history, administration, organization, or other details necessary to understanding the nature of its records. Indexed by names, organizations, and subjects. Accessions and the opening of records are reported in *Prologue: Journal of the National Archives* (1969– , quarterly), which also prints articles on holdings. The bulk of this massive accumulation of documents relates to administrative matters, but there is considerable material on individuals that is too rarely explored by literary biographers. Although lacking the tradition of important discoveries made in the Public Record Office and thus not as well known to literary researchers, the National Archives is an obligatory stop for biographers of writers associated with the federal government, whether by election, through employment, or under surveillance.

Prucha, *Handbook for Research in American History* (entry 3185), has a useful overview of the National Archives (pp. 101–06), and Sears, *Using Government Publications* (3190), outlines strategies for searching National Archives materials (vol. 2, pp. 157–61).

See also

Sec. E: Libraries and Library Catalogs/Research Libraries/Guides to Libraries.
Fraser, *Children's Authors and Illustrators* (5465).
Royal Commission on Historical Manuscripts (1360).
Schatz, *Directory of Afro-American Resources* (3730).

Guides to Collections

Union Catalogs

295 *National Union Catalog of Manuscript Collections (NUCMC)*. Library of Congress Catalogs. Washington: Library of Congress, 1962– . Annual. Z6620.U5.N3.

A union catalog of collections of manuscripts held in public or quasi-public libraries, archives, historical societies, museums, and other institutions in the United

States. Users must remember that *NUCMC* is not a catalog of individual manuscripts (although a few exceptions are made for important items) but of collections of papers formed about an individual, subject, or organization, or by an individual, group, or institution. Although encompassing many periods and countries, the bulk of the collections are of English-language materials. Along with original manuscripts, transcripts, photocopies, microforms, facsimiles, and transcripts of sound recordings are included. Before the volume for 1962, descriptions are entered randomly; later volumes are organized alphabetically by repository (but usually in four or five sequences), then by collections. A typical entry includes person, family, organization, or collector who formed the collection or is its focus; collection title; physical description in linear feet or number of items; repository; location of original manuscripts if the collection consists of copies; description of scope and content, mentioning principal subjects and individuals (including sometimes the writers and recipients of letters); and notes on restrictions, provenance, and available descriptions, catalogs, indexes, or calendars. Entries for some extensive collections merely refer users to published finding aids. Indexed by persons, places, and subjects in each volume; cumulative indexes for volumes covering 1959–62, 1963–66, 1967–69, 1970–74, 1975–79, 1980–84. Scholars searching for manuscripts by or about individuals should begin with *Index to Personal Names in the* National Union Catalog of Manuscript Collections, *1959–1984*, 2 vols. (Alexandria: Chadwyck-Healey, 1988), which incorporates numerous corrections and additions to the interim indexes. RLIN (230) is exploring the feasibility of integrating *NUCMC* records into its archive and manuscript file.

Prepared from reports, indexes, and other sources, the entries vary considerably in detail, sophistication, and accuracy. Inevitably, the length of many descriptions is disproportionate to their content. Although collections at numerous major repositories are either omitted or incompletely reported, the breadth of coverage—especially of little-known or uncataloged collections—makes *NUCMC* one of the indispensable sources for locating manuscripts and letters by (and sometimes about) authors and literary-related subjects.

See also

Union List of Manuscripts in Canadian Repositories (4590).

Catalogs of Major Collections

300 *Index of Manuscripts in the British Library*. 10 vols. Cambridge: Chadwyck-Healey, 1984–86. Z921.L553.B74.

A person and place index to manuscripts acquired through 1950 by the British Library Department of Manuscripts. The *Index* is an amalgamation of the indexes in the printed catalogs and unprinted working indexes as well as cards for collections first indexed herein. Although edited for consistency and corrected as much as possible, the entries reflect the variations in accuracy, thoroughness, and cataloging practices of their sources (each of which is assessed in the introduction). Users must study the clear Instructions for Use (especially before searching for rulers, members of the nobility, and places) and remember that the siglum identifying a collection is printed above an entry or group of entries. Because the *Index of*

Manuscripts reproduces only those subject entries that could be incorporated under a geographical location, users needing subject access will still have to consult the indexes of the individual published catalogs.

A valuable time-saving compilation that corrects many entries in the printed catalogs and that indexes some collections for the first time, the work is an essential source for searching the holdings of one of the world's great collections of manuscripts.

Manuscripts acquired after 1960 are listed in *"Rough Register" of Acquisitions of the Department of Manuscripts, British Library, 1961–1965*, List and Index Society Special Series 7 (London: Swift, 1974, 172 pp.); *1966–1970*, List and Index Society Special Series 8 (1975, n.pag.); *1971–1975*, List and Index Society Special Series 10 (1977, 246 pp.); *1976–1980*, List and Index Society Special Series 15 (1982, 242 pp.).

The most current guide to the catalogs and other finding aids (especially for manuscripts acquired after 1950) is M. A. E. Nickson, *The British Library: Guide to the Catalogues and Indexes of the Department of Manuscripts*, 2nd ed. (London: British Library, 1982, 24 pp.). Somewhat fuller descriptions are in T. C. Skeat, *The Catalogues of the Manuscript Collections, The British Museum*, rev. ed. (London: British Museum, 1962, 45 pp.).

The largest collection in the Department of Manuscripts is the Additional Manuscripts, which includes acquisitions since 1756 (except for some separately cataloged closed collections). The Additional Manuscripts, except for the Sloane Collection, are described in *Catalogue of Additions to the Manuscripts [1756–]: Additional Manuscripts [4104–]* (London: British Library, 1843– ; irregular). The individual volumes vary in cataloging practices, accuracy, and thoroughness, but recent ones provide full descriptions of collections and individual documents. Manuscripts acquired after 1950 are listed or described in various handlists and looseleaf catalogs in the Department of Manuscripts. For a description of the collection of plays submitted to the Lord Chamberlain, see entry 1540.

Part of the Bodleian collection, which includes a substantial number of literary manuscripts, is cataloged in Falconer Madan et al., *A Summary Catalogue of Western Manuscripts in the Bodleian Library at Oxford*, 7 vols. (Oxford: Clarendon, 1895–1953). To sort out the various catalogs and classification schemes, users must consult vol. 1, which also includes lists of current and obsolete shelfmarks. Two indexes in vol. 7: persons, places, some subjects; owners.

See also

Sec. E: Libraries and Library Catalogs/Research Libraries.

Crum, *First-Line Index of English Poetry, 1500–1800, in Manuscripts of the Bodleian Library* (1590).

General Indexes

See

American Book Prices Current (5415).

Book Auction Records (5420).

Periodicals

305 *Manuscripta.* 1957– . 3/yr. Z6602.M36 091.

Publishes articles, notes, and reviews on medieval and Renaissance manuscripts (although reviews in recent volumes cover studies and editions of modern manuscripts). Some volumes since 7 (1963) print "A Review of English Renaissance Textual Studies," which surveys textual and bibliographical scholarship and editions. Indexed in every fifth volume.

310 *Manuscripts (MSS).* 1948– . Quarterly. Former title: *Autograph Collectors' Journal* (1948–53). Z41.A2.A925 091.505.

Publishes articles on collecting, editing, and preserving manuscripts; transcripts and descriptions of individual documents; reports on auctions; and notes on acquisitions. Coverage extends to several periods and countries, but the majority of the articles focus on American literary and historical manuscripts. Although addressed to collectors, *Manuscripts* prints numerous articles of interest to literary researchers. Annual index; cumulative index: vols. 1–28 (n.d., 51 pp.).

See also

Library (5310).
Papers of the Bibliographical Society of America (5315).
Studies in Bibliography (5320).

G

Serial Bibliographies, Indexes, and Abstracts

This section includes works covering more than one national literature or discipline. Works devoted to a single national literature or subject appear in appropriate sections of the *Guide*. Although there is considerable overlapping among the following sources, each—because of its scope, organization, or indexing features—cites studies omitted from or not readily accessible in the others. (The extent of duplication in literature serial bibliographies has never been satisfactorily established. The existing studies are based on seriously flawed methodologies and an inadequate grasp of the scope, editorial principles, and taxonomies of the major bibliographies. See, for example, Lewis Sawin, "The Integrated Bibliography for English Studies: Plan and Project," *Pennsylvania Library Association Bulletin* 19 [1964]: 7–19; Abigail A. Loomis, "Dickens Duplications: A Study of Overlap in Serial Bibliographies in Literature," *RQ* 25 [1986]: 348–57.)

Bibliographies of Bibliographies

325 Wortman, William A. *A Guide to Serial Bibliographies for Modern Literatures*. Selected Bibliographies in Language and Literature 3. New York: MLA, 1982. 124 pp. Z6519.W67 [PN695] 016.805.

A guide to serial bibliographies published separately or in journals (generally excluding those which ceased publication before c. 1960). Organized in divisions for comprehensive bibliographies and general indexes, literatures in English, non-English literatures, subjects, and authors, the 700 titles include bibliographies for periods, genres, subjects, themes, and literature-related topics (such as psychology, music, art, and religion). Many sections are preceded by a helpful evaluative overview. A typical annotation briefly describes scope and basic organization, but the confusing use of "comprehensive" (see p. 6) can easily mislead a user, and discontinued bibliographies are not always identified. Wortman is the best source for identifying specialized serial bibliographies which are frequently more extensive in coverage than—or at least essential supplements to—comparable parts of standard general works such as *MLAIB* (335) and *ABELL* (340).

Bibliographic Index (145) lists new serial bibliographies as well as a number of discontinued ones omitted by Wortman. Richard A. Gray, comp., *Serial Bibliographies in the Humanities and Social Sciences* (Ann Arbor: Pierian, 1969, 345 pp.), covers philosophy, religion, the social sciences, language, the arts, history, and literature, but is now outdated.

Serial Bibliographies

Surveys of Research

330 *Year's Work in English Studies* (*YWES*). London: Murray; Atlantic Highlands: Humanities for the English Assn., 1921– . Annual. PE58.E6 820.9.

A selective, evaluative review of scholarship on English, American, and some other literatures in English. Coverage of American literature began in vol. 35 (for 1954); a chapter on African, Caribbean, and Canadian literature in English was added in vol. 63 (for 1982) and expanded to include Australian, New Zealand, and Indian literature in vol. 64 (for 1983). Each volume is organized by individual essays devoted (currently) to periods, national literatures, major authors (Chaucer, Shakespeare, Milton), or subjects (English language, literary history and criticism, literary theory). The scope of some chapters varies over the years.

Coverage is necessarily selective (sometimes erratic, idiosyncratic, or restricted because of the unavailability of works) and emphasizes Anglo-American scholarship. The quality, objectivity, rigor of evaluation, and breadth of individual chapters vary, depending on the contributor(s), but most attempt to evaluate judiciously the most significant scholarship. To offer representative coverage of the steadily increasing number of studies, contributors in recent volumes tend to be more succinct in discussing an individual work. Citations to books and articles do not include complete bibliographical information. A volume now appears about three years after the year of scholarship it covers; however, a classified list of books received for future review was added in vol. 64 (for 1983). Two indexes: critics; subjects and literary authors. Since vol. 47 (for 1966) the subject indexing has been more detailed and includes titles of literary works.

Because it offers the most comprehensive evaluative survey of important studies, *YWES* can be an invaluable guide to significant scholarship (particularly in English literature; *American Literary Scholarship* [3265] provides more exhaustive coverage of American literature). Together, the annual volumes offer an incomparable record of scholarly and critical trends as well as of the fluctuations of academic reputations of literary works and authors.

Literature Bibliographies

335 *MLA International Bibliography of Books and Articles on the Modern Languages and Literatures* (*MLAIB*; sometimes called *PMLA Bibliography*). New York: MLA, 1922– . Annual. Z7006.M676 016.8.

A classified bibliography of literary, linguistic, and folklore scholarship published throughout the world. Its scope is extensive: *all* human languages (living and dead) and many invented ones; *all* literatures (except classical Greek and Latin, which are covered in *L'année philologique* [4890]); *all* aspects of folklore. Although many bibliographies listed in this *Guide* offer more exhaustive coverage of a single literature, period, genre, or subject, many achieve their superiority by relying heavily on the *MLAIB*, and none approaches its breadth and few its currency.

Effective use of the *Bibliography* requires close familiarity with the many alterations over the years in editorial policy, scope, and organization. Because of the extensive changes instituted with the 1981 *Bibliography* and the general similarity of the organization of the earlier volumes, a separate consideration of the two periods is appropriate.

MLAIB for 1921–80. Originally titled the "American Bibliography," published in essay format, nominally limited to scholarship by Americans, and covering English, Romance, Germanic, and American languages and literatures, the bibliography gradually expanded its scope to cover other literatures and languages, and to become "international" in the volume for 1956. Volumes covering 1921–68 were published as a part of *PMLA* (725); however, many libraries will have these volumes in the separate reprints published by Kraus or New York University Press. With the 1969 volume the *Bibliography* became a separate publication issued in four parts (each with its separate index of scholars). Pt. 1: General, English, American, Medieval and Neo-Latin, and Celtic Literatures; pt. 2: General Romance, French, Italian, Spanish, Portuguese and Brazilian, Romanian, General Germanic, German, Netherlandic, Scandinavian, Modern Greek, Oriental, African, and East European Literatures; pt. 3: Linguistics; pt. 4: ACTFL Annual Bibliography on Pedagogy in Foreign Languages. (Most libraries will have the bound library edition.) In the 1970 volume, Folklore became a separate section in pt. 1; pt. 4 was discontinued after the 1972 *MLAIB.*

The continual expansion was accompanied by numerous changes in the organization of sections and refinements in the classification of entries (especially in the bibliographies for 1926, 1928, 1953, 1956, 1957, 1967, and 1969); consequently, users must be certain to check the table of contents at the beginning of each volume. In general, scholarship on literary works is organized by national literature, then (after a general section) by period, and then by genre and literary author; some literatures, however, are grouped by language rather than geography (e.g., Cornish and Welsh are under Celtic Literatures; French-Canadian and West Indian are listed with French Literature). Studies not assignable to a national literature, general discussions of themes or genres, and works about criticism and theory are listed in the General Literature section (which for many years also served as a catchall and included several national literatures, folklore, and general linguistics). Folklore scholarship is classified by broad topics (e.g., Folk Poetry, Folk Games and Toys, Material

Culture), then by types (e.g., Folk Poetry includes headings for Oral Epics, Ballads, Songs, and Rhymes and Verses), and then continent. (Folklore scholarship appears in the various national literature divisions through the volume for 1927 and in the General division in the volumes for 1928–68; even after Folklore became a separate division, several national literatures continued to include a Folklore section.) The Linguistics part includes classified sections for linguistic topics (e.g., Theoretical and Descriptive Linguistics includes a subdivision for Grammar which is further subdivided into General and Miscellaneous, Morphophonemics, Morphology, Syntax, Word Classes and Categories, and Discourse Analysis) and language groups (subdivided by specific languages, with further subdivisions for general studies, Bibliography, Dialectology, Graphemics, Lexis, Morphology, Onomastics, Phonology, Semantics, Stylistics, Syntax, and Translation). Until the volume for 1967 (which marks the beginning of systematic coverage of linguistic studies), linguistic scholarship was included with individual languages; general linguistic studies were listed in the General section.

A publication is listed only once in each part, with up to five cross-references; any work that requires more is relegated, without cross-references, to the most appropriate general heading (e.g., a book on several English plays, medieval through modern, would usually be listed only under Drama in the General section of the English Literature division; an article surveying plays from several national literatures would usually appear only under Drama in the General IV: Themes and Types section). Thus scholars must be certain to search appropriate general sections.

Most journals and series are cited by acronyms keyed to the Master List of Periodicals found at the front of each part. (Serials on the Master List are fully described in *MLA Directory of Periodicals* [615].) Essays from a collection or festschrift (identifiable by a bracketed number preceded by F) are keyed to the Festschriften and Other Analyzed Collections entries at the beginning of each part. In the volumes for 1970–75, an asterisk preceding an entry number means that an abstract is printed in the corresponding volume of *MLA Abstracts of Articles in Scholarly Journals* (New York: MLA, 1972–77, annual). Indexed by scholar in most volumes since 1948.

MLAIB for 1981– . Since the introduction of a sophisticated computerized classification and indexing system in the volume for 1981, the *Bibliography* has been published in five parts, each available with self-contained subject and scholar indexes. Pt. 1: British Isles, British Commonwealth, English-Caribbean, and American Literatures; pt. 2: European, Asian, African, and South American [i.e., Latin American] Literatures; pt. 3: Linguistics; pt. 4: General Literature and Related Topics; pt. 5: Folklore. Most libraries will subscribe to the library edition, which includes all five parts and comprehensive scholar and subject indexes.

National literature sections are classified chronologically in parts 1 and 2; depending on the scholarship covered in a volume, chronological spans range from a single century to several centuries. For example, a book on English drama from the Renaissance to the modern period would appear in a division headed "English Literature/1500–1999"; an article on Black Mountain poets would appear in "American Literature/1900–1999." Chronological divisions encompassing more than a century include subdivisions for general studies and genres; those limited to a century or, for some literatures, a broader early period (e.g., Old English, medieval, Old Russian, Ch'ing Dynasty period) are further classified by literary author. Individual authors have subdivisions for general studies, bibliographies, genres, and literary works. In general, the post-1980 volumes are more consistent than their predecessors in distinguishing national literatures. The remaining inconsistencies—for example, there are no separate sections for Swiss, Austrian, or East German literature—are generally ameliorated by the national literature headings in the subject index.

Studies on General Literature and Related Topics are classified in pt. 4 under nine broad divisions: General Literature, Literary Movements, Bibliographical, Criticism, Literary Theory, Genres, Literary Forms, Professional Topics, Themes and Figures. Each includes appropriate subdivisions, again depending on the nature of the scholarship covered in a given volume (e.g., the Poetry subdivision of the Genres division might include headings for Concrete Poetry, Elegy, Haiku, Lyric Poetry, and Prose Poem).

Linguistic scholarship is organized by broad topics (Language, History of Linguistics, Theory of Linguistics, Areal Linguistics, Comparative Linguistics, Diachronic Linguistics, Language Interaction, Mathematical Linguistics, Paralinguistics, Psycholinguistics, Sociolinguistics, Topics of Professional Interest), by aspects of language (Dialectology, Grammar, Lexicology, Morphology, Onomastics, Phonetics, Phonology, Pragmatics, Prosody, Semantics, Stylistics, Syntax, Translation, Writing Systems), and by specific language. Each section includes appropriate divisions and subdivisions (e.g., Sociolinguistics has subdivisions for Ethnolinguistics, Language Attitudes, Language Policy, Social Dialects, and Speech Registers; Stylistics has subdivisions for Metrics and Rhetoric).

Folklore studies are listed in pt. 5 under general studies and under headings for History and Study of Folklore, Folk Literature, Ethnomusicology, Folk Belief Systems, Folk Rituals, and Material Culture. Each is subdivided by type or genre and then by geographical area (continent, region, country), for example, Folk Literature has subdivisions for Folk Speech Play, Folk Narrative, and Folk Poetry (the last with headings for such forms as ballad, epic, and folk song.

A study is listed only once in each part; there are no cross-references, since the subject index provides access to related authors, genres, or subjects. Acronyms are still used for most journal and series titles, but an entry for an essay from a collection provides full bibliographical information (and thus does away with the [F] numbers that mystified so many users). Since index terms are printed within brackets following a citation, researchers can usually get some sense of the content of a study.

Of most benefit is the subject indexing made possible by the new system. Each separately published part includes self-contained subject and scholar indexes, but for comprehensive searches users must consult the integrated indexes to the library edition. All searches should begin with the subject index because the classified listings include no cross-references. The subject index provides access to literary authors, genres, groups, themes, literary movements, motifs, literary characters, theories, critics, scholars, linguistic features, techniques (such as characterization, allusion), languages, folklore genres, literary features (e.g., structure, point of view), and processes (e.g., textual revision). Each subject heading is followed by the citations in which it appears. Since each citation prints its full list of subject terms, a user can frequently judge the probable relevance of a book or article before looking it up in the classified listing. Many subject headings also refer users to related headings.

MLAIB Data Base. As of late 1988, the volumes for 1964 to the present (about 890,000 citations) can be searched online through Dialog (520). Updated eight times each year, the data base is more current than the printed *Bibliography*, and, since 1981, entries are retrievable by scholarly approach only through the data base. When retrospective coverage through 1921 is complete, more than one million citations will be available for retrieval.

Volumes from 1981 to the present can also be searched through WILSONLINE (525). Earlier volumes will eventually be available through the Wilson data base, which is updated eight times a year. Bibliographies since 1981 are available on CD-ROM through WILSONDISC, which offers much of the flexibility of an online search but with the advantage of menu-driven access at four levels of expertise. The discs are updated quarterly, and subscribers have unlimited access to the *MLAIB* data base through WILSONLINE, which includes the most recent additions to the file. Volumes before 1981 will eventually be available on CD-ROM.

The lack of subject indexing has always been a major impediment to use of the volumes for 1921 through 1980. Now, however, free text searching of the data base makes some subject access possible (e.g., searchers can retrieve all studies with "Joyce" and "*Ulysses*" in their respective titles).

Online searching of post-1980 entries offers some advantages (besides speed) over manual searches of the printed classified listings and subject indexes. Using combinations of "supercoded descriptors" (e.g., codes for genre, literary technique, theme, place, or time period), a researcher can narrow a search to various levels (e.g., one could quickly isolate journal articles written in English between 1982 and 1985 and employing an archetypal approach to Joyce's use of the journey motif in *Ulysses*). Although some descriptors are being added and classification discrepancies resolved when listings from 1921 through 1980 are added to the data base, online searching of these entries will never allow the flexibility and specificity possible with post-1980 citations. Those using the online file should watch the *MLA Newsletter* for updates on search techniques (see, e.g., "On-Line with the MLA," 16.2 [1984]: 4; "New Software for Bibliographic Search," 17.1 [1985]: 5).

Despite the dramatic increase in accessibility to the post-1980 listings, a search of the printed subject indexes or online file must be supplemented by a reading of appropriate sections in the classified volumes. Although the number of entries given index terms has grown steadily each year, not all works are or can be indexed. Many broad studies can be described in only the most general terms, and some publications, lacking a thesis or any discernible focus, cannot be given any descriptors. Subject indexing, at its best, is an imperfect art. A book or essay usually requires an MLA bibliographer to choose among a range of indexing possibilities, and no two people are likely to index any but the most straightforward study in the same way.

No reference work of this magnitude, especially one that relies heavily on a network of volunteer contributors, is without its limitations and faults. Before 1956 the *Bibliography* was generally restricted to scholarship by American authors. Although it became "international" in 1956 and includes books, essays from edited collections, journal articles, review essays (but not reviews), and published abstracts of dissertations, coverage has never been exhaustive. The classification system—sometimes maddeningly quirky and inconsistent—requires considerable time to master. Until 1981 there is no convenient way of determining what serials listed in the Master List of Periodicals are actually covered in a given volume (now an asterisk preceding an acronym in the Master List denotes that at least one issue of the journal or volume in the series is covered; those with access to the data base can search by journal and year to determine which volumes were actually covered); issues of journals whose coverage lapses for a year or more are frequently left unanalyzed. New journals are not always added in a timely manner; when they are, retrospective coverage is haphazard. Since contributors must actually have a work in hand before listing it, studies are overlooked or entered years after publication. And there are the inevitable number of outright errors. Yet no researcher can afford to ignore the *MLAIB*.

Although the *MLAIB* is frequently the single most valuable aid to research, its coverage must be supplemented with other serial bibliographies and reference works. (For a comparison of *MLAIB* and *ABELL*, see the following entry.)

The Modern Language Association and Research Libraries Group are planning a research-in-progress data base that will record articles accepted for publication in selected journals and grants funded through the NEH Research Programs Division. The data base will be available through RLIN (230) in 1989.

340 *Annual Bibliography of English Language and Literature* (*ABELL*; sometimes called *MHRA Bibliography*). London: Modern Humanities Research Assn., 1921– . Annual. Z2011.M69 016.82.

An international bibliography of scholarship about the English language and literatures in English (British, American, Canadian, Australian, African, Asian). Although a number of subdivisions have been added over the years (especially in vols. 48 [for 1973] and 51 [for 1976]), the scope and basic organization have remained fairly stable. Entries are currently organized in divisions for general works; festschriften and other collections; bibliography; scholarly method; language, literature, and the computer; newspapers and other periodicals; English language; folklore and folklife; English literature. This last has sections for general studies and periods (Old English, Middle English and fifteenth century, then by century), with subsections for general studies, genres, anthologies, literary history and criticism, related studies, and individual authors. Entries are efficiently cross-referenced and uninformative titles are occasionally glossed. Two indexes: subjects; scholars.

Coverage is reasonably thorough, but publication lags about three years. The broad subject classifications, failure to distinguish among national literatures (the sections for the nineteenth and twentieth centuries are particularly unwieldy), inadequate subject indexing (essentially listings of the classification and author heads), and lack of online access make this a cumbersome work to search for studies other than those restricted to a specific author.

The more detailed classification system, subject indexing in recent volumes, and online access render *MLAIB* (335) a more efficient source to search; however, every volume of *ABELL* includes scores of works omitted in the *MLAIB*, and vice versa. Precise comparison of coverage of areas common to the two serial bibliographies is difficult because of differences in scope and organization. Comparing the number of entries in similar sections is an invalid measure, since *ABELL* numbers separately all cross-references and entries for books reviewed and does not distinguish among national literatures in literary period sections. Before 1956—when *MLAIB* was generally restricted to scholarship by American authors—the duplication is frequently quite low. Although recent volumes of *MLAIB* are overall more comprehensive than *ABELL* in their common areas of coverage, *ABELL* lists British theses and some reviews (which *MLAIB* does not index); its coverage of books published solely in Great Britain and smaller British journals is superior; and it includes a selective list of related studies for each historical period. Used together, *ABELL* and *MLAIB* will lead researchers to the bulk of scholarship since 1921 on the English language and literatures in English.

345 *Bulletin signalétique, 523: Histoire et sciences de la littérature*. Paris: Centre de Documentation Sciences Humaines, Centre Nationale de la Recherche Scientifique, 1947– . 5/yr., inc. cumulative index. Former titles: *Bulletin analytique* (1947–55); *Bulletin signalétique: Philosophie, sciences humaines* (1956–60); *Bulletin signalétique C (19–24): Sciences humaines* (1961–68). Z6513.B82 800.

A bibliography of articles published in journals and collections on European, African, and North and South American literatures, as well as literary history and theory. The descriptively annotated entries are organized in three extensively classified divisions: general studies, sciences of literature (including literary theory, genre studies, and comparative literature), history of literature (with sections for general studies, literary periods and movements, and national literatures). Four indexes: subjects; literary authors and anonymous works; scholars and critics; journals listed. Entries since 1972 can be searched through the FRANCIS data base (available in the United States through Questel, Inc.). Although especially useful for its extensive coverage of French publications and subject indexing, *Bulletin signalétique* is much less comprehensive than *MLAIB* (335) and (for British and American literature) *ABELL* (340).

350 *Literary Criticism Register: A Monthly Listing of Studies in English and American Literature*. Deland: Literary Criticism Register, 1983– . Monthly. Z2011.L76 [PR83] 016.82'09.

A selective list of English-language studies (since c. 1982) of English and American literature, critical theory, and (occasionally) composition. Each issue consists of three lists: contents (excluding reviews) of journals (drawn from a list of some three hundred major ones), organized alphabetically by journal title, then issue; books in *American Book Publishing Record* (4110), organized by issue, then by broad subject heading; dissertations in *Dissertation Abstracts International* (465), organized by issue. Two indexes, with semiannual and annual cumulations: subjects; scholars. Because of its restricted coverage, ineffective organization, inadequate subject indexing, and overlap with superior indexes, the best that can be said for this work is that it is reasonably current and culls out many works on English and American literature from *ABPR* and *DAI*. *Current Contents* (365a) offers a more thorough list of more journals.

355 *Literature and Language Bibliographies from the* American Year Book, *1910–1919*. Introd. and indexes by Arnold N. Rzepecki. Cumulated Bibliography Series 1. Ann Arbor: Pierian, 1970. 259 pp. Z7001.L57 [P121] 016.41.

A convenient reprint of the annual surveys, useful now because they cover a period before publication of *MLAIB* (335) and *ABELL* (340). The highly selective essay reviews, restricted largely to American scholarship, cover classical and European languages and literatures. The American literature sections treat creative, rather than scholarly, works. The one-page subject index lists only literature and language divisions; the "Personal Name and Main Entry" index, contrary to its title, includes only scholars, literary authors, and an occasional anonymous work.

See also

"Anglo-German Literary Bibliography," *JEGP: Journal of English and Germanic Philology* (690).
"Bibliography of Critical Arthurian Literature," *Modern Language Quarterly* (695).
"Check List of Explication," *Explicator* (685).
LLBA: Linguistics and Language Behavior Abstracts (6015).

General Bibliographies

Although the following indexes are much less comprehensive in their coverage of language and literature studies, their interdisciplinary scope and subject indexing make them important complements to *MLAIB* (335) and *ABELL* (340).

360 *American Humanities Index* (*AHI*). Troy: Whitston, 1976– . Quarterly, with annual cumulation. AI3.A278 016.051.

An author and subject index to English language articles and creative works in about 230 journals (currently). Despite its title, *AHI* is not limited to American journals or subjects, and its focus is overwhelmingly on literature. Except for a few little magazines and author newsletters, periodicals covered are more adequately indexed by the other serial bibliographies. The extensive duplication and imprecise, superficial subject indexing make this the least useful index in this section.

365 *Arts and Humanities Citation Index, [1976–]* (*AHCI*). Philadelphia: Institute for Scientific Information, 1978– . 3/yr., with annual cumulation and an expanded quinquennial one covering 1975–79 (14 vols., 1987). AI3.A63 016.05.

Subject, author, and citation indexes to journals (currently 1,300) and a few books in archaeology, dance, history, music, architecture, film, language, philosophy, art, television, radio, linguistics, theater, classics, folklore, religion, and literature. (An additional 5,600 journals surveyed for *Science Citation Index* [1961–] and *Social Sciences Citation Index* [1966–] are selectively covered.) The contents of *AHCI* are indexed in four ways:

1. The Source Index, to which entries in the other three indexes are keyed, is an author list of articles, reviews, notes, illustrations, letters, and creative works. Each entry includes basic publication information, the author's address (a useful feature for those wishing to request an offprint), and a list of works cited. The latter sometimes indicates the focus of an article and yields sources relevant to its topic.
2. The Permuterm Subject Index indexes key words in titles of entries in the Source Index. Although "title enrichment terms" are added for uninformative titles, the value of this part as a subject index is restricted because of the reliance on title words for index terms.
3. The Citation Index lists (by author or artist) books, articles, dissertations, reviews, works of art, music, and films mentioned in the text, notes, or bibliography of works in the Source Index. Thus users can identify (a) scholarship relevant to a topic by locating studies that cite a pertinent book or article; (b) discussions of literary authors buried in vaguely titled or broad studies. Because indexers do not discriminate between passing references and substantial discussions, users frequently will waste time tracking down insignificant citations (especially in the case of a major, frequently cited author). Also, the uncritical reliance on endnotes and footnotes results in numerous misattributions and variant titles.
4. The Corporate Index, which lists authors in the Source Index by organizational affiliation (e.g., a department in a university), is useful principally when a researcher knows that a particular organization is involved in work relevant to a search.

Entries from 1980 are searchable online through BRS (515); coverage is updated every two weeks. Weekly issues of *Current Contents: Arts and Humanities* (1979–) keep *AHCI* up to date by printing a title keyword index to reproductions of contents pages from journals. *Index to Social Sciences and Humanities Proceedings* (*ISSHP*) (1980– , quarterly with annual cumulation) indexes the published proceedings of conferences, seminars, and symposia by author or editor, topic, permuterm subject, sponsor, and geographic area. The publisher offers a reprint service for indexed journal articles published after 1980 and for some papers listed in *ISSHP*.

The numerous errors and false leads, very small print, abbreviated entries and cross-references, and the need to refer continually to the Source Index make *AHCI* a cumbersome, time-consuming work to use. Although *AHCI* represents a largely unsuccessful attempt to apply science and social science indexing practices to the humanities, its citation index occasionally uncovers important discussions of individuals buried in obscurely titled articles. Review: Sandy Petrey, *French Review* 54 (1980): 117–21.

370 *British Humanities Index* (*BHI*). London: Library Assn., 1963– . Quarterly, with annual cumulation and author index. AI3.B7 011'.34.

A subject index to about three hundred British and Commonwealth periodicals that continues *Subject Index to Periodicals* (1915–62). *BHI* is useful because of its good subject indexing (with plentiful cross-references) and inclusion of several publications not covered by other bibliographies in this section.

375 *Cumulative Book Index: A World List of Books in the English Language* (*CBI*). New York: Wilson, 1898– . 11/yr., with quarterly, annual, and larger cumulations. Z1219.M78 015.73.

An author, title, and subject bibliography of books in English that continues *United States Catalog: Books in Print* (1898–1928). Although *CBI* is international in scope, coverage of works published outside the United States is not particularly thorough. For literary researchers, especially those with access to OCLC (225) or RLIN (230) terminals, *CBI* is principally useful as a subject index and occasionally as a title index to the *National Union Catalogs* (235, 240, and 245). Entries since January 1982 can be searched through WILSONLINE (525) and on CD-ROM through WILSONDISC.

International Books in Print (4370) offers more extensive international coverage. Although limited to cataloging records created by the British Library and Library of Congress, *Books in English* (London: British Library, Bibliographic Services Division, 1971– , 6/yr., with annual and larger cumulations, microfiche only) includes ephemeral and local publications, which are excluded from *CBI*.

380 *Essay and General Literature Index* (*EGLI*). New York: Wilson, 1931– Semiannual, with annual, quinquennial, and larger cumulations extending coverage to 1900. AI3.E752 080.1'6.

An author and subject index to essays and chapters in books and some annual publications, with emphasis on the humanities and social sciences. Entries for literary authors include works by and about a writer (with the latter classified by literary work). Books indexed are listed in the back of each issue; a cumulative list was published in 1972 (Essay and General Literature Index: *Works Indexed, 1900–1969* [New York: Wilson, 1972, 437 pp.]). Although highly selective and limited to English-language publications, *EGLI* is the only serial bibliography devoted to the indexing of chapters of books and essays in a collection by a single author. It is also a good source for locating a reprint of an essay.

English-language books before 1900 are indexed by subject in *The "A.L.A." Index: An Index to General Literature: Bibliographical, Historical, and Literary Essays and Sketches, Reports and Publications of Boards and Societies Dealing with Education, Health, Labor, Charities, and Corrections, Etc., Etc.*, 2nd ed., by William I. Fletcher (Boston: American Library Assn., 1901, 679 pp.). Some of the books in the *Supplement, 1900–1910* (Chicago: American Library Assn., 1914, 223 pp.) are reindexed in *EGLI*. For authors, see *A.L.A. Index to General Literature Cumulative Author Index*, comp. and ed. C. Edward Wall, Cumulative Author Index Series 4 (Ann Arbor: Pierian, 1972, 192 pp.).

385 *Humanities Index*. New York: Wilson, 1975– . Quarterly, with annual cumulation. (An expanded continuation of humanities coverage in *Social Sciences and Humanities Index* [1966–74], itself a continuation of *International Index to Periodicals* [1916–65, with coverage beginning with 1907].) AI3.H85 016.0013.

An author and subject index to English-language articles, creative works, and reviews in about 300 journals (currently) devoted to folklore, history, language, literature, performing arts, philosophy, religion, and classical studies. Book reviews, listed by author of the book reviewed, are grouped separately at the back. Since 1974, author and title (but not subject) entries for short stories are repeated in *Short Story Index* (1085). Listings since February 1984 can be searched through WILSONLINE (525) and on CD-ROM through WILSONDISC. Although highly selective, the work is useful for its interdisciplinary coverage and subject indexing.

387 InfoTrac. Foster City: Information Access, 1985– . CD-ROM system.

A data base that offers author and subject indexing of a variety of popular, general interest, and scholarly periodicals through the following systems:

1. The General Periodicals Index, the largest of the systems, is available in two versions: the Academic Library Edition, which covers about 1,100 general and scholarly periodicals in several fields, and the Public Library Edition, which indexes approximately 1,100 popular magazines and journals, including those in Magazine Index Plus. Both editions include the current four years of data as well as the latest two months of *New York Times* and *Wall Street Journal*, are updated monthly, and offer a backfile of at least four years of data (with coverage beginning in 1981 and 1980, respectively).
2. The Academic Index indexes the most current four years of about 390 general interest journals, all of which are included in the Academic Library Edition of the General Periodicals Index. Coverage begins January 1985.
3. The Magazine Index Plus covers the most current four years of *New York Times* and about 400 popular magazines, all of which are covered in the Public Library Edition of the General Periodicals Index. A backfile extends coverage to 1980.
4. The National Newspaper Index, which is updated monthly, indexes the most recent four years of *New York Times*, *Wall Street Journal*, *Christian Science Monitor*, *Washington Post*, and *Los Angeles Times*. For earlier coverage see *National Newspaper Index* (3420), the print version.
5. LegalTrac covers about 800 legal publications, beginning with January 1980.

6. The Government Publications Index indexes the *Monthly Catalog* of the Government Printing Office since 1976.

Although searches cannot be narrowed as effectively as in more sophisticated data bases, the breadth of coverage, user-friendliness, excellent subject access, attached printer, and speed make InfoTrac the best periodical index for searching general interest and some scholarly periodicals since around 1980. Unfortunately, many unsophisticated library users—and even some reference librarians—have come to regard InfoTrac as the only general periodical index worth searching; its severely limited and unrepresentative coverage of many subject areas (especially language and literature) means that it must be supplemented by other indexes in this section.

390 *Internationale Bibliographie der Zeitschriftenliteratur aus allen gebieten des Wissens/International Bibliography of Periodical Literature Covering All Fields of Knowledge/Bibliographie internationale de la littérature périodique dans tous les domaines de la connaissance [1965–]* (*IBZ*, Dietrich). Osnabrück: Dietrich, 1965– . 2 multivol. pts./yr. (A merger of *Internationale Bibliographie der Zeitschriftenliteratur.* Abteilung A: *Bibliographie der deutschen Zeitschriftenliteratur* [1896–1964] and Abteilung B: *Bibliographie der fremdsprachigen Zeitschriftenliteratur* [1911–64].) AI9.I5 016.

An international bibliography of periodical articles on all subjects. Coverage, now extending to several thousand serials published worldwide, emphasizes those in English and German and excludes only those in Oriental languages. Currently each half-year part has four main divisions:

1. The Subject Index is a keyword index to article titles. Author, title, and publication information are listed only under German headings, with cross-references in English and French. Periodical titles are keyed by number to the periodical index. The keyword and author indexes refer to subject headings in this index.
2. The Keyword Index is a list by field of knowledge of the headings and cross-references used in the Subject Index. Of most interest to literature scholars are the general, book and documentation, literature and linguistics, and fine arts fields. Because of the vagaries of subject indexing, the Keyword Index is a necessary complement to the Subject Index. The *Register der Schlagwörter/Index of Key-Words/Index des mots-clef, 1896–1974*, 2 vols. (1975) lists all keywords used from 1896 through 1974 but identifies volumes in which they appear for only 1965 through 1974.
3. The Author Index consists of an alphabetical list of authors of articles cited in the Subject Index. An author entry cites the heading under which the article is listed.
4. The Periodical Index contains an alphabetical list of periodicals cited in the Subject Index.

The most useful feature is the subject indexing; however, researchers must devote considerable time to mastering terminology and identifying appropriate headings and must remember that indexing is dependent on title words. Usability would be enhanced if the journal title were included with the main entry for an article.

The criteria governing selection of journals and articles have never been explained; coverage of a journal is often erratic; many issues are incompletely indexed;

and the compilation procedures and editing (as described by Broadwin—see below) hardly inspire confidence in accuracy or thoroughness. However, the breadth of coverage—the most wide-ranging of any single index—makes *IBZ* an occasionally useful complement to the other works in this section. Currently, however, coverage of English and American literature is not particularly thorough.

For a discussion of editorial procedures and evaluation of *IBZ*, see John A. Broadwin, "An Analysis of the *Internationale Bibliographie der Zeitschriftenliteratur*," *Journal of Documentation* 32 (1976): 26–31; and B. J. McMullin, "Indexing the Periodical Literature of Anglo-American Bibliography," *Studies in Bibliography* 33 (1980): 1–17. The publisher plans to make *IBZ* available online.

395 *Internationale Jahresbibliographie der Festschriften/International Annual Bibliography of Festschriften/Bibliographie internationale annuelle des mélanges [1980–] (IJBF)*. Osnabrück: Dietrich, 1982– . Annual. Z1033.F4.I67.

An international index to festschriften in all subjects. Each annual bibliography has five divisions:

1. The festschriften list by honoree is an index with publication information for the collection and a list of contents. The following divisions are keyed to this one.
2. The festschriften list by fields of knowledge classifies the collections in sixteen fields of knowledge, including general, book and documentation, literature and linguistics, and fine arts.
3. The subject index is a keyword index, in German with English and French cross-references, to titles of contributions.
4. The keyword index lists, by field of knowledge, the headings used in the subject index.
5. The author index is an index of contributors listed in the festschriften entries.

The most useful feature is the subject indexing; however, researchers must devote considerable time to mastering terminology and identifying appropriate headings and must remember that indexing is dependent on title words.

Although *IJBF* is marred by compilation and editorial procedures which hardly inspire confidence in accuracy or thoroughness, by the lack of an adequate explanation of scope and criteria governing selection, and by awkward organization, the breadth of the work makes it a potentially useful source for identifying essays on language and literature appearing in festschriften in disciplines other than language and literature. Indexing is now about three years in arrears. *MLAIB* (335) offers superior and more current coverage of collections devoted to language and literature.

The publisher plans to make *IJBF* available online and has announced publication of a complementary series, *Internationale Jahresbibliographie der Kongressberichte*.

Festschriften published through 1979 are indexed in Otto Leistner, *Internationale Bibliographie der Festschriften von den Anfängen bis 1979 mit Sachregister/International Bibliography of Festschriften from the Beginnings until 1979 with Subject-Index*, 2nd enl. ed., 2 vols. (Osnabrück: Biblio, 1984–86). The first part lists collection by honoree; the second indexes volumes (but not individual essays) by subject under German and English headings. Although more limited in scope, Charles Szabo, Christopher Kleinhenz, and James Brewer, *Bibliography of Articles in the Humanities: British and American Festschriften through 1980*,

2 vols. (White Plains: Kraus, scheduled for 1989) helpfully offers subject access to articles from approximately 10,000 festschriften published in North America, the United Kingdom, New Zealand, and Australia. Coverage includes language, literature, history, art history, philosophy, logic, library science, and history of science. For other bibliographies of festschriften, see Bewsey, "Festschriften Bibliographies and Indexes" (165).

400 *Readers' Guide to Periodical Literature: An Author and Subject Index* (*RG*; *Readers' Guide*). New York: Wilson, 1901– . 18/yr., with annual cumulation. AI3.R4 051.

An author, title, and subject index to about 180 popular magazines (currently) published in English. Users searching for reviews should consult the "Suggestions for . . . Use" section on the verso of the front cover for indexing practices. Since 1974, author and title (but not subject) entries for short stories are repeated in *Short Story Index* (1085). Listings from January 1983 can be searched online through WILSONLINE (525) and on CD-ROM through WILSONDISC. *Readers' Guide Abstracts* (1986– , 8/yr. and cumulated within each issue, microfiche only) includes full indexing as well as abstracts. Vol. 1 provides retrospective coverage to September 1984.

Among indexes to popular magazines, *Readers' Guide* offers the most extensive retrospective coverage; however, the following recently established indexes include a greater number of publications:

Abstrax. Galway, Ireland: Information Sources, 1984– . Fully cumulated every six weeks on microfiche. Offers subject access to abstracts of articles and reviews from 225 popular magazines in English. Coverage begins December 1982, and listings are searchable through BRS (515).

Access: The Supplementary Index to Periodicals. Evanston: Burke, 1976– . 3/yr., with annual cumulation. Indexes, by author and subject, about 140 periodicals not covered by *Readers' Guide*.

Alternative Press Index: An Index to Alternative and Radical Publications. Baltimore: Alternative Press Center, 1970– . Quarterly. Indexes about 400 English-language magazines by subject.

Magazine Index. Belmont: Information Access, 1978– . Monthly, with various cumulations; microform. Indexes more than 400 English-language magazines by author, title, and subject. Coverage begins January 1977, and entries can be searched through Dialog (520); entries since January 1980 are included in the Magazine Index Plus system in the InfoTrac data base (387).

For nineteenth-century periodicals, see Helen Grant Cushing and Adah V. Morris, eds., *Nineteenth Century Readers' Guide to Periodical Literature, 1890–1899: With Supplementary Indexing, 1900–1922*, 2 vols. (New York: Wilson, 1944); *Wellesley Index* (2545); and *Poole's Index to Periodical Literature* (4150).

These sources are occasionally useful to literary researchers for locating creative works, articles, interviews, and reviews of books, films, and plays in periodicals not covered by the standard literature indexes.

See also

Poole's Index to Periodical Literature (4150).

Bibliographies of Work in Progress

405 *Current Research in Britain: The Humanities [1985–].* Boston Spa: British Library Document Supply Centre, 1985– . Annual. Former title: *Research in British Universities, Polytechnics, and Colleges* (1979–84). AZ188.G7.C87 001.3'072041.

A register of research in progress by faculty and graduate students at universities, colleges, and other institutions in the United Kingdom. Organized by institution, then department, and then person, entries provide a brief description of projects, beginning and estimated concluding dates, proposed form of publication, and grants or other support. Three indexes: researchers; subjects; keywords in descriptions. Based on responses to questionnaires, *Current Research* is inevitably incomplete and records some projects now abandoned, but it is the best source for identifying work in progress by faculty at institutions of higher learning in the United Kingdom.

Unfortunately, nothing comparable exists for work in progress in the United States, although the Modern Language Association and Research Libraries Group are planning a data base that will record work accepted for publication in selected journals and grants funded through the NEH Research Programs Division. The data base will be available through RLIN (230) in 1989.

Book Review Indexes

Bibliographies of Bibliographies

410 Gray, Richard A., comp. *A Guide to Book Review Citations: A Bibliography of Sources.* Ohio State University Libraries Publications 2. Columbus: Ohio State UP, 1968. 223 pp. Z1035.A1.G7 016.0281.

A bibliography of serial bibliographies and indexes, closed bibliographies, and other works (through the mid-1960s) that cite reviews from more than one periodical. The 512 entries are organized by author or title in eight variously classified subject divisions: general works (including general book review indexes); philosophy and psychology; religion; social sciences (with a section for anthropology and folklore); ancient, Oriental, and African civilizations; modern languages, philology, and literature; geography and history; fine arts (with sections for the performing arts and theater and drama); and science and technology. In the language and literature division, sections for general indexes, comparative literature, and periods are followed by sections for various languages, with that for English subdivided by period. Additions are printed on pp. 194–97. Annotations first describe the general scope of a work, then the organization of review citations. Five indexes: subjects; persons who are the subjects of bibliographies; titles; works indexing reviews before 1900 and before 1800; country of origin (listing works that review or cite periodicals published in a single country). The lack of headings for sections leaves readers unable to skim effectively or locate a work easily, but the full descriptions and international coverage make Gray an indispensable guide to identifying sources that index reviews. A revised, updated edition that evaluates sources is badly needed, however.

Indexes

415 *Book Review Index*. Detroit: Gale, 1965–69, 1972– . 6/yr., with annual cumulation and one for 1965–84. Z1035.A1.B6.

An index of reviews of books and serials in about 460 (currently) newspapers, library and popular periodicals, and scholarly journals. Books reviewed are listed by author or editor; periodicals and some reference works, by title. Although it is more current than *Index to Book Reviews in the Humanities* (425), this work indexes numerous brief mentions and uncritical summaries, and covers far fewer serials that offer substantial and substantive evaluations of scholarly books. It is, however, the best source for identifying reviews of creative works and thus tracing their critical reception. Reviews since 1969 can be searched through Dialog (520). Entries for children's books are repeated in *Children's Book Review Index* (5495), but this clone and two recent cumulations—*Book Review Index: Reference Books, 1965–1984* (1986, 700 pp.) and *Book Review Index: Periodical Reviews, 1976–1984* (1987, 295 pp.)—are hardly essential for those with access to the 1965–84 cumulation.

To locate reviews before 1965, see *Book Review Digest* (New York: Wilson, 1905– , 10/yr., with annual cumulation). Because of its weak coverage of the humanities, limited scope (currently, about 80 periodicals, most of them popular), and numerous restrictions—books must be published or distributed in the United States, reviews must appear within 18 months of publication, a nonfiction work must have two reviews (fiction, four) in the periodicals indexed—*Book Review Digest* is more useful for identifying reviews of popular fiction and nonfiction than of scholarly works. Since brief excerpts from three or four reviews are reprinted and citations indicate the approximate number of words, users are generally spared from searching out the brief uncritical summaries. Cumulatively indexed in *Author/Title Index, 1905–1974*, ed. Leslie Dunmore-Leiber, 4 vols. [1976] and *1975–1984* [1986, 1,488 pp.]. Entries since April 1983 can be searched through WILSONLINE (525).

420 *Combined Retrospective Index to Book Reviews in Humanities Journals, 1802–1974*. Ed. Evan Ira Farber et al. 10 vols. Woodbridge: Research Publications, 1982–84. Z6265.C65 [AZ221] 001.3.

An index to reviews in about 150 philosophy, classics, folklore, linguistics, music, and (primarily) literature journals, all but a few of them published in English in Great Britain or North America. Although the criteria determining the choice of journals are never revealed, most of the important literature journals are indexed. The work excludes brief summaries or annotated listings, and—unfortunately—review articles whose titles do not cite the books reviewed. Organized alphabetically by primary authors or editors and then by book titles, reviews are listed by journal title and cite publication information and reviewer. Users searching for anything other than a single-author monograph should begin with the title index (vol. 10), because names are not thoroughly edited for consistency, critical editions are inconsistently entered under author or editor, authors are confused (see, e.g., Robert Herrick), reference works are usually listed by primary editor, and there are no cross-references. Unfortunately, there are numerous omissions of reviews in journals that are supposedly fully indexed. Although flawed in organization and untrustworthy in coverage, *Combined Retrospective Index* is undeniably valuable as the only source offering retrospective indexing of reviews in a significant number of scholarly humanities journals. For reviews published between 1960 and 1974, *Index to Book*

Reviews in the Humanities (425) usually offers fuller, more accurate indexing. Researchers should also check *ABELL* (340) for reviews of scholarly books.

Some additional reviews can be found in *Combined Retrospective Index to Book Reviews in Scholarly Journals, 1886–1974*, ed. Evan Ira Farber, 15 vols. (Arlington: Carrollton, 1979–82), which indexes about one million reviews in 459 scholarly periodicals in history, political science, and sociology.

425 *An Index to Book Reviews in the Humanities [1960–]*. Williamstown: Phillip Thomson, 1960– . Annual. Z1035.A1.I63 028.1.

An index to reviews in about 440 (currently) scholarly journals devoted to literature (primarily), language, philosophy, the arts, travel, biography, dance, folklore, and sports and pastimes. Coverage underwent a major change with vol. 12 (for 1971): history and social science journals were dropped; journals in major foreign languages were added; the emphasis became more literary; and except for those of children's books, all reviews—not just of humanities books—were indexed. Organized for the most part by author or editor—but occasionally by title for some reference works, with cross-references for compilers or editors—entries cite title and reviews. (Since names of authors are taken from reviews and not edited for consistency, users must check all forms of a name, including pseudonyms.) An asterisk following a title indicates that reviews are cited in the preceding volume. Since most review citations identify journals by a number code (with many omitting the *MLAIB* [335] acronym that the compiler claims to use when possible) and cite date but not volume number, users must continually flip to the prefatory list of journals (and issues) indexed and then waste time hunting out issues by date rather than the more convenient volume number. Although it omits numerous important journals, is difficult to scan in the volumes printed from uppercase computer printout, is inconsistent in covering titles, and lacks an adequate statement of criteria governing the selection of journals, *Index to Book Reviews in the Humanities* is by far the best, most trustworthy source for locating scholarly reviews of books on language and literature.

430 *Internationale Bibliographie der Rezensionen Wissenschaftlicher Literatur/International Bibliography of Book Reviews of Scholarly Literature/Bibliographie internationale des recensions de la littérature savante* (*IBR*). Osnabrück: Dietrich, 1971– . 2/yr. Z5051.I64 [AS9] 001.2.

An international index to book reviews (published since c. 1969) in journals on all subjects. Coverage extends to more than 10,000 journals published worldwide, excluding only those in Oriental languages. Currently each half-year part has five divisions:

1. The Subject Index is a keyword index to titles of books reviewed. Author, title, publication information, and reviews are listed under German headings, with cross-references in English and French. Periodicals are identified by a number keyed to the Periodical Index.
2. The Keyword Index lists, by field of knowledge, the headings and cross-references used in the Subject Index. Of most interest to literature scholars are the general, book and documentation, literature and linguistics, and fine arts fields. Because of the vagaries of subject indexing, this is a necessary complement to the Subject Index.
3. The Works Reviewed is an author index to the books listed in the Subject Index. Each author entry cites the heading under which the book is listed.

4. The Reviewers Index provides access to names of reviewers listed in the Subject Index. Each entry cites the heading under which the review is listed.
5. The Periodicals Index is an alphabetical list of periodicals cited in the Subject Index.

The work is needlessly complicated and time-consuming to use, since a researcher must consult three indexes to locate all publication information for a review. The criteria governing selection of journals and reviews have never been explained; coverage of a journal is often erratic and issues incompletely indexed; and the compilation procedures and editing hardly inspire confidence in the accuracy and thoroughness. However, the breadth of coverage—the most wide-ranging of any single index—makes *IBR* a useful complement to the other review indexes in this section. Online access is planned.

IBR continues *Internationale Bibliographie der Zeitschriftenliteratur*, Abteilung C: *Bibliographie der Rezensionen [1900–1943]*, 77 vols. (Osnabrück: Dietrich, 1901–44), which inconsistently covers non-German periodicals.

See also

Sec. G: Serial Bibliographies, Indexes, and Abstracts/Serial Bibliographies/General Bibliographies.
ABELL (340): Coverage of reviews is neither thorough nor consistent, however.
Index to Book Reviews in Religion (6350a).
Index to Reviews of Bibliographical Publications (5295).

Abstracts

The following include summaries of scholarship on more than one national literature. Those limited to a single national literature or subject will be found under the heading Abstracts in appropriate sections.

One of the major lacunae in reference works for literatures in English is a thorough, current, fully indexed abstract. Because of the discontinuation of *MLA Abstracts of Articles in Scholarly Journals* (335a) and the dim prospect that libraries could afford to support a private venture, language and literature scholars will likely never enjoy a resource comparable to *Psychological Abstracts* (6530).

435 *Abstracts of English Studies* (*AES*). Calgary: U of Calgary, 1958– . Quarterly. PE25.A16 820'.5.

Abstracts of articles published in a core list of about 750 journals (currently), all but a few publishing in English. Originally restricted to articles on English and American literature, coverage now extends to world literature in English and related literatures (defined by the editors as any "literature that has had marked influence on English literature and language"). With vol. 13 (1969), the unwieldy organization of entries by journal was replaced by a classified arrangement in four divisions (currently, general, Britain, United States, and world literature in English and related languages). Users should consult the front matter of each volume for the then current organization. The descriptive summaries tend to be brief, but frequently alert researchers to discussions of authors or topics buried in vaguely titled or general studies. Two indexes (subjects; scholars) in each issue; cumulated annually in the last issue, which also prints a list of journals abstracted in the volume. Except for literary authors and titles of anonymous works, the subject indexing is inadequate. Coverage is erratic (with unfilled gaps for many major periodicals), includes few articles in foreign languages, and is usually quite slow. Still, *AES* is currently the only general abstracting service devoted to language and literature.

440 *English and American Studies in German: Summaries of Theses and Monographs: A Supplement to* Anglia. Tübingen: Niemeyer, 1969– . Annual. PE3.A6 420'.5.

Publishes English summaries of dissertations, collections of essays, and books (primarily in German) on the English language and literatures in English. Coverage begins with 1967. Currently organized in four sections: language, English literature (British as well as other literatures in English and comparative studies), American literature (including Canadian literature), and teaching of English. Indexed by author and subject. Since *English and American Studies in German* relies on authors and editors for abstracts, coverage is incomplete but does include many studies overlooked in the standard bibliographies.

See also

Because of their international, interdisciplinary scope, the following works abstract a considerable number of literature- and language-related studies not included or inadequately indexed in standard literature and language bibliographies: *America: History and Life* (3310), *Historical Abstracts* (6500), *Psychological Abstracts* (6530), *Sociological Abstracts* (6475), *Women's Studies Abstracts* (6610).

Children's Literature Abstracts (5490).

H

Guides to Dissertations and Theses

This section includes bibliographies, indexes, and abstracts of dissertations on more than one national literature. Those devoted to a single literature, period, or topic appear in appropriate sections.

Bibliographies of Bibliographies

455 Reynolds, Michael M. *A Guide to Theses and Dissertations: An International Bibliography of Bibliographies*. Rev. and enl. ed. Phoenix: Oryx, 1985. 263 pp. Z5053.A1.R49 011'.7.

A bibliography of bibliographies, abstracts, and indexes (through mid-1984) of dissertations and theses. Reynolds includes separately published works as well as periodical contributions, but excludes general lists of theses and dissertations accepted by a single institution. The entries are generally organized by date of publication within 19 classified divisions; of most interest to language and literature scholars are the universal and national divisions (with the latter classified by country), which list the general indexes, abstracts, and bibliographies; area studies (with a section for Anglo-American studies); special and racial groups; fine arts (with a section on theater); and language and literature, with sections for general lists, African languages and literature, Anglo-American language and literature (subdivided by country), Arabic literature, Austronesian linguistics, Chinese linguistics, children's literature, classical studies, comparative literature, folklore, Germanic languages and literature, Hebrew literature, Indian languages and literature, Japanese language and literature, languages and linguistics, Philippine literature, Romance languages and literature, science fiction, Slavic and East European languages and literature, speech, and individual authors. The annotations clearly describe scope, organization, and content. Three indexes: institutions; names and journal titles;

subjects. Although the introduction is unduly murky, *Guide to Theses and Dissertations* is the essential, time-saving source for identifying both the well-known and the obscure indexes, bibliographies, and abstracts that must be searched for theses and dissertations relevant to a topic.

General Indexes

460 *Comprehensive Dissertation Index, 1861–1972* (*CDI*). 37 vols. Ann Arbor: Xerox, 1973. Annual supplements, with cumulation for 1973–82. Z5053.X47 013'.379.

A keyword index to the titles of a majority of the doctoral dissertations accepted by institutions in the United States and Canada (along with a very few dissertations from other countries). Entries are organized by broad subject divisions, then alphabetically by keyword, then chronologically by date (with the most recent first), then alphabetically by institution, and then alphabetically by author. An entry cites title, author, degree, date, institution, number of pages, source of entry, and University Microfilms International (UMI) order number for those microfilmed. Indexed by dissertation author in each cumulation and annual issue. Although *CDI* is an invaluable index to parts A and B of *Dissertation Abstracts International* (465), *American Doctoral Dissertations* (see below), *List of American Doctoral Dissertations Printed* (see below), *Canadian Theses* and its predecessors (470), and numerous institutional abstracts and indexes, users must bear in mind the following:

1. The subject organization has changed during the course of publication (e.g., in the 1861–1972 cumulation, theater is a subdivision of communications and the arts, and folklore a subdivision of social sciences; in the 1973–82 cumulation and subsequent issues, theater and folklore studies are incorporated into the language and literature division).
2. Because of the sources, there are duplicate and misclassified entries as well as numerous errors.
3. Cumulations and annual issues correct earlier entries and offer some retrospective coverage (e.g., *Canadian Theses* and its predecessors are first indexed in the 1973–82 cumulation).
4. Because *CDI* is an index of title keywords, users must check for variant spellings of names or terms, must keep in mind that many titles do not lend themselves to keyword indexing, and, if possible, search for narrow rather than broad terms (e.g., in 1861–1972, "novel" and related terms occupy 37 columns).

Doctoral dissertations and master's theses in the data base of University Microfilms International can be searched online through three services, each of which allows users to narrow a search by combining or excluding keywords and to limit it by degree date or institution:

Datrix Direct, which is updated monthly, is limited to titles in *CDI* and *Masters Abstracts International* (465a). The cost is currently $20 ($30 for those outside North America) for up to 500 citations. Search request forms are available at many libraries or from University Microfilms International, 300 North Zeeb Rd., Ann Arbor, MI 48106.

Dissertation Abstracts Online, which is updated monthly and is available through BRS (515) and Dialog (520), allows keyword searches of all of the records in Datrix Direct as well as abstracts since vol. 41 (1980) in pts. A and B of *Dissertation Abstracts International* (465).

Dissertation Abstracts Ondisc is a CD-ROM version of Dissertation Abstracts Online; however, the current system is frustrating to master, time-consuming to search, and updated only once a year.

Although an eye-straining and occasionally frustrating work to use, *CDI* offers unparalleled, time-saving subject and author access to all but a few North American doctoral dissertations.

CDI and its data bases supersede the following:

American Doctoral Dissertations [1933–] (ADD). Ann Arbor: University Microfilms International, 1934– . Annual. Former titles: *Index to American Doctoral Dissertations [1955–63]* (1957–64); *Doctoral Dissertations Accepted by American Universities [1933–55] (DDAU)*.

A List of American Doctoral Dissertations Printed in [1912–38]. Washington: GPO, 1913–40.

General Abstracts

465 *Dissertation Abstracts International* (*DAI*). Ann Arbor: University Microfilms International, 1938– . Monthly. Former titles: *Dissertation Abstracts* (*DA*) (1952–69); *Microfilm Abstracts* (1938–51). Z5053.D57 011'.7.

Pt. A: The Humanities and Social Sciences. 1966– . Monthly.
Pt. B: The Sciences and Engineering. 1966– . Monthly.
Pt. C: European Abstracts. 1976– . Quarterly.

Abstracts of doctoral dissertations accepted by North American and some foreign institutions. *DAI* now abstracts most United States and Canadian dissertations, but coverage in the early years is considerably less thorough, and some universities still do not submit abstracts or dissertations for microfilming. Coverage of dissertations outside North America is superficial. A list of participating institutions (along with the year each began sending dissertations) is printed at the beginning of each issue.

The abstracts are now organized in classified subject divisions. Currently, the language and literature division is in two parts: (1) language, with sections for general studies, ancient languages, linguistics, and modern languages; (2) literature, with sections for general, classical, comparative, medieval, modern, African, American, Asian, Canadian, English, Germanic, Latin American, Middle Eastern, Romance, and Slavic and East European literatures. Theater and cinema appear as sections in the communication and the arts division; folklore, in the social sciences division. Since placement is determined by the dissertation author, subject classification is frequently inconsistent or imprecise. Within each section, abstracts are printed in no particular order.

An entry consists of title, UMI order number, author, degree, institution, date of degree, number of pages, sometimes the dissertation advisor, and an abstract written by the author. Pt. C adds an English translation of a foreign language title and ISBN for a published dissertation or information on location or availability of a reference copy if the work is unavailable from University Microfilms. In recent years, *DAI*'s rigorous enforcement of a 350-word limit results in some abstracts being cut off in mid-sentence.

Since vol. 30 (1969), each issue has keyword title and dissertation author indexes, with the latter cumulated at the end of a volume. Earlier issues and volumes have a dissertation author index, and vols. 22–29 (1961–69) are indexed by subject. *Dissertation Abstracts International Retrospective Index, Volumes I–XXIX*, 9 vols. (Ann Arbor: Xerox, 1970) is superseded by *Comprehensive Dissertation Index* (460), Dissertation Abstracts Online (460a), or Dissertation Abstracts Ondisc (460a); however, none of these indexes pt. C. The two data bases allow keyword searches of all titles in pts. A and B of *DAI* as well as abstracts since vol. 41 (1980). The keyword access to abstracts is particularly welcome because of the sometimes imprecise subject classification of *DAI* and the recent trend toward uninformative, imprecise dissertation titles.

Copies of dissertations filmed by UMI can be purchased in microform or on paper. (See the front matter of the most recent issue of *DAI* for prices and ordering instructions.) Some dissertations are restricted and others must be ordered from the degree-granting institution; Canadian dissertations must be obtained from the National Library in Ottawa (470). For information on how to obtain British and Irish dissertations and theses, see *Index to Theses* (475). D. H. Borchardt and J. D. Thawley, comps., *Guide to the Availability of Theses*, IFLA Publications 17 (München: Saur, 1981, 443 pp.), and G. G. Allen and K. Deubert, comps., *Guide to the Availability of Theses, II: Non-University Institutions*, IFLA Publications 29 (1984, 124 pp.), outline policies governing the borrowing or copying of theses and dissertations accepted by 750 institutions in 85 countries.

Although frequently imprecise in subject classification and incomplete in coverage, *DAI* offers an invaluable service in making available abstracts of so many dissertations.

North American dissertations not abstracted in *DAI* are listed in *American Doctoral Dissertations* (460a).

Masters Abstracts International (Ann Arbor: University Microfilms, 1962– , quarterly) is similar in organization to *DAI* but abstracts a relatively small percentage of the annual output of master's theses even in the United States. Each volume has cumulative author and subject indexes, and titles can be searched by keyword through UMI's data bases.

National Bibliographies and Abstracts

470 *Canadian Theses/Thèses canadiennes [1961–]*. Ottawa: National Library of Canada, 1963– . 2/yr., with cumulative index. Microfiche only since *1980–1981* (1984–). *1947–1960*. 2 vols. 1973. Z5055.C2 013'.375'0971.

A bibliography of theses and dissertations accepted by Canadian institutions since 1947 or microfilmed by the National Library since 1981 and, beginning with the *1980–1981* volumes, foreign theses and dissertations by Canadians or related to Canada. Currently, entries are listed in processing order in two parts: works accepted by Canadian institutions; those by Canadians or about the country accepted by foreign institutions. Entries cite author, title, degree, institution, and date. Access to the parts is provided by five indexes (which cumulate with each issue): author and title; title keywords; Dewey Decimal Classification; Canadian theses on microfiche series number; ISBN. Before *1980–1981*, entries are organized by Dewey Decimal Classification.

This work continues *Canadian Graduate Theses in the Humanities and Social Sciences, 1921–1946/Thèses des gradués canadiens dans les humanités et les sciences sociales* (Ottawa: Cloutier, 1951, 194 pp.). Together, the two sources provide the fullest coverage of theses and dissertations accepted by Canadian institutions; however, researchers will find those on literature easier to identify in Antoine Naaman and Léo A. Brodeur, *Répertoire des thèses littéraires canadiennes de 1921 à 1976*, Collection "Bibliographies" 3 (Sherbrooke: Naaman, 1978, 453 pp.), a subject list that includes a few works in progress as of March 1976 and some written by Canadians at foreign universities. Canadian theses and dissertations on Canadian literature are covered by Gabel, *Canadian Literature* (4660); several on British or American literature are listed in McNamee, *Dissertations in English and American Literature* (490). Many Canadian dissertations are listed in *American Doctoral Dissertations* (460a) and abstracted in *Dissertation Abstracts International* (465). For other bibliographies of Canadian dissertations and theses, see Denis Robitaille and Joan Waiser, *Theses in Canada: A Bibliographic Guide/Thèses au Canada: Guide bibliographique* (Ottawa: National Library of Canada, 1986, 72 pp.).

The quickest way to search *Canadian Theses* and its predecessor is through *Comprehensive Dissertation Index* (beginning with the 1973–82 cumulation, which also has retrospective coverage), Datrix Direct, Dissertation Abstracts Online, or Dissertation Abstracts Ondisc (460).

475 *Index to Theses with Abstracts Accepted for Higher Degrees by the Universities of Great Britain and Ireland and the Council for National Academic Awards*. London: Aslib, 1953– . Quarterly. Title varies slightly. Z5055.G69.A84 013'.379'0941.

A list of bachelor's, master's, and doctoral theses accepted since 1950 by academic institutions in the British Isles. Currently, entries are listed alphabetically by author within classified subject divisions, including one for arts and humanities, with subdivisions for theater, cinema, and broadcasting; linguistics; and literature. The last has sections for general, classical, English (divided by period), American, Celtic, Romance (divided by language), Germanic (divided by language), Icelandic and Old Norse, Slavonic, and other languages. The organization has changed over the years. An entry includes title, author, institution, degree, date, and—since vol. 35 (1986)—an abstract. Variations in institutional policies mean that the date can refer to submission, acceptance, or award of degree. Two indexes in each issue: authors; subjects. Prefacing an issue is a guide to each institution's policies governing access to its theses. This source is the essential index to British and Irish theses after 1950.

Since 1988, many British doctoral dissertations are abstracted in *Dissertation Abstracts International* (465) and available through University Microfilms International. The best general source for copies, however, remains the British Document Supply Centre, Boston Spa, Wetherby, West Yorkshire, Eng. LS23 7BQ.

Retrospective coverage is offered by *Retrospective Index to Theses of Great Britain and Ireland, 1716–1950*, ed. Roger R. Bilboul, vol. 1: *Social Sciences and Humanities* (Santa Barbara: ABC-Clio, 1975, 393 pp.) and *Addenda* (1977, 26 pp.). Entries citing author, title, degree, date, and institution appear in two parts: (1) a subject index, which is based largely but not exclusively on title keywords, offers liberal cross-references, and provides several multiple entries; and (2) an author list. Since *Retrospective Index* is compiled from information supplied by institutions, there are inconsistencies and errors; however, it is the best index to pre-1951 British and Irish theses on language and literature.

480 *Union List of Higher Degree Theses in Australian University Libraries: Cumulative Edition to 1965*. Hobart: U of Tasmania Library, 1967. 568 pp. *Supplement, [1966–]*. 1971– . Irregular. Since the supplement for 1974, the main title omits *University*. Z5055.A698 011'.7.

A union list of master's theses and doctoral dissertations accepted by Australian universities and held by at least one Australian university library. Works are organized alphabetically by author within extensively classified subject divisions (including, in recent supplements, folklore, language, literature, and theater). Two indexes: authors; subject headings (the supplements have an additional one for title keywords). Although the subject classification is sometimes imprecise because it is based largely on titles, and although coverage is not exhaustive, *Union List* offers the fullest record of theses and dissertations accepted by Australian universities.

The prefatory matter of the most recent supplement discusses the availability of theses in Australian university libraries. For additional information, see *How to Locate Australian Theses: A Guide to Theses in Progress or Completed at Australian Universities and the University of Papua New Guinea* (Canberra: Library, Australian National U, 1979, 41 pp.).

See also

English and American Studies in German (440).

Other Bibliographies

485 Gabel, Gernot U., and Gisela R. Gabel, comps. *Dissertations in English and American Literature: Theses Accepted by Austrian, French, and Swiss Universities, 1875–1970*. Hamburg: Gabel, 1977. 198 pp. *Dissertations in English and American Literature: A Bibliography of Theses Accepted by Austrian, French, and Swiss Universities: Supplement, 1971–1975, and Additions*. Köln: Gemini, 1982. 56 pp. Z2011.G25 [PR83] 016.82.

A bibliography of 2,588 doctoral-level theses compiled from the standard national dissertation bibliographies (and university lists in the case of Austria) of the three countries. Dissertations are listed chronologically in nine classified divisions: general literary history and criticism, Old and Middle English literature, then by century for English literature, American literature to 1900, and twentieth-century American literature. The period divisions have sections for general studies or individual authors. Two indexes: scholars; literary authors and anonymous works (with fuller subject indexing in the supplement). A time-saving compilation that offers the single fullest list of dissertations on English and American literature accepted by universities in the three countries.

490 McNamee, Lawrence F. *Dissertations in English and American Literature: Theses Accepted by American, British, and German Universities, 1865–1964*. New York: Bowker, 1968. 1,124 pp. *Supplement One, 1964–1968*. 1969. 450 pp. *Supplement Two: Theses Accepted by American, British, British Commonwealth, and German Universities, 1969–1973*. 1974. 690 pp. Z5053.M32 016.82.

A subject bibliography of dissertations written in English departments of institutions in the United States, Great Britain, East and West Germany, Canada (beginning in the first supplement and including retrospective coverage), Australia (beginning in the first supplement), and New Zealand (in the second supplement). Derived from lists supplied or checked by the institutions, the 25,953 entries are organized by date of acceptance in 35 classified divisions: Anglo-Saxon; English language and linguistics; Chaucer; Middle English; Renaissance; Shakespeare; seventeenth century; Milton; eighteenth century; Romantic period; Victorian period; twentieth century; drama and theater; English novel; poetry; comparative literature; literary criticism, rhetoric, and genre studies; creative dissertations; teaching of English; Empire literature; magazines, newspapers, and publishing; religion and literature; Colonial American; National period; post–Civil War period; twentieth-century American literature; American novel and fiction; American drama and theater; literary criticism in the United States; language in the United States; regional literature; African-American literature; American poetry; American literary relationships; miscellaneous topics in American literature. Most divisions are extensively classified by subjects, groups, genres, movements, or ˙ndividual authors. An entry consists of author, title, date of acceptance, a code number that identifies the institution, and, in the 1969–73 supplement, number of pages. Two indexes in each volume: a cross-index of literary authors in the titles of multiple-author studies; dissertation writers.

McNamee must be used with due regard for its numerous limitations and deficiencies:

1. The work falls far short of the complete list it claims to be. Restricted to studies written in English departments, it ignores numerous dissertations on English and American literature produced in history, comparative literature, and (especially) theater or drama departments. And there are many omissions of dissertations accepted by English departments.
2. Dissertations are frequently difficult to locate because titles determine placement in divisions and classified sections, many of which are insufficiently exclusive. Particularly vexing are the numerous classified sections which are frequently imprecise in heading, inconsistent across divisions, and organized in no discernible manner (e.g., related topics are rarely grouped together). Because a dissertation is listed in only one section and multiple-author studies are placed under the first author mentioned, users searching for dissertations on specific writers must be certain to check the cross-index of authors, which is unhelpfully keyed to the numbered sections rather than to pages. The vagueness and inconsistencies in subject classifications and inadequate indexing mean that researchers must exercise considerable ingenuity to locate dissertations.
3. There are numerous typographical errors, and the combination of uppercase computer print and poor layout makes for inefficient scanning.

Because of these serious limitations and deficiencies, McNamee is now principally useful for identifying the occasional dissertation overlooked in a search of the more thorough and easily accessible *Comprehensive Dissertation Index* (460) and the other bibliographies and abstracts in this section.

495 Mummendey, Richard. *Language and Literature of the Anglo-Saxon Nations as Presented in German Doctoral Dissertations, 1885–1950/Die Sprache und Literatur der Angelsachsen im Spiegel der deutschen Universitätsschriften, 1885–1950*. Bonn: Bouvier; Charlottesville: Bibliographical Soc. of the U of Virginia, 1954. 200 pp. Z2011.M8 016.82.

A classified list of doctoral dissertations on the English language and literature in English accepted by German universities between 1885 and 1950, by the University of Strassburg to 1918, and by Austrian universities from 1938 to 1945. The approximately 3,000 entries are organized in three divisions: linguistics, with dissertations listed by year of acceptance within sections for general studies, phonetics, orthography, morphology, etymology, syntax, dialect and slang, stylistics, and prosody; literature, with sections for Great Britain (including subsections for genres, motifs and topics, influences, and individual periods), the Commonwealth, and the United States (including subsections for general studies and individual periods); theater. In the literature and theater divisions, dissertations are organized alphabetically by a title keyword, which is set in spaced type. An entry cites author, title, number of pages, publication information for dissertations published in a series or periodical, an indication of manuscript ("HS") or typescript ("MS") for those not printed, institution, and year of acceptance. Indexed by dissertation authors and title keywords.

The subject indexing by title keyword is frequently imprecise or misleading (and the spaced type is not immediately recognizable), but the poor subject indexing is a minor deficiency in comparison to the frequent errors in citations and numerous omissions. (In *Guide to Doctoral Dissertations in Victorian Literature* [2510], Altick reports that he discovered about 130 dissertations overlooked by Mummendey.) While useful for compiling a preliminary list of German dissertations on a topic, Mummendey must be supplemented by a laborious search through *Jahresverzeichnis der Hochschulschriften der DDR, der BRD und Westberlins [1885–]* (Leipzig: VEB Bibliographisches Institut, 1887– ; title varies).

See also

Dundes, *Folklore Theses and Dissertations in the United States* (5885).
Fielding, *Bibliography of Theses and Dissertations on the Subject of Film, 1916–1979* (5795).
Gilbert, *Women's Studies: A Bibliography of Dissertations, 1870–1982* (6615).

I

Data Bases

The following vendors offer access to computer-readable files of several reference sources in this *Guide*. Subscribing libraries employ trained personnel who can help a researcher define search strategies and in some instances do the actual search. Individual users should contact vendors for current rates, software requirements, and guides to searching specific data bases. For current descriptions of new and existing data bases, consult the most recent issue of *Directory of Online Databases* (1979– ; quarterly).

Researchers should also watch for CD-ROM versions of data bases. Among those currently available are *MLAIB* (335), ERIC (5590), *Books in Print* (4225), *Psychological Abstracts* (6530), *Dissertation Abstracts International* (465), and several Wilson indexes (525).

510 BLAISE-LINE. British Library, Bibliographic Services Division, 2 Sheraton St., London W1V 4BH.

Offers access to the following data bases of interest to language and literature scholars: *British Books in Print* (2770), Conference Proceedings Index (publications since the nineteenth century, with fuller coverage since 1964); DPB (works published since 1971 and acquired since 1976 by the British Library Department of Printed Books; see 250a); *ESTC* (2230); ISTC (Incunable Short Title Catalogue) (1820a); LC MARC (235a); SIGLE ("grey" literature, including theses, proceedings, and research reports); UK MARC (the online equivalent of *British National Bibliography* [2775], with bibliographic records for British books and serials published since 1950). The *BLAISE Newsletter* keeps users informed of new data bases and system features. Data bases can be searched by author, title word(s), series, Dewey and Library of Congress classification numbers, and subject. Researchers without direct access to BLAISE-LINE can have searches performed by the Bibliographic Services Division.

515 BRS Information Technologies. 1200 Rte. 7, Latham, NY 12110. 800–345–4277.

BRS/SEARCH service offers access to the following data bases of interest to language and literature scholars: *Arts and Humanities Citation Index* (365), *Books in Print* (4225), Bowker's International Serials Database (625a), Dissertation Abstracts Online (460a), ERIC (5590), *Guide to Microforms in Print* (6210), *LLBA:*

Linguistics and Language Behavior Abstracts (6015), *Magazine Index* (400a), OCLC subject search (225), PsycINFO (6530), *Religion Index* (6350), Social SciSearch (6470a), and *Sociological Abstracts* (6475). For individual subscribers BRS publishes a user's manual that outlines search strategies and fully describes each data base. The bimonthly *BRS Bulletin* informs users about new data bases and refinements to existing ones.

520 Dialog Information Services, Inc. 3460 Hillview Ave., Palo Alto, CA 94304. 415–858–3810.

Offers access to the largest variety of data bases useful to language and literature researchers: *America: History and Life* (3310), *American Library Directory* (200a), *ARTbibliographies Modern* (5140), *Biography and Genealogy Master Index* (565), *Book Review Index* (415), *Books in Print* (4225), Bowker's International Serials Database (625a), *British Books in Print* (2770), Dissertation Abstracts Online (460a), *Encyclopedia of Associations* (5085), ERIC (5590), *Historical Abstracts* (6500), LC MARC (235a), *LLBA: Linguistics and Language Behavior Abstracts* (6015), *Magazine Index* (400a), *Who's Who* (3395), *MLAIB* (335), *National Newspaper Index* (3420), *Philosopher's Index* (6275), PsycINFO (6530), REMARC (235a), *RILA* (5155), *RILM Abstracts* (6240), *Religion Index* (6350), Social SciSearch (6470a), and *Sociological Abstracts* (6475). *Chronolog*, a monthly newsletter, keeps users informed about new and updated data bases.

525 WILSONLINE. H. W. Wilson Co., 950 University Ave., Bronx, NY 10452. 800–367–6770.

Offers online access to several of the popular Wilson indexes: *Art Index* (5145), *Bibliographic Index* (145), *Biography Index* (540), *Book Review Digest* (415a), *Cumulative Book Index* (375), *Education Index* (5590a), *Humanities Index* (385), and *Readers' Guide* (400). Data bases are updated twice each week and include an online thesaurus. In addition, WILSONLINE offers access to *MLAIB* (335) beginning with the volume for 1981.

Many of these sources are also available on CD-ROM through WILSONDISC. Although the discs are updated only quarterly, subscribers to a disc receive unlimited free searching of the data base through WILSONLINE.

J

Biographical Sources

This section includes the important general bibliographies, indexes, and biographical dictionaries. Those devoted to residents of a single country are listed with the appropriate national literature.

General Bibliographies and Indexes

Serial Bibliographies

540 *Biography Index: A Quarterly Index to Biographical Material in Books and Magazines*. New York: Wilson, 1946– . Quarterly, with annual and larger cumulations. Z5301.B5 016.92.

A biographee index to biographical material and obituaries in (currently) about 2,600 periodicals (almost all in English and covered by other Wilson indexes), a few books (including chapters therein), and some collective biographies and biographical dictionaries. A majority of the individuals covered are Americans. Indexed in each issue and cumulation by professions and occupations. Highly selective and providing no explanation of the criteria governing the selection process, the source is useful principally for locating biographical material in periodicals. Entries since July 1984 can be searched through WILSONLINE (525) and on CD-ROM through WILSONDISC. Entries are also indexed in the 1981–85 cumulation and later volumes of *Biography and Genealogy Master Index* (565).

Other Bibliographies

545 *Bibliography of Biography, 1970–1984.* London: British Library Bibliographic Services Division, 1985. Annual supplements. Microfiche.

A bibliography of some 95,000 biographical books published worldwide between 1970 and 1984 and cataloged by the British Library Bibliographic Services or the Library of Congress. Entries (which reproduce full cataloging information) are organized alphabetically by biographee. Indexed by biographers and titles. Although covering a limited number of years, this work is a useful starting point for locating recent biographies.

550 *Biographical Books, 1876–1949.* New York: Bowker, 1983. 1,768 pp. Z5301.B48 [CT104] 016.92'002. *Biographical Books, 1950–1980.* New York: Bowker, 1980. 1,557 pp. Z5301.B68 [CT104] 016.92'002.

A biographee and subject index to biographical books (including biographies, autobiographies, collective biographies, collections of letters, diaries, journals, and biographical dictionaries) published, reprinted, or distributed in the United States between 1876 and 1980. Each entry prints card catalog copy as it appears in Bowker's *American Book Publishing Record* (4110) data base. Three indexes: vocations (at the beginning); authors; titles. (The *1950–1980* volume prints a superfluous list of books in print.) The total reliance on card catalog tracings to generate biographee and subject headings leads to the placement of numerous books under vague or general subject heads, the failure to list many works under biographees, the needless duplication of entries, and an incomplete index of vocations. The uncritical reliance on computer generated indexing and utter lack of editing has produced a seriously flawed work that, while occasionally useful, cannot be relied on to identify biographical books about an individual.

555 Jarboe, Betty M. *Obituaries: A Guide to Sources.* Boston: Hall, 1982. 370 pp. Z5305.U5.J37 [CT214] 016.929'373.

A bibliography of indexes through c. 1980—including serial publications, books, articles, and a few manuscripts—of obituaries in newspapers and periodicals. Although international in coverage, *Obituaries* emphasizes indexes of American sources. Entries are organized alphabetically (usually by title, but sometimes by author or corporate author) in three divisions: international sources, United States (with sections for general studies and for each state), and foreign (with sections for Great Britain, France, Germany, and other countries). Bibliographical information is incomplete for several works; a few entries are accompanied by a brief description of scope. An appendix lists by state the location of obituary card files for the United States. Two indexes: subjects; authors. Although the work is inconsistent in organizing and presenting information—with several entries based on other works rather than on personal examination—and sketchy in covering foreign sources, Jarboe leads researchers to the major—as well as several obscure and local—indexes to obituaries.

Biographical Dictionaries

There is no adequate evaluative guide to the hundreds of biographical dictionaries that compete for space on library shelves. Sheehy, *Guide to Reference Books* (60), pp. 279–313, and Walford, *Walford's Guide to Reference Material* (65), vol. 2, pp. 491–519, describe—but too rarely compare or evaluate—major current and retrospective ones. For dictionaries published since c. 1965 and still in print, Bohdan S. Wynar, ed. *ARBA Guide to Biographical Dictionaries* (Littleton: Libraries Unlimited, 1986, 444 pp.), offers some guidance. It is composed largely of entries from *American Reference Books Annual* (745); neither selection nor evaluation is as rigorous as it should be.

Bibliographies

560 Slocum, Robert B., ed. *Biographical Dictionaries and Related Works: An International Bibliography of More Than 16,000 Collective Biographies, Bio-Bibliographies, Collections of Epitaphs, Selected Genealogical Works, Dictionaries of Anonyms and Pseudonyms, Historical and Specialized Dictionaries, Biographical Materials in Government Manuals, Bibliographies of Biography, Biographical Indexes, and Selected Portrait Catalogs*. 2nd ed. 2 vols. Detroit: Gale, 1986. Z5301.S55 [CT104] 016.92.

An international bibliography of collective biographies, principally biographical dictionaries of more than 100 entries, but also including related kinds of works. Slocum omits most collections devoted to a limited geographical area or unit of a national government. Works are listed alphabetically by author or title in three divisions: universal biographies, national or geographical area works (variously subdivided by country, then region, state, or city), and vocational biographies (subdivided by vocation, then geographical area). When necessary, the divisions and subdivisions begin with sections for bibliographies and indexes, dictionaries of anonyms and pseudonyms, and general works. Entries cite author or editor, title, and publication information; most are accompanied by a brief description of scope or content and a note on other editions or related works. Three indexes: authors and editors; titles; subjects. Although largely uncritical in annotations, not always accurate in its information, and covering Western Europe and North America more fully than the rest of the world, Slocum is the most complete list of these numerous dictionaries.

Indexes

565 *Biography and Genealogy Master Index: A Consolidated Index to More Than 3,200,000 Biographical Sketches in over 345 Current and Retrospective Biographical Dictionaries*. Ed. Miranda C. Herbert and Barbara McNeil. 2nd ed. 8 vols. Gale Biographical Index Series 1. Detroit: Gale, 1980. Annual supplements, with quinquennial cumulations. Also published in microfiche as *Bio-Base*. Z5305.U5.B56 [CT214] 920'.073.

A name index to entries in a wide variety of popular and scholarly English-language biographical dictionaries, most of which are regularly updated compilations published in the United States. As of 1987, some six million entries on living and dead individuals, the majority of whom are American or British, are listed. An entry provides name, birth and death dates, and a coded list of dictionaries. Since variations in the form and spelling of names and discrepancies in dates are not edited for consistency, numerous individuals have several entries; thus users must be certain to check all variant spellings, discrepancies in birth and death dates, and combinations of prename, middle name, initials, and surname. Although accessibility would be improved by some judicious editing and although the *Master Index* omits some of the major retrospective works (such as the main volumes of *Dictionary of National Biography* [1425]), it is a valuable, time-saving source for determining in which of the numerous general and specialized biographical dictionaries an individual would be found. Coverage of literary figures is especially strong. Entries are searchable through Dialog (520). Review: Bruce Bonta and Frances Cable, *RSR: Reference Services Review* 10.1 (1982): 25–33.

Gale has used this data base to produce several clones, some of which include additional entries; those of most interest to literary researchers are the following:

Artist Biographies Master Index. Ed. Barbara McNeil. 1986. 700 pp.

Author Biographies Master Index. Ed. McNeil and Miranda C. Herbert. 2nd ed. 2 vols. 1984. *Supplement*. Ed. McNeil. 1987. 409 pp.

Biography Almanac: A Comprehensive Reference Guide to More Than 24,000 Famous and Infamous Newsmakers from Biblical Times to the Present as Found in over 550 Readily Available Biographical Sources. 3rd ed. Ed. Susan L. Stetler. 3 vols. 1987. Incl. chronological, geographical, and occupation indexes.

Children's Authors and Illustrators (5500).

Historical Biographical Dictionaries Master Index. Ed. McNeil and Herbert. 1980. 1,003 pp.

Performing Arts Biography Master Index. Ed. McNeil and Herbert. 2nd ed. 1982. 701 pp.

Twentieth-Century Author Biographies Master Index. Ed. McNeil. 1984. 519 pp.

Writers for Young Adults: Biographies Master Index (5500a).

Although the work has largely been superseded, Patricia Pate Havlice, *Index to Literary Biography*, 2 vols. (Metuchen: Scarecrow, 1975) and *First Supplement*, 2 vols. (1983), does index some biographical dictionaries of foreign authors that are omitted from *Biography and Genealogy Master Index*.

570 *IBN: Index Bio-Bibliographicus Notorum Hominum* (*IBN*). Ed. Jean-Pierre Lobies, Denise Masson-Steinbart, and François-Pierre Lobies. 5 pts. Osnabrück: Biblio, 1972– . Z5301.L7 [CT104] 016.92.

Pars A: *Allgemeine Einführung/General Introduction/Introduction générale*. In progress.

Pars B: *Liste der ausgewerteten bio-bibliographischen Werke/List of the Evaluated Bio-Bibliographical Works/Liste des ouvrages bio-bibliographiques dépouillés*. 1973– .

Pars C: *Corpus Alphabeticum*.

I. *Sectio Generalis*. 1974– .

II. *Sectio Islamica*.

III. *Sectio Armeniaca*. 1982– .

IV. *Sectio Indica.*
V. *Sectio Japonica.*
VI. *Sectio Sinica.* 1976– .
Pars D: *Supplementum.*
Pars E: *Gesamtregister der Verweisungen/General Index of References/ Table générale des renvois.*

A massive index to entries in several thousand universal and specialized biographical dictionaries published throughout the world. The sources are listed in pt. B, with periodic supplements in volumes of the *Corpus Alphabeticum* (see *Sectio Generalis*, pp. 23–25). In the *Corpus Alphabeticum*, a typical entry cites name; birth and death dates; occupation, residence, birthplace, or other information that distinguishes between persons with the same name; and coded references to the sources listed in *List of the Evaluated Bio-Bibliographical Works*. Supplementary listings for the portion of the alphabet already covered appear at intervals in volumes of *Corpus Alphabeticum* (see *Sectio Generalis*, pp. 9–12 and 27–30). Entries follow sources in forms of names, with cross-references for variant forms and pseudonyms. Because the *General Introduction* (which will explain principles of compilation, guidelines for using the work, and transliteration practices) has not been published, the scope, organization, and criteria governing selection of sources remain unclear. It appears that *Corpus Alphabeticum: Sectio Generalis* covers persons of all nationalities other than those accorded a separate *sectio*. In contrast to *Biography and Genealogy Master Index*, *IBN* emphasizes retrospective dictionaries rather than regularly updated compilations and is far more international in scope; however, publication of *Corpus Alphabeticum: Sectio Generalis* had reached only the middle of *C* by 1986. When finished, *IBN* will provide an invaluable, time-saving source for identifying which biographical dictionaries print an entry on an individual.

See also

Arnim, *Internationale Personalbibliographie* (160).
Wearing, *American and British Theatrical Biography* (1175).

General Biographical Dictionaries

RETROSPECTIVE DICTIONARIES

575 *Biographie universelle (Michaud) ancienne et moderne, ou histoire, par ordre alphabétique, de la vie publique et privée de tous les hommes qui se sont fait remarquer par leurs écrits, leurs actions, leurs talents, leurs vertus ou leurs crimes* (Michaud). [Ed. J. F. Michaud, L. G. Michaud, and E. E. Desplaces.] New ed. 45 vols. Paris: Desplaces; Leipzig: Brockhaus, 1843–65. CT143.M5.

An extensive universal biographical dictionary of eminent and notorious persons. The signed articles, ranging from a few lines to several pages, frequently include a list of works by the entrant. Although badly dated, Michaud is the best of the older universal dictionaries and remains a useful source of information on numerous minor figures.

Less trustworthy but including more minor figures through the letter *M* is *Nouvelle biographie générale depuis les temps les plus reculés jusqu'à nos jours*, ed. [Jean Chrétien Ferdinand] Hoefer, 46 vols. (Paris: Didot, 1857–66).

For a detailed evaluation and comparison of the two works—along with a summary of the legal action brought by Michaud and Desplaces against Didot for plagiarism—see [R. C. Christie, "Biographical Dictionaries,"] *Quarterly Review* 157 (1884): 187–230.

580 *Webster's New Biographical Dictionary*. Springfield: Merriam-Webster, 1983. 1,130 pp. CT103.W4 920'.02.

A compilation of biographical data on some 30,000 dead individuals who were "important, celebrated, or notorious" from c. 3100 BC to the twentieth century. A revision of the venerable *Webster's Biographical Dictionary* (Springfield: Merriam, with several revised printings from 1943 to 1980), the later work now omits living persons and increases coverage of non-English-speaking countries, especially in the Third World. The brief entries provide surname (indicating end-of-line division and pronunciation); prename; titles, epithets, pseudonyms, or nicknames; birth and death dates; nationality or ethnic group; occupations; birthplace (primarily for Americans and Canadians); and brief career details. Concludes with a guide to pronunciation of name elements, titles, and prenames. Although vague about criteria determining selection, *New Biographical Dictionary* remains the best desktop source of basic biographical information and pronunciation of names for important individuals.

Chambers Biographical Dictionary, ed. J. O. Thorne and T. C. Collocott, rev. ed. (Cambridge: Cambridge UP, 1984, 1,493 pp.) covers only about 15,000 persons but offers fuller, albeit not always accurate, information.

CURRENT DICTIONARIES

585 *Current Biography*. New York: Wilson, 1940– . 11/yr., with annual cumulation and revision as *Current Biography Yearbook*. CT100.C8 920'.009'04.

Biographies of persons throughout the world who are currently "prominent in the news." Issues also include revised biographies and obituaries of previous entrants. Based on popular sources and information from the biographees, the approximately 2,500 word sketches provide basic biographical data, address, an interpretative account of the person's career and achievements, and a list of sources. The annual cumulations classify entrants by profession and provide a cumulative index for the current decade. Cumulatively indexed in *Current Biography Cumulated Index, 1940–1985*, ed. Mary E. Kiffer (1986, 125 pp.); the yearbooks are also indexed in *Biography and Genealogy Master Index* (565). Although formulaic in organization, predictable in style, and usually uncritical in interpretation, *Current Biography* does treat a substantial number of writers from throughout the world.

590 *The International Who's Who*. London: Europa, 1935– . Annual. CT120.I5 920.01.

A biographical dictionary of living notable and eminent individuals from throughout the world (including some 18,000 persons in the 52nd ed., 1988). The compact entries provide basic biographical and career information, selected publications and awards, and address. A list of reigning royal families appears at the beginning. Some volumes are indexed in *Biography and Genealogy Master Index* (565). This work is generally accounted the best of the who's who dictionaries that attempt international coverage. Among others of this kind, *Who's Who in the World* (Wilmette: Marquis, 1970– , biennial) is sometimes useful.

See also

Directory of American Scholars (5070a).

Dictionaries of Writers

595 *Contemporary Authors: A Bio-Bibliographical Guide to Current Writers in Fiction, General Nonfiction, Poetry, Journalism, Drama, Motion Pictures, Television, and Other Fields*. Detroit: Gale, 1962– . Z1224.C6 928.1.

A dictionary of twentieth-century writers, scholars, and critics whose books have been published by legitimate publishers in the United States. Although emphasizing living authors who write in English, *Contemporary Authors* includes foreigners whose works have been translated into English as well as many persons who died since 1900. (Until vol. 104 [1982], the only deceased persons included were those who died after 1959.) Entries are of three types:

1. Sketches are full entries that provide basic biographical and career information; home, office, and/or agent address; memberships; awards and honors; publications; work in progress; sidelights (e.g., a comment by the biographee or quotations from reviews or criticism); avocational interests; selected biographical and critical sources; and occasionally an interview.
2. Brief entries give basic biographical details and a list of selected publications; many of the brief entries are expanded into sketches in subsequent volumes.
3. Obituaries of both previous entrants and other writers include references to obituaries in other publications or biographical sources; many obituaries are expanded or revised as sketches in subsequent volumes.

All entries in vols. 1–44 are revised or reprinted in *Contemporary Authors: First Revision*, 44 vols. (1967–79). A few early entries for writers who later died or became inactive are revised or reprinted in *Contemporary Authors: Permanent Series*, 2 vols. (1975–78). Revised or updated entries now appear in *Contemporary Authors: New Revision Series* (1981–). All these sources are complemented by the following:

Contemporary Authors: Autobiography Series. 1984– . A collection of extensively illustrated autobiographical essays of 10,000 words written especially for the series.

Contemporary Authors: Bibliographical Series (4245).

Because of the numerous series and frequent revisions, users must consult the cumulative index in the most recent even-numbered volume of *Contemporary Authors: A Bio-Bibliographical Guide* to locate the most current entry on a writer. (The cumulative index also includes other Gale biographical dictionaries such as

Dictionary of Literary Biography [600].) The biographical entries are also indexed in *Biography and Genealogy Master Index* (565).

Although a majority of the entries are based on information supplied (and subsequently checked) by a biographee, agent, or family member, there are omissions and errors; however, currency and scope make *Contemporary Authors* a valuable source for information about and addresses of living British and American writers.

Other useful, but less comprehensive, sources for biographical information on writers include the following:

International Authors and Writers Who's Who. [Ed. Adrian Gaster. 9th ed.]; *International Who's Who in Poetry.* [Gen. ed. Ernest Kay. 6th ed.] Cambridge: International Biographical Centre, 1982. 1,093 pp. Made up of quite compact biographical entries, this work is most useful as a source of addresses. Indexed in *Biography and Genealogy Master Index* (565).

Twentieth Century Authors: A Biographical Dictionary of Modern Literature. Ed. Stanley J. Kunitz and Howard Haycraft. New York: Wilson, 1942. 1,577 pp. *First Supplement.* Ed. Kunitz and Vineta Colby. 1955. 1,123 pp. The work is continued as *World Authors, 1950–1970*, ed. John Wakeman, Authors Series (1975, 1,594 pp.); *World Authors, 1970–1975*, ed. Wakeman, Wilson Authors Series (1980, 894 pp.); *World Authors, 1975–1980*, ed. Colby, Wilson Authors Series (1985, 829 pp.). Selection in the preceding works is based on importance or popularity. Others in the series—*American Authors, 1600–1900: A Biographical Dictionary of American Literature*, ed. Kunitz and Haycraft (1938, 846 pp.); *British Authors before 1800: A Biographical Dictionary*, ed. Kunitz and Haycraft (1952, 584 pp.); *British Authors of the Nineteenth Century*, ed. Kunitz and Haycraft (1936, 677 pp.); and *European Authors, 1000–1900: A Biographical Dictionary of European Literature*, ed. Kunitz and Colby, Authors Series (1967, 1,016 pp.)—are too dated to be of much value. All the preceding works are indexed in *Index to the Wilson Author Series* (1986, 104 pp.) and in *Biography and Genealogy Master Index* (565).

600 *Dictionary of Literary Biography* (*DLB*). Detroit: Gale, 1978– . PS221.D5.

Vol. 1: *The American Renaissance in New England.* Ed. Joel Myerson. 1978. 224 pp.

Vol. 2: *American Novelists since World War II.* Ed. Jeffrey Helterman and Richard Layman. 1978. 557 pp.

Vol. 3: *Antebellum Writers in New York and the South.* Ed. Myerson. 1979. 383 pp.

Vol. 4: *American Writers in Paris, 1920–1939.* Ed. Karen Lane Rood. 1980. 426 pp.

Vol. 5: *American Poets since World War II.* Ed. Donald J. Greiner. 2 pts. 1980.

Vol. 6: *American Novelists since World War II: Second Series.* Ed. James E. Kibler, Jr. 1980.

Vol. 7: *Twentieth-Century American Dramatists.* Ed. John MacNicholas. 2 pts. 1981.

Vol. 8: *Twentieth-Century American Science-Fiction Writers*. Ed. David Cowart and Thomas L. Wymer. 2 pts. 1981.
Vol. 9: *American Novelists, 1910–1945*. Ed. James J. Martine. 3 pts. 1981.
Vol. 10: *Modern British Dramatists, 1900–1945*. Ed. Stanley Weintraub. 2 pts. 1982.
Vol. 11: *American Humorists, 1800–1950*. Ed. Stanley Trachtenberg. 2 pts. 1982.
Vol. 12: *American Realists and Naturalists*. Ed. Donald Pizer and Earl N. Harbert. 1982. 486 pp.
Vol. 13: *British Dramatists since World War II*. Ed. Weintraub. 2 pts. 1982.
Vol. 14: *British Novelists since 1960*. Ed. Jay L. Halio. 2 pts. 1983.
Vol. 15: *British Novelists, 1930–1959*. Ed. Bernard Oldsey. 2 pts. 1983.
Vol. 16: *The Beats: Literary Bohemians in Postwar America*. Ed. Ann Charters. 2 pts. 1983.
Vol. 17: *Twentieth-Century American Historians*. Ed. Clyde N. Wilson. 1983. 519 pp.
Vol. 18: *Victorian Novelists after 1885*. Ed. Ira B. Nadel and William E. Fredeman. 1983. 392 pp.
Vol. 19: *British Poets, 1880–1914*. Ed. Donald E. Stanford. 1983. 486 pp.
Vol. 20: *British Poets, 1914–1945*. Ed. Stanford. 1983. 431 pp.
Vol. 21: *Victorian Novelists before 1885*. Ed. Nadel and Fredeman. 1983. 417 pp.
Vol. 22: *American Writers for Children, 1900–1960*. Ed. John Cech. 1983. 412 pp.
Vol. 23: *American Newspaper Journalists, 1873–1900*. Ed. Perry J. Ashley. 1983. 392 pp.
Vol. 24: *American Colonial Writers, 1606–1734*. Ed. Emory Elliott. 1984. 415 pp.
Vol. 25: *American Newspaper Journalists, 1901–1925*. Ed. Ashley. 1984. 385 pp.
Vol. 26: *American Screenwriters*. Ed. Robert E. Morsberger, Stephen O. Lesser, and Randall Clark. 1984. 382 pp.
Vol. 27: *Poets of Great Britain and Ireland, 1945–1960*. Ed. Vincent B. Sherry, Jr. 1984. 393 pp.
Vol. 28: *Twentieth-Century American-Jewish Fiction Writers*. Ed. Daniel Walden. 1984. 367 pp.
Vol. 29: *American Newspaper Journalists, 1926–1950*. Ed. Ashley. 1984. 410 pp.
Vol. 30: *American Historians, 1607–1865*. Ed. Wilson. 1984. 382 pp.
Vol. 31: *American Colonial Writers, 1735–1781*. Ed. Elliott. 1984. 421 pp.
Vol. 32: *Victorian Poets before 1850*. Ed. Fredeman and Nadel. 1984. 417 pp.
Vol. 33: *Afro-American Fiction Writers after 1955*. Ed. Thadious M. Davis and Trudier Harris. 1984. 350 pp.
Vol. 34: *British Novelists, 1890–1929: Traditionalists*. Ed. Thomas F. Staley. 1985. 378 pp.
Vol. 35: *Victorian Poets after 1850*. Ed. Fredeman and Nadel. 1985. 437 pp.
Vol. 36: *British Novelists, 1890–1929: Modernists*. Ed. Staley. 1985. 387 pp.
Vol. 37: *American Writers of the Early Republic*. Ed. Elliott. 1985. 374 pp.
Vol. 38: *Afro-American Writers after 1955: Dramatists and Prose Writers*. Ed. Davis and Harris. 1985. 390 pp.

Vol. 39: *British Novelists, 1660–1800*. Ed. Martin C. Battestin. 2 pts. 1985.
Vol. 40: *Poets of Great Britain and Ireland since 1960*. Ed. Vincent B. Sherry, Jr. 2 pts. 1985.
Vol. 41: *Afro-American Poets since 1955*. Ed. Harris and Davis. 1985. 401 pp.
Vol. 42: *American Writers for Children before 1900*. Ed. Glenn E. Estes. 1985. 441 pp.
Vol. 43: *American Newspaper Journalists, 1690–1872*. Ed. Ashley. 1986. 527 pp.
Vol. 44: *American Screenwriters: Second Series*. Ed. Clark. 1986. 464 pp.
Vol. 45: *American Poets, 1880–1945: First Series*. Ed. Peter Quartermain. 1986. 490 pp.
Vol. 46: *American Literary Publishing Houses, 1900–1980: Trade and Paperback*. Ed. Peter Dzwonkoski. 1986. 465 pp.
Vol. 47: *American Historians, 1886–1912*. Ed. Wilson. 1986. 427 pp.
Vol. 48: *American Poets, 1880–1945: Second Series*. Ed. Quartermain. 1986. 510 pp.
Vol. 49: *American Literary Publishing Houses, 1638–1899*. Ed. Dzwonkoski. 2 pts. 1986.
Vol. 50: *Afro-American Writers before the Harlem Renaissance*. Ed. Harris and Davis. 1986. 369 pp.
Vol. 51: *Afro-American Writers from the Harlem Renaissance to 1940*. Ed. Harris and Davis. 1987. 386 pp.
Vol. 52: *American Writers for Children since 1960: Fiction*. Ed. Estes. 1986. 488 pp.
Vol. 53: *Canadian Writers since 1960: First Series*. Ed. W. H. New. 1986. 445 pp.
Vol. 54: *American Poets, 1880–1945: Third Series*. Ed. Quartermain. 2 pts. 1987.
Vol. 55: *Victorian Prose Writers before 1867*. Ed. William B. Thesing. 1987. 379 pp.
Vol. 56: *German Fiction Writers, 1914–1945*. Ed. James Hardin. 1987. 382 pp.
Vol. 57: *Victorian Prose Writers after 1867*. Ed. Thesing. 1987. 571 pp.
Vol. 58: *Jacobean and Caroline Dramatists*. Ed. Fredson Bowers. 1987. 370 pp.
Vol. 59: *American Literary Critics and Scholars, 1800–1850*. Ed. John W. Rathbun and Monica M. Grecu. 1987. 406 pp.
Vol. 60: *Canadian Writers since 1960: Second Series*. Ed. New. 1987. 470 pp.
Vol. 61: *American Writers for Children since 1960: Poets, Illustrators, and Non-Fiction Authors*. Ed. Estes. 1987. 430 pp.
Vol. 62: *Elizabethan Dramatists*. Ed. Bowers. 1987. 492 pp.
Vol. 63: *Modern American Critics, 1920–1955*. Ed. Gregory S. Jay. 1988. 384 pp.
Vol. 64: *American Literary Critics, 1850–1880*. Ed. Rathbun and Grecu. 1988. 352 pp.
Vol 65: *French Novelists, 1900–1930*. Ed. Catharine Savage Brosman. 1988. 381 pp.
Vol. 66: *German Fiction Writers, 1885–1913*. Ed. Hardin. 2 pts. 1988.
Vol. 67: *Modern American Critics since 1955*. Ed. Jay. 1988. 397 pp.
Vol. 68: *Canadian Writers, 1920–1959: First Series*. Ed. New. 1988. 417 pp.

Vol. 69: *Contemporary German Fiction Writers: First Series*. Ed. Wolfgang D. Elfe and Hardin. 1988. 413 pp.
Vol. 70: *British Mystery Writers, 1860–1919*. Ed. Bernard Benstock and Thomas F. Staley. 1988. 389 pp.
Vol. 71: *American Literary Critics and Scholars, 1880–1900*. Ed. Rathbun and Grecu. 1988. 374 pp.
Vol. 72: *French Novelists, 1930–1960*. Ed. Brosman. 1988. 478 pp.
Vol. 73: *American Magazine Journalists, 1741–1850*. Ed. Sam G. Riley. 1988. 430 pp.
Vol. 74: *American Short-Story Writers before 1880*. Ed. Bobby Ellen Kimbel. 1988.
Vol. 75: *Contemporary German Fiction Writers: Second Series*. Ed. Elfe and Harding. 1988. 367 pp.
Vol. 76: *Afro-American Writers, 1940–1955*. Ed. Harris and Davis. 1988. 389 pp.
Vol. 77: *British Mystery Writers, 1920–1939*. Ed. Benstock and Staley. 1988. 414 pp.
Vol. 78: *American Short-Story Writers, 1880–1910*. Ed. Kimbel. Scheduled for 1989.
Vol. 79: *American Magazine Journalists, 1850–1900*. Ed. Riley. Scheduled for 1989.
Vol. 82: *Chicano Writers: First Series*. Ed. Francisco A. Lomelí and Carl R. Shirley. Scheduled for 1989.

Additional volumes are in progress on the following groups: Austrian writers, American short story writers, hardboiled mystery writers, and Canadian writers before 1920.

Contains collections of separately authored biographical essays that trace the careers of selected authors. Ranging from 1,000 to 15,000 words, the extensively illustrated discussions integrate biographical information with brief synopses and critical estimates of major works within the designated genre, describe the author's importance and reputation, note manuscripts, and list primary works and selected scholarship. Each volume concludes with a list of important general studies. Because of the organization by genre within a period, some writers appear in more than one volume. Cumulatively indexed by writer (along with the *Yearbook*s and *Documentary Series*—see below) in each volume; volumes are also indexed in *Biography and Genealogy Master Index* (565) and in *Contemporary Authors* (595). Although varying widely in quality, the essays are generally superior to those in similar collections, offer a convenient summary of a writer's career, and for several minor authors provide the fullest available discussions.

Dictionary of Literary Biography: Yearbook [1980–] (1981–) updates some entries, adds new ones to published volumes, and includes reports on conferences, discussions of literary prizes, interviews, obituaries, and surveys of the year's publication in fiction, poetry, drama, and biography. Cumulatively indexed (along with the *Dictionary* and the *Documentary Series*) in each volume. *Dictionary of Literary Biography: Documentary Series: An Illustrated Chronicle* (1982–) reprints biographical and background materials (including letters, diary entries, interviews, book reviews, and excerpts from criticism) on selected authors or topics. Cumulatively indexed by author (along with the *Dictionary* and *Yearbook*s) in each volume. *The Concise Dictionary of American Literary Biography*, 6 vols. (1987–), a collection of updated *DLB* articles on major authors, is designed for high school and junior college libraries. In preparation is *A Guide, Chronology, and Glossary* *for American Literature*, which will essentially be an analytical index to the *DLB* volumes on American literature.

See also

Allibone, *Critical Dictionary of English Literature* (1430).
Writers Directory (5075).

K

Periodicals

This section is limited to works not restricted to a national literature, genre, or subject.

Directories

615 *MLA Directory of Periodicals: A Guide to Journals and Series in Languages and Literatures [1978–]*. New York: MLA, 1979– . Biennial. P1.A1.M62 [Z7006.M58] 016'.405.

A directory to the serials currently included in the *MLAIB* Master List of Periodicals (335a), and thus does not cover all journals and series publishing language and literary studies. (The separately published paperbound edition, which lists only serials published in the United States and Canada, is of limited value, since it excludes so many major journals and series.) Entries, arranged alphabetically by title, typically include editorial address, subscription and publication information (including circulation and *MLAIB* acronym), editorial description (scope, inclusion of reviews, languages published), and submission requirements (manuscript length and number of copies required, style manual, time interval between submission and editorial decision and between acceptance and publication, number of referees, and number of manuscripts submitted, accepted, and published each year). Since some editors do not respond to requests for verification, information carried over from earlier volumes may be outdated. Four indexes: editorial personnel; languages published (excluding English, French, German, Italian, and Spanish); sponsoring organizations; subjects (keyed to descriptions of scope and titles). Although not comprehensive, the *MLA Directory* is the best source for identifying serials that specialize in an author or topic and for determining where to submit a manuscript. Authors should, of course, verify submission requirements by consulting the most recent copy of the serial. (Unfortunately, no similar guide exists for university and other scholarly presses.) Review: (1978–79 ed.) Michael West, *College English* 41 (1980): 903–23 (including a tentative rank-ordering of selected journals), with responses, 42 (1980): 399–419.

A. J. Walford, ed., *Walford's Guide to Current British Periodicals in the Humanities and Social Sciences* (London: Library Assn., 1985, 473 pp.), is much less informative but includes journals omitted from the *MLA Directory*. See also Patterson, *Author Newsletters and Journals* (620) and *Ulrich's International Periodicals Directory* (625).

620 Patterson, Margaret C. *Author Newsletters and Journals: An International Annotated Bibliography of Serial Publications Concerned with the Life and Works of Individual Authors*. American Literature, English Literature, and World Literatures in English: An Information Guide Series 19. Detroit: Gale, 1979. 497 pp. Z6513.P37 [PN4836] 016.809.

A bibliography of 1,129 currently published and defunct serials, arranged alphabetically by author (with additions on pp. 357–65). Entries typically include bibliographical, editorial, and subscription information; description of contents; languages published; reprint availability; and indexing information (in both the publication and standard serial bibliographies and abstracts). Seven appendixes analyze listings in a variety of ways (e.g., by centuries and authors, and by indexing and abstracting services). Title index. Updated by Patterson's "*Author Newsletters and Journals*: Supplement 1 [2]," *Serials Review* 8.4 (1982): 61–72; 10.1 (1984): 51–59. Patterson provides a wealth of detail on specialized serials, many of which are not indexed by the standard serial bibliographies and indexes in section G of this *Guide*. Another supplement will be needed before long.

625 *Ulrich's International Periodicals Directory: A Classified Guide to Current Periodicals, Foreign and Domestic*. New York: Bowker, 1932– . Annual. Z6941.U5 011.

Irregular Serials and Annuals: An International Directory. 1967– . Annual. Z6941.I78 016.05.

These sources are updated between editions by *Bowker International Serials Database Update* (1985– ; quarterly); all three are published on CD-ROM as *Ulrich's Plus*.

The two directories and the quarterly update comprise Bowker's International Serials Database. *Ulrich's* classifies by subject periodicals currently publishing at least two issues per year. Each entry provides basic editorial and subscription information, along with an incomplete and frequently inaccurate list of serial bibliographies that index the publication. There is a separate list of journals that have ceased publication since the previous edition. *Irregular Serials and Annuals* records basic subscription and editorial information for serials issued less frequently than twice a year. Both works are indexed by titles. Although the Bowker Database offers the most comprehensive coverage of currently published serials, it contains numerous errors and omissions. Entries can be searched through Dialog (520) and BRS (515).

Additional periodicals are listed in *The Serials Directory: An International Reference Book* (Birmingham: Ebsco, 1986– ; irregular; also available on CD-ROM). *The Standard Periodical Directory* (New York: Oxbridge, 1965– ; biennial) is also useful for publication and subscription information on serials published in the United States and Canada. More current (although not always accurate) information on publication and editorial changes, cessations, and new periodicals can sometimes be found in the monthly issues of *Serials Updating Service* (Westwood: Faxon, 1973–).

Given the ephemerality of many periodicals, the ease with which they begin and cease publication, and their proneness to frequent changes in editorial personnel or publisher, it is hardly surprising that the general directories are so full of errors or outdated information and omit so many publications.

See also

Anson, "Journals in Composition" (5605).

Related Works

630 *Periodical Title Abbreviations: Covering Periodical Title Abbreviations in Science, the Social Sciences, the Humanities, Law, Medicine, Religion, Library Science, Engineering, Education, Business, Art, and Many Other Fields*. Comp. and ed. Leland G. Alkire, Jr. 5th ed. 3 vols. Detroit: Gale, 1986. Z6945.A2 [PN4832] 050'.148.

A dictionary of periodical acronyms and abbreviations used by some of the major serial bibliographies, indexes, and abstracts. Coverage is limited primarily to North American and British publications, and does not include all works in section G: Serial Bibliographies, Indexes, and Abstracts. Vol. 1 is an acronym list; vol. 2, a title list; and vol. 3 consists of interedition supplements. Although coverage is far from exhaustive, the work is occasionally useful for interpreting the acronym or abbreviated title for a journal not included in the lists in *MLAIB* (335), *ABELL* (340), or other standard language or literature bibliography.

Acronyms and abbreviations of journals in classical studies are more fully covered in Wellington, *Dictionary of Bibliographic Abbreviations Found in the Scholarship of Classical Studies* (4890a). A useful supplement for foreign journals is Otto Leistner, *ITA: Internationale Titelabkürzungen von Zeitschriften, Zeitungen, wichtigen Handbüchern, Wörterbüchern, Gesetzen, usw./International Title Abbreviations of Periodicals, Newspapers, Important Handbooks, Dictionaries, Laws, etc.*, 3rd ed., 2 vols. (Osnabrück: Biblio, 1981).

Periodicals about Periodicals

635 *Serials Review*. 1975– . Quarterly. PN4832.S47 016.05.

Although addressed to the serials librarian, *Serials Review* is useful to the literature scholar for its frequent surveys of little magazines, occasional articles on major literature periodicals, reviews of serials, regular column that reviews indexes to individual periodicals, and (since vol. 10 [1984]) index to reviews of serials. The reviews are not very rigorous, but *Serials Review* is one of the few sources that regularly evaluate periodicals and reference works on serials. Index in each issue; cumulative index: Linda Gabel, comp., "*Serials Review*: Cumulative Index of Titles Reviewed in Volumes 1 through 5, 1975–1979," 6.1 (1980): 18 pp. printed between pp. 38 and 39.

Union Lists

Many library consortia or state associations produce regional union lists of serials. A reference or interlibrary loan librarian is usually the best source for information on the local lists.

Although now dated, Ruth S. Freitag, comp., *Union Lists of Serials: A Bibliography* (Washington: Reference Dept., Library of Congress, 1964, 150 pp.), is still useful for identifying union lists published before c. 1962.

640 *New Serial Titles: A Union List of Serials Held by Libraries in the United States and Canada* (*NST*). Washington: Library of Congress, 1953– . Monthly, with quarterly, annual, and larger cumulations for 1950–70, 1971–75, 1976–80, 1981–85. Available on microfiche since 1984. Z6945.U5.S42 [PN4832] 016.05.

A title list of serials from throughout the world held by libraries in the United States and Canada. Until 1981, *NST* includes only works first published after 1949; since 1981, it admits newly cataloged serials regardless of initial date of publication. *NST* continues *Union List of Serials in Libraries of the United States and Canada* (*ULS*), ed. Edna Brown Titus, 3rd ed., 5 vols. (New York: Wilson, 1965), which records holdings for more than 156,000 serials published before 1950. *NST* and *ULS* are essential for identifying libraries that own lengthy or complete runs (but there are numerous errors and omissions in the records of holdings). OCLC (225) and RLIN (230), although offering more current information on libraries that own a particular serial, do not record specific holdings. For subject access, see *New Serial Titles, 1950–1970: Subject Guide*, 2 vols. (New York: Bowker, 1975).

645 *Serials in the British Library*. London: British Library Bibliographic Services Division, 1981– . Quarterly, with annual and larger cumulations. Z6945.B874 [PN4832] 011.34.

From 1987 on, this source is restricted to new serials acquired by the British Library, with entries providing title, publication details, and ISSN. Indexed by subject. From 1981 through 1986, it is a union list of serials acquired since 1976 by the British Library and 16 other major libraries in the United Kingdom and Republic of Ireland. *Serials in the British Library* succeeds *British Union-Catalogue of Periodicals Incorporating* World List of Scientific Periodicals*: New Periodical Titles* (London: Butterworths, 1964–81, quarterly, with annual and larger cumulations), which records periodicals that were first published, began a new series, or ceased publication from 1960 through 1980, and lists the holdings of a significantly larger number of libraries. The holdings of earlier periodicals are recorded in *British*

Union-Catalogue of Periodicals: A Record of the Periodicals of the World, from the Seventeenth Century to the Present Day, in British Libraries (*BUCOP*), ed. James D. Stewart, 4 vols. (New York: Academic; London: Butterworths, 1955–58); a supplement (1962) extends coverage to 1960.

Scholarly Journals

The following list is limited to major journals not restricted to a national literature, genre, or subject.

650 *Anglia: Zeitschrift für Englische Philologie* (*Anglia*). 1878– . 2/yr. PE3.A6 420.05.

Publishes articles and notes, in German and English, on all aspects of the English language and British, American, and Commonwealth literature. Recent volumes emphasize English literature through the eighteenth century. Reviews are frequently lengthy and appear some years after publication dates. For the annual supplement *English and American Studies in German: Summaries of Theses and Monographs*, see 440. Cumulative indexes: vols. 1–50, H. Füchsel, supplement to vol. 54 (1930, 65 pp.); vols. 51–75, Th. Stemmler (1961, 45 pp.).

655 *Archiv für das Studium der neueren Sprachen und Literaturen* (*Archiv*). 1848– . 2/yr. PB3.A5 405.

Publishes articles and notes (in German and English, and occasionally French, Italian, and Spanish) on Western European, British, and American languages and literatures. Reviews sometimes appear as long as five years after publication dates. Cumulative indexes: vols. 1–50, Ludwig Herrig, *General-Register* (Braunschweig: Westermann, 1874, 172 pp.); vols. 51–100, Hermann Springer, *General-Register* (1900, 285 pp.); vols. 101–10 (n.d., 28 pp.); vols. 111–20 (n.d., 39 pp.); vols. 121–30, *Register* (1913, 56 pp.); vols. 131–40, Fritz Fiedler, *Register* (1921, 24 pp.).

660 *Bulletin of Bibliography* (*BB*). 1897– . Quarterly. (Title varies.) Z1007.B94 011'.34.

Publishes enumerative bibliographies on topics in the humanities, social sciences, and arts, and (since 39.4 [1982]) reviews of bibliographies and books about books. Annual index. Cumulative indexes: Eleanor Cavanaugh Jones and Margaret L. Pollard, comp., *Cumulative Index (1897–1975) to the* Bulletin of Bibliography and Magazine Notes (Westwood, MA: Faxon, 1977, 137 pp); Sandra Conrad, comp., *Cumulative Index (1976–1980) to the* Bulletin of Bibliography (Westwood, MA: Faxon, 1981, 10 pp).

665 *Bulletin of Research in the Humanities* (*BRH*). 1897– . Quarterly. Former title: *Bulletin of the New York Public Library* (1897–1977). Z881.N6 001.3'05.

Publishes articles on literature, music, and art, with recent volumes emphasizing British topics from the late eighteenth to the early twentieth centuries. Annual index; cumulative indexes: vols. 1–40, Daniel E. Haskell (1937, 197 pp.); vols. 41–50, Haskell (1948, 64 pp.); vols. 51–66, David H. Stam (1963, 50 pp.).

670 *ELH*. 1934– . Quarterly. Former title: *ELH: A Journal of English Literary History* (1934–55). PR1.E5 820.9.

Publishes historical and critical articles on English and American literature, but emphasizing the former. The consistent quality of the articles and rigorous editorial standards rank *ELH* among the most distinguished scholarly literature journals. Vols. 4–16 (1937–49) print "The Romantic Movement: A Selective and Critical Bibliography for [1936–48]" (see entry 2485).

675 *English Language Notes* (*ELN*). 1963– . Quarterly. PE1.E53 420'.5.

Publishes short articles and notes, emphasizing explication and source study, as well as reviews on English and American language and literature. "The Romantic Movement: A Selective and Critical Bibliography for [1964–78]" (2485) appears as a supplement to vols. 3–17 (1965–79).

680 *Etudes anglaises: Grande-Bretagne, Etats-Unis* (*EA*). 1937– . Quarterly. PR1.E8 820.9.

Publishes articles, notes, documents (unpublished letters and short manuscripts), and reviews on English and American literature and (occasionally) language. Since vol. 28 (1975), *EA* prints English and French abstracts of articles. An extensive Revue des Revues section lists contents of journals received. Particularly useful is the Chronique section, which prints summaries of dissertations and theses accepted by French universities and lists of contents of proceedings and collections of essays published by French research centers and learned societies; many of these works are not covered by the standard bibliographies in section G.

685 *Explicator* (*Expl*). 1942– . Quarterly. PR1.E9 820.5.

Prints concise explications of passages in works from a variety of national literatures. Selected contributions are reprinted in *The Explicator Cyclopedia*, ed. Charles Child Walcutt and J. Edwin Whitesell, 3 vols. (Chicago: Quadrangle, 1966–68). Since vol. 3 (1944–45), *Explicator* publishes an annual "Check List of Explication," which is limited to explications of "unquestioned . . . merit and substance." Originally confined to English and American poetry and fiction, the checklist now includes film, drama, and (since the list for 1983, in vol. 44 [1985]) a few foreign authors. Annual index; cumulative indexes: vols. 1–20, J. Edwin Whitesell (1962, n.pag.); vols. 21–30, J. Edwin Whitesell and Virginia B. Whitesell (1973, n.pag.); vols. 31–42, as 43.4 (1985).

690 *JEGP: Journal of English and Germanic Philology* (*JEGP*). 1897– . Quarterly. Former title: *Journal of Germanic Philology* (1897–1902). PD1.J7 420.

Publishes articles and reviews on English and Germanic literatures and languages, with an emphasis on German and British literature before 1900. Until the 1960s, *JEGP* printed occasional bibliographies and surveys of research. Vols. 34–70 (1935–71) include the "Anglo-German Literary Bibliography [1933–70]," an unannotated list of scholarship. Annual index; cumulative index: vols. 1–50, supplement to vol. 61 (1962).

695 *Modern Language Quarterly* (*MLQ*). 1940– . Quarterly. PB1.M642 405.

Publishes articles and reviews on a wide range of topics in English, American, Romance, Germanic, and comparative literatures, with an emphasis on English and American. Vols. 1–24 (1940–63) include "A Bibliography of Critical Arthurian Literature for the Year 1936[–1962]," a continuation of John J. Parry and Margaret Schlauch, *A Bibliography of Critical Arthurian Literature for the Years 1922–1929 [1930–1935]*, 2 vols. (New York: MLA, 1931–36), and continued by *Bulletin Bibliographique de la Société Internationale Arthurienne* (1949– , annual).

700 *Modern Language Review* (*MLR*). 1905– . Quarterly. PB1.M65 405.

Publishes articles and reviews, principally on European and North American literatures. Articles submitted on literatures in English are also considered for publication in the annual *Yearbook of English Studies* (1971–), which has focused on a topic or theme since vol. 8. Cumulative indexes: vols. 1–10, as 10.4 (1915, 69 pp.); vols. 11–20 (1926, 76 pp.); vols. 21–30, Winifred Husbands (1938, 99 pp.); vols. 31–50, Husbands (Cambridge: Cambridge UP, 1960, 216 pp.); vols. 51–60, R. L. Smallwood (1969, 223 pp.).

705 *Modern Philology: A Journal Devoted to Research in Medieval and Modern Literature* (*MP*). 1903– . Quarterly. PB1.M7 405.

Publishes articles, notes, documents, review essays, and reviews on a variety of literatures but with a decided emphasis on English and American topics. Vols. 30–54 (1933–57) include the annual "Victorian Bibliography for [1932–56]" (2500).

710 *Neuphilologische Mitteilungen: Bulletin de la Société Néophilologique/Bulletin of the Modern Language Society* (*NM*). 1899– . Quarterly. PB10.N415 410'.5.

Publishes articles, notes, and reviews on English, Romance, and Germanic languages and literatures, with an emphasis on linguistic analysis and Old and Middle English topics. Of particular importance are the three annual surveys of research in progress: "Old English Research in Progress [1964–]," 66 (1965)– ; "Middle English Research in Progress [1963–]," 65 (1964)– ; "Chaucer Research in Progress [1968–]," 70 (1969)– (adapted from the annual bibliography in *Chaucer Review*).

715 *Papers on Language and Literature: A Journal for Scholars and Critics of Language and Literature* (*PLL*). 1965– . Quarterly. Former title: *Papers on English Language and Literature* (1965). PR1.P3 820'.5.

Publishes articles, notes, and occasional review essays on "literary history, theory, and interpretation" of a wide range of national literatures but with an emphasis on English and American. Welcomes "original materials such as letters, journals, and notebooks," but few have been printed. Annual index; cumulative indexes: vols. 1–15 (n.d., 41 pp.); vols. 16–20, in 20 (1984): 461–72.

720 *Philological Quarterly* (*PQ*). 1922– . Quarterly. P1.P55 410'.5.

Publishes articles, notes, and reviews on an eclectic range of literatures, classical to modern. For many years *PQ* hosted two important serial bibliographies: "The Romantic Movement: A Selective and Critical Bibliography for the Year [1949–63]," vols. 29–43 (1950–64) (see entry 2485); "The Eighteenth Century: A Current Bibliography for [1927–74]," vols. 5–54 (1926–75) (see entry 2245). Vols. 55–58 (1976–79) include a yearly issue devoted to critical surveys of research on Restoration and eighteenth-century English literature; occasional surveys of a period or genre appear through 62.3 (1983). Cumulative index: vols. 1–25 (1950, 172 pp.). Noted for its consistently rigorous editorial standards.

725 *PMLA: Publications of the Modern Language Association of America* (*PMLA*). 1886– . 6/yr. PB6.M6 809.2.

Publishes articles and occasional special issues on language and (principally) literature, without restrictions on methodological or theoretical approach. According to the current editorial policy, "The ideal *PMLA* essay exemplifies the best of its kind, whatever the kind; addresses a significant problem; draws out clearly the implications of its findings; and engages the attention of its audience through a concise, readable presentation." Although sometimes damned for "pedantry" or "narrowness," *PMLA* submits manuscripts to the most rigorous review of any literature journal, and its preeminence is evidenced by its rank as the most frequently cited journal in its field. John H. Fisher, "Remembrance and Reflection: *PMLA* 1884–1982," *PMLA* 99 (1984): 398–407, surveys the history of the journal, its contents, and changes in editorial policy.

Each issue (except the annual Program) includes an extensive list of forthcoming meetings and conferences as well as a "Professional Notes and Comments" section, which prints news of awards, requests for information for or submissions to works in progress, notes on new journals and forthcoming special issues, and reports on meetings of MLA committees and governing bodies.

The Directory issue (5060) prints several useful lists: members (with addresses); administrators of language and literature departments, ethnic studies programs, women's studies programs, and language and area studies programs; and fellowships and grants supporting research in language and literature. The Program issue is a guide to the meetings at the annual convention. Cumulative indexes: vols. 1–50 (1936, 240 pp.); vols. 51–79, Bayard Quincy Morgan (1966, 94 pp.)

For the annual bibliography that appears in vols. 37–84 (1922–69), see entry 335.

The *MLA Newsletter* (1969– , quarterly) provides additional information on activities of the association and a list of topics for meetings at forthcoming conventions.

730 *Texas Studies in Literature and Language: A Journal of the Humanities* (*TSLL*). 1911– . Quarterly. Former title: *Texas Studies in English* (1911–58). AS30.T4 820.5.

Publishes articles and occasional special issues on literature and American studies, with a decided emphasis on American and British literature. Annual index.

735 *University of Toronto Quarterly: A Canadian Journal of the Humanities* (*UTQ*). 1931– . Quarterly. AP5.U58 378.1.

Publishes articles and reviews on all aspects of the humanities, with an emphasis on English literature and some attention to Canadian topics. For the annual "Letters in Canada," see entry 4610. W. J. Keith and B.-Z. Shek, "A Half-Century of *UTQ*," 50 (1980): 146–56, trace the history of the journal.

740 *World Literature Today: A Literary Quarterly of the University of Oklahoma* (*WLT*). 1927– . Quarterly. Former title: *Books Abroad: A Quarterly Publication Devoted to Comment on Foreign Books* (1927–76). Z1007.B717 028.1.

Publishes articles, frequent special issues, and numerous reviews on recent literary works in all the major and many minor languages of the world. Annual index. For the history of the journal, see the several articles and reminiscences in 50.4 (1976). *World Literature Today* offers the most extensive coverage of any periodical of new belles lettres (including biography and criticism) published throughout the world.

Book Reviews

Included in this section are serials whose primary content is reviews.

745 *American Reference Books Annual [1970–]* (*ARBA*). Littleton: Libraries Unlimited, 1970– . Annual. Z1035.1.A55 011.02.

Prints brief reviews (150–400 words) of English-language reference books published or distributed in the United States or Canada (with decent coverage of the latter beginning in vol. 18 [1987]). Hyperbolically claiming to be a "comprehensive" source that "reviews *all* reference books," *ARBA* actually overlooks or ignores a substantial number of major works each year. Reviews are organized in four extensively classified divisions: general reference works (organized by types of works, including bibliographies, biographical sources, directories, encyclopedias, and indexes), social sciences (including sections for ethnic studies and anthropology; genealogy; history; library science, publishing, and bookselling; and women's studies), humanities (including general works; language and linguistics; literature; mythology, folklore, and popular customs; and performing arts), and science and technology. The literature section has subdivisons for general works, children's literature, classical literature, drama, fiction, poetry, and national literatures (with each of the national literatures having sections, as needed, for general works, genres, and individual authors). Most reviews conclude with citations to others in library journals. Two indexes: authors and titles; subjects. Cumulative indexes: Joseph W. Sprug, *Index to* American Reference Books Annual, *1970–1974: A Cumulative Index to Subjects, Authors, and Titles* (1974, 364 pp.); Christine L. Wynar, *1975–1979* (1979, 407 pp.); Ruth Blackmore, *1980–1984* (1984, 402 pp.). Although the quality of the reviews has improved a bit over the years, the majority remain essentially descriptive, and many that attempt evaluation are simply inaccurate. Omitting too many significant publications within its scope and insufficiently rigorous in evaluations, *ARBA* is primarily useful for alerting researchers to some new reference books and to changes in serial ones (which are examined at intervals).

Selected reviews are reprinted in *Best Reference Books, 1970–1980: Titles of Lasting Value Selected from* American Reference Books Annual, ed. Susan Holte and Bohdan S. Wynar (1981, 480 pp.) and *1981–1985*, ed. Wynar (1986, 504 pp.); neither fulfills the claim of the works' common title and subtitle.

750 *Choice: Current Reviews for College Libraries*. 1964– . 11/yr. Z1035.C5 028.

A selection guide for undergraduate libraries, each issue prints approximately 600 brief notices of English-language books published or distributed in North America, a few new journals, and some nonprint materials. (For the most recent statement of editorial policies, see 21 [1983]: 29–40.) Most issues also feature an extended bibliographical essay on a topic of current interest, and the May issue lists "Outstanding Academic Books and Nonprint Materials" drawn from works reviewed during the past year. The notices, which have been signed only since vol. 22 (1984), are organized by subject areas, including the humanities, language and literature (classified by language), performing arts (with sections for film and theater), and reference works (although coverage of the last is weak). Two indexes in each issue (authors; titles); annual cumulative index. The notices are seldom by recognized scholars; reviewers are allowed insufficient space for more than a cursory report; and too many important books are ignored or overlooked. Nonetheless, the sheer number of publications noticed, coupled with the abundance of publishers' advertisements, makes *Choice* one of the better sources for identifying new and forthcoming English-language books published in North America.

755 *The New York Review of Books* (*NYRB*). 1963– . 22/yr. AP2.N655 028.1'05.

Each issue typically consists of a few extensive, signed reviews and review essays of books from a variety of fields, but with a preference for the humanities; an essay on a literary, political, or social topic; letters; and queries from biographers, editors, and other scholars. Although less broad in scope and reviewing fewer books per issue than *TLS* (765), *NYRB* offers more depth in its reviews. Cumulative index: The New York Review of Books*: Ten-Year Cumulative Index, February 1963–January 1973* (New York: Arno, 1973, 90 pp.). Stephen Fender, "*The New York Review of Books*," *Yearbook of English Studies* 16 (1986): 188–202, analyzes the mixture of politics and criticism in the work.

760 *Review* (*Rev*). Charlottesville: UP of Virginia, 1979– . Annual. PR1.R32 820.9.

Publishes lengthy, usually exacting signed reviews of representative critical studies, biographies, textual editions, bibliographies, and reference works in British and American literature. Because the commissioned reviews are subjected to a refereeing process, *Review* prints some of the most considered, rigorous evaluations of any periodical. Unfortunately, the proportion of bibliographies and reference works has fallen in recent volumes. For a discussion of editorial policy and procedures, and comments on academic book reviewing, see James O. Hoge and James L. W. West III, "Academic Book Reviewing: Some Problems and Suggestions," *Scholarly Publishing* 11 (1979): 35–41.

765 *TLS: Times Literary Supplement* (*TLS*). 1902– . Weekly. Former title: *Times Literary Supplement* (1902–68). AP4.T45 072'.1.

Publishes reviews of books in a variety of fields (but with a decided emphasis on the humanities, especially literature) and, in recent years, of art exhibitions, television programs, movies, operas, and productions of plays; occasional essays on literary and other topics; a lively, sometimes contentious, letters section; reports on book auctions; requests for information from biographers, editors, and other scholars; and, since 1987, an extensive list of books received. Since 7 June 1974, reviews are signed. Long regarded as the best general review publication, *TLS* is valuable for its broad, literate coverage; however, it frequently still betrays a British bias, and the quality of reviews varies considerably, with those in recent years being overall less rigorous. Author index in each issue. Although *TLS* is indexed since 1973 in The Times *Index* (1450), fuller, more convenient access is offered by the cumulative indexes: The Times Literary Supplement *Index, 1902–1939*, 2 vols. (Reading: Newspaper Archive Developments, 1978); *1940–1980*, 3 vols. (Reading: Research Publications, 1982); and *1981–1985* (1986, 407 pp.).

The *Times Higher Education Supplement* (1971– , weekly) also reviews a number of books of interest to literature researchers.

Little Magazines

Histories and Surveys

770 Hoffman, Frederick J., Charles Allen, and Carolyn F. Ulrich. *The Little Magazine: A History and a Bibliography*. 2nd ed. Princeton: Princeton UP, 1947. 450 pp. PN4836.H6 052.

A survey rather than a history proper of selected little magazines published since c. 1912, principally in the United States but also including a few from Great Britain and Ireland. The narrative part emphasizes the place of these publications in literary and cultural history, with chapters on individual magazines, types of publications, poetry, regionalism, politics, and psychoanalysis. The selective bibliography of United States, Canadian, British, and Irish magazines (from 1891 through 1946) is organized chronologically by date of first issue. Entries provide title; publication information; frequency; a record of mergers and suspensions; editors; and notes on history, scope, editorial policy, important contributors, and contents (although some information is taken from sources other than the magazines themselves). The bibliography includes a supplementary list of periodicals that are similar to little magazines. (For some additions to both lists, see Carolyn F. Ulrich and Eugenia Patterson, comps., "Little Magazines," *Bulletin of the New York Public Library* 51 [1947]: 3–25.) Concludes with a list of secondary sources, which must be supplemented by Charles L. P. Silet, "An Annotated Checklist of Articles and Books on American Little Magazines," *Bulletin of Bibliography* 34 (1977): 157–66, 208. Indexed by persons, titles, and a few subjects. This remains the fullest survey and bibliography of little magazines. Reviews: Louis Filler, *American Literature* 18 (1947): 334–35; Robert Wooster Stallman, *Poetry* 70 (1947): 274–78.

Although many supplements or new histories have been contemplated, none has appeared. For magazines since c. 1940, the best general source is Elliott Anderson and Mary Kinzie, eds., *The Little Magazine in America: A Modern Documentary History* (Yonkers: Pushcart, 1978, 770 pp.; also published as *TriQuarterly* 43 [1978], 750 pp., but without the index), a collection of essays, interviews, and memoirs treating individual titles and kinds of magazines. *The Little Magazine in America* also includes an annotated bibliography (modeled on the one in Hoffman) of eighty-four little magazines since c. 1950, with a valuable preliminary discussion of sources for the study of little magazines in the United States.

Guides to Primary Works

Despite the importance of little magazines in twentieth-century literature, their use is hampered by the lack of an adequate bibliography of magazines and indexes to their content. Consequently, researchers must depend heavily on incomplete collections in various libraries. Willard Fox, "The Archives: An Analysis of Little Magazine Collections in the United States and Canada" (forthcoming in *American Literary Magazines: The Twentieth Century* [3410]), offers an overview of the collections, finding aids, and complementary holdings of 28 repositories.

The fullest—but by no means comprehensive—list of little magazines is *Catalog of Little Magazines: A Collection in the Rare Book Room, Memorial Library, University of Wisconsin–Madison*, comp. and ed. Robert F. Roeming (Madison: U of Wisconsin P, 1979, 137 pp.).

DIRECTORIES

775 *The International Directory of Little Magazines and Small Presses*. Paradise: Dustbooks, 1965– . Annual. Former title: *Directory of Little Magazines and Small Presses* (1965–73). Z6944.L5.D5 015'.025.

A directory of English-language little magazines and small presses, the majority of them in the United States and Canada. Presses and magazines are listed alphabetically by name or title, with a typical entry recording press or publisher (for magazines), editor(s), address, telephone number, type of material published, notes (on content of recent issues or publications, contributors, editorial policies, and sometimes artistic credos or pleas for submissions), submission requirements, production method, and subscription information. Based on information supplied by publishers or editors, entries vary in fullness, accuracy, and currency. Two indexes: subjects; regional (by state, then zip code; foreign countries follow states). The *Directory* is the best source for identifying current little magazines and active small presses; earlier editions remain valuable for information about defunct publications and presses, especially alternative and underground ones. Between editions, new listings appear in *Small Press Review* (1967– , monthly).

Two complementary publications based on the *Directory* are *Directory of Small Press and Magazine Editors and Publishers* (1971– , annual) and *Directory of Poetry Publishers* (1985– , annual).

For earlier English-language little magazines and small presses, *Trace* (1952–70) remains a valuable source of information, although locating within issues the variously titled "Directory" and its supplements is exasperating.

See also

Serials Review (635).
Sullivan, *British Literary Magazines* (1445).
Warwick, *Commonwealth Literature Periodicals* (4385).

INDEXES

780 *Access: The Index to Little Magazines, [1976–78]*. N.p.: Burke, 1977–79. Annual. AI3.A24.

Author, title, and subject indexes to selected little magazines published, for the most part, in the United States. The title index covers only fiction and poetry; the subject index is limited to nonfiction, including book reviews which are listed by the author of the book. Offering no explanation of the criteria governing selection, covering a very limited number of magazines (69 in the 1978 volume), and weak in its subject indexing, *Access* is principally useful because no other bibliography indexes most of the magazines for these years.

785 Bloomfield, B. C. *An Author Index to Selected British "Little Magazines," 1930–1939*. London: Mansell, 1976. 153 pp. AI3.B56 052.

An author index to 73 little magazines, all but one of them published in Great Britain. Magazines not included—those indexed in general periodical indexes, without literary merit, or unlocated—are listed on pp. vii-viii. The approximately 11,000 entries cite title, publication information, and type of work (verse, prose, illustration); at the end of each author entry is a list of books by that author reviewed in magazines indexed. Although lacking subject access (except for the heading "Films Reviewed") and encompassing only 73 magazines within a decade, Bloomfield is valuable for the access it provides to magazines otherwise unindexed.

790 *Comprehensive Index to English-Language Little Magazines, 1890–1970: Series One*. Ed. Marion Sader. 8 vols. Millwood: Kraus, 1976. Z6944.L5.S23 [PN4836] 016.051.

An author index to 100 periodicals, 59 of which are published in the United States and most of the remainder in Great Britain. Ostensibly limited to the "best" works, the *Index* does include several publications (such as *Modern Fiction Studies* [845] and *Twentieth Century Literature* [2825]) that hardly qualify as "little magazines." Under each author, primary works appear first, followed by works about the author (including reviews). In addition to recording basic publication information, each entry identifies the type of work (see vol. 1, p. xv for a list of abbreviations). Since unsigned works that cannot be attributed are omitted, Sader is not the "comprehensive" index claimed by the title; however, it does offer the fullest access to a minuscule number of twentieth-century little magazines.

795 *Index to Commonwealth Little Magazines, 1964–1965*. By Stephen H. Goode. New York: Johnson Reprint, 1966. 187 pp. *1966–1967*. 1968. 251 pp. *1968–1969*. Troy: Whitston, 1970. 216 pp. *1970–1973*. 1975. 550 pp. *1974–1975*. Comp. Sarah V. Grey. 1976. 491 pp. *1976–1979*. 2 vols. 1984. *1980–1982*. 1986. 926 pp. *1983–1984*. 1987. 575 pp. *1985–1986*. (In progress.) AI3.I48 051.

A highly selective author and subject index to articles, original works, review essays, and substantial reviews in 34 to 42 English-language little magazines, many of them published in the British Isles. Canadian publications are excluded. Although offering no explanation of the criteria governing selection, including some periodicals that hardly qualify as little magazines, and utilizing inexact subject headings, the work at least provides access to a few little magazines indexed nowhere else. Reviews: (1964–65) Charles L. Dwyer, *English Literature in Transition, 1880–1920* 10 (1967): 96; (1974–75) Joan Stockard, *Literary Research Newsletter* 3 (1978): 186–90.

800 *Index to Little Magazines [1948–67]*. Chicago: Swallow, 1949–70. (Compilers and frequency vary.) AI3.I54.

Retrospective volumes have been compiled by Stephen H. Goode:

Index to Little Magazines, 1943–1947. Denver: Swallow, 1965. 287 pp.

Index to Little Magazines, 1940–1942. New York: Johnson Reprint, 1967. 234 pp.

Index to American Little Magazines, 1920–1939. Troy: Whitston, 1969. 346 pp.

Index to American Little Magazines, 1900–1919: To Which Is Added a Selected List of British and Continental Titles for the Years 1900–1950, Together with Addenda and Corrigenda to Previous Indexes. 3 vols. Troy: Whitston, 1974.

Contains author and subject indexes to selected little magazines, the majority published in the United States. Volumes typically cover between 31 and 57 important magazines not indexed by general periodical bibliographies such as *Readers'*

Guide (400) and *Humanities Index* (385). Besides covering 102 magazines, the *1900–1919* index supplements and corrects Goode's other volumes. The subject indexing is usually too imprecise to be of much use; book reviews are not always indexed; and the coverage extends to only a small percentage of little magazines published before 1967. Still, these works remain the only indexes to many of the magazines.

See also

American Humanities Index (360).
Annual Index to Poetry in Periodicals (4325a).
Index of American Periodical Verse (4325).
Index to Poetry in Periodicals (4325a).
Messerli, *Index to Periodical Fiction in English, 1965–1969* (1085a).

Guides to Scholarship and Criticism

See

Chielens, *Literary Journal in American, 1900–1950* (4250).

Periodicals about Periodicals

805 *Literary Magazine Review*. 1982– . Quarterly. PN4878.3.L48 810'.9.
The only source that consistently reviews issues of a variety of little magazines. Cumulative index in each volume.

See also

Serials Review (635).

L

Genres

Only works that encompass more than one national literature are included here. Works limited to a single literature are listed in the genre portion of national literature sections. All of the guides to scholarship and criticism in this section should be supplemented by the serial bibliographies, indexes, and abstracts in section G.

General

Guides to Scholarship and Criticism

820 Ruttkowski, Wolfgang. *Bibliographie der Gattungspoetik für den Studenten der Literaturwissenschaft: Ein abgekürztes Verzeichnis von über 3000 Büchern, Dissertationen, und Zeitschriftenartikeln in Deutsch, Englisch, und Französisch/Bibliography of the Poetics of Literary Genres for the Student of Literature: A Short-Title Catalogue of More Than 3000 Books, Dissertations, and Articles in English, French, and German/Bibliographie de la poétique des genres littéraires pour l'étudiant de la littérature: Une bibliographie de plus que 3000 livres, thèses, et articles en français, en allemand, et en anglais.* München: Hueber, 1973. 246 pp. Z6511.R86.

A selective bibliography of studies on genres and forms. Ruttkowski emphasizes English, French, and German publications from 1940 to 1970, but includes, albeit unsystematically, earlier studies as well as works in other European languages. Entries are arranged alphabetically by author in three sections: literary dictionaries containing articles on genres, general and multiple genre studies, and works on particular genres. Since the last section is classified by German terminology for genres and forms, use of the trilingual genre index is mandatory. Many entries are taken from other bibliographies; both selection and classification seem based primarily on title keywords; and the extensive use of abbreviations, especially in titles, requires constant reference to the list of abbreviations. Two indexes: genres (which indexes only the classified section on individual forms and genres); authors. Although the work is uneven in coverage, inadequately subject-indexed, and now badly dated—given the attention accorded genre study since 1970—Ruttkowski provides the most extensive list of studies on genres and forms, and thus offers a convenient starting point for research.

See also

ABELL (340): [English] Literature/General through the volume for 1972, Literary History and Criticism division in the volume for 1973, and English Literature/General in later volumes.

"Check List of Explication," *Explicator* (685).

MLAIB (335): General VII: Literature, General and Comparative in the volumes for 1953–55; General II: Literature, General and Comparative in the volume for 1956; General IV in the volumes for 1957–80; and the Genres and Literary Forms divisions in pt. 4 of the later volumes.

Periodicals

825 *Genre: A Quarterly Devoted to Generic Criticism* (*Genre*). 1968– . Quarterly. PN80.G4 801.95.

As the editorial policy stipulates, *Genre* "publishes articles dealing with questions of genre in relation to interpretation of major literary texts, historical development of specific genres, and theoretical discussion of the concept of genre itself." The work also publishes reviews and frequent special issues. Annual index.

Background Reading

830 Fowler, Alastair. *Kinds of Literature: An Introduction to the Theory of Genres and Modes*. Cambridge: Harvard UP, 1982. 357 pp. PN45.5.F6 801'.95.

Focuses generally on English literature in examining concepts, names, formation, transformation, function, systems, and hierarchies of genres. Reviews: Brian Corman, *University of Toronto Quarterly* 54 (1984): 101–06; Laurence Lerner, *Modern Language Review* 79 (1984): 888–90; Harry Levin, *Comparative Literature* 36 (1984): 258–60.

Fiction

General

GUIDES TO PRIMARY WORKS

835 *Fiction Catalog*. Ed. Juliette Yaakov. 11th ed. Standard Catalog Series. New York: Wilson, 1986. 951 pp. Annual supplements. Z5916.W74 [PN3451] 016.823008.

A highly selective author, title, and subject index to 5,131 English-language works (including translations). Although emphasizing novels, *Fiction Catalog* includes some short story and novella collections. Pt. 1 is an author catalog; entries include publication information, plot summary or list of contents, and occasionally extracts from reviews. Pt. 2 is a title and subject index (with headings for themes, geographical settings, and historical eras). Designed as a selection aid for libraries and thus emphasizing established authors, *Fiction Catalog* is useful to the literary researcher needing to identify novels about a topic. Earlier editions cite works subsequently dropped.

A useful complement for works published since 1945 is *Cumulated Fiction Index, 1945–1960*, comp. G. B. Cotton and Alan Glencross (London: Assn. of Assistant Librarians, 1960, 552 pp.); *1960–1969*, comp. Raymond Ferguson Smith (1970, 307 pp.); *1970–1974*, comp. Smith and Antony John Gordon (1975, 192 pp.); *1975–1979*, comp. Marilyn E. Hicken (1980, 225 pp.); *1980–1984*, comp. Hicken ([1986?], 167 pp.); with annual supplements between cumulations: *Fiction Index*

[1945–]: A Guide to Works of Fiction Available during the Year and Not Previously Indexed in the Fiction Index Series (1952–). Although *Cumulated Fiction Index* covers more titles than *Fiction Catalog*, many subject headings are vague, the criteria governing selection are unclear, and entries unhelpfully cite only author and abbreviated title.

GUIDES TO SCHOLARSHIP AND CRITICISM

See

ABELL (340): [English] Literature/General through the volume for 1967; Literature, General/Literary History/Fiction, and Literature, General/Literary Criticism/Fiction in the volumes for 1968–72; Literary History and Criticism/Fiction in the volume for 1973; and English Literature/General/Fiction in later volumes.

"Check List of Explication," *Explicator* (685).

MLAIB (335): General VII: Literature, General and Comparative in the volumes for 1953–55; General II: Literature, General and Comparative in the volume for 1956; General IV/Prose Fiction in the volumes for 1957–80; and the Literary Forms division and Genres/Fiction section in pt. 4 of the later volumes. Researchers must also check the "Fiction" heading in the subject index to post-1980 volumes.

PERIODICALS

840 *Journal of Narrative Technique* (*JNT*). 1971– . 3/yr. PE1425.J68 820.9.

JNT is devoted to narrative theory and practice in both prose and verse, but the bulk of the articles and notes emphasize British and American fiction of the past three centuries. Annual index; cumulative indexes: vols. 1–10, in 10 (1980): 205–13; vols. 11–14, in 14 (1984): 223–27.

845 *Modern Fiction Studies* (*MFS*). 1955– . Quarterly. PS379.M55 809.3.

As its editorial policy indicates, the articles, notes, and reviews are "devoted to criticism, scholarship, and bibliography of fiction in all languages since about 1880." The spring and autumn numbers are special issues on individual writers or subjects (and include a bibliography or survey of research on the author or topic). Annual index; cumulative index: Brooke K. Horvath, comp., *A Cumulative Index to* Modern Fiction Studies *(1955–1984), Volumes 1–30* (West Lafayette: Modern Fiction Studies, 1985, 270 pp.).

Gothic and Horror Fiction

Many works in section L: Genres/Fiction/Science and Fantasy Fiction are useful for research in horror fiction.

GUIDES TO PRIMARY WORKS

860 Bleiler, Everett F. *The Guide to Supernatural Fiction: A Full Description of 1,775 Books from 1750 to 1960, Including Ghost Stories, Weird Fiction, Stories of Supernatural Horror, Fantasy, Gothic Novels, Occult Fiction, and Similar Literature*. Kent: Kent State UP, 1983. 723 pp. PN56.S8.B57 809.3'937.

A collection of summaries of about 7,200 stories. Books are organized by author, editor, or title of anonymous work, then chronologically by publication date, with a separate summary for each story within a collection. Most summaries conclude with a brief evaluative comment. Three indexes: motifs and story types; persons; titles. Offering fuller but less discriminating coverage than Tymn, *Horror Literature* (865), Bleiler is primarily valuable for its extensive indexing of motifs and story types.

Although unreliable, Montague Summers, *A Gothic Bibliography* (London: Fortune, 1941, 620 pp.), includes some works not in Bleiler. Far inferior is Elsa J. Radcliffe, *Gothic Novels of the Twentieth Century: An Annotated Bibliography* (Metuchen: Scarecrow, 1979, 272 pp.), which is too inconsistent, idiosyncratic, and error-ridden to recommend to researchers.

865 Tymn, Marshall B., ed. *Horror Literature: A Core Collection and Reference Guide*. New York: Bowker, 1981. 559 pp. Z2014.H67.H67 [PR830.T3] 016.823'0872.

A selective guide emphasizing Anglo-American horror literature, with chapters on primary works and scholarship (through the late 1970s) as well as allied topics. The bulk of the collection consists of historical surveys accompanied by annotated lists of the most important primary works in the gothic romance, 1762–1820; the residual gothic impulse, 1824–73; psychological, antiquarian, and cosmic horror, 1872–1919; modern horror, 1920–80; horror pulps, 1933–40; and poetry. Along with lists of periodicals, societies and organizations, awards, and research collections are two incomplete, poorly organized, annotated guides to secondary sources and reference works (both superseded by Frank, *Guide to the Gothic* [875]). Indexed by author and title. Designed as a guide to library acquisitions, Tymn is useful to the literary researcher principally for its annotated lists of major primary works. Fuller, but less discriminating, coverage is offered by Bleiler, *Guide to Supernatural Fiction* (860).

More extensive summaries of five hundred representative English gothic romances from 1764 to the 1820s are available in Frederick S. Frank, *The First Gothics: A Critical Guide to the English Gothic Novel*, Garland Reference Library of the Humanities 710 (New York: Garland, 1987), 496 pp.

GUIDES TO SCHOLARSHIP AND CRITICISM

Serial Bibliographies

870 "The [1978–] Bibliography of Gothic Studies." Irregular supplements to *Gothic* (880) ns 1 (1986)– .

Earlier issues appear as:

1980: Comp. Gary William Crawford et al. Gothic Chapbooks 1. Baton Rouge: Gothic, 1983. 20 pp.

1978–79: *Gothic* 1–2 (1979–80).

An annotated bibliography of scholarship on literary gothicism and related supernatural literature of several countries and periods. Includes dissertations and some master's theses, but excludes reviews, interviews, and regular columns in magazines. Studies are listed alphabetically by author in three divisions: bibliographical and textual studies, general studies, and works about individual authors. The brief annotations are descriptive, although a few include evaluative phrases. Coverage is spotty, especially of foreign-language publications, but the works are useful for their inclusion of parts of books and studies overlooked by the standard serial bibliographies and indexes in section G. Coverage, however, is far in arrears.

See also

ABELL (340): [English] Literature/General through the volume for 1967; Literature, General/Literary History/Fiction, and Literature, General/Literary Criticism/Fiction in the volumes for 1968–72; Literary History and Criticism/Fiction in the volume for 1973; and English Literature/General/Fiction in later volumes.

Hall, *Science Fiction and Fantasy Research Index* (1005).

MLAIB (335): General VII: Literature, General and Comparative in the volumes for 1953–55; General II: Literature, General and Comparative in the volume for 1956; General IV/Prose Fiction in the volumes for 1957–80; and Genres/Fiction/Gothic Fiction and Genres/Novel/Gothic Novel sections in pt. 4 of the later volumes. Researchers must also check the headings beginning "Gothic" in the subject index to post-1980 volumes.

Other Bibliographies

875 Frank, Frederick S. *Guide to the Gothic: An Annotated Bibliography of Criticism*. Metuchen: Scarecrow, 1984. 421 pp. Z5917.G66.F7 [PN3435] 016.8093'872.

A descriptively annotated guide to criticism from 1900 to 1982. The approximately 2,500 entries are organized in classified divisions for bibliographies, national literatures (English, American, Canadian, French, and German, with sections for individual authors listed chronologically), and subjects (e.g., parodies, vampire, death by spontaneous combustion, film). Two indexes: critics; authors, artists, actors. This is the most complete guide to twentieth-century criticism on the genre.

Some additional studies through 1987 are listed in Frank, *Gothic Fiction: A Master List of Twentieth Century Criticism and Research*, Meckler's Bibliographies on Science Fiction, Fantasy, and Horror 3 (Westport: Meckler, 1988, 193 pp.), which rearranges entries (minus annotations) from *Guide to the Gothic* (without, of course, acknowledging its ancestry).

See also

Inge, *Handbook of American Popular Culture* (6295).
Spector, *English Gothic* (2345).
Tymn, *Horror Literature* (865).

PERIODICALS

880 *Gothic*. 1979–80; 1986– . Annual. PR830.T3.G67 823'.0872.

Publishes articles and reviews on all aspects of literary gothicism, especially in British and American literature. "The Bibliography of Gothic Studies" (870) now appears as an irregular supplement.

Historical Fiction

GUIDES TO PRIMARY WORKS

There is no adequate general guide to historical fiction; the following are the best reference sources available.

885 Baker, Ernest A. *A Guide to Historical Fiction*. London: Routledge; New York: Macmillan, 1914. 566 pp. Z5917.H6.B2 016.80883'81.

A selective guide, arranged by chronological periods within country divisions, mainly to novels in English (including translations). The bulk of the entries are devoted to British, American, and French history. The summary annotations are frequently quite full. Indexed by authors, titles, and subjects. Like Nield, *Guide to the Best Historical Novels and Tales* (900), Baker is dated but still useful for its subject indexing.

890 Gerhardstein, Virginia Brokaw. *Dickinson's American Historical Fiction*. 5th ed. Metuchen: Scarecrow, 1986. 352 pp. Z1231.F4.D47 [PS374.H5] 016.813'081.

A selective guide to 3,048 English-language works (principally novels) published for the most part between 1917 and 1984 and depicting some aspect of American history. The briefly annotated entries are classified by historical period. Two indexes: authors and titles; subjects. Although lacking any explanation of criteria governing selection, Gerhardstein is useful for its subject indexing, which allows identification by ethnic group, geographical location, and historical figure.

Some additional works on American history are listed in the following:

Coan, Otis W., and Richard G. Lillard. *America in Fiction: An Annotated List of Novels That Interpret Aspects of Life in the United States, Canada, and Mexico*. 5th ed. Palo Alto: Pacific, 1967. 232 pp. A selective guide to English-language novels, volumes of short stories, and folklore collections that treat some aspect of American life. Other than a preference for "substantial, realistic books over those that are romantic or sentimental or melodramatic or that merely broke ground," criteria governing selection are vague. Works are listed by author in seven variously classified divisions: pioneering, farm and village life, industrial America, politics and institutions, religion, minority ethnic groups, and Mexico. A brief descriptive annotation accompanies each entry. Indexed by authors.

VanDerhoof, Jack. *A Bibliography of Novels Related to American Frontier and Colonial History*. Troy: Whitston, 1971. 501 pp. Although VanDerhoof offers more thorough coverage of novels treating Colonial and frontier history, the lack of subject classification or indexing means that a user must search all 6,439 entries to locate works on a particular topic.

895 McGarry, Daniel D., and Sarah Harriman White. *World Historical Fiction Guide: An Annotated, Chronological, Geographical, and Topical List of Selected Historical Novels*. 2nd ed. Metuchen: Scarecrow, 1973. 629 pp. Z5917.H6.M3 016.80883'81.

A list of about 6,400 English-language works and translations (almost exclusively novels) organized by geographical area within chronological periods up to 1900. The one-sentence annotations are frequently inaccurate and rarely provide an adequate sense of content. Indexed by authors and titles, but not by subjects. Leonard B. Irwin, comp., *A Guide to Historical Fiction for the Use of Schools, Libraries, and the General Reader*, 10th ed., McKinley Bibliographics 1 (Brooklawn: McKinley, 1971, 255 pp.), exhibits similar inadequacies.

900 Nield, Jonathan. *A Guide to the Best Historical Novels and Tales*. 5th ed. New York: Macmillan, 1929. 424 pp. Z5917.H6.N6 016.80883'81.

A chronological guide, largely devoted to novels in English (including translations). Entries do not provide complete bibliographical information, but the succinct summaries clearly delineate content. Includes a brief bibliography of publications on historical fiction. Three indexes: authors; titles; subjects. Like Baker, *Guide to Historical Fiction* (885), Nield is dated but still useful for its subject indexing.

GUIDES TO SCHOLARSHIP AND CRITICISM

See

ABELL (340): [English] Literature/General through the volume for 1967; Literature, General/Literary History/Fiction, and Literature, General/Literary Criticism/Fiction in the volumes for 1968–72; Literary History and Criticism/Fiction in the volume for 1973; and English Literature/General/Fiction in later volumes.

Inge, *Handbook of American Popular Culture* (6295).

MLAIB (335): General VII: Literature, General and Comparative in the volumes for 1953–55; General II: Literature, General and Comparative in the volume for 1956; General IV/Prose Fiction in the volumes for 1957–80; and the Genres/Fiction/Historical Fiction and Genres/Novel/Historical Novel sections in pt. 4 of the later volumes. Researchers must also check the "Historical Fiction" and "Historical Novel" headings in the subject index to post-1980 volumes.

Mystery Fiction

LITERARY HANDBOOKS, DICTIONARIES, AND ENCYCLOPEDIAS

905 Steinbrunner, Chris, and Otto Penzler, eds. *Encyclopedia of Mystery and Detection*. New York: McGraw, 1976. 436 pp. P96.D4.E5 808.83'872'0321.

Includes about 600 entries on authors, characters, types of works, and films. Author entries include a checklist of primary works. Breen (920a) rates this as indispensable.

GUIDES TO PRIMARY WORKS

910 Cook, Michael L., comp. *Monthly Murders: A Checklist and Chronological Listing of Fiction in the Digest-Size Mystery Magazines in the United States and England*. Westport: Greenwood, 1982. 1,147 pp. Z1231.F4.C67 [PS374.D4] 016.813'0872'08.

A list of the stories published in American and English mystery magazines from 1941 through 1980. Magazines are organized alphabetically by title, with stories listed chronologically by issue. Two indexes: titles of magazines (including variant and alternate titles); authors (followed by titles of stories). Although not comprehensive, *Monthly Murders* is the fullest single index to the contents of these periodicals.

915 Hubin, Allen J. *Crime Fiction, 1749–1980: A Comprehensive Bibliography*. Garland Reference Library of the Humanities 371. New York: Garland, 1984. 712 pp. *1981–1985 Supplement*. Garland Reference Library of the Humanities 766. 1988. 260 pp. Z2014.F4.H82 [PR830.D4] 016.823'0872.

Indexes about 67,000 separately published English-language novels, collections of short stories or novellas, plays, and poems of mystery, detective, suspense, thriller, romantic suspense, police, and spy fiction. The author index lists works by name on title page with cross-references between pseudonym and real name; each work is identified by genre, setting, and series character. In the 1749–1980 volume, the title, setting, series and series character, and series character chronology indexes are keyed to the author list; the supplement adds indexes for screenwriters and directors. Besides new works and corrections to the original bibliography, the supplement adds a list of films based on any work recorded in either volume. Breen (920a) calls this an indispensable work. Review: (1749–1980) B. C. Bloomfield, *Library* 6th ser. 8 (1986): 96–98.

Albert J. Menendez, *The Subject Is Murder: A Selective Guide to Mystery Fiction*, Garland Reference Library of the Humanities 627 (New York: Garland, 1986, 332 pp.), classifies about 3,800 works under 25 subjects (e.g., academe, literary people, bookshops and libraries, weddings and honeymoons, and gardening).

See also

"Mystery, Detective, and Suspense Fiction Published in the U. S.," *Armchair Detective* (930).

GUIDES TO SCHOLARSHIP AND CRITICISM

920 Albert, Walter. *Detective and Mystery Fiction: An International Bibliography of Secondary Sources*. Madison: Brownstone, 1985. 781 pp. Z5917.D5.A4 [PN3448.D4].

A classified, annotated international bibliography of studies (published before c. 1984) on crime, detective, mystery, suspense, and espionage fiction that incorporates the *Armchair Detective* bibliographies (930a) but excludes Sherlockiana. Entries are arranged alphabetically by scholar in four divisions: reference works; general studies; dime novels, juvenile series, and pulps; and authors. Annotations are frequently extensive and evaluative. Indexed by scholars, authors, series characters, magazines, and publishers. The most thorough bibliography of the subject, *Detective and Mystery Fiction* is superior to the following:

Breen, Jon L. *What about Murder? A Guide to Books about Mystery and Detective Fiction*. Metuchen: Scarecrow, 1981. 157 pp. Supplemented by "What about Murder," Breen's regular column in *Armchair Detective* (930) 18 (1984–). This work remains valuable for its detailed evaluations.

Johnson, Timothy W., and Julia Johnson, eds. *Crime Fiction Criticism: An Annotated Bibliography*. Garland Reference Library of the Humanities 233. New York: Garland, 1981. 423 pp.

Skene Melvin, David, and Ann Skene Melvin, comps. *Crime, Detective, Espionage, Mystery, and Thriller Fiction and Film: A Comprehensive Bibliography of Critical Writing through 1979*. Westport: Greenwood, 1980. 367 pp.

See also

ABELL (340): [English] Literature/General through the volume for 1967; Literature, General/Literary History/Fiction, and Literature, General/Literary Criticism/Fiction in the volumes for 1968–72; Literary History and Criticism/Fiction in the volume for 1973; and English Literature/General/Fiction in later volumes.

"Bibliography of Secondary Sources," *Armchair Detective* (930).

Inge, *Handbook of American Popular Culture* (6295).

MLAIB (335): General VII: Literature, General and Comparative in the volumes for 1953–55; General II: Literature, General and Comparative in the volume for 1956; General IV/Prose Fiction in the volumes for 1957–80; and the Genres/Fiction/Detective Fiction, Genres/Fiction/Mystery Fiction, Genres/Novel/Detective Novel, and Genres/Novel/Mystery Novel sections in pt. 4 of the later volumes. Researchers must also check the headings beginning "Detective" and "Mystery" in the subject index to post-1980 volumes.

PERIODICALS

Guides to Primary Works

925 Cook, Michael L., [ed.]. *Mystery, Detective, and Espionage Magazines*. Historical Guides to the World's Periodicals and Newspapers. Westport: Greenwood, 1983. 795 pp. PN3448.D4.C56 809.3'872.

A collection of separately authored profiles of English-language fiction and nonfiction magazines (including scholarly journals and fanzines) published in North America and England, along with selective overviews of foreign-language periodicals. Excludes publications restricted to members of Sherlock Holmes organizations. Organized alphabetically by title (with cross-references for variants), the entries for the English-language periodicals include a discussion of publishing history and general content; a selected list of studies, indexing sources, and locations (with many citing only private collections); and information on title changes, volume and issue numbering and dates, publisher(s), editor(s), price, size and pagination, and current status. Two other divisions offer basic overviews and lists by country of foreign-language magazines, and discussions of book clubs. Seven appendixes: United States, English, and Canadian magazines, classified by country, then format for fiction and subject for nonfiction publications; major writers and the magazines which published them; chronology of English-language periodicals and book clubs; American true-detective magazines; Canadian true-detective magazines; Sherlock Holmes scion society periodicals; other periodicals of interest to the collector. Concludes with a selected bibliography. The index of titles, persons, publishers, and some subjects excludes the division listing foreign-language magazines. Given the ephemeral nature and short lives of many of these publications, the lack of publishing details and few locations for many entries is not surprising. Although the essays vary substantially in quality and accuracy, Cook is the single best guide to the important English-language periodicals. Review: Fred Erisman, *Resources for American Literary Study* 13 (1983): 109–11.

Scholarly Journals

930 *Armchair Detective* (*ArmD*). 1967– . Quarterly. PS374.D4.A75 813.

Publishes articles, interviews, collector's guides, and bibliographies on mystery, suspense, and detective fiction. Each issue includes several regular columns and reviews, as well as a checklist of "Mystery, Detective, and Suspense Fiction Published in the U.S." The annual "Bibliography of Secondary Sources," which appears in vols. 7–16 (1973–83), is incorporated into Albert, *Detective and Mystery Fiction* (920). Cumulative index: Steven A. Stilwell, comp., *The* Armchair Detective *Index: Volumes 1–10, 1967–1977* (New York: Armchair Detective, 1979, 64 pp.).

935 *Clues: A Journal of Detection* (*Clues*). 1980– . 2/yr. PN3448.D4.C6 808.

Although open to studies of detection "in all the media and in all aspects of culture," articles emphasize twentieth-century mystery and detection fiction. *Clues* also publishes reviews of books by and about detection.

Picaresque Fiction

GUIDES TO SCHOLARSHIP AND CRITICISM

950 Laurenti, Joseph L. *Bibliografía de la literatura picaresca: Desde sus orígenes hasta el presente/A Bibliography of Picaresque Literature: From Its Origins to the Present.* Metuchen: Scarecrow, 1973. 262 pp. *Bibliografía de la literatura picaresca (suplemento)/A Bibliography of Picaresque Literature (Supplement).* New York: AMS, 1981. 163 pp. Z5917.P5.L35 [PN3428] 016.80883'87.

A bibliography of editions and translations of Spanish picaresque fiction first published between 1554 and 1743 and of studies through 1978 of picaresque fiction worldwide. Entries are listed chronologically in sections on bibliographies, anthologies, etymology of *pícaro*, general studies, literary relations (subdivided by country), and individual Spanish novels (with subdivisions for editions, translations [grouped by language], and studies). Entries for primary works locate copies in North American libraries. Indexed by scholars, authors, editors, and translators. Organization, layout, and minimal indexing make Laurenti a frustrating work to use, but no other source collects so handily the widely dispersed scholarship on the picaresque.

See also

ABELL (340): [English] Literature/General through the volume for 1967; Literature, General/Literary History/Fiction, and Literature, General/Literary Criticism/Fiction in the volumes for 1968–72; Literary History and Criticism/Fiction in the volume for 1973; and English Literature/General/Fiction in later volumes.

MLAIB (335): General VII: Literature, General and Comparative in the volumes for 1953–55; General II: Literature, General and Comparative in the volume for 1956; General IV/Prose Fiction in the volumes for 1957–80; and the Genres/Fiction/Picaresque Fiction and Genres/Novel/Picaresque Novel sections in pt. 4 of the later volumes. Researchers must also check the headings beginning "Picaresque" in the subject index to post-1980 volumes.

Science and Fantasy Fiction

This section lists only the major general reference works on science and fantasy fiction. It excludes works devoted to film and television; illustration; chronological periods; a single national literature; and individual forms, types, or themes. For these specialized reference works, consult Tymn, *Research Guide to Science Fiction Studies* (1015a); "Year's Scholarship in Fantastic Literature" (1010); Hall, *Science Fiction and Fantasy Research Index* (1005); and Barron, *Anatomy of Wonder* (1015).

HISTORIES AND SURVEYS

For an evaluative annotated list of histories and surveys, see Neil Barron, "History and Criticism" (pp. 609–35), in Barron, *Anatomy of Wonder* (1015); and Marshall B. Tymn, "Science Fiction: A Brief History and Review of Criticism," *American Studies International* 23.1 (1985): 41–66.

955 Aldiss, Brian W., and David Wingrove. *Trillion Year Spree: The History of Science Fiction*. New York: Atheneum, 1986. 511 pp. PR830.S35.A38 823'.0876'09.

A critical history from Shelley's *Frankenstein* through the mid-1980s that locates the origin of science fiction in the gothic romance and emphasizes its development as a genre (primarily in Britain and the United States). Indexed by author, title, and some subjects. Although some assertions are controversial and although the treatment of post-1970 works is not up to the standard of the earlier part, *Trillion Year Spree* remains the fullest history of science fiction and a worthy successor to Aldiss, *Billion Year Spree: The True History of Science Fiction* (Garden City: Doubleday, 1973, 339 pp.). Reviews: John Clute, *Times Literary Supplement* 31 Oct. 1986: 1223; Veronica Hollinger, *Science-Fiction Studies* 15 (1988): 102–05.

960 Suvin, Darko. *Metamorphoses of Science Fiction: On the Poetics and History of a Literary Genre*. New Haven: Yale UP, 1979. 317 pp. PN3448.S45.S897 809.3'876.

An attempt to legitimatize science fiction by establishing a poetics of the genre and tracing its early evolution. Based on Marxist ideology, the first part presents the theoretical foundation, which defines science fiction as "the literature of cognitive estrangement" and emphasizes utopian literature while largely excluding myth and fantasy. The second part traces the evolution of European and American science fiction from More through Wells, with a brief excursion into early twentieth-century Russian works and a chapter on Karel Čapek. Concludes with a selected bibliography. Indexed by person. Although reviewers justifiably find the discussion of poetics too restrictive, most agree that Suvin is an important, provocative contribution to the study of the genre. Reviews: Dagmar Barnouw, *MLN* 95 (1980): 1461–66; John R. Reed, *Modern Philology* 78 (1981): 338–40; George Slusser, *Nineteenth-Century Fiction* 35 (1980): 73–76.

LITERARY HANDBOOKS, DICTIONARIES, AND ENCYCLOPEDIAS

965 Nicholls, Peter, gen. ed. *The Science Fiction Encyclopedia*. Garden City: Doubleday, 1979. 672 pp. British ed.: *The Encyclopedia of Science Fiction: An Illustrated A to Z* (London: Granada, 1979, 672 pp.). PN3448.S45.S29 809.3'876.

Prints more than 2,800 signed entries on authors, themes, films and television programs, magazines and fanzines, illustrators, editors, critics, filmmakers, publishers, pseudonyms, series, anthologies, comics, terminology, and awards. A useful source of general information. Review: Robert M. Philmus, *Science-Fiction Studies* 7 (1980): 217–21.

James Gunn, ed., *The New Encyclopedia of Science Fiction* (New York: Viking, 1988, 524 pp.), emphasizes American and British science fiction in signed entries for writers and others (such as illustrators, film directors, and actors), organizations, films, serial publications, and a variety of related topics. Gunn is overall more selective (but more current) than Nicholls.

970 Wolfe, Gary K. *Critical Terms for Science Fiction and Fantasy: A Glossary and Guide to Scholarship*. New York: Greenwood, 1986. 162 pp. PN3435.W64 809.3'876.

A dictionary of genres, subgenres, forms, some themes, techniques, effects, and other terms important to the description of science fiction and fantasy. Entries provide basic definitions, usually accompanied by examples and references to important scholarship. Indexed by writers cited. The work, which is based on extensive acquaintance with the criticism, offers an essential guide to the use and interpretation of terminology for analyzing science fiction and fantasy.

GUIDES TO PRIMARY WORKS

Serial Bibliographies

975 Brown, Charles N., and William G. Contento. *Science Fiction, Fantasy, and Horror [1985–]: A Comprehensive Bibliography of Books and Short Fiction Published in the English Language*. Oakland: Locus, 1986– . Annual. Former title: *Science Fiction in Print* (1986). PN3433.8.S4.

A list of science fiction anthologies, collections, magazines, and novels, as well as books about the subject, published since December 1984 and received by *Locus* magazine. Works are indexed in six divisions: an author list of books, collections, and magazines (including contents); a title list of books; an author list of books and stories first published during the year; a list of new books classified by broad subject, form, or genre; an author list of stories in collections and magazines; and a title list of stories. Most of the entries cite publication information and type of work. Concludes with a statistical summary of the year's publishing trends and a directory of small publishers. Users should be alert for the corrected sheets that the publisher promises to buyers. Although it is far from "comprehensive," is not an actual books in print, and employs some vague categories and needless lists, Brown and Contento is the closest we have to a list of currently available science fiction publications and a useful continuation of Contento, *Index to Science Fiction Anthologies and Collections* (985).

980 *N.E.S.F.A. Index to the Science Fiction Magazines and Original Anthologies*. Cambridge: New England Science Fiction Assn., 1973– . Annual. (Title varies.) Z5917.S36.I55 [PN3433] 813'.0876'016.

An author, title, and magazine or anthology index to English-language publications. *N.E.S.F.A. Index* is now the standard index, but publication is far in arrears. Coverage begins with 1971; for earlier magazines see the following:

Index to the Science Fiction Magazines, 1966–1970. Cambridge: New England Science Fiction Assn., 1971. 82 pp.

Strauss, Erwin S., comp. *The MIT Science Fiction Society's Index to the*

S-F Magazines, 1951–1965. Cambridge: MIT Science Fiction Soc., 1965. 207 pp. Superior to Norm Metcalf, comp., *The Index of Science Fiction Magazines, 1951–1965* (El Cerrito: Stark, 1968, 249 pp.).

Day, Donald B., comp. *Index to the Science Fiction Magazines, 1926–1950*. Rev. ed. Reference Publication in Science Fiction. Boston: Hall, 1982. 289 pp.

Other Bibliographies

985 Contento, William. *Index to Science Fiction Anthologies and Collections*. 2 vols. Reference Publication in Science Fiction. Boston: Hall, 1978–84. Z1231.F4.C65 [PS374.S35] 016.813'0876'08.

An author and title index to the contents of English-language collections, anthologies, and novels developed out of three or more stories. Vol. 1 (covering works published through June 1977) is restricted to science fiction which deals "with social and technical extrapolation and invention," but the second volume (primarily covering works published from July 1977 through December 1983) admits more horror, weird, and fantasy fiction. The second volume offers a significantly improved layout, but both volumes are plagued by an unduly confusing system of abbreviations. Although not comprehensive, Contento is the best single index to science fiction anthologies and collections.

Continued by Brown, *Science Fiction, Fantasy, and Horror* (975) for collections published after December 1984.

990 Reginald, R. *Science Fiction and Fantasy Literature: A Checklist, 1700–1974, with Contemporary Science Fiction Authors II*. 2 vols. Detroit: Gale, 1979. *Science Fiction and Fantasy Literature: A Twelve-Year Supplement, 1975–1986, with Contemporary Science Fiction Authors III*. 2 vols. Scheduled for 1989. Z5917.S36.R42 [PN3448.S45] 016.823'0876.

Vol. 1 lists 15,884 English-language first editions by author, with accompanying title and series indexes. (The supplement will add about 12,000 first editions, as well as include corrections and additions to the original checklist.) Although Reginald offers the most comprehensive coverage of separately published fantasy, science, and weird supernatural fiction, it does not completely supersede E. F. Bleiler, *The Checklist of Science-Fiction and Supernatural Fiction* (Glen Rock: Firebell, 1978, 266 pp.). L. W. Currey, *Science Fiction and Fantasy Authors: A Bibliography of First Printings of Their Fiction and Selected Nonfiction* (Boston: Hall, 1979, 571 pp.), is the most accurate source for identifying first printings through 1977 of separately published works by 215 writers.

Vol. 2, a revision of *Contemporary Science Fiction Authors* (New York: Arno, 1975, 365 pp.), provides biographical information on 1,443 twentieth-century authors. (The supplement will print about 2,000 biographies, replacing or updating the original ones where possible.) Since details were compiled from questionnaires and *Contemporary Authors* (595), entries are uneven.

995 Schlobin, Roger C. *The Literature of Fantasy: A Comprehensive, Annotated Bibliography of Modern Fantasy Fiction*. Garland Reference Library of the Humanities 176. New York: Garland, 1979. 425 pp. Z2014.F4.S33 [PR830.F3] 016.823'0876.

A selective guide to major works published between 1837 and April 1979 by English and American authors and a few foreign writers important to the Anglo-American tradition. *Literature of Fantasy* includes primarily adult prose fiction published in book form in English. The first part is a list of novels and collections—as well as bibliographies—accompanied by summaries, with occasional evaluative comments, for novels and lists of contents for collections. The second part lists anthologies (along with contents) alphabetically by editor. Two indexes: authors, compilers, editors, translators; titles. Although hardly the comprehensive bibliography claimed in the subtitle, Schlobin is the fullest guide to important fantasy fiction.

For a more selective annotated guide that covers about 240 major works of fantasy published in English between 1854 and 1978, see chapter 3 of Marshall B. Tymn, Kenneth J. Zahorski, and Robert H. Boyer, *Fantasy Literature: A Core Collection and Reference Guide* (New York: Bowker, 1979, 273 pp.), which also includes lists of major North American and British periodicals, societies and organizations, literary awards, and American and Canadian library collections. (The indexing is untrustworthy, however.) The chapter on selected critical studies and reference works is superseded by Tymn, *Research Guide to Science Fiction Studies* (1015a) and especially Neil Barron, "General Reference Works" (pp. 593–608) and "History and Criticism" (pp. 609–35) in Barron, *Anatomy of Wonder* (1015).

1000 Tuck, Donald H. *The Encyclopedia of Science Fiction and Fantasy through 1968*. 3 vols. Chicago: Advent, 1974–82. Z5917.S36.T83 016.80883'876.

Vols. 1 and 2 constitute an international who's who of science, fantasy, and weird fiction. Entries include basic biographical information, but the focus of each is a bibliography of collections (including contents), novels (originally published or reprinted 1945–68), and translations. (For earlier novels see Reginald, *Science Fiction and Fantasy Literature* [990].) Vol. 2 prints a title index to the listings. Vol. 3 includes a title bibliography of magazines (with publication and historical information on many ephemeral periodicals); an author list of paperback editions from the 1940s through 1968; a list of paperback publishers with titles published under imprints; a pseudonym and real name list; and a list of series, connected stories, and sequels. Tuck records a wealth of information, although parts are superseded by recent bibliographies of primary works in this section and by more current but less comprehensive biographical dictionaries such as Curtis C. Smith, ed., *Twentieth-Century Science-Fiction Writers*, 2nd ed., Twentieth-Century Writers Series (Chicago: St. James, 1986, 933 pp.), which must be used with care because of numerous errors and omissions.

See also

Barron, *Anatomy of Wonder* (1015).
Bleiler, *Guide to Supernatural Fiction* (860).
"Cross-Referenced Index of Short Fiction Anthologies," *Studies in Short Fiction* (1100). Science fiction anthologies have been included since the index for 1978–79 in 16.2 (1979).

GUIDES TO SCHOLARSHIP AND CRITICISM

Serial Bibliographies

1005 Hall, Hal W., comp. *Science Fiction and Fantasy Research Index* (*SFFRI*). Westport: Meckler, 1981– . Annual. Former title: *Science Fiction Research Index* (1981). Z5917.S36.H37 016.8093876.

The volumes for 1981–85 are cumulated and augmented in the following:

Hall, Hal W., ed. *Science Fiction and Fantasy Reference Index, 1878–1985: An International Author and Subject Index to History and Criticism.* 2 vols. Detroit: Gale, 1987.

Subject and author indexes of books, articles, parts of books, and newspaper materials on science, fantasy, and horror fiction. Each volume provides broad chronological and international coverage (including, it seems, whatever the compiler recently discovered). The subject index, based largely on titles, utilizes some imprecise headings, has inconsistencies, and does not adequately represent the content of many entries (some of which are taken from other sources). *Science Fiction and Fantasy Research Index* offers fuller but more erratic coverage of scholarship and criticism than "Year's Scholarship in Fantastic Literature" (1010) and the standard serial bibliographies and indexes in section G. Reviews: C[harles] E[lkins], *Science-Fiction Studies* 9 (1982): 100–02; Robert M. Philmus, *Science-Fiction Studies* 11 (1984): 204–09.

Science Fiction and Fantasy Reference Index includes approximately 19,000 works, the majority of which are English-language publications between 1945 and 1985. Entries are organized in two indexes: authors of books and articles; subjects. Although the editor claims that 95% of the works were personally examined, the subject indexing is not much improved over that in *Science Fiction and Fantasy Research Index.* Coverage of foreign-language scholarship is weak, but *Science Fiction and Fantasy Reference Index* is the fullest retrospective bibliography of studies of science fiction and supersedes Hall, *Science Fiction Index: Criticism* (Bryan: the author, 1980, microfiche), and the augmented cumulation of *Science Fiction and Fantasy Research Index* in Hall, *Science Fiction and Fantasy Book Review Index, 1980–1984* (1020), pp. 347–761.

1010 "The Year's Scholarship in Fantastic Literature [1972–79, 1983–]." *Extrapolation* (entry 1030). 17–22, 26– (1975–81, 1985–). (Title varies.)

Tymn, Marshall B., ed. *The Year's Scholarship in Science Fiction, Fantasy, and Horror Literature, [1980, 1981, 1982].* Kent: Kent State UP, 1983–84.

The bibliographies for 1972–79 are cumulated and expanded as the following:

Tymn, Marshall B., and Roger C. Schlobin, eds. *The Year's Scholarship in Science Fiction and Fantasy, 1976–1979.* Serif Series 41. Kent: Kent State UP, 1982. 251 pp.

———. *The Year's Scholarship in Science Fiction and Fantasy, 1972–1975.* Serif Series 36. 1979. 222 pp.

An annual bibliography limited to English-language studies and emphasizing American scholarship. Entries are currently divided among seven sections: bibliography and reference, history and criticism, author studies, writing and publishing, film and television, art and artists, and teaching resources. The bibliography has undergone a number of changes in title, scope, and form since its first appearance in 17 (1975): 78–96 as "A Checklist of American Critical Works on SF, 1972–1973." In the 1984–85 bibliographies, the annotations are replaced by an inadequate subject index to only the history and criticism section; with the 1986 bibliography, the index was dropped and some entries are again briefly annotated. Although limited in scope, the bibliographies remain the most widely consulted annual list of scholarship on science and fantasy fiction. Hall, *Science Fiction and Fantasy Research Index* (1005) offers fuller coverage.

See also

ABELL (340): [English] Literature/General through the volume for 1967; Literature, General/Literary History/Fiction, and Literature, General/Literary Criticism/Fiction in the volumes for 1968–72; Literary History and Criticism/Fiction in the volume for 1973; and English Literature/General/Fiction in later volumes.

MLAIB (335): General VII: Literature, General and Comparative in the volumes for 1953–55; General II: Literature, General and Comparative in the volume for 1956; General IV/Prose Fiction in the volumes for 1957–80; and the Genres/Fiction/Fantasy Fiction, and Genres/Fiction/Science Fiction sections in pt. 4 of the later volumes. Researchers must also check the "Fantasy Fiction" and "Science Fiction" headings in the subject index to post-1980 volumes.

"Relations of Literature and Science" (6440).

Other Bibliographies

1015 Barron, Neil, ed. *Anatomy of Wonder: A Critical Guide to Science Fiction*. 3rd ed. New York: Bowker, 1987. 874 pp. Z5917.S36.A52 [PN3433.8] 016.80883'876.

A selective, evaluative guide to primary works, scholarship, and reference sources. The first part consists of chapters on periods (the beginnings to 1920s, 1918–38, 1938–63, 1964–86), works for children, and foreign-language science fiction (German, French, Russian, Italian, Japanese, Danish, Swedish, Norwegian, Dutch, Belgian, Romanian, Yugoslav, and Hebrew, with most chapters commenting on reference works). Each chapter begins with a historical survey and is followed by critical summaries of the most important works. The second part is devoted to lists of research aids, with chapters on library selection; general reference works; history and criticism; books about individual authors; film and television; illustration; teaching materials; magazines; and library and private collections. The full annotations are rigorously evaluative and frequently offer helpful comparisons. (In both parts an asterisk denotes an especially significant work.) Two indexes: authors and subjects; titles. Usually judicious in selection and pointed in evaluation, *Anatomy of Wonder* is the best guide to important scholarship and reference works.

Although now dated, the following selective guides remain occasionally useful:

Clareson, Thomas. *Science Fiction Criticism: An Annotated Checklist*. Serif Series 23. Kent: Kent State UP, 1972. 225 pp. The work remains useful for its inclusion of articles, which both Barron and Tymn (see below) omit.

Tymn, Marshall B., Roger C. Schlobin, and L. W. Currey, comps. and eds. *A Research Guide to Science Fiction Studies: An Annotated Checklist of Primary and Secondary Sources for Fantasy and Science Fiction*. Garland Reference Library of the Humanities 87. New York: Garland, 1977. 165 pp. A selective, classified guide to about 400 important bibliographies, reference works, biographical dictionaries, indexes, surveys and histories, studies of individual authors, and periodicals published in the United States and England through 1976. The annotations are only occasionally evaluative but usually indicate when a work supersedes an earlier one. (The separate list of North American dissertations, compiled by Douglas R. Justus, is not annotated.)

See also

Inge, *Handbook of American Popular Culture* (6295).
Schatzberg, *Relations of Literature and Science* (6445).

Review Indexes

1020 *SFBRI: Science Fiction Book Review Index*. Comp. Hal W. Hall. Bryan: SFBRI, 1970– . Annual. Z5917.S36.S19 809.3'876.

The work is cumulated and augmented in the following:

Hall, Hal W. *Science Fiction and Fantasy Book Review Index, 1980–1984*. Detroit: Gale, 1985. 761 pp.

———. *Science Fiction Book Review Index, 1974–1979*. 1981. 391 pp.

———. *Science Fiction Book Review Index, 1923–1973*. 1975. 438 pp.

An author list, with title index, of works reviewed in science fiction and a few additional periodicals. Although entries do not include full bibliographical information and many are taken from other indexes, *SFBRI* is the fullest guide to reviews of science fiction works and scholarship. The cumulation of *Science Fiction and Fantasy Research Index*, vols. 1–5 (1005) in the 1980–84 cumulation of *SFBRI* is superseded by Hall, *Science Fiction and Fantasy Reference Index, 1878–1985* (1005a). Review: (1980–84) Gary K. Wolfe, *Science-Fiction Studies* 14 (1987): 252–60.

See also

Sec. G: Serial Bibliographies, Indexes, and Abstracts/Book Review Indexes.

BIOGRAPHICAL DICTIONARIES

For an evaluatively annotated list of biographical reference works, see Neil Barron, "General Reference Works" (pp. 593–608) and "Author Studies" (pp. 636–71) in Barron, *Anatomy of Wonder* (1015).

See also

Contemporary Authors (595).
Dictionary of Literary Biography (600).
Nicholls, *Science Fiction Encyclopedia* (965).
Reginald, *Science Fiction and Fantasy Literature*, vol. 2 (990).
Tuck, *Encyclopedia of Science Fiction and Fantasy through 1968* (1000).

PERIODICALS

For an evaluative, but highly selective, list of reference works and periodicals, see H. W. Hall, "Science Fiction Magazines" (pp. 721–33), in Barron, *Anatomy of Wonder* (1015).

Guides to Primary Works

1025 Tymn, Marshall B., and Mike Ashley, eds. *Science Fiction, Fantasy, and Weird Fiction Magazines*. Historical Guides to the World's Periodicals and Newspapers. Westport: Greenwood, 1985. 970 pp. PN3433.T9 809.3'876.

A guide to magazines, fanzines, and scholarly journals from 1882 through 1983. The entries are organized in four divisions: 279 English-language magazines, 15 paperback English-language anthology series associated with magazines, 72 scholarly journals and major fanzines, and 184 foreign-language magazines. The first three divisions are organized alphabetically by title (with cross-references for variant titles); the last by country, then title. In the first and second divisions, the separately authored profiles consist of a discussion of publishing history, editorial policies, contents, personnel, and significance; a selective list of scholarship, indexing sources, reprints, and locations; and details of title changes, volume and issue data, publisher(s), editor(s), format, and price. Entries in the other divisions offer much less detailed information on scope, contents, beginning and ending dates, and publishing information. Concludes with two appendixes (index to major cover artists; chronology of English-language magazines from 1882 through 1983) and a selective bibliography. The persons, titles, and awards index excludes foreign-language magazines. Although the entries vary in amount of detail and degree of assessment, Tymn and Ashley offers the fullest guide to the important magazines. Review: Gary K. Wolfe, *Science-Fiction Studies* 14 (1987): 252–60.

Scholarly Journals

1030 *Extrapolation*. 1959– . Quarterly. PN3448.S45.E9 808.83'876'05.

Publishes articles, bibliographies, reviews, and occasional special issues on science, fantasy, and horror fiction. Annual index. See entry 1010 for the annual "The Year's Scholarship in Fantastic Literature."

1035 *Foundation: The Review of Science Fiction* (*Foundation*). 1972– . 3/yr. PS374.S35.F68 813'.0876'09.

Publishes articles, reviews, and occasional special issues on all aspects of science, fantasy, and horror fiction.

1040 *Science-Fiction Studies* (*SFS*). 1973– . 3/yr. PN3448.S45.S34 809.3'876.

Like *Extrapolation* (1030), *Science-Fiction Studies* publishes articles, notes, and reviews on science and utopian fiction (with occasional sections devoted to special topics), but offers more emphasis on theory, more reviews and review articles, and fewer bibliographies. Annual index; cumulative index: vols. 1–10, in 10 (1983): 364–88.

Utopian Fiction

Many works in the preceding part on science and fantasy fiction are important for research in utopian literature.

GUIDES TO PRIMARY WORKS

1055 Sargent, Lyman Tower. *British and American Utopian Literature, 1516–1985: An Annotated, Chronological Bibliography*. Garland Reference Library of the Humanities 831. New York: Garland, 1988. 559 pp. Z2014.U84.S28 [PR149.U8] 016.82'08'0372.

An annotated list of utopias, arranged chronologically by year of first publication. Entries include a brief descriptive annotation and locate one or two copies in British and American libraries. Two indexes: authors; titles. An expanded, revised version of *British and American Utopian Literature, 1516–1975: An Annotated Bibliography*, Reference Publication in Science Fiction (Boston: Hall, 1979, 324 pp.), the new edition omits the first edition's list of scholarship (whose usefulness, however, is mitigated by the fact that books, articles, and dissertations are divided into separate alphabetical listings and by the lack of any indexing). Sargent offers the best guide to English-language utopias.

Although Glenn Negley, *Utopian Literature: A Bibliography, with a Supplementary Listing of Works Influential in Utopian Thought* (Lawrence: Regents P of Kansas, 1977, 228 pp.), includes European fiction, it is more restrictive in defining utopian literature and marred by a number of deficiencies (for which see the review by R. D. M[ullen], *Science-Fiction Studies* 5 [1978]: 184–86).

See also

MLAIB (335): Themes and Figures/Utopia section of pt. 4 of the post-1980 volumes. Researchers must also check the headings beginning "Utopia," "Utopian," and "Utopianism" in the subject index to post-1980 volumes.

Novel

GUIDES TO PRIMARY WORKS

1060 Wright, R. Glenn, comp. *Author Bibliography of English Language Fiction in the Library of Congress through 1950*. 8 vols. Boston: Hall, 1973.

Chronological Bibliography of English Language Fiction in the Library of Congress through 1950. 8 vols. 1974. *Title Bibliography of English Language Fiction in the Library of Congress through 1950.* 9 vols. 1976. Z5918.W74 016.823'008.

Reproductions of catalog cards from the Library of Congress shelflist PZ3 classification, which lists individual works of English-language prose fiction, including translations, by authors whose first work was published before 31 December 1950. The *Author Bibliography* arranges cards alphabetically under the author's nationality (Australia, Canada, East and Southeast Asia, Europe, Latin America, New Zealand, South Africa, United Kingdom, United States, and unknown). Vol. 7 includes a pseudonym index; vol. 8 is an author list of English-language translations (with a translator index).

The *Chronological Bibliography* is also organized by nationality of the author and then by date of edition (although many editions are actually classified by country of publication). Vol. 7 includes an index of joint authors, and lists of pseudonyms, real names, and unidentified pseudonymous authors (all classified by nationality); vol. 8 prints chronological indexes to translations and translators, and alphabetical indexes to joint authors of translations and joint translators.

Like the other works, the *Title Bibliography* is organized by nationality of the author, then alphabetically by title, with cross-references for variant titles; however, many works are actually classified by country of publication. Vol. 8 includes an index of joint authors, list of pseudonyms, list of real names, list of unidentified pseudonymous authors and their works, and index of translations; vol. 9 has an index of translators and joint translators.

Wright's compilations are principally useful as catalogs of American editions of English-language novels (largely by Americans) but limited by their restriction to the Library of Congress holdings, which are extensive but not comprehensive. The *Author* and *Title* bibliographies are superseded by OCLC (225), RLIN (230), and more specialized works such as Wright, *American Fiction* (4180). The *Chronological Bibliography* is a convenient preliminary source for charting trends in the publishing of fiction in the United States (particularly in the twentieth century); however, its ascriptions of nationality cannot be trusted.

GUIDES TO SCHOLARSHIP AND CRITICISM

See

ABELL (340): [English] Literature/General through the volume for 1967; Literature, General/Literary History/Fiction, and Literature, General/Literary Criticism/Fiction in the volumes for 1968–72; Literary History and Criticism/Fiction in the volume for 1973; and English Literature/General/Fiction in later volumes.

MLAIB (335): General VII: Literature, General and Comparative in the volumes for 1953–55; General II: Literature, General and Comparative in the volume for 1956; General IV/Prose Fiction in the volumes for 1957–80; and Genres/Novel section in pt. 4 of the later volumes. Researchers must also check the headings beginning "Novel" in the subject index to post-1980 volumes.

PERIODICALS

1065 *Novel: A Forum on Fiction* (*Novel*). 1967– . 3/yr. PN3311.N65 813.
Publishes articles and reviews on theory, forms, and history of the novel, but emphasizes theory and English and American works since 1800. Annual index; cumulative index: vols. 1–5, in 5 (1972): 278–92.

1070 *Studies in the Novel* (*SNNTS*). 1969– . Quarterly. PN3311.S82 809.3'3'05.
Emphasizes studies of individual post-1800 English and American novels, with less attention than *Novel* (1065) to theory. Early volumes include a number of special issues with accompanying bibliographies. *Studies in the Novel* also publishes reviews and review essays. Annual index.

See also

Journal of Narrative Technique (840).
Modern Fiction Studies (845).

Short Fiction (Short Story, Novella)

GUIDES TO PRIMARY WORKS

1085 *Short Story Index: An Index to Stories in Collections and Periodicals* (*SSI*). New York: Wilson, 1953– . Annual, with quinquennial and other cumulations extending coverage to 1900. Z5917.S5.C62 016.80883'1.
An author, title, and subject index to more than 154,000 (as of the volume covering 1986) short stories published in anthologies and (since 1974) in periodicals covered by *Readers' Guide* (400) and *Humanities Index* (385). (Those from periodicals are not indexed by subject.) The coverage emphasizes established authors. Entries are keyed to a list of anthologies at the back and in the cumulation *Short Story Index: Collections Indexed, 1900–1978*, ed. Juliette Yaakov (1979, 349 pp.). *SSI* is the best source for identifying stories on a theme or subject and for locating reprints.
Less comprehensive but occasionally useful are the following:

Chicorel, Marietta, ed. *Chicorel Index to Short Stories in Anthologies and Collections*. 4 vols. Chicorel Index Series 12. New York: Chicorel, 1974. Supplement: *1975/76*. 2 vols. 1977. An author and title list only.

Messerli, Douglas, and Howard N. Fox, comps. *Index to Periodical Fiction in English, 1965–1969*. Metuchen: Scarecrow, 1977. 746 pp. An author list of 11,077 works of short fiction in a variety of journals (popular and little magazines, university reviews, scholarly journals) published throughout the world (but emphasizing American publications). Although several periodicals are not fully searched and coverage is restricted to five years, a majority of the entries are not indexed elsewhere.

See also

Sec. K: Periodicals/Little Magazines.
American Humanities Index (360).
Arts and Humanities Citation Index (365).
"Cross-Referenced Index of Short Fiction Anthologies," *Studies in Short Fiction* (1100).
Humanities Index (385).
Readers' Guide (400).

GUIDES TO SCHOLARSHIP AND CRITICISM

1090 Walker, Warren S., comp. *Twentieth-Century Short Story Explication: Interpretations 1900–1975 of Short Fiction since 1800*. 3rd ed. Hamden: Shoe String, 1977. 880 pp. *Supplement I*. 1980. 257 pp. *Supplement II*. 1984. 348 pp. *Supplement III*. 1987. 486 pp. Z5917.S5.W33 [PN3373] 016.8093'1.

A selective bibliography of articles and parts of books (primarily in English and published from 1900 through 1984) on short stories printed after 1800 by some 1,767 authors worldwide. Since the focus is explication ("interpretation or explanation of the meaning of a story, including observations on theme, symbol, and sometimes structure"), source, biographical, and background studies are excluded. Entries are organized by writer, then by individual work, with citations to books keyed to a list at the back. For abbreviations of journal titles in the main volume, users must consult the list in the first supplement. *Twentieth-Century Short Story Explication* incorporates listings from the annual bibliography in *Studies in Short Fiction* (1100). Although far from thorough, Walker is a useful starting point for research, especially since it indexes parts of books.

See also

ABELL (340): [English] Literature/General through the volume for 1967; Literature, General/Literary History/Fiction, and Literature, General/Literary Criticism/Fiction in the volumes for 1968–72; Literary History and Criticism/Fiction in the volume for 1973; and English Literature/General/Fiction in later volumes.
"Annual Bibliography of Short Fiction Interpretation," *Studies in Short Fiction* (1100).
MLAIB (335): General VII: Literature, General and Comparative in the volumes for 1953–55; General II: Literature, General and Comparative in the volume for 1956; General IV/Prose Fiction in the volumes for 1957–80; and the Genres/Fiction, Novella, and Short Story sections in pt. 4 of the later volumes. Researchers must also check the "Novella" and "Short Story" headings in the subject index to post-1980 volumes.
Thurston, *Short Fiction Criticism* (3480a).

PERIODICALS

1095 *Journal of the Short Story in English/Les Cahiers de la nouvelle (JSSE).* 1983– . 2/yr. PN3373.C33.

Limited to articles, in French and English, on the short story, principally British and American, *Journal of the Short Story* prints occasional special issues or sections.

1100 *Studies in Short Fiction (SSF).* 1963– . Quarterly. PN3311.S8 813.

Although *Studies in Short Fiction* is international in scope, the articles, notes, and brief reviews emphasize British and American works since 1800. The highly selective "Annual Bibliography of Short Fiction Interpretation" supplements Walker, *Twentieth-Century Short Story Explication* (1090) and Weixlmann, *American Short-Fiction Criticism* (3480). The "Cross-Referenced Index of Short Fiction Anthologies" (7.1 [1970]; 8 [1971]: 351–409; updated annually since 13 [1976]) indexes contents by author and anthology. Annual index; cumulative index: vol. 1–20, as 22.1 (1985).

See also

Journal of Narrative Technique (840).
Modern Fiction Studies (845).

Drama and Theater

Guides to Reference Works

1115 Bailey, Claudia Jean. *A Guide to Reference and Bibliography for Theatre Research.* 2nd ed. Columbus: Publications Committee, Ohio State U Libraries, 1983. 149 pp. Z5781.B15 [PN1620.A1] 016.792.

A classified, descriptively annotated guide to general and specialized reference works on drama and theater. Although the emphasis is overwhelmingly on the United States and Western Europe, and the annotations are sometimes less thorough than they could be, Bailey is the standard introduction to reference works for theater research. Review: Robert H. Hethmon, *Theatre Research International* 9 (1984): 260–61.

1120 Whalon, Marion K. *Performing Arts Research: A Guide to Information Sources.* Performing Arts Information Guide Series 1. Detroit: Gale, 1976. 280 pp. Z6935.W5 [PN1584] 016.7902.

A selective guide to reference works (in several languages and published through 1973) useful to research in the performance aspects of theater, dance, music, musical theater, film, and other entertainments. Entries are organized alphabetically in seven variously classified divisions for types of works: basic guides and general reference works; dictionaries, encyclopedias, and handbooks; directories of organizations, institutions, and persons; play indexes and finding lists; sources for reviews of plays and films; bibliographies, indexes, and abstracts; sources for illustrations and audiovisual material. The numerous cross-references compensate somewhat for imprecise classification of several entries. Many of the descriptive annotations offer helpful evaluative comments. Indexed by authors, titles, and subjects. Although it lacks an adequate statement of scope and explanation of criteria governing selections, omits some important works, and is now dated, *Performing Arts Research* remains the best general guide to reference works important to research in the performing arts.

Literary Handbooks, Dictionaries, and Encyclopedias

1125 *Cambridge Guide to World Theatre*. Ed. Martin Banham. Cambridge: Cambridge UP, 1988. 1,104 pp. PN2035.C27 792'.0321.

An international dictionary of theater, classical to contemporary, that emphasizes performance. The entries cover traditions, theories, acting companies, playwrights, performers, designers, directors, movements, folk drama, types of performance, television and radio drama, and the theatrical aspects of ballet and opera.

1130 *Enciclopedia dello spettacolo*. Ed. Silvio d'Amico and Francesco Savio. 9 vols. Roma: Maschere, 1954–62. *Aggiornamento, 1955–1965*. Roma: Unione, 1966. 1,292 cols. *Indice-Repertorio*. 1968. 1,024 pp. *Cinema, teatro, balletto, tv*. Roma: Garzanti, 1978. 782 pp. PN1625.E7 792.03.

An international encyclopedia of all forms of dramatic and musical theater, opera, cinema, television, and circus from classical antiquity to 1965. Concerts, sports, and civil and religious ceremonies are excluded. The more than 30,000 signed entries encompass dramatists, composers, librettists, performers, cinematographers, directors, producers, critics, various other theater personnel, terminology, genres and forms, national and ethnic literatures, places, technical matters, movements, groups, and themes. The entries, which range from a paragraph to several pages, are organized alphabetically by Italian-language term; most conclude with a brief bibliography, and many are accompanied by illustrations. Indexed by title in the index volume. Entries in *Appendice di aggiornamento: Cinema* (Roma: Istituto per la Collaborazione Culturale, 1963, 178 cols.) are revised in the supplement for 1955–65, but the former includes some different plates. Although now dated, the *Enciclopedia* and companion volumes remain the fullest international guide to all aspects of the theatrical arts.

1135 *An International Dictionary of Theatre Language*. Gen. ed. Joel Trapido. Greenwood: Westport, 1985. 1,032 pp. PN2035.I5 792'.03'21.

A dictionary of some 10,000 English-language and 5,000 foreign-language terms, historical and current, covering drama and theater worldwide. Definitions are very brief but do cite works in the accompanying bibliography that offer fuller definitions or discussions. "A Brief History of Theatre Glossaries and Dictionaries" (pp. xxxiii-xxxvi) surveys related works. Although not exhaustive—since only foreign-language terms "used in the English-speaking world" are admitted and since some technical aspects of production are excluded (see the detailed explanation of scope in the prefatory matter)—the work is the most extensive dictionary of drama and theater terminology.

1140 *The Oxford Companion to the Theatre.* Ed. Phyllis Hartnoll. 4th ed. Oxford: Oxford UP, 1983. 934 pp. PN2035.O9 792'.03'21.

Emphasizes established legitimate theater, classical to contemporary, with factual entries on actors, actresses, producers, directors, designers, dramatists, groups, movements, theatrical techniques and technology, theaters, acting companies, and national drama. Concludes with a highly selective bibliography. Coverage of ballet, opera, and dance was dropped, and several entries were condensed in the fourth edition, but this volume remains a standard source for quick reference. Because they are riddled with errors, earlier editions must be used with care.

Among the numerous other encyclopedic works on drama and theater, the following are reasonably trustworthy:

The Encyclopedia of World Theater. Ed. Martin Esslin. New York: Scribner's, 1977. 320 pp. A translation and revision of Karl Gröning and Werner Kliess, *Friedrichs Theaterlexikon*, ed. Henning Rischbieter (Hannover: Friedrich, 1969, 462 pp.), that covers theater, classical to contemporary, in brief entries on performers, theatrical personnel, forms, genres, theaters, movements, terms, groups, characters and character types, and critics.

McGraw-Hill Encyclopedia of World Drama. Ed. Stanley Hochman. 2nd ed. 5 vols. New York: McGraw, 1984. Emphasizes dramatists but also includes entries on terms, anonymous plays, genres, national literatures, and movements. The lengthy entries on major dramatists include biographical information, critical commentary, synopses of selected plays, a list of plays, and selected bibliography.

The Reader's Encyclopedia of World Drama. Ed. John Gassner and Edward Quinn. New York: Crowell, 1969. 1,030 pp. Emphasizes drama rather than theater in signed entries on playwrights, plays, countries, forms, and genres; however, there are numerous factual errors and inconsistencies (see the review by Daniel C. Gerould, *Educational Theatre Journal* 26 [1974]: 119–32).

1145 *Piper's Enzyklopädie des Musiktheaters.* Ed. Carl Dalhaus and Sieghart Döhring. 8 vols. München: Piper, 1986– . (Scheduled for completion in 1994.) ML102.O6.P5 782'.03'31.

An encyclopedia of musicals, melodramas, ballets, operas, and operettas in the modern repertory as well as some works of historical importance. Although the work emphasizes European theater, there is substantial coverage of the rest of the world. In vols. 1–5, signed entries on about three thousand works are organized by author, composer, or choreographer. When possible, an entry identifies the author and source of the libretto, composer of the music, date and place of premiere and later important versions, characters, and orchestral requirements; provides a lengthy synopsis; analyzes the historical or current significance of the work; traces influence; locates the original manuscript and important copies; and cites printed versions, copyright holders, and selected scholarship. Indexed by titles in each volume; vol. 6 is a cumulative index of titles and persons. Vols. 7–8 constitute a handbook of terminology relating to all aspects of musical theater. Offering considerably more detail than one typically encounters in an encyclopedic work, *Piper's* is the fullest single guide to international musical theater.

Guides to Primary Works

1150 Connor, Billie M., and Helene G. Mochedlover. *Ottemiller's Index to Plays in Collections: An Author and Title Index to Plays Appearing in Collections Published between 1900 and 1985*. 7th ed. Metuchen: Scarecrow, 1988. 564 pp. Z5781.O8 [PN1655] 016.80882.

An author index to 6,548 titles in various languages (including translations) by 2,555 authors in 1,350 collections published for the most part in the United States or England. Plays are keyed by an awkward system of symbols to the list of anthologies. Indexed by title. Similar indexes include the following:

Chicorel, Marietta, ed. *Chicorel Theater Index to Plays in Anthologies, Periodicals, Discs, and Tapes*. 2 vols. New York: Chicorel, 1970–71. *Chicorel Theater Index to Plays in Anthologies and Collections, 1970–1976*. Chicorel Index Series 25. 1977. 479 pp. An author and title list, with minimal subject indexing, of English-language plays.

Samples, Gordon. *The Drama Scholars' Index to Plays and Filmscripts: A Guide to Plays and Filmscripts in Selected Anthologies, Series, and Periodicals*. 2 vols. Metuchen: Scarecrow, 1974–80. A selective author and title index to plays and scripts of radio, television, and film productions in a variety of languages. Entries are keyed to lists of periodicals and collections. A useful complement to the other indexes listed in this entry, since coverage extends from eighteenth-century collections through 1977 and includes periodicals; however, the number of entries is needlessly swollen by the indexing of many standard collected editions of individual authors. Poor typography and layout make this a frustrating work to use.

There is considerable overlapping among these indexes, which are principally useful for locating anthologized reprints of plays.

Dean H. Keller, *Index to Plays in Periodicals*, rev. ed. (Metuchen: Scarecrow, 1979, 824 pp.), an author list with title index, supplements periodical coverage of the preceding works and locates many plays not separately published or anthologized.

1155 *Play Index*. New York: Wilson, 1953– . Irregular. Z5781.P53 016.80882.

A selective author, title, and subject index to English-language plays and translations—classical through contemporary—published separately or in collections since 1949. Entries, which include a brief plot summary and production specifications, are keyed to a list of collections at the back. Although it overlaps with the sources listed in entry 1150, this is the only work of its kind that indexes plays by subject (although some subject headings are too broad to be useful). Ina Ten Eyck Firkins, comp., *Index to Plays, 1800–1926* (New York: Wilson, 1927, 307 pp.) and *Supplement* (1935, 140 pp.), selectively cover plays first published between 1800 and 1934.

Guides to Scholarship and Criticism

SERIAL BIBLIOGRAPHIES

1160 *International Bibliography of Theatre [1982–].* New York: Theatre Research Data Center, Brooklyn Coll., City U of New York, 1985– . Annual. Z6935.I53 [PN1561] 016.79'02.

A bibliography of books, articles, dissertations, and other documents on all aspects of theatrical performance worldwide. Reviews of books and performances are excluded, as are literary studies without a substantial discussion of performance. Entries are currently organized in nine divisions: general, dance, dance-drama, drama, media, mime, mixed entertainment, music-drama, and puppetry. Each is subdivided by type or genre and then by geographical area within an elaborate classification system outlined in the prefatory matter. An entry consists of author, title, publication information, geographical and chronological classification, type of document, and brief descriptive annotation. Three indexes: subjects; geographical (subdivided chronologically); scholars. The indexing of themes and topics is incomplete and coverage of some parts of the world remains weak, but both are gradually improving. Effective use requires considerable familiarity with the complicated but insufficiently refined taxonomy, and publication lags about three years behind the year of coverage; nevertheless, the *International Bibliography* is an important addition to reference works for the study of theater. Particularly noteworthy is the emphasis on performance, an area not effectively covered by the serial bibliographies and indexes in section G of this *Guide*. Reviews: Thomas Postlewait, *Theatre History Studies* 6 (1986): 200–10; 8 (1988): 234–37.

See also

ABELL (340): [English] Literature/General through the volume for 1967; Literature, General/Literary History/Drama and Theatre History, and Literature, General/Literary Criticism/Drama [and Theatre History] in the volumes for 1968–72; Literary History and Criticism/Drama and Theatre History in the volume for 1973; and English Literature/General/Drama and the Theatre in later volumes.

Carpenter, *Modern Drama Scholarship and Criticism* (2875).

"Check List of Explication," *Explicator* (685).

"Graduate Theses in Theatre," *Theatre Journal* (1205).

MLAIB (335): General VII: Literature, General and Comparative in the volume for 1953–55; General II: Literature, General and Comparative in the volume for 1956; General IV/Drama in the volumes for 1957–80; and the General Literature/Theater, and Genres/Drama sections in pt. 4 of the later volumes. Researchers must also check the headings beginning "Theater" or "Drama" in the subject index to post-1980 volumes.

"Modern Drama Studies: An Annual Bibliography," *Modern Drama* (2870).

RILM Abstracts (6240).

OTHER BIBLIOGRAPHIES

1165 *Cumulated* Dramatic Index, *1909–1949: A Cumulation of the F. W. Faxon Company's* Dramatic Index. 2 vols. Boston: Hall, 1965. Z5781.C8 016.8082.

Reprints, in a single alphabetical sequence, the annual *Dramatic Index* subject indexes to English-language books and articles, illustrations, and plays published in about 150 British and American periodicals between 1909 and 1949. Opera, dance, and ballet as well as plays are covered. Except for play titles and dramatists, the subject headings are quite general. Three appendixes: author list of books; title list of plays; author list of plays. Although there are numerous errors, the work is useful for locating reviews and articles in periodicals not indexed in standard bibliographies and indexes in section G. Coverage continues through August 1953 in *Bulletin of Bibliography* (660).

1170 Palmer, Helen H., comp. *European Drama Criticism, 1900–1975*. 2nd ed. Hamden: Shoe String; Folkestone: Dawson, 1977. 653 pp. Z5781.P2 [PN1721] 016.809'2.

A selective bibliography of articles, parts of books, and abstracts from *Dissertation Abstracts International* (465) in a variety of languages on plays, classical through modern, by "outstanding" playwrights (except Shakespeare). Except for the limitation to studies, regardless of merit, devoted to a play as a whole, the entries seem to represent what the compiler could locate. Studies are listed under individual plays arranged alphabetically by dramatist; citations to parts of books are keyed to a list at the back. A separate list of journals does not identify volumes actually searched. Indexed by playwrights and plays. Although selection criteria are vague, the bibliography is useful for its indexing of parts of books.

Less comprehensive and current but occasionally supplementing Palmer are the following:

Adelman, Irving, and Rita Dworkin. *Modern Drama: A Checklist of Critical Literature on 20th Century Plays* (2875a).

Breed, Paul F., and Florence M. Sniderman, comps. and eds. *Dramatic Criticism Index: A Bibliography of Commentaries on Playwrights from Ibsen to the Avant-Garde* (2875a).

Coleman, Arthur, and Gary R. Tyler. *Drama Criticism*. Vol. 1: *A Checklist of Interpretation since 1940 of English and American Plays*. Vol. 2: *A Checklist of Interpretation since 1940 of Classical and Continental Plays* (2875a).

For scholarship between 1966 and 1980 on twentieth-century drama, researchers should begin with Carpenter, *Modern Drama Scholarship and Criticism* (2875).

See also

Wildbihler, *The Musical: An International Annotated Bibliography* (4295).

REVIEW INDEXES

See

Salem, *Guide to Critical Reviews* (4300).

Biographical Dictionaries

INDEXES

1175 Wearing, J. P. *American and British Theatrical Biography: A Directory.* Metuchen: Scarecrow, 1979. 1,007 pp. PN2285.W42 792'.0295.

A finding list of entries on dramatists and theatrical personnel in about 55 popular and scholarly biographical dictionaries and reference works from the mid-eighteenth century to the late 1970s. Each entry includes name, cross-references to married or stage name or pseudonym, dates of birth and death, nationality, theatrical occupation, and coded references to the dictionaries and reference works. Because of the works indexed, coverage is fuller for those who lived after c. 1800. A time-saving source for determining which of the numerous standard biographical sources include an individual. Reviews: Sandra Billington, *Theatre Research International* 7 (1982): 152–53; Joseph Donohue, *Theatre Journal* 32 (1980): 406–08; Cecil Price, *Notes and Queries* ns 28 (1981): 569–70.

See also

Sec. J: Biographical Sources/Biographical Dictionaries/Indexes.

DICTIONARIES

See

Contemporary Theatre, Film, and Television (4305).

Microform Collections

1180 Wells, Henry W., ed. *Three Centuries of Drama.* New York: Readex, 1960–62. Microopaque.

Reproduces widely scattered early editions of 5,350 British (1500–1800) and American (1714–1830) plays, including the Larpent manuscripts (now at the Huntington Library). Indexed in G. William Bergquist, ed., *Three Centuries of English and American Plays: A Checklist: England, 1500–1800; United States, 1714–1830* (New York: Hafner, 1963, 281 pp.); when appropriate, entries cite Greg, *Bibliography of the English Printed Drama to the Restoration* (2135) and Gertrude L. Woodward and James G. McManaway, comps., *A Check List of English Plays, 1641–1700* (Chicago: Newberry Library, 1945, 155 pp.).

Periodicals

1185 *Comparative Drama* (*CompD*). 1967– . Quarterly. PN1601.C66 809.2.

Seeks "studies which are international in spirit and interdisciplinary in scope," but articles and reviews emphasize medieval and Renaissance English drama. Annual index.

1190 *Modern Drama* (*MD*). 1958– . Quarterly. PN1861 809.2'005.

Along with articles, reviews, frequent special issues, and occasional bibliographies on North American and European drama from 1850 to the present, publishes the annual "Modern Drama Studies: An Annual Bibliography" (2870).

1195 *New Theatre Quarterly*. 1971–81, 1985– . Quarterly. Former title: *Theatre Quarterly* (1971–81). PN2001.T435 792'.05.

Publishes articles and bibliographies on theater, classic to contemporary, but with an emphasis on the United States and Great Britain.

1200 *Theatre History Studies*. 1981– . Annual. PN2000.T49 792'.09.

Focuses on theater and stage history in articles and reviews, with an emphasis on nineteenth- and twentieth-century British and American topics.

1205 *Theatre Journal* (*TJ*). 1949– . Quarterly. Former title: *Educational Theatre Journal* (1949–78). PN3171.E38 792'.05.

Publishes historical, critical, and theoretical studies of theater arts (e.g., acting, theater and stage history, staging), as well as book and production reviews, and frequent special issues. The annual "Doctoral Projects in Progress in Theatre Arts" classifies United States dissertations by geographical area of topic. In vols. 3–15 (1951–63), "Graduate Theses in Theatre" lists theses and dissertations accepted by American universities. Annual index; cumulative index: David Welker, Educational Theatre Journal: *A Ten-Year Index, 1949–1958* (East Lansing: AETA, n.d., 81 pp).

1210 *Theatre Research International* (*ThR*). 1958– . 3/yr. Former title: *Theatre Research/Recherches théâtres* (1958–74). PN2001.T436 790.2'05.

Emphasizes the "historical, critical and theoretical study of documentation of drama," with articles on costume, stage and theater history, theatrical personnel, and staging. Reviews. Annual index.

1215 *Theatre Survey: The American Journal of Theatre History* (*ThS*). 1960– . 2/yr. PN2000.T716 792'.05.

Publishes articles, notes, documents, and reviews, with an emphasis on British and American topics. Cumulative index: vols. 1–20, by Constance F. Gremore, 20.2 (1979): 73–134.

See also

Journal of Aesthetics and Art Criticism (5970).

Poetry

Literary Handbooks, Dictionaries, and Encyclopedias

1230 *Princeton Encyclopedia of Poetry and Poetics*. Ed. Alex Preminger. Enl. ed. Princeton: Princeton UP, 1974. 992 pp. (In progress is a completely revised third edition, edited by Preminger and T. V. F. Brogan.) PN1021.E5 808.1'03.

A guide to "the history, theory, technique, and criticism of poetry from earliest times to the present." The approximately 1,000 signed entries, ranging from 20 to 20,000 words, cover the history of poetry (by language, school, movement, and country), technique, genres, forms, prosody, poetic theory and criticism (including critical terminology), related forms, and the relationship of poetry to other fields (e.g., music, religion, philosophy). A typical entry includes a definition, discussion of historical development, examples, and a brief bibliography. The enlarged edition treats subjects overlooked in and some developments since the original edition in a separate alphabetical sequence (pp. 909–92). The most thorough and authoritative of the numerous poetry encyclopedias, the *Princeton Encyclopedia* is an essential companion for serious readers and scholars and a model for similar, much needed encyclopedias of drama and fiction. Selected entries on prosodic and poetic terms are reprinted or revised and 10 new entries and a selective reading list added in *The Princeton Handbook of Poetic Terms*, ed. Alex Preminger (Princeton: Princeton UP, 1986, 309 pp.). The third edition will revise nearly every one the existing entries, completely rewrite many of the lengthier ones, and add about 100 new entries.

Although neither as comprehensive nor as thorough as the *Princeton Encyclopedia*, the following are also useful:

Deutsch, Babette. *Poetry Handbook: A Dictionary of Terms*. 4th ed. New York: Funk, 1974. 203 pp.

Myers, Jack, and Michael Simms. *Longman Dictionary and Handbook of Poetry*. Longman English and Humanities Series. New York: Longman, 1985. 366 pp.

Turco, Lewis. *The New Book of Forms: A Handbook of Poetics*. Hanover: UP of New England, 1986. 280 pp.

Williams, Miller. *Patterns of Poetry: An Encyclopedia of Forms*. Baton Rouge: Louisiana State UP, 1986. 203 pp. Stanza patterns and poetic forms—including a few not in *Princeton Encyclopedia*—are more fully illustrated in this and the preceding work.

See also

Malof, *Manual of English Meters* (1585).
Shapiro, *Prosody Handbook* (1585a).

Guides to Primary Works

1235 *Granger's Index to Poetry*. Ed. William F. Bernhardt. 8th ed. New York: Columbia UP, 1986. 2,014 pp. PN1022.G7 016.80881.

Title and first-line, author, and subject indexes to some 50,000 English-language poems (including translations) in 405 of the most accessible anthologies published through 30 June 1985. Subject indexing, although expanded in this edition to include forms and genres, remains too broad in many instances. The indexes are cumbersome to use because the author and subject listings are keyed to the title and first-line entries, which are in turn keyed to the list of anthologies. Since the current edition is not fully cumulative, earlier editions are still useful. *A Compilation of Works Listed in* Granger's Index to Poetry, *1904–1978* (Great Neck: Granger, 1980, 217 pp.) indexes anthologies by Granger symbol, title, and editor or compiler. Although highly selective and emphasizing established writers, *Granger's Index* is valuable for identifying poems on a topic or anthologized reprints.

For fuller coverage of recent anthologies, see *Poetry Index Annual* (1240); for European and Latin American poetry (including English translations) see Herbert H. Hoffman, *Hoffman's Index to Poetry: European and Latin American Poetry in Anthologies* (Metuchen: Scarecrow, 1985, 672 pp.), which includes some 14,000 poems from about 100 readily available anthologies but offers no subject index.

1240 *Poetry Index Annual: A Title, Author, First Line, and Subject Index to Poetry in Anthologies*. Great Neck: Poetry Index, 1982– . Annual. PN1022.P63 808.81'0016.

An author, title, first-line, and subject index to English language anthologies published during the year. Subject headings are frequently too broad and the typography does not allow for quick distinction of types of entries in the single alphabetical sequence. Although more thorough and current than *Granger's Index* (1235), especially in covering small-press publications, *Poetry Index Annual* hardly achieves the exhaustiveness it claims ("*all* poetry anthologies as they are published"). It is useful for identifying poems on a subject or anthologized reprints, especially of works by lesser-known contemporary writers.

See also

American Humanities Index (360).
Humanities Index (385).
Index to Children's Poetry (5540).
Readers' Guide (400).

Guides to Scholarship and Criticism

1245 Coleman, Arthur. *Epic and Romance Criticism*. 2 vols. Searingtown: Watermill, 1973–74. Z7156.E6.C64 016.8091.

Vol. 1: *A Checklist of Interpretations, 1940–1972, of English and American Epics and Metrical Romances*. 1973. 387 pp.

Vol. 2: *A Checklist of Interpretations, 1940–1973, of Classical and Continental Epics and Metrical Romances.* 1974. 368 pp.

A selective bibliography of English-language articles and parts of books organized by title of poem. Inconsistencies abound in the inclusion of several works that can hardly be classified as epic or romance, in the alphabetization of titles, and in the transcription of bibliographical information. Despite the inconsistencies, errors, and omissions, the focus on long poems makes Coleman—if used with considerable caution—a useful complement to Kuntz, *Poetry Explication* (1255), Cline, *Index to Criticisms of British and American Poetry* (1255a), and Alexander, *American and British Poetry* (1255a). Review: John Keith Wikeley, *Literary Research Newsletter* 1 (1976): 117–21.

1250 Donow, Herbert S., comp. *The Sonnet in England and America: A Bibliography of Criticism.* Westport: Greenwood, 1982. 477 pp. Z2014.S6.D66 [PR509.S7] 821'.042'09.

A bibliography of studies, anthologies, and editions of British and American sonneteers from the Renaissance through the nineteenth century. Coverage of English, French, and German scholarship is reasonably thorough; that of other languages is admittedly less so. Entries are listed alphabetically in four classified sections: general studies and anthologies, Renaissance, Shakespeare, and eighteenth and nineteenth centuries; the period sections have subdivisions for general studies, anthologies, and poets. Approximately half of the 4,191 entries are annotated, but usually with a brief sentence that rarely offers an adequate indication of content. Of the three indexes (scholars, poets, subjects) only the first is adequate: neither the poet index—essential to discovering studies that discuss more than one writer—nor the subject index, which utilizes unconventional headings, is thorough. Despite its shortcomings, Donow is a valuable compilation of the widely scattered scholarship on the sonnet.

1255 Kuntz, Joseph M., and Nancy C. Martinez. *Poetry Explication: A Checklist of Interpretation since 1925 of British and American Poems Past and Present.* [3rd ed.] Boston: Hall, 1980. 570 pp. Z2014.P7.K8 [PR502] 016.821'009.

A selective list of English-language articles and parts of books (published between 1925 and 1977) that explicate a poem of generally less than 500 lines. Contemporary authors who are not widely recognized are not included. Entries are classified by poet, then by title, with parts of books keyed to a list at the back (which also identifies volumes of journals searched). The focus is explication; therefore, source, analogue, and most metrical studies are excluded, as are studies devoted to only part of a poem or books limited to one author. A standard source, *Poetry Explication* is particularly useful because of its indexing of parts of books.

Similar indexes that supplement Kuntz and Martinez include Gloria Stark Cline and Jeffrey A. Baker, *An Index to Criticisms of British and American Poetry* (Metuchen: Scarecrow, 1973, 307 pp.), covering studies published between 1960 and 1970 in 30 journals and a few books; and Harriet Semmes Alexander, comp., *American and British Poetry: A Guide to the Criticism, 1925–1978* (Athens: Swallow, 1984, 486 pp.), whose approximately 20,000 entries include articles and parts of books that range beyond explication but are based on an unstated selection policy. For studies of long poems, see Coleman, *Epic and Romance Criticism* (1245).

See also

ABELL (340): [English] Literature/General through the volume for 1967; [English] Literature/General/[Study of] Metre in the volumes for 1926–72; Literature, General/Literary History/Poetry, and Literature, General/Literary Criticism/Poetry in the volumes for 1968–72; Literary History and Criticism/Poetry, and Literary History and Criticism/Versification in the volume for 1973; and English Literature/General/Poetry in later volumes.

"Check List of Explication," *Explicator* (685).

MLAIB (335): General VII: Literature, General and Comparative in the volumes for 1953–55; General II: Literature, General and Comparative in the volume for 1956; General IV/Poetry in the volumes for 1957–80; and the Literary Forms division and Genres/Poetry section in pt. 4 of the later volumes. Researchers must also check the headings beginning "Poetry" in the subject index to post-1980 volumes.

RILM Abstracts (6240).

Prose

General

GUIDES TO SCHOLARSHIP AND CRITICISM

See

ABELL (340): [English] Literature/General through the volume for 1967; Literature, General/Literary History/Prose, and Literature, General/Literary Criticism/Prose in the volumes for 1968–72; Literary History and Criticism/Prose in the volume for 1973; and English Literature/General/Prose in later volumes.

MLAIB (335): General VII: Literature, General and Comparative in the volumes for 1953–55; General II: Literature, General and Comparative in the volume for 1956; General IV/Prose in the volumes for 1957–80; and the Literary Forms division and Genres/Prose section in pt. 4 of the later volumes. Researchers must also check the headings beginning "Prose" in the subject index to post-1980 volumes.

PERIODICALS

1270 *Prose Studies (PSt)*. 1977– . 3/yr. Former title: *Prose Studies, 1800–1900* (1977–79). PR750.P76 828'.08.

Publishes articles, reviews, and occasional special issues dealing with theoretical concerns, genres, and specific works of nonfictional prose. Emphasizes nineteenth-century British topics.

Biography and Autobiography

RESEARCH METHODS

1275 Edel, Leon. *Writing Lives: Principia Biographica.* New York: Norton, 1984. 270 pp. CT21.E33 808'.06692.

An exploration of the theory and problems of writing a biography of a literary author. Successive chapters examine the basic principles of biography since c. 1920, the relationship between biographer and subject, the search for materials, the role of criticism in biography, the application of psychoanalytic concepts to biography, and types of biographies. An appendix reprints some papers on Edel's research for his biography of James. Indexed by persons, titles, and subjects. An expansion of *Literary Biography*, rpt. of rev. ed., with new foreword (Bloomington: Indiana UP, 1973, 170 pp.), *Writing Lives* is one of the best introductions to the art of literary biography by one of its masters.

1280 Runyan, William McKinley. *Life Histories and Psychobiography: Explorations in Theory and Method.* New York: Oxford UP, 1982. 288 pp. BF38.5.R86 155.

An examination of the methodological and conceptual problems of psychobiography, with particular attention to descriptive, conceptual, and interpretive issues. The chapters are organized in three parts: problems of description and explanation (with discussions of alternate explanations in biographies, social influences, and the structure of biographical narrative), models for conceptualization of the life course, and theory and method in the study of individual lives (with examinations of the case-study, idiographic, and psychobiographic methods). Indexed by persons and subjects. Although addressed to psychologists and social scientists, Runyan is important preliminary reading for the literary biographer who would employ psychobiography or the reader evaluating a product of the approach.

GUIDES TO SCHOLARSHIP AND CRITICISM

There is no adequate bibliography of scholarship on the theory and practice of biography and autobiography. Given the increasing interest in life-writing, such a bibliography is a major desideratum.

1285 "Bibliography of Works about Life-Writing for [1977–]." *Biography* (entry 1290) 1 (1978)– .

A selective list of studies, mostly in English, about biography, autobiography, and related topics. Since vol. 9 (1986), works are organized in three author lists: dissertations; periodicals, articles, and reviews; and books. In most installments, entries are accompanied by brief descriptive annotations. Although far from comprehensive—with several entries based on advertisements or sources other than the works themselves—this bibliography does isolate studies that are sometimes difficult to identify in the standard serial bibliographies and indexes in section G.

See also

ABELL (340): Biography [and Autobiography] division through the volume for 1974; and English Literature/General/Biography and Autobiography in later volumes.

MLAIB (335): General IV/Biography [and Autobiography] in the volumes for 1957–80; and Genres/Autobiography and Biography sections in pt. 4 of the later volumes. Researchers must also check the headings beginning "Autobiography" or "Biography" in the subject index to post-1980 volumes.

PERIODICALS

1290 *Biography: An Interdisciplinary Quarterly* (*Biography*). Honolulu: U of Hawaii P for Biographical Research Center, 1978– . Quarterly. CT100.B54 920'.005.

Publishes articles on the theory and practice of biography, occasional bibliographies of scholarship on life-writing within a country, reviews and review essays on biographies and related scholarship, an annual "Bibliography of Works about Life-Writing" (1285), and, beginning in 10.3 (1987), a section quoting from selected reviews of biographies and works about life-writing. Annual index; cumulative indexes: vols. 1–3, in 3 (1980): 371–76; vols. 4–6, in 6 (1983): 370–73.

Travel Writing

GUIDES TO PRIMARY WORKS

1295 Cox, Edward Godfrey. *A Reference Guide to the Literature of Travel: Including Voyages, Geographical Descriptions, Adventures, Shipwrecks, and Expeditions.* 3 vols. University of Washington Publications in Language and Literature 9–10, 12. Seattle: U of Washington P, 1935–49. Z6011.C87 016.91.

Vol. 1: *The Old World.* 1935. 404 pp.
Vol. 2: *The New World.* 1938. 591 pp.
Vol. 3: *Great Britain.* 1949. 732 pp.

A bibliography of travel literature printed before 1800 in Great Britain. Cox includes English-language translations, some European-language versions of English works, and accounts written before 1800 but first published later. Vol. 3 goes beyond separately published works to cite a host of letters, diaries, and miscellaneous documents printed in larger works or collections. Each volume is organized by topical or geographical divisions; within each division, works are listed chronologically by publication date. Many entries are accompanied by a note that variously refers to translations or other editions, offers biographical information, or comments on contents. Many notes quote from other sources, some of them of dubious authority. Indexed by persons (vols. 1–2 in vol. 2, vol. 3 in 3). The projected volume on Ireland was never published. Organization by date of publication combined with a lack of subject indexing makes the work less accessible than it should be. Despite the numerous errors and heavy reliance on other sources, Cox remains the best guide to travel literature in English before 1800.

M

English Literature

Section M includes works devoted primarily to literature in England or the British Isles generally. Works limited to Irish, Scottish, or Welsh literature will be found in their respective sections.

General

This part includes works that encompass several periods of English literature. Works limited to a movement, century, or period will be found in the appropriate parts of section M. Users should note that most of the reference works in sections A-K of the *Guide* are useful to research in English literature.

Histories and Surveys

1310 *The Oxford History of English Literature* (*OHEL*). Ed. F. P. Wilson et al. 13 vols. Oxford: Clarendon, 1945– . PR823.09 820.9.

Vol. 1, pt. 1: Pope, J. C. *English Literature before the Norman Conquest.* In progress.
Vol. 1, pt. 2: Bennett, J. A. W. *Middle English Literature.* Ed. and completed by Douglas Gray. 1986. (1785).
Vol. 2, pt. 1: Bennett, H. S. *Chaucer and the Fifteenth Century.* 1947. (1780).
Vol. 2, pt. 2: Chambers, E. K. *English Literature at the Close of the Middle Ages.* 2nd impression with corrections. 1947. (1790).
Vol. 3: Lewis, C. S. *English Literature in the Sixteenth Century Excluding Drama.* 1954. (1975).
Vol. 4, pt. 1: Wilson, F. P. *The English Drama, 1485–1585.* Ed. G. K. Hunter. 1969. (2125).
Vol. 4, pt. 2: Hunter, G. K. *The English Drama, c. 1586–1642.* In progress.
Vol. 5: Bush, Douglas. *English Literature in the Earlier Seventeenth Century, 1600–1660.* 2nd ed. rev. 1962. (1970).
Vol. 6: Sutherland, James. *English Literature of the Late Seventeenth Century.* 1969. (2215).
Vol. 7: Dobrée, Bonamy. *English Literature in the Early Eighteenth Century, 1700–1740.* Corrected rpt. 1964. (2210).
Vol. 8: Butt, John. *The Mid-Eighteenth Century.* Ed. and completed by Geoffrey Carnall. 1979. (2205).
Vol. 9: Renwick, W. L. *English Literature, 1789–1815.* 1963. (2460).
Vol. 10: Jack, Ian. *English Literature, 1815–1832.* 1963. (2455).
Vol. 11, pt. 1: Turner, Paul. *English Poetry in the Mid-Nineteenth Century.* In progress.
Vol. 11, pt. 2: Horeman, Alan. *English Prose in the Mid-Nineteenth Century.* In progress.
Vol. 12: Stewart, J. I. M. *Eight Modern Writers.* 1963. 704 pp. PR461.S8 820.904.
Vol. 13: Robson, Wallace. *English Literature, 1890–1945.* In progress.

A traditional history of English literature, with each volume by a distinguished scholar. Most volumes open with a chapter on the social, scientific, political, and religious background; examine major and minor writers; include a chronology (with sections for public events, literary history, verse, prose, and drama); and conclude with a highly selective bibliography (with sections for reference works, collections and anthologies, literary history and criticism, studies of topics and subjects, background studies, and authors). Indexed by persons, anonymous works, and a few subjects. Although their bibliographies are dated in varying degrees, many volumes rank among the better histories of their respective periods; a few are classics (especially those by Bush and Lewis); but others, such as those by Dobrée and Butt, have met with a mixed reception or are clearly inadequate (such as those by Stewart and Renwick). When complete, the *OHEL* will offer the most comprehensive history of English literature. See the individual entries for fuller discussions of each volume (except vol. 12, whose manifold inadequacies are detailed in the review by Robert Martin Adams, *Hudson Review* 16 [1963–64]: 594–600).

Some of the individual chapters in the *Cambridge History of English Literature* (*CHEL*), ed. A. W. Ward and A. R. Waller, 15 vols. (Cambridge: Cambridge UP, 1907–27) have never been completely superseded, although the work as a whole is outdated. George Sampson, *The Concise Cambridge History of English Literature*, rev. R. C. Churchill, 3rd ed. (Cambridge: Cambridge UP, 1970, 976 pp.), is a revised digest of *CHEL* that extends coverage to the mid-twentieth century for British literature and adds discussions of Commonwealth and American literature (through James).

1315 Baugh, Albert C., ed. *A Literary History of England*. 2nd ed. New York: Appleton-Century-Crofts, 1967. 1,605 pp. PR83.B3 820.9.

A traditional history in four books written (and then updated with bibliographical supplements) by eminent scholars: Kemp Malone and Albert C. Baugh, the Middle Ages (to 1500); Tucker Brooke, Renaissance (1500–1660), supplemented by Matthias A. Shaaber; George Sherburn, Restoration and eighteenth century (1660–1789), supplemented by Donald F. Bond; Samuel C. Chew, nineteenth century and after (1789–1939), supplemented by Richard D. Altick. The second edition reprints with minor corrections the text of the 1948 edition with bibliographical supplements at the back. Indexed by authors and titles. Although dated in many respects, the work is still the best single-volume history of English literature. Review: René Wellek, *Modern Philology* 47 (1949): 39–45.

1320 *The New History of Literature*. 10 vols. New York: Bedrick, 1987– . (A partial revision of *History of Literature in the English Language*, 10 vols. [London: Barrie, 1970–75].)

Vol. 1: *The Middle Ages*. Ed. W. F. Bolton. 1987. 436 pp. PR166.M53 820'.9'001.

Vol. 2: *English Poetry and Prose, 1540–1674*. Ed. Christopher Ricks. 1987. 468 pp. PR533.E5 820'.9'003.

Vol. 3: *English Drama to 1710*. Ed. Ricks. 1987. 465 pp. PR625.E5 822'.009.

Vol. 4: *Dryden to Johnson*. Ed. Roger Lonsdale. 1987. 450 pp. PR442.D79 820'.9'005.

Vol. 5: *Literature of the Romantic Period*. Ed. David B. Pirie. Scheduled for 1989.

Vol. 6: *The Victorians*. Ed. Arthur Pollard. 1987. 569 pp. PR463.V55 820'.9'008.
Vol. 7: *The Twentieth Century*. Ed. Martin Dodsworth. Scheduled for 1989.
Vol. 8: *American Literature to 1900*. Ed. Marcus Cunliffe. 1987. 400 pp. PS88.A44 810'.9.
Vol. 9: *American Literature since 1900*. Ed. Cunliffe. 1987. 489 pp. PS221.A65 810'.9'0052.
Vol. 10: *The English Language*. Ed. Bolton and David Crystal. 1987. 362 pp. PE1072.E55 420.

A collection of essays on major authors, genres, movements, and a few literature-related topics rather than a connected history of literature. Each volume concludes with a highly selective bibliography and short chronology; the bibliographies vary considerably in quality and currency. Indexed in each volume by persons, anonymous works, and a few subjects. Rarely do the editors or authors reveal whether or how extensively an essay has been revised for the new edition, and too seldom are the bibliographies adequately updated. Like the *New Pelican Guide* (1325), the essays vary considerably in quality and currency, and together fail to offer the perspective and breadth of an organized, coherent history.

1325 *The New Pelican Guide to English Literature*. Ed. Boris Ford. 9 vols. Harmondsworth: Penguin, 1982–84. (A partial revision of *The Pelican Guide to English Literature*, 7 vols. [1959–61].) PR83.N49 820'.9.

Vol. 1, pt. 1: *Medieval Literature: Chaucer and the Alliterative Tradition*. 1982. 647 pp.
Vol. 1, pt. 2: *Medieval Literature: The European Inheritance*. 1983. 623 pp.
Vol. 2: *The Age of Shakespeare*. 1982. 576 pp.
Vol. 3: *From Donne to Marvell*. 1982. 411 pp.
Vol. 4: *From Dryden to Johnson*. 1982. 527 pp.
Vol. 5: *From Blake to Byron*. 1982. 429 pp.
Vol. 6: *From Dickens to Hardy*. 1982. 528 pp.
Vol. 7: *From James to Eliot*. 1983. 592 pp.
Vol. 8: *The Present*. 1983. 619 pp.
A Guide for Readers to The New Pelican Guide to English Literature. 1984. 545 pp.

Rather than a connected history of literature, the *New Pelican Guide* offers a series of critical essays by eminent scholars. Each volume consists of four parts: a discussion of the social context; a broad survey of the literature; a series of essays on movements, genres, language, special topics, and major writers; and a bibliographical appendix, with sections on the social and cultural setting, general literature, and individual authors. Rarely is it clear which essays are new, revised, or merely reprinted from the earlier edition. Indexed by literary author and subject. The *Guide for Readers* prints revised bibliographical appendixes, which are further revised in subsequent printings of individual volumes and the *Guide for Readers*.

Although the essays are uneven in quality and sometimes badly dated, some offer provocative assessments of individual authors but at the expense of the perspective and breadth offered by a connected narrative.

Literary Handbooks, Dictionaries, and Encyclopedias

1330 *The Oxford Companion to English Literature*. Ed. Margaret Drabble. 5th ed. Oxford: Oxford UP, 1985. 1,155 pp. PR19.D73 820'.9.

A wide-ranging encyclopedia, with entries for authors (born before 1940), works, characters, literary prizes, movements, critical theories, periods, groups, historical figures and foreign writers important to English literature, critics, theaters, periodicals, terminology, places, prosody, and allusions (although the last two are treated less fully than in the 4th ed.). Entries emphasize information rather than critical evaluation, although the latter is inevitably present. Discussions of authors are very inconsistent in directing readers to standard editions and critical works. Three appendixes: "Censorship and the Law of the Press"; "Notes on the History of English Copyright"; "The Calendar," with tables for the Gregorian and Julian calendars, movable feast days, and saints' days—all essential to dating documents. Despite omissions, errors, and inconsistencies, the *Oxford Companion* retains its stature as the most reliable and readable single source for essential information on English literary culture. Reviews: Basil Cottle, *Review of English Studies* ns 37 (1986): 620–23; Harold Fromm, *American Scholar* 55 (1986): 410–18; James R. Kincaid, *New York Times Book Review* 14 July 1985: 1+; Iain McGilchrist, *TLS: Times Literary Supplement* 26 Apr. 1985: 455–56. Although an abridgment, *The Concise Oxford Companion to English Literature*, ed. Margaret Drabble and Jenny Stringer (Oxford: Oxford UP, 1987, 632 pp.) does add some entries and revise others.

1335 Eagle, Dorothy, and Hilary Carnell, comps. and eds. *The Oxford Illustrated Literary Guide to Great Britain and Ireland*. Rev. by Dorothy Eagle. Oxford: Oxford UP, 1981. 312 pp. PR109.E18 914.1'048570248.

An alphabetical guide to places, real and imaginary, associated with some 900 dead authors. The entries, which are keyed to a series of maps and accompanied by numerous illustrations, succinctly identify associations with writers and works (occasionally quoting relevant passages) and provide directions for locating places. Indexed by authors. Based on visits to most of the places described, the work offers the fullest, most authoritative general guide to British literary topography.

A useful complement for the literary pilgrim is Lois H. Fisher, *A Literary Gazetteer of England* (New York: McGraw, 1980, 740 pp.). Although it is restricted to England, the *Literary Gazetteer* offers more discursive descriptions (along with frequent quotations and occasional illustrations).

1340 Goode, Clement Tyson, and Edgar Finley Shannon. *An Atlas of English Literature*. New York: Century, 1925. 136 pp. PR109.G6 820'.9.

A series of historical maps, each accompanied by a list of writers and associated places. The maps and lists for England and Wales are organized by period (449–1066, 1066–1500, 1500–1660, 1660–1798, and 1798–1900); a single map and list covers each of the following: Scotland, Ireland, London, and Italian locales associated with British authors. Two indexes: places (with authors listed under each); authors. Although in need of revision, the *Atlas* remains useful for identifying the literary associations of locales as they existed in various periods.

Although lacking this historical perspective, Michael Hardwick, *A Literary Atlas and Gazetteer of the British Isles* (Detroit: Gale, 1973, 216 pp.), prints detailed county maps (keyed to terse explanatory notes on literary associations) and is more current.

See also

Cambridge Guide to Literature in English (125).

Annals

LITERATURE

1345 *Annals of English Literature, 1475–1950: The Principal Publications of Each Year Together with an Alphabetical Index of Authors with Their Works.* [Ed. R. W. Chapman and W. K. Davin.] 2nd ed. rpt. with corrections. Oxford: Clarendon, 1965. 380 pp. (A revised edition, edited by Douglas Matthews, is in progress.) Z2011.A5 016.82.

A chronology of important literary and major nonliterary works, births and deaths of authors, and selected historical events. Although it includes American and Commonwealth authors and works, the *Annals* emphasizes British literature. The standard chronology essential for placing a British author or work within a literary, historical, cultural, or intellectual milieu. Superior coverage of American literature is offered by Ludwig, *Annals of American Literature* (3220).

Samuel J. Rogal, *A Chronological Outline of British Literature* (Westport: Greenwood, 1980, 341 pp.), spans the period 516–1979 but offers less satisfying coverage of intellectual and social history.

RELATED TOPICS

1350 *Handbook of British Chronology*. Ed. E. B. Fryde et al. 3rd ed. Royal Historical Society Guides and Handbooks 2. London: Royal Historical Soc., 1986. 605 pp. DA34.P6 942.002.

A chronology of rulers, officers of state, archbishops, and bishops to 1985 and of peers, parliaments, and church councils for earlier periods. Entries are organized in six divisions: rulers (by country, with details of "parentage, birth, accession, death [or removal], marriage and issue" as well as changes in titles and regents); officers of state (by country, office, then ruler, with dates of assumption and demission); archbishops and bishops (by country, see, then date of accession); dukes, marquesses, and earls (by country, then title, but covering only 1066 to 1714 for England); English and British parliaments and related assemblies to 1832; and provincial and national councils of the church in England, c. 600–1536. An introduction to each division (and to many sections) fully explains content, organization, limitations, and sources. Although access is hampered by the lack of an index and information is provisional for the period to 1066, the *Handbook* is the standard chronology and an indispensable source for dating documents.

Bibliographies of Bibliographies

1355 Howard-Hill, T. H. *Index to British Literary Bibliography*. Oxford: Clarendon, 1969– . Z2011.A1.H68 [PR83] 016.82.

Vol. 1: *Bibliography of British Literary Bibliographies*. 2nd ed., rev. and enl. 1987. 886 pp.
Vol. 2: *Shakespearian Bibliography and Textual Criticism: A Bibliography*. 1971. 322 pp.
Vol. 3: *British Bibliography to 1890: A Bibliography*. In progress.
Vol. 4: *British Bibliography and Textual Criticism: A Bibliography*. 1979. 732 pp.
Vol. 5: *British Bibliography and Textual Criticism: A Bibliography (Authors)*. 1979. 488 pp.
Vol. 6: *British Bibliography and Textual Criticism, 1890–1969: An Index*. 1980. 409 pp.
Vol. 7: *British Literary Bibliography, 1970–1979*. In progress.
Vol. 8: *Dissertations on British Literary Bibliography to 1980*. In progress.

Also planned are decennial supplements covering 1980–2000 and an index to all volumes.

The work is a broad-ranging index of bibliographies and bibliographical and textual studies originally

> intended to cover books, substantial parts of books, and periodical articles written in English and published in the English-speaking Commonwealth and the United States after 1890, on the bibliographical and textual examination of English manuscripts, books, printing and publishing, and any other books published in English in Great Britain or by British authors abroad, from the establishment of printing in England, except for material on modern (post-1890) printing and publishing not primarily of bibliographical or literary interest.

Among kinds of publications initially excluded are bibliographical and textual discussions in editions, catalogs of manuscripts, and most library, auction, booksellers', and private library catalogs. During the course of publication, Howard-Hill has included some studies in foreign languages and on foreign-language books published in Britain; has added coverage of manuscripts before 1475 by authors for whom studies of printed books are listed; has included some material on some modern private presses, studies published before 1890, and discussions in editions; and has modified organization and citation form. For a full discussion of changes in scope, see his "The *Index to British Literary Bibliography*," *TEXT: Transactions of the Society for Textual Scholarship* 2 (1985): 1–12.

In general, entries are organized by date of publication within sections. The brief descriptive annotations frequently note contents and selected reviews. Since a work is usually entered only once and seldom cross-referenced, users must check the index volume (vol. 6) to locate all entries relevant to an author or topic.

Vol. 1 classifies enumerative bibliographies (published c. 1890–1969) in divisions for general bibliographies, periods, regions (generally works printed at or written by inhabitants of—rather than those about—a place), book production and distribution, forms and genres (e.g., ballads, emblem books, forgeries, poetry, unfinished books), subjects (e.g., alchemy, circus, fencing, tobacco, witchcraft), and authors. Under some literary authors, the bibliographies of primary works are preceded by a selective list of bibliographies of scholarship; both are organized by date of publication, and the latter sometimes admits works belonging to the former list. The brief descriptive annotations frequently note organization, type of bibliography, content of bibliographical descriptions, revised editions or supplements published after 1969, and reviews. Indexed by persons and subjects; vol. 6 also indexes most entries in the revised edition of vol. 1. Vol. 2 prints a now obsolete supplement to the first edition of vol. 1.

Vol. 2 is misleadingly titled, for nearly half of it (pp. 179–322) is a now obsolete supplement to the first edition of vol. 1. The earlier part of the volume organizes Shakespearean textual and bibliographical research (published c. 1890–c. 1969) in divisions for general bibliographies and guides, editions (with sections on quartos and the various folios), and textual studies (with sections on handwriting and palaeography, collected emendations, and individual works). Bibliographies appear first in each section, followed by studies in chronological order. Vol. 5 prints additions (pp. 374–88). Indexed by persons, publishers, and subjects (pp. 161–77); vol. 6 also indexes vol. 2.

Vols. 4 and 5 classify bibliographical and textual studies (published c. 1890–c. 1969) on printed works and manuscripts in divisions for bibliography and textual criticism; general and period bibliography; regional bibliography; book production and distribution; forms, genres, and subjects; and authors. Only a very few entries are annotated. Corrections appear in vol. 6 (pp. xvii-xix).

Vol. 6 indexes vols. 1 (including most entries in the revised edition), 2, 4, and 5 in two sequences: persons and titles of anonymous works; subjects. The organization of the subject index requires considerable study before it can be used efficiently, as it must be if all entries on an author or subject are to be located.

Mastering indexing principles and changes in scope and organization amply rewards a user's perseverance because Howard-Hill offers the fullest single guide to bibliographical scholarship on and bibliographies of English literature. Review: (vols. 4–6) Peter Davison, *Library* 6th ser. 4 (1982): 185–87.

For bibliographies published before 1890, see Besterman, *World Bibliography of Bibliographies* (155); for those after 1969, see *Bibliographic Index* (145); for recent bibliographical and textual studies, see *ABHB: Annual Bibliography of the History of the Printed Book* (5275) and *Bibliographie der Buch- und Bibliotheksgeschichte* (5280).

See also

Sec. D: Bibliographies of Bibliographies.

Guides to Primary Works

MANUSCRIPTS

1360 Royal Commission on Historical Manuscripts (Historical Manuscripts Commission; HMC). Quality House, Quality Court, Chancery Lane, London WC2A 1HP. 1869– .

The Royal Commission on Historical Manuscripts was established by Royal Warrant in 1869 to locate and publish or describe nongovernmental manuscripts of historical or literary interest held by individuals, families, or institutions. Since 1870, the commission has published an important but bewildering array of reports, appendixes, calendars, and editions of collections. The best conspectus of these publications through 1982 is offered by Mullins, *Texts and Calendars* (1375). In addition, three guides broadly index places and persons mentioned in documents described or calendared in published volumes:

A Guide to Reports on Collections of Manuscripts of Private Families, Corporations, and Institutions in Great Britain and Ireland. Pt. 1: *Topographical*. London: HMSO, 1914. 233 pp.

Guide to the Reports of the Royal Commission on Historical Manuscripts, 1870–1911. Pt. 2: *Index of Persons*. Ed. Francis Bickley. 2 vols. 1935–38.

Guide to the Reports of the Royal Commission on Historical Manuscripts, 1911–1952. Pt. 2: *Index of Persons*. Ed. A. C. S. Hall. 3 vols. 1966.

Users must remember that these works are only general indexes and not cumulations of indexes in individual volumes. The reports on collections range from hastily prepared brief descriptions in haphazard order to full calendars that carefully transcribe entire documents or generous extracts. Although varying widely in accuracy and thoroughness, the guides and reports provide the best access to important private collections (some of which are now in public repositories) and many preserve the only record of documents subsequently destroyed, lost, or inaccessible to researchers. For current locations, researchers should consult *Guide to the Location of Collections Described in the Reports and Calendars Series, 1870–1980*, Guides to Sources for British History 3 (London: HMSO, 1982, 69 pp.).

In 1945 the Royal Commission on Historical Manuscripts established the National Register of Archives to collect and index lists and reports of private collections. These finding aids vary considerably in detail and sophistication, and the only complete set exists at the National Register.

Although the bulk of the documents calendared or indexed are historical, no literary researcher or biographer can afford to ignore the published HMC volumes or the unpublished reports indexed by the National Register.

1365 *Index of English Literary Manuscripts*. Ed. P. J. Croft, Theodore Hofmann, and John Horden. 5 vols. London: Mansell; New York: Bowker, 1980– . Z6611.L7.I5 [PR83] 016.82'08.

Vol. 1: *1450–1625*. Comp. Peter Beal. 2 pts. 1980. (1985).
Vol. 2: *1625–1700*. Comp. Beal. 2 pts. 1987– . (1985).
Vol. 3: *1700–1800*. Comp. Margaret M. Smith. 1986– . (2225).
Vol. 4: *1800–1900*. Comp. Barbara Rosenbaum and Pamela White. 1982– . (2465).
Vol. 5: *Indexes of Titles, First Lines, Names, Repositories*. In progress.

A descriptive catalog of extant literary manuscripts by about 300 British and Irish writers who flourished between 1450 and 1900. The authors included are essentially those listed in *Concise Cambridge Bibliography of English Literature, 600–1950*, ed. George Watson, 2nd ed. (Cambridge: Cambridge UP, 1965, 270 pp.). The emphasis is on *literary* manuscripts, including an author's typescripts, corrected proof sheets, diaries, notebooks, and marginalia in printed books, but excluding letters; scribal copies to c. 1700 are also included. The individual volumes are organized alphabetically by author, with entries listed as the nature of the surviving manuscripts and canon demands. An introduction to each author describes the manuscripts generally, summarizes scholarship, alerts researchers to special problems, comments on nonliterary papers, discusses canon, and concludes with an outline of the arrangement of entries. A typical entry provides a physical description, dates composition of the manuscript, lists editions and facsimiles, notes provenance, cites relevant scholarship, and identifies location (with shelfmark). Queries about privately owned manuscripts should be addressed to the *Index* in care of Mansell. Additions and corrections will be printed in vol. 5. Since some entries are based on inquiries to libraries and collectors, on bibliographies and other reference works, and on booksellers' and auction catalogs, rather than on personal examination by a compiler, the descriptions vary in fullness and accuracy. Terminology and format also vary somewhat from volume to volume. Although there are inevitable errors and omissions, and although the scope is unduly restricted by reliance on the *Concise Cambridge Bibliography*, the *Index* has brought to light a number of significant unrecorded manuscripts and is an essential, if limited, source for the identification and location of manuscripts. It must, however, be supplemented by the works listed in section F: Guides to Manuscripts and Archives.

1370 Location Register of English Literary Manuscripts and Letters. The Library, P.O. Box 223, U of Reading, Whiteknights, Reading, England RG6 2AE.

A machine-readable union catalog of manuscripts and letters by British authors since 1700. Only materials publicly accessible in the British Isles are included. Originally the Location Register of Twentieth-Century English Literary Manuscripts and Letters (2765a). Retrospective coverage began in 1987. The editors anticipate that this second phase will require at least five years and that the data base will eventually be available through OCLC (225) and RLIN (230).

1375 Mullins, E. L. C. *Texts and Calendars: An Analytical Guide to Serial Publications*. Rpt. with corrections. Royal Historical Society Guides and Handbooks 7. London: Royal Historical Soc., 1978. 674 pp. *Texts and Calendars II: An Analytical Guide to Serial Publications, 1957–1982*. Royal Historical Society Guides and Handbooks 12. 1983. 323 pp. Z2016.M82 [DA30] 016.941.

An annotated guide to the contents of serial publications issued by government bodies or learned societies since the eighteenth century and devoted to printing texts or calendars of records and documents important to the history of England and Wales. The serials are grouped by issuing body in four divisions: official bodies (including the Public Record Office [285] and Royal Commission on Historical Manuscripts [1360]), national societies (e.g., Hakluyt Society), English local societies (including records, antiquarian, historical, and archaeological societies), and Welsh societies. Vol. 2 adds a division for series begun after 1957. The citation to each publication is accompanied by a full description of contents and, in vol. 2, a summary of prefatory matter. Corrections to the corrected reprint appear in vol. 2, pp. 317–20. Indexed in each volume by persons, places, subjects, and types of documents. Besides being the only source that indexes many of these volumes, *Texts and Calendars* offers an invaluable conspectus of the numerous publications of the Public Record Office and Royal Commission on Historical Manuscripts.

See also

Sec. F: Guides to Manuscripts and Archives.
Storey, *Primary Sources for Victorian Studies* (2450).

PRINTED WORKS

1380 Records of the Worshipful Company of Stationers and Newspaper Makers. Stationers' Hall, London EC4M 7DD.

The records, which date from 1554, are in three main groups: the court books (valuable for biographical research on printers and publishers, and essential sources for publishing history), miscellaneous documents, and—of primary interest to literary researchers—the registers of printed books, usually called the Stationers' Register (SR). The registers are virtually complete for 1554–1911, when compulsory registration halted. For 1554–1708, the registers consist of works entered for ownership by a member of the company; for 1710–1911, of works entered for copyright. Registers after 1920 are not available to researchers. Arranged chronologically, the registers identify the member claiming ownership or copyright, title (frequently descriptive in the early registers), author (but infrequently in the early years), and registration fee.

The records of the company are available to researchers at Stationers' Hall, in microfilm (Robin Myers, ed. *Records of the Stationers' Company, 1554–1920* [Cambridge: Chadwyck-Healey, 1984–]), or in various published transcripts:

1554–1640: *Transcript of the Registers of the Company of Stationers* (2000).
1640–1708: *Transcript of the Registers of the Worshipful Company of Stationers* (2005).

(David Foxon has unfortunately had to abandon his transcript of the registers for the period 1710–46.)

Since the records are the property of the company, scholars should seek permission to cite them in books and articles. To facilitate the exchange of information among researchers, the Honorable Archivist (currently Robin Myers) maintains a register of those working on aspects of the records.

For a description of the records and an annotated list of published and unpublished catalogs, indexes, and transcripts, see Robin Myers, "The Records of the Worshipful Company of Stationers and Newspaper Makers (1554–1912)," *Archives* 16 (1983): 28–38 (rpt. *Publishing History* 13 [1983]: 89–104). This article will be superseded by Myers, *Guide to the Archives of the Stationers' Company from 1554* (Cambridge: Chadwyck-Healey, in progress), which includes an analytical catalog of the contents of the Muniment Room and a glossary. For a history of the company, see Cyprian Blagden, *The Stationers' Company: A History, 1403–1959* (Cambridge: Harvard UP, 1960, 321 pp.).

Researchers must remember that the registers are records of ownership or copyright by members of the company and thus do not include everything actually printed or published in England, and that many works entered were never published or appeared under a different title. See entry 2000 for a further discussion of problems in the use of the early registers. The records—many of which await adequate exploration—are essential sources for identifying lost works, aiding in dating composition or publication, and researching all aspects of printing or publishing history.

See also

Sec. U: Literature-Related Topics and Sources/Anonymous and Pseudonymous Works/Dictionaries.

Guides to Scholarship and Criticism

OTHER BIBLIOGRAPHIES

1385 *The New Cambridge Bibliography of English Literature* (*NCBEL*). Ed. George Watson and I. R. Willison. 5 vols. Cambridge: Cambridge UP, 1969–77. (A new edition is in progress.) Z2011.N45 [PR83] 016.82.

Vol. 1: *600–1660*. Ed. Watson. 1974. 2,476 cols. (1675, 1840, and 2035).
Vol. 2: *1660–1800*. Ed. Watson. 1971. 2,082 cols. (2255).
Vol. 3: *1800–1900*. Ed. Watson. 1969. 1,948 cols. (2505).
Vol. 4: *1900–1950*. Ed. Willison. 1972. 1,408 cols. (2785).
Vol. 5: *Index*. Comp. J. D. Pickles. 1977. 542 pp.

A selective, but extensive, bibliography of works by and about "literary authors native to or mainly resident in the British Isles" from the Old English period through those established by 1950. Because of the scope, coverage of scholarship is necessarily selective and excludes unpublished dissertations, ephemeral publications, encyclopedia articles, insignificant notes, and superseded studies. Parts of books are omitted from the lists of secondary materials, thus leading researchers to overlook important studies. Otherwise, the thoroughness of coverage and terminal date (from c. 1962 to 1969) vary widely from section to section, with only extended use revealing how adequate an individual part is.

Entries are organized by literary period and then by six major divisions (each extensively subdivided and classified as its subject and the period require): introduction, poetry, novel, drama, prose, and Scottish or Anglo-Irish. For a fuller account of the organization of each period, see entries for the individual volumes.

Listings under individual authors are divided into bibliographies, collections, primary works, and secondary materials. Headnotes sometimes locate manuscripts or unique items. The full entry for an author who writes in several genres appears under the genre with which he or she is most closely associated; briefer entries emphasizing primary works usually appear under other genres or forms. Since these entries are not always cross-referenced, users must check the index volume (vol. 5) to locate all listings for an author.

In the various subdivisions and author entries, primary and secondary works are listed chronologically by date of publication. Editions and translations follow, in chronological order, a primary work. When a list of secondary materials includes more than one study by a scholar, the chronological sequence is unnecessarily violated by grouping all the studies under the earliest publication date of those cited. This practice, which requires considerable backtracking in lengthy lists (since scholars are not indexed), is almost universally condemned by reviewers and users.

Scholars are identified by surname and initial(s); titles are short titles, with only the first word capitalized and no designation of a title within a title; bibliographical information is incomplete. Although these conventions save space and create an uncluttered page, they also frequently prolong searches of card catalogs and volumes of journals.

The index (vol. 5) lists literary authors, major anonymous works, and some headings for subdivisions, but is insufficiently detailed to provide adequate access to the wealth of information in vols. 1–4. To be certain of locating all sections on an author, form, or genre, users must consult vol. 5 rather than the provisional index in each volume.

Although the *NCBEL* is a revision of *The Cambridge Bibliography of English Literature* (*CBEL*), ed. F. W. Bateson, 4 vols. (Cambridge: Cambridge UP, 1940), and *Supplement*, ed. George Watson (1957), the *CBEL* is still occasionally useful for its sections on political and social background and Commonwealth literature dropped from the *NCBEL*. See the entries on individual volumes for details of differences in coverage. For a discussion of the significance and history of *CBEL* and *NCBEL*, see George Watson, *CBEL: The Making of the Cambridge Bibliography* (Los Angeles: School of Library Service, U of California, 1965, 13 pp.).

Despite its unevenness, errors, inconsistencies, and deficiencies in organization, *NCBEL* is frequently the best starting point for research, especially for authors, forms, genres, and subjects that are not themselves subjects of bibliographies.

Reviews: (vol. 1) Fred C. Robinson, *Anglia* 97 (1979): 511–17; (vol. 2) *TLS: Times Literary Supplement* 15 Oct. 1971: 1296; Eric Rothstein, *Modern Philology* 71 (1973): 176–86; (vol. 3) Richard D. Altick, *JEGP: Journal of English and Germanic Philology* 70 (1971): 139–45; (vol. 4) *TLS: Times Literary Supplement* 29 Dec. 1972: 1582; T. A. Birrell, *Neophilologus* 59 (1975): 306–15.

Addressed to the student and general reader, *The Shorter New Cambridge Bibliography of English Literature*, ed. George Watson (Cambridge: Cambridge UP, 1981, 1,612 cols.) emphasizes the traditional canon of English literature by reprinting, with few changes, the sections on primary works by major authors and several minor ones, listing only a very few basic studies about each author, and completely cutting or severely trimming other sections. Although the *Shorter NCBEL* includes a few additions and corrections, it is, as Peter Davison points out in his review, "an unimaginative scissors-and-paste job which shows little thought for the needs of" its intended audience (*Library* 6th ser. 4 [1982]: 188–89).

1390 Baer, Florence E. *Folklore and Literature of the British Isles: An Annotated Bibliography*. Garland Reference Library of the Humanities 622: Garland Folklore Bibliographies 11. New York: Garland, 1986. 355 pp. Z2014.F6.B34 [PR149.F64] 016.82'09.

A bibliography of studies that discuss folklore elements in literary works written in English in the British Isles. Baer includes scholarly and popular studies (all but a few in English and published between 1890 and 1980) as well as dissertations after 1950, but excludes most of the standard reference works. Listed alphabetically by scholar, the 1,039 entries are accompanied by descriptive annotations offering clear, informative summaries that isolate significant elements of a study; cite tale-types, motifs, or Child numbers for ballads; provide appropriate cross-references; and sometimes include an astute evaluation. Because of the organization, users must approach the contents through the detailed general index, which covers literary and folklore genres, literary authors, titles, subjects, theoretical approaches, titles, subjects, and theorists. Three additional indexes cover tale-types, folklore motifs, and Child ballad numbers. Although the work is not comprehensive, the careful annotations and thorough indexing make it a valuable, time-saving source for identifying studies of the folklore content and relationships of British literature. Until *MLAIB* for 1981 (335), such studies are not easily identified in the standard serial bibliographies and indexes in section G.

See also

Secs. G: Serial Bibliographies, Indexes, and Abstracts; and U: Literature-Related Topics and Sources/Folklore/Guides to Scholarship.

ABELL (340): English Literature division.
Bailey, *English Stylistics* (6080).
"Current Literature," *English Studies* (1470).
Hayes, *Sources for the History of Irish Civilisation* (2980).
Horner, *Historical Rhetoric* (5600).
Horner, *Present State of Scholarship in Historical and Contemporary Rhetoric* (5565).
Kallendorf, *Latin Influences on English Literature from the Middle Ages to the Eighteenth Century* (4895).
Kirby, *America's Hive of Honey* (4190).
MLAIB (335): English Language and Literature (or English Literature) division through the volume for 1980, and the English Literature and Literature of the British Isles divisions in the later volumes. Researchers must also check the "English Literature" and "Literature of the British Isles" headings in the subject index to post-1980 volumes.
Ross, *Film as Literature, Literature as Film* (5800).
Schwartz, *Articles on Women Writers* (6605).
YWES (330) has a chapter on general literary history and criticism.

DISSERTATIONS AND THESES

1395 Howard, Patsy C., comp. *Theses in English Literature, 1894–1970.* Ann Arbor: Pierian, 1973. 387 pp. Z2011.H63 [PR83] 016.82.

A list of baccalaureate and masters' theses accepted by American and some foreign institutions. Includes a limited number of institutions (whether completely is unclear) and apparently only theses on an identifiable author. Entries are organized alphabetically under literary authors. Cross-references identify studies of multiple authors. Two indexes: subject (inadequate); thesis author. Although marred by an inadequate explanation of scope and coverage, *Theses in English Literature* will save some hunting through elusive institutional lists. A companion volume is devoted to *Theses in American Literature* (3315).

See also

Sec. H: Guides to Dissertations and Theses.

RELATED TOPICS

1400 *Annual Bibliography of British and Irish History: Publications of [1975–].* Brighton: Harvester, for Royal Historical Soc.; New York: St. Martin's, 1976– . Annual. Z2016.A55 [DA30] 016.941'005.

A selective list of books and articles (mostly in English) on all aspects of British and Irish history from Roman times to the present. Entries are organized in 13 classified divisions: auxiliary works (including bibliographies, reference works, and historiography), general studies, Roman Britain, periods of British history, medieval Wales, Scotland before the Union, Ireland to c. 1640, and Ireland since c. 1640.

Although variously classified, most period divisions have sections for general studies; politics; constitution, administration, and law; external affairs; religion; economics; social structure and population; naval and military; intellectual and cultural history; visual arts; and topography. Two indexes: scholars; subjects. Although the *Bibliography* is highly selective in coverage, with many entries taken at second hand, it offers the most current list of publications on British history and is useful for literature researchers because of its inclusion of several literary studies from periodicals not covered by the standard bibliographies and indexes in section G.

Before 1975, publications on British history are covered by the following:

Writings on British History, [1946–74]: A Bibliography of Books and Articles on the History of Great Britain from about 450 A.D. to 1939. 12 vols. London: Institute of Historical Research, U of London, 1973–86.

Writings on British History, [1934–45]: A Bibliography of Books and Articles on the History of Great Britain from about 450 A.D. to 1914, Published during the Year [1934–45], with an Appendix Containing a Select List of Publications . . . on British History since 1914. Comp. Alexander Taylor Milne. 8 vols. London: Cape, 1937–60.

Writings on British History, 1901–1933: A Bibliography of Books and Articles on the History of Great Britain from about 400 A.D. to 1914, Published during the Years 1901–1933 Inclusive, with an Appendix Containing a Select List of Publications in These Years on British History since 1914. 5 vols. London: Cape, 1968–70. An important complementary work is E. L. C. Mullins, comp., *A Guide to the Historical and Archaeological Publications of Societies in England and Wales, 1901–1933* (London: Athlone, 1968, 850 pp.).

Language

GUIDES TO PRIMARY WORKS

1405 Alston, R. C., comp. *A Bibliography of the English Language from the Invention of Printing to the Year 1800: A Systematic Record of Writings on English, and on Other Languages in English, Based on the Collections of the Principal Libraries of the World*. 20 vols. N.p.: Privately printed, 1965– . Z2015.A1.A4.

Vol. 1: *English Grammars Written in English and English Grammars Written in Latin by Native Speakers*. 1965. 119 pp.

Vol. 2: *Polyglot Dictionaries and Grammars; Treatises on English Written for Speakers of French, German, Dutch, Danish, Swedish, Portuguese, Spanish, Italian, Hungarian, Persian, Bengali, and Russian*. 1967. 311 pp.

Vol. 3, pt. 1: *Old English, Middle English, Early Modern English: Miscellaneous Works; Vocabulary*. 1970. 205 pp.

Vol. 3, pt. 2: *Punctuation, Concordances, Works on Language in General, Origins of Language, Theory of Grammar*. 1971. 66 pp.

Vol. 4: *Spelling Books*. 1967. 277 pp.

Vol. 5: *The English Dictionary*. 1966. 195 pp.

Vol. 6: *Rhetoric, Style, Elocution, Prosody, Rhyme, Pronunciation, Spelling Reform*. 1969. 202 pp.

Vol. 7: *Logic, Philosophy, Epistemology, Universal Language.* 1967. 115 pp.
Vol. 8: *Treatises on Short-Hand.* 1966. 152 pp.
Vol. 9: *English Dialects, Scottish Dialects, Cant and Vulgar English.* 1971. 178 pp.
Vol. 10: *Education and Language-Teaching.* 1972. 75 pp.
Supplement: *Additions and Corrections, Volume I–X; List of Libraries; Cumulative Indexes.* 1973. 117 pp.
Vol. 11: *Place Names and Personal Names.* 1977. 148 pp.
Vol. 12, pt. 1: *The French Language: Grammars, Miscellaneous Treatises, Dictionaries.* 1985. 208 pp.
Vol. 12, pt. 2: *The Italian, Spanish, Portuguese, and Romansh Languages: Grammars, Dictionaries, Miscellaneous Treatises.* 1987. 55 pp.
Vol. 13: *Germanic Languages: Grammars, Dictionaries, Glossaries, Spelling, Pronunciation.*
Vol. 14: *Other Languages: Grammars, Dictionaries, Glossaries, Spelling, Pronunciation.*
Vol. 15: *Latin Language (1500–1650).*
Vol. 16: *Latin Language (1651–1800); Greek Language.*
Vol. 17: *Vocabulary of Science, Technology, Arts, Crafts, Sports, Pastimes.*
Vol. 18: *Periodical Literature: Essay Material.*
Vol. 19: *Material in Manuscript.*
Vol. 20: *Indexes.*

(The compiler's annotated copies of vols. 1–10 were reprinted, without the facsimiles, in a single volume [Ilkley: Janus, 1974]. The corrections and additions are incorporated into the printed supplement to the first ten volumes.)

A massive bibliography of English-language works through 1800 related to the history of the English language. Works are organized by publication date within various subject classifications; subsequent editions follow, in chronological order, the first. A typical entry provides author, short title, publication information, format, pagination, citations to standard bibliographies, locations, references to important scholarship and contemporary reviews, and occasional notes on content. Most volumes print several facsimiles of title pages and other printed material. Each volume has up to four indexes: titles; authors; subjects and other persons; places. Based on research in an extensive number of libraries, Alston is an indispensable guide to the identification and location of works essential for the study of the early history of the English language. Review: (reprint of vols. 1–10) *TLS: Times Literary Supplement* 8 Nov. 1974: 1267.

When complete, Alston will supersede (for publications before 1800) Arthur G. Kennedy, *A Bibliography of Writings on the English Language from the Beginning of Printing to the End of 1922* (Cambridge: Harvard UP; New Haven: Yale UP, 1927, 517 pp.).

GUIDES TO SCHOLARSHIP

See also

Sec. U: Literature-Related Topics and Sources/Linguistics and Literature/Guides to Scholarship.
ABELL (340): English Language division.

MLAIB (335): English Language and Literature division in the volumes for 1922–25; English Language and Literature I/Linguistics in the volumes for 1926–66; Indo-European C/Germanic Linguistics IV/English in those for 1967–80; and Indo-European Languages/West Germanic Languages/English Language in later volumes. Researchers must also check "British English Dialect" in the subject index to post-1980 volumes.

DICTIONARIES

1410 *The Oxford English Dictionary* (*OED*). Ed. James A. H. Murray et al. 12 vols. and supplement. Oxford: Clarendon, 1933. (A corrected reissue of *A New English Dictionary on Historical Principles* [*NED*], originally published in 125 fascicles between 1884 and 1928.) Also published in CD-ROM. (A CD-ROM version incorporating the *Supplement* is in progress.) PE1625.N53 423.

A Supplement to the Oxford English Dictionary. Ed. R. W. Burchfield. 4 vols. Oxford: Clarendon, 1972–86.

The Compact Edition of the Oxford English Dictionary. 3 vols. Oxford: Oxford UP, 1971–87. (A micrographic reprint of the 1933 reissue and *Supplement*.)

Oxford English Dictionary. Ed. J. A. Simpson and E. S. C. Weiner. 2nd ed. 20 vols. Oxford: Clarendon, 1989. (A third edition is planned.)

New Oxford English Dictionary (*NOED*). Ed. E. S. C. Weiner. Oxford: Clarendon. In progress.

The Shorter Oxford English Dictionary on Historical Principles. Rev. and ed. C. T. Onions. 3rd ed., with revised etymologies and addenda. Oxford: Clarendon, 1973. 2,672 pp.

A historical dictionary that attempts to record all English words (including obsolete ones, dialect terms before 1500, and archaisms, as well as a considerable number of scientific, technical, and slang terms) used since c. 1150. Words obsolete by 1150 and dialect terms new after 1500 are excluded. Although the *OED* emphasizes standard British usage and vocabulary, both the original volumes and (especially) the *Supplement* admit meanings and senses used in English worldwide.

The entries for about 478,000 words in the main volumes and *Supplement* are based on several million excerpts from written works (a majority of which are belles lettres). There are three classifications of headwords: main words (all single words, whether radical or derivative, as well as compounds requiring separate treatment), subordinate words (mostly obsolete and variant forms, irregular inflections, or alleged words), and combined forms. Entries for subordinate words and combinations typically refer users to related main words for fuller information. A typical entry for a main word consists of four parts: (1) identification, with the headword appearing in its current or most usual spelling, pronunciation, part of speech, any specification of vocation, status, earlier spellings (with indication of chronological range), and inflected forms; (2) morphology, with etymology, history of the form, and notes on the history of the word; (3) signification, with senses organized from the earliest to most recent; (4) dated illustrative quotations listed chronologically (averaging one per century in the main volumes and one per decade in the *Supplement*). Each grammatical form of a main word is accorded a separate entry. (The

CD-ROM version can be searched by any combination of headword, definition, etymology, usage labels, and date, author, source, or text of quotations.)

The 1933 corrected reissue adds a supplement that records new words and senses, corrections, and spurious words, and lists the sources of illustrative quotations. Except for the list of sources, the 1933 supplement is superseded by the four-volume *Supplement*, which records new words or senses since 1884–1928 to 1965–85 (depending on when the part of the alphabet was sent to the printer), includes several words (especially "taboo" terms) and senses omitted from or overlooked in the original volumes, and offers more substantial coverage of colloquialisms and English outside the British Isles. The necessity of having the original volumes in hand for effective use of the *Supplement* is remedied by the second edition, which integrates (but does not correct or revise) the original volumes and *Supplement*, adds 5,000 new words or senses, and converts Murray's phonetic system to the International Phonetic Alphabet. The printed *OED* will eventually be superseded by the *New Oxford English Dictionary* data base, which will allow continual revision and updating as well as the incorporation of material not suitable or practical for a printed dictionary. The data base, which Oxford hopes to have ready by the early 1990s, will offer an unparalleled resource whose flexibility will allow numerous kinds of studies impossible with the printed version. (The data base will be available through vendors and probably in a CD-ROM version.) For a description of the *NOED* data base, see E. S. C. Weiner, "The *New Oxford English Dictionary*: Progress and Prospects," *Dictionaries of English: Prospects for the Record of Our Language*, ed. Richard W. Bailey (Ann Arbor: U of Michigan P, 1987) 30–48; J. C. Gray, "Creating the Electronic *New Oxford English Dictionary*," *Computers and the Humanities* 20 (1986): 45–49; N. C. Hultin and H. M. Logan, "The *New Oxford English Dictionary* Project at Waterloo," *Dictionaries* 6 (1984): 128, 183–98; and John Stubbs and Frank Wm. Tompa, "Waterloo and the *New Oxford English Dictionary* Project," *Editing, Publishing, and Computer Technology*, ed. Sharon Butler and William P. Stoneman (New York: AMS, 1988) 19–44.

To make effective use of the *OED*—and eventually the *NOED*—users must study the introductory explanation (in both the 1933 reissue and *Supplement*) of principles of compilation and editorial practices, and keep in mind the following points:

1. The *OED* is not exhaustive in its coverage of standard vocabulary, and is limited in its treatment of slang, dialect, scientific, and technical terms; thus, it must be supplemented by more specialized dictionaries such as Eric Partridge, *A Dictionary of Slang and Unconventional English: Colloquialisms and Catch-Phrases, Solecisms and Catachreses, Nicknames and Vulgarisms*, ed. Paul Beale, 8th ed. (New York: Macmillan, 1984, 1,400 pp.); *Dictionary of Old English* (1690); *Middle English Dictionary* (1860); *Dictionary of the Older Scottish Tongue* (3090); *Scottish National Dictionary* (3095); *Dictionary of American English* (3355); *Dictionary of Americanisms* (3360); *Webster's Second* and *Third* (3365); *Dictionary of American Regional English* (3350); and *English Dialect Dictionary* (1415).
2. Each grammatical form of a main word has a separate entry; thus, explicators in search of a definition must be certain to locate the entry for the grammatical form of the word as it is used in the literary work.
3. Subsequent research has corrected several etymologies; since erroneous ones are not revised in the *Supplement*, users must consult a good etymological dictionary such as *The Oxford Dictionary of English Etymology*, ed.

C. T. Onions, G. W. S. Friedrichsen, and R. W. Burchfield, rpt. with corrections (Oxford: Clarendon, 1969, 1,024 pp.).

4. Dates of first recorded uses are frequently incorrect (for an important study of the unreliability of first citations, see Jürgen Schäfer, *Documentation in the* O.E.D.*: Shakespeare and Nashe as Test Cases* [Oxford: Clarendon, 1980, 176 pp.]).
5. Additions of new words and senses, corrections, and antedatings are regularly published in a variety of journals (especially *Notes and Queries* [1475] and *American Speech* [3375]; several of these are indexed in Wall, *Words and Phrases Index* [6025]); the *Supplement* does not record antedatings before 1820.

One of the truly great dictionaries, the *OED* is an indispensable source for the historical study of the English language and for the explication of literary works. Reviews of *Supplement*: (vol. 1) Fred C. Robinson, *Yale Review* 62 (1973): 450–56; Donald B. Sands, *College English* 37 (1976): 710–18; (vol. 2) Robinson, *Yale Review* 67 (1977): 94–99; (vol. 3) Roy Harris, *TLS: Times Literary Supplement* 3 Sept. 1982: 935–36; Thomas M. Paikeday, *American Speech* 60 (1985): 74–79; (vol. 4) Pat Rogers, *TLS: Times Literary Supplement* 9 May 1986: 487–88.

An informative and entertaining account of the inception, editing, and publication of *OED* is K. M. Elizabeth Murray, *Caught in the Web of Words: James A. H. Murray and the* Oxford English Dictionary (New Haven: Yale UP, 1977), 386 pp.

In addition to those noted above, the following are important complementary works:

Bailey, *Michigan Early Modern English Materials* and *Early Modern English: Additions and Antedatings* (2055a).

The Barnhart Dictionary Companion (3365a) updates several standard dictionaries, including the *OED*, *Supplement*, and Partridge, *Dictionary of Slang*.

Fowler, H. W. *A Dictionary of Modern English Usage*. Rev. Ernest Gowers. 2nd ed. New York: Oxford UP, 1965. 725 pp. Although idiosyncratic and unrelentingly prescriptive, Fowler offers a fuller guide than the *OED* to usage. Because of the numerous arbitrary headings, locating a word or phrase usually requires J. Arthur Greenwood, *Find It in Fowler: An Alphabetical Index to the Second Edition (1965) of H. W. Fowler's* Modern English Usage (Princeton: Wolfhart, 1969, 113 pp.). A good complement to Fowler, which remains the standard guide, is Eric Partridge, *Usage and Abusage: A Guide to Good English*, new ed. (London: Hamilton, 1965, 392 pp.).

The best single-volume dictionary of British English is *Chambers 20th Century Dictionary*, ed. E. M. Kirkpatrick, new ed. (Edinburgh: Chambers, 1983, 1,583 pp.).

1415 *The English Dialect Dictionary: Being the Complete Vocabulary of All Dialect Words Still in Use, or Known to Have Been in Use during the Last Two Hundred Years*. Ed. Joseph Wright. 6 vols. London: Frowde; New York: Putnam's, 1898–1905. (Originally issued in parts.) PE1766.W8.

A dictionary of dialect terms (as distinct from those appearing in "the literary language") and Americanisms used in Great Britain and Ireland. A typical entry consists of headword, geographical area, variant spellings, pronunciation, definitions organized by parts of speech, illustrative dated quotations taken from printed sources and organized by area, and etymology. Vol. 6 includes a supplement (179 pp.), bibliography of sources (59 pp.), and grammar of English dialect (187 pp.). Although incomplete and dated, the work remains the fullest English dialect dictionary and, for literary scholars, an essential source for explicating dialect terms in English literature.

A useful complement for illustrating the geographical distribution of phonological, lexical, morphological, and syntactic features is Harold Orton, Stewart Sanderson, and John Widdowson, eds., *The Linguistic Atlas of England* (London: Croom Helm; Atlantic Highlands: Humanities, 1978, n.p.).

THESAURUSES

1420 *The Historical Thesaurus of English*. Ed. M. L. Samuels et al. London: Oxford UP. Tentatively scheduled for 1991.

A historical thesaurus of standard British English words arranged according to sense and with synonymous forms dated and listed in chronological order. The *Historical Thesaurus* differs from Roget and other modern thesauruses by including Old and Middle English as well as obsolete words and senses from Modern English. It will eventually be accessible online. For a description of the project and sample entry, see Christian J. Kay, "The Historical Thesaurus of English," *LEXeter '83 Proceedings*, ed. R. R. K. Hartmann, Lexicographica Series Maior 1 (Tübingen: Niemeyer, 1984) 87–91. When published, the *Historical Thesaurus* will be a valuable tool for studying the evolution of meaning of words as well as explicating literary works.

Biographical Dictionaries

1425 *Dictionary of National Biography from the Earliest Times to 1900* (*DNB*). Ed. Leslie Stephen and Sidney Lee. 22 vols. London: Oxford UP, 1967–68. (Originally published in 63 parts between 1885–1900.) DA28.D4 920.042.

Supplement. Ed. Sidney Lee. 3 vols. London: Smith, Elder, 1901. (Reissued as vol. 22 of the 1967–68 ed.)
Second Supplement. Ed. Lee. 3 vols. 1912.
1912–1921. Ed. H. W. C. Davis and J. R. H. Weaver. London: Oxford UP, 1927. 623 pp.
1922–1930. Ed. Weaver. 1937. 962 pp.
1931–1940. Ed. L. G. Wickham Legg. 1949. 968 pp.
1941–1950. Ed. Legg and E. T. Williams. 1959. 1,031 pp.
1951–1960. Ed. Williams and Helen M. Palmer. 1971. 1,150 pp.
1961–1970. Ed. Williams and C. S. Nicholls. 1981. 1,178 pp.
1971–1980. Ed. Lord Blake and Nicholls. 1986. 1,010 pp.
Compact Edition of the Dictionary of National Biography. 2 vols. London: Oxford UP, 1975. (A reduced-print reprint of the original dictionary and supplements through 1960.)

The Dictionary of National Biography: The Concise Dictionary: From the Beginnings to 1911, Being an Epitome of the Main Work and Its Supplement, to Which Is Added an Epitome of the Supplement 1901–1911. London: Oxford UP, 1920, 1,456 and 129 pp.

The Dictionary of National Biography: The Concise Dictionary. Pt. 2, *1901–1970.* Oxford: Oxford UP, 1982. 747 pp.

A biographical dictionary of dead individuals of some eminence or notoriety in Great Britain and the colonies. The original dictionary includes 29,120 individuals—from criminals to rulers, with a severe bias against women—in entries ranging from 49 pages for Shakespeare to a few sentences. After the 1912–21 supplement, selection is less catholic (although increasingly less biased in favor of men) and entries much shorter. Many of the signed entries are based on unpublished materials, private information, or personal knowledge as well as published documents; all conclude with a bibliography that in the original *DNB* frequently cites works not elsewhere indexed. Although the entries stress factual information, unflattering details were frequently suppressed in the original dictionary and early supplements. Recent supplements are more candid about the foibles of entrants. For an important discussion of biases, editorial intervention in the original contributions, and unacknowledged revisions made in successive printings, see Laurel Brake, "Problems in Victorian Biography: The *DNB* and the *DNB* 'Walter Pater,'" *Modern Language Review* 70 (1975): 731–42. Corrections and new facts are collected in *Corrections and Additions to the* Dictionary of National Biography*: Cumulated from the* Bulletin of the Institute of Historical Research, *University of London, Covering the Years 1923–1963* (Boston: Hall, 1966, 212 pp.), with information keyed to the 1908–09 issue; corrections to the supplements are incorporated into the *Concise Dictionary*. Indexed by name in each volume; each supplement has a cumulative index extending back to 1901; the *Concise Dictionary* is useful as an index to the entire work. David Bank, *A Chronological and Occupational Index to the* Dictionary of National Biography (Oxford: Oxford UP), announced for publication in 1985, has been delayed until at least 1990.

Although many entries require revision or supplementing in light of new information or reinterpretation of existing facts, the *DNB* remains an indispensable initial source for details of the lives of the eminent and notorious (many of which receive their fullest biographies herein), a major quarry for less comprehensive biographical dictionaries, and a model for national biographical dictionaries of other countries.

Among major dictionaries that cover a more restricted period but incorporate recent findings and additional lives, the most important are the following:

Baylen, Joseph O., and Norbert J. Gossman, eds. *Biographical Dictionary of Modern British Radicals [1770–1914].* 3 vols. Hassocks: Harvester; Atlantic Highlands: Humanities, 1979– . Vol. 1 covers 1770–1830; vol. 2, 1830–70; and vol. 3 (scheduled for 1989), 1870–1914, with many entries for individuals not in the *DNB*.

Boase, Frederic. *Modern English Biography: Containing Many Thousand Concise Memoirs of Persons Who Have Died between the Years 1851–1900.* 6 vols. Truro: Netherton, for the author, 1892–1921. Among the approximately thirty thousand brief sketches are many for names not in the *DNB*. Indexed by subject in each volume; women are indexed in Peter Bell, comp., *Index to Biographies of Women in Boase's* Modern English Biography (Edinburgh: Bell, 1986, n.pag.).

Valentine, Alan. *The British Establishment, 1760–1784: An Eighteenth-Century Biographical Dictionary*. 2 vols. Norman: U of Oklahoma P, 1970. About one-half of the approximately three thousand entries are for people not in the *DNB*.

For members of the aristocracy, see:

C[okayne], G[eorge] E[dward], ed. *Complete Baronetage*. 5 vols. Exeter: Pollard, 1900–06. Covers only the period 1611–1800.

Cokayne, George Edward, ed. *The Complete Peerage of England, Scotland, Ireland, Great Britain, and the United Kingdom, Extant, Extinct, or Dormant*. Ed. Vicary Gibbs et al. New ed. 13 vols. London: St. Catherine P, 1910–59. Records "particulars of the parentage, birth, honours, orders, offices, public services, politics, marriage, death and burial, of every holder of a Peerage."

1430 Allibone, S. Austin. *A Critical Dictionary of English Literature, and British and American Authors, Living and Deceased, from the Earliest Accounts to the Middle of the Nineteenth Century*. 3 vols. Philadelphia: Lippincott; London: Trübner, 1859–71.

Kirk, John Foster. *A Supplement to Allibone's Critical Dictionary of English Literature and British and American Writers*. 2 vols. Philadelphia: Lippincott, 1892. Z2010.A44 820.3

A dictionary of British and American writers through 1888. The approximately 83,000 entries provide biographical details, a list of books by the entrant, and references to other biographical dictionaries, all interspersed with biographical and critical comments extracted from the major nineteenth-century periodicals and other sources. The supplement provides less biographical information and fewer extracts. Indexed by broad topic in vol. 3 of the original dictionary; the supplement is not indexed. Although saddled with one of the most tedious introductions of any reference work, riddled with inaccuracies (partly because of its heavy reliance on untrustworthy sources), and thoroughly outdated in its treatment of authors of any note, Allibone remains occasionally useful for its inclusion of a host of minor writers nowhere else listed and extracts from nineteenth-century periodicals. Information taken from Allibone must always be verified.

1435 *Who's Who: An Annual Biographical Dictionary*. London: Black, 1849– . Annual. CT773.W6282 [DA28.W6] 920.042.

A biographical dictionary of living persons of distinction and influence primarily in the British Isles and current and former Commonwealth countries. The compact entries provide basic biographical, family, and career information; a list of publications, awards, and honors; and address. Indexed in *Biography and Genealogy Master Index* (565). This is the best general source for biographical data and addresses of notable residents of the British Isles.

Biographies of dead entrants are reprinted with corrections in *Who Was Who: A Companion to* Who's Who *Containing the Biographies of Those Who Died during the Period [1897–]* (London: Black, 1920–). Volumes are now issued for each decade; several early volumes have been published in revised editions. Cumulatively indexed in *Who Was Who: A Cumulated Index, 1897–1980* (1981, 746 pp.).

See also

Dictionary of Literary Biography (600).
Oxford Companion to English Literature (1330).

Periodicals

See section K: Periodicals for general directories and union lists of periodicals.

GUIDES TO PRIMARY WORKS

Bibliographies

1440 *Bibliography of British Newspapers*. Gen. ed. Charles A. Toase. London: British Library, 1975– . Z6956.G6.B5 [PN5114] 016.079'41.

Vol. 1: *Wiltshire*. Ed. R. K. Bluhm. 1975. 28 pp.
Vol. 2: *Kent*. Ed. Winifred E. Bergess, Barbara R. M. Riddell, and John Whyman. 1982. 139 pp.
Vol. 3: *Durham and Northumberland*. Ed. F. W. D. Manders. 1982. 65 pp.
Vol. 4: *Derbyshire*. Ed. Anne Mellors and Jean Radford. 1987. 74 pp.
Vol. 5: *Nottinghamshire*. Ed. Michael Brook. 1987. 62 pp.

A bibliography of current and defunct newspapers, with individual volumes devoted to a single county or related counties according to boundaries before the 1974 reorganization (and in the case of greater London, the pre-1965 boundaries). Titles are organized geographically by "main area of news coverage or . . . principal area of circulation," then (depending on the volume) chronologically by date of first issue or alphabetically by title. Defunct newspapers are listed by earliest title; others by current title. A typical entry records place of publication, publisher, address (if still being published), dates of publication, mergers and name changes, locations of copies (with information on completeness of holdings), and references to historical studies. Two indexes: places; titles. When complete, this bibliography will offer the fullest, most current general record of British newspapers and the locations of copies.

Until then, the only reasonably full list is *Tercentenary Handlist of English and Welsh Newspapers, Magazines, and Reviews* [comp. J. G. Muddiman] (London: The Times, 1920, 324 pp.), which covers 1620 through 1919. Based on the British Library holdings, the *Handlist* is far from complete (especially for the eighteenth century) and lists titles chronologically by date of the first issue extant in the library's collection. Numerous additions and corrections are scattered throughout *Notes and Queries* 12th ser. 8 (1921), 12th ser. 10 (1922), and 161 (1931). Although covering briefer periods, the following are superior in thoroughness and accuracy:

Crane, *Census of British Newspapers and Periodicals, 1620–1800* (2270).
Nelson, *British Newspapers and Periodicals, 1641–1700* (2060).
Ward, *Index and Finding List of Serials Published in the British Isles, 1789–1832* (2535).
Wolff, *Waterloo Directory of Victorian Periodicals, 1824–1900* (2540).

1445 Sullivan, Alvin, ed. *British Literary Magazines*. 4 vols. Historical Guides to the World's Periodicals and Newspapers. Westport: Greenwood, 1983–86. PN5124.L6.B74 820'.8.

Vol. 1: *The Augustan Age and the Age of Johnson, 1698–1788*. 1983. 427 pp.
Vol. 2: *The Romantic Age, 1789–1836*. 1983. 491 pp. (Errata in vol. 3, p. xii.)
Vol. 3: *The Victorian and Edwardian Age, 1837–1913*. 1984. 560 pp.
Vol. 4: *The Modern Age, 1914–1984*. 1986. 628 pp.

Profiles of major and representative minor literary magazines. Each volume includes an introductory survey, essays on 80 to 90 magazines, and a chronology of social and literary events and literary magazines; vols. 1 and 3 list other magazines with literary content, and vol. 4, Scottish literary periodicals and magazines with short runs. The individual essays, which vary widely in quality, survey publishing history, characterize content, note important literary contributions, and provide publication details (title changes, volume and issue data, frequency of publication, publishers, and editors) and selective lists of studies, indexes, reprints, and locations. Indexed by persons and magazine titles. Although the lack of clear criteria governing selection leads to the inclusion of some magazines that can hardly qualify as literary, Sullivan is a serviceable compilation of basic information on a number of periodicals. Reviews: (vols. 1–2) G. E. Bentley, Jr., *Victorian Periodicals Review* 17 (1984): 109–13; (vol. 3) Charles Brownson, *English Literature in Transition, 1880–1920* 29 (1986): 340–42; Rosemary T. VanArsdel, *Victorian Periodicals Review* 18 (1985): 99–101.

Indexes

1450 The Times *Index [1906–]*. Reading: Research Publications, 1907– . Monthly, with annual cumulations. Former titles: *The Annual Index to the* Times (1907–13); *The Official Index to* The Times (1914–57). AI21.T46 072'.1.

A subject and author index to the final editions of *The Times* and, since 1973, *Sunday Times*, *TLS: Times Literary Supplement*, *Times Educational Supplement*, *Times Educational Supplement Scotland*, and *Times Higher Education Supplement*. Users should watch for changes in coverage and indexing practices over the years, and note that annual cumulations do not begin until 1977. In most volumes, books reviewed are listed by title under the heading "Books" as well as under the authors. The *Index* offers the best access to one of the world's great newspapers, which for literature scholars is a valuable source of biographical information (especially in obituaries). And, like other indexes of major newspapers, the source can be used to narrow dates for searching unindexed papers.

For issues before 1906, see *Palmer's Index to* The Times *Newspaper [10 October 1790–30 June 1941]* (Corsham: Palmer, 1868–1943), which is much less thorough and more idiosyncratic in indexing practices, and The Times *Index [1785–90]*, 6 vols. (Reading: Newspaper Archive Developments, 1978–84). Times Literary Supplement *Index* (765a) offers superior access to *TLS: Times Literary Supplement* (765).

Doreen Morrison, "Indexes to *The Times* of London: An Evaluation and Comparative Analysis," *Serials Librarian* 13.1 (1987): 89–106, offers a useful comparison of the two indexes and discussion of the difficulties in using *Palmer's Index*.

GUIDES TO SCHOLARSHIP AND CRITICISM

1455 Linton, David, and Ray Boston, eds. *The Newspaper Press in Britain: An Annotated Bibliography*. London: Mansell, 1987. 361 pp. Z6956.G6.L56 [PN5114] 016.072.

A bibliography of published studies (through c. 1985), dissertations, theses, and a few manuscripts (although the latter are inadequately identified and unlocated). The approximately 2,900 entries are listed alphabetically by author. Unfortunately the citations do not record pagination for articles or essays in collections, and many of the brief descriptive annotations fail to provide an adequate sense of contents. Two appendixes: a chronology of British newspaper history from 1476 through 1986; locations of papers and archives of newspapers and persons connected with the trade. Indexed by subjects (including newspapers). Although it is the fullest general list of scholarship on British newspapers, the lack of a classified organization, frequently inadequate annotations, and insufficiently thorough subject indexing make the work far less accessible than it should be.

1460 White, Robert B. *The English Literary Journal to 1900: A Guide to Information Sources*. American Literature, English Literature, and World Literatures in English: An Information Guide Series 8. Detroit: Gale, 1977. 311 pp. Z6956.G6.W47 [PN5114] 016.81'05.

An annotated bibliography of English-language studies (published between c. 1890 and c. 1973) and modern critical editions of literary periodicals. Entries are organized in five chapters: bibliographies, general studies, periodicals, persons (including authors), and places. Few annotations are adequately informative, and many entries are unannotated. Of the four indexes (authors, periodicals, persons, places), only the first is necessary; the others merely repeat classified listings without incorporating cross-references. Because the lack of clarity in the selection policy and definition of the term *literary periodical* results in considerable unevenness of coverage (which is more thorough for eighteenth- than nineteenth-century periodicals), White is little more than a place to begin research. For nineteenth-century periodicals, see Madden, *Nineteenth-Century Periodical Press* (2560). Reviews: Richard Haven, *Analytical and Enumerative Bibliography* 1 (1977): 250–55; Lionel Madden, *Victorian Periodicals Newsletter* 11 (1978): 108–10; Joanne Shattock, *Yearbook of English Studies* 10 (1980): 230–32.

SCHOLARLY JOURNALS

The following works publish on a variety of periods in English literature; those limited to a period, movement, or genre of English literature are listed in appropriate parts of section M: English Literature. All journals listed in section K: Periodicals/Scholarly Journals and under the heading Scholarly Journals in section L: Genres publish on English literature.

1465 *English*. 1936– . 3/yr. PR5.E5 820'.9.

Since vol. 25 (1976), *English* emphasizes major British writers and works in articles, and critical studies in reviews (with brief notices of editions and scholarly works in the Editorial Miscellany section). Annual index in some volumes before vol. 25 (1976).

1470 *English Studies: A Journal of English Language and Literature* (*ES*). 1919– . 6/yr. PE1.E55 420.5.

Publishes articles, notes, occasional surveys of recent research on an author, and reviews primarily on English language and literature. The highly selective annual survey of "Current Literature" (since vol. 8 [1926]) is now divided into two parts: one reviews British, American, and occasionally Commonwealth fiction, poetry, and drama; the other surveys editions, biographies, literary histories, works of literary theory, and criticism principally on English literature. Cumulative indexes: vols. 1–40 (1960, 97 pp.); vols. 41–60, J. De Smet-D'hondt, comp., *Index to Volumes 41–60* (1979, 63 pp.).

1475 *Notes and Queries: For Readers and Writers, Collectors and Librarians* (*N&Q*). 1849– . Quarterly. AG305.N7 032.

Publishes notes, queries, replies, and reviews on "English language and literature, lexicography, history, and scholarly antiquarianism." Frequently prints additions, corrections, and antedatings to the *Oxford English Dictionary* (1410); source, influence, biographical, textual, and philological notes; and unpublished letters and poems. Annual index; cumulative indexes: to each of the first 12 series; vols. 145–56 (n.d., 219 pp.); vols. 157–68 (n.d., 183 pp.); vols. 169–92 (1955, 215 pp.). *Notes and Queries* is more substantial and significant than the similar *ANQ: A Quarterly Journal of Short Articles, Notes, and Reviews* (1988– , quarterly), successor to *American Notes and Queries* (1962–86).

1480 *Review of English Studies: A Quarterly Journal of English Literature and the English Language* (*RES*). 1925– . Quarterly. PR1.R4 820'.9.

Publishes articles, notes, and reviews on all aspects of English literature and language (with a decided emphasis on literature). Recent issues tend to be divided fairly evenly between articles and reviews. A useful feature is the "Summary of Periodical Literature" that lists contents of journals received. Annual index. Noted for the quality of its articles and reviews.

1485 *Studies in English Literature, 1500–1900* (*SEL*). 1961– . Quarterly. PR1.S82 820'.9.

Publishes historical and critical essays and surveys of recent studies, with the winter issue devoted to the English Renaissance (2015), the spring issue to Elizabethan and Jacobean drama (2150), the summer issue to the Restoration and eighteenth century (2240), and the autumn issue to the nineteenth century (2480). The surveys are highly selective (and too frequently limited to books received for review), with wide variation in quality from contributor to contributor.

1490 *Studies in Philology* (*SP*). 1906– . Quarterly. P25.S8 405.

Since vol. 85 (1988), *SP* publishes articles on British literature before 1900. Earlier volumes encompass classical through modern literature, with a decided emphasis on the Middle Ages and Renaissance (especially in England). "Literature of the Renaissance in [1917–68]: A Bibliography" (2030) appears in vols. 14–66 (1917–69). Since vol. 68 (1979), an annual Text and Studies issue prints a reference work or edition. Cumulative index: vols. 1–50 [Loraine Anderson, comp.], *Index Volumes I–L* (Chapel Hill: U of North Carolina P, 1954, 124 pp.)

Background Reading

1495 *The Oxford History of England.* Ed. George N. Clark. 16 vols. Oxford: Clarendon, 1936–86.

Vol. 1a: Salway, Peter. *Roman Britain.* 1981. 824 pp. DA145.S26 936.1'04.
Vol. 1b: Myres, J. N. L. *The English Settlements.* 1986. 248 pp. DA152.M97 942.01. (This and the preceding volume replace R. G. Collingwood and Myres, *Roman Britain and the English Settlements,* 2nd ed. [1937, 515 pp.].)
Vol. 2: Stenton, F. M. *Anglo-Saxon England.* 3rd ed. 1971. 765 pp. DA152.S74 942.01.
Vol. 3: Poole, Austin Lane. *From Domesday Book to Magna Carta, 1087–1216.* 2nd ed. 1955. 541 pp. DA175.P6 942.02.
Vol. 4: Powicke, Maurice. *The Thirteenth Century, 1216–1307.* 2nd ed. 1962. 829 pp. DA225.P65 942.034.
Vol. 5: McKisack, May. *The Fourteenth Century, 1307–1399.* 1959. 598 pp. DA230.M25 942.037.
Vol. 6: Jacob, E. F. *The Fifteenth Century, 1399–1485.* 1961. 775 pp. DA245.J3 942.04.
Vol. 7: Mackie, J. D. *The Earlier Tudors, 1485–1558.* Rpt. with corrections. 1978. 699 pp. DA325.M3.
Vol. 8: Black, J. B. *The Reign of Elizabeth, 1558–1603.* 2nd ed. 1959. 539 pp. DA355.B65 942.055.
Vol. 9: Davies, Godfrey. *The Early Stuarts, 1603–1660.* 2nd ed. 1959. 458 pp. DA390.D3 942.06.
Vol. 10: Clark, George N. *The Later Stuarts, 1660–1714.* 2nd ed., rpt. with corrections. 1961. 479 pp. DA435.C55 942.06.
Vol. 11: Williams, Basil. *The Whig Supremacy, 1714–1760.* 2nd ed., rev. C. H. Stuart. 1962. 504 pp. DA498.W5 942.071.
Vol. 12: Watson, J. Steven. *The Reign of George III, 1760–1815.* 1960. 637 pp. DA505.W38 942.073.
Vol. 13: Woodward, Llewellyn. *The Age of Reform, 1815–1870.* 2nd ed. 1962. 681 pp. DA530.W6 942.07.
Vol. 14: Ensor, R. C. K. *England, 1870–1914.* 1936. 634 pp. DA560.E6 942.08.
Vol. 15: Taylor, A. J. P. *English History, 1914–1945.* 1965. 708 pp. DA566.T38 942.083.

A general economic, social, political, and military history. Individual volumes are variously organized, but each includes a selective bibliography, maps, and an index of persons and subjects. Although some volumes are now outdated, the work remains the most authoritative general history of England. It will, however, be superseded by the *New Oxford History of England,* ed. J. M. Roberts (scheduled to begin publication in 1989).

1500 *The Victoria History of the Counties of England* (*Victoria County History, VCH*). Oxford: Oxford UP for Institute of Historical Research, 1900– . DA670 942.

A collaborative history, with several volumes devoted to each county. Among the topics covered are the physical environment, prehistory, archaeology, schools, industries, sports and pastimes, topography (with descriptions of manors, estates, and other places), and natural, political, social, and economic history. Some volumes have an index of persons, places, and subjects; a cumulative index is planned for each county when all the volumes are published. The quality of the essays varies considerably, but coverage has generally become more thorough over the years; however, there is no consistency in the publication schedule of volumes for each county. Although frequently pedestrian, the volumes offer an incomparable accumulation of local history. The *General Introduction*, ed. R. B. Pugh (1970, 282 pp.) offers a thorough discussion of the origin and history of the project; an overview of changes in titles, publishers, and printers; and a detailed list of contents of all volumes published by 1970.

Genres

Most of the works in section L: Genres are useful for research in English literature.

FICTION

Most of the works in section L: Genres/Fiction are important to research in English fiction.

Histories and Surveys

1505 Baker, Ernest A. *The History of the English Novel.* 10 vols. London: Witherby, 1924–39. PR821.B3 823.09.

Vol. 1: *The Age of Romance; from the Beginnings to the Renaissance.* 1924. 336 pp.
Vol. 2: *The Elizabethan Age and After.* 1929. 303 pp.
Vol. 3: *The Later Romances and the Age of Realism.* 1929. 278 pp.
Vol. 4: *Intellectual Realism: From Richardson to Sterne.* 1930. 297 pp.
Vol. 5: *The Novel of Sentiment and the Gothic Romance.* 1934. 300 pp.
Vol. 6: *Edgeworth, Austen, Scott.* 1929. 277 pp.
Vol. 7: *The Age of Dickens and Thackeray.* 1936. 404 pp.
Vol. 8: *From the Brontës to Meredith: Romanticism in the English Novel.* 1937. 411 pp.
Vol. 9: *The Day before Yesterday.* 1938. 364 pp.
Vol. 10: *Yesterday.* 1939. 420 pp.
Vol. 11: Stevenson, Lionel. *Yesterday and After.* New York: Barnes, 1967. 431 pp.

A descriptive history, ranging from Anglo-Saxon fiction through the mid-twentieth century, with an emphasis on major authors. Each volume includes a highly selective bibliography (now outdated) and is indexed by author, anonymous work, and subject. Although pedestrian and predictable, Baker remains the most comprehensive general history of the English novel.

More compact surveys include Lionel Stevenson, *The English Novel: A Panorama* (Boston: Houghton, 1960, 539 pp.); Edward Wagenknecht, *Cavalcade of the English Novel* (New York: Holt, 1954, 686 pp., with a supplementary bibliography); and Walter Allen, *The English Novel: A Short Critical History* (New York: Dutton, 1955, 454 pp.). Major desiderata are a multivolume history that would replace Baker and a good general compact history of the novel.

Guides to Scholarship and Criticism

Surveys of Research

1510 Dyson, A. E., ed. *The English Novel: Select Bibliographical Guides*. London: Oxford UP, 1974. 372 pp. Z2014.F5.D94 016.823'03.

A collection of evaluative surveys of the best editions, critical studies, biographies and collections of letters, bibliographies, and background studies (published through the early 1970s) for twenty-two novelists: Bunyan, Defoe, Swift, Richardson, Fielding, Sterne, Smollett, Scott, Austen, Thackeray, Dickens, Trollope, the Brontë sisters, Eliot, Hardy, James, Conrad, Forster, Lawrence, and Joyce. The quality of individual essays varies widely, but Dyson is a serviceable guide to important scholarship published through the early 1970s. See *Year's Work in English Studies* (330) for evaluations of later works. Review: David Leon Higdon, *Modern Fiction Studies* 20 (1974–75): 607–08.

Other Bibliographies

1515 Bell, Inglis F., and Donald Baird. *The English Novel, 1578–1956: A Checklist of Twentieth-Century Criticisms*. Denver: Swallow, 1958. 168 pp. Z2014.F4.B4 016.82309.

Continued by: Palmer, Helen H., and Anne Jane Dyson, comps. *English Novel Explication: Criticisms to 1972*. Hamden: Shoe String, 1973. 329 pp. *Supplement I*. Comp. Peter L. Abernethy, Christian J. W. Kloesel, and Jeffrey R. Smitten. 1976. 305 pp. *Supplement II*. Comp. Kloesel and Smitten. 1981. 326 pp. *Supplement III*. Comp. Kloesel. 1986. 533 pp. Z2014.F5.P26 [PR821] 016.823'009.

Bell and Baird provide a highly selective list of English-language books, parts of books, and articles published from c. 1900 to c. 1957, with entries organized alphabetically by novelist and then by novel. The emphasis is rather loosely on explication, but the criteria for selection are unclear. The degree of selectivity, typographical errors, lack of indexing, and inadequate explanation of editorial policy render Bell and Baird the least useful of these checklists.

Palmer and Dyson interpret "novel" more broadly, range beyond explication, extend coverage back to Malory's *Morte Darthur*, and include dissertation abstracts, some book reviews, and foreign-language criticism. Their work covers studies published between 1958 and 1972, with selection apparently based on what the compilers could discover. Indexed by literary authors and novel titles.

The first supplement lists books, parts of books, and articles published between 1972 and 1974 (with some earlier works and some from 1975), is more precisely limited to explication, and coordinates coverage with Walker, *Twentieth-Century Short Story Explication* (1090). The second supplement extends coverage through 1979; the third, through 1985.

Although *English Novel* and *English Novel Explication* (and supplements) make a handy set of volumes for preliminary work (especially because of the inclusion of parts of books), many novelists are more adequately treated in author bibliographies.

1520 *The English Novel: Twentieth Century Criticism*. Vol. 1: *Defoe through Hardy*. Ed. Richard J. Dunn. Chicago: Swallow, 1976. 202 pp. Vol. 2: *Twentieth Century Novelists*. Ed. Paul Schlueter and June Schlueter. Athens: Swallow-Ohio UP, 1982. 380 pp. Z2014.F4.E53 [PR821] 016.823'91'09.

Highly selective lists of English-language books, parts of books, and articles (published through 1974 in vol. 1; 1975 in vol. 2). Vol. 1 covers general studies of the novel and 45 novelists, each with sections for general studies (an alphabetical hodgepodge), bibliographies, and works on individual novels. Vol. 2 covers eighty established writers, each with sections for bibliographies, interviews, general studies, and works on individual novels. Both volumes fail to clarify selection criteria, and the second hardly bears out its editors' claim as "the most nearly complete bibliography of criticism of the twentieth century British novel yet published." Although these volumes are occasionally useful as a starting point, most of the novelists included are more adequately treated in period and author bibliographies.

See also

ABELL (340): English Literature/General/Fiction section.
MLAIB (335): English III/Prose Fiction section in pre-1981 volumes; and the English Literature/Fiction and English Literature/Novel sections in pt. 1 of the later volumes.

DRAMA AND THEATER

Most works in section L: Genres/Drama are important to research in English drama.

Histories and Surveys

1525 Nicoll, Allardyce. *A History of English Drama, 1660–1900*. 6 vols. Cambridge: Cambridge UP, 1952–59. PR625.N52 822.09.

Vol. 1: *Restoration Drama*. 4th ed. 1952. (2360).
Vol. 2: *Early Eighteenth Century Drama*. 3rd ed. 1952. (2360).
Vol. 3: *Late Eighteenth Century Drama, 1750–1800*. 2nd ed. 1952. (2360).
Vol. 4: *Early Nineteenth Century Drama, 1800–1850*. 2nd ed. 1955. (2670).

Vol. 5: *Late Nineteenth Century Drama, 1850–1900.* 2nd ed. 1959. (2670).
Vol. 6: *A Short-Title Alphabetical Catalogue of Plays Produced or Printed in England from 1660 to 1900.* 1959. (1545).

Emphasizes the history of the stage and dramatic forms of the legitimate and popular theater. Each volume includes a chapter on the theater, discussions of genres or kinds of dramatic entertainments, an appendix on playhouses, and an author list of plays first printed or produced during the respective period. Readers should watch for the supplementary sections containing revisions that could not be incorporated into the text. Each volume is indexed by persons and subjects; vol. 6 indexes by title plays in the author list to each volume and includes numerous additions and corrections. Although the history of the stage is now dated and the production details for 1660–1800 are now largely superseded by *London Stage* (2370), the volumes include a wealth of information, especially on minor writers, not readily available elsewhere. Continued by Nicoll, *English Drama, 1900–1930* (2855). See the individual entries for a fuller description of each volume. Reviews: Rudolf Stamm, *English Studies* 37 (1956): 220–22; 42 (1961): 46–48.

1530 *The Revels History of Drama in English.* Gen. eds. Clifford Leech, T. W. Craik, and Lois Potter. 8 vols. London: Methuen, 1975–83. PR625.R44 822'.009.

Vol. 1: *Medieval Drama.* 1983. (1910).
Vol. 2: *1500–1576.* 1980. (2120).
Vol. 3: *1576–1613.* 1975. (2120).
Vol. 4: *1613–1660.* 1981. (2120).
Vol. 5: *1660–1750.* 1976. (2365).
Vol. 6: *1750–1880.* 1975. (2675).
Vol. 7: *1880 to the Present Day.* 1978. (2860).
Vol. 8: *American Drama.* 1977. (3495).

Each volume includes a chronology; essays that examine the social and/or literary context, actors and the stage, and the plays and playwrights; an evaluative survey of important scholarship; and an index of authors, titles, and subjects. The *Revels History* offers a useful synthesis of scholarship rather than a connected history of the drama, with many volumes justly faulted for unevenness and inconsistencies. For fuller descriptions, see the individual entries.

Annals

1535 Harbage, Alfred. *Annals of English Drama, 975–1700: An Analytical Record of All Plays, Extant or Lost, Chronologically Arranged and Indexed by Authors, Titles, Dramatic Companies, &c.* Rev. by S. Schoenbaum. Philadelphia: U of Pennsylvania P, 1964. 321 pp. Schoenbaum. *Supplement to the Revised Edition.* Evanston: Department of English, Northwestern U, 1966. 19 pp. *Second Supplement to the Revised Edition.* 1970. 19 pp. (A third edition, by Sylvia S. Wagonheim, will be published by Methuen in 1989.) Z2014.D7.H25.

A chronology of dramatic and quasidramatic works (including translations) written in England or by English writers in other countries. Entries are organized according to the known or probable date of first performance: under each century (to 1495) or year (1495–1700), plays of known authorship are listed alphabetically by author, followed by anonymous plays listed by title. Information is presented in tabular format, with columns for author, title, date of first performance (when known), type of play, auspices of first production (including acting company and place), date of first edition or manuscript, and date of most recent modern edition (which is not always the best edition). To decipher information in the columns, users must refer continually to the explanation of symbols in the introduction. Following the chronology are various supplementary lists: extant plays, lost plays omitted because of uncertain date or identity, editions referred to in the list of most recent editions, editions in dissertations, theaters. An appendix lists extant play manuscripts, with location and shelf number. Five indexes: English playwrights; English plays; foreign playwrights; foreign plays translated or adapted; dramatic companies. The third edition incorporates scholarship since 1964 but remains as conservative as its predecessor in dating and attributing works. It retains the same format, but adds a selective list of editions of medieval drama texts, details of collected works to the index of English playwrights, and lists of editions in the index of English plays. The *Annals* is an authoritative accumulation of factual information and an essential source for investigating the environment of a play or the evolution of the early drama (but superseded by *London Stage, 1660–1800* [2370] for 1660–1700). Kawachi, *Calendar of English Renaissance Drama* (2130) offers more detailed and current coverage of productions between 1558 and 1642.

For an instructive discussion of how the *Annals* led to the discovery of a "lost" play, see Arthur H. Scouten and Robert D. Hume, eds., introd., The Country Gentleman: *A "Lost" Play and Its Background* (Philadelphia: U of Pennsylvania P, 1976) 10–17.

Guides to Primary Works

Manuscripts

1540 *Catalogue of Additions to the Manuscripts: Additional Manuscripts 42865–43038: Plays Submitted to the Lord Chamberlain, 1824–1851*. London: British Museum, 1964. 357 pp. Z6621.B8422 016.091.

One result of the Licensing Act of 1737, which required that every play intended for performance be approved by the Lord Chamberlain, is an unrivaled collection of manuscripts and printed acting copies and editions documenting English theater and drama since the early eighteenth century. Unfortunately, the collection is split between the Huntington Library and the British Library, and only plays submitted between 1737 and 1851 have published catalogs. Some copies submitted during the nineteenth century are reproduced in *English and American Drama of the Nineteenth Century* (2695).

1737–January 1824. Held in the Huntington Library and cataloged in *Catalogue of the Larpent Plays in the Huntington Library*, comp. Dougald MacMillan, Huntington Library Lists 4 (San Marino: Huntington Library, 1939, 442 pp.). Plays in the Larpent collection are reproduced in Wells, *Three Centuries of Drama* (1180).

February 1824–December 1851. Held in the Department of Manuscripts, British Library. The catalog lists plays in order of submission, with a typical entry recording manuscript title, any alternate title, author (frequently taken from Nicoll, *History of English Drama*, vol. 4 [2670]), and the presence of an autograph copy. Two indexes: authors; titles.

1852–1967. Held in the Department of Manuscripts, British Library, and indexed by title in a card index there.

1968– . Since 1968, plays no longer must be licensed, but a copy of the script of every play produced in Great Britain must be deposited in the Department of Manuscripts. Indexed by authors and titles in a card index there.

An invaluable collection that preserves hundreds of unique copies of dramatic presentations, legitimate and popular, London and provincial, and whose existence is too little known among researchers.

Printed Works

1545 Nicoll, Allardyce. *A Short-Title Alphabetical Catalogue of Plays Produced or Printed in England from 1660 to 1900*. Vol. 6 of *A History of English Drama, 1660–1900* (1525). Cambridge: Cambridge UP, 1959. 565 pp. PR625.N52 822.09.

More than a title index to the author lists of plays in vols. 1–5, this is an independent record of plays and dramatic entertainments (excluding most Italian operas and "the repertoire of the French and Italian comedians") first produced or printed in England from 1660 to 1900. The entries, which identify authors and dates of first productions, include corrections and additions to the individual lists. Of particular value is the inclusion of alternate titles and subtitles along with main titles. Although not exhaustive and partly superseded by *London Stage* (2370) for the period 1660–1800, the *Catalogue* remains the most complete list of dramatic works for the period 1660–1900.

1550 Stratman, Carl J., C.S.V., comp. and ed. *Bibliography of English Printed Tragedy, 1565–1900*. Carbondale: Southern Illinois UP; London: Feffer, 1966. 843 pp. Z2014.D7.S83 016.822051.

A bibliography of editions published between 1565 and the early 1960s of 1,483 tragedies written in English and first printed between 1565 and 1900. Stratman excludes Shakespeare's tragedies (but includes adaptations of them), translations, one-act plays unless the author also wrote full-length plays, and works existing only in manuscript. Plays are organized alphabetically by author, then title, with editions listed chronologically. Additions and corrections appear on pp. 837–43. An entry typically includes title, imprint, pagination, notes (principally bibliographical or textual, with references to standard bibliographies), and locations. Useful features include a list of anthologies and collections, a chronological list of plays by date of first edition, and a list of locations of manuscripts of works included in the bibliography. Indexed by titles. Although not comprehensive (especially for nineteenth-century works), Stratman is valuable for identifying and locating editions and for studying the genre. Review: Inga-Stina Ewbank, *Shakespeare Studies* 5 (1969): 366–69.

Guides to Scholarship and Criticism

Surveys of Research

1555 Wells, Stanley, ed. *English Drama (Excluding Shakespeare): Select Bibliographical Guides*. London: Oxford UP, 1975. 303 pp. Z2014.D7.E44 [PR625] 822'.009.

A collection of essays that delineate trends in criticism, evaluate the best editions and studies published through the early 1970s, and frequently suggest work that needs to be undertaken on medieval through contemporary drama. Chapters are devoted to reference works and general studies; medieval drama; Tudor and early Elizabethan drama; Marlowe; Jonson and Chapman; Marston, Middleton, and Massinger; Beaumont and Fletcher, Heywood, and Dekker; Webster, Tourneur, and Ford; the court masque; Davenant, Dryden, Lee, and Otway; Etherege, Shadwell, Wycherley, Congreve, Vanbrugh, and Farquhar; Gay, Goldsmith, Sheridan, and other eighteenth-century dramatists; nineteenth-century drama; Shaw; the Irish School; English drama, 1900–45; and English drama since 1945. Shakespeare occupies a separate volume: *Shakespeare: Select Bibliographical Guides*, ed. Stanley Wells (London: Oxford UP, 1973, 300 pp). Indexed by dramatists and anonymous plays. The judicious (sometimes pointed) evaluations serve as useful guides through the mass of scholarship. See *Year's Work in English Studies* (330) for evaluations of works published after c. 1970, and Logan and Smith (2145) for more thorough treatment of Renaissance dramatists.

Other Bibliographies

1560 Arnott, James Fullarton, and John William Robinson. *English Theatrical Literature, 1559–1900: A Bibliography Incorporating Robert W. Lowe's* A Bibliographical Account of English Theatrical Literature *Published in 1888*. London: Soc. for Theatre Research, 1970. 486 pp. Z2014.D7.A74 016.792'0942.

A bibliography of works published between 1559 and 1900 on British theater (including opera, pantomime, and music hall, but not ballet or circus). Studies are organized chronologically within classified divisions for bibliography, government regulation of the theater, theater arts (e.g., acting, costume, playwriting), general history, London theater, theater out of London, a national theater, opera, irregular forms (pantomime, music hall, etc.), societies, amateur theater, biography, theory and criticism, periodicals (see Stratman, *Britain's Theatrical Periodicals* [1565] for a fuller list of periodicals). Only British editions are fully described; only one location is cited for each work; and the notes generally deal with bibliographical matters. Three indexes: authors; titles; places of publication. The classified organization and cross-references do not compensate for the absence of a subject index. Although limited by its exclusion of articles (unless also separately printed) and terminal date, Arnott is still the best single guide to early publications, many of which are indexed nowhere else.

See also

ABELL (340): English Literature/General/Drama and the Theatre section.
MLAIB (335): English III/Drama section in the pre-1981 volumes; and the English Literature/Drama and English Literature/Theater sections in the later volumes.

Biographical Dictionaries

Indexes

See

Wearing, *American and British Theatrical Biography* (1175).

Periodicals

Guides to Primary Works

1565 Stratman, Carl J., C.S.V. *Britain's Theatrical Periodicals, 1720–1967: A Bibliography*. 2nd ed. New York: New York Public Library, 1972. 160 pp. Z6935.S76 016.792'0942.

A chronological bibliography of periodicals devoted to the theater and published in Great Britain between 1720 and 1967. Entries are listed by date of original issue and include title, publication information, and locations. Indexed by titles, editors, and places of publication. *Britain's Theatrical Periodicals* remains useful for identifying periodicals and locating complete (or the most complete) runs. For additional locations, consult OCLC (225), RLIN (230), *New Serial Titles* (640), *Union List of Serials* (640a), and *Serials in the British Library* (645). Review: J. W. Robinson, *Victorian Periodicals Newsletter* 8 (1975): 109–10.

Scholarly Journals

Most journals in section K: Periodicals/Scholarly Journals, and all in section L: Genres/Drama and Theater/Periodicals publish materials on English drama and theater.

1570 *Theatre Notebook: A Journal of the History and Technique of the British Theatre* (*TN*). 1945– . 3/yr. PN2001.T37 792.

Publishes articles, notes, queries, and reviews, with an emphasis on the eighteenth and nineteenth centuries. Annual index.

POETRY

Most of the works listed in section L: Genres/Poetry are important to research in English poetry.

Histories and Surveys

1575 Courthope, W. J. *A History of English Poetry*. 6 vols. New York: Macmillan, 1895–1910. PR502.C8 821.09.

A historical survey of the development of poetry (including dramatic poetry) through the Romantic movement. In treating poetry as an aspect of intellectual history, Courthope emphasizes the impact of political and social history but gives little attention to minor figures. Cumulative index of authors and titles in vol. 6. Although uneven in places and generally superseded by surveys limited to individual periods, the work remains the most extensive connected history of English poetry.

1580 *The Routledge History of English Poetry*. Gen. ed. R. A. Foakes. 7 vols. London: Routledge, 1977– . PR502.R58 821'.009.

Vol. 1: Pearsall, Derek. *Old English and Middle English Poetry*. 1977. (1735).
Vol. 2: Leslie, Michael. *Sixteenth-Century Poetry*. In progress.
Vol. 2a: Post, Jonathan. *Seventeenth-Century Poetry to the Restoration*. In progress.
Vol. 3: Rothstein, Eric. *Restoration and Eighteenth-Century Poetry, 1660–1780*. 1981. (2410).
Vol. 4: Jackson, J. R. de J. *Poetry of the Romantic Period*. 1980. (2705).
Vol. 6: Armstrong, Isobel. *Victorian Poetry*. In progress.
Vol. 7: Kelly, John. *Modern Poetry*. In progress.

A critical history whose aim "is not to provide merely another account of the major figures, but to reassess the development of English poetry." Other than the inclusion of a chronology, there is no attempt at consistency or continuity between volumes. The authors do give attention to minor as well as major figures, but the *History* overall has been faulted for dense passages consisting largely of names and titles. For fuller descriptions, see the entries for individual volumes. As a history of poetry, this does not completely supersede Courthope, *History of English Poetry* (1575).

Literary Handbooks, Dictionaries, and Encyclopedias

1585 Malof, Joseph. *A Manual of English Meters*. Bloomington: Indiana UP, 1970. 236 pp. PE1505.M3 426.

A technical manual of metrical forms and techniques of scansion. After a preliminary discussion of basic terms and symbols, chapters define and illustrate the patterns and forms of foot verse, stress verse, syllabic verse, and free verse; a section on the application of scansion in critical reading concludes the body of the manual. Appendixes include common stanza forms, checklist of rhymes, glossary of additional terms, selected bibliography, and summary of metrical forms. Indexed by subjects. Clear explanations combined with aptly chosen examples make Malof the best manual for learning scansion.

A useful complementary handbook for the analysis of English prosody is Karl Shapiro and Robert Beum, *A Prosody Handbook* (New York: Harper, 1965, 214 pp.), which moves from syllable to stanza.

Guides to Primary Works

1590 Crum, Margaret, ed. *First-Line Index of English Poetry, 1500–1800, in Manuscripts of the Bodleian Library, Oxford.* 2 vols. Oxford: Clarendon, 1969. Z2014.P7.F5 821'.0016.

An index to poems in manuscripts acquired before April 1961. Entries, arranged alphabetically according to the initial word of the first line, include first and last line, author, title of poem, references to printed versions, and a list of Bodleian manuscripts containing the poem. Five indexes: Bodleian manuscripts by shelf marks; poets; names mentioned; authors of works translated, paraphrased, or imitated; composers of settings and of tunes named or quoted. Crum is the essential index to the most important collection of English poetry manuscripts of the three centuries. Significant manuscripts acquired after April 1961 are described in the "Notable Acquisitions" section of *Bodleian Library Record* (1938– , 2/yr.).

Guides to Scholarship and Criticism

Surveys of Research

1595 Dyson, A. E., ed. *English Poetry: Select Bibliographical Guides.* London: Oxford UP, 1971. 378 pp. Z2014.P7.E53 016.821.

A collection of essays that evaluate the best editions, critical studies, biographies and collections of letters, bibliographies, and background studies published before 1970 on twenty major poets (Chaucer, Spenser, Donne, Herbert, Milton, Marvell, Dryden, Pope, Blake, Wordsworth, Coleridge, Byron, Shelley, Keats, Tennyson, Browning, Arnold, Hopkins, Yeats, and Eliot). *English Poetry* remains useful for its generally judicious evaluations of scholarship before 1970. See *Year's Work in English Studies* (330) for later editions and studies.

Other Bibliographies

1600 Brogan, T. V. F. *English Versification, 1570–1980: A Reference Guide with a Global Appendix.* Baltimore: Johns Hopkins UP, 1981. 794 pp. Z2015.V37.B76 [PE1505] 016.821'009.

A classified annotated bibliography of studies published from 1570 through 1979 on all aspects of versification in British and American poetry in English. An appendix selectively annotates major studies on versification in other languages. Pt. 1 treats modern poetry (since Wyatt), with sections, classified as the topic requires, on histories and bibliographies, general studies, sound, rhythm, meter, syntax and grammar, stanza structures, visual structures, and the poem in performance. Pt. 2 divides studies between sections for Old and Middle English verse. The appendix has sections for other languages as well as comparative studies, poetry and music, and classical versification. The lengthy annotations usually offer a trenchant evaluation, place a work in its theoretical or historical context, and cite selected reviews. Two indexes: British and American poets and anonymous works; scholars. Since classifications are sometimes ambiguous, access would be improved by a subject index (even though liberal cross-references conclude each section). An authoritative guide with admirably full coverage, *English Versification* deserves the acclaim of all those working in a field heretofore plagued by a lack of bibliographical control and standardized terminology.

Some additions and corrections appear in Brogan, "Addenda and Corrigenda to *English Versification, 1570–1980*," *Modern Philology* 81 (1983): 50–52. Coverage is continued by Brogan as "Studies of Verseform [1979–]," *Eidos: The International Prosody Bulletin* 1 (1984)– . Originally called "Current Bibliography," "Studies of Verseform" is not annotated but provides fuller coverage of other languages.

See also

ABELL (340): English Literature/General/Poetry section.
MLAIB (335): English III/Poetry section in the pre-1981 volumes; and the English Literature/Poetry section in later volumes.

PROSE

Many works listed in section L: Genres/Prose are important to research in English prose.

Biography and Autobiography

Histories and Surveys

1605 Stauffer, Donald A. *English Biography before 1700*. Cambridge: Harvard UP, 1930. 392 pp. CT34.G7.S7 920.002.

A critical history of published biographical works in prose and verse by English writers in any language to 1700. Emphasizing the place of biography in English literature and focusing on works important in themselves or to the development of biography, chapters treat the Middle Ages, Renaissance, ecclesiastical biography, Izaak Walton, intimate biography, autobiography, and biography as a form. The extensive bibliography is divided into two parts. The first is an author list, with cross-references to subjects, of biographical works before 1700. Each entry cites the most important modern edition; several entries provide notes on the importance, quality, or content of a work. The second part is a selected, evaluatively annotated list of scholarship. Concludes with a chronology of the most important biographies. Indexed by names and some titles. Although its bibliographies are incomplete and outdated, Stauffer is still the most comprehensive treatment of early English biography.

Continued by Stauffer, *Art of Biography in Eighteenth Century England* (2430).

Guides to Primary Works

1610 Matthews, William, comp. *British Autobiographies: An Annotated Bibliography of British Autobiographies Published or Written before 1951.* Berkeley: U of California P, 1955. 376 pp. Z2027.A9.M3 016.920042.

A bibliography of English-language autobiographies, published and in manuscript, written by British subjects and treating a significant portion of the writer's life. Matthews excludes works restricted to a single event (such as religious conversion), fiction, and discussions of life in Canada, South Africa, New Zealand, Australia, and the United States. The majority of the works date from the nineteenth and twentieth centuries. Listed alphabetically by autobiographer or title of anonymous work, entries provide title, publication information or location of manuscript, dates of coverage, and a very brief note on content. Most descriptions are based on personal examination, but some are taken from reviews. Indexed by subjects (but utilizing headings that are sometimes too general). Although incomplete and offering briefer notes on content than Matthews's other compilations (1615, 3540a, and 4765), this work remains an important initial source for identifying British autobiographies. Autobiographies by British subjects are also included in Matthews, *Canadian Diaries and Autobiographies* (4765) and Arksey, *American Diaries* (3540).

Susan Groag Bell and Barbara Kanner are preparing *British Women's Autobiographies, 1790–1950: An Annotated Bibliography*, which will offer thematic indexes that identify "work patterns, professions, life-styles, spirituality, [and] politics."

1615 Matthews, William, comp. *British Diaries: An Annotated Bibliography of British Diaries Written between 1442 and 1942.* Berkeley: U of California P, 1950. 339 pp. Z5305.G7.M3 016.920042.

An annotated bibliography of published and manuscript English-language diaries written by British citizens in the British Isles, in Europe, and on the high seas, and by foreigners traveling in the British Isles. Besides diaries by British travelers in the United States (listed in Arksey, *American Diaries* [3540]), it excludes works that are not primarily daily accounts, explorers' journals, ships' logs, and parliamentary diaries. Although the majority of the works have been published separately or in periodicals, Matthews includes several manuscripts in public collections and private hands. Entries are organized chronologically by the New Style calendar according to the year of initial entry and then alphabetically by diarist. Annotations cite type of diary and inclusive dates, briefly describe content (major places, persons, and events), sometimes evaluate style or coverage, and give publication information or location of manuscript (including shelf number). Two indexes: diaries extending more than 10 years (at the beginning); diarists (at the end). Although incomplete (especially in its record of unpublished diaries) and lacking a subject index, it remains the fullest record of British diaries and an essential source for identifying where they were published or are held in manuscript. Reviews: T. A. Birrell, *English Studies* 33 (1952): 264–66; Hilary Jenkinson, *American Historical Review* 56 (1951): 552–54.

For manuscript diaries between 1800 and 1899, Matthews is superseded by John Stuart Batts, *British Manuscript Diaries of the Nineteenth Century: An Annotated Listing* (Totowa: Rowman, 1976, 345 pp.), a chronological list of unpublished diaries held primarily in public collections in Great Britain. There are numerous errors and inconsistencies in the entries, however.

Some additional published British diaries are listed in Patricia Pate Havlice,

And So to Bed: A Bibliography of Diaries Published in English (Metuchen: Scarecrow, 1987, 698 pp.); however, its chief feature is the combined index of diarists in Matthews, *British Diaries*; *American Diaries* (3540a); and *Canadian Diaries* (4765).

Old English Literature

Many works listed in section M: English Literature/General are useful for research in Old English literature. In "Anglo-Saxon Studies: Present State and Future Prospects," *Mediaevalia* 1.1 (1975): 62–77, Fred C. Robinson suggests a number of reference works still needed by Anglo-Saxonists.

Research Methods

See

Powell, *Medieval Studies* (1755).

Histories and Surveys

For an evaluative review of literary histories and surveys from the seventeenth century through 1977, see Daniel G. Calder, "Histories and Surveys of Old English Literature: A Chronological Review," *Anglo-Saxon England* 10 (1982): 201–44. Particularly valuable are Calder's analysis of trends in scholarship and trenchant evaluations of individual works.

1635 Greenfield, Stanley B., and Daniel G. Calder. *A New Critical History of Old English Literature*. With a Survey of the Anglo-Latin Background by Michael Lapidge. New York: New York UP, 1986. 370 pp. PR173.G73 829'.09.

A critical history of Anglo-Saxon poetry and prose that incorporates important scholarship and criticism in its readings of texts. Chapters are devoted to the Anglo-Latin background; Alfredian translations and related prose; Ælfric, Wulfstan, and other late prose; the nature and quality of Old English poetry; secular heroic poetry; the Christian saint as hero; Christ as poetic hero; Old Testament narrative poetry; miscellaneous religious and secular poetry; lore and wisdom verse; and elegiac poetry. The extensive list of works cited also serves as the best selective bibliography of scholarship on Old English literature. Indexed by literary authors and anonymous works (but unfortunately not by scholars). Like its predecessor—Greenfield, *A Critical History of Old English Literature* (New York: New York UP, 1965, 237 pp.)—this is an authoritative history that will have a profound impact on Old English scholarship. Review: E. G. Stanley, *Comparative Literature* 40 (1988): 286–89.

See also

Sec. M: English Literature/General/Histories and Surveys.
Greenfield, *Bibliography of Publications on Old English Literature* (1670) lists histories and surveys (entries 530–611 in Greenfield).

Literary Handbooks, Dictionaries, and Encyclopedias

1640 *Reallexikon der germanischen Altertumskunde*. Ed. Heinrich Beck et al. 2nd ed. 20 vols. Berlin: de Gruyter, 1968– . (Published in parts and not scheduled for completion until after 2000.) DD51.R42.

An encyclopedia of pre-Christian Germanic culture, including Anglo-Saxon England. The signed entries—predominantly in German, but with some in English and a few lengthy ones in a mixture of the two languages—range from single paragraphs to extensive essays on persons, places, material culture, folklore, languages, archaeological discoveries, literary works, numismatics, religion, historical events, commerce, domestic matters, art works, and politics. The lengthy entries are helpfully subdivided and sometimes consist of separately authored divisions. All conclude with references to important scholarship. Generous cross-references guide users to appropriate headings. When complete, the *Reallexikon* will offer the fullest encyclopedic coverage of Anglo-Saxon culture. Until then, the earlier edition edited by Johannes Hoops (4 vols., Strassburg: Trübner, 1911–19) remains useful but is badly dated. *Lexikon des Mittelalters* (entry 1800) and *Dictionary of the Middle Ages* (entry 1795) include some Anglo-Saxon topics.

See also

Dictionary of the Middle Ages (1795).
Lexikon des Mittelalters (1800).

Bibliographies of Bibliographies

See

Rouse, *Serial Bibliographies for Medieval Studies* (1805).

Guides to Primary Works

1645 Ker, N. R. *Catalogue of Manuscripts Containing Anglo-Saxon*. Oxford: Clarendon, 1957. 567 pp. Z6605.A56.K4 016.829.

A descriptive catalog of more than 400 manuscripts written before c. 1200 entirely or partly in Old English. Ker includes fragments, Latin–Old English glossaries, and Latin manuscripts that contain even a single gloss (other than a tag phrase) in Old English, but excludes cartularies and charters. Entries are organized alphabetically by the city in which a collection is located or the surname of private owner, then by title of collection, then by shelfmark. Concludes with a section listing lost and untraced manuscripts and an appendix with brief descriptions of "manuscripts containing Anglo-Saxon written by foreign scribes." Manuscripts entirely or substantially in Old English receive full descriptions, with references to significant scholarship and editions, and discussion of date, content, physical characteristics, script and decorations, and provenance. Necessary supplements are Ker, "A Supplement to *Catalogue of Manuscripts Containing Anglo-Saxon*," *Anglo-Saxon England* 5 (1976): 121–31; and Mary Blockley, "Addenda and Corrigenda to N. R. Ker's 'A Supplement to *Catalogue of Manuscripts Containing Anglo-Saxon*,'" *Notes and Queries* ns 29 (1982): 1–3.

The *Catalogue of Manuscripts Containing Anglo-Saxon* is the essential source for information about the location, dating, localization, and palaeographic details of Anglo-Saxon manuscripts. Like Ker's *Medieval Manuscripts in British Libraries* (1810), it is a magisterial achievement informed by an incomparable knowledge of early manuscripts. Reviews: Kenneth Sisam, *Review of English Studies* ns 10 (1959): 68–71; Rudolph Willard, *JEGP: Journal of English and Germanic Philology* 59 (1960): 129–37.

For complementary lists, especially of Latin manuscripts, see Helmut Gneuss, "A Preliminary List of Manuscripts Written or Owned in England up to 1100," *Anglo-Saxon England* 9 (1981): 1–60 (a revision is promised in *Anglo-Saxon England* c. 1989) and "Liturgical Books in Anglo-Saxon England and Their Old English Terminology," *Learning and Literature in Anglo-Saxon England: Studies Presented to Peter Clemoes on the Occasion of His Sixty-Fifth Birthday*, ed. Michael Lapidge and Helmut Gneuss (Cambridge: Cambridge UP, 1985) 91–141. Both of these works represent preliminary stages in the compilation of "an inventory of all texts available to Anglo-Saxon readers"; for a description of the project, see Gneuss, "A Handlist of Anglo-Saxon Manuscripts," *Sources of Anglo-Saxon Culture*, ed. Paul E. Szarmach, Studies in Medieval Culture 20 (Kalamazoo: Medieval Institute Publications, Western Michigan U, 1986) 433–35. Until completion of that project, J. D. A. Ogilvy, *Books Known to the English, 597–1066* (Cambridge: Mediaeval Academy of America, 1967, 300 pp.) and "*Books Known to the English, A.D. 597–1066*: Addenda et Corrigenda," *Mediaevalia* 7 (1981): 281–325 (rpt. in *Old English Newsletter* 11, subsidia [1985]), offer the fullest record. For iconographic descriptions of illustrations, see Thomas H. Ohlgren, comp. and ed., *Insular and Anglo-Saxon Illuminated Manuscripts: An Iconographic Catalogue, c. A.D. 625 to 1100*, Garland Reference Library of the Humanities 631 (New York: Garland, 1986, 400 pp.); a supplement is in progress. Other major catalogs of Anglo-Saxon manuscripts are listed in Greenfield, *Bibliography of Publications on Old English Literature* (1670), entries 108–28.

1650 Cameron, Angus. "A List of Old English Texts." *A Plan for the* Dictionary of Old English. Ed. Roberta Frank and Angus Cameron. Toronto: U of Toronto P in association with Centre for Medieval Studies, U of Toronto, 1973. 25–306. PE273.P5 429'.3.

Prepared as a list of manuscripts and editions on which the *Dictionary of Old English* will be based, this is the most complete record of extant Old English works. Entries are organized in six sections: poetry, prose, interlinear glosses, glossaries, runic inscriptions, and vernacular inscriptions in the Latin alphabet. Each entry identifies the known manuscripts (or object, for inscriptions), facsimiles, and the most important editions. For additions and corrections, see the review by T. F. Hoad, *Review of English Studies* ns 26 (1975): 322–24.

Guides to Scholarship and Criticism

SURVEYS OF RESEARCH

1655 "The Year's Work in Old English Studies, [1967–]." *Old English Newsletter* (entry 1725). 2 (1968)– .

An evaluative survey of research based on the "Old English Bibliography" (1665). The commentary by various scholars is arranged in eight classified divisions: general, language, literature, Anglo-Latin and ecclesiastical works, manuscripts and illumination, history and culture, onomastics, and archaeology and numismatics. Each section concludes with a list of works not seen, which may be discussed in a following survey. Like the "Old English Bibliography" and the annual bibliography in *Anglo-Saxon England* (1660), "The Year's Work in Old English Studies" is an essential source for current scholarship and one that is more thorough, critical, and timely than the chapter on Old English literature in *Year's Work in English Studies* (330).

See also

YWES (330) has a chapter on Old English literature.

SERIAL BIBLIOGRAPHIES

1660 "Bibliography for [1971–]." *Anglo-Saxon England* (entry 1720). 1 (1972)– .

An international classified bibliography of books, articles, and significant reviews on all aspects of Anglo-Saxon studies. Entries are classified in 10 divisions: general; Old English language; Old English literature; Anglo-Latin, liturgy, and other ecclesiastical texts; palaeography, diplomatics, and illumination; history; numismatics; onomastics; archaeology; reviews. Although less timely than "Old English Bibliography" (1665) and "The Year's Work in Old English Studies" (1655), this work, like them, is an essential source for current scholarship.

1665 "Old English Bibliography [1969–]." *Old English Newsletter* (entry 1725). 3 (1970)– .

An international bibliography of scholarship on England before 1066 in 10 divisions: general, language, literature, Anglo-Latin and ecclesiastical works, manuscripts and illumination, history and culture, names, archaeology and numismatics, reviews, and works forthcoming and in progress. Many of the works are subsequently evaluated in "The Year's Work in Old English Studies" (1655). More timely than the annual bibliography in *Anglo-Saxon England* (1660), this work is an essential source for current scholarship that offers fuller coverage than the serial bibliographies and indexes in section G.

See also

Sec. G: Serial Bibliographies, Indexes, and Abstracts.

ABELL (340): English Literature/Old English section and, through the volume for 1933, English Literature/Old and Middle English: Subsidiary.

International Medieval Bibliography (1835).

MLAIB (335): English Language and Literature division in the volumes for 1921–25; English V in the volumes for 1926–56; English IV in the volumes for 1957–80; and the English Literature/400–1099: Old English section (as well as any larger chronological sections encompassing the period) in later volumes. Researchers must also check the headings beginning "English Literature" in the subject index to post-1980 volumes.

"Old English Research in Progress," *Neuphilologische Mitteilungen* (710).

OTHER BIBLIOGRAPHIES

1670 Greenfield, Stanley B., and Fred C. Robinson. *A Bibliography of Publications on Old English Literature to the End of 1972.* Toronto: U of Toronto P, 1980. 437 pp. (Carl T. Berkhout is preparing a supplement covering 1973–82.) Z2012.G83 [PR173] 016.829.

The closest we are likely to come to an exhaustive bibliography of books, editions, articles, notes, and reviews published from the fifteenth century through 1972 (with a few later publications) on Old English literature. Since the focus is literature in Old English, Greenfield and Robinson exclude discussions of Anglo-Latin literature as well as linguistic, historical, and archaeological studies which do not bear directly on an Old English literary text; they also exclude unpublished dissertations as well as general anthologies and surveys of English literature. Entries are listed chronologically in three variously classified divisions: general works, poetry, and prose. Many entries are accompanied by a brief annotation which clarifies the topic or place of a study in a scholarly controversy; entries for books list reviews. The liberal cross-references exclude works within the same section and standard texts in collections. Two indexes: authors and reviewers; subjects. A magisterial achievement whose accuracy and comprehensiveness fully deserve the praise accorded it by reviewers. Reviews: Carl T. Berkhout, *Speculum* 57 (1982): 897–99; Donald K. Fry, *Analytical and Enumerative Bibliography* 6 (1982): 183–86; Fry, *English Language Notes* 20 (1982): 11–20.

A discursive examination of "the changing aims and achievements of [Anglo-Saxon] scholars" occasioned by the Greenfield and Robinson *Bibliography*, E. G. Stanley's "The Scholarly Recovery of the Significance of Anglo-Saxon Records in Prose and Verse: A New Bibliography," *Anglo-Saxon England* 9 (1981): 223–62, notes important sources for research in areas outside Greenfield and Robinson's scope (as does *New Cambridge Bibliography of English Literature* [1675]). For supplementary coverage of prose (principally by King Alfred and his circle), see Carl T. Berkhout, "Research on Early Old English Literary Prose, 1973–1982," *Studies in Earlier Old English Prose*, ed. Paul E. Szarmach (Albany: State U of New York P, 1986) 401–09. For studies published after 1972, see the annual bibliographies in *Anglo-Saxon England* (1660) and *Old English Newsletter* (1655 and 1665). North American dissertations through 1986 are conveniently found in Phillip Pulsiano, *An Annotated Bibliography of North American Doctoral Dissertations on Old English*

Language and Literature, Medieval Texts and Studies 3 (East Lansing: Colleagues, 1988, 317 pp.).

1675 *The New Cambridge Bibliography of English Literature* (*NCBEL*). Vol. 1: *600–1660*. Ed. George Watson. Cambridge: Cambridge UP, 1974. 2,476 cols. Z2011.N45 [PR83] 016.82.

(For a full discussion of *NCBEL*, see entry 1385.) The part devoted to the Anglo-Saxon period (to 1100) has two major divisions: Old English Literature and Writings in Latin. The first includes sections for general works (subdivided by bibliographies, histories, anthologies, general studies, and ancillary studies), poetry (dictionaries, collections, manuscript studies, general criticism, and individual poems and authors), and prose (collections, general criticism, major translators of King Alfred's reign, major writers of the later period, other religious prose, chronicles, laws and charters, and secular prose). Writings in Latin includes sections for general works, British Celtic writers, Irish writers, and Anglo-Saxon writers. The general introduction for the volume as a whole lists bibliographies, histories, anthologies, and works about prosody, prose rhythm, and language that include the Anglo-Saxon period. Vol. 1 of *Cambridge Bibliography of English Literature* (1385a) is still occasionally useful for its coverage of the social and political background (which *NCBEL* drops).

Users must familiarize themselves with the organization, remember that there is considerable unevenness of coverage in subdivisions, and consult the index volume (vol. 5) rather than the provisional index in vol. 1. Review: Fred C. Robinson, *Anglia* 97 (1979): 511–17.

Although Greenfield, *Bibliography of Publications on Old English Literature* (1670) is *the* source for research on Old English literature, *NCBEL* is still useful for studies outside the scope of the former.

RELATED TOPICS

1680 Rosenthal, Joel T. *Anglo-Saxon History: An Annotated Bibliography, 450–1066*. AMS Studies in the Middle Ages 7. New York: AMS, 1985. 177 pp. Z2017.R67 [DA152] 016.94201.

A highly selective bibliography of primary and secondary sources for the study of Anglo-Saxon history. Confined largely to English-language works published through the early 1980s, *Anglo-Saxon History* excludes most Celtic and literary topics. Entries are organized alphabetically in 11 variously classified divisions: reference works and collections of essays; primary sources and scholarship on them (including chronicles, biography and hagiography, and constitutional and administrative history); general and political history (including secular biography and Vikings); constitutional and administrative history; ecclesiastical history; social and economic history; science, technology, and agriculture; place and personal names; numismatics; archaeology; and fine arts, arts, and crafts (including manuscripts). Rarely do annotations adequately describe a work (although some do offer evaluative comments). Indexed by person. Although highly selective, poorly organized in many divisions, and lacking an adequate statement of editorial policy, the work is the most current guide to scholarship on Anglo-Saxon history. For more thorough coverage of recent scholarship on some topics, see "Old English Bibliography" (1665), "The Year's Work in Old English Studies" (1655), and the annual bibliography in *Anglo-Saxon England* (1660).

Older bibliographies still of value are the following:

Altschul, Michael. *Anglo-Norman England, 1066–1154*. Conference on British Studies Bibliographical Handbooks. Cambridge: Cambridge UP for the Conference on British Studies, 1969. 83 pp. Coverage extends through mid-1968.

Bonser, Wilfrid. *An Anglo-Saxon and Celtic Bibliography (450–1087)*. 2 vols. Berkeley: U of California P, 1957. Coverage extends through 1953.

See also

Annual Bibliography of British and Irish History (1400).
Graves, *Bibliography of English History to 1485* (1845).

Language

GUIDES TO SCHOLARSHIP

1685 Cameron, Angus, Allison Kingsmill, and Ashley Crandell Amos. *Old English Word Studies: A Preliminary Author and Word Index*. Toronto Old English Series 8. Toronto: U of Toronto P in association with Centre for Medieval Studies, U of Toronto, 1983. 192 pp. and 5 microfiche. Z2015.S4.C35 [PE265] 016.429.

An interim bibliography of Old English vocabulary studies (published through 1980) compiled as part of the *Dictionary of Old English* project (1690). Entries are listed by author in three sections: sixteenth- and seventeenth-century manuscript dictionaries; dictionaries, encyclopedias, concordances, and glossaries; and vocabulary studies. The third section is indexed (in the accompanying microfiche) by words discussed (see pp. xiv-xv for an explanation of the indexing of variant forms). Although not exhaustive, *Old English Word Studies* is an essential source for the study of Old English vocabulary. A revised edition is planned after publication of the *Dictionary*. Reviews: Susan Cooper, *Medium Ævum* 54 (1985): 290–91; Constance B. Hieatt, *English Studies in Canada* 11 (1985): 231–32; Ilkka Mönkkönen, *Neuphilologische Mitteilungen* 86 (1985): 599–601.

1687 Tajima, Matsuji, comp. *Old and Middle English Language Studies: A Classified Bibliography, 1923–1985*. Amsterdam Studies in the Theory and History of Linguistic Science, Ser. 5: Library and Information Sources in Linguistics 13. Amsterdam: Benjamins, 1988. 391pp. Z2015.A1.T3 [PE123] 016.429.

A bibliography of studies, including dissertations and book reviews but excluding works in Slavic languages and most Japanese studies, published between 1923 and 1985 about Old and Middle English language. The approximately 3,900 entries are organized in 14 divisions (each with sections for general or historical studies, Old English, and Middle English): bibliographies; dictionaries, concordances, and glossaries; histories of the English language; grammars; general works; studies of the language of individual authors or works (however, numerous author studies appear without cross-references in other sections); orthography and punctuation; phonology and phonetics; morphology; syntax; lexicology, lexicography, and word formation; onomastics; dialectology; and stylistics. A few entries include a brief note on content or a list of later editions and reprints. Indexed by scholars. The lack of a subject index and cross-references means that users searching for studies of an author, anonymous work, or topic will find themselves skimming all entries. Although less accessible than it should be (with some entries not seen by the compiler), Tajima provides the fullest list of twentieth-century scholarship on Old and Middle English language.

See also

ABELL (340): Old English heading in the subdivisions of the English Language section.

MLAIB (335): English Language and Literature division in the volumes for 1922–25; Old English headings in English I/Linguistics section in the volumes for 1926–66; Indo-European C/Germanic Linguistics IV/English/Old English section in the volumes for 1967–80; and the Indo-European Languages/West Germanic Languages/English Language/English Language (Old) section in pt. 3 of the later volumes. Researchers should also check the "English Language (Old)" heading in the subject index to post-1980 volumes.

YWES (330): The chapter on English language covers Old English.

DICTIONARIES

1690 *Dictionary of Old English* (*DOE*). Ed. Angus Cameron et al. Toronto: Pontifical Institute of Mediaeval Studies for Dictionary of Old English Project, Centre for Medieval Studies, U of Toronto, 1987– . Microfiche. (Publication began with fascicle *D*; when complete, *DOE* will be issued in hardcopy.)

A dictionary of Old English that excludes only place and personal names. There are three types of entries: common words receive full entries; rarer words, exhaustive ones; and grammar words, special entries. A full entry consists of headword (usually in late West-Saxon spelling), grammatical details, variant spellings, occurrence and usage information, definitions, illustrative citations (keyed to the accompanying *List of Texts and Index of Editions*), Latin equivalents in the same manuscript, typical collocations, and references to the *Middle English Dictionary* (1860), *English Dialect Dictionary* (1415), *Dictionary of the Older Scottish Tongue* (3090), and *Oxford English Dictionary* (1410). Editorial practices are briefly outlined in the *Preface* (1987, 14 pp.). Progress reports appear regularly in *Old English Newsletter*; a discussion of the research for and possible uses of the *Dictionary* may be found in Ashley Crandell Amos, "*The Dictionary of Old English*," *Sources of Anglo-Saxon Culture*, ed. Paul E. Szarmach, Studies in Medieval Culture 20 (Kalamazoo: Medieval Institute Publications, Western Michigan U, 1986) 407–13. When complete, *DOE* will supersede the Bosworth-Toller *Dictionary* (1695).

The *DOE* project has been the source of other important reference works: a machine-readable corpus of Old English works; Cameron, "A List of Old English Texts" (1650); Cameron, *Old English Word Studies* (1685); and Venezky, *Microfiche Concordance to Old English* (1705).

1695 Bosworth, Joseph. *An Anglo-Saxon Dictionary*. Ed. and enl. by T. Northcote Toller. 4 pts. Oxford: Clarendon, 1882–98. Rpt. in 1 vol., 1898. 1,302 pp. Toller. *Supplement.* 3 pts. 1908–21. Rpt. in 1 vol., 1921. 768 pp. Alistair Campbell. *Enlarged Addenda and Corrigenda to the* Supplement. 1972. 68 pp. PE279.B5 429.3.

The most complete Anglo-Saxon dictionary currently available. A typical entry includes part of speech, definition, Latin equivalents, illustrative passages (with modern English translation), etymology, and cross-references to variant and related forms. Campbell's *Enlarged Addenda* incorporates Toller's additions published in *Modern Language Review* 17 (1922): 165–66; 19 (1924): 200–04. Inconsistencies and unevenness in treatment occur, since editorial practices changed during the course of publication (e.g., in the *Dictionary* different forms are listed separately in the earlier part of the alphabet but grouped under a single form in the latter part); there are errors and omissions; and definitions of rare or difficult words are not always accurate. But until *Dictionary of Old English* (1690) is complete, Bosworth-Toller remains the most authoritative dictionary. Reviews: Edward M. Brown, *JEGP: Journal of English and Germanic Philology* 3 (1901): 505–09; Otto B. Schlutter, *JEGP: Journal of English and Germanic Philology* 18 (1919): 137–43.

The best concise dictionary is John R. Clark Hall, *A Concise Anglo-Saxon Dictionary*, 4th ed. (Cambridge: Cambridge UP, 1960, 432 pp.), which includes a supplement by Herbert D. Meritt.

Until completion of *Dictionary of Old English*, the best source for etymology is F. Holthausen, *Altenglisches Etymologisches Wörterbuch*, Germanische Bibliothek, Reihe 4: Wörterbücher 7 (Heidelberg: Winter, 1934, 428 pp.), with additions and corrections in Alfred Bammesberger, *Beiträge zu einem etymologischen Wörterbuch des Altenglischen*, Anglistische Forschungen 139 (Heidelberg: Winter, 1979, 156 pp.).

1700 *Dictionary of Medieval Latin from British Sources*. Ed. R. E. Latham and D. R. Howlett. London: Oxford UP for British Academy, 1975– . (Published in fascicles.) PA2891.L28 473'.21.

A dictionary of the Latin language used in Great Britain from c. 550 to c. 1550, but excluding most personal and place names as well as Irish sources before 1200 because of their inclusion in *Dictionary of Medieval Latin from Celtic Sources* (in progress) and covering Welsh sources very selectively. Classical Latin words used with little change are given brief entries; fuller treatment is accorded post-classical words and usages, with the fullest entries going to distinctly British words and usages. An entry provides basic meaning(s), accompanied by an extensive list of quotations to illustrate nuances of meaning. The indispensable source for interpreting early British writings in Latin. Until the work is complete, R. A. Latham, ed. *Revised Medieval Latin Word-List from British and Irish Sources* (London: Oxford UP for British Academy, 1965, 524 pp.), provides basic meanings for words. Review: (fasc. 1) A. B. Scott, *Medium Ævum* 46 (1977): 105–08.

See also

Greenfield, *Bibliography of Publications on Old English Literature* (1670) lists other dictionaries (entries 52–82).

CONCORDANCES

1705 Venezky, Richard L., and Antonette diPaolo Healey, comps. *A Microfiche Concordance to Old English.* Newark: U of Delaware, 1980. Microfiche. Venezky, Richard L., and Sharon Butler, comps. *A Microfiche Concordance to Old English: The High-Frequency Words.* 1983. Microfiche.

An unlemmatized concordance based on the machine-readable Old English corpus prepared for the *Dictionary of Old English* (1690). For each headword, there is a frequency count and citations (with generous contexts) for each occurrence in the corpus, which encompasses all Old English texts (but not all manuscripts; hence some spellings are not represented). Users should note that homographs are not differentiated. Editorial policies are explained and sources listed in the accompanying guides: Healey and Venezky, comps., *A Microfiche Concordance to Old English: The List of Texts and Index of Editions*, rpt. with revisions, Publications of the Dictionary of Old English 1 (Toronto: Pontifical Institute of Mediaeval Studies for Dictionary of Old English Project, 1985, 202 pp.), and Venezky and Butler, comps., *A Microfiche Concordance to Old English: The High-Frequency Words*, Publications of the Dictionary of Old English 2 (1985, 20 pp.). Encompassing all known Old English texts, these concordances are unparalleled sources for linguistic studies, thematic investigations, and stylistic analyses. Review: Donald K. Fry, *English Language Notes* 20 (1982): 11–20.

STUDIES OF LANGUAGE

1710 Mitchell, Bruce. *Old English Syntax.* 2 vols. Oxford: Clarendon, 1985. PE213.M5 429'.5.

A detailed study of the principles of Old English syntax using "the formal descriptive approach and traditional Latin-based grammar." Vol. 1 examines concord, parts of speech, and sentence parts; vol. 2, subordinate clauses, other sentence elements and their order, and problems specifically related to poetry. An afterword (pp. 1000–05) prints additions to vol. 2. Throughout, Mitchell examines problems of interpretation in literary texts, emphasizes areas needing further study, and rigorously evaluates existing scholarship (which will be more fully surveyed in his *A Critical Bibliography of Publications on Old English Syntax to the End of 1984* [Oxford: Blackwell; in progress]). Includes a selective bibliography, a general index to each volume, and two cumulative indexes (words and phrases; passages discussed). A seminal work, *Old English Syntax* admirably fulfills the author's intent to provide a basis for definitive studies of individual topics and eventually "an authoritative *Old English Syntax.*" Reviews: R. D. Fulk, *Philological Quarterly* 66 (1987): 279–83; Willem Koopman, *Neophilologus* 71 (1987): 460–66; T. A. Shippey, *TLS: Times Literary Supplement* 28 June 1985: 716.

1715 Campbell, A. *Old English Grammar.* Oxford: Clarendon, 1959. 423 pp. PE131.C3 429.5.

A detailed historical grammar of Old English, covering phonology, morphology, and almost all other aspects and features of the language except syntax (for which, see Mitchell, *Old English Syntax* [1710].) Concludes with a selective bibliography and an index of words discussed. *Old English Grammar* is the authoritative work on the subject. Reviews: C. E. Bazell, *Medium Ævum* 29 (1960): 27–30; Norman E. Eliason, *Speculum* 35 (1960): 435–38.

More suitable for beginners is Bruce Mitchell and Fred C. Robinson, *A Guide to Old English*, 4th ed. (Oxford: Blackwell, 1986, 354 pp.).

Periodicals

Many journals listed in sections K: Periodicals/Scholarly Journals and M: English Literature/General/Periodicals/Scholarly Journals publish articles on Old English topics.

1720 *Anglo-Saxon England* (*ASE*). 1972– . Annual. DA152.2.A75 942.01'05.

Publishes articles, bibliographies, and occasional surveys of research on all aspects of Anglo-Saxon studies, including Anglo-Latin, ecclesiastical history, archaeology, Old English language and literature, history, numismatics, and manuscripts. Since its inception, the journal has included an annual bibliography of Anglo-Saxon studies (see entry 1660). Cumulative indexes: vols. 1–5, in 5 (1976): 281–320; vols. 6–10, in 10 (1982): 285–326; vols. 11–15, in 15 (1986): 255–79. The most important journal in its field.

1725 *Old English Newsletter* (*OENews*). 1967– . 2/yr. 829'.09.

Publishes announcements of meetings, notes about new and forthcoming publications, reports on work in progress, abstracts of convention papers, occasional articles, and two important annual bibliographies: "Old English Bibliography" (1665) and "The Year's Work in Old English Studies" (1655).

See also

Neuphilologische Mitteilungen (710).

Background Reading

1730 Hill, David. *An Atlas of Anglo-Saxon England*. Toronto: U of Toronto P, 1981. 180 pp. G1812.21.S2.H5 912'.42.

A series of maps, tables, diagrams, chronologies, and graphs that organize information on topography, demography, physical geography, historical events and periods, political administration, the economy, and the church. Indexed by place. An essential complement to narrative histories. Reviews: Rebecca V. Colman, *Canadian Journal of History* 17 (1982): 515–16; Simon Keynes, *Antiquity* 57 (1983): 66–67.

Genres

POETRY

Histories and Surveys

1735 Pearsall, Derek. *Old English and Middle English Poetry*. Vol. 1 of *The Routledge History of English Poetry* (1580). Gen ed. R. A. Foakes. London: Routledge, 1977. 352 pp. PR502.R58 821'.009.

Emphasizes poetry as a social, rather than artistic, phenomenon in a critical history of poetry to c. 1500. Ranging broadly through the poetic corpus, Pearsall offers chapters on "*Beowulf* and the Anglo-Saxon Poetic Tradition," "Anglo-Saxon Religious Poems," "Late Old English Poetry and the Transition," "Poetry in the Early Middle English Period," "Some Fourteenth-Century Books and Writers," "Alliterative Poetry," "Court Poetry," and "The Close of the Middle Ages." Concludes with an appendix listing technical terms (mostly describing metrics) and a chronology (with sections for historical events, poems by composition date, and the most important poetry manuscripts). Indexed by persons, anonymous works, and a few subjects. Although reviewers have pointed out errors in translations, objected to a number of interpretations, and faulted the density of many passages, they generally commend the breadth and learning of the work. Reviews: Daniel G. Calder, *Anglo-Saxon England* 10 (1982): 243–44; Margaret E. Goldsmith, *English* 27 (Spring 1978): 33–37; Stanley B. Greenfield, *Modern Philology* 77 (1979): 188–91; Fred C. Robinson, *Modern Language Review* 76 (1981): 651–54.

Concordances

1740 Bessinger, J. B., Jr., ed. *A Concordance to* The Anglo-Saxon Poetic Records. Programmed by Philip H. Smith, Jr. Cornell Concordances. Ithaca: Cornell UP, 1978. 1,510 pp. PR1506.B47 829'.1.

A concordance based on George Philip Krapp and Elliott Van Kirk Dobbie, eds., *The Anglo-Saxon Poetic Records: A Collective Edition*, 6 vols. (New York: Columbia UP, 1931–53), plus one other poem, "Instructions for Christians." Bessinger omits some runes and does not differentiate variant spellings, homographs, and word families. Separate or final elements of compounds are separately indexed by Michael W. Twomey, and an appendix lists headwords in order of frequency. Although not a definitive concordance, the work is indispensable to research on Old English poetry. Researchers should also consult Venezky, *Microfiche Concordance to Old English* (1705). Reviews: Thomas Elwood Hart, *Computers and the Humanities* 13 (1979): 229–35 (an important discussion of limitations and uses); Bruce Mitchell, *Notes and Queries* ns 26 (1979): 347–49; E. G. Stanley, *Review of English Studies* ns 30 (1979): 328–31; Joseph B. Trahern, Jr., *JEGP: Journal of English and Germanic Philology* 78 (1979): 242–44.

Madeleine M. Bergman, "Supplement to *A Concordance to* The Anglo-Saxon Poetic Records," *Mediaevalia* 8 (for 1982): 9–52, concords an additional 113 lines of verse and runic inscriptions.

Middle English Literature

Many works listed in section M: English Literature/General are important to research in Middle English literature.

Research Methods

GENERAL GUIDES

1755 Powell, James M., ed. *Medieval Studies: An Introduction*. Syracuse: Syracuse UP, 1976. 389 pp. (A revised edition is in progress.) D116.M4 940.1'07'2.

A collection of introductions to research in Latin palaeography, diplomatics, numismatics, prosopography, computer-assisted analysis of statistical documents (outdated now), chronology, English literature (with some inaccuracies and errors of judgment), Latin philosophy, art, and music. Each essay outlines the historical development of its field, identifies major reference tools and important studies, explains research methods, and ends with a selective bibliography. Indexed by authors, scholars, and anonymous works. Although addressed to "the beginner in medieval studies," the volume offers expert orientations to research in unfamiliar fields. Review: Joseph R. Strayer, *Speculum* 53 (1978): 183–84.

MANUSCRIPTS

General Guides

1760 Moorman, Charles. *Editing the Middle English Manuscript*. Jackson: UP of Mississippi, 1975. 107 pp. PR275.T45.M6 820'.9'001.

A manual intended as a practical introduction for the neophyte, with chapters on palaeography, the East Midland dialect, textual criticism (including discussions of collation, recension, transcription, and emendation), and the content of an edition. Concludes with a brief bibliography. Indexed by persons, titles, and subjects. Although the work is a highly simplified discussion that is sometimes naive and will not turn a reader into an accomplished editor, it is an accessible overview of the process of editing a Middle English manuscript. For corrections and alternatives to Moorman's views, see the following reviews: E. Talbot Donaldson, *Modern Philology* 77 (1979): 84–86; Richard F. Giles, *Literary Research Newsletter* 2 (1977): 31–38 (including a reply by Moorman); R. J. Schoeck, *Speculum* 55 (1980): 410–11.

Palaeography

1765 Johnson, Charles, and Hilary Jenkinson. *English Court Hand, A.D. 1066 to 1500, Illustrated Chiefly from the Public Records*. 2 vols. Oxford: Clarendon, 1915. Z115.E5.J6 421'.7.

A manual for those learning to read English court hand. Vol. 1 traces the evolution of the hand, outlines methods of abbreviations (with a helpful list of common ones), offers practical hints on transcription, provides a selected bibliography, traces the development of individual forms (with valuable dated illustrations of letters, runes, abbreviations, signs, numerals, and other marks), and concludes with extensively annotated transcriptions of the plates in vol. 2. The detailed illustrations of various forms make this the best introduction to court hand and an essential companion for those who work with medieval English documents.

Hands from the fifteenth through seventeenth centuries are described and illustrated in Jenkinson, *Later Court Hands in England* (entry 1965).

1770 Parkes, M. B. *English Cursive Book Hands, 1250–1500*. Corrected rpt. Oxford Palaeographical Handbooks. Berkeley: U of California P, 1980. 26 pp. Z115.E5.P37 745.6'1.
Wright, C. E. *English Vernacular Hands from the Twelfth to the Fifteenth Centuries*. Oxford Palaeographical Handbooks. Oxford: Clarendon, 1960. 24 pp. Z115.E5.W7 421.7.

Each work prints a series of plates with accompanying transcriptions and notes that illustrate the different types of hands used in England for writing books. The plates are arranged chronologically to show the development of each hand. Although lacking a discussion of abbreviations used by scribes, Parkes and Wright are convenient sources for identifying and learning to read the hands used for writing the majority of Middle English literary manuscripts. Reviews: (Parkes) Ruth J. Dean, *Speculum* 46 (1971): 177–80; (Wright) A. I. Doyle, *Medium Ævum* 30 (1961): 117–20.

See also

Jenkinson, *Later Court Hands in England* (1965).

Guides to Scholarship

1775 Braswell, Laurel Nichols. *Western Manuscripts from Classical Antiquity to the Renaissance: A Handbook*. Garland Reference Library of the Humanities 139. New York: Garland, 1981. 382 pp. Z105.B73 091.

A selective annotated bibliography of reference works and scholarship (published through the late 1970s) on the identification, study, and editing of early manuscripts from the ninth through the mid-fifteenth centuries, principally in Romance and Germanic languages, with particular attention to medieval English literary and scientific manuscripts. The 2,074 entries are listed alphabetically in 15 classified sections: bibliographies, libraries, microforms, incipits, subjects, palaeography, diplomatics and archives, fragments and booklets, decoration and illumination, music, codicology, reference works, contexts of manuscripts, journals, and textual criticism. Although importance is the main criterion determining selection, a number of works of dubious value are admitted, and there are some notable omissions. The descriptive annotations are neither as precise nor as accurate as they might be, but there are some judicious brief evaluations. Indexed by person and anonymous title. Despite the errors and some lack of balance among sections, Braswell is a serviceable basic guide to scholarship on early manuscripts. Reviews: Revilo P. Oliver, *Classical Journal* 78 (1983): 367–69; Germaine Warkentin, *University of Toronto Quarterly* 52 (1983): 403–04.

Histories and Surveys

The best guides to literary histories and surveys are Robert W. Ackerman, "Middle English Literature to 1400" (pp. 73–123), in Fisher, *Medieval Literature of Western Europe* (entry 1830), and John H. Fisher, "English Literature" (pp. 1–54), in Cooke, *The Present State of Scholarship in Fourteenth-Century Literature* (1830a).

1780 Bennett, H. S. *Chaucer and the Fifteenth Century*. Corrected rpt. Vol. 2, pt. 1 of *The Oxford History of English Literature* (1310). Gen. eds. John Buxton and Norman Davis. Oxford: Clarendon, 1979. 348 pp. PR255.B43 821.17.

A critical history with chapters on fourteenth-century London, Chaucer, religion, the intellectual background, author-audience relationships, verse, and prose, as well as a chronology and selective bibliography (now outdated). Indexed by authors, anonymous works, and subjects. (The corrected reprint makes only minor corrections to the text of the 1947 edition but provides a much better index and updates the bibliography to c. 1970.) Bennett is an important history, although reviewers have argued with some interpretations and justifiably faulted the division of coverage between this volume and Chambers, *English Literature at the Close of the Middle Ages* (1790)—a division that, for example, isolates Chaucer from his contemporaries. Reviews: *Times Literary Supplement* 17 Apr. 1948: 221; Francis Lee Utley, *Speculum* 26 (1951): 370–75.

1785 Bennett, J. A. W. *Middle English Literature*. Ed. and completed by Douglas Gray. Vol. 1., pt. 2 of *The Oxford History of English Literature* (1310). Gen. eds. John Buxton and Norman Davis. Oxford: Clarendon, 1986. 496 pp. PR255.B45 820'.9'001.

A critical history organized in chapters devoted to genres and major authors: pastoral and comedy, didactic and homiletic verse, Layamon, romances, poems of the Gawain manuscript, prose, lyrics, Gower, and Langland. Concludes with a chronology and selected bibliography through 1984 (but the latter excludes some important works). Indexed by persons and works. Although the volume lacks any synthesis and gives little attention to historical and intellectual contexts, most chapters offer substantial—and, depending on one's perspective, occasionally brilliant or opinionated—discussions of major authors and works. *Middle English Literature* will likely become one of the standard works on the period. Reviews: Charles Blyth, *Essays in Criticism* 37 (1987): 321–29; A. J. Minnis, *TLS: Times Literary Supplement* 6 Feb. 1987: 140.

1790 Chambers, E. K. *English Literature at the Close of the Middle Ages*. 2nd impression with corrections. Vol. 2, pt. 2 of *The Oxford History of English Literature* (1310). Gen. eds. F. P. Wilson and Bonamy Dobrée. Oxford: Clarendon, 1947. 247 pp. PR291.C5 820.902.

Unlike other volumes of the *Oxford History of English Literature* (1310), Chambers is comprised of four independent essays on the drama (an updated distillation of his *Mediaeval Stage* [1905]), the carol and fifteenth-century lyric, popular narrative poetry and the ballad, and Malory. Concludes with a selective bibliography (now outdated). Indexed by authors, anonymous works, and subjects. Although composed of erudite, balanced discussions, the volume does not offer a literary history of the period. This and Bennett, *Chaucer and the Fifteenth Century* (1780) have been justifiably faulted for the division of coverage. Reviews: A. C. Baugh, *JEGP: Journal of English and Germanic Philology* 46 (1947): 304–07; Beatrice White, *Modern Language Review* 41 (1946): 426–28.

See also

Sec. M: English Literature/General/Histories and Surveys.

Literary Handbooks, Dictionaries, and Encyclopedias

1795 *Dictionary of the Middle Ages*. Ed. Joseph R. Strayer. 12 vols. New York: Scribner's, 1982– . D114.D5 909.07.

Covers the intellectual, ecclesiastical, political, and literary history, material culture, and geography of "the Latin West, the Slavic World, Asia Minor, the lands of the caliphate in the East, and the Muslim-Christian areas of North Africa" from the period 500 to 1500. The projected 5,000 entries, ranging from brief identifications and definitions to major articles by established scholars, treat places, persons, art works, events, literary forms and genres, national literatures, and a variety of miscellaneous topics. Brief bibliographies, largely confined to English-language scholarship, conclude most entries. The *Interim Index* (1985, 190 pp.) to vols. 1–5 will eventually be superseded by a comprehensive one. There is an occasional imbalance in the treatment of similar topics, but readable discussions and solid scholarship make this a useful source of quick information and basic surveys. Complemented by *Lexikon des Mittelalters* (1800), which is more scholarly but less broad in coverage. Review: (vols. 1–5) Charles T. Wood, *Speculum* 60 (1985): 967–71.

1800 *Lexikon des Mittelalters*. München: Artemis, 1977– . (Published in fascicles.) D101.5.L49 940.1'05.

A dictionary of the history and culture of the European Middle Ages from c. 300 to c. 1500. Entries, ranging from brief definitions or identifications to lengthy articles by an international group of scholars, treat individuals, forms and genres, material culture, places, and events. Each concludes with a brief bibliography. The extensive use of symbols and abbreviations makes for slow reading, and there is some imbalance in the treatment of similar topics. Authoritative and scholarly, *Lexikon des Mittelalters* and *Dictionary of the Middle Ages* (1795) provide medievalists with essential information on a wide range of topics. Review: (vol. 1.1–5) Joseph R. Strayer, *Speculum* 55 (1980): 627–28.

Bibliographies of Bibliographies

1805 Rouse, Richard H. *Serial Bibliographies for Medieval Studies*. Publications of the Center for Medieval and Renaissance Studies 3. Berkeley: U of California P, 1969. 150 pp. Z6203.R66 016.016914'03'1.

A classified, descriptive guide to 294 current and defunct serial bibliographies covering medieval studies from the advent of Christianity to c. 1500. Rouse omits standard general indexes and national bibliographies but includes bibliographic essays, lists of contents of recent periodicals, accessions lists of special libraries, and reports of work in progress. Entries are classified in 11 divisions: general bibliographies; national and regional bibliographies; Byzantine, Islamic, and Judaic studies; archival and auxiliary studies; art and archaeology; ecclesiastical history; economic, social, and institutional history; intellectual history; literature and linguistics; music; science, technology, and medicine. Since the description of each bibliography is based primarily on a single volume published between 1964 and 1967, variations in scope, editorial policy, and organization are not always noted. An asterisk denotes an important work. Two indexes: title; editor. Although dated, Rouse remains useful for identifying essential serial bibliographies outside the field of literature (for which Wortman, *Guide to Serial Bibliographies* [325], generally provides more thorough coverage).

See also

Sec. D: Bibliographies of Bibliographies.

Guides to Primary Works

MANUSCRIPTS

1810 Ker, N. R. *Medieval Manuscripts in British Libraries*. 5 vols. Oxford: Clarendon, 1969- . Z6620.G7.K4 011.

A catalog of manuscripts written before c. 1500 in Latin or Western European languages and held in public collections that have not been previously or adequately cataloged. Thus Ker does not include private collections or major libraries (such as the British Library or the Bodleian), although researchers are directed to the standard catalogs of institutional collections. Vol. 1 covers London; vols. 2–4 list collections alphabetically by city; vol. 5 will be a general index. The detailed descriptions of uncataloged items—informed by Ker's incomparable knowledge of medieval manuscripts—include short title; date; contents; bibliographical, palaeographical, and codicological information; and provenance. (Manuscripts adequately described elsewhere receive summary treatment and references to published catalogs.) Besides making known for the first time a number of manuscripts, *Medieval Manuscripts* is an invaluable source for finding iconographic and palaeographical information, identifying texts and provenance, and locating manuscripts. One of the truly great catalogs. Reviews: (vol. 2) Christopher de Hamel, *Medium Ævum* 50 (1981): 101–04; Jean F. Preston, *Review* 1 (1979): 223–31.

1815 Ricci, Seymour de. *Census of Medieval and Renaissance Manuscripts in the United States and Canada.* 3 vols. New York: Wilson, 1935–40. C. U. Faye and W. H. Bond. *Supplement.* New York: Bibliographical Soc. of America, 1962. 626 pp. Z6620.U5.R5.

Essentially a finding list of Western manuscripts before 1600 owned by institutions and private collectors. Except for Greek and Latin papyri, the work includes all written documents, but because of their number, letters, charters, and deeds are usually not described separately. Entries are organized alphabetically by state, then by city, then by institution or collector; Canadian listings appear in vol. 2, pp. 2201–38, and are followed by a lengthy list of errata and corrections (vol. 2, pp. 2239–343). Since Ricci is not intended to be a definitive catalog and since many descriptions are supplied by owners, an entry provides only basic information: author, title or incipit, brief physical description, place of composition, provenance, and references to scholarship. Vol. 3 is made up of six indexes (general index of names, titles, and headings; scribes, illuminators, and cartographers; incipits; Gregory numbers for Greek New Testament manuscripts; present owners; previous owners) but does not include the planned lists of unlocated manuscripts or those held by dealers. The *Supplement* (compiled almost exclusively from questionnaires) adds new manuscripts, records changes in ownership, and prints corrections. Although not comprehensive and now dated, the work remains an important starting point for locating manuscripts in collections that have not been fully cataloged and for tracing provenance. A major desideratum is a descriptive catalog (such as Ker, *Medieval Manuscripts in British Libraries* [1810]) for medieval manuscripts in North American collections.

See also

Sec. F: Guides to Manuscripts and Archives.
Index of English Literary Manuscripts, vol. 1 (1985).
Severs, *Manual of the Writings in Middle English* (1825).

PRINTED WORKS

1820 *Gesamtkatalog der Wiegendrucke* (*GKW*). Vols. 1–7. 2nd ed. 1968. Vol. 8– . Stuttgart: Hiersemann; New York: Kraus, 1972– . (The 2nd ed. reprints, with additions and corrections, the volumes published 1925–38.) Z240.G39.

An analytical bibliography that attempts to describe every extant edition printed in fifteenth-century Europe. Listed alphabetically by author or title of anonymous work, the detailed entries include author, short title, editor, translator, corrector, commentator, place of printing, printer, publisher, date, format, collation, notes on typography, transcription of title and colophon, contents, references to standard bibliographies, and locations of copies. (See vol. 8 for a description in English [pp. *101–08], German, French, Russian, and Italian of the parts of an entry.) Vols. 1–7 locate no more than 10 copies, but the later ones attempt a complete census. Since the editors must frequently work from photographic copies, format and collation are not always accurately described; and there are errors in the identification of printers. *GKW* is an essential source for identifying editions (and their contents and sometimes complex textual relationships), authors, and printers; for localizing and dating books; and for locating copies. Reviews: John L. Flood, *Library* 5th ser. 30 (1975): 339–44; Paul Needham, *TLS: Times Literary Supplement* 15 Aug. 1980: 922.

When complete, *GKW* will supersede the numerous existing general bibliographies of incunabula, of which the most important are the following:

Catalogue of Books Printed in the XVth Century Now in the British Museum. London: British Library, 1908– .

Goff, Frederick R., comp. and ed. *Incunabula in American Libraries: A Third Census of Fifteenth-Century Books Recorded in North American Collections*. New York: Bibliographical Soc. of America, 1964. 798 pp. *Supplement*. 1972. 104 pp. A photographic reprint of Goff's annotated copy was published by Kraus in 1973. Although the annotated copy served as the working copy for the *Supplement*, the latter does not include Goff's notes on dealers' and auction prices. The entries, along with additions and corrections, are incorporated into the ISTC data base.

Hain, Ludwig. *Repertorium Bibliographicum, in Quo Libri Omnes ab Arte Typographica Inventa usque ad Annum MD. Typis Expressi Ordine Alphabetico vel Simpliciter Enumerantur vel Adcuratius Recensentur*. 2 vols. in 4 pts. Stuttgart: Cotta; Paris: Lutetiae, 1826–38. The work is indexed by K. Burger, *Ludwig Hain's* Repertorium Bibliographicum: *Register*, Zentralblatt für Bibliothekswesen 8 (Leipzig: Harrassowitz, 1891, 427 pp.). Copinger, W. A. *Supplement to Hain's* Repertorium Bibliographicum. 2 pts. Berlin: Altmann, 1926 (with *Index* by Konrad Burger).

ISTC (Incunable Short Title Catalogue) data base. London: British Library. An online catalog which intends to record every copy of every extant edition. The data base, which can be searched through BLAISE-LINE (510), is currently the single most comprehensive list of incunabula. Although entries are based largely on printed catalogs and do not provide the detail of *GKW*, the data base can be searched in a variety of ways (e.g., by author, place, printer, date, or title words). For a description of ISTC, see John Goldfinch, "Searching the ISTC on BLAISE-LINE," *Bibliography and the Study of 15th-Century Civilisation*, ed. Lotte Hellinga and John Goldfinch, British Library Occasional Papers 5 (London: British Library, 1987) 12–34; several other essays in this collection suggest uses of the data base.

Proctor, Robert. *An Index to the Early Printed Books in the British Museum: From the Invention of Printing to the Year 1500. With Notes of Those in the Bodleian Library*. London: Holland, 1960. 908 pp. A convenient reprint of the original two volumes and four supplements, 1898–1906.

Reichling, Dietrich. *Appendices ad Hainii-Copingeri* Repertorium Bibliographicum*: Additiones et Emendationes*. 6 fascicles and index. München: Rosenthal, 1905–11. *Supplement*. Monasterii Guestphalorum, 1914. 109 pp.

See also

"Bibliography of Editions and Translations in Progress," *Medium Ævum* (1875).

Pollard, *Short-Title Catalogue* (1990).

Severs, *Manual of the Writings in Middle English* (1825).

Guides to Scholarship and Criticism

SURVEYS OF RESEARCH

1825 Severs, J. Burke, and Albert E. Hartung, gen. eds. *A Manual of the Writings in Middle English, 1050–1500.* 10 vols. New Haven: Archon-Shoe String, for Connecticut Acad. of Arts and Sciences, 1967– . PR255.M3 016.820'9'001.

Chapters are published as they are completed in consecutively paginated volumes:

Vol. 1: Romances. 1967. (Supplemented by Joanne A. Rice, *Middle English Romance: An Annotated Bibliography, 1955–1985*, Garland Reference Library of the Humanities 545 [New York: Garland, 1987, 626 pp.], although there are numerous omissions of studies published outside the United States.)

Vol. 2: *Pearl* Poet; Wyclyf and His Followers; Translations and Paraphrases of the Bible, and Commentaries; Saints' Legends; Instructions for Religious. 1970.

Vol. 3: Dialogues, Debates, and Catechisms; Thomas Hoccleve; Malory and Caxton. 1972.

Vol. 4: Middle Scots Writers; Chaucerian Apocrypha. 1973.

Vol. 5: Dramatic Pieces [miracle, mystery, morality, and folk plays]; Poems Dealing with Contemporary Conditions. 1975.

Vol. 6: Carols; Ballads; John Lydgate. 1980. (See A. S. G. Edwards, "Additions and Corrections to the Bibliography of John Lydgate," *Notes and Queries* ns 32 [1985]: 450–52.)

Vol. 7: John Gower; *Piers Plowman*; Travel and Geographical Writings; Works of Religious and Philosophical Instruction. 1986.

Chapters are planned for tales; chronicles; homilies; proverbs, precepts, and monitory pieces; science, information, and documents; letters; legal writings; Rolle and his followers; lyrics; and miscellaneous prose.

The work is a survey of scholarship and bibliography that revises and expands John Edwin Wells, *A Manual of the Writings in Middle English, 1050–1400* (New Haven: Connecticut Acad. of Arts and Sciences, 1916, 941 pp.), and its nine supplements (1919–51). Each chapter (and sometimes sections thereof) has two parts: (1) the commentary, which for each work discusses content, manuscripts, date, dialect, source, and form, and summarizes scholarship and critical trends; (2) a classified bibliography (with sections for manuscripts, editions, textual matters, language, versification, date, authorship, sources, literary criticism, and bibliography). Many entries are briefly annotated. Coverage is less thorough in vols. 1–3 ("all serious studies down through 1955 . . . and all important studies from 1955 to" one or two years before publication); the later volumes strive to include "all serious studies" up to one or two years before publication. (See the preface to each volume—especially vol. 5—for specific terminal dates.) Reviewers have, however, noted a number of omissions in some chapters; and following Wells's organization while expanding his scope has led to some inconsistent groupings in chapters. Indexed by authors, titles, early printers, and subjects; a master index is planned upon completion. Although the early chapters are now dated and some works and authors are now more exhaustively treated in separate bibliographies, Severs and Hartung remains an indispensable starting point for most research in medieval literature. Reviews: (vol. 1) Norman Davis, *Review of English Studies* ns 21 (1970): 72–74; (vol. 2) Anne Hudson, *Medium Ævum* 43 (1974): 199–201; (vol. 3) Davis, *Review of English Studies* ns 25 (1974): 67–69; (vol. 4) Davis, *Review of English Studies* ns 26 (1975): 325–27; (vol. 5) Hudson, *Yearbook of English Studies* 9 (1979): 361–62.

1830 Fisher, John H., ed. *The Medieval Literature of Western Europe: A Review of Research, Mainly 1930–1960*. Revolving Fund Series 22. New York: New York UP, for MLA. London: U of London P, 1966. 432 pp. PN671.F5 809.02.

Surveys of research from c. 1930 to c. 1964 on medieval Latin, Old English, Middle English (to 1400), French, German, Old Norse, Italian, Spanish, Catalan, Portuguese, and Celtic literatures. Addressed to advanced graduate students and scholars not specializing in the literatures, chapters typically examine bibliographical and reference works; background, language, and general studies; literary histories; and research on major forms, works, and authors. (The essay "Middle English Literature to 1400" [pp. 73–123], by Robert W. Ackerman, has sections for bibliographies, general and background studies, works of religious instruction, mysticism, translations and didactic works, poetry, romance, drama, *Piers Plowman*, Chaucer, and Gower.) Indexed by scholars and authors. Although now badly dated, *Medieval Literature of Western Europe* is still useful for its sensible evaluations of important studies published during the period. Review: A. A. Heathcote, Johanna H. Torringa, and R. M. Wilson, *Modern Language Review* 63 (1968): 141–42.

Essential supplements are *Year's Work in English Studies* (330), *Year's Work in Modern Language Studies* (4855), and especially the surveys and bibliographies of English, French, German, Italian, Latin, and Spanish literature in Thomas D. Cooke, ed., *The Present State of Scholarship in Fourteenth-Century Literature* (Columbia: U of Missouri P, 1982, 319 pp.). The essay by John H. Fisher on English literature (pp. 1–54) surveys bibliographies and research tools, anthologies and translations, facsimiles, thematic studies, language, major authors, works, and genres, and concludes with a selective classified bibliography of 386 books published since the early 1960s.

See also

YWES (330): Chapters for Middle English Literature; Chaucer.

SERIAL BIBLIOGRAPHIES

1835 *International Medieval Bibliography [1967–]* (*IMB*). Leeds: U of Leeds, 1968– . 2/yr. Z6203.I63 016.914'03'1.

An international bibliography of articles and notes in journals, festschriften, and collections of essays on Europe and the Byzantine Empire from 500 to 1500. Books, reviews, and (as of 1983) collections of previously published articles are excluded. Entries are classified by country or area under several divisions, which currently include ones for language; literature (with sections for general studies, drama, prose, and verse); manuscripts and palaeography; myth, folklore, and magic; printing; history; and women's studies. Since these divisions have changed markedly over the years, users must consult the contents list in respective volumes. Two indexes: scholars; subjects (selective). Although the work is not comprehensive, its breadth makes it a useful supplement to the standard serial bibliographies and indexes in section G. Review: B. D. H. Miller, *Review of English Studies* ns 29 (1978): 78–79.

The following defunct serial bibliographies are still useful:

International Guide to Medieval Studies: A Continuous Index to Periodical Literature. 12 vols. Darien: American Bibliographic Service, 1963–78. International coverage of articles from 1961 to 1973, with scholar and subject indexes.

Progress of Medieval and Renaissance Studies in the United States and Canada. 25 nos. Boulder: U of Colorado, 1921–60. Lists publications, dissertations, and work in progress, 1922–59.

For other serial bibliographies, see Rouse, *Serial Bibliographies for Medieval Studies* (1805).

See also

Sec. G: Serial Bibliographies, Indexes, and Abstracts.

ABELL (340): English Literature/Middle English through the volume for 1972; English Literature/Old and Middle English: Subsidiary through the volume for 1933; English Literature/Fifteenth Century in the volumes for 1927–72; and English Literature/Middle English and Fifteenth Century in later volumes.

"Bibliography of American Periodical Literature," *Medium Ævum* (1875).

MLAIB (335): English Language and Literature division in the volumes for 1921–25; English VI in the volumes for 1926–56; English V in the volumes for 1957–80; and English Literature/1100–1499: Middle English Period section (as well as any larger chronological sections encompassing the period) in the later volumes. Some studies treating Middle English literature appear in General/Medieval in the volume for 1928; General II: Medieval Literature in the volumes for 1929–32; General/Medieval Literature in the volumes for 1933–52: General VII: Literature, General and Comparative/Medieval Literature in the volumes for 1953–55; General II: Literature, General and Comparative/Medieval Literature in the volume for 1956; and General III: Literature, General and Comparative/Medieval Literature in the volumes for 1957–80. Researchers must also check the headings beginning "English Literature" in the subject index to post-1980 volumes.

"Middle English Research in Progress" and "Chaucer Research in Progress," *Neuphilologische Mitteilungen* (710).

OTHER BIBLIOGRAPHIES

1840 *The New Cambridge Bibliography of English Literature* (*NCBEL*). Vol. 1: *600–1660*. Ed. George Watson. Cambridge: Cambridge UP, 1974. 2,476 cols. Z2011.N45 [PR83] 016.82.

(For a full discussion of *NCBEL*, see entry 1385.) The part devoted to the Middle English period (1100–1500) has six major divisions, each subdivided and classified as its subject requires: introduction, Middle English literature to 1400 (with sections for romances, literature, Chaucer, education), the fifteenth century (English Chaucerians, Middle Scots poets, English prose, miscellaneous verse and prose), songs and ballads, medieval drama, and writings in Latin. The general introduction for the volume as a whole lists bibliographies, histories, anthologies, and works about prosody, prose rhythm, and language important to the study of the Middle English period. Users must familiarize themselves with the organization, remember that there is considerable unevenness of coverage among subdivisions, and consult the index volume (vol. 5) rather than the provisional index in vol. 1. Review: Fred C. Robinson, *Anglia* 97 (1979): 511–17.

Vol. 1 of the *Cambridge Bibliography of English Literature* (1385a) is still occasionally useful for its coverage of the social and political background (which *NCBEL* drops).

See also

Kallendorf, *Latin Influences on English Literature from the Middle Ages to the Eighteenth Century* (4895).

RELATED TOPICS

1845 Graves, Edgar B., ed. *A Bibliography of English History to 1485*. Oxford: Clarendon, 1975. 1,103 pp. Z2017.B5 [DA130] 016.942.

An extensive, albeit selective, bibliography of primary works and scholarship on English (not British) history from prehistoric times to 1485 that revises Charles Gross, *The Sources and Literature of English History from the Earliest Times to about 1485*, 2nd ed. (London: Longmans, 1915, 820 pp.). Graves covers publications through December 1969 on the pre-Norman era, and through December 1970 (along with some later works) on the period 1066–1485. Entries are organized in five classified divisions: general (with sections for bibliographies, journals, and ancillary areas such as philology, archaeology, and art); archives, source collections, and modern narratives (including a section on local history); prehistory to Anglo-Saxon conquest; Anglo-Saxon period; the period 1066–1485 (with sections on a variety of topics such as chronicles, public records, military and naval history, urban society, the church, and intellectual interests). Many annotations are evaluative or refer to related works; unfortunately, several entries are not annotated or inadequately so. Indexed by persons and subjects. The authoritative guide to historical scholarship on the period, Graves is especially useful for cross-disciplinary research.

For broader geographical coverage, see Paetow, *Guide to the Study of Medieval History* (1855) and Crosby, *Medieval Studies* (1850). Convenient highly selective bibliographies are Bertie Wilkinson, *The High Middle Ages in England, 1154–1377*, Conference on British Studies Bibliographical Handbooks (Cambridge: Cambridge UP for the Conference on British Studies, 1978, 130 pp.), and Delloyd J. Guth, *Late-Medieval England, 1377–1485*, Conference on British Studies Bibliographical Handbooks (Cambridge: Cambridge UP for the Conference on British Studies, 1976, 143 pp.).

1850 Crosby, Everett U., C. Julian Bishko, and Robert L. Kellogg. *Medieval Studies: A Bibliographical Guide*. Garland Reference Library of the Humanities 427. New York: Garland, 1983. 1,131 pp. Z5579.5.C76 [CB351] 016.9401.

A classified, annotated, selective bibliography of books and serials on all aspects of medieval studies from the period 200 to 1500. The approximately 9,000 entries are organized in 138 divisions covering reference works, the arts, sciences, social sciences, religion, laws, languages, literatures, numismatics, and heraldry. The broader topics have sections devoted to geographical areas, and each is subdivided as its subject requires. The brief annotations—many of them evaluative—are generally accurate and helpful. Two indexes: authors and editors; topics. Given the breadth of coverage, the organization of the work is clear and the selection judicious, but access is inhibited by the lack of a subject index. Still, *Medieval Studies* is useful for identifying important reference works and studies, and for interdisciplinary research.

1855 Paetow, Louis John. *A Guide to the Study of Medieval History*. Rev. and corrected ed. with errata by Gray C. Boyce and an addendum by Lynn Thorndike. Millwood: Kraus, 1980. 643 pp. Gray Cowan Boyce, comp. and ed. *Literature of Medieval History, 1930–1975: A Supplement to Louis John Paetow's* A Guide to the Study of Medieval History. 5 vols. Millwood: Kraus, 1981. Z6203.P25 [D117] 016.9401.

A selective bibliography emphasizing studies in English, French, and German (with some in Spanish and Italian) published through 1975 on Western Europe. Entries are organized in three divisions, each elaborately classified: general works (with chapters for bibliographies, reference works, subjects related to the study of medieval history, general modern historical works, and collections of original sources), general history of the Middle Ages, and medieval culture (to 1300 in Paetow, 1500 in Boyce). In Paetow, most sections begin with an outline, followed by a list of the most important works, and then a general bibliography. (See pp. xxi-li for errata and pp. liii-cxii for the addendum.) Indexed by scholars, collection titles, and subjects. Boyce generally follows Paetow's organization (omitting the introductory outlines and providing a straightforward author list of studies) but offers more thorough coverage of scholarship and expands the section on medieval culture to 1500. Indexed by persons. Although poorly organized, both works are valuable guides to scholarship on literature-related subjects. Review (Boyce): C. Warren Hollister, *American Historical Review* 87 (1982): 1064–66.

See also

Annual Bibliography of British and Irish History (1400).

Language

GUIDES TO SCHOLARSHIP

See

ABELL (340): Middle English headings in the subdivisions of the English Language section.

MLAIB (335): English Language and Literature division in the volumes for 1922–25; Middle English headings in English I/Linguistics section of the volumes for 1926–66; Indo-European C/Germanic Linguistics IV/English/Middle English section in the 1967–80 volumes; and the Indo-

European Languages/West Germanic Languages/English Language/English Language (Middle) section in pt. 3 of the later volumes. Researchers should also check the "English Language (Middle)" heading in the subject index to post-1980 volumes.

Tajima, *Old and Middle English Language Studies* (1687).

DICTIONARIES

1860 *Middle English Dictionary* (*MED*). Ed. Hans Kurath et al. Ann Arbor: U of Michigan P, 1952– . PE679.M54 427.02.

A dictionary of Middle English from c. 1100 to 1475. Entries, based on the Southeast Midland dialect, cite variant and grammatical forms, part of speech, etymology, meanings (grouped by semantic relationship), and illustrative quotations. For a detailed description of editorial procedures and a bibliography of the manuscripts and printed editions from which passages are drawn, see *Plan and Bibliography* (1954, 105 pp.) and *Plan and Bibliography: Supplement I* (1984, 36 pp.), which updates the bibliography in the original *Plan*; for an account of compilation methods and procedures, see Sherman M. Kuhn, "On the Making of the *Middle English Dictionary*," *Dictionaries* 4 (1982): 14–41. When complete, the *MED* will largely supersede the Middle English entries in *Oxford English Dictionary* (1410) and Francis Henry Stratmann, *A Middle-English Dictionary*, rev. Henry Bradley (Oxford: Oxford UP, 1891, 708 pp.), the only complete Middle English dictionary. Justly praised for accuracy and reliability, *MED* is the indispensable source for the study of Middle English and for explication of the literature of the period.

Representative of the numerous reviews that suggest additions and corrections are those appearing in *Medium Ævum*: B. D. H. Miller, 37 (1968): 332–36; 42 (1973): 73–81; 44 (1975): 181–90; 46 (1977): 343–48; 47 (1978): 351–56; R. L. Thompson, 34 (1965): 269–74; Martyn Wakelin, 54 (1985): 292–95. *English Studies* and *Review of English Studies* also regularly review volumes. In addition, there are a number of corrections and additions: F. Th. Visser, "Three Suggested Emendations of the *Middle English Dictionary*," *English Studies* 36 (1955): 23–24, and "*The Middle English Dictionary* (Parts A, B1–4, E, and F)," *English Studies* 40 (1959): 18–27; Hans Kurath, "Some Comments on Professor Visser's Notes on the *Middle English Dictionary*," *English Studies* 41 (1960): 253–54 (with a response by Visser, 254–55); Hans Käsmann, "Anmerkungen zum *Middle English Dictionary*," *Anglia* 77 (1959): 65–74; Autumn Simmons, "A Contribution to the *Middle English Dictionary*: Citations from the English Poems of Charles, Duc d'Orléans," *Journal of English Linguistics* 2 (1968): 43–56; Lilo Moessner, "Some Remarks on the *MED*," *Neuphilologische Mitteilungen* 83 (1982): 150–51.

An important complement for the localization of English from c. 1350 to c. 1450 is Angus McIntosh, M. L. Samuels, and Michael Benskin, *A Linguistic Atlas of Late Mediaeval English*, 4 vols. (Aberdeen: Aberdeen UP, 1986). Although full of information, it is a difficult work to use.

See also

Dictionary of Medieval Latin from British Sources (1700).

STUDIES OF LANGUAGE

1865 Brunner, Karl. *An Outline of Middle English Grammar.* Trans. Grahame Johnston. Cambridge: Harvard UP, 1963. 111 pp. PE531.B713 427.02.

A basic overview of the phonology and inflexions of Middle English from c. 1100 to c. 1500. Indexed by lexical items. Terse but clear, Brunner is a basic introductory outline of the language.

Fernand Mossé, *A Handbook of Middle English*, trans. James A. Walker (Baltimore: Johns Hopkins P, 1952, 495 pp.), is a good complement because of its somewhat fuller explanations and generous selection of annotated illustrative texts.

Periodicals

For an annotated list of serials devoted to medieval studies, see Christopher Kleinhenz, "Medieval Journals et Publications Series in North America," *Medieval Studies in North America: Past, Present, and Future*, ed. Francis G. Gentry and Christopher Kleinhenz (Kalamazoo: Medieval Inst., 1982) 120–78. Many journals listed in sections K: Periodicals/Scholarly Journals and M: English Literature/General/Periodicals/Scholarly Journals publish articles on Middle English topics.

1870 *Mediaeval Studies* (*MS*). 1939– . Annual. D111.M44 901.92.

Publishes edited texts and articles on the European Middle Ages. Cumulative indexes: vols. 1–25, *General Index* (n.d., 202 pp.); vols. 26–30, *General Index: First Supplement* (n.d., 61 pp.); vols. 31–40, Catherine G. Monahan, Kathryn Ann Taglia, and Ron B. Thomson, *General Index: Second Supplement* (n.d., 164 pp.). Index for vols. 26–50 is in progress.

1875 *Medium Ævum* (*MÆ*). 1932– . 2/yr. PB1.M4 405.

Emphasizes British topics and lesser-known works in articles, notes, and reviews on language and medieval literature. Cumulative index: *General Index to* Medium Ævum, *Volumes I–XXV, 1932–1957* (Oxford: Blackwell, 1958, 35 pp.).

1880 *Speculum: A Journal of Medieval Studies* (*Speculum*). 1926– . Quarterly. PN661.S6 809.2.

Publishes articles, notes, documents, reviews, and review essays on all aspects of medieval studies. Includes two serial bibliographies—the quarterly "Bibliography of American Periodical Literature" (vols. 9–47 [1934–72]) and the annual "Bibliography of Editions and Translations in Progress" (48 [1973]–)—as well as an extensive list of books received in each issue. Noted for the quality of its articles and rigorous reviews.

1885 *Studies in the Age of Chaucer* (*SAC*). 1979– . Annual. PR1901.S88 820'.9'001.

In addition to the annual "An Annotated Chaucer Bibliography [1975–]," publishes articles and reviews on Chaucer, his contemporaries, and the historical, religious, intellectual, literary, and other backgrounds of their works. Although most articles are on Chaucer, the reviews cover books on several authors and topics. The bibliography and the articles and reviews are separately indexed in each volume.

1890 *Traditio: Studies in Ancient and Medieval History, Thought, and Religion* (*Traditio*). 1943– . Annual. D111.T7 940.1058.

Publishes articles on topics from classical antiquity through the Middle Ages, with occasional bibliographies and surveys of research.

See also

Neuphilologische Mitteilungen (710).

Background Reading

The best guides to background studies are Robert W. Ackerman, "Middle English Literature to 1400" (pp. 73–123) in Fisher, *Medieval Literature of Western Europe* (1830); and John H. Fisher, "English Literature" (pp. 1–54), in Cooke, *Present State of Scholarship in Fourteenth-Century Literature* (1830a). Bateson, *Guide to English and American Literature* (85) has a chapter on medieval literature (pp. 26–40).

1895 Ackerman, Robert W. *Backgrounds to Medieval English Literature.* Random House Study in Language and Literature 7. New York: Random, 1966. 171 pp. PR255.A3 820.9'001.

An introduction to the cultural and intellectual background of English literature from *Beowulf* to c. 1500, with a decided emphasis on the Middle English period. The overview is organized in five chapters: social and religious backgrounds of the Old English period, social and religious backgrounds of the Middle English period, the English language in the Middle Ages, popular Christian doctrine, and the world view of the Middle Ages. An appendix outlines critical approaches to medieval literature. Each chapter, the appendix, and the book conclude with a brief list of recommended readings (now dated). Indexed by persons, titles, and subjects. Ackerman remains a helpful introduction for readers lacking a basic knowledge of the background of Middle English literature.

1900 Lewis, C. S. *The Discarded Image: An Introduction to Medieval and Renaissance Literature.* Cambridge: Cambridge UP, 1964. 232 pp. PN671.L4 809.02.

An overview of the organization of theology, science, and history into the model of the universe integral to medieval and Renaissance thought. Lewis outlines the classical and pagan background of the model, operations and inhabitants of the heavens and earth, parts of the soul and the human body, and the impact of the model on literature. Indexed by persons, subjects, and anonymous works. Perceptive and learned, *Discarded Image* remains the classic exposition of the cosmology underlying medieval and Renaissance literature. Tillyard, *Elizabethan World Picture* (2085) is a useful complement. Reviews: D. C. Allen, *English Language Notes* 2 (1965): 133–35; John Burrow, *Essays in Criticism* 15 (1965): 207–11; M. A. Shaaber, *Renaissance News* 18 (1965): 19–20.

See also

Oxford History of England (1495).

Genres

DRAMA AND THEATER

Histories and Surveys

1905 Chambers, E. K. *The Mediaeval Stage.* 2 vols. Oxford: Oxford UP, 1903. PN2152.C4 792.094.

A history of the development of the stage to 1558, in four parts: minstrelsy, folk drama, religious drama, and interludes. A variety of appendixes print documents or extracts from dramatic works, amplify points in the text, or provide bibliographies. The pioneering, seminal work on the topic, Chambers has never been completely superseded but must be supplemented by later histories and specialized studies such as the following:

Hardison, O. B., Jr.. *Christian Rite and Christian Drama in the Middle Ages: Essays in the Origin and Early History of Modern Drama.* Baltimore: Johns Hopkins P, 1965. 328 pp.

Revels History of Drama, vols. 1–2 (1910 and 2120) and a number of the works cited in the bibliographies (vol. 1, pp. 303–36; vol. 2, pp. 259–82).

Wickham, *Early English Stages* (1915).

Young, Karl. *The Drama of the Medieval Church.* 2 vols. Oxford: Clarendon, 1933. On the importance of Young's study, see C. Clifford Flanigan, "Karl Young and the Drama of the Medieval Church: An Anniversary Appraisal," *Research Opportunities in Renaissance Drama* 27 (1984): 157–66.

For an updated distillation, see the essay on drama in Chambers, *English Literature at the Close of the Middle Ages* (1790); continued by his *Elizabethan Stage* (2115).

1910 *The Revels History of Drama in English* (1530). Gen. ed. Lois Potter. Vol. 1: *Medieval Drama.* London: Methuen, 1983. 348 pp. PR625.R44 822'.009.

Includes a chronology; essays on staging, religious drama, and early moral plays and secular drama; an appendix listing "Manuscripts and Contents of the Extant English Cycles"; and an evaluative survey of important studies. Indexed by authors, titles, and subjects. Like other volumes of *Revels History*, this volume is a useful synthesis of scholarship but not a connected history of the drama and theater.

1915 Wickham, Glynne. *Early English Stages, 1300 to 1660.* 4 vols. London: Routledge; New York: Columbia UP, 1963– . PN2587.W53 792'.0941.

Vol. 1: *1300 to 1576.* 2nd ed. 1980. 428 pp. (Originally published, 1959.)
Vol. 2: *1576–1660.* 2 pts. 1963–72.
Vol. 3: *Plays and Their Makers to 1576.* 1981. 357 pp.
Vol. 4: In progress.

Traces the evolution of the drama, emphasizing visual elements in organizing the survey on the theory that festival is the basis for drama. Vol. 1 examines open-air and indoor entertainments, and dramatic theory and practice; vol. 2, regulation of the theater, the emblematic tradition, playhouses and theaters, and stages and stage directions; vol. 3, the occasions of drama, emblems, and comedy and tragedy.

A variety of appendixes print documents and texts. Indexed by persons, subjects, works, and places (in a single index in vols. 1 and 2 but separately in 3). Reviewers note many factual errors but generally agree that Wickham is an important, provocative work. Reviews: (vol. 1) Hardin Craig, *Speculum* 34 (1959): 702–05; (vol. 2, pt. 1) *Times Literary Supplement* 15 March 1963: 180; (vol. 3) Clifford Davidson, *Comparative Drama* 16 (1982): 86–88; Gordon Kipling, *Renaissance Quarterly* 36 (1983): 654–59.

Important complementary works are Chambers, *Mediaeval Stage* (1905) and *Elizabethan Stage* (2115); *Revels History of Drama*, vols. 1–4 (1910 and 2120); and Bentley, *Jacobean and Caroline Stage* (2110).

Annals

See

Harbage, *Annals of English Drama* (1535).

Guides to Primary Works

1920 *Records of Early English Drama* (*REED*). Gen. ed. Alexandra F. Johnston. Toronto: U of Toronto P, 1979– .

York. 2 vols. Ed. Alexandra F. Johnston and Margaret Rogerson. 1979. (Covers 1370–1642.) PN2596.Y6.Y6 790.2'09428'43.

Chester. Ed. Lawrence M. Clopper. 1979. 591 pp. (Covers 1268–1642.) PN2596.C48.C4 790.2'09427'14.

Coventry. Ed. R. W. Ingram. 1981. 712 pp. (Covers 1392–1642.) PN2596.C68.C6 790.2'09424'98.

Newcastle upon Tyne. Ed. J. J. Anderson. 1982. 216 pp. (Covers 1427–1641.) PN2596.N4.N48 790.2'09428'76.

Norwich, 1540–1642. Ed. David Galloway. 1984. 501 pp. PN2596.N6.N67 790.2'09426'15.

Cumberland, Westmorland, Gloucestershire. Ed. Audrey Douglas and Peter Greenfield. 1986. 547 pp. (Covers 1345–1643, 1537–1642, 1283–1643, respectively.) PN2589.C86 790.2'09427'8.

Devon. Ed. John M. Wasson. 1986. 623 pp. (Covers 1444–1637.) PN2596.D48.D48 790.2'09423'5.

Cambridge. Ed. Alan Nelson. 2 vols. Scheduled for 1989.

Transcribes—but does not interpret—civic, guild, and ecclesiastical records, wills, and antiquarians' compilations that relate to dramatic, ceremonial, or minstrel activity before 1642. Each volume includes a general introduction to the urban center or county (with the latter following pre-1642 boundaries), its dramatic activities, and the nature of the records; transcriptions of the pertinent documents (arranged chronologically in the city volumes, by place in the county ones); various appendixes (including one with English translations of Latin-language documents); a glossary; and an index of persons, places, subjects, and titles.

These volumes are incomparable sources of raw material for theatrical, dramatic, and musical history. Reviews: (York) Barrie Dobson, *Renaissance and Refor-*

mation ns 6 (1982): 47–55; Sheila Lindenbaum, *Modern Philology* 80 (1982): 80–83; (Chester) Peter Clark, *Renaissance and Reformation* ns 5 (1981): 237–39; Alan H. Nelson, *Modern Language Review* 78 (1983): 131–33.

The *Records of Early English Drama Newsletter* (*REEDN*) (1976– , 2/yr.) prints news of the project, additions and corrections to published volumes, brief articles, transcriptions of records, and (every second year since 1978) the "Annotated Bibliography of Printed Records of Early British Drama and Minstrelsy [for 1976–]."

1925 Lancashire, Ian. *Dramatic Texts and Records of Britain: A Chronological Topography to 1558*. Studies in Early English Drama 1. Toronto: U of Toronto P, 1984. 633 pp. PN2587.L36 792'.0941.

A calendar and finding list of references to "a text . . . or the record of a dramatic representation or show, a playing place, a playwright, visits of acting troupes, an official act of control over playing, or other evidence relating to plays and their production" from Roman times to 1558. Entries are organized chronologically under specific sites in separate sections for England, Wales, Scotland, and Ireland. An entry includes a brief summary of a record along with references to the most reliable printed editions or manuscript sources. The chronological list of published and unpublished dramatic works refers to editions and important scholarship. The mass of information is best approached through the several indexes: playing companies (two indexes: place; patron or player); playwrights; playing places and buildings (chronological); salient dates and entry numbers; general index of places, persons, and subjects. (Unfortunately, users must contend with five different number systems.) The emphasis is on collecting rather than interpreting evidence, but the introduction provides a brief history of dramatic activity and suggestions for further research. (Confusing, though, is the use of italic numbers to refer to the list of bibliographical abbreviations, since numbers in the list are hidden at the end of citations.) *Dramatic Texts and Records* is a valuable systematic guide to widely scattered primary evidence and scholarship that serves as an important complement to *Records of Early English Drama* (1920). Continued by the biennial "Annotated Bibliography of Printed Records of Early British Drama and Minstrelsy [for 1976–]" (1920a).

Guides to Scholarship and Criticism

1930 Stratman, Carl J., C.S.V. *Bibliography of Medieval Drama*. 2nd ed. rev. and enl. 2 vols. New York: Ungar, 1972. Z5782.A2.S8 016.80882'02.

A bibliography of manuscripts, editions, and studies of liturgical, mystery, morality, and miracle plays, interludes, and folk drama written before c. 1600, principally in England; there is very selective coverage of Continental and Byzantine works. Entries are organized in 10 variously classified divisions: general studies, festschriften, liturgical Latin, and English, Byzantine, French, German, Italian, Low Countries', and Spanish drama. The English division has sections for bibliographies, collections of plays, general studies, mystery and miracle plays, moralities and interludes, and folk drama. Plays are organized alphabetically by title, with listings for manuscripts, editions, and studies (with the last arranged chronologically and including theses and dissertations). Entries are not annotated, but important studies are marked by an asterisk, and library locations are provided for manuscripts and books. Indexed by scholars, dramatists, titles, and subjects. The lack of clear organization within some divisions is compounded by poor layout and typography. Although untrustworthy because of the numerous errors and omissions, the *Bibliography of Medieval Drama* is useful as a preliminary list of works published before 1970. Reviews: Lorrayne Y. Baird, *Speculum* 50 (1975): 155–58; J. W. Robinson, *Theatre Research International* 1 (1975): 47–48.

Supplemented by Jim Villani, Lorrayne Y. Baird, Alice Crosetto, and Mary Sandra Moller, "Musical Texts, Recordings, Films, and Filmstrips for Medi[e]val Drama," *Studies in Medieval and Renaissance Teaching* 10.1 (1983): 3–8. For a more complete and trustworthy guide to English drama c. 1495–1580, see White, *Early English Drama* (2165).

Continued by Maria Spaeth Murphy and James Hoy, eds., "Bibliography of Medieval Drama, 1969–1972," *Emporia State Research Studies* 34.4 (1986): 44 pp., and Murphy, Carole Ferguson, and Hoy, "Bibliography of Medieval Drama, 1973–1976," 35.1 (1986): 41 pp. Entries are organized chronologically (with separate lists of books, articles, and dissertations under each year); most are accompanied by a descriptive annotation. Coverage will continue through 1980.

See also

Lancashire, *Dramatic Texts and Records* (1925).
John Leyerle, "Medieval Drama," pp. 19–28, in Wells, *English Drama* (1555).

Periodicals

1935 *Medieval and Renaissance Drama in England: An Annual Gathering of Research, Criticism, and Reviews* (*MRDE*). 1984– . Annual. PR621.M65 822'.009.

Publishes articles, review essays, and reviews on all aspects of drama in England before 1640 (generally excluding Shakespeare). Annual index.

See also

Medieval Supplement, *Research Opportunities in Renaissance Drama* (2175).

POETRY

Histories and Surveys

See

Pearsall, *Old and Middle English Poetry* (1735).

Guides to Primary Works

1940 Brown, Carleton, and Rossell Hope Robbins. *The Index of Middle English Verse*. New York: Columbia UP, for the Index Soc., 1943. 785 pp. Robbins and John L. Cutler. *Supplement*. Lexington: U of Kentucky P, 1965. 551 pp. Z2012.B86 016.821'1.

A first-line index to poems, for the most part in manuscripts and written before 1500. The *Supplement* extends coverage to early printed texts and beyond 1500 to encompass, e.g., the Scottish Chaucerians and songbooks. Each entry identifies extant manuscripts and modern editions. Acephalous poems occupy a separate section, and an appendix lists manuscripts in private hands. The *Index* and *Supplement* must be used together, since the latter includes nearly 1,500 new entries and prints additions and corrections to nearly half of the original ones and the index. Indexed by subjects and titles. Although not exhaustive (especially for verse buried in larger manuscript collections or early printed texts) and being superseded by Severs, *Manual of the Writings in Middle English* (1825), *Index of Middle English Verse* is still indispensable for identifying and locating texts of poems not yet covered in the *Manual*. (The Brown-Robbins-Cutler numbers are the standard references for Middle English verse.)

Among the more important lists of additions and corrections are Linne R. Mooney, "Additions and Emendations to *The Index of Middle English Verse* and Its *Supplement*," *Anglia* 99 (1981): 394–98; Ralph Hanna III, "*The Index of Middle English Verse* and Huntington Library Collections: A Checklist of Addenda," *Papers of the Bibliographical Society of America* 74 (1980): 235–58; Siegfried Wenzel, "Unrecorded Middle English Verses," *Anglia* 92 (1974): 55–78. Many reviews also include additions and corrections, e.g., Morton W. Bloomfield, *Speculum* 42 (1967): 548–50; Curt F. Bühler, *Papers of the Bibliographical Society of America* 37 (1943): 161–65; Norman Davis, *Review of English Studies* ns 18 (1967): 444–48.

See also

Ringler, *Bibliography and Index of English Verse Printed 1476–1500 and 1501–1558* (2190).

PROSE

Guides to Primary Works

1945 *The Index of Middle English Prose*. Gen. ed. A. S. G. Edwards. In progress since 1977.

An attempt to locate and identify all Middle English printed and manuscript prose texts (except letters and legal documents) composed between c. 1200 and c. 1500 (as well as later transcripts). The project and editorial procedures are outlined in A. S. G. Edwards, "Towards an *Index of Middle English Prose*," and Robert E. Lewis, "Editorial Technique in the *Index of Middle English Prose*," *Middle English Prose: Essays on Bibliographical Problems*, ed. A. S. G. Edwards and Derek Pearsall (New York: Garland, 1981) 23–41, 43–64. Preparation of the comprehensive index is proceeding in a number of stages:

Lewis, R. E., N. F. Blake, and A. S. G. Edwards. *Index of Printed Middle English Prose*. Garland Reference Library of the Humanities 537. New York: Garland, 1985. 362 pp. An index of literary prose written from c. 1150 to c. 1500; entries include first line, title, and lists of printed editions and manuscripts.

A series of bibliographical catalogs of genres and authors.
Handlists to major collections, of which the following have appeared under the main title *The Index of Middle English Prose*:

Handlist I: A Handlist of Manuscripts Containing Middle English Prose in the Henry E. Huntingdon [sic] Library. By Ralph Hanna III. Cambridge: Brewer, 1984. 81 pp.

Handlist II: A Handlist of Manuscripts Containing Middle English Prose in the John Rylands University Library of Manchester and Chetham's Library, Manchester. By G. A. Lester. 1985. 112 pp.

Handlist III: A Handlist of Manuscripts Containing Middle English Prose in the Digby Collection, Bodleian Library, Oxford. By Patrick J. Horner. 1986. 86 pp.

Handlist IV: A Handlist of Douce Manuscripts Containing Middle English Prose in the Bodleian Library, Oxford. By Laurel Braswell. 1987. 110 pp.

Entries, organized by the library's shelfmark, include incipit and explicit (for each item in a collection), physical description, and references to other manuscripts, reference works, and scholarship.

If editorial problems involving dates of coverage and handling of items such as recipes and macaronic texts can be solved, the *Index* could exert an influence on the study of prose similar to that of the Brown, Robbins, and Cutler *Index of Medieval English Verse* (entry 1940) on poetry. Review: Peter J. Lucas, *Analytical and Enumerative Bibliography* 6 (1982): 253–55.

Guides to Scholarship and Criticism

1950 Edwards, A. S. G., ed. *Middle English Prose: A Critical Guide to Major Authors and Genres*. New Brunswick: Rutgers UP, 1984. 452 pp. PR255.M52 828'.108'09.

Surveys of scholarship and editions, with essays on *Ancrene Wisse*, the Katherine Group, and the *Wohunge* Group; Richard Rolle and related works; *The Cloud of Unknowing* and Walter Hilton's *Scale of Perfection*; Nicholas Love; Julian of Norwich; Margery Kempe; Mandeville; John Trevisa; minor devotional writings; sermon literature; historical prose; Wycliffite prose; romances; Chaucer; medical prose; utilitarian and scientific prose; Caxton; and works of religious instruction. (Malory is omitted because of the existence of recent author bibliographies such as Page West Life, *Sir Thomas Malory and the* Morte Darthur: *A Survey of Scholarship and Annotated Bibliography* [Charlottesville: UP of Virginia, for Bibliographical Soc. of U of Virginia, 1980, 297 pp.].) Each essay concludes with a selective bibliography of manuscripts, editions, and studies. Indexed by authors, scholars, and anonymous works. Although the essays are uneven in covering dissertations and editions, their perceptive evaluations of scholarship and suggestions for further study make *Middle English Prose* an essential starting point for research on prose works. Review: Siegfried Wenzel, *Anglia* 104 (1986): 478–81.

Renaissance Literature (1500–1660)

Many works listed in section M: English Literature/General are useful for research in Renaissance literature.

Research Methods

1965 Jenkinson, Hilary. *The Later Court Hands in England from the Fifteenth to the Seventeenth Century: Illustrated from the Common Paper of the Scriveners' Company of London, the English Writing Masters, and the Public Records*. 2 vols. Cambridge: Cambridge UP, 1927. Z115.E5.J57 745.6'1.

A manual for reading the hands used in documents from c. 1400 to c. 1700. Vol. 1 consists of succinct discussions of the development of the hands; forms of documents; languages used in English archives; the teaching and practice of handwriting in England; letter forms current in the fifteenth century; runes; abbreviations, ligatures, conjoined letters, and elisions; the letter forms of each of the hands; dating court hands; personal marks, paraphs, and signatures; symbols and ciphers; numerals; punctuation, accents, and the apostrophe; paragraph marks and other conventional divisions; alterations and corrections; decoration; and hints on reading, interpreting, transcribing, and describing hands. Concludes with a selective bibliography and annotated transcriptions of the plates in vol. 2. Among the plates are alphabets for each of the hands. Indexed in vol. 1 by persons and subjects. Although more detailed in its treatment of the fifteenth and sixteenth centuries, it remains the best introduction to the reading of the hands commonly used between 1400 and 1700. For earlier hands, see Johnson, *English Court Hand* (1765).

Anthony G. Petti, *English Literary Hands from Chaucer to Dryden* (Cambridge: Harvard UP, 1977, 133 pp.), which emphasizes manuscripts after 1500, must be consulted with care because of its oversimplifications and errors (see the review by M. C. Seymour, followed by Petti's response, *Library* 5th ser. 33 [1978]: 343–49).

Useful for tracing the later development of English handwriting is P. J. Croft, comp. and ed., *Autograph Poetry in the English Language: Facsimiles of Original Manuscripts from the Fourteenth to the Twentieth Century*, 2 vols. (London: Cassell, 1973), which reproduces and transcribes examples from holograph manuscripts by 146 poets.

Histories and Surveys

1970 Bush, Douglas. *English Literature in the Earlier Seventeenth Century, 1600–1660*. 2nd ed. rev. Vol. 5 of *The Oxford History of English Literature* (1310). Gen. eds. Bonamy Dobrée, Norman Davis, and F. P. Wilson. Oxford: Clarendon, 1962. 680 pp. PR431.B8 820.903.

A literary history of the period organized by "types of writing and modes of thought," with chapters on the background of the age; popular literature and translations; successors of Spenser, song books, and miscellanies; Jonson, Donne, and their successors; travel literature; essays and characters; history and biography; political thought; science; religion; heroic verse; and Milton. Concludes with a chronology and a now outdated selective bibliography (both omitted in the 1973 paperback edition). Indexed by authors and subjects. A magisterial work that fully merits its reputation as the best volume of the *Oxford History* and a model of traditional literary history. Review: Arthur E. Barker, *JEGP: Journal of English and Germanic Philology* 62 (1963): 617–28 (a detailed examination of revisions).

1975 Lewis, C. S. *English Literature in the Sixteenth Century Excluding Drama.* Vol. 3 of *The Oxford History of English Literature* (1310). Gen. eds. F. P. Wilson and Bonamy Dobrée. Oxford: Clarendon, 1954. 696 pp. PR411.L4 820.903.

A literary history covering the latter part of the fifteenth century to 1600. After an initial chapter outlining the background of the age, divides the literature into three periods: late medieval, "drab," and "golden"—a division that has not gained wide acceptance. Includes a chronology and a now outdated selective bibliography (both omitted in the 1973 paperback edition). Indexed by authors, subjects, and anonymous works. A provocative, opinionated, sometimes brilliant work that has occasioned widespread controversy. Reviews: Donald Davie, *Essays in Criticism* 5 (1955): 159–64; Charles T. Harrison, *Sewanee Review* 63 (1955): 153–61; Yvor Winters, *Hudson Review* 8 (1955): 281–87.

See also

Sec. L: English Literature/General/Histories and Surveys.

Literary Handbooks, Dictionaries, and Encyclopedias

1980 Ruoff, James E. *Crowell's Handbook of Elizabethan and Stuart Literature.* New York: Crowell, 1975. 468 pp. British ed.: *Macmillan's Handbook of Elizabethan and Stuart Literature.* London: Macmillan, 1975. PR19.R8 820'.9'003.

A handbook to the period 1558–1660, with entries for authors, works, genres, movements, and literary terms. Author entries include biographical information, a brief career survey, and a summary critical evaluation. Entries for works note details of composition, date, and source, and offer a brief synopsis and critical evaluation. Those for genres survey major developments and works. Most entries conclude with a very brief list of standard editions, reference works, and major critical studies. Although a useful compendium, whose commentary is frequently more illuminating than one expects in a handbook, the work must be used with care, since there are inexplicable omissions, questionable evaluations, untrustworthy or outdated bibliographies, and numerous factual errors. Reviews: J. Max Patrick, *Seventeenth-Century News* 35 (1977): 26–27; Warren W. Wooden, *Literary Research Newsletter* 3 (1978): 135–37.

Bibliographies of Bibliographies

For a survey and selected list of bibliographies published before 1700, see Archer Taylor, *Renaissance Guides to Books: An Inventory and Some Conclusions* (Berkeley: U of California P, 1945, 130 pp.).

See

Sec. D: Bibliographies of Bibliographies.
Howard-Hill, *Index to British Literary Bibliography* (1355).

Guides to Primary Works

MANUSCRIPTS

1985 *Index of English Literary Manuscripts* (1365). Ed. P. J. Croft, Theodore Hofmann, and John Horden. Vol. 1: *1450–1625*. 2 pts. Comp. Peter Beal. Vol. 2: *1625–1700*. 2 pts. Comp. Beal. London: Mansell; New York: Bowker, 1980– . Z6611.L7.I5 [PR83] 016.82'08.

A descriptive catalog of extant literary manuscripts. Vol. 1 covers 72 British and Irish authors who flourished between 1450 and 1625, with the bulk dating from the latter years of the period; vol. 2, pt. 1, covers 27 authors from the years 1625–1700. The authors are essentially those listed in *Concise Cambridge Bibliography of English Literature, 600–1950* (1365a). The emphasis is (rather loosely at times) on literary manuscripts, including scribal copies. Letters are excluded, although the introductions to individual authors list either individual ones or collections. Moreover, the introductions alert researchers to special problems and relevant scholarship, point out additional manuscripts, discuss canon, and conclude with an outline of the arrangement of entries. A typical entry provides a physical description, identifies the hand(s), dates composition of the manuscript, includes any necessary commentary (as well as references to editions or scholarship), and identifies location (with shelfmark). Queries about privately owned manuscripts should be addressed to the *Index* in care of Mansell. Additions and corrections will be printed in vol. 5. Since some entries are based on inquiries to libraries and collectors, bibliographies and other reference works, booksellers' and auction catalogs, rather than personal examination by the compiler, descriptions vary in fullness and accuracy. Also, terminology and format vary somewhat from part to part.

Although there are errors and omissions, and the scope is unduly restricted by reliance on the *Concise Cambridge Bibliography*, these volumes have brought to light a number of significant unrecorded manuscripts and are an essential, if limited, source for the identification and location of manuscripts. They must, however, be supplemented by the works listed in section F: Guides to Manuscripts and Archives. Reviews: (vol. 1) Hilton Kelliher, *Library* 6th ser. 4 (1982): 435–40; Anthony G. Petti, *Analytical and Enumerative Bibliography* 5 (1981): 153–56.

See also

Sec. F: Guides to Manuscripts and Archives.
Ricci, *Census of Medieval and Renaissance Manuscripts* (1815).

PRINTED WORKS

1990 Pollard, A. W., and G. R. Redgrave, comps. *A Short-Title Catalogue of Books Printed in England, Scotland, and Ireland, and of English Books Printed Abroad, 1475–1640* (*RSTC*, *NSTC*). Rev. Katharine F. Pantzer, W. A. Jackson, and F. S. Ferguson. 2nd ed., rev. and enl. 3 vols. London: Bibliographical Soc., 1976– . (Vol. 3, which will include cumulative additions and corrections, an index of printers and booksellers, and concordances with selected bibliographies, is in progress.) Z2002.P77 015'.42.

A bibliography of extant editions, impressions, issues, and occasionally states and variants of books and other printed matter published or printed in the British Isles and of books in English, Irish, or Welsh printed abroad from c. 1473 through 1640. Although it lists a few unique items seen by the compilers but now destroyed or untraceable, *RSTC* is not a bibliography of all works actually printed during the period.

The work revises—more precisely, transforms—the venerable *Short-Title Catalogue* (*STC*), comp. Pollard and Redgrave (London: Bibliographical Soc., 1926, 609 pp.), by adding some 10,000 entries, including fuller transcriptions of titles, and providing considerably expanded bibliographical detail and helpful cross-references. (For a full account of the revision and the history of *STC* and *RSTC*, see the preface to vol. 1 and "*STC*: The Scholar's Vademecum," *Book Collector* 33 [1984]: 273–304.) As far as possible, *RSTC* retains the *STC* numbers, which have become the standard of reference for printed works of the period.

Entries, based largely on personal examination of copies or extensive correspondence with librarians and scholars, are arranged by author; corporate heading (with extensive sections such as "England" or "Liturgies" clearly subdivided); or, for anonymous works, by author's initials, proper noun or adjective, or first noun. (See vol. 1, pp. xxx-xxxi for a fuller explanation of the handling of anonymous works. A useful aid to locating entries for attributed works in English is Halkett, *Dictionary of Anonymous and Pseudonymous Publications* [5110], which includes *RSTC* references as well as a concordance of *RSTC* numbers.) A typical entry includes author, title, format, imprint, Stationers' Register entry, locations, references to standard bibliographies, and editorial information (which offers sometimes extensive bibliographical detail and references to scholarship). Each volume concludes with a list of additions and corrections, which will be cumulated, along with additional ones, in vol. 3. Users should study the admirably clear explanation of parts of an entry and procedures in the introduction to vol. 1.

Each entry lists up to five locations in Europe (principally in the British Isles) and five in North America (primarily), Australia, or New Zealand. A plus sign signifies that additional copies are known. Most locations are institutions or libraries, although a few private collections are listed. For the location "Private Owner," a query addressed to the secretary of the (London) Bibliographical Society will be forwarded to the owner. (For the secretary's address, see the current issue of *Library* [5310].) Additional locations for entries in the *STC* may be found in William Warner Bishop, comp., *A Checklist of American Copies of* Short-Title Catalogue *Books*, 2nd ed. (Ann Arbor: U of Michigan P, 1950, 201 pp.), and David Ramage, comp., *A Finding-List of English Books to 1640 in Libraries in the British Isles (Excluding the National Libraries and the Libraries of Oxford and Cambridge)* (Durham, Eng.: Council of the Durham Colls., 1958, 101 pp.). Scholars seeking further locations should send a letter listing *all* locations known to them to the *STC* office, Houghton

Library, Harvard University, Cambridge, MA 02138. Researchers should also note that most *STC* works are being made available on microfilm through *Early English Books, 1475–1640* (Ann Arbor: University Microfilms International). Reels are indexed by *STC* numbers, some of which are changed in *RSTC*. Under discussion is a machine-readable union catalog, 1475–1800, that would expand and edit *RSTC* and Wing entries and combine them with ESTC (2230) and NAIP (4010) records. For details, see Henry L. Snyder, "The English Short Title Catalogue," *Papers of the Bibliographical Society of America* 82 (1988): 333–36.

Until the index of printers and booksellers appears in vol. 3, consult Paul G. Morrison, *Index of Printers, Publishers, and Booksellers*, 2nd impression with corrections (Charlottesville: Bibliographical Soc. of the U of Virginia, 1961, 82 pp.). Philip R. Rider is preparing a chronological index (a printout of entries in vol. 2 is on deposit in several research libraries). Some title access is offered by A. F. Allison and V. F. Goldsmith, *Titles of English Books (and of Foreign Books Printed in England): An Alphabetical Finding-List by Title of Books Published under the Author's Name, Pseudonym, or Initials*, vol. 1: *1475–1640* (Hamden: Archon-Shoe String, 1976, 176 pp.). This source must be used with care, however, since it omits anonymous works and is based on unauthorized use of an unrevised draft of vol. 1 and proof of vol. 2 of *RSTC*. (For details, see the review by Peter Davison, *Library* 5th ser. 31 [1976]: 273.) Writers of prefatory matter and dedicatees are indexed in Franklin B. Williams, Jr., *Index of Dedications and Commendatory Verses in English Books before 1641* (London: Bibliographical Soc., 1962, 256 pp.), and "Dedications and Verses through 1640: Addenda," a 19-page supplement printed at the end of *Library* 5th ser. 30.1 (1975). Works of American interest are identified in Jackson Campbell Boswell, *A Check List of Americana in* A Short-Title Catalogue of Books Printed in England, Scotland, and Ireland and of English Books Printed Abroad, 1475–1640, Supplement to *Early American Literature* 9.2 (1974), 124 pp.

RSTC is the indispensable source for identifying and locating extant works (and various editions, issues, variants, and impressions). Exemplary thoroughness in searching out material and precision in its analysis make the *RSTC* one of the truly monumental reference works. Like its predecessor, *RSTC* is the essential basis for scholarship of the period. Continued by Wing, *Short-Title Catalogue, 1641–1700* (1995). Reviews: (vol. 1) *Book Collector* 35 (1986): 417–30; Arthur Freeman, *TLS: Times Literary Supplement* 13 Feb. 1987: 170; Freeman, *Library* 6th ser. 9 (1987): 289–92; (vol. 2): R. C. Alston, *Papers of the Bibliographical Society of America* 71 (1977): 391–95; James L. Harner, *Seventeenth-Century News* 36 (1978): 24–25; David Rogers, *TLS: Times Literary Supplement* 27 Aug. 1976: 1061; William P. Williams, *Review* 1 (1979): 249–54.

A useful complement is M. A. Shaaber, *Check-List of Works by British Authors Printed Abroad, in Languages Other Than English, to 1641* (New York: Bibliographical Soc. of America, 1975, 168 pp.).

1995 Wing, Donald, comp. *Short-Title Catalogue of Books Printed in England, Scotland, Ireland, Wales, and British America and of English Books Printed in Other Countries, 1641–1700* (Wing). 2nd ed., rev. and enl. New York: MLA, 1972– . Z2002.W52 015.42.

Vol. 1: *A1–E2926*. 1972. 622 pp. A revised edition is in progress.
Vol. 2: *E2927–O1000*. Ed. Timothy J. Crist. 1982. 690 pp.
Vol. 3: *P1–Z28*. Ed. John J. Morrison et al. 1988. 766 pp.

(Additional volumes, which will consist of title, chronological, printer, publisher, and bookseller indexes, are in preparation.)

Continues the *Short-Title Catalogue* (1990), employing the same basic organization but providing less comprehensive coverage and much less bibliographical detail. Like *RSTC*, Wing is an enumerative bibliography of extant works printed in the British Isles and North America, and in English elsewhere in the world. Vols. 2 and 3 do include a few unique items destroyed during World War II; other than annuals, periodicals, which are listed in Nelson, *British Newspapers and Periodicals* (2060), are excluded.

Works are entered by author, corporate author, or title of anonymous work. Until the volume with the title index appears, the title index in *Accessing* Early English Books (see below) provides some help in locating anonymous works, those listed by corporate author, and ones for which a researcher knows only the title; *Dictionary of Concealed Authorship* (5110) will cite Wing references.

A typical entry provides author, short title, imprint, format, references to standard bibliographies, and locations. Researchers should note that "anr. ed." (another edition) refers indiscriminately to edition, issue, or state, and "var." merely indicates that undifferentiated variants exist. The revised vol. 3 provides somewhat fuller descriptions and is more precise in identifying editions and variants. There are occasional duplicate entries.

Up to 10 copies are located in libraries and a few private collections: five in the British Isles, and five in North America (primarily), New Zealand, Australia, or the Continent. (Several entries actually provide more than 10 locations.) Additions and corrections are printed in *Studies in Bibliography* 29 (1976): 386–87; 30 (1977): 276–80; 31 (1978): 266–71; and in works listed in vol. 1, p. ix. Like *RSTC*, Wing is not a census of copies; however, information on additional locations—as well as some details of bibliographical references, provenance, and auction records—can be obtained by writing the editor (Wing *STC* Revision Project, Yale U Library, Box 1603A, New Haven, CT 06520).

The revised vol. 1 (which eventually will be published in a further revised edition) must be used cautiously because of serious flaws arising from the reassignment of 7–8% of the original numbers which serve as standard references in bibliographies, catalogs, studies, and editions, and are essential to locating microfilmed works in University Microfilms International's *Early English Books, 1641–1700* collection. Several entries were cancelled without notice or moved without cross-reference, and typographical errors abound. These problems are not fully redressed by the list of changes in vol. 2, pp. 669–90. Vol. 2 seldom reassigns numbers and vol. 3 never does; both scrupulously note cancelled or moved entries.

The Wing *STC* has spawned a number of useful supplementary works:

Accessing Early English Books, 1641–1700: *A Cumulative Index to Units 1–32 of the Microfilm Collection*. 4 vols. Ann Arbor: University Microfilms International, 1981–82. Author, title, subject, and reel-position-Wing number indexes to the first 25,000 titles in the microfilm collection. The title index expands the short titles in Wing and is sometimes useful in locating anonymous works in the catalog; the subject index, based on Library of Congress headings, is not adequate for most narrow subject searches. The indexes must be used with the original edition of vol. 1. The handlists to the later microfilm units are not indexed. Works filmed are being cataloged in the MARC data base (235a) and are searchable through OCLC (225).

Allison, A. F., and V. F. Goldsmith. *Titles of English Books (and of Foreign Books Printed in England): An Alphabetical Finding-List by Title of Books Published under the Author's Name, Pseudonym, or Initials.* Vol. 2: *1641–1700.* Hamden: Archon-Shoe String, 1977. 318 pp. Only marginally useful because of the exclusion of anonymous works and the failure to include many entries in the revised vol. 1. Better title access to many entries is offered by the title index to *Accessing* Early English Books.

Morrison, Paul G. *Index of Printers, Publishers, and Booksellers in Donald Wing's* Short-Title Catalogue. Charlottesville: U of Virginia P, for the Bibliographical Soc. of the U of Virginia, 1955. 217 pp. The *Index* must be used with the original edition of vol. 1, and will eventually be superseded by indexes printed in the revised edition.

Wing, Donald. *A Gallery of Ghosts: Books Published between 1641–1700 Not Found in the* Short-Title Catalogue. New York: Index Committee of the MLA, 1967. 225 pp. A catalog of works and editions listed in bibliographies and dealers' or auction catalogs but not identified or located. Those found are incorporated in the revised edition.

Despite its faults, Wing is an essential guide to the identification and location of works published during the period. Although Wing has had a major impact on scholarship, scholars now need a catalog that will equal the *RSTC* (1990) and *ESTC* (2230) in coverage and sophistication. Entries are now being computer-stored to produce title, chronological, and printer, publisher, or bookseller indexes and to provide a convenient means of correcting, adding, and expanding entries in a subsequent edition. Under discussion is a machine-readable union catalog, 1475–1800, that would expand and edit *RSTC* and Wing entries and combine them with *ESTC* (2230) and NAIP (4010) records. For details, see Henry L. Snyder, "The English Short Title Catalogue," *Papers of the Bibliographical Society of America* 82 (1988): 333–36.

For an account of the compilation of the first edition, see Donald G. Wing, "The Making of the *Short-Title Catalogue, 1641–1700*," *Papers of the Bibliographical Society of America* 45 (1951): 59–69; for the revision, see Timothy Christ [i.e., Crist], "The Wing *STC* Revision Project: A Progress Report," *Literary Research Newsletter* 4 (1979): 67–72.

Reviews: (vol. 1) *TLS: Times Literary Supplement* 26 Jan. 1973: 100 (and the subsequent correspondence by James M. Osborn and the reviewer, 23 Mar.: 325; and Peter Grant, 6 Apr.: 395); B. J. McMullin, *Papers of the Bibliographical Society of America* 72 (1978): 435–54 (with a reply by Timothy J. Crist, 73 [1979]: 273–75); (vol. 2) D. F. McKenzie, *TLS: Times Literary Supplement* 17 Dec. 1982: 1403; Alexandra Mason, *Papers of the Bibliographical Society of America* 80 (1986): 255–62.

2000 *A Transcript of the Registers of the Company of Stationers of London, 1554–1640 A.D.* Ed. Edward Arber. 5 vols. London and Birmingham: Privately printed, 1875–1894. Z2002.S79 655.442.

An edited transcript of part of the surviving records relating to the ownership of written works or to members of the company, as well as a number of miscellaneous documents. (See entry 1380 for a discussion of the records of the company.) Of principal interest to literary scholars are the registers of copies entered and records of fines for unlawful printing. In the registers, entries are listed chronologically according to the Old Style calendar and include the member entering the work (or being fined), a descriptive "title" (sometimes accompanied by the author's name), and registration fee. (For the typographical distinctions of parts of an entry, see vol. 1, pp. 27–30.) Users must remember that (1) the registers are records of ownership claims by members of the company; (2) they were never intended as a record of authorized publication; (3) an entry does not automatically mean the work actually existed at that date; (4) many works entered were never published (or intended to be, as in the case of "blocking entries" used to prevent unauthorized printing of plays) or are no longer extant; (5) many works were printed with a different title; (6) sometimes a year or more elapsed between entry and publication; (7) later editions, unless a transfer of ownership occurred, were typically not entered; (8) a considerable number of works actually printed were never entered; (9) Register B and Arber's transcript of it includes entries forged by John Payne Collier (see Franklin Dickey, "The Old Man at Work: Forgeries in the Stationers' Registers," *Shakespeare Quarterly* 11 [1960]: 39–47).

Because the *Transcript* is incomplete, confusingly organized, and inadequately indexed, it must be supplemented by the following:

Short-Title Catalogue (1990), which includes references to entries in the register and thus serves as a handy index to extant publications that were entered.

Greg, *Bibliography of the English Printed Drama* (2135), which prints a superior transcription of all entries relating to the drama.

Greg, W. W., ed. *A Companion to Arber: Being a Calendar of Documents in Edward Arber's* Transcript. . . . Oxford: Clarendon, 1967. 451 pp. A calendar and index to the illustrative documents scattered haphazardly through the *Transcript*, as well as documents from other sources.

Greg, W. W., and E. Boswell, eds. *Records of the Court of the Stationers' Company, 1576 to 1602, from Register B.* London: Bibliographical Soc., 1930. 144 pp.

Jackson, William A., ed. *Records of the Court of the Stationers' Company, 1602 to 1640.* London: Bibliographical Soc., 1957. 555 pp. This and the preceding work transcribe documents Arber was not allowed to publish.

Rollins, Hyder E., comp. *An Analytical Index to the Ballad-Entries (1557–1709) in the Registers of the Company of Stationers of London.* 1924. Rpt., with some corrections in a foreword by Leslie Shepard. Hatboro: Tradition, 1976. 324 pp.

Of major value would be a published index to the early records.

Despite its faults, the *Transcript* offers the most convenient access to records essential for identifying lost works, researching publishing history, and dating composition (but the evidence must be carefully evaluated, since entry in the register establishes only a possible terminus ad quem for composition and only a possible terminus a quo for publication). Some research will require the use of the original records at Stationers' Hall or the microfilm (1380a). For a description of the records and a useful annotated list of published and unpublished catalogs, indexes, and transcripts, see Robin Myers, "The Records of the Worshipful Company of Stationers and Newspaper Makers (1554–1912)," *Archives* 16 (1983): 28–38 (rpt. *Publishing History* 13 [1983]: 89–104).

2005 *A Transcript of the Registers of the Worshipful Company of Stationers from 1640–1708 A.D.* [Ed. George Edward Briscoe Eyre, Charles Robert Rivington, and Henry Robert Plomer.] 3 vols. London: Privately printed, 1913–14. PR1105.R7.

A transcript that continues the 1554–1640 *Transcript* (2000) to March 1709 and employs the same typographic conventions to print entries. See entry 2000 for a discussion of the organization and use of the registers and entry 1380 for the records of the Stationers' Company. Fortunately for scholars, the *Transcript* has been indexed by printers, publishers, authors, editors, translators, compilers, and titles in William P. Williams, ed., *Index to the Stationers Register, 1640–1708: Being an Index to* A Transcript of the Registers of the Worshipful Company of Stationers from 1640–1708 A.D., *Edited by Eyre, Rivington, and Plomer (1913–1914)* (La Jolla: McGilvery, 1980, 67 pp. and 2 microfiche). Ballad entries are indexed in Rollins, *Analytical Index to the Ballad-Entries* (2000a).

See also

New Cambridge Bibliography of English Literature, vol. 1: *600–1660* (2035).

Guides to Scholarship and Criticism

SURVEYS OF RESEARCH

2010 "Recent Studies in the English Renaissance." *English Literary Renaissance* (entry 2065) 1 (1971)– .

Most issues of *English Literary Renaissance* conclude with a survey of recent research on an author, topic, or group of related works from 1485 to 1674. Modeled on those in Logan and Smith (2145) and based on *MLAIB* (335), *ABELL* (340), and *Year's Work in English Studies* (330), the surveys typically examine biographical and general works, editions, studies of special topics and individual works, canon and text, and the current state of scholarship. Each survey concludes with a bibliography of works not discussed in the text. Coverage and evaluation vary with the individual contributor, but the general quality is high and the series treats a number of authors who are not the subject of a more comprehensive author bibliography. The individual surveys are conveniently indexed in *MLAIB* (335), *ABELL* (340), and *Bibliographie internationale de l'Humanisme et de la Renaissance* (2025), and are available as separate reprints.

2015 "Recent Studies in the English Renaissance." *Studies in English Literature, 1500–1900* (entry 1485) 1 (1961)– . Annually in the winter issue.

A commissioned survey by an established scholar of studies on nondramatic literature, with recent ones emphasizing full-length critical and historical works. (The drama is covered in the spring issue [2150].) The essays vary considerably in soundness and rigor of assessment. Although it is the most current annual survey, the work is generally limited to books submitted for review and must be supplemented by the chapters in *Year's Work in English Studies* (330) on the nondramatic literature of the period.

Broader authoritative surveys include the following:

Hamilton, A. C. "The Modern Study of Renaissance English Literature: A Critical Survey." *Modern Language Quarterly* 26 (1965): 150–83.

Schoeck, Richard J. "English Literature." *The Present State of Scholarship in Sixteenth-Century Literature*. Ed. William M. Jones. Columbia: U of Missouri P, 1978. 111–68.

Summers, Joseph H. "Notes on Recent Studies in English Literature of the Earlier Seventeenth Century." *Modern Language Quarterly* 26 (1965): 135–49.

Tuve, Rosemond. "Critical Survey of Scholarship in the Field of English Literature of the Renaissance." *Studies in Philology* 40 (1943): 204–55.

See also

"Review of English Renaissance Textual Studies," *Manuscripta* (305).

YWES (330): Chapters for Sixteenth Century: Excluding Drama after 1550; Shakespeare; Renaissance Drama: Excluding Shakespeare; Earlier Seventeenth Century: Excluding Drama; Milton.

SERIAL BIBLIOGRAPHIES

2020 "Shakespeare: Annotated World Bibliography for [1949–]." *Shakespeare Quarterly* 1 (1950)– . PR2885.S63 822.3'3.

An annotated bibliography of Shakespearean scholarship and productions that lists a significant number of works important to Renaissance literature generally. The international coverage encompasses books, articles, dissertations, productions, films, and reviews of the foregoing—in short, anything that is related to the study of Shakespeare. The bibliography is currently organized in two divisions: general Shakespeareana and studies of particular works. The first includes classified sections for festschriften and collections, bibliographies, biography and milieu, editions, reference works, textual studies, language, Shakespeare and his stage, productions and stage history, conferences and colloquia, and general studies. The second has classified sections for apocrypha, genres, and individual works. Most entries are now descriptively annotated. Four indexes: scholars; theater people; writers and other individuals; subjects. The extensive coverage, clear organization, and thorough indexing make this work the indispensable bibliography of Shakespeare studies and an important guide to scholarship on Renaissance literature generally.

The annual bibliographies for 1949–57 are incorporated into Smith (see below). Two annual surveys that complement the "World Bibliography" are "The Year's Contributions to Shakespearian Study" (*Shakespeare Survey* 1 [1948]–) and the Shakespeare chapter in *Year's Work in English Studies* (330). Earlier studies are listed in the following:

Ebisch, Walther, and Levin L. Schücking. *A Shakespeare Bibliography*. Oxford: Clarendon, 1931. 294 pp.

———. *Supplement for the Years 1930–1935 to* A Shakespeare Bibliography. Oxford: Clarendon, 1937. 104 pp.

Smith, Gordon Ross. *A Classified Shakespeare Bibliography, 1936–1958.* University Park: Pennsylvania State UP, 1963. 784 pp.

The Cumulative Shakespeare Bibliography, ed. Harrison T. Meserole (in progress) will cumulate and augment the above from 1900–79 in printed bibliographies for 1900–57 and 1958–79, as well as a data base that will accommodate custom searches. On the planning and organization, see Harrison T. Meserole and John B. Smith, " 'Yet there is method in it': *The Cumulative Shakespeare Bibliography*: A Product of Project Planning in the Humanities," *Editing, Publishing, and Computer Technology*, ed. Sharon Butler and William P. Stoneman (New York: AMS, 1988) 65–80. The best selective bibliography of Shakespeare scholarship is Larry S. Champion, *The Essential Shakespeare: An Annotated Bibliography of Major Modern Studies*, Reference Publication in Literature (Boston: Hall, 1986, 463 pp.).

2025 *Bibliographie internationale de l'Humanisme et de la Renaissance* (*BIHR*). Genève: Droz, 1966– . Annual. Z6207.R4.B5 016.9402'1.

An international, interdisciplinary bibliography of scholarship on all aspects of Humanism and the Renaissance that continues and expands "Bibliographie des articles relatifs à l'histoire de l'Humanisme et de la Renaissance [1956–64]," *Bibliothèque d'Humanisme et Renaissance* 20–27 (1958–65). Coverage in *BIHR* begins with 1963. Entries are currently organized in seven divisions: studies of individuals and anonymous works; general studies; history (including political, social, and economic history, and geography); religion, philosophy, politics, and law; general literary studies, linguistics, and bibliography; the arts (including music and dance); science and technology. Except in the first division, which is organized alphabetically by writer, historical personage, or anonymous work, studies are grouped by country or geographical area, then listed alphabetically by author. Two indexes: scholars; writers and other individuals not separately classified in the first division. Researchers would benefit from a more refined classification system and greater currency (the lag is currently four years). Although coverage of British literature is overall not as thorough as in *MLAIB* (335) or *ABELL* (340), the interdisciplinary scope and more extensive survey of European publications make *BIHR* an essential complement to these standard serial bibliographies.

For a discussion of the editorial difficulties which have beset *BIHR* and the unsuccessful attempt to establish an *Annual Bibliography of Early Modern Europe*, see John B. Dillon, "Renaissance Bibliography in the Electronic Age: Recent Work on a Computer-Produced Annual Bibliography of Studies on Early Modern Europe," *Collection Development* 6.1–2 (1984): 217–26.

2030 "Literature of the Renaissance in [1917–68]: A Bibliography." *Studies in Philology* (entry 1490) 14–66 (1917–69).

An annual bibliography originally limited to English literature but expanded in vol. 36 (1939) to encompass French, Germanic, Italian, Spanish, and Portuguese literature. At its demise, coverage was international and included dissertations and some reviews as well as books and articles. Entries in the English division are listed by author in nine sections: general; history, manners, and customs; drama and stage; Shakespeare; nondramatic literature; More; Spenser; Donne; Milton. Indexed by persons. Although never comprehensive, it includes many works omitted from the other standard bibliographies such as *MLAIB* (335) and *ABELL* (340).

See also

Secs. G: Serial Bibliographies, Indexes, and Abstracts; and H: Guides to Dissertations and Theses.

ABELL (340): English Literature/Sixteenth Century and Seventeenth Century sections.
"Abstracts of Recent Articles," *Seventeenth-Century News* (2080).
MLAIB (335): English Language and Literature division in the volumes for 1921–25; English VII and VIII in the volumes for 1926–56; English VI and VII in the volumes for 1957–80; and English Literature/1500–1599 and 1600–1699 sections (as well as any other larger chronological section encompassing either century) in the later volumes. Researchers must also check the headings beginning "English Literature" in the subject index to post-1980 volumes.
Progress of Medieval and Renaissance Studies (1835a).
"Renaissance Books," *Renaissance Quarterly* (2075).

OTHER BIBLIOGRAPHIES

2035 *The New Cambridge Bibliography of English Literature* (*NCBEL*). Vol. 1: *600–1660*. Ed. George Watson. Cambridge: Cambridge UP, 1974. 2,476 cols. Z2011.N45 [PR83] 016.82.

(For a full discussion of *NCBEL*, see entry 1385.) The part devoted to Renaissance literature (1500–1660) has seven divisions, each subdivided and classified as its subject requires: introduction (general works, literary relations with the Continent, book production and distribution); poetry (general works, Tudor poetry, Elizabethan sonnet, minor Tudor poetry, Jacobean and Caroline poetry, Milton, minor Jacobean and Caroline poetry, emblem books, epigrams and formal satire, song books); drama (general works, theaters and actors, Puritan attack on the stage, moralities, early comedies, early tragedies, later Elizabethan drama, minor Elizabethan drama, Shakespeare, Jacobean and Caroline drama, minor Jacobean and Caroline drama, university plays); religion (Humanists and reformers, English Bible, Prayer Book, versions of the Psalms, sermons and devotional writings, Richard Hooker, Marprelate controversy, Caroline divines); popular and miscellaneous prose (pamphleteers and miscellaneous writers, minor popular literature, character books and essays, prose fiction, news sheets and newsbooks, travel, translations into English); history, philosophy, science and other forms of learning (historians, biographers, and antiquaries; letters, diaries, autobiographies, and biographies; economics and politics; law; scholarship; literary criticism; philosophy; science; education); and Scottish literature (general works, poetry and drama, prose). The general introduction for the volume as a whole lists bibliographies, histories, anthologies, and works about prosody, prose rhythm, and language important to the study of the Renaissance period. Vol. 1 of the *Cambridge Bibliography of English Literature* (1385a) is still occasionally useful for its coverage of the social and political background (which *NCBEL* drops).

Users must familiarize themselves with the organization, remember that there is considerable unevenness of coverage among subdivisions, and consult the index volume (vol. 5) rather than the provisional index in vol. 1. Despite its shortcomings (see entry 1385), *NCBEL* offers the best general coverage of both primary and secondary works for the study of Renaissance literature, but it must be supplemented by the other works in this section and by *MLAIB* (335), *ABELL* (340), and *Year's Work in English Studies* (330). Review: Fred C. Robinson, *Anglia* 97 (1979): 511–17.

The best selective bibliographies remain the following volumes in the

Goldentree Bibliographies in Language and Literature series: John L. Lievsay, comp., *The Sixteenth Century: Skelton through Hooker* (New York: Appleton, 1968, 132 pp.); and Arthur E. Barker, comp., *The Seventeenth Century: Bacon through Marvell* (Arlington Heights: AHM, 1979, 132 pp.). Each is badly dated, however.

2040 Tannenbaum, Samuel A., and Dorothy R. Tannenbaum. *Elizabethan Bibliographies*. 10 vols. Port Washington: Kennikat, 1967. Z2012.T3 016.8208'003.

A convenient reprint of the 41 volumes and seven supplements privately printed in limited numbers between 1937 and 1950. The individual volumes—devoted to a variety of Renaissance writers, some of Shakespeare's works, and Mary Stuart—vary in organization but typically include sections for editions, selections, biography and commentary, and bibliography. Indexed by person and subject. The highly abbreviated entries rarely transcribe a title exactly, include a number of inessential passing notices, and are replete with errors.

The Tannenbaums also compiled the annual "Shakespeare and His Contemporaries (A Classified Bibliography for [1925–48])," *Shakespeare Association Bulletin* 1–24 (1924–45), which supplements their Elizabethan Bibliographies series. Many of the volumes are updated and new authors added in *Elizabethan Bibliographies Supplements*, gen. ed. Charles A. Pennel, 17 vols. (London: Nether, 1967–71). Entries are listed chronologically and indexed by scholar and title.

The Tannenbaum and Pennel volumes are convenient starting points for research on a writer who has not been the subject of a recent author bibliography. Neither series, however, offers comprehensive coverage.

See also

Kallendorf, *Latin Influences on English Literature from the Middle Ages to the Eighteenth Century* (4895).

RELATED TOPICS

2045 Davies, Godfrey, ed. *Bibliography of British History: Stuart Period, 1603–1714*. Ed. Mary Frear Keeler. 2nd ed. Oxford: Clarendon, 1970. 734 pp. Z2018.D25 016.9142.

An extensive, albeit selective, bibliography of primary and secondary materials published for the most part before 1963. Entries are organized in 15 classified divisions: general reference works, politics, constitutional history, law, ecclesiastical history, military history, naval history, economics, social history, cultural history (e.g., fine arts, music, science, and education), local history, colonization, Wales, Scotland, and Ireland. Annotations are largely descriptive, with frequent references to related studies, but many entries lack annotation. Indexed by persons and subjects. The authoritative guide to historical studies on the period and a valuable resource for cross-disciplinary research. Review: J. P. Cooper, *English Historical Review* 89 (1974): 118–22.

A useful supplement because of its pointed evaluations and inclusion of works published to mid-1979 is J. S. Morrill, *Seventeenth-Century Britain, 1603–1714*,

Critical Bibliographies in Modern History (Folkestone: Dawson; Hamden: Archon-Shoe String, 1980, 189 pp.). Coverage is highly selective and for articles does not extend before 1957.

2050 Read, Conyers, ed. *Bibliography of British History: Tudor Period, 1485–1603.* 2nd ed. Oxford: Clarendon, 1959. 624 pp. Z2018.R28 016.94205.

An extensive, albeit rigorously selective, bibliography of primary and secondary materials published largely before 1 January 1957. Entries are organized in 14 classified divisions: general studies (including reference works); political history; constitutional history; political theory; law; ecclesiastical history; economics; discovery, exploration, and colonization; military and naval history; cultural and social history (e.g., education, music, science, and fine arts); local history; Scotland; Ireland; and Wales. Several annotations are helpfully evaluative or refer to related studies; unfortunately, many entries are inadequately annotated or not at all. Indexed by persons and subjects (with several errors in the indexing). The authoritative guide to historical studies on the period and a valuable resource for cross-disciplinary research.

A very selective but useful supplement with coverage through 1 September 1966 is Mortimer Levine, *Tudor England, 1485–1603*, Conference on British Studies Bibliographical Handbooks (Cambridge: Cambridge UP, 1968, 115 pp.), with frequent brief but pointed annotations.

See also

Annual Bibliography of British and Irish History (1400).

Language

DICTIONARIES

2055 *Early Modern English Dictionary, 1475–1700.* In progress.

A historical dictionary that will offer more extensive coverage of early modern English than the *OED* (1410). Although actual editing will await completion of the *Middle English Dictionary* (1860), many citations are accessible in the Michigan Early Modern English Material (MEMEM) data base (which can be purchased from the Oxford University Computing Service Text Archive) and in Richard W. Bailey et al., *Michigan Early Modern English Materials* (Ann Arbor: Xerox University Microfilms, 1975, microfiche), an index to some 38,000 citations. Bailey has also edited *Early Modern English: Additions and Antedatings to the Record of English Vocabulary 1475–1700* (Hildesheim: Olms, 1978, 367 pp.), which is based on MEMEM materials. For a history of the project, see Richard W. Bailey, "Charles C. Fries and the *Early Modern English Dictionary*," *Toward an Understanding of Language: Charles Carpenter Fries in Perspective*, ed. Peter Howard Fries, Amsterdam Studies in the Theory and History of Linguistic Science, Ser. 4: Current Issues in Linguistic Theory 40 (Amsterdam: Benjamins, 1985) 171–204.

See also

Dictionary of Medieval Latin from British Sources (1700).

Biographical Dictionaries

The *Dictionary of National Biography* (1425) remains the standard general source of biographical information for the period. Additional details, especially about less prominent individuals, may be found in Mark Eccles, *Brief Lives: Tudor and Stuart Authors*, Texts and Studies, 1982, *Studies in Philology* 79.4 (1982): 135 pp.; and J. W. Saunders, *A Biographical Dictionary of Renaissance Poets and Dramatists, 1520–1650* (Brighton: Harvester; Totowa: Barnes, 1983, 216 pp.). The latter suffers from a lack of balance and numerous errors. Neither fulfills the need for a reliable and thorough biographical dictionary of Renaissance authors.

See

Dictionary of Literary Biography (600).
Ruoff, *Crowell's Handbook of Elizabethan and Stuart Literature* (1980).

Periodicals

GUIDES TO PRIMARY WORKS

2060 Nelson, Carolyn, and Matthew Seccombe, comps. *British Newspapers and Periodicals, 1641–1700: A Short-Title Catalogue of Serials Printed in England, Scotland, Ireland, and North America*. Index Society Fund Publications. New York: MLA, 1987. 724 pp. Z6956.G6.N44 [PN5115] 015.41034.

An enumerative bibliography and finding list of extant issues of serials printed between 1641 and 1700, with a supplementary checklist extending coverage through March 1702. The approximately 700 titles encompass newspapers, newsbooks, miscellanies, official journals, trade bulletins, and other publications with numbered or dated issues bearing uniform titles and formats and published at intervals of less than a year. (Annuals are included in Wing, *Short-Title Catalogue* [1995].) The serials are organized alphabetically by title of the first number, followed by issues in chronological order, with separate entries for different editions or versions; variant, general, and later titles are thoroughly cross-referenced to main entries. Preceding the list of issues is a headnote that includes, when known, variant titles, inclusive dates, format, average length of issue, frequency, price, author or editor, notes on variants, and references to standard bibliographies. The entry for an issue cites, when appropriate, title, volume number, issue number, date (in New Style), imprint, variants, standard bibliographies, and up to twenty locations (with those in the British Isles to the left of the semicolon, and those elsewhere in the world to the right). An extensive appendix on variants identifies different typesettings of selected serials after June 1642; variants in earlier publications are described in the main list. Descriptions are based on personal examination of at least one copy of nearly every issue. Six indexes: chronological by month; publishers and printers; editors and authors; subjects; places of publication other than London; foreign languages. Users must be certain to study the full explanation of organization and editorial policies and remember that, like Wing, this work is not a census of copies and that the identification of authors and editors is based on *New Cambridge Bibliography of English Literature* (2035 and 2255), which is not trustworthy in many of its ascriptions. The first reliable guide to the identification and location of issues, *British Newspapers and Periodicals* provides the necessary groundwork for further bibliographical investigations and studies of authorship, editorship, and content.

For a preliminary analysis of publishing practices, along with suggestions for further research on serial publications, see Nelson and Seccombe, *Periodical Publications, 1641–1700: A Survey with Illustrations*, Occasional Papers of the Bibliographical Society 2 (London: Bibliographical Soc., 1986, 109 pp.).

GUIDES TO SCHOLARSHIP AND CRITICISM

See

Linton, *Newspaper Press in Britain* (1455).
Weed, *Studies of British Newspapers and Periodicals* (2285).

SCHOLARLY JOURNALS

Many journals in sections K: Periodicals/Scholarly Journals and M: English Literature/General/Periodicals/Scholarly Journals publish articles on Renaissance literature.

2065 *English Literary Renaissance* (*ELR*). 1971– . 3/yr. PR1.E43 820.9'002.

Publishes essays, edited texts, surveys of research, and occasional special issues on literature from 1485 to 1674. Of particular note is "Recent Studies in the English Renaissance" (2010), a survey of research and bibliography on an author, group of works, or topic that concludes nearly every issue. Annual index (with abstracts). Although a relative newcomer, *ELR* has established a reputation for publishing quality scholarship.

2070 *Renaissance and Reformation/Renaissance et Réforme* (*Ren&R*). 1964– . Quarterly. Former title: *Renaissance and Reformation: A Bulletin for Scholars in the Toronto Area* (1964–69). CB359.R45 [PN720] 940.2'1.

Publishes articles and reviews on all aspects of the European Renaissance and Reformation, with emphasis on literature and history. Annual index; cumulative index: vols. 1–3 (n.d., 4 pp.).

2075 *Renaissance Quarterly* (*RenQ*). 1948– . Quarterly. Former title: *Renaissance News* (1948–66). CB361.R45 940.

Publishes articles and reviews on all aspects of the European Renaissance (emphasizing history and literature), with typically more than half of an issue devoted to reviews. Each issue from 5.2 to 33.4 (1954–74) prints a list of "Renaissance Books" compiled from national bibliographies and volumes submitted for review. The annual *Studies in the Renaissance* (1954–74) was subsumed in *RenQ* with 28.4 (1975).

Annual index since vol. 26 (1973); earlier volumes are cumulatively indexed every two or three years.

2080 *Seventeenth-Century News* (*SCN*). 1942– . Quarterly. Former title: *Seventeenth Century News Letter* (1942–50). PR1.S47.

Publishes reviews and occasional brief articles on all aspects of seventeenth-century culture in Europe and North America, with an emphasis on British and American literature and history. Each issue since 6.3 (1948) includes a highly selective "Abstracts of Recent Articles"; a separate section of "American Abstracts" began in 45.3 (1987). Beginning with 12.2 (1954), *SCN* incorporates *Neo-Latin News*, which reviews scholarship on Latin literature since 1500.

See also

Studies in English Literature, 1500–1900 (1485).
Studies in Philology (1490).

Background Reading

The chapter on the Renaissance (pp. 54–100) in Bateson, *Guide to English and American Literature* (85) offers a good overview of important background studies. See also the surveys of research in entries 2010 and 2015.

2085 Tillyard, E. M. W. *The Elizabethan World Picture*. New York: Macmillan, 1944. 108 pp. PR428.P5.T5 820.903.

An explanation of the commonplaces regarding human, political, and cosmic order that underlie much of Renaissance literature. The discussions of order, sin, the great chain of being, correspondences between the macrocosm and microcosm, and the cosmic dance are admirably clear; however, Tillyard's overall model is not so readily accepted as it once was.

Complemented by Lewis, *Discarded Image* (1900). The great chain of being is more exhaustively explored in Arthur O. Lovejoy, *The Great Chain of Being: A Study of the History of an Idea* (Cambridge: Harvard UP, 1936, 382 pp.), which remains a classic in the history of ideas. Related topics are given straightforward explanations in Isabel Rivers, *Classical and Christian Ideas in English Renaissance Poetry: A Students' Guide* (London: Allen, 1979, 231 pp.). A corrective to the simplifications of Tillyard and useful synthesis of the relationship between literature and society, religion, education, the court, and views of nature is Julia Briggs, *This Stage-Play World: English Literature and Its Background, 1580–1625*, OPUS Book (Oxford: Oxford UP, 1983, 225 pp.).

See also

Oxford History of England (1495).

Genres

FICTION

Histories and Surveys

2090 Salzman, Paul. *English Prose Fiction, 1558–1700: A Critical History*. Oxford: Clarendon, 1985. 391 pp. PR836.S24 823'.3'09.

A critical history of the development of prose fiction, organized by genre or type and including an extended critical analysis of at least one example of each. Concludes with a two-part bibliography of extant works: pt. 1 is an author list of Elizabethan fiction; pt. 2 classifies seventeenth-century fiction in 25 types. Although the bibliography is not comprehensive, it does complement Mish, *English Prose Fiction* (2095) and O'Dell, *Chronological List of Prose Fiction* (2100). Indexed by persons, genres, and titles (but with some inconsistencies in the last). Salzman is by far the best survey, with especially perceptive treatment of seventeenth-century fiction. Reviews: Jerry C. Beasley, *Studies in the Novel* 17 (1985): 303–10; John J. O'Connor, *Renaissance Quarterly* 39 (1986): 130–32.

For fiction before 1558, Margaret Schlauch, *Antecedents of the English Novel, 1400–1600 (from Chaucer to Deloney)* (Warszawa: PWN; London: Oxford UP, 1963, 264 pp.), remains useful although colored by an anachronistic search for realism.

See also

Baker, *History of the English Novel*, vols. 1–2 (1505).

Guides to Primary Works

2095 Mish, Charles C., comp. *English Prose Fiction, 1600–1700: A Chronological Checklist*. Charlottesville: Bibliographical Soc. of the U of Virginia, 1967. 110 pp. Z2014.F4.M5.

A chronological short-title list of editions of original fictional works and translations that depends heavily on the *Short-Title Catalogues* (1990 and 1995) and Arundell Esdaile, *A List of English Tales and Prose Romances Printed before 1700* (London: Blades, for the Bibliographical Soc., 1912, 329 pp.). Editions are listed alphabetically by author or title of anonymous work under the year of publication (although the dating of many editions is conjectural). Indexed by authors and titles. Although Mish is more conservative than O'Dell (2100) in defining fiction and generally superior to his *Chronological List* for editions after 1599, both works are bedeviled by the difficulty in determining what constitutes prose fiction before the eighteenth century. Mish supersedes Esdaile but must be supplemented by the bibliography in Salzman, *English Prose Fiction* (2090).

2100 O'Dell, Sterg. *A Chronological List of Prose Fiction in English Printed in England and Other Countries, 1475–1640*. Cambridge: Technology P of M.I.T., 1954. 147 pp. Z2014.F5.O33 016.823.

A chronological list of editions of original works and translations that is based largely on *Short-Title Catalogue* (1990), *Transcript of the Registers of the Company of Stationers* (2000), and Esdaile, *List of English Tales and Prose Romances* (2095a). Editions are listed alphabetically by author or title of anonymous work under the year of publication (or entry in the Stationers' Register for nonextant editions). Entries include *Short-Title Catalogue* or Stationers' Register references, locations of copies (superseded by the revised *Short-Title Catalogue*), and occasional citations to modern editions (superseded by Harner, *English Renaissance Prose Fiction* [2105]). Indexed by authors and anonymous works. Although it is the fullest bibliography of early fiction, O'Dell is swollen by the inclusion of many works that cannot qualify as fiction and several bibliographical ghosts. O'Dell supersedes Esdaile, but Mish, *English Prose Fiction* (2095), is generally preferable as a guide to editions printed after 1599; see also the bibliography in Salzman, *English Prose Fiction* (2090).

Guides to Scholarship and Criticism

2105 Harner, James L. *English Renaissance Prose Fiction, 1500–1660: An Annotated Bibliography of Criticism.* A Reference Publication in Literature. Boston: Hall, 1978. 556 pp. *English Renaissance Prose Fiction, 1500–1660: An Annotated Bibliography of Criticism (1976–1983).* A Reference Publication in Literature. 1985. 228 pp. (Another supplement is in progress.) Z2014.F4.H37 [PR833] 016.823'009.

An annotated bibliography of studies and editions since 1800 of English-language fiction (including translations) written or printed in England from 1500 to 1660. The descriptively annotated entries are arranged in four divisions: bibliographies; anthologies; general studies; and authors, translators, and titles. The last is organized alphabetically, with anonymous works entered (sometimes awkwardly) by title of the earliest extant edition. Each author, translator, or title includes sections for bibliographies, editions, and studies. Indexed by persons, anonymous works, and subjects (with the supplement more fully indexed). Although conservative in defining prose fiction and overlooking some studies, *English Renaissance Prose Fiction* offers the most thorough coverage of international scholarship on the topic. Reviews: Jane Belfield, *Library* 6th ser. 3 (1981): 73–74; Charles C. Mish, *Seventeenth-Century News* 38 (1980): 10; Robert Yeager, *Studies in the Novel* 13 (1981): 340–41.

DRAMA AND THEATER

Several works in sections L: Genres/Drama and Theater and M: English Literature/General/Genres/Drama and Theater are useful for research in Renaissance literature.

Histories and Surveys

2110 Bentley, Gerald Eades. *The Jacobean and Caroline Stage.* 7 vols. Oxford: Clarendon, 1941–68. PN2592.B4 792.0942.

Vols. 1–2: *Dramatic Companies and Players*. 1941.
Vols. 3–5: *Plays and Playwrights*. 1956.
Vol. 6: *Theatres*. 1968. 309 pp.
Vol. 7: *Appendixes to Volume VI; General Index*. 1968. 390 pp.

A massive cumulation of factual information on all aspects of the stage from 1616 to 1642, designed to continue Chambers, *Elizabethan Stage* (2115). Vols. 1–2 trace the history of each of the London dramatic companies (with lists of actors and repertory) and the career of each known actor (quoting in chronological order "every scrap of biographical evidence"); appendixes transcribe various documents. Vols. 3–5 collect biographical details on dramatists and bibliographical information on plays. A typical entry for a play lists editions, scholarship, and seventeenth-century records, and evaluates what is known of its date, authorship, source(s), allusions, and performance. Vol. 6 examines the private and public London theaters. Vol. 7 prints appendixes to vol. 6 (among which is a chronology of theatrical affairs) and a detailed analytical index of plays, authors, scholars, actors, places, and subjects. The careful evaluation of primary evidence and scholarship makes Bentley the essential source for facts about acting companies, players, playwrights, plays, and theaters. Reviews: (vols. 1–2) K. M. Lea, *Review of English Studies* 18 (1942): 491–96; (vols. 3–5) Harold Jenkins, *Review of English Studies* ns 9 (1958): 196–202; (vols. 6–7) Jenkins, *Review of English Studies* ns 20 (1969): 222–24.

2115 Chambers, E. K. *The Elizabethan Stage*. 4 vols. Rpt. with corrections. Oxford: Clarendon, 1951. PN2589.C4 792.0942.

Continues his *Mediaeval Stage* (1905) in a history of the development of the Elizabethan stage that emphasizes the social and economic conditions affecting the drama from 1558 to 1616. Detailed examinations of court entertainments, the control of the stage, acting companies, playhouses, and plays and playwrights are supplemented by extensive appendixes (a calendar of court entertainments, extracts from records and texts, and bibliographies of academic, printed, lost, and manuscript plays). For additions, see his "Elizabethan Stage Gleanings," *Review of English Studies* 1 (1925): 75–78, 182–86. Four indexes: plays; persons; places; subjects; more fully indexed by Beatrice White, comp., *An Index to* The Elizabethan Stage *and* William Shakespeare *by Sir Edmund Chambers* (Oxford: Clarendon, 1934, 161 pp.). An indispensable source, *Elizabethan Stage* has never been superseded but must be supplemented with other histories (such as *Revels History of Drama* [2120]) and specialized studies such as those listed in the bibliographies of the *Revels History*, vol. 2, pp. 259–82; vol. 3, pp. 475–508. Continued by Bentley, *Jacobean and Caroline Stage* (2110).

2120 *The Revels History of Drama in English* (1530). Gen. eds. Clifford Leech, T. W. Craik, and Lois Potter. Vol. 2: *1500–1576*; vol. 3: *1576–1613*; vol. 4: *1613–1660*. London: Methuen, 1975–81. PR625.R44 822'.09.

Each volume includes a chronology; essays on the social context, staging, theaters and actors, and plays and playwrights; an evaluative survey of important studies; and an index of authors, titles, and subjects. Like other volumes of *Revels History*, these offer a useful synthesis of scholarship but not a connected history of the drama. Reviews: (vol. 3) David M. Bergeron, *Modern Language Review* 73 (1978): 380–82; Richard Proudfoot, *English* 25 (1976): 33–38; (vol. 4) Catherine M. Shaw, *Medieval and Renaissance Drama in England* 2 (1985): 334–36.

2125 Wilson, F. P. *The English Drama, 1485–1585*. Ed. G. K. Hunter. Vol. 4, pt. 1 of *The Oxford History of English Literature* (1310). Gen. eds. Bonamy Dobrée and Norman Davis. Oxford: Clarendon, 1969. 244 pp. PR641.W58 822'.2'09.

A critical history of the morality, interlude, masque, pageant, entertainment, sacred drama, comedy, and tragedy, with a chapter on the major dramatic companies. Includes a chronology and a now dated selective bibliography. Indexed by authors, titles, and subjects. A judicious, authoritative account that remains one of the better introductions to the drama of the period. The *Oxford History* volume on the drama c. 1586–1642 is in preparation by G. K. Hunter. Reviews: Norman Sanders, *Shakespeare Studies* 6 (1970): 389–91; S. Schoenbaum, *Yearbook of English Studies* 1 (1971): 226–27.

See also

Chambers, *Mediaeval Stage* (1905).
Wickham, *Early English Stages, 1300 to 1660* (1915).

Annals

2130 Kawachi, Yoshiko. *Calendar of English Renaissance Drama, 1558–1642*. Garland Reference Library of the Humanities 661. New York: Garland, 1986. 351 pp. PN2589.K36 792'.0941.

A daily calendar of performances of plays, masks, entertainments, and other theatrical presentations, and of tours of acting companies in England. Modeled on Harbage, *Annals of English Drama* (1535), and borrowing many of its conventions and symbols (along with a good bit of information), the *Calendar* presents details in tabular format, with columns for date of production (according to the New Style calendar), information (such as licensing or entry in Stationers' Register [1380 and 2000]) that qualifies the preceding date, acting company, location of performance or tour (including patrons or other important persons in the audience), title, type of play, author(s), date of manuscript or earliest printed text, and sources of information. Deciphering an entry requires constant reference to the explanations of abbreviations and symbols (pp. x-xvi). Three indexes: titles of plays; playwrights; dramatic companies (classified by types of companies). Although the lack of running heads makes the year difficult to ascertain and articles used as sources are not identified (e.g., the code "K" stands for twenty-three different journals), Kawachi is valuable for its compilation and organization of widely scattered scholarship. The daily record of performances allows for more precise studies of dramatic trends, stage history, and repertory than does its complement, Harbage, *Annals of English Drama* (1535).

See also

Harbage, *Annals of English Drama, 975–1700* (1535).

Guides to Primary Works

2135 Greg, W. W. *A Bibliography of the English Printed Drama to the Restoration*. 4 vols. Illustrated Monographs 24: 1–4. London: Bibliographical Soc., 1939–59. Z2014.D7.G78 016.822.

A descriptive bibliography of all editions, issues, and variants to 1700 of dramatic works (including many translations) "written before the *end* of 1642 . . . and printed before the *end* of 1700 . . . together with those written after 1642 but printed before the *beginning* of 1660." After an initial section that transcribes extracts relating to drama from the records of the Stationers' Company (1380), plays are described in four divisions: individual plays, Latin plays, lost plays, and collected editions. Individual and Latin plays are listed chronologically by publication date of the earliest extant edition (with issues, variants, and later editions following in order of printing); lost plays, by date of presumed publication; and collected editions, by author. Additions and corrections appear in vol. 4, pp. 1643–711.

An entry for a printed play includes the Greg number (now the standard reference number); a full analytical description for each edition, issue, and variant, with notes on bibliographical and textual matters; references to advertisements and bibliographies; and locations in a limited number of British and American libraries (see the revised *Short-Title Catalogue* [1990] and Wing, *Short-Title Catalogue* [1995] for current and additional locations). Users must consult the lengthy introduction (vol. 4, pp. i-clxxiv) for a detailed explanation of scope, content, and procedures.

Vol. 3 prints several useful appendixes—advertisements in newspapers, prefatory matter and actor lists from editions, contemporary lists of plays—as well as 18 indexes (e.g., prologues and epilogues; acting companies; court performances; printers, publishers, and booksellers; and general indexes of persons and titles, and of subjects mentioned in descriptions and commentary). Vol. 4 provides a title index to the entire work.

A cornucopia of historical, bibliographical, and textual detail derived from meticulous examination of copies, Greg is the authoritative source for information on the publication and identification of early texts and the foundation for much of the important research on Renaissance drama. Reviews: (vols. 3–4) *Times Literary Supplement* 15 Jan. 1960: 40; Harold Jenkins, *Review of English Studies* ns 12 (1961): 201–04.

2140 Berger, Thomas L., and William C. Bradford, Jr. *An Index of Characters in English Printed Drama to the Restoration*. Englewood: Microcard Editions Books, 1975. 222 pp. PR1265.3.B4 822'.009'27016.

An index to characters (including animals and inanimate objects represented by actors, such as Wall in *Midsummer Night's Dream*) who appear in printed English plays listed in Greg, *Bibliography of the English Printed Drama* (2135). Characters are indexed by surname, given name, nationality, occupation, religion, psychological state (e.g., melancholic), and type (e.g., poisoner, tyrant, magician). Plays are identified by Greg number (a finding list is appended). Effective use requires close familiarity with the description of scope and procedures in the introduction. Although the indexing by psychological state and type is sometimes inexact, surname and given name are not indexed together, and variants of the same name are entered separately, the work is a time-saving resource for character studies of the drama. Reviews: G. K. Hunter, *Yearbook of English Studies* 9 (1979): 297–99; J. L. Simmons, *Research Opportunities in Renaissance Drama* 18 (1975): 25–28.

See also

Lancashire, *Dramatic Texts and Records* (1925).
Records of Early English Drama (1920).

Guides to Scholarship and Criticism

Surveys of Research

2145 Logan, Terence P., and Denzell S. Smith, eds. *The Predecessors of Shakespeare.* Lincoln: U of Nebraska P, 1973. 348 pp. Z2014.D7.L83 [PR646] 016.822'3'09.

——. *The Popular School.* 1975. 299 pp. Z2014.D7.L82 [PR651] 016.822'3'09.
——. *The New Intellectuals.* 1977. 370 pp. Z2014.D7.N29 [PR671] 016.822'3.
——. *The Later Jacobean and Caroline Dramatists.* 1978. 279 pp. Z2014.D7.L816 [PR671] 016.822'3'09.
(Each volume bears the subtitle *A Survey and Bibliography of Recent Studies in English Renaissance Drama.*)

Selective surveys of research and bibliographies for dramatists (excluding Shakespeare) and plays from 1580 to 1642. Coverage extends from 1923 to 1968–76, supplemented by some important earlier and later publications (see the preface to each volume for details of coverage). Each volume consists of chapters on individual major writers, anonymous works, and minor dramatists. Those on individual authors are in three parts: (1) a survey of biographical and general studies of the plays as well as nondramatic works; (2) a survey of criticism of individual plays (with plays awkwardly arranged in order of critical importance) and a summary of the state of scholarship; (3) a survey of scholarship on canon, dating, and textual studies, and a critique of editions. A selective bibliography of studies not discussed concludes each chapter. Anonymous plays are grouped by date of performance in a single chapter with sections, when necessary, on editions, authorship, date, source, genre, and general studies. The chapter on minor dramatists consists of an annotated bibliography of studies and editions. Two indexes: persons; plays. Although the extent and quality of evaluation vary from contributor to contributor and although many playwrights are now the subjects of more thorough author bibliographies, these volumes remain important for their evaluative surveys of scholarship. Reviews: (*Popular School*) Michael Shapiro, *Literary Research Newsletter* 3 (1978): 79–83; (*New Intellectuals*) David M. Bergeron, *Shakespeare Quarterly* 31 (1980): 443–44; Philip R. Rider, *Analytical and Enumerative Bibliography* 2 (1978): 63–71; (*Later Jacobean*) Rider, *Analytical and Enumerative Bibliography* 4 (1980): 49–54.

Coverage should be supplemented with *Year's Work in English Studies* (330), Wells, *English Drama* (1555), "Recent Studies in Elizabethan and Jacobean Drama" (2150), "Shakespeare: Annotated World Bibliography" (2020), and the following:

Fordyce, Rachel. *Caroline Drama: A Bibliographic History of Criticism.* A Reference Publication in Literature. Boston: Hall, 1978. 203 pp. Although occasionally useful for its inclusion of early scholarship, the work is badly marred by poor organization and numerous omissions and errors.

Lidman, Mark J. *Studies in Jacobean Drama, 1973–1984: An Annotated Bibliography*. Garland Reference Library of the Humanities 597. New York: Garland, 1986. 278 pp. Updates Logan and Smith's coverage of English-language scholarship on Chapman, Dekker, Heywood, Tourneur, Marston, Middleton, Webster, Massinger, Ford, Brome, and Shirley.

The best selective bibliographies are Brownell Salomon, *Critical Analyses in English Renaissance Drama: A Bibliographic Guide*, 2nd ed., Garland Reference Library of the Humanities 588 (New York: Garland, 1985, 198 pp.); and Irving Ribner and Clifford Chalmers Huffman, comps., *Tudor and Stuart Drama*, 2nd ed., Goldentree Bibliographies in Language and Literature (Arlington Heights: AHM, 1978, 121 pp.), with coverage through 1975.

2150 "Recent Studies in Elizabethan and Jacobean Drama." *Studies in English Literature, 1500–1900* (entry 1485) 1 (1961)– . Annually in the spring issue.

A commissioned survey by an established scholar, with recent ones emphasizing full-length critical and historical studies. (Nondramatic literature is covered in the winter issue [2015].) The essays vary considerably in soundness and rigor of assessment. Although the most current annual survey, the work is generally limited to books received for review and must be supplemented by the chapters in *Year's Work in English Studies* (330) on Renaissance drama and Shakespeare. The broader surveys listed in entry 2015 also treat drama.

See also

YWES (330): Chapters for Shakespeare; Renaissance Drama: Excluding Shakespeare.

Other Bibliographies

2155 Bergeron, David M. *Twentieth-Century Criticism of English Masques, Pageants, and Entertainments, 1558–1642*. With a supplement on the folk play and related forms by Harry B. Caldwell. Checklists in the Humanities and Education. San Antonio: Trinity UP, 1972. 67 pp. Z2014.D7.B44 016.822'3.

A selective bibliography of English-language studies published through 1971. Entries are arranged alphabetically in five divisions: general studies, Ben Jonson (including works on Inigo Jones), Milton's *Comus*, other writers, and folk plays, with additions to the first four parts on pp. 39–40. Two indexes: authors; subjects. Although in need of updating, sometimes superseded by author bibliographies (especially the sections on Jonson and *Comus*), and limited by the exclusion of foreign-language criticism, Bergeron remains useful as a starting point for research on the masque and related dramatic forms.

2160 Stevens, David. *English Renaissance Theatre History: A Reference Guide*. A Reference Guide to Literature. Boston: Hall, 1982. 342 pp. Z2014.D7.S78 [PN2589] 016.792'0942.

An annotated bibliography of scholarship published between 1664 and 1979 on theater history from 1558 through 1642. The descriptively annotated entries, arranged chronologically, include (for example) studies of acting, playhouses, the stage, audience, actors and other theater personnel, finance, government regulation, and music. Indexed by playwrights, scholars, and subjects. There are errors and omissions, and reviewers have criticized the inadequate coverage of music and repertory, but Stevens offers the best starting point for research on many aspects of theater history of the period. Reviews: David M. Bergeron, *Shakespeare Quarterly* 35 (1984): 253–54; Reavley Gair, *Analytical and Enumerative Bibliography* 7 (1983): 239–42.

2165 White, D. Jerry. *Early English Drama,* Everyman *to 1580: A Reference Guide.* A Reference Guide to Literature. Boston: Hall, 1986. 289 pp. Z2014.D7.W48 [PR641] 016.822'2'09.

An extensive, although not comprehensive, bibliography of studies and scholarly editions (published from 1691 to 1982, with a few later items) on plays from c. 1495 to 1580 by British playwrights. Biographical material not related to plays is excluded, as are studies of folk drama, pageants, entertainments, masques, and John Skelton, since they are the subjects of other bibliographies (see Stevens, *English Renaissance Theatre History* [2160], Bergeron, *Twentieth-Century Criticism of English Masques* [2155], and Robert S. Kinsman, *John Skelton, Early Tudor Laureate: An Annotated Bibliography, c. 1488–1977*, A Reference Publication in Literature [Boston: Hall, 1979, 179 pp.]). The succinctly annotated entries are listed chronologically in divisions for bibliographies, collections, general studies, and authors, translators, or anonymous works; the last has sections for bibliographies and editions and studies. Since there are few multiple listings, users must consult the index to locate all studies on an author or work. Indexed by authors, scholars, anonymous works, and subjects. Breadth, accuracy, and clear annotations make this an essential starting point for research on the early drama.

See also

Kallendorf, *Latin Influences on English Literature from the Middle Ages to the Eighteenth Century* (4895).
Lancashire, *Dramatic Texts and Records* (1925).
Stratman, *Bibliography of Medieval Drama* (1930).

Microform Collections

See

Wells, *Three Centuries of Drama* (1180).

Periodicals

2170 *Renaissance Drama* (*RenD*). 1956– . Annual. PN1785.R4 809.2'09'02.

Open to essays on Renaissance drama, its precursors and successors throughout Europe, but the overwhelming emphasis is on England. Most volumes after ns 1 (1968) are devoted to a specific topic.

2175 *Research Opportunities in Renaissance Drama* (*RORD*). 1956– . Annual. With a Medieval Supplement since vol. 10 (1967). PR621.M75 822'.2'09.

Publishes articles, reports on conferences and work in progress, censuses of productions, occasional review essays, and numerous surveys of research and bibliographies of primary and secondary materials. Cumulative index: Christopher J. Thaiss, "An Index to Volumes I–XVI of *Research Opportunities in Renaissance Drama*," 17 (1974): 35–44. *RORD* is an important source of bibliographies that supplement published ones or treat subjects too narrow for a monograph.

See also

Medieval and Renaissance Drama in England (1935).
Studies in English Literature, 1500–1900 (1485).

POETRY

Many works in sections L: Genres/Poetry and M: English Literature/General/Genres/Poetry are important to research in Renaissance poetry.

Histories and Surveys

Lewis, *English Literature in the Sixteenth Century* (1975) and Bush, *English Literature in the Earlier Seventeenth Century* (1970) remain the best general histories of Renaissance poetry. Gary Waller, *English Poetry of the Sixteenth Century*, Longman Literature in English Series (London: Longman, 1986, 315 pp.), employs new theoretical approaches in a revisionist history that emphasizes major writers.

Guides to Primary Works

2180 Case, Arthur E. *A Bibliography of English Poetical Miscellanies, 1521–1750*. London: Oxford UP, for the Bibliographical Soc., 1935. 386 pp. Z2014.P7.C3 016.8210822.

An analytical bibliography of 481 collections of miscellaneous verse (including translations) by British writers in any language and printed in any country. Case excludes song and hymn books but otherwise lists any volume with "a fairly considerable section devoted to miscellaneous verse." Collections are listed chronologically by date of earliest known edition, followed by later editions to 1750 (with additions on p. 344). An entry includes title, collation, brief indication of content (but not a list of individual poems), bibliographical notes, and a few locations (superseded by the *Short-Title Catalogue*s [1990, 1995, and 2230]); for additional locations of eighteenth-century editions, see Richard C. Boys, "A Finding-List of English Poetical Miscellanies, 1700–48, in Selected American Libraries," *ELH: A Journal of English Literary History* 7 (1940): 144–62. Five indexes: titles; chronological index of editions other than the earliest known ones; places of publication (other than London); persons; printers and publishers. The descriptions are accurate, but researchers would benefit from a published list of first lines (a first-line index compiled by Boys and Arthur Mizener is held by the Dept. of Special Collections, Kenneth Spencer Research Library, U of Kansas, Lawrence 66045). Review: *Times Literary Supplement* 10 Oct. 1935: 626.

2185 Frank, Joseph. *Hobbled Pegasus: A Descriptive Bibliography of Minor English Poetry, 1641–1660.* Albuquerque: U of New Mexico P, 1968. 482 pp. Z2014.P7.F7 016.821'4'08.

A bibliography of English-language poetry written and printed in the British Isles from March 1641 to 29 May 1660 (with a few additional works to June 1661). Frank excludes plays and any work of which more than half is in prose. The approximately 800 entries, listed chronologically by date of first publication, give Wing, *Short-Title Catalogue* (1995), and Case, *Bibliography of English Poetical Miscellanies* (2180), numbers; short title; author; length (see p. 29 for an explanation of the abbreviations); publication details; subsequent editions to 1700; political or religious classification, "literary category," and subject (see pp. 5–12 for an explanation); meter or stanza form; illustrative extract; content; an incomplete list of reprints; and references to related poems, scholarship, and bibliographies. Additions appear on p. 462. Two indexes: authors; titles. There are numerous inconsistencies and inaccuracies in transcribing details; the lack of a first-line index seriously inhibits use; and most editions are listed in Wing, *Short-Title Catalogue*. Even so, *Hobbled Pegasus* is a time-saving compilation for researchers interested in this body of mostly second-rate poetry. Review: Charles Clay Doyle, *Eighteenth-Century Studies* 2 (1969): 490–93.

2190 Ringler, W. A., Jr. *A Bibliography and Index of English Verse Printed 1476–1500 and 1501–1558.* London: Mansell. In press.

A first-line index to more than 2,700 English-language poems printed between 1476 and 1558 (regardless of date of composition). Entries cite the first printing, the best edition, and facsimiles. Concludes with several useful indexes: refrains; burdens; verse forms and rhyme schemes; English poets; historical persons and events; religious topics; subjects; titles; fictitious names; translations and adaptations.

For 1476 to 1558, Ringler completely supersedes Nancy A. Gutierrez, *English Historical Poetry, 1476–1603: A Bibliography*, Garland Reference Library of the Humanities 410 (New York: Garland, 1983, 429 pp.), which is virtually useless because of its organization by date of topic and lack of a subject index. (See the review by James L. Harner, *Analytical and Enumerative Bibliography* 8 [1984]: 32–35.)

In progress at Ringler's death were two complementary volumes: *A Bibliography and Index of English Verse Transcribed, 1501–1558* and *1559–1603*, which indexed by first line any poem, regardless of date of composition, transcribed by hand during the period.

See also

Crum, *First-Line Index of English Poetry, 1500–1800* (1590).

Guides to Scholarship and Criticism

There is no adequate general bibliography of scholarship on Renaissance poetry; however, most poets, major and minor, are the subjects of author bibliographies, and studies of poetry are well covered in the guides to scholarship and criticism listed at the beginning of the Renaissance literature section.

See

Brogan, *English Versification, 1570–1980* (1600).
Donow, *Sonnet in England and America* (1250).
Kuntz, *Poetry Explication* (1255).

Restoration and Eighteenth-Century Literature

Many works listed in section M: English Literature/General are useful for research in Restoration and eighteenth-century literature.

Histories and Surveys

2205 Butt, John. *The Mid-Eighteenth Century*. Ed. and completed by Geoffrey Carnall. Vol. 8 of *The Oxford History of English Literature* (1310). Gen. eds. John Buxton and Norman Davis. Oxford: Clarendon, 1979. 671 pp. PR441.B83 820'.9'006.

A literary history of the period 1740–89, with chapters on Johnson; poetry (1740–60 and 1760–89); Scottish poetry; drama; history; travel literature, memoirs, and biography; essays, letters, dialogues, and speeches; major novelists (Richardson, Fielding, Smollett, Sterne); and other prose fiction. Concludes with a chronology and a selective bibliography. Indexed by authors, artists, and some subjects. *Mid-Eighteenth Century* received a mixed reception with its "traditional" approach to literary history eliciting much of the negative criticism. Reviews: P. N. Furbank, *Listener* 12 July 1979: 61–62; Donald Greene, *English Language Notes* 18 (1980): 139–46; Ronald Paulson, *Modern Language Review* 76 (1981): 674–75; Pat Rogers, *Review of English Studies* ns 32 (1981): 83–86; G. S. Rousseau, *Eighteenth-Century Studies* 14 (1980–81): 181–93.

2210 Dobrée, Bonamy. *English Literature in the Early Eighteenth Century, 1700–1740*. Corrected rpt. Vol. 7 of *The Oxford History of English Literature* (1310). Gen. eds. Bonamy Dobrée and F. P. Wilson. Oxford: Clarendon, 1964. 701 pp. PR445.D6 820.903.

Emphasizes Defoe, Swift, and Pope but does not scant minor figures, in a three-part literary history of the period. Pt. 1 covers the period 1700–20 in chapters on the background of the age, Defoe to 1710, Swift to 1709, essayists and controversialists, poetry, and Pope to 1725; pt. 2 treats the period 1700–40 in chapters on drama (a weak discussion), philosophers, critics and aestheticians, and miscellaneous prose; pt. 3 covers the period 1720–40 in chapters on Defoe (1715–31), Swift (1715–45), poetry, and Pope (1725–44). Concludes with a chronology and an inadequate (and now outdated) selective bibliography. Indexed by authors and a few subjects. This work received a mixed reception, with some reviewers praising its thoroughness and critical sympathy and others censuring it as prejudiced and unreliable. Some of the numerous factual errors are corrected in the 1964 printing. Reviews: Donald F. Bond, *Modern Philology* 60 (1962): 138–41; Kathleen Williams, *Modern Language Notes* 76 (1961): 356–59.

2215 Sutherland, James. *English Literature of the Late Seventeenth Century*. Vol. 6 of *The Oxford History of English Literature* (1310). Gen. eds. Bonamy Dobrée and Norman Davis. Oxford: Clarendon, 1969. 589 pp. PR437.S9 820.9'004.

A critical history of the period 1660–1700, with chapters on the background of the age; drama; poetry; fiction; essays, letters, and journals; biography, history, and travel writings; religious literature; philosophy, politics, and economics; science; and criticism. Includes a chronology and a selective bibliography (with numerous errors and now outdated). Indexed by author, anonymous work, and subject. A good, sensible history but sometimes dated in its critical discussions. Review: *TLS: Times Literary Supplement* 5 June 1969: 611–12.

See also

Sec. M: English Literature/General/Histories and Surveys.

Bibliographies of Bibliographies

2220 Lund, Roger D. *Restoration and Early Eighteenth-Century English Literature, 1660–1740: A Selected Bibliography of Resource Materials*. Selected Bibliographies in Language and Literature 1. New York: MLA, 1980. 42 pp. Z2012.L88 [PR43] 016.82.

A highly selective list of important bibliographies, concordances, and current journals published through 1978. Entries are listed alphabetically by author, editor, or title in divisions for current journals; annual bibliographies; general bibliographies; poetry; drama; fiction; literary criticism and language study; translation; publishing and bookselling; newspapers and periodicals; art and music; history, biography, and autobiography; religious literature; miscellaneous bibliographies; and individual authors. A brief descriptive annotation accompanies many works. Indexed by persons. A convenient, judicious guide to essential reference sources. Review: J. M. Armistead, *Literary Research Newsletter* 5 (1980): 189–91.

See also

Sec. D: Bibliographies of Bibliographies.
Howard-Hill, *Index to British Literary Bibliography* (1355).

Guides to Primary Works

MANUSCRIPTS

2225 *Index of English Literary Manuscripts* (1365). Ed. P. J. Croft, Theodore Hofmann, and John Horden. Vol. 3: *1700–1800*. Comp. Margaret M. Smith. London: Mansell, 1986– . Z6611.L715 [PR83] 016.82'08.

A descriptive catalog of extant literary manuscripts by 55 major English, Scottish, and Irish authors. The emphasis is on literary manuscripts, including diaries, notebooks, marginalia, and some scribal copies. Letters are excluded, but the introductions to individual authors identify collections of them. In addition, the introductions alert researchers to special problems and relevant scholarship, point out additional manuscripts and transcripts, discuss canon, note the disposition of any personal library, and conclude with an outline of the arrangement of entries. A typical entry provides a physical description, dates composition of the manuscript, includes any necessary commentary (as well as references to sale catalogs, editions, or scholarship), and identifies location (with shelfmark). Queries about privately owned manuscripts should be addressed to the *Index* in care of Mansell.

Additions and corrections will be printed in vol. 5. Since some entries are based on inquiries to libraries and collectors, bibliographies, other reference works, and booksellers' and auction catalogs rather than personal examination by the compiler, descriptions vary in fullness and accuracy.

Although there are errors and omissions, and the scope is unduly restricted by reliance on the *Concise Cambridge Bibliography* (1365a), the *Index* is an essential, if limited, source for the identification and location of manuscripts. It must, however, be supplemented by the works listed in sections F: Guides to Manuscripts and Archives and M: English Literature/General/Guides to Primary Works/Manuscripts.

PRINTED WORKS

2230 *The Eighteenth-Century Short-Title Catalogue* (*ESTC*). Ed. Robin Alston. London: British Library; Baton Rouge: Louisiana State U. In progress. (A provisional first edition on microfiche is projected for 1989.)

A computer-readable bibliography and union list of editions, issues, impressions, and variant states of books, pamphlets, and single sheets printed in any language in the British Isles, North America, and British territories, and in English throughout the rest of the world between 1701 and 1800. Excludes engraved single sheets without letterpress, forms intended to be completed in manuscript, trade cards, bookplates, tickets, playbills, concert and theater programs, playing cards, maps, and games. The data base, which also includes records of the North American Imprints Program (4010), will eventually provide access to approximately 500,000 titles.

A typical record includes author; title; edition; imprint; pagination; illustrations; format; notes on authorship, language, type of work, subject and content (if not clear from the title), and bibliographical and publication details; references to other bibliographies; and locations (with call number or shelfmark and notes on provenance or imperfections). The amount of detail and degree of bibliographical sophistication vary, with fuller entries for items held by the British Library. Users should be aware that information included in entries is frequently not precise enough to identify reprints and variant issues. For a convenient summary of cataloging practices, see the introduction to the catalog of the British Library collection (reprinted as R. C. Alston, *The First Phase: An Introduction to the Catalogue of the British Library Collections for* ESTC, Occasional Paper 4, *Factotum: Newsletter of the XVIIIth Century STC* [London: British Library, 1983, 29 pp.]); fuller details are provided in J. C. Zeeman, *The Eighteenth Century Short Title Catalogue: The Cataloguing Rules*, 1986 ed. (London: British Library, 1986, 114 pp.).

The *ESTC* data base can be searched through RLIN (230) and BLAISE-LINE (510) by Library of Congress card number, title word(s) or phrase, place or date of publication, publisher, bookseller, or printer. Boolean operators (i.e., "and," "or," or "not") allow for narrow searches—for example, books printed in Stirling between 1740 and 1760, French-language tragedies printed in London in 1714, or travel books on China. Searchers should consult the most recent RLIN or BLAISE-LINE guide for search instructions. Simplified guides are available from *ESTC*: R. C. Alston, *Searching ESTC on BLAISE-LINE: A Brief Guide*, Occasional Paper 1, *Factotum: Newsletter of the XVIIIth Century STC* (London: British Library, 1982, 29 pp.; revision in progress); and David Hunter, *Searching ESTC on RLIN*, Occasional Paper 5 (1987, 22 pp.).

Some 200,000 volumes will eventually be available on microfilm in *The Eighteenth Century* (Woodbridge: Research Publications, 1982–). The contents are indexed by main entry, title, and one of eight broad subject heads in *The Eighteenth Century: Guide to the Microform Collection* (1984–), a cumulative index that eventually supersedes the temporary guide accompanying each unit. In addition, RLIN and BLAISE-LINE records cite reel and item numbers for works and editions filmed.

The holdings of the British Library have been published as R. C. Alston, ed., *The Eighteenth Century Short Title Catalogue: The British Library Collections* (London: British Library, 1983, microfiche). *Factotum: Newsletter of the XVIIIth Century STC* (1978– , 2/yr.) carries progress reports as well as notes derived from research in *ESTC* records. (From 1978 to 1980, *ESTC Facsimile: The Newsletter of the Eighteenth-Century Short Title Catalogue in America* recorded the progress of the North American group.) For a history of the project and examples of research based on *ESTC*, see M. Crump and M. Harris, eds., *Searching the Eighteenth Century: Papers Presented at the Symposium on the* Eighteenth Century Short Title Catalogue *in July 1982* (London: British Library in association with Dept. of Extra-Mural Studies, U of London, 1983, 104 pp.).

The *ESTC* is the most sophisticated and accessible of the short-title catalogs. Since the data base can be searched in a variety of ways and continually updated to reflect corrections and additions, it offers an incomparable source for identifying extant works by an author, about a topic, or in a genre, and for locating copies. A major international cooperative project that has already unearthed a number of unknown works and unrecorded editions, the *ESTC* is effecting a major revolution in all areas of eighteenth-century studies and has precipitated similar projects such as the ISTC (1820a). Under discussion is a machine-readable union catalog, 1475–1800, that would combine NAIP (4010) records and expanded, edited *RSTC* (1990) and Wing (1995) entries with the *ESTC* data base. For details, see Henry L. Snyder, "The English Short Title Catalogue," *Papers of the Bibliographical Society of America* 82 (1988): 333–36.

Review: C. Y. Ferdinand, *Analytical and Enumerative Bibliography* 8 (1984): 242–47.

The *ESTC* must not be confused with the following inferior, badly flawed compilations: F. J. G. Robinson et al., *Eighteenth-Century British Books: An Author Union Catalogue Extracted from the* British Museum General Catalogue of Printed Books, *the Catalogues of the Bodleian Library, and of the University Library, Cambridge*, 5 vols. (Folkestone: Dawson, 1981); G. Averley et al., *Eighteenth-Century British Books: A Subject Catalogue Extracted from the* British Museum General Catalogue of Printed Books, 4 vols. (1979); Robinson et al., *Eighteenth-Century British Books: An Index to the Foreign and Provincial Imprints in the Author Union Catalogue* (Newcastle: Avero, 1982, 320 pp.).

2235 Arber, Edward, ed. *The Term Catalogues, 1668–1709 A.D.; with a Number for Easter Term, 1711 A.D.* 3 vols. London: Privately printed, 1903–06. Z2002.A31 015.42.

An edition of the quarterly lists of books printed in London, Oxford, and Cambridge for London booksellers. Since the catalogs are advertising lists, not all books published during the period are included. Works are classified under various headings, such as divinity, physic, histories (including novels), humanity, poetry and plays, Latin books, music, miscellanies, law, and reprints. Entries record title (frequently descriptive rather than exact), author (but only occasionally), size, price, and the bookseller(s) for whom the work was printed. Two indexes in each volume: titles (accompanied by author); names, places, and subjects. An important source for identifying works and editions no longer extant, researching publishing history, establishing approximate publication dates, and studying the environment of a work.

The catalog of Michaelmas Term 1695 is reproduced as *The "Missing" Term Catalogue: A Facsimile of the Term Catalogue for Michaelmas Term 1695 with a List of Identified Books*, Occasional Publication 20 (Oxford: Oxford Bibliographical Soc., 1987, n.pag.).

See also

New Cambridge Bibliography of English Literature, vol. 2: *1660–1800* (2255).
Transcript of the Registers of the Worshipful Company of Stationers from 1640–1708 A.D. (2005).
Wing, *Short-Title Catalogue* (1995).

Guides to Scholarship and Criticism

SURVEYS OF RESEARCH

2240 "Recent Studies in the Restoration and Eighteenth Century." *Studies in English Literature, 1500–1900* (entry 1485). 1 (1961)– . Annually in the summer issue.

A commissioned survey by established scholars, with recent surveys emphasizing full-length critical and historical studies. The essays vary considerably in soundness and rigor of assessment. Although highly selective and now generally limited to books received for review, the work is the most current annual survey, but it must be supplemented by the chapters in *Year's Work in English Studies* (330) on the period.

See also

YWES (330): Later Seventeenth Century and Eighteenth Century chapters.

SERIAL BIBLIOGRAPHIES

2245 *The Eighteenth Century: A Current Bibliography for [1925–]* (*ECCB*). NS 1– . New York: AMS, 1978– . Annual. Z5579.6.E36 [CB411] 016.909.

1925–74: *Philological Quarterly* (entry 720) 5–54 (1926–75). (Title varies: [1925–26] "English Literature of the Restoration and Eighteenth Century: A Current Bibliography"; [1927–69] "English Literature, 1660–1800: A Current Bibliography"; [1970–74] "The Eighteenth Century: A Current Bibliography.")

(The bibliographies for 1925–70 are reprinted, with a few corrections and cumulative indexes in every second volume, as *English Literature, 1660–1800: A Bibliography of Modern Studies*, 6 vols. [Princeton: Princeton UP, 1950–72].)

A selective international bibliography of books, articles, and reviews that now offers interdisciplinary coverage of the period in Europe and the New World. Until the bibliography for 1970, *ECCB* emphasized English literature but always included numerous studies in other disciplines and national literatures. Both scope and criteria governing selection have varied over the years and within individual disciplines (see, e.g., the forewords to the bibliographies for 1970 [50 (1971): 321–23]; for 1975 [ns 1: n.pag.]; and for 1982 [ns 8: i-iv]), but have generally included important studies in English, French, German, Italian, and Spanish (with other languages covered less systematically).

Currently, entries are listed alphabetically by scholar in six divisions: printing and bibliographical studies; historical, social, and economic studies; philosophy, science, and religion; fine arts; general literary studies; and individual writers (although works on individual authors are also incorporated in the preceding divisions). Many articles are descriptively annotated (and frequently evaluated); significant books are stringently reviewed by specialists (although the overall quality and authoritativeness of the reviewing have declined somewhat in recent volumes). Indexed since 1970 by persons.

For a history of the bibliography, see Donald Greene, " 'More than a necessary chore': *The Eighteenth-Century Current Bibliography* in Retrospect and Prospect," *Eighteenth-Century Studies* 10 (1976): 94–110; and O M Brack, "Curt Zimansky: A Reminiscence," *ECCB* ns 7 (for 1981): ix-xvii.

Although users would benefit from subject indexing and classified sections in the first five divisions as well as more timely publication, *ECCB* is an indispensable resource that fully deserves its long-standing reputation as the best period serial bibliography. Review (ns 3–4) Paula R. Backscheider, *Modern Language Review* 80 (1985): 681–84.

Since coverage is selective and omits dissertations, researchers must also consult the other bibliographies in this section as well as in sections G: Serial Bibliographies, Indexes, and Abstracts and H: Guides to Dissertations and Theses. Waldo Sumner Glock, *Eighteenth-Century English Literary Studies: A Bibliography*

(Metuchen: Scarecrow, 1984, 847 pp.), a selective annotated list of studies from 1925 to 1980 on 25 authors, is an occasionally serviceable compilation of listings from *ECCB*, *MLAIB* (335), *ABELL* (340), and *Year's Work in English Studies* (330). Earlier scholarship is selectively covered in James E. Tobin, *Eighteenth Century English Literature and Its Cultural Background: A Bibliography* (New York: Fordham UP, 1939, 190 pp.), with additions in a review by Donald F. Bond, *Library Quarterly* 10 (1940): 446–50.

The best general selective bibliographies remain the two compiled by Donald F. Bond for the Goldentree Bibliographies in Language and Literature series: *The Age of Dryden* (New York: Appleton, 1970, 103 pp.) and *The Eighteenth Century* (Northbrook: AHM, 1975, 180 pp). Both are now dated, however.

2250 "Some Current Publications." *Restoration: Studies in English Literary Culture, 1660–1700* (*Restoration*). Knoxville: U of Tennessee, 1977– . 2/yr. PR437.R47 820'.9'004.

A selective bibliography by a different compiler in each issue. The descriptively annotated entries are classified under sections for individual authors; bibliography; drama; nondramatic literature; social sciences, natural sciences, religion; colonies; and sister arts. The criteria governing selection are unclear and the quality of annotations and coverage varies with the contributor, but the work is sometimes a useful source for identifying recent scholarship.

See also

Sec. G: Serial Bibliographies, Indexes, and Abstracts; and H: Guides to Dissertations and Theses.

ABELL (340): English Literature/Seventeenth Century and Eighteenth Century sections.

"Abstracts of Recent Articles," *Seventeenth-Century News* (2080).

"Abstracts of Recent Dissertations," *Eighteenth-Century Life* (2300).

MLAIB (335): English Language and Literature division in the volumes for 1921–25; English VIII and IX in the volumes for 1926–56; English VII and VIII in the volumes for 1957–80; and English Literature/1600–1699 and 1700–1799 sections (as well as any larger chronological section encompassing either century) in the later volumes. Researchers must also check the headings beginning "English Literature" in the subject index to post-1980 volumes.

OTHER BIBLIOGRAPHIES

2255 *The New Cambridge Bibliography of English Literature* (*NCBEL*). Vol. 2: *1660–1800*. Ed. George Watson. Cambridge: Cambridge UP, 1971. 2,082 cols. Z2011.N45 [PR83] 016.82.

(For a full discussion of *NCBEL*, see entry 1385.) Primary works and scholarship are organized in six major divisions (each subdivided and classified as its subject requires): introduction (general works, literary theory, literary relations with the Continent, medieval influences, book production and distribution), poetry (histories, collections, 1660–1700, 1700–50, 1750–1800), drama (theaters and actors,

1660–1700, 1700–50, 1750–1800, adaptations and translations), novel (principal novelists, minor fiction, children's books), prose (essayists and pamphleteers; periodicals; travel; English-language translations; sport; letters, diaries, autobiographies, and memoirs; religion; history; literary studies; classical and oriental studies; philosophy; science; law; education), and Scottish literature. Vol. 2 of the *Cambridge Bibliography of English Literature* (1385a) is still occasionally useful for its coverage of the social and political background (most of which *NCBEL* drops).

Users must familiarize themselves with the organization, remember that there is considerable unevenness of coverage among sections, and consult the index volume (vol. 5) rather than the provisional index in vol. 2. Reviews: *TLS: Times Literary Supplement* 15 Oct. 1971: 1296; Eric Rothstein, *Modern Philology* 71 (1973): 176–86.

See also

Kallendorf, *Latin Influences on English Literature from the Middle Ages to the Eighteenth Century* (4895).

RELATED TOPICS

2260 Pargellis, Stanley, and D. J. Medley, eds. *Bibliography of British History: The Eighteenth Century, 1714–1789*. Oxford: Clarendon, 1951. 642 pp. (A supplement by A. Newman and A. T. Milne is in progress.) Z2018.P37 [DA498] 016.94207.

A selective bibliography, with significantly fuller coverage of primary than secondary materials, of publications before 1941 than after, and of books than articles. The 4,558 entries are variously organized under 17 extensively classified divisions: general reference works; political, constitutional, legal, ecclesiastical, economic, military, naval, social, cultural, and local history; Scotland; Ireland; Wales; American Colonies; India; and Historical Manuscripts Commission reports. Annotations are generally descriptive and cite numerous related studies, but many entries lack annotation. Indexed by persons and some subjects. Although now badly dated and marred by an inadequate explanation of selection criteria, the *Bibliography* is still useful as a starting point for cross-disciplinary research. Reviews: E. R. Adair, *Canadian Historical Review* 32 (1951): 384–86; D. B. Horn, *English Historical Review* 66 (1951): 594–97.

Convenient selective bibliographies are Robert A. Smith, *Late Georgian and Regency England, 1760–1837*, Conference on British Studies Bibliographical Handbooks (Cambridge: Cambridge UP, for the Conference on British Studies, 1984, 114 pp.), with coverage through 1980, and William L. Sachse, *Restoration England, 1660–1689*, Conference on British Studies Bibliographical Handbooks (Cambridge: Cambridge UP, for the Conference on British Studies, 1971, 115 pp.), with coverage through 1968.

See also

Annual Bibliography of British and Irish History (1400).
Brown, *Bibliography of British History, 1789–1851* (2515).
Davies, *Bibliography of British History: Stuart Period, 1603–1714* (2045).

Biographical Dictionaries

Although the *Dictionary of National Biography* (1425) remains the standard general source of biographical information for the period, its entries for Restoration and eighteenth-century theatrical personnel (including dramatists who were also actors or managers) are superseded by Highfill, *Biographical Dictionary* (2400), and for female authors by Todd, *Dictionary of British and American Women Writers* (2265).

2265 Todd, Janet, ed. *A Dictionary of British and American Women Writers, 1660–1800.* Totowa: Rowman, 1985. 344 pp. PR113.D5 820'.9'9287.

A biographical dictionary of women who wrote published or unpublished literary or nonliterary works between 1660 and 1800. A writer is entered under her most commonly used name or title, with index entries for a married or family name used in her writing. Entries provide biographical details, a list (usually complete) of known works, and a brief assessment that sometimes includes contemporary critical comments. Unfortunately, unpublished works are not located. Indexed by names, periodicals, and a few subjects. Fuller subject indexing—especially of genres—would improve the utility of the work. Although it is selective—especially for authors in prolific nonbelletristic genres—the *Dictionary* is an indispensable guide to Restoration and eighteenth-century women writers, few of whom are accorded entries in the standard biographical dictionaries such as *Dictionary of National Biography* (1425) and *Dictionary of American Biography* (3380). Of special importance are the numerous discussions of unpublished writers.

See also

Valentine, *British Establishment, 1760–1784* (1425a).

Microform Collections

See

Eighteenth Century (2230a).

Periodicals

GUIDES TO PRIMARY WORKS

Bibliographies

2270 Crane, R. S., and F. B. Kaye. *A Census of British Newspapers and Periodicals, 1620–1800.* Chapel Hill: U of North Carolina P, 1927. 205 pp. (A reprint of *Studies in Philology* 24 [1927]: 1–205.) Z6956.E5.C8.

A preliminary checklist in two parts: a finding list based on the holdings of 37 United States libraries; a list, compiled largely from other works, of periodicals and newspapers not found in the United States. Organized alphabetically (with cross-references for variant titles), entries supply title, variants, place of publication, beginning and ending dates, editor(s), publisher(s), printer(s), frequency, and (in the first part) locations (occasionally specifying the length of runs). Two indexes: chronological; geographical (excluding London). Compiled largely from institutional reports and published bibliographies, the *Census* is not comprehensive and many entries are inaccurate or incomplete. As the fullest single list of newspapers and periodicals of the period, it remains a useful preliminary guide, but it has been superseded by the union lists in section K: Periodicals for locations and by the following for various periods:

Nelson, *British Newspapers and Periodicals, 1641–1700* (2060).

Ward, *Index and Finding List of Serials Published in the British Isles, 1789–1832* (2535).

A second edition was planned but never published, but several additions and corrections by J. G. Muddiman et al. appear as "The History and Bibliography of English Newspapers," *Notes and Queries* 160 (1931): 3–6, 21–24, 40–43, 57–59, 174–75, 207–09, 227–30, 264, 298–300, 336–38, 375–76, 391, 442–43; 161 (1931): 337. Several periodicals are reproduced in two microfilm series published by University Microfilms International: *Early British Periodicals, 1681–1921* and *English Literary Periodicals, 1681–1914*. Review: Walter Graham, *Journal of English and Germanic Philology* 28 (1929): 303–07.

In progress is Robert N. Gosselink, *Early British Periodicals (1700–1800)*, a bibliography of serials and newspapers whose entries typically cite title and subtitle, inclusive dates, editor(s), publication information, frequency, price, size, locations, and variant and other titles.

See also

Sec. K: Periodicals/Union Lists.

Bibliography of British Newspapers (1440).

Sullivan, *British Literary Magazines*, vols. 1–2 (1445).

Indexes

2275 Forster, Antonia. *Index to Book Reviews in England, 1749–1774*. Carbondale: Southern Illinois UP. Scheduled for 1989.

An index to reviews of poetry, fiction, and drama that appear in 16 English periodicals between 1749 and 1774. Excludes newspapers and reviews of dramatic productions. The 3,021 entries are listed alphabetically by author, translator, adapter, or anonymous title of the work reviewed, with cross-references for original authors of translated works or adaptations; a female is entered under her most generally used surname. A typical entry cites title, place and date of publication, format, price, bookseller, location of copy examined, and reviews. For most works, the title, place of publication, and date are based on personal examination of a copy; format, price, and bookseller are taken from the reviews. The introduction examines the theory and practice of reviewing during the period. Although restricted to 16 periodicals, the *Index* promises to be an important source for locating reviews and studying the critical reception of belles lettres during the period.

2280 Ward, William S., comp. *Literary Reviews in British Periodicals, 1789–1797: A Bibliography: With a Supplementary List of General (Non-Review) Articles on Literary Subjects*. Garland Reference Library of the Humanities 172. New York: Garland, 1979. 342 pp. Z2013.W36 [PR442] 016.820'9'006.

A bibliography of reviews of books published between 1789 and 1797 by British and American literary authors. Works reviewed are organized alphabetically by author, then chronologically by date of publication, followed by reviews listed alphabetically by periodical title. Nonreview articles are divided among five appendixes: (A) general articles on contemporary authors and works; (B, which consists of five separate lists) volumes of general and genre criticism reviewed, general criticism, and articles on poetry, fiction, and drama and theater; (C) reviews of studies of contemporary authors and their works; (D) reviews of books and articles dealing with selected authors before 1789 (with separate sections for Shakespeare, Milton, Pope, and Johnson); (E) reviews of operas and musical dramas. The preface offers some general suggestions for further research. An essential source for investigating the contemporary critical reception of an author or work and for locating early criticism. Continued by Ward, *Literary Reviews in British Periodicals, 1798–1820* and *1821–1826* (2550).

GUIDES TO SCHOLARSHIP AND CRITICISM

See James E. Tierney, "The Study of the Eighteenth-Century British Periodical," *Papers of the Bibliographical Society of America* 69 (1975): 165–86, for an assessment of the state of scholarship that surveys reference works, editions, and critical and historical studies; comments on difficulties researchers face; and offers detailed suggestions for topics needing investigation.

2285 Weed, Katherine Kirtley, and Richmond Pugh Bond. *Studies of British Newspapers and Periodicals from Their Beginning to 1800: A Bibliography*. *Studies in Philology* extra ser. 2. Chapel Hill: U of North Carolina P, 1946. 233 pp. Z6956.E5.W4.

A bibliography of studies (essentially through 1940, but with some as late as 1945) of serials published through 1800 in Great Britain and a few other countries. The approximately 2,100 entries are organized alphabetically in seven divisions: bibliographies and bibliographical studies; corantos, newsbooks, and newsletters; general studies; works on individual newspapers and periodicals, editors, authors, publishers, towns, and counties (classified by newspaper, editor, etc.); subjects; newspapers and periodicals in Europe (classified by country); newspapers and periodicals in North America (classified by country, then province or state). The last three divisions are highly selective. Several entries are accompanied by brief descriptive annotations, which include citations to selected reviews. Indexed by authors (excluding those who appear as a heading in the fourth division). Although the work is badly dated, its coverage of pre-1941 scholarship on serials published before 1789 remains unsuperseded. For studies of periodicals published after 1789, see Ward, *British Periodicals and Newspapers, 1789–1832* (2565). *New Cambridge Bibliography of English Literature* (2255) and Linton, *Newspaper Press in Britain* (1455), offer the best coverage of post-1940 scholarship. Review: Donald F. Bond, *Modern Philology* 45 (1947): 65–66.

See also

White, *English Literary Journal to 1900* (1460).

SCHOLARLY JOURNALS

Most journals listed in sections K: Periodicals/Scholarly Journals and M: English Literature/General/Periodicals/Scholarly Journals publish articles on the Restoration and eighteenth century.

2290 *British Journal for Eighteenth-Century Studies*. 1978– . 2/yr. CB411.B75 900.

Publishes articles, reviews, and review articles, especially on British and French topics and emphasizing literature.

2295 *The Eighteenth Century: Theory and Interpretation* (*ECent*). 1959– . 3/yr. Former titles: *Burke Newsletter* (1959–67); *Studies in Burke and His Time* (1967–78). DA506.B9.B86 909.7.

Now publishes articles, review essays, critical rejoinders, and occasional special issues on British, American, and Continental culture from 1660 to 1800. Since 1979, *The Eighteenth Century* has a special interest in the application of twentieth-century critical theories and methodologies. Cumulative indexes: vols. 1–5 (n.d., 14 pp.); vols. 6–13 (n.d., 34 pp.); vols. 14–19 in 19 (1978): 279–88.

2300 *Eighteenth-Century Life* (*ECLife*). 1974– . 3/yr. HN1.E42 309.1'03.

Publishes articles, review essays, and special issues on all areas of American, British, and Continental life, with some emphasis on English literature. Since ns 9 (1984), includes a forum on films about the period. Each volume since vol. 6 (1980) prints "Abstracts of Recent Dissertations" (based largely on *Dissertation Abstracts International* [465]).

2305 *Eighteenth-Century Studies* (*ECS*). 1967– . Quarterly. NX452.E54 700.5.

Emphasizes interdisciplinary studies in essays, reviews, and occasional special issues on all aspects of the Restoration and eighteenth century. Of the journals in this section, *ECS* is the most consistently international in coverage. Cumulative index: vols. 1–20, Eighteenth-Century Studies*: A Cumulative Index, 1967–1987*, comp. and ed. Ann F. Scheuring (Northfield: American Soc. for Eighteenth-Century Studies, 1988, 145 pp.).

2310 *The Scriblerian and the Kit-Cats* (*Scriblerian*). 1968– . 2/yr. Former title: *The Scriblerian: A Newsletter Devoted to Pope, Swift, and Their Circle* (1968–71). PR445.S39 820.5.

Publishes notes and reviews (of both books and articles) on the Scriblerians, Kit-Cats, and their acquaintances. Regular features include "Scribleriana Transferred" (news of manuscripts and books sold at auction, offered by antiquarian bookdealers, or acquired by libraries) and "Scribleriana" (featuring miscellaneous notes on new publications and exhibitions). Quinquennial cumulative index and bibliography of notes published and articles and books reviewed.

See also

Restoration: Studies in English Literary Culture, 1660–1700 (2250).
Seventeenth-Century News (2080).
Studies in English Literature, 1500–1900 (1485).

Background Reading

The chapter on the period 1650–1800 in Bateson, *Guide to English and American Literature* (85) offers an overview of important histories, surveys, and critical studies (pp. 111–37). See also "Recent Studies in the Restoration and Eighteenth Century" (2240).

2315 Sambrook, James. *The Eighteenth Century: The Intellectual and Cultural Context of English Literature, 1700–1789.* Longman Literature in English Series. London: Longman, 1986. 290 pp. PR441.S33 820'.9'005.

An introduction to the intellectual and cultural backgrounds of eighteenth-century literature, with chapters on science, religion, philosophy, politics and history, aesthetics, visual arts (architecture, sculpture, painting, and landscape gardening), and cultural models (Roman, Grecian, Gothic, Oriental, and savage); the final chapter suggests some connections between the preceding ones. Concludes with a chronology of literary works, other publications, and historical and cultural events; and an evaluatively annotated bibliography, with sections for general studies, each of the chapters, and selected major authors. Indexed by persons, topics, and anonymous titles. The clear summaries of major theories, ideas, and works make Sambrook the best guide to the backgrounds necessary for an understanding of eighteenth-century literature.

Donald Greene, *The Age of Exuberance: Backgrounds to Eighteenth-Century English Literature* (New York: Random, 1970, 182 pp.), is still a good introduction "to the salient historical, ideological, and aesthetic events and circumstances" in Britain from 1660 to the 1780s. Underlying the chapters on Britain and its people, history, ideas and attitudes, and the arts is an insistence on the energy and bold imagination of the age. Indexed by persons and subjects.

See also

Oxford History of England (1495).

Genres

Several works in sections L: Genres and M: English Literature/General/Genres are useful for research in Restoration and eighteenth-century English literature.

FICTION

Some works in sections L: Genres/Fiction and M: English Literature/General/Genres/Fiction are useful for research in Restoration and eighteenth-century English literature.

Histories and Surveys

See

Baker, *History of the English Novel*, vols. 3–5 (1505).
Salzman, *English Prose Fiction, 1558–1700* (2090).

Guides to Primary Works

There is no adequate bibliography of fiction published between 1770 and the end of the century (although eventually it will be possible to extract a list of extant works from the *ESTC* [2230]). Leonard Orr, *A Catalogue Checklist of English Prose Fiction, 1750–1800* (Troy: Whitston, 1979, 204 pp.), compiled almost exclusively from other sources, is riddled with errors and omissions. (See the reviews by Edward W. Pitcher, *Analytical and Enumerative Bibliography* 5 [1981]: 56–60; and Jerry C. Beasley, *Literary Research Newsletter* 5 [1980]: 140–47.) Andrew Block, *The English Novel, 1740–1850: A Catalogue Including Prose Romances, Short Stories, and Translations of Foreign Fiction*, rev. ed. (London: Dawsons, 1961, 349 pp.), is, as Richard Altick points out, "one of the worst such compilations published in modern times—inaccurate, incomplete, wholly dependent on secondary sources and not even using them in any systematic way" (*Librarianship and the Pursuit of Truth* [New Brunswick: Rutgers U, Graduate School of Library Science, 1974] 11). For particulars, see the following reviews: *Times Literary Supplement* 25 Mar. 1939: 180; Robert A. Colby, *Nineteenth-Century Fiction* 16 (1962): 354–59.

2320 Beasley, Jerry C., comp. *A Check List of Prose Fiction Published in England, 1740–1749*. Charlottesville: UP of Virginia, for the Bibliographical Soc. of the U of Virginia, 1972. 213 pp. Z2014.F4.B37 016.823'5'08.

An enumerative bibliography of original works, reprints, and English translations that continues McBurney, *Check List of English Prose Fiction, 1700–1739* (2325). Although admitting histories, lives, voyages, or collections of letters with a narrative line, Beasley excludes chapbooks, jestbooks, and magazine fiction (for the last, see Mayo, "Catalogue of Magazine Novels" [2330]). Works are organized by year of initial publication; under each year are separate alphabetical lists of anonymous publications, works of known authorship, and translations. A typical entry includes author, short title, imprint, pagination or number of volumes, format, price, location of at least one copy, a descriptive annotation that identifies subject matter and type of work, and a list of subsequent editions through 1749. Appendixes list unverified editions of authentic works and unauthenticated titles. Indexed by titles, authors, and members of the book trade. Although limited to a decade, *Check List of Prose Fiction* is an accurate source for identifying works by subject or type, locating copies, and studying the environment of some of the major novels of the century. Several works are available on microfilm in *Early British Fiction: Pre-1750* (Woodbridge: Research Publications, 1980). Beasley's checklist is complemented by his analysis of narrative forms in *Novels of the 1740s* (Athens: U of Georgia P, 1982, 238 pp.).

2325 McBurney, William Harlin, comp. *A Check List of English Prose Fiction, 1700–1739*. Cambridge: Harvard UP, 1960. 154 pp. Z2014.F4.M3 016.8235.

A bibliography of fictional prose narratives, by English writers or translators, first published in England between 1700 and 1739. McBurney omits reprints of earlier fiction, chapbooks, jestbooks, pamphlets, and periodical fiction. Works are listed chronologically by year of first publication; under each year are sections for original works and translations, each organized alphabetically by author or title of anonymous work. A typical entry includes author, complete title, imprint, pagination, format, price, location of at least one copy, translator and original title (for translations), miscellaneous notes, and a chronological list of subsequent editions through 1739. Dubious or unauthenticated titles occupy a separate section at the back. Indexed by authors, titles, translators, printers, publishers, and booksellers. The selection policy could be clearer and transcriptions more accurate, but McBurney is the standard bibliography for identifying and locating works, establishing the fictional environment of a novel, and charting trends in fiction (although the last two tasks are made difficult because subsequent editions are not cross-referenced to years of publication and because periodical fiction and reprints of pre-1700 works are excluded). Reviews: Donald F. Bond, *Modern Philology* 59 (1962): 231–34; C. J. Rawson, *Notes and Queries* ns 9 (1962): 468–71; Andrew Wright, *Library* 5th ser. 17 (1962): 273.

Several titles are available on microfilm in *Early British Fiction: Pre-1750* (Woodbridge: Research Publications, 1980). Continued by Beasley, *Check List of Prose Fiction Published in England, 1740–1749* (2320).

2330 Mayo, Robert D. "A Catalogue of Magazine Novels and Novelettes, 1740–1815." *The English Novel in the Magazines, 1740–1815: With a Catalogue of 1375 Novels and Novelettes*. Evanston: Northwestern UP; London: Oxford UP, 1962. 431–677. PR851.M37 823.09.

A bibliography of narrative prose works of more than 5,000 words printed in serial publications (except newspapers). Includes translations, abridgments of and self-contained excerpts from novels, as well as travels, voyages, biographies, and histories that are predominantly fictional. Works are listed alphabetically by title (with identical texts listed under the title of the first magazine appearance); additions appear on p. 647. Entries identify the periodical, number of parts (and approximate number of words), and, when possible, author or translator, reprints, source, alternate titles, and related works. Users should note that the bibliography is indexed separately in three parts: authors, editors, translators, titles, alternative titles, and series titles; publication date; periodicals. Although not exhaustive, Mayo is the indispensable pioneering guide to fiction previously ignored in histories and bibliographies. Numerous additions and corrections are printed in a series of articles and notes by Edward W. Pitcher: "Robert Mayo's *The English Novel in the Magazines, 1740–1815*: New Facts," *Library* 5th ser. 31 (1976): 20–30; "The Short Story in Anthology and Miscellany, 1750–1800: A Response to Robert Mayo," *Studies in Short Fiction* 14 (1977): 1–11; "Robert Mayo's *The English Novel in the Magazines,*

1740–1815: More Emendations and New Facts," *Library* 6th ser. 2 (1980): 326–32; "Robert Mayo's *The English Novel in the Magazines, 1740–1815*: Further Emendations," *Library* 6th ser. 9 (1987): 162–64. Reviews: Richard D. Altick, *Library Quarterly* 34 (1964): 131–32; J. M. S. Tompkins, *Review of English Studies* ns 15 (1964): 208–10.

2335 Raven, James. *British Fiction, 1750–1770: A Chronological Check-List of Prose Fiction Printed in Britain and Ireland*. Newark: U of Delaware P; London: Associated U Presses, 1987. 349 pp. Z2014.F4.R34 [PR851] 016.823'6'08.

A checklist of editions of prose fiction—original works, reprints, and translations extant as well as lost—printed in the British Isles and Ireland between 1750 and 1770. Although emphasizing the novel, *British Fiction* includes representative examples of imaginary voyages, fictional biographies, and miscellanies; it excludes jestbooks, children's books, chapbooks, reports of crimes, and serial and magazine fiction. The 1,363 entries are organized by year of actual publication (which sometimes differs from imprint date); under each year, anonymous works are listed alphabetically by title, followed by works of known or attributed authorship (alphabetically by author, with translations listed by original author), and then a selection of miscellanies, imaginary voyages, and fictional biographies. A typical entry includes author, title, imprint, number of pages or volumes, format, price, references to reviews and standard bibliographies, notes on authorship, other editions, cross-references, and locations in selected British and American libraries. Two indexes: authors and translators; titles. Although much of the information is taken secondhand, Raven is an indispensable source for locating copies and charting trends in prose fiction during the two decades. It must, however, be supplemented with *ESTC* (2230).

See also

Mish, *English Prose Fiction, 1600–1700* (2095).

Guides to Scholarship and Criticism

2340 Beasley, Jerry C. *English Fiction, 1660–1800: A Guide to Information Sources*. American Literature, English Literature, and World Literatures in English: An Information Guide Series 14. Detroit: Gale, 1978. 313 pp. Z2014.F5.B42 [PR851] 016.823.

A highly selective annotated bibliography restricted largely to English-language scholarship published through the mid-1970s. Entries are organized in two divisions: general studies (with sections for background sources, general histories and surveys of the English novel, genre studies, history and criticism of the novel from 1660–1800, bibliographies, and background reading) and individual bibliographies of 29 authors (with sections under each for editions, letters, bibliographies, biographies, and critical studies). A majority of the entries are descriptively annotated (with occasional evaluative comments). Indexed by authors, scholars, and short titles of works cited. Although many of the writers are subjects of author bibliographies, *English Fiction, 1660–1800* remains useful for its generally judicious selectivity.

Reviews: James T. Boulton, *Notes and Queries* ns 26 (1979): 577–78; C. J. Rawson, *Yearbook of English Studies* 11 (1981): 268–70.

Some additional coverage is offered by H. George Hahn and Carl Behm III, *The Eighteenth-Century British Novel and Its Background: An Annotated Bibliography and Guide to Topics* (Metuchen: Scarecrow, 1985, 392 pp.), a less than successful attempt to index scholarship through 1984 by topic. The criteria governing selection are unclear and the annotations inadequate.

2345 Spector, Robert Donald. *The English Gothic: A Bibliographic Guide to Writers from Horace Walpole to Mary Shelley*. Westport: Greenwood, 1984. 269 pp. Z2014.H67.S66 [PR830.T3] 016.823'0872'09.

An evaluative survey of the most important English-language publications on the genre and major authors. After a lengthy introduction that treats the definition and development of the genre, an initial chapter examines bibliographies; genre, influence, and critical reception studies; and scholarship on several minor writers. The remaining four chapters range beyond gothic fiction in evaluating biographies, editions, and scholarship on pairs of related authors: Walpole and Reeve, Charlotte Smith and Radcliffe, Lewis and Beckford, Maturin and Mary Shelley. The index of subjects and authors is seriously marred by inconsistencies and numerous omissions. Although highly selective and inadequately indexed, *English Gothic* is valuable for its extensive evaluations of studies and surveys of critical trends.

Less selective but provisionally complete through only 1971 is Dan J. McNutt, *The Eighteenth-Century Gothic Novel: An Annotated Bibliography of Criticism and Selected Texts* (New York: Garland, 1975, 330 pp.). There are numerous omissions in the background sections; foreign-language studies are relegated (unannotated) to an appendix; and the indexing is inadequate. Nevertheless, the clearly annotated entries include studies omitted by Spector.

See also

Frank, *Guide to the Gothic* (875).

Background Reading

2350 Watt, Ian. *The Rise of the Novel: Studies in Defoe, Richardson, and Fielding*. Berkeley: U of California P, 1957. 319 pp. PR851.W3.

An analysis of the influence of formal realism, the growth of a middle-class reading public, and social, economic, and religious conditions on the development of the novel. Although serious deficiencies of method are now evident, *Rise of the Novel* remains an influential work that has not been superseded. For its composition, reception, and shortcomings, see Watt, "Serious Reflections on *The Rise of the Novel*," *Novel* 1 (1968): 205–18; on the impact of the work and its relationship to recent critical theories, see Daniel R. Schwarz, "The Importance of Ian Watt's *The Rise of the Novel*," *Journal of Narrative Technique* 13 (1983): 59–73. Reviews: Irving Howe, *Partisan Review* 25 (1958): 145–50; Alan D. McKillop, *Modern Philology* 55 (1958): 208–10.

DRAMA AND THEATER

Many works in sections L: Genres/Drama and Theater and M: English Literature/General/Genres/Drama and Theater are useful to research in Restoration and eighteenth-century drama and theater.

Histories and Surveys

2355 Hume, Robert D. *The Development of English Drama in the Late Seventeenth Century*. Oxford: Clarendon, 1976. 525 pp. PR691.H8 822'.4'09.

A study of the development of the drama from 1660 to 1710 in two parts: an examination of the dramatic types in theory and practice; and a decade-by-decade analysis of theatrical fashions, particularly as they are influenced by political and social change. Two indexes: names and subjects; plays. A provocative, scholarly work on a neglected period of the drama, but Hume's categorization of types of plays and individual readings have elicited some controversy. Reviews: Anne Barton, *TLS: Times Literary Supplement* 10 Sept. 1976: 1110–11; Maximillian E. Novak, *Eighteenth-Century Studies* 10 (1977): 512–16; Eric Rothstein, *Modern Language Quarterly* 38 (1977): 191–94.

2360 Nicoll, Allardyce. *Restoration Drama, 1660–1700*. 4th ed. *Early Eighteenth Century Drama*. 3rd ed. *Late Eighteenth Century Drama, 1750–1800*. 2nd ed. Vols. 1–3 of *A History of English Drama, 1660–1900* (1525). Cambridge: Cambridge UP, 1952. PR625.N52 822.09.

Emphasizing the history of the stage and dramatic forms, each volume includes chapters on the theater, tragedy, comedy, and (except vol. 1) miscellaneous dramatic forms. Appendixes treat playhouses and government documents related to the stage. Each volume concludes with an author list of plays, operas, and other dramatic forms written during the period, with information on performances, printed editions, and manuscripts (although the last are sketchily treated). Revisions that could not be incorporated readily into the text are printed as supplementary sections. Indexed by persons and subjects; the lists of plays (excluding most Italian operas and "the repertoire of the French and Italian comedians") are indexed and supplemented in vol. 6 (entry 1545). (Further additions are printed in Raymond A. Biswanger, Jr., "Additions to Allardyce Nicoll's 'Hand-List of Plays, 1700–1750,'" *Restoration and 18th Century Theatre Research* 15.1 [1976]: 46–60; 15.2: 60.) Although in need of updating (most notably by reference to *London Stage, 1660–1800* [2370]), the volumes contain a wealth of information not available elsewhere and the most complete bibliographies of dramatic works for the period.

2365 *The Revels History of Drama in English* (1530). Gen. ed. T. W. Craik. Vol. 5: *1660–1750*. London: Methuen, 1976. 331 pp. PR625.R44 822'.009.

Includes a chronology; essays on the social and literary context, theaters and actors, and plays and playwrights; and an evaluative survey of important studies. Indexed by authors, titles, and subjects. Although uneven in quality, the essays complement Nicoll, *History of English Drama* (2360). Vol. 6 covers the period 1750–1880 (2675). Like other volumes of *Revels History*, this offers a useful synthesis of scholarship rather than a connected history of the drama. Reviews: John Barnard, *English* 26 (1977): 233–39; John Kenyon, *TLS: Times Literary Supplement* 28 Jan. 1977: 102.

Annals

See

Harbage, *Annals of English Drama, 975–1700* (1535).

Guides to Primary Works

2370 *The London Stage, 1660–1800: A Calendar of Plays, Entertainments, and Afterpieces Together with Casts, Box-Receipts, and Contemporary Comment: Compiled from the Playbills, Newspapers, and Theatrical Diaries of the Period.* 5 pts. and index in 12 vols. Carbondale: Southern Illinois UP, 1960–79. PN1582.G72.L65 792'.09421.

Part 1: 1660–1700. Ed. William Van Lennep. 1965. 532 pp. (A revision by Judith Milhous and Robert D. Hume is in progress, with publication possibly in the mid-1990s.)
Part 2: 1700–1729. 2 vols. Ed. Emmett L. Avery. 1960. (A revision by Judith Milhous and Robert D. Hume is in progress, with publication possibly in the mid-1990s.)
Part 3: 1729–1747. 2 vols. Ed. Arthur H. Scouten. 1961.
Part 4: 1747–1776. 3 vols. Ed. George Winchester Stone, Jr. 1962.
Part 5: 1776–1800. 3 vols. Ed. Charles Beecher Hogan. 1968.
Index to The London Stage, 1660–1800. Comp. Ben Ross Schneider, Jr. 1979. 939 pp.

A calendar of spoken and in some instances sung dramatic entertainments, organized by theatrical season and then by date of performance. A typical entry identifies date, theater, title, afterpiece, cast (a full list for the initial performance, with changes noted for subsequent ones), prologues, epilogues, dancing, singing, music, or other entertainment; a concluding section notes "benefits, requests for particular plays, box office receipts, the presence of royalty and other persons named in the bills, and references to or quotations from contemporary documents which throw light upon the evening's whole entertainment." Entries vary in fullness, depending on the available information.

Each season is prefaced by a brief summary, and each part begins with an extensive general introduction that typically examines the playhouses and their organization, finances, management, advertising, costumes, scenery, repertory, players, music, production details, audience, and contemporary criticism. (These important introductions have been separately published as *The London Stage*, 5 vols. [Carbondale: Southern Illinois UP; London: Feffer, 1968].)

Entries—but not the introductions—are indexed by titles, names, places, theaters, and some subjects in Schneider's *Index*, which cumulates and expands the index in each volume; however, the index volume must be used very cautiously, since there are innumerable errors and misidentifications. (For important strictures on the use of the *Index*, see Langhans's review.)

The London Stage Information Bank, the data base used to prepare the index volume, is unfortunately not accessible at present. Ben Ross Schneider, Jr., is exploring the feasibility of publishing the data base on optical disc for use with personal computers but has no plans to update it. The Harvard Theatre Collection (Harvard College Library, Cambridge, MA 02138) is arranging to convert the tapes to a modern operating system and is exploring the possibility of linking the data base to materials in its collection. (For a description of the London Stage Information Bank, see the introduction to the *Index*.)

Users must remember that (1) completeness and accuracy vary markedly from part to part; (2) editorial policy changes somewhat from part to part; (3) performance records are very incomplete in the early years; (4) before 1705, dates are frequently those of publication rather than performance; (5) an advertised play or entertainment was not necessarily performed or acted by the announced cast; (6) many additions and corrections have been made (see, for example, William J. Burling and Robert D. Hume, "Theatrical Companies at the Little Haymarket, 1720–1737," *Essays in Theatre* 4 [1986]: 98–118; and the following by Judith Milhous and Robert D. Hume in *Harvard Library Bulletin*: "Dating Play Premières from Publication Data," 22 [1974]: 374–405; "Lost English Plays, 1660–1700," 25 [1977]: 5–33; and "Attribution Problems in English Drama, 1660–1700," 31 [1983]: 5–39).

In spite of its flaws, *London Stage* is an indispensable source for research on theater and stage history, repertory, acting careers, theater personnel, trends in drama, reception history—in short, on nearly every aspect of the drama and stage of the period. Researchers must also consult Highfill, *Biographical Dictionary* (2400), whose entries make numerous corrections and additions to *London Stage*. Until the revisions of parts 1 and 2 are published (probably in the mid-1990s), scholars should also see Milhous, *Register of English Theatrical Documents* (2380). Reviews: (pt. 1) Arthur Sherbo, *JEGP: Journal of English and Germanic Philology* 65 (1966): 194–96; (pt. 2) Sherbo, 60 (1961): 299–305; (pt. 3) Sherbo, 61 (1962): 926–31; (pt. 4) Sherbo, 63 (1964): 365–69; (pt. 5) Robert D. Hume, *Philological Quarterly* 50 (1971): 389–90; (index) Edward A. Langhans, *Eighteenth-Century Studies* 14 (1980): 72–78 (including a list of entries in the *Biographical Dictionary* [2400] corrected by the *Index*).

2375 Bowers, Fredson. *A Bibliography of the English Printed Drama, 1660–1700*. In progress.

A descriptive bibliography of all editions, issues, and states of plays published between 1660 and 1700 that are excluded from Greg, *Bibliography of the English Printed Drama* (2135). Titles are arranged according to date of publication. Each entry provides a full bibliographical description based on personal examination of multiple copies, with extensive notes on printing, dating, advertisements, and identification of printers. Indexes include printers, publishers, dedicatees, writers of prologues and epilogues, first lines of epilogues and prologues, and first lines of songs.

2380 Milhous, Judith, and Robert D. Hume, comps. *A Register of English Theatrical Documents, 1660–1737*. Carbondale: Southern Illinois UP. Scheduled for 1990.

A chronological calendar of manuscript and printed documents related to the management and regulation of the theater, principally in London, from 1660 through 1737. Entries are organized by theatrical season, then by date (but users must study the introductory discussion of how certain kinds of documents, such as lawsuits, are dated). Each entry provides date, location, title (descriptive in the case of manuscripts), description of content (with a full transcription in many instances; some documents will be printed in full or excerpted in the revision of pts. 1 and 2 of *London Stage* [2370]), and notes (amplifying location information, giving bibliographical details for printed works, and referring to other copies, published transcriptions, or scholarship). Five appendixes list documents not assignable to a single season, undatable bills from Drury Lane (1713–16), documents spanning more than one season, documents misdated by earlier authorities, and Chancery suits by Public Record Office number. The work is an invaluable compilation that carefully describes and locates a mass of widely scattered documents, corrects numerous published accounts, and adds much that is new. By ordering what is known, the *Register* should stimulate the identification and publication of additional material.

See also

Nicoll, *History of English Drama*, vols. 1–3 (2360).

Guides to Scholarship and Criticism

Surveys of Research

2385 Hume, Robert D. "English Drama and Theatre, 1660–1800: New Directions in Research." *Theatre Survey* 23.1 (1982): 71–100.

A summary of the state of scholarship, with evaluations of reference works, bibliographies, critical studies, and histories; comments on research methodologies; and valuable suggestions for further research.

Other Bibliographies

2390 Link, Frederick M. *English Drama, 1660–1800: A Guide to Information Sources*. American Literature, English Literature, and World Literatures in English: An Information Guide Series 9. Detroit: Gale, 1976. 374 pp. Z2014.D7.L55 [PR701] 016.822.

A selective survey of "every substantial book and article" through 1973 (along with a few from 1974). The emphasis is on English-language studies, and researchers must read the prefatory list of topics excluded before consulting the guide. Unlike other volumes in the series, this one consists of a series of surveys of research in two divisions. The first examines general works in sections for reference works, collections, playhouses and audience, biography, dramatic theory, history of drama, general criticism, and antecedents and influences. The second treats a variety of playwrights, major and minor. The commentary tends toward brief description, with occasional incisive evaluations and perceptive suggestions for research. The format—more effective for the treatment of individual authors than for general topics—

does not accommodate scanning. Two indexes: persons; play titles. Accuracy, judicious selectivity and evaluation, clear organization, and broad coverage make *English Drama, 1660–1800* a useful starting point, especially for minor writers, but it must be supplemented by Stratman, *Restoration and Eighteenth Century Theatre Research* (2395); *Eighteenth Century: A Current Bibliography* (2245); and *Year's Work in English Studies* (330). Review: David Mann, *Analytical and Enumerative Bibliography* 1 (1977): 246–50.

2395 Stratman, Carl J., C.S.V.; David G. Spencer; and Mary Elizabeth Devine, eds. *Restoration and Eighteenth Century Theatre Research: A Bibliographical Guide, 1900–1968*. Carbondale: Southern Illinois UP; London: Feffer, 1971. 811 pp. Z2014.D7.S854 016.822'5'09.

An annotated bibliography of editions and studies (including dissertations and master's theses) through 1967 on all aspects of drama and theater in the British Isles. The approximately 6,000 entries are listed chronologically under 780 alphabetically arranged subject headings, with those for playwrights having separate lists of editions and studies. By the editors' count, 81.6% of the entries are descriptively annotated. The work is indexed by persons and subject headings, but because of the insufficiently refined headings and lack of cross-references, it is difficult to locate studies of specific topics. The numerous errors and omissions make this an untrustworthy source, yet it offers the most extensive single list of scholarship on the topic. Reviews: Hilbert H. Campbell, *Papers of the Bibliographical Society of America* 67 (1973): 200–03; D. F. McKenzie, *Notes and Queries* ns 21 (1974): 237–39; Geoffrey Marshall, *Seventeenth-Century News* 31 (1973): 18–19.

This work incorporates the "Restoration and 18th Century Theatre Research Bibliography for [1961–67]" (2405a); for post-1967 publications, see "Restoration and 18th Century Theatre Research Bibliography" (2405a); "Some Current Publications," *Restoration* (2250); *Eighteenth Century: A Current Bibliography* (2245); "Recent Studies in the Restoration and Eighteenth Century," *Studies in English Literature, 1500–1900* (2240); and the serial bibliographies and indexes in section G. For a selective bibliography, see Link, *English Drama, 1660–1800* (2390).

See also

"Restoration and 18th Century Theatre Research Bibliography," *Restoration and 18th Century Theatre Research* (2405).

Biographical Dictionaries

2400 Highfill, Philip H., Jr., Kalman A. Burnim, and Edward A. Langhans. *A Biographical Dictionary of Actors, Actresses, Musicians, Dancers, Managers, and Other Stage Personnel in London, 1660–1800*. 16 vols. Carbondale: Southern Illinois UP, 1973– . PN2597.H5 790.2'092'2.

A biographical dictionary of about 8,500 persons (and some animals) associated with professional dramatic entertainments. Entries include "actors and actresses, dancers, singers, instrumental musicians, scene painters, machinists, management officials, prompters, acrobats, contortionists, pyrotechnists, magicians, dwarfs, freaks, animal trainers, strong men, public orators, mimics, dressers, callers, concessionaires, and also members of certain trades operating on salary and within the physical confines of the theatres—such employees as tailors, carpenters, and barbers." Excludes dramatists except those who were also actors, managers, or otherwise connected with the theater. The informative, well-written entries, which vary from a single line to more than a hundred pages and include at least one portrait if any exists, are based on extensive research in primary sources. Although many biographies are the most authoritative available, entries lack full documentation—the only major flaw and one that will not be rectified by a bibliography volume. There are omissions and errors (but the majority of corrections and additions have come to light only because of the publication of the biographies); nevertheless, the *Biographical Dictionary* is undeniably a major achievement that, along with *London Stage* (2370), has already stimulated much research. Reviews: (vols. 1–2) Robert D. Hume, *Eighteenth-Century Studies* 8 (1975): 510–17; (vols. 3–4) Judith Milhous, *Eighteenth Century: A Current Bibliography* ns 2 (1976): 162–65.

Microform Collections

See

Wells, *Three Centuries of Drama* (1180).

Periodicals

2405 *Restoration and 18th Century Theatre Research* (*RECTR*). 1962–77, 1986– . Quarterly. Former title: *17th and 18th Century Theatre Research* (1962). PN2592.R46 792.

Publishes articles, bibliographies, and occasional reviews on drama and theater, primarily in England. The annual "Restoration and 18th Century Theatre Research Bibliography [1961–75]" (vols. 1–15 [1962–76]), a descriptively annotated subject bibliography, has not reappeared as of 2nd ser. 2.1 (1987). The bibliographies for 1961–67 are incorporated into Stratman, *Restoration and Eighteenth Century Theatre Research* (2395), and are cumulated in Carl J. Stratman, C.S.V., ed., and Edmund A. Napieralski and Jean E. Westbrook, comps., *Restoration and 18th Century Theatre Research Bibliography, 1961–1968* (Troy: Whitston, 1969, 241 pp.). Although subject headings are not as refined as they might be and coverage is not comprehensive, this work is a useful complement to *Eighteenth Century: A Current Bibliography* (2245) and the serial bibliographies and indexes in section G.

Background Reading

Hume, "English Drama and Theatre" (2385) surveys important criticism and background studies. See also the bibliography in *Revels History of Drama*, vols. 5–6 (2365 and 2675).

POETRY

Some works in sections L: Genres/Poetry and M: English Literature/General/Genres/Poetry are useful for research in Restoration and eighteenth-century English poetry.

Histories and Surveys

2410 Rothstein, Eric. *Restoration and Eighteenth-Century Poetry, 1660–1780.* Vol. 3 of *The Routledge History of English Poetry* (1580). Gen. ed. R. A. Foakes. Boston: Routledge, 1981. 242 pp. PR502.R58 [PR561] 821'.009.

A critical history that emphasizes the continuity of the period in chapters on poetry (1660–1720), style, uses of the past, and poetry (1720–80). A chronology features commentary on principal poems and collections by minor poets, and summaries of important historical events, especially political ones. Indexed by authors and anonymous works. Although sometimes lapsing into dense lists of authors and poems, the volume is overall an intelligent, well-organized, authoritative treatment of both major and minor writers. Reviews: John M. Aden, *Eighteenth Century: A Current Bibliography* ns 7 (for 1981): 371–72; James Engell, *Modern Philology* 79 (1982): 438–41.

Guides to Primary Works

2415 Foxon, D. F. *English Verse, 1701–1750: A Catalogue of Separately Printed Poems with Notes on Contemporary Collected Editions.* 2 vols. Cambridge: Cambridge UP, 1975. Z2014.P7.F69 [PR551] 016.821.

A short-title catalog of separately published verse, translations, and collections by a single author, in any language, written and printed between 1701 and 1750 in the British Isles. Since Foxon is not a catalog of all poems written and printed during the period, it excludes miscellanies (see Case, *Bibliography of English Poetical Miscellanies* [2180]), periodical verse, popular broadside ballads, slip songs, chapbooks, engraved sheets with music or cartoons, oratorios, and libretti (but see vol. 1, pp. xii-xiii, for some exceptions).

Entries are listed alphabetically by author, translator, or title of anonymous work; under each author, collected editions are listed chronologically, with separately published poems following in alphabetical order. An entry for a single work includes short title, imprint, collation, bibliographical notes (which distinguish editions, issues, impressions, or states; describe watermark; and cite standard bibliographies), first line, notes on authorship and subject matter, and locations (up to five libraries in the British Isles and five in the United States). Collected editions receive abbreviated descriptions. Six indexes: first lines; first editions (listed chronologically); imprints; bibliographical notes; epithets describing authors of anonymous books; subjects (including forms and genres).

Inevitably there are omissions, but the accuracy and detail of the descriptions (based almost exclusively on personal examination of multiple copies) make this an indispensable source for textual study, publishing history, and the identification and location of editions. Thorough coverage, detailed indexes (which open new approaches to the poetry), and numerous attributions render this a landmark catalog that lays the groundwork for definitive studies. For some additions and corrections, see Bryan Coleborne, "Some Notes on D. F. Foxon's *English Verse 1701–1750*," *Bibliographical Society of Australia and New Zealand Bulletin* 7 (1983): 45–48, as well as the following reviews: L. J. Harris, *Library* 5th ser. 31 (1976): 158–64; James Woolley, *Modern Philology* 75 (1977): 59–73.

2420 Jackson, J. R. de J. *Annals of English Verse, 1770–1835: A Preliminary Survey of the Volumes Published*. Garland Reference Library of the Humanities 535. New York: Garland, 1985. 709 pp. Z2039.P6.J32 [PR502] 016.821'6.

A chronological catalog of volumes of poems and verse drama published in the United Kingdom (along with a few volumes published elsewhere but intended for a British audience) in English and other languages except Gaelic and Welsh. Jackson excludes hymn books (except for some that print original hymns), books of songs not intended to be read, annuals, reprints of works originally published before 1770 (except for significant new editions), volumes of fewer than eight pages, "stage adaptations of plays, operas, textbooks, [and] foreign works in foreign languages." Entries, organized alphabetically by title under year of publication, record short title, editor or translator, publication information, edition if other than the first, format, number of volumes, pagination for single-volume works, price, author, and source(s) of the citation. Two indexes: authors; anonymous works.

Compiled from secondary sources (principally *Cambridge Bibliography of English Literature* [1385a], *New Cambridge Bibliography of English Literature* [1385], British Museum *General Catalogue of Printed Books* [250a], and *National Union Catalog, Pre-56 Imprints* [235]), *Annals of English Verse* is intended as a preliminary list. Although it repeats the errors of its sources, perpetuates ghosts, and omits works and editions, it is nonetheless a useful compilation for situating a play or volume of verse in its literary context and for preliminary identification of editions (especially of minor works). For the period 1770–1800, researchers should also consult *ESTC* (2230). Review: Anne McWhir, *University of Toronto Quarterly* 56 (1986): 99–101.

See also

Case, *Bibliography of English Poetical Miscellanies* (2180).
Crum, *First-Line Index of English Poetry, 1500–1800* (1590).

Guides to Scholarship and Criticism

2425 Mell, Donald C., Jr. *English Poetry, 1660–1800: A Guide to Information Sources*. American Literature, English Literature, and World Literatures in English: An Information Guide Series 40. Detroit: Gale, 1982. 501 pp. Z2014.P7.M44 [PR551] 016.821.

A selective bibliography of English-language scholarship (primarily from the 1930s through 1979) organized in two divisions: general studies and individual authors. The first lists works in three classified sections: reference materials; background studies of English literature, 1660–1800; and general studies of poetry,

1660–1800 (with subsections for themes, genres, poetic forms and structures, and language and versification). The second is devoted to 31 poets, each with separate lists of major editions; correspondence; bibliographies, textual studies, and concordances; collections of studies; biographical works; and critical studies. Annotations to the 2,264 entries are occasionally evaluative (but not always reliably so). Indexed by persons and titles of works listed. The established canon is emphasized, and subject indexing is lacking; nonetheless, the judicious selection of studies and clear annotations make his work, as Mell says, "imperfect yet useful." Review: David L. Vander Meulen, *Literary Research Newsletter* 9 (1984): 29–31.

See also

Donow, *Sonnet in England and America* (1250).
Kuntz, *Poetry Explication* (1255).

PROSE

Some works in sections L: Genres/Prose and M: English Literature/General/Genres/Prose are useful for research in Restoration and eighteenth-century prose.

Biography and Autobiography

Histories and Surveys

2430 Stauffer, Donald A. *The Art of Biography in Eighteenth Century England.* Princeton: Princeton UP; London: Oxford UP, 1941. 572 pp. *Bibliographical Supplement* (entry 2435). 1941. CT34.G7.S67 808.06.

A critical history of eighteenth-century English biography that emphasizes its place in the literature of the period. Chapters are devoted to biography and the drama, biography and the novel, biography and the Romantic spirit, lives of eccentrics and antiquaries, inner life, major biographers, and trends of biography. Indexed by persons and a few titles. Although now dated, this work remains the fullest history of biography during the century. Reviews: James R. Sutherland, *Review of English Studies* 18 (1942): 350–54; René Wellek, *Modern Philology* 39 (1942): 432–36.

Art of Biography continues Stauffer, *English Biography before 1700* (1605). For the *Bibliographical Supplement*, see entry 2435.

Guides to Primary Works

2435 Stauffer, Donald A. *The Art of Biography in Eighteenth Century England: Bibliographical Supplement.* Princeton: Princeton UP; London: Oxford UP, 1941. 293 pp. CT34.G7.S67 808.06.

A bibliography of biographies written or translated in England from 1700 through 1800 and of important scholarship on the genre. The bulk of the work consists of an author list of biographies, with cross-references to subjects. Each entry cites editions through 1800, along with an occasional modern one. Works not discussed in the text of *Art of Biography in Eighteenth Century England* (2430) are accompanied by a brief description of content or evaluative comment. The second part is a selective list of important studies. Concludes with a chronology of the most important biographies from 1700 through 1800. Although incomplete and including some works more properly classified as fiction, the *Supplement* remains the most complete list of biographies of the period.

Nineteenth-Century Literature

Many works listed in section M: English Literature/General are important for research in nineteenth-century literature. See also sections N: Irish Literature; O: Scottish Literature; P: Welsh Literature; and U: Literature-Related Topics and Sources/Children's Literature.

Research Methods

2450 Storey, Richard, and Lionel Madden. *Primary Sources for Victorian Studies: A Guide to the Location and Use of Unpublished Materials*. London: Phillimore, 1977. 81 pp. Storey. *Primary Sources for Victorian Studies: An Updating*. Occasional Papers in Bibliography. Leicester: Victorian Studies Centre, U of Leicester, 1987. 38 pp. Z2019.S86 [DA550] 016.941081.

A basic guide to the location and use of manuscripts and records. Except for a very brief discussion of guides to collections outside Britain, the work emphasizes British resources in chapters on the Royal Commission on Historical Manuscripts (1360) and National Register of Archives (1360a), national repositories, local repositories, general published guides, and special topics (such as art, education, literature, and religious history), terminology, and practical hints to researchers. Indexed by subjects. A clear, practical introduction whose usefulness as a guide to locating and using unpublished materials extends well beyond the Victorian period.

Histories and Surveys

2455 Jack, Ian. *English Literature, 1815–1832*. Vol. 10 of *The Oxford History of English Literature* (1310). Gen. eds. Bonamy Dobrée, Norman Davis, and F. P. Wilson. Oxford: Clarendon, 1963. 643 pp. PR457.J24 820.903.

A history of the period, with chapters on the literary scene in 1815; Byron; Shelley; Keats; Clare and minor poets; the Waverley romances; Peacock; Galt and minor prose fiction; Hazlitt; Lamb; De Quincey; miscellaneous prose; history, biography, and autobiography; the interest in foreign and earlier English literature; and the literary scene in 1832. Includes a chronology and an outdated selective bibliography. Indexed by persons and a few titles. A solid but not critically adventuresome work, whose accuracy, range, lucidity, and clarity of style cause reviewers to rate this work as one of the better *Oxford History* volumes. Reviews: Geoffrey Carnall, *Essays in Criticism* 14 (1964): 310–18; John Jones, *Review of English Studies* ns 16 (1965): 319–20.

The earlier Romantic writers are treated in a separate, unsatisfactory volume by Renwick (2460).

2460 Renwick, W. L. *English Literature, 1789–1815*. Vol. 9 of *The Oxford History of English Literature* (1310). Gen. eds. Bonamy Dobrée, Norman Davis, and F. P. Wilson. Oxford: Clarendon, 1963. 293 pp. PR447.R4 820.903.

Covers the full careers of writers whose "most characteristic work was published between 1789 and 1815" in eight chapters: background of the period; political works; science and travel writing; novels; writers of the early 1790s; Wordsworth, Coleridge, and Southey; Scottish literature; and drama and historical writing. Concludes with a chronology and an outdated bibliography. Indexed (inadequately) by person. A frequently impenetrable style, imbalances in discussions of important figures, and a lack of synthesis make this one of the least successful *Oxford History* volumes. Reviews: *Times Literary Supplement* 1 Mar. 1963: 154; Robert Martin Adams, *Hudson Review* 16 (1963–64): 594–600; Anne Kostelanetz, *Minnesota Review* 4 (1964): 532–43.

The later Romantic writers are more adequately treated by Jack, *English Literature, 1815–1832* (2455).

See also

Sec. M: English Literature/General/Histories and Surveys.

Bibliographies of Bibliographies

See

Sec. D: Bibliographies of Bibliographies.
Howard-Hill, *Index to British Literary Bibliography* (1355).

Guides to Primary Works

MANUSCRIPTS

2465 *Index of English Literary Manuscripts* (1365). Ed. P. J. Croft, Theodore Hofmann, and John Horden. Vol. 4, *1800–1900*. Comp. Barbara Rosenbaum and Pamela White. London: Mansell, 1982– . Z6611.L7.I5 [PR83] 016.82'08.

A descriptive catalog of extant literary manuscripts by a limited number of major British and Irish authors drawn from among those in *Concise Cambridge Bibliography of English Literature, 600–1950* (1365a). The emphasis is on literary manuscripts, including diaries, notebooks, and marginalia. Letters are excluded, although the introductions to individual authors identify important collections. In addition, the introductions alert researchers to special problems and relevant scholarship, point out additional manuscripts, discuss canon, note the disposition of an author's library, and conclude with an outline of the arrangement of entries. A typical entry provides a physical description of the manuscript, dates its composition, includes any necessary commentary (as well as references to editions, facsimiles, sale catalogs, or scholarship), and identifies its location (with shelfmark). Queries about privately owned manuscripts should be addressed to the *Index* in care of Mansell. Additions and corrections appear in pt. 1, pp. 825–31; others will be printed in vol. 5. Since some entries are based on inquiries to libraries and collectors, bibliographies, other reference works, and booksellers' and auction catalogs rather than personal examination by the compilers, the descriptions vary in fullness and precision.

Although restricted in the number of authors covered, this volume is an essential source for identifying and locating manuscripts. It must, however, be supplemented by the works listed in sections F: Guides to Manuscripts and Archives and M: English Literature/General/Guides to Primary Works/Manuscripts. Reviews: (pt. 1) T. A. J. Burnett, *TLS: Times Literary Supplement* 4 Feb. 1983: 120; Philip Collins, *Library* 6th ser. 5 (1983): 309–12.

See also

Secs. F: Guides to Manuscripts and Archives and M: English Literature/General/Guides to Primary Works/Manuscripts.

PRINTED WORKS

2470 *The English Catalogue of Books [1801–1968]*. Irregular, with various cumulations and index volumes. London: Publishers Circular, 1858–1969. Z2001.E52 015.42.

An author, title, and subject list of books published in Great Britain, American books imported or issued in England, and English-language books published on the Continent. Since the lists are augmented compilations of various trade catalogs, there are several ghosts and coverage is not thorough, especially for provincial British, American, and Continental publications. Through 1905, series are listed in an appendix, as are publications of learned societies (through 1941). Subject indexing is largely confined to title keywords. Separate subject indexes were published through 1889; thereafter, subject heads appear in the main alphabetic sequence. Entries vary in details but usually cite publisher, edition, size, and price. Although superseded in many respects by the union and national library catalogs in section E, the *English Catalogue*, as the most complete record of books published in Great Britain during the nineteenth century, is occasionally useful as a limited subject guide and for identifying and dating editions. Beginning in 1874, *Reference Catalogue of Current Literature* (2770) is an important supplement; after 1924, more thorough coverage of works published or issued in Great Britain is provided by *Whitaker's Cumulative Book List* (2770a) and after 1950 by *British National Bibliography* (2775).

2475 *Nineteenth Century Short Title Catalogue* (*NSTC*). Newcastle-upon-Tyne: Avero, 1984– . Z2013.N7 011.221.

Series I, Phase I, 1801–1815. 6 vols. 1984–86.
Series II, Phase I, 1816–1870. 55 vols. 1986– .

An attempt to record all books (and other unspecified letterpress material) printed between 1801 and 1918 in Great Britain, the colonies, and the United States; in English throughout the rest of the world; and in translation from English. *NSTC* plans a series of increasingly complete listings: the first phase is limited to a series of author catalogs based on the holdings of a few major libraries; phase two will draw upon the catalogs of specialist libraries. The *NSTC* data base will eventually be made available for computer searches.

Series I, Phase I, 1810–1815 is a union list derived from the published and in-house catalogs of the Bodleian; British Library; Library of Trinity College, Dublin; National Library of Scotland; and University Libraries of Cambridge and Newcastle. (A supplement listing the holdings of the Harvard libraries and the Library of Congress may be issued.) An entry cites *NSTC* number, author, short title, as many as three Dewey Decimal Classification numbers (the bases for the subject index), date and place of publication (but not printer or publisher), format, bibliographical notes, number of volumes, locations (with a complete list only in the main entry), and cross-references. Although cataloging generally follows the practices of the British Museum *General Catalogue of Printed Books* (250a), the entries are subject to the limitations, errors, and vagaries of the individual catalogs. Vols. 1–4 are author catalogs, each with imprint (i.e., place of publication only) and subject indexes (which are cumulated in vol. 5). Vol. 5 includes subject listings (essentially taken over from the British Museum *General Catalogue of Printed Books*) for England, Ireland, London, Scotland, directories, ephemerides, and periodical publications, with separate imprint and subject indexes for each; a title index to the subject listings; a supplement to vols. 1–4, listing British Library accessions from 1976 to 1984; imprint and subject indexes to the supplement; and cumulative imprint and subject indexes to the first four volumes. (London is omitted from all the imprint indexes.) Vol. 6 is a cumulative title index to vols. 1–4 and the supplement in vol. 5. Although five of the six libraries included are copyright deposit libraries, coverage of works published in Great Britain is not comprehensive (especially for provincial and ephemeral publications); that for the rest of the world is much less so. For United States imprints, bibliographies listed in section Q: American Literature/Nineteenth Century/Guides to Primary Works offer superior coverage. Because of an inadequate explanation of scope, users cannot be certain what kinds of publications are excluded.

Series II, Phase I, 1816–1870 provides better coverage of American imprints by incorporating the catalogs of the Library of Congress and Harvard University Libraries, and transcribes titles and imprints more fully, but otherwise retains the features of the first series. Subject and imprint (i.e., place of publication only) indexes appear in every fifth volume; cumulative title, imprint, and subject indexes will be published when the series is complete.

The main volumes are useful primarily as a union list (although it appears that locations are incomplete for many entries); the imprint indexes are important tools for identifying works printed in a locale other than London; and the title indexes are essential to locating entries for anonymous works; but the subject indexes, based on and organized by Dewey classifications, are too unrefined, especially for literary topics (e.g., the English Poetry entry in *1801–1815* consists of 10 densely packed columns of *NSTC* numbers).

News of the project and progress reports are published in *Nineteenth Century Short Title Catalogue (NSTC) Newsletter* (1983– , irregular). Chadwyck-Healey is publishing microform collections based on selected subject categories from the *NSTC*.

The larger scope, greater number of publications, and reliance on library catalog entries rather than examination of copies mean that *NSTC* will never attain the comprehensiveness, sophistication, and level of accuracy of the other *Short-Title Catalogues* (1990, 1995, and 2230). Because of its limited scope, need for considerable editorial refinement, and steep price, libraries may be unable to justify purchasing future series in hard copy. More accessible, affordable, and appropriate for the present state of the project would be publication as a data base that could be continually refined and expanded. Reviews: (1801–15): Robin Alston, *TLS: Times Literary Supplement* 6 Apr. 1984: 381–82; Patricia Fleming, *Victorian Periodicals Review* 19 (1986): 68–69; (1801–15 and 1816–70) David McKitterick, *TLS: Times Literary Supplement* 8 May 1987: 497.

See also

Sec. E: Libraries and Library Catalogs.
Records of the Worshipful Company of Stationers (1380).
British Books in Print (2770).
Halkett, *Dictionary of Anonymous and Pseudonymous English Literature* (5110).
New Cambridge Bibliography of English Literature, vol. 3 (2505).

Guides to Scholarship and Criticism

SURVEYS OF RESEARCH

2480 "Recent Studies in the Nineteenth Century." *Studies in English Literature, 1500–1900* (entry 1485). 1 (1961)– . Annually in the autumn issue.

A commissioned survey by an established scholar, with recent issues emphasizing book-length critical and historical studies. The essays vary considerably in breadth as well as soundness and degree of assessment. Now generally limited to books received for review, this work must be supplemented by *Romantic Movement* (2485) and the chapters in *Year's Work in English Studies* (330) on the Romantic and Victorian periods.

SERIAL BIBLIOGRAPHIES

2485 *The Romantic Movement: A Selective and Critical Bibliography for [1936–]*. New York: Garland, 1980– . Annual. Z6514.R6.R63 [PN603] 016.809'9145.

1964–78: Supplement to *English Language Notes* (entry 675) 3–17 (1965–79).

1949–63: *Philological Quarterly* (entry 720) 29–43 (1950–64).
1936–48: *ELH: A Journal of Literary History* (entry 670) 4–16 (1937–49).
(The bibliographies for 1936–70 are reprinted, with cumulative indexes, as A. C. Elkins and L. J. Forstner, eds. *The Romantic Movement Bibliography, 1936–1970: A Master Cumulation*, 7 vols. [Ann Arbor: Pierian in association with Bowker, 1973].)

A bibliography of significant books, articles, and reviews on the Romantic Movement in Great Britain and Western Europe. Although this work includes minor items that fall outside the scope of *MLAIB* (335) and studies of American Romanticism that relate to the European movement, it makes no attempt at comprehensiveness. The scope has altered over the years and within individual sections so that recent volumes are more critical and selective. (For an overview of changes, see David V. Erdman's foreword to the reprint of the 1936–70 bibliographies [vol. 1, pp. vii-xi].) Entries are organized in six major divisions: general, English, French, German, Italian, and Spanish (at various times there were divisions for other national literatures such as Portuguese, Russian, and Scandinavian); each national literature has sections for bibliographies, general studies, and individual authors. The chronological scope varies from country to country and alters to reflect changes in critical perspectives (e.g., while the English section has remained fairly stable at 1789–1837, the German one has undergone some major shifts in chronological coverage). Most entries are now annotated: many descriptively, several critically, with a number of books receiving full reviews. Recent volumes quote from other reviews. Since the 1961 bibliography, reviews of previously listed books, composite reviews, and review essays are grouped at the end of a section. Although recent annual volumes unfortunately provide no indexes, the reprint of the 1936–70 bibliographies offers three cumulative indexes: authors, main entries, reviewers; subjects: personal names; and subjects: categories. Timely coverage and judicious selection and evaluation make this the best guide to significant scholarship on the Romantic movement. Since it makes no attempt at comprehensiveness, scholars must also consult "Current Bibliography" in *Keats-Shelley Journal* (2495) and the standard serial bibliographies in section G.

2490 *Annual Bibliography of Victorian Studies, [1976–]*. Edmonton: LITIR Database, 1980– . Irregular. Z2019.A64 [DA533] 016.941.

The *Annual Bibliography* is cumulated and expanded as the following:
Chaudhuri, Brahma, comp. and ed. *A Comprehensive Bibliography of Victorian Studies, 1970–1984.* 3 vols. Edmonton: LITIR Database, 1984–85.
Vol. 1: *1970–1974*. 1984. 470 pp.
Vol. 2: *1975–1979*. 1985. 757 pp.
Vol. 3: *1980–1984*. 1985. 1,077 pp.

These works are further augmented and corrected:
Chaudhuri, Brahma, comp. and ed. *Cumulative Bibliography of Victorian Studies, 1970–1984.* 2 vols. Edmonton: Access Elite, 1988.

A classified bibliography of books, articles, and dissertations, primarily in English, on Great Britain from c. 1830 to 1914. Selected reviews are cited only in the *Annual Bibliography*, which the *Comprehensive Bibliography* otherwise expands and corrects (and which in turn is corrected and expanded in the *Cumulative Bibliography*). This work emphasizes studies of language and literature, with some attention to other subjects; for transitional authors, it includes only those studies treating the Victorian period. Entries are listed alphabetically by scholar in seven classified divisions: general and reference works, fine arts, philosophy and religion, history, social sciences, science and technology, and language and literature. The last has sections for general works, reference works, drama and theater, poetry, prose, fiction, children's literature, and individual authors (with lists of general works, bibliographies, biography and correspondence, general criticism, and studies of individual works). Some entries are accompanied by brief descriptive annotations. Users searching for publications on a minor author must be sure to use the subject index, since writers who are the subject of fewer than three studies are lumped together under "Other Authors" in the classified listings. Four indexes in each *Annual Bibliography* (subjects; scholars; reviewers; titles of works); each volume of the *Comprehensive Bibliography* has three indexes (subjects; scholars; titles of works), and those in vol. 3 are cumulative; the *Cumulative Bibliography* offers the same three indexes. The subject indexing, while useful, is limited to literary authors and title keywords (with some significant omissions). Although a useful compilation, it is slow and erratic in publication, and the 1970–84 cumulation is far short of the "comprehensive bibliography" claimed by the title (as is the *Cumulative Bibliography*, even though it adds more than 3,500 entries). Researchers must also consult the other bibliographies listed in this section and in section G: Serial Bibliographies, Indexes, and Abstracts, as well as "Victorian Periodicals" (2555) and "Guide to the Year's Work in Victorian Poetry" (2720).

2495 "Current Bibliography [1 July 1950–]." *Keats-Shelley Journal* (entry 2585) 1 (1952–).

The work is cumulated as the following:

Hartley, Robert A., ed. *Keats, Shelley, Byron, Hunt, and Their Circles: A Bibliography: July 1, 1962–December 31, 1974*. Lincoln: U of Nebraska P, 1978. 487 pp.

Green, David Bonnell, and Edwin Graves Wilson, eds. *Keats, Shelley, Byron, Hunt, and Their Circles: A Bibliography: July 1, 1950–June 30, 1962*. Lincoln: U of Nebraska P, 1964. 323 pp.

An annotated bibliography that attempts comprehensive coverage of Byron, Shelley, Keats, Hunt, and their circles. This excludes textbooks, but otherwise includes substantial references as well as reprints or translations of even a single poem and (between 1 July 1955 and 31 December 1972) phonograph recordings. The early numbers list publications from 1940 through 1950 that were omitted from other standard bibliographies. Entries are organized in five divisions: general works (with sections for bibliographies and general studies of English Romanticism), Byron, Hunt (Hunt and Hazlitt since the bibliography for 1984), Keats, and Shelley. In the author sections, primary works appear first, followed by an alphabetical list of studies on the writer and his circle. Entries are accompanied by brief descriptive annotations (with several works left unannotated in the early volumes) and review citations. Indexed by names and works referred to in annotations or titles and by scholars. The two reprints cumulate the individual indexes. Because the makeup of the various circles is not consistent throughout the volumes, users should consult the index to locate studies of individuals other than the four principal authors. This offers fuller coverage of the four writers and their circles than *Romantic Movement* (2485) or the serial bibliographies and indexes in section G.

2500 "Victorian Bibliography for [1932–]." *Victorian Studies* (entry 2610) 1 (1958)– .

1932–56: *Modern Philology* (entry 705) 30–54 (1933–57).

Reprinted, with cumulative indexes, as follows:

Freeman, Ronald E., ed. *Bibliographies of Studies in Victorian Literature for the Ten Years 1965–1974*. New York: AMS, 1981. 876 pp.

Slack, Robert C., ed. *Bibliographies of Studies in Victorian Literature for the Ten Years 1955–1964*. Urbana: U of Illinois P, 1967. 461 pp.

Wright, Austin, ed. *Bibliographies of Studies in Victorian Literature for the Ten Years 1945–1954*. Urbana: U of Illinois P, 1956. 310 pp.

Templeman, William D., ed. *Bibliographies of Studies in Victorian Literature for the Thirteen Years 1932–1944*. Urbana: U of Illinois P, 1945. 450 pp.

A selective international bibliography of "noteworthy" publications, including reviews, on Victorian England. Over the years, coverage has become more inclusive but with a corresponding decrease in annotations, so that recent bibliographies offer only an occasional brief explanation of an uninformative title. (Early volumes offer more substantial commentary, including some full reviews and quotations from others; however, evaluations during the first two decades are far less rigorous than they should be.) The bibliographies for 1932–74 list works alphabetically in four divisions: bibliographical materials; economic, political, religious, and social environment; movements of ideas, literary forms, and anthologies; individual authors. With the 1975 bibliography, entries appear in one of six divisions: bibliographical materials; histories, biographies, autobiographies, and historical documents; economic, educational, political, religious, scientific, and social environment; fine arts, household arts, performing arts, and city planning; literary history, literary forms, literary ideas; individual authors. Since the bibliography for 1966, listings under transitional figures such as Conrad and Shaw are restricted to studies dealing with the Victorian period. Articles in author journals and newsletters are awkwardly grouped under a single entry for the periodical, and users would benefit from a more refined classification system and better cross-referencing. Until recently, the annual issues (and subsequent cumulations) are seriously marred by a multitude of typographical errors, inaccurate citations, and faulty cross-references. The four volumes of reprints provide useful cumulative indexes: of Victorian authors in the 1932–44 volume; of scholars, Victorian figures, and some topics in the others. The cumulation for 1965–74 corrects some errors (pp. 739–42) and provides an introductory statistical and narrative survey of trends in scholarship for the period. In spite of its faults, the work offers the fullest, most current list of scholarship on the period, but scholars must also consult *Annual Bibliography of Victorian Studies* (2490), "Victorian Periodicals" (2555), "Guide to the Year's Work in Victorian Poetry" (2720), and the standard serial bibliographies and indexes in section G.

Although it is incomplete, poorly organized, and sometimes inaccurate, Thomas G. Ehrsam, Robert H. Deily, and Robert M. Smith, comps., *Bibliographies of Twelve Victorian Authors* (New York: Wilson, 1936, 362 pp.), offers the best coverage of studies—especially contemporary reviews—through July 1934 of Arnold, E. B. Browning, Clough, FitzGerald, Hardy, Kipling, Morris, C. G. and D. G. Rossetti, Stevenson, Swinburne, and Tennyson. Supplemented by Joseph G. Fucilla, "*Bibliographies of Twelve Victorian Authors*: A Supplement," *Modern Philology* 37 (1939): 89–96.

A convenient but dated selective bibliography is Jerome H. Buckley, comp., *Victorian Poets and Prose Writers*, 2nd ed., Goldentree Bibliographies in Language and Literature (Arlington Heights: AHM, 1977, 96 pp.), with coverage through early 1975.

See also

Sec. G: Serial Bibliographies, Indexes, and Abstracts.
ABELL (340): English Literature/Nineteenth Century section.
MLAIB (335): English Language and Literature division in the volumes for 1921–25; English X in the volumes for 1926–56; English IX in the volumes for 1957–80; and English Literature/1800–1899 (as well as any larger chronological sections encompassing the century) in later volumes. Researchers must also check the headings beginning "English Literature" in the subject index to post-1980 volumes.

OTHER BIBLIOGRAPHIES

2505 *The New Cambridge Bibliography of English Literature* (*NCBEL*). Vol. 3: *1800–1900*. Ed. George Watson. Cambridge: Cambridge UP, 1969. 1,948 cols. Z2011.N45 [PR83] 016.82.

(For a full discussion of *NCBEL*, see entry 1385.) Primary works and scholarship are organized in six divisions (each subdivided and classified as its subject requires): introduction (general studies, book production and distribution, literary relations with the Continent), poetry (1800–35, 1835–70, 1870–1900), novel (1800–35, 1835–70, 1870–1900, children's books), drama (1800–35, 1835–70, 1870–1900), prose (1800–35, 1835–70, 1870–1900, history, philosophy, religion, English studies, travel, sport, education, periodicals), Anglo-Irish literature (through 1916). Vol. 3 of the *Cambridge Bibliography of English Literature* (1385a) is still occasionally useful for its coverage of the intellectual, social, and political background; education; and Commonwealth literature (which *NCBEL* drops).

Users must familiarize themselves with the organization, remember that there is considerable unevenness of coverage among subdivisions, and consult the index volume (vol. 5) rather than the provisional index in vol. 3. Review: Richard D. Altick, *JEGP: Journal of English and Germanic Philology* 70 (1971): 139–45.

See also

McKenna, *Irish Literature, 1800–1875* (2985).

DISSERTATIONS AND THESES

2510 Altick, Richard D., and William R. Matthews, comps. *Guide to Doctoral Dissertations in Victorian Literature, 1886–1958*. Urbana: U of Illinois P, 1960. 119 pp. Z2013.A4 016.82'09'008.

A classified bibliography of 2,105 dissertations entirely or partly on British literature from c. 1837 to 1900. Coverage extends through 1957 for France, 1956 for the United Kingdom and Germany, and 1958 for Austria, Switzerland, and the United States. Dissertations are listed alphabetically by writer in nine sections: general topics, themes and intellectual influences, fiction, drama, poetry, literary criticism, periodicals, foreign relations, and individual authors. Indexed by dissertation writers. Although compiled largely from printed institutional and national lists (which are themselves not always accurate or complete), the *Guide* also includes several dissertations which have otherwise escaped notice. Thorough but not exhaustive, this work significantly reduces the time researchers would otherwise spend poring over the bibliographies in section H: Guides to Dissertations and Theses. A supplement would be welcomed by scholars.

See also

Sec. H: Guides to Dissertations and Theses.

RELATED TOPICS

2515 Brown, Lucy M., and Ian R. Christie, eds. *Bibliography of British History, 1789–1851.* Oxford: Clarendon, 1977. 759 pp. Z2019.B76 [DA520] 016.94107'3.

An extensive, albeit rigorously selective, bibliography of primary and secondary materials published through the early 1970s. Because of the multitude of publications on the era, Brown emphasizes reference sources. The 4,782 entries are listed chronologically (for the most part) in fifteen extensively classified divisions: general reference works; political, constitutional, legal, ecclesiastical, military, naval, economic, social, cultural, and local history; Wales; Scotland; Ireland; and British Empire. A majority of the entries are descriptively annotated and frequently cite several related studies. Indexed by persons and a few subjects. An essential guide for cross-disciplinary research. Review: John Saville, *Victorian Studies* 22 (1979): 203–04.

Continued by Hanham, *Bibliography of British History, 1851–1914* (2520). A convenient, more selective bibliography is Smith, *Late Georgian and Regency England, 1760–1837* (2260a).

2520 Hanham, H. J., comp. and ed. *Bibliography of British History, 1851–1914.* Oxford: Clarendon, 1976. 1,606 pp. Z2019.H35 [DA530] 016.942.

A massive, yet selective, bibliography of primary and secondary works (through 1973) organized in 13 extensively classified divisions: general reference works and studies, political and constitutional history, colonies and foreign relations, armed forces, legal system, religion, economic history, social history, intellectual and cultural history, local history, Wales, Scotland, and Ireland. A majority of the entries are annotated, many with judicious evaluative comments and citations to related studies (which nearly double the 10,829 numbered entries). Indexed by persons and subjects. An indispensable guide to historical scholarship on the period (and one of the better volumes of this important series). The earlier half of the century is covered in Brown, *Bibliography of British History, 1789–1851* (2515). Review: Josef L. Altholz, *Victorian Studies* 21 (1977): 108–09.

Convenient, more selective bibliographies are Josef L. Altholz, *Victorian England, 1837–1901*, Conference on British Studies Bibliographical Handbooks (Cambridge: Cambridge UP, for the Conference on British Studies, 1970, 100 pp.); and David Nicholls, *Nineteenth-Century Britain, 1815–1914*, Critical Bibliographies in Modern History (Folkestone: Dawson; Hamden: Archon, 1978, 170 pp.). Altholz is decidedly more thorough and authoritative, cites articles as well as books (through 1967), but offers only an occasional brief descriptive comment. Nicholls is current through 1977 and provides evaluative annotations, but cites only books and is designed for the undergraduate.

See also

Annual Bibliography of British and Irish History (1400).
Smith, *Late Georgian and Regency England, 1760–1837* (2260a).

Biographical Dictionaries

The *Dictionary of National Biography* (1425) remains the standard general source of biographical information for the nineteenth century; however, Boase, *Modern English Biography* (1425a) is an important supplement.

See also

Sec. J: Biographical Sources.
Dictionary of Literary Biography (600).

Periodicals

CONTEMPORARY PERIODICALS

Research Methods

2525 Vann, J. Don, and Rosemary T. VanArsdel, eds. *Victorian Periodicals: A Guide to Research.* 2 vols. New York: MLA, 1978– . 188 pp. (Vol. 2 is scheduled for 1989.) PN5124.P4.V5 052.

Vol. 1 is a guide to research methods and reference works (to 1977) essential to the study of periodicals (primarily elite British ones) from 1824 to 1900. Individual essays treat bibliographies and inventories, finding lists, biographical resources, general histories of the press, histories and studies of individual periodicals, identification of authors, and circulation and the Stamp Tax. Contributors typically outline their subject, describe (with occasional evaluative comments) essential reference sources (but without complete citations), discuss research strategies, and sometimes suggest topics for further work. Indexed by persons and titles. Individual essays vary in accuracy (in both citations and evaluations of reference works), but, overall, *Victorian Periodicals* is an essential guide for those working in this expanding field. Review: John Bush Jones, *Analytical and Enumerative Bibliography* 4 (1980): 107–23.

Vol. 2 is both a companion and supplement to the earlier one. Along with appendixes updating the essays on finding lists, biographical resources, general histories, and histories and studies of individual periodicals, it has chapters on Irish, Scottish, Welsh, feminist, religious, and children's periodicals, the radical press, publishers' archives, periodicals of the 1890s, serialized novels, periodicals and art history, and desiderata to the twenty-first century.

Guides to Primary Works

For other guides, indexes, lists, and bibliographies, see Scott Bennett, "The Bibliographic Control of Victorian Periodicals," *Victorian Periodicals* (2525) 1: 35–51. Many nineteenth-century periodicals have been reproduced in microfilm in two series by University Microfilms International: *Early British Periodicals, 1681–1921* and *English Literary Periodicals, 1681–1914*.

Union Lists

2530 Fulton, Richard D., and C. M. Colee, gen. eds. *Union List of Victorian Serials: A Union List of Selected Nineteenth-Century British Serials Available in United States and Canadian Libraries*. Garland Reference Library of the Humanities 530. New York: Garland, 1985. 732 pp. Z6956.G6.F85 [PN5124.P4] 011'.34.

A union list of periodicals published between 1824 and 1900 and listed in *New Cambridge Bibliography of English Literature* (2505) (augmented by about one hundred science and technology titles). Compiled from regional union lists, library lists, and reports by volunteers who examined actual holdings, the *Union List* records the holdings of 376 libraries (predominantly in the United States), especially major regional libraries and those with important Victorian serials collections. (There are some notable omissions, however.) A typical entry provides *Waterloo Directory* number (entry 2540), *NCBEL* reference, bibliographical information, notes (which may include title, series, and volume changes; details of conflicting information in standard references; and numbering irregularities), and locations (with exact holdings—accurate and complete for 1824–1900 only—including microform copies or reprints, and notes on special copies or cataloging problems). While many questions of dates and titles remain unsolved, entries alert researchers to conflicting information in standard reference sources. Although neither comprehensive nor definitive, this work is more thorough and reliable in its bibliographical descriptions and locations than *Union List of Serials* (640a), *British Union-Catalogue of Periodicals* (645a), or *New Cambridge Bibliography of English Literature*. See OCLC (225) and RLIN (230) for other locations and *Waterloo Directory of Irish Newspapers and Periodicals* (3000) for more thorough and accurate information on Irish serials. Review: Kathryn Chittick, *Victorian Periodicals Review* 18 (1985): 149–51.

2535 Ward, William S., comp. *Index and Finding List of Serials Published in the British Isles, 1789–1832*. Lexington: U of Kentucky P, 1953. 180 pp. Z6956.E5.W27 016.052.

——— . "*Index and Finding List of Serials Published in the British Isles, 1789–1832*: A Supplementary List." *Bulletin of the New York Public Library* 77 (1974): 291–97.

A list of periodicals and newspapers held by some 475 libraries and newspaper offices in the United States and Great Britain. Serials are listed by title (or by institution or learned society for publications lacking a distinctive title) and accompanied by minimal bibliographical information. Ward is designed to be used with *Union List of Serials* (640a); *Union Catalogue of the Periodical Publications in the University Libraries of the British Isles*, comp. Marion G. Roupell (London: Joint Standing Committee on Library Co-operation, National Central Library, 1937, 712 pp.); and *British Union-Catalogue of Periodicals* (645a); therefore, only additional or corrected holdings are recorded (but imprecisely in many instances). Although it offers numerous additions to the standard union lists, Ward must be supplemented by OCLC (225), RLIN (230), *Serials in the British Library* (645), and (for serials continuing beyond 1832) Fulton, *Union List of Victorian Serials* (2530). For Irish serials after 1824, see *Waterloo Directory of Irish Newspapers and Periodicals* (3000). A new edition, with full bibliographical information and details of holdings, would be welcome.

See also

Sec. K: Periodicals/Union Lists.

Bibliographies

2540 Wolff, Michael, John S. North, and Dorothy Deering. *The Waterloo Directory of Victorian Periodicals, 1824–1900: Phase I*. Waterloo: Wilfrid Laurier UP, for U of Waterloo, [1976]. 1,187 pp. Z6956.G6.W63 [PN5124.P4] 011'.34.

A bibliography of 24,500 newspapers and periodicals published between 1824 and 1900 in England, Scotland, Ireland, and Wales, as well as a few related ones published after 1900. A partial conflation of several major union catalogs and bibliographies—including *Union List of Serials* (640a), *British Union-Catalogue of Periodicals* (645a), and *Tercentenary Handlist of English and Welsh Newspapers, Magazines, and Reviews* (1440a)—*Phase I* is a preliminary handlist for a comprehensive directory that will quadruple the number of entries and be based on actual examination of copies. The second phase is in course of publication: North, *Waterloo Directory of Irish Newspapers and Periodicals, 1800–1900* (3000) appeared in 1986; the volume on Scotland, with about 6,000 entries, is in progress; and the approximately 20 volumes on England are planned for 1989.

Serials are listed alphabetically by the earliest known title, with extensive (but not thorough) cross-references for variant and related titles and sponsoring bodies. A main entry records the following (depending on available information and citing conflicting details in sources): title; subtitle; series, volume, and issue numbering; publication dates; editor(s); place of publication; publisher; printer; price; size; frequency; illustrations; issuing body; indexing sources; notes on content; mergers; alternate titles. Most entries provide only minimal details. Researchers should

(1) study carefully the prefatory explanation of organization, alphabetization, cross-referencing, and content of entries; and (2) read John North, "*The Waterloo Directory of Victorian Periodicals*: A Report," *Victorian Periodicals Newsletter* 8 (1975): 69–78, a discussion of the compilation and limitations of *Phase I* and preliminary work on the second phase. A subject index is in progress.

Although it is flawed by an unclear explanation of limitations and incomplete assimilation of sources, is not comprehensive, and perpetuates the errors of existing works, *Phase I* is useful for its compilation of scattered information and extensive cross-referencing, which allows for the identification of variant titles and publications issued by an organization. Reviews: William E. Fredeman, *English Studies in Canada* 4 (1978): 238–46; H. B. de Groot, *Victorian Studies* 21 (1978): 291–94; Lionel Madden, *Library* 5th ser. 32 (1977): 272–77; Sheila Rosenberg, *Victorian Periodicals Newsletter* 10 (1977): 71–76 (an important discussion of limitations).

For Irish publications, this work is superseded by *Waterloo Directory of Irish Newspapers and Periodicals* (3000). Fuller, more accurate information on some periodicals can be found in Fulton, *Union List of Victorian Serials* (2530), and Houghton, *Wellesley Index* (2545); for locations, consult Fulton (2530); Ward, *Index and Finding List* (2535); *Union List of Serials* (640a); *British Union-Catalogue of Periodicals* (645a); *Serials in the British Library* (645); OCLC (225); and RLIN (230).

For a list of periodicals addressed to women and of articles about women in other serials, see E. M. Palmegiano, *Women and British Periodicals, 1832–1867: A Bibliography*, Garland Reference Library of the Humanities 55 (New York: Garland, 1976, 118 pp.)—also published as *Victorian Periodicals Newsletter* 9 (1976): 1–36—with additions in Anne Lohrli, "Women in British Periodicals," *Victorian Periodicals Newsletter* 9 (1976): 128–30.

See also

Bibliography of British Newspapers (1440).
Sullivan, *British Literary Magazines* (1445).

Indexes

2545 Houghton, Walter E., Esther Rhoads Houghton, and Jean Harris Slingerland, eds. *Wellesley Index to Victorian Periodicals, 1824–1900.* 5 vols. Toronto: U of Toronto P; London: Routledge, 1966– . AI3.W45 052'.016.

An index to the prose contents of 43 major periodicals. Poetry is excluded—unfortunately, but understandably so, because of the quantity and insurmountable problems in attributing authorship. Vols. 1 through 4 each consists of three parts. Organized by periodical, pt. A is an issue-by-issue list of contents that explains uninformative titles, identifies reprints, and attributes authorship (citing evidence) for individual articles and reviews. The list for each periodical is prefaced by a summary of publishing history and editorial policy, discussion of sources for attribution of authorship, and a bibliography. Pt. B is an author bibliography of works listed in pt. A. Pt. C indexes initials and pseudonyms. Additions and corrections to vol. 1 appear in vol. 2, pp. 1181–221; to vols. 1 and 2, in vol. 3, pp. 977–1012; and to vols. 1–3, in vol. 4, pp. 765–826. Vol. 5 (scheduled for publication in 1989) will cumulate pts. B and C and print additions and corrections to the preceding volumes.

The high degree of accuracy and reliability makes the *Wellesley Index* an indispensable source for efficiently scanning the contents of journals (especially inaccessible ones), for gauging the spirit of the age as reflected in a range of leading periodicals, for comparing the contents of influential serials, for determining the authorship of a majority of the numerous unsigned or pseudonymous contributions (although attributions cannot be automatically accepted, since some are based on unauthenticated sources or internal evidence), and for identifying pseudonyms used in periodicals, which Halkett, *Dictionary of Anonymous and Pseudonymous English Literature* (5110), does not cover. A monumental scholarly work that has revolutionized the study of Victorian periodicals. Reviews: (vol. 1) Robert A. Colby, *Modern Philology* 65 (1968): 411–14; Ian Jack, *Review of English Studies* ns 19 (1968): 228–31; (vol. 2) Colby, *Modern Philology* 71 (1974): 455–59; Jack, *Review of English Studies* ns 25 (1974): 491–93; (vol. 3) William S. Ward, *JEGP: Journal of English and Germanic Philology* 79 (1980): 454–57.

2550 Ward, William S., comp. *Literary Reviews in British Periodicals, 1798–1820: A Bibliography: With a Supplementary List of General (Non-Review) Articles on Literary Subjects.* 2 vols. New York: Garland, 1972.

———. *Literary Reviews in British Periodicals, 1821–1826: A Bibliography: With a Supplementary List of General (Non-Review) Articles on Literary Subjects.* Garland Reference Library of the Humanities 60. New York: Garland, 1977. 301 pp. Z2013.W36 [PR453] 016.809'034.

A bibliography of reviews of belles lettres, criticism, and other writings by literary authors published between 1798 and 1826. Books are organized alphabetically by author, then by publication date, with reviews following alphabetically by periodical title. Nonreview articles are relegated to various appendixes: appendix A includes general articles about authors appearing in the reviews section; appendix B is in five parts: (1) volumes of general criticism reviewed, (2) general criticism articles, and articles on (3) poetry, (4) fiction, and (5) drama and theater; appendix C (in *1798–1820* only) lists reviews of operas. The prefaces offer general suggestions for further research. These two works are essential sources for investigating the contemporary critical reception of an author or work and for locating early criticism. For earlier coverage, see Ward, *Literary Reviews in British Periodicals, 1789–1797* (2280).

Most reviews published between 1793 and 1824 of books by Wordsworth, Coleridge, Byron, Shelley, and Keats (along with a few reviews of other writers) are conveniently reproduced in Donald H. Reiman, ed., *The Romantics Reviewed: Contemporary Reviews of British Romantic Writers*, 9 vols. (New York: Garland, 1972).

See also

Poole's Index to Periodical Literature (4150).
Times *Index* (1450).

Guides to Scholarship and Criticism

Serial Bibliographies

2555 "Victorian Periodicals [1971–]: A Checklist of Criticism." *Victorian Periodicals Review* (entry 2570) 6 (1973)– .

An annotated author list of books, dissertations, articles, and reviews about periodicals published between 1800 and 1914 in the United Kingdom and its colonies (with some coverage of English-language periodicals from the rest of the world). Three indexes: name; subject; periodical. For earlier scholarship, see Madden, *Nineteenth-Century Periodical Press in Britain* (2560). Although this work is the standard serial bibliography, its coverage is far from exhaustive.

Other Bibliographies

2560 Madden, Lionel, and Diana Dixon, comps. *The Nineteenth-Century Periodical Press in Britain: A Bibliography of Modern Studies, 1901–1971*. Supplement to *Victorian Periodicals Newsletter* 8.3 (1975). Toronto: Victorian Periodicals Newsletter, 1975. 76 pp. Also published as Garland Reference Library of the Humanities 53. New York: Garland, 1976. 280 pp. Z6956.G6.M3 [PN5117] 016.072.

An annotated bibliography of books, articles, dissertations, and theses devoted to the history, editing, and publication of general interest periodicals. Madden excludes examinations of a periodical's treatment of specific topics, literary history studies, and attributions of individual works (however, such exclusions are not rigorously observed). The 2,632 entries are organized in four liberally cross-referenced divisions: reference works (listed chronologically), general histories of periodicals and newspapers (listed chronologically), studies of individual periodicals (listed alphabetically by the earliest nineteenth-century title, then chronologically), and studies and memoirs of proprietors, editors, journalists, and contributors (listed alphabetically by person, then chronologically). Indexed by names. Although carelessly compiled—with numerous omissions, uneven annotations, inconsistencies in coverage, and far too many errors in the citations and index—and less than efficiently organized, this work is the most complete guide to scholarship on the topic. It must be supplemented, however, by the serial bibliographies and indexes in section G and by Ward, *British Periodicals and Newspapers, 1789–1832* (2565). For studies published after 1971, see the annual "Victorian Periodicals: A Checklist of Criticism" (2555). Reviews: Walter E. Houghton, *Library* 5th ser. 32 (1977): 386–87; John Bush Jones, *Analytical and Enumerative Bibliography* 4 (1980): 107–23 (with several additions and corrections).

2565 Ward, William S. *British Periodicals and Newspapers, 1789–1832: A Bibliography of Secondary Sources*. Lexington: UP of Kentucky, [1972]. 386 pp. Z6956.G6.W37 016.052.

A bibliography of books, articles, theses, and dissertations (through the late 1960s) about periodicals and newspapers listed in Ward, *Index and Finding List of Serials* (2535). Entries are listed in six divisions: general bibliographies and bibliographical studies, general studies, periodicals, people, places, and special subjects. Brief descriptive annotations accompany some entries. Three indexes: scholars; subjects (completely inadequate); library catalogs and union lists. Ward offers generally better coverage than Madden, *Nineteenth-Century Periodical Press* (2560) of the early decades of the nineteenth century, especially for studies of topics and literary authors; however, the organization, paucity of cross-references, and utterly inadequate subject indexing make it a frustrating work to search. For recent scholarship, see "Victorian Periodicals: A Checklist of Criticism" (2555).

See also

Linton, *Newspaper Press in Britain* (1455).
Vann, *Victorian Periodicals* (2525).
White, *English Literary Journal to 1900* (1460).

Scholarly Journals (Devoted to Contemporary Periodicals)

2570 *Victorian Periodicals Review* (*VPR*). 1968– . Quarterly. Former title: *Victorian Periodicals Newsletter* (1968–78). PN5124.P4.V52 016.052.

Publishes articles, notes, and reviews on critical, historical, and bibliographical topics, as well as indexes and descriptions of work in progress, dealing with English-language periodicals (including newspapers) published from 1800 to 1914 (but emphasizing those from the Victorian period in Great Britain and Ireland). Beginning in vol. 6 (1973), *Victorian Periodicals Review* includes the annual "Victorian Periodicals: A Checklist of Criticism" (2555). For a history of the journal, see N. Merrill Distad, "The Origins and History of *Victorian Periodicals Review*, 1954–1984," 18 (1985): 86–98. Annual index in vols. 8–16; cumulative index: Bruce A. White, "Index for the First Ten Years [1968–77] of *VPN-VPR*," 18 (1985): 102–32.

Background Reading

General and specialized studies are conveniently surveyed in Joanne Shattock, "General Histories of the Press" (pp. 81–98) and Lionel Madden and Diana Dixon, "Histories and Studies of Individual Periodicals" (pp. 99–122), in Vann, *Victorian Periodicals* (2525).

SCHOLARLY JOURNALS

Many journals in sections K: Periodicals/Scholarly Journals and M: English Literature/General/Periodicals/Scholarly Journals publish articles on nineteenth-century literature.

2575 *Browning Institute Studies: An Annual of Victorian Literary and Cultural History* (*BIS*). 1973– . Annual. PR4229.B77a 821'.8'05.

Since vol. 7 (1979), *Browning Institute Studies* publishes articles on a variety of topics related to Victorian literary and cultural history. It also prints the annual

"Robert and Elizabeth Barrett Browning: An Annotated Bibliography for [1971–]," 1 (1973)– .

2580 *English Literature in Transition, 1880–1920* (*ELT*). 1957– . Quarterly. Former title: *English Fiction in Transition (1880–1920)* (1957–62). PR1.E55.

Publishes articles, reviews, surveys of research, bibliographies, descriptions of library collections, and occasional special issues dealing with English literature and culture from 1880 to 1920. Noteworthy for its many bibliographies, especially of minor authors. For the early history of the journal, see Helmut E. Gerber, "*ELT*: An Autobiography," pp. ix-xv in the cumulative index. Cumulative index: Mary Ellen Quint and Bernard Quint, comps. and eds., ELT *Index: Volume 1 (1957)–Volume 15 (1972)* (Tempe: [Dept. of English, Arizona State U], 1975, n.pag.).

2585 *Keats-Shelley Journal: Keats, Shelley, Byron, Hunt, and Their Circles* (*KSJ*). 1952– . Annual. (Subtitle varies.) PR4836.A145 821.705.

Publishes articles, notes, and reviews on the early English Romantics, especially the four principal writers. For the annual bibliography, see entry 2495.

2590 *Keats-Shelley Review* (*KSMB*). 1910–13, 1950– . Annual. Former Title: *Keats-Shelley Memorial Bulletin* (1910–13, 1950–85). PR4836.A15.

Although emphasizing Keats and Shelley, the articles, reviews, and occasional special issues treat a variety of early English Romantic writers.

2595 *Nineteenth-Century Contexts*. 1975– . 2/yr. Former titles: *Milton and the Romantics* (1975–80); *Romanticism Past and Present* (1981–86). PR3579.M47 821'.4.

Beginning in vol. 11 (1987), the journal publishes articles and reviews on all aspects of nineteenth-century Britain, with an emphasis on interdisciplinary studies. Each issue also prints one or two surveys of the state of research in a field or topic.

2600 *Nineteenth-Century Literature* (*NCF*). 1945– . Quarterly. Former titles: *The Trollopian: A Journal of Victorian Fiction* (1945–49); *Nineteenth-Century Fiction* (1949–86). PR451.N56 823.

Publishes articles, notes, occasional special issues, and reviews chiefly on British and American works. Annual index; cumulative index: G. B. Tennyson and Elizabeth J. Tennyson, comps., *An Index to* Nineteenth-Century Fiction, *Volumes 1–30, Summer 1945–March 1976* (1977, 196 pp.). Unfortunately, inadequate subject indexing, inconsistencies, errors, and omissions seriously mar the index; see the review by Dianna Vitanza, *Analytical and Enumerative Bibliography* 3 (1979): 59–62. G. B. Tennyson and Thomas Wortham, "*Nineteenth-Century Literature*: Forty Years," 41 (1986): 1–8, traces the history of the journal.

2605 *Studies in Romanticism* (*SIR*). 1961– . Quarterly. PN751.S8 809'.91'4.

Publishes articles, book reviews (since vol. 10 [1977]), and frequent special issues on all aspects of Romanticism in Europe and the United States (with some emphasis on British literature and preference for interdisciplinary approaches). Annual index; cumulative index: vols. 1–10 (n.d., 16 pp.).

2610 *Victorian Studies: A Quarterly Journal of the Humanities, Arts, and Sciences* (*VS*). 1957– . Quarterly. PR1.V5 820'.9'008.

Publishes articles, reviews, and occasional special issues on the humanities, arts, and sciences in Victorian Britain. For the annual "Victorian Bibliography," see entry

2500. Annual index; cumulative index: vols. 1–20, by David Slayden, vol. 20, supplement (1977): 176 pp. (including an annotated checklist of articles). The history of the journal is detailed in Michael Wolff and Martha Vicinus, "Retrospectives," 20, supplement (1977): 6–12, which is complemented by reminiscences of former editors and staff in "*Victorian Studies*, 1957–1987: An Editorial Birthday Party," 31 (1987): 79–102.

2615 *The Wordsworth Circle* (*WC*). 1970– . Quarterly. PR1.W67 820'.9'14.

Publishes articles and notes on Wordsworth, Coleridge, Hazlitt, De Quincey, Lamb, Austen, Scott, and minor writers of the early nineteenth century in England. Since vol. 4 (1973), one issue per year is devoted to reviews of works on English and (occasionally) Continental Romanticism. Annual index in many volumes.

Background Reading

The chapters on "General Materials" in Faverty, *Victorian Poets* (entry 2715), DeLaura, *Victorian Prose* (2740), and Ford, *Victorian Fiction* (2665) survey important background studies. See also the chapter on 1800–1970 (pp. 153–221) in Bateson, *Guide to English and American Literature* (85) and "Recent Studies in the Nineteenth Century" (2480). Although directed to the undergraduate new to the subject, David Nicholls, "Nineteenth-Century English History: Materials for Teaching and Study (Great Britain)," *Victorian Studies* 19 (1976): 345–77, is a useful evaluative survey for the literary scholar unfamiliar with general histories and specialized studies on economic, political, social, cultural, and religious history.

2620 Altick, Richard D. *The English Common Reader: A Social History of the Mass Reading Public, 1800–1900*. Chicago: U of Chicago P, 1957. 430 pp. Z1003.A57 028.9.

A historical study of the role of religion, education, public libraries, the book trade, and periodicals in the growth of a mass reading public in an industrial, democratic society. The appendix listing best-sellers chronologically by type of work is supplemented by Altick, "Nineteenth-Century English Best-Sellers: A Further List," *Studies in Bibliography* 22 (1969): 197–206, and "Nineteenth-Century English Best-Sellers: A Third List," *Studies in Bibliography* 39 (1986): 235–41. Another appendix records newspaper and periodical circulation (supplemented in the first list, above). Indexed by persons, anonymous titles, and some subjects. Review: R. K. Webb, *Victorian Studies* 1 (1958): 286–88.

2625 Houghton, Walter E. *The Victorian Frame of Mind, 1830–1870*. New Haven: Yale UP, for Wellesley Coll.; London: Oxford UP, 1957. 467 pp. DA533.H85 942.081.

Draws largely from literary works to explore "those general ideas and attitudes about life which a Victorian of the middle and upper classes would have breathed in with the air." Among these ideas and attitudes are optimism, anxiety, the critical spirit, anti-intellectualism, dogmatism, rigidity, the commercial spirit, worship of force, earnestness, enthusiasm, hero worship, love, and hypocrisy. Indexed by persons and subjects. An authoritative overview. Reviews: Perry Miller, *New England Quarterly* 30 (1957): 407–09; Lionel Stevenson, *Modern Language Quarterly* 21 (1960): 273–75; Geoffrey Tillotson, *Victorian Studies* 1 (1957): 184–85.

2630 Young, G. M. *Portrait of an Age: Victorian England.* Annotated ed. by George Kitson Clark. London: Oxford UP, 1977. 423 pp. DA550.Y6 941.081.

An analysis of the changes from 1831 to 1901 in religion, politics, history, social reform, commerce, education, economics, agriculture, art, and literature, written from the perspective of a member of "the highly educated, moderately liberal, professional middle class." Because of Young's extraordinary allusiveness and the lack of documentation in the original edition (1936, 213 pp.) or the second edition (1953, 219 pp.), all but a few readers will need Clark's annotations, which identify sources and correct quotations and facts. Indexed by persons and subjects. Despite its age, *Portrait of an Age* is still a classic introduction to the period. Review: John Clive, *TLS: Times Literary Supplement* 20 Jan. 1978: 50–52.

See also

Oxford History of England (1495).

Genres

Many works in section L: Genres and most in section M: English Literature/General/Genres are useful for research in nineteenth-century literature.

FICTION

Sections L: Genres/Fiction and M: English Literature/General/Genres/Fiction include several works useful for research in nineteenth-century fiction.

Guides to Primary Works

2635 Sadleir, Michael. *XIX Century Fiction: A Bibliographical Record Based on His Own Collection.* 2 vols. London: Constable; Berkeley: U of California P, 1951. Z2014.F4.S16 016.8237.

A descriptive catalog of Sadleir's collection—now at the University of California, Los Angeles—with some additions (identified by an asterisk) from other sources to complete the list of first editions for authors not previously subjects of bibliographies. Reflecting Sadleir's tastes and interests, the collection emphasizes rare and unusual editions of British authors between 1800 and 1899, especially "Silver Fork" novels and those published in two or three volumes; generally excludes major novelists and those who published fiction before 1800; and includes a few foreign writers notable for the rarity of their English editions and some British novels published after 1900. The novels are organized in three divisions: an author catalog of first editions as well as variant issues, later editions of textual significance, and multiple copies; the Yellow-Back collection (books issued in colored noncloth bindings); and principal series of fiction and novels. Only the author catalog fully describes editions by recording title, subtitle, number of volumes and pagination, imprint, binding, provenance, notes on bibliographical points, and references to other bibliographies. A headnote indicates the completeness of each author list. (Users should note that entry numbers skip from 2099 to 3000.) Indexed by titles in vol. 1, by titles and by authors in vol. 2. Although the catalog includes only a small fraction of the novels published during the century, the careful descriptions and numerous unique items make Sadleir a valuable source of bibliographical and textual information, a significant contribution to the much needed record of fiction published during the nineteenth century, and one of the monumental catalogs of a private collection. Supplemented by Wolff, *Nineteenth-Century Fiction* (2660), which Sadleir's catalog inspired, and by *English Catalogue of Books* (2470), which remains the most complete list of novels published during the century. The subject index described by Bradford A. Booth ("An Analytical Subject-Index to the Sadleir Collection," *Nineteenth-Century Fiction* 23 [1968]: 217–20) has apparently not survived. Reviews: Hugh G. Dick, *Nineteenth-Century Fiction* 6 (1951): 209–17; *Times Literary Supplement* 13 Apr. 1951: 234.

2640 Grimes, Janet, and Diva Daims. *Novels in English by Women, 1891–1920: A Preliminary Checklist.* Garland Reference Library of the Humanities 202. New York: Garland, 1981. 805 pp. (Work on the volume covering 1781–1890 has been postponed.) Z2013.5.W6.G75 [PR1286] 016.823'912.

An author list of 15,174 titles (including translations) by 5,267 authors, primarily published in England and the United States. Excludes most juvenile fiction and novels by joint authors when one is male. Entries are arranged by author in three divisions: verified entries, novels by anonymous or pseudonymous authors whose gender could not be determined, and unverified novels. Approximately 75% of the entries are annotated with what are aptly described as "working notes not originally intended for publication," which consist principally of quotations from or rough paraphrases of reviews. Indexed by titles. Although it is a reproduction of a printout of a minimally edited working copy based on secondary sources, *Novels in English by Women* does record the bulk of novels written by women during the period (as well as reviews of them in several major periodicals).

The potential value of these working notes is illustrated by Daims and Grimes, *Toward a Feminist Tradition: An Annotated Bibliography of Novels in English by Women, 1891–1920*, Garland Reference Library of the Humanities 201 (New York: Garland, 1982, 885 pp.), which extracts entries for novels offering "unconventional treatment of women characters which focuses attention either on the efforts of women to control their lives or on social attitudes and conditions functioning as counterforces to that achievement." The annotations have been edited, but readers must consult *Novels in English* for sources of the reviews. Indexed by titles. Although neither comprehensive nor based on first-hand knowledge of the works, *Toward a Feminist Tradition* is nonetheless an important source for studying attitudes toward women, especially in British novels.

Intended as a companion to *Novels in English* and *Toward a Feminist Tradition*, Doris Robinson, *Women Novelists, 1891–1920: An Index to Biographical and Autobiographical Sources*, Garland Reference Library of the Humanities 491 (New York: Garland, 1984, 458 pp.), lists separately published autobiographies and biographies as well as entries in collective biographies for 1,565 of the women.

2645 Harris, Wendell V. *British Short Fiction in the Nineteenth Century: A Literary and Bibliographic Guide.* Detroit: Wayne State UP, 1979. 209 pp. PR861.H35 823'.01.

The "Bibliographic Appendix" (pp. 164–203) is an author list of collections of short fiction made by the author, standard collections published after the author's death, and selected other collections. *British Short Fiction* lists contents of collections not analyzed in *New Cambridge Bibliography of English Literature* (1385) or *Short Story Index* (1085) and, for all authors, cites standard general and author bibliographies that list short fiction. Harris, *NCBEL*, and *Short Story Index* combined provide the best guide to the collected short fiction during the century. Review: Robert A. Colby, *Victorian Studies* 24 (1981): 254–55.

2650 Leclaire, Lucien. *A General Analytical Bibliography of the Regional Novelists of the British Isles, 1800–1950*. Rev. ed. Collection d'histoire et de littérature étrangères. Paris: Belles Lettres, 1969. 399 pp. Z2014.F4.L4 016.823.

A bibliography of novels with some regional association (other than London), organized by author in three chronological divisions: 1800–30, 1830–70, 1870–1950 (with the last subdivided). Placement in a division depends on the date of a writer's first "regional" novel. A typical author entry includes a biographical headnote, a highly selective list of studies and bibliographies, and a chronological list of regional novels (including an incomplete list of subsequent editions), with a note identifying the setting of each. A map places authors by region. Three indexes: authors (alphabetical); authors (regional by country, then area); place names. Although it is not comprehensive and although organization by region and fuller, more consistent notes on setting would better serve the user, Leclaire remains the best source for identifying novels associated with a place other than London in the British Isles. Review: (first edition) Gwyn Jones, *Review of English Studies* ns 8 (1957): 102–04.

For a fuller list of fiction (through c. 1910) associated with Ireland, see Brown, *Ireland in Fiction* (3025).

2655 Vann, J. Don. *Victorian Novels in Serial*. Index Society Fund Publications. New York: MLA, 1985. 181 pp. Z2014.F4.V36 [PR871] 016.823'8.

Identifies the date of publication and content of each installment of 192 serialized novels by Ainsworth, Collins, Dickens, Eliot, Gaskell, Hardy, Kingsley, Kipling, Bulwer-Lytton, Marryat, Meredith, Reade, Stevenson, Thackeray, Trollope, and Ward. Under each author, Vann lists novels by date of publication of the first part, and for each installment cites date of publication and identifies, as precisely as possible, its content in relation to the separately published volume. The introduction discusses the history of serialization, its effect on authorship, the impact of the form on plot (especially the ending of an installment), and publishing practices. Concludes with a selected bibliography of scholarship on serial novels. Since the periodicals are frequently difficult to obtain and few modern editions identify installments, Vann offers essential information to those studying the initial reception and structure of the more important Victorian serial novels. Reviews: Michael Lund, *Studies in the Novel* 19 (1987): 503–05; Rosemary T. VanArsdel, *Victorian Periodicals Review* 19 (1986): 78–79.

2660 Wolff, Robert Lee, comp. *Nineteenth-Century Fiction: A Bibliographical Catalogue Based on the Collection Formed by Robert Lee Wolff*. 5 vols. Garland Reference Library of the Humanities 261, 331–34. New York: Garland, 1981–86. Z2014.F4.W64 [PR861] 016.823'8.

A descriptive author catalog of Wolff's extensive collection of novels published between 1837 and 1901 (as well as other works written by novelists during the period, novels before 1837 and after 1901 by novelists published between those years, and related manuscripts and letters). The collection—now owned by the Harry Ransom Humanities Research Center, University of Texas at Austin—complements Sadleir's, since Wolff sought the minor authors not favored by collectors. Effective use of the catalog requires a copy of *XIX Century Fiction* (2635) at hand, because Wolff assumes familiarity with Sadleir's procedures and records only significant variants and details of provenance for editions fully described by Sadleir. The 7,938 titles (plus numerous editions thereof and duplicates) are listed alphabetically by author, then title; there are separate alphabetic sequences for unattributed anonymous works, pseudonymous works, and multiple-author collections, annuals, and periodical fiction in vol. 5. Letters relating to novels are fully transcribed; manuscripts receive extensive descriptions. Entries vary in content but typically include title; imprint; description of binding; number of volumes and pagination; bibliographical notes, with information on condition, provenance, and references to standard bibliographies; and a variety of miscellaneous notes, including publishing history, content, and frequently eccentric critical observations. Indexed by title in vol. 5. Wolff corrected only the entries from A to mid-D before his death; hence, many errors and incomplete references remain, and most entries would benefit from considerable pruning. Although the work is not one of the monumental catalogs of a private collection, its emphasis on minor novels, the several corrections to standard author bibliographies, and descriptions of numerous unique items, variant editions, manuscripts, and association copies make Wolff an essential complement to Sadleir and an important contribution toward a much needed comprehensive list of Victorian novels. Review: (vol. 1) Walter E. Smith, *Papers of the Bibliographical Society of America* 76 (1982): 481–88.

See also

Bleiler, *Guide to Supernatural Fiction* (860).
Hubin, *Crime Fiction, 1749–1980* (915).
Mayo, *English Novel in the Magazines, 1740–1815* (2330).
Sargent, *British and American Utopian Literature* (1055).
Tymn, *Horror Literature* (865).
Wright, *Author [Chronological; Title] Bibliography of English Language Fiction* (1060).

Guides to Scholarship and Criticism

Surveys of Research

2665 Ford, George H., ed. *Victorian Fiction: A Second Guide to Research.* New York: MLA, 1978. 401 pp. PR871.V5 823'.8'09.

Stevenson, Lionel, ed. *Victorian Fiction: A Guide to Research.* Cambridge: Harvard UP, 1964. 440 pp. PR873.S8 823.809.

Evaluative surveys of research on established novelists. The original volume covers scholarship from the 1930s through 1962 (with some important earlier and later studies) in chapters on general works, Disraeli and Bulwer-Lytton, Dickens,

Thackeray, Trollope, the Brontës, Gaskell and Kingsley, Collins and Reade, Eliot, Meredith, Hardy, and Moore and Gissing. The *Second Guide* continues coverage through 1974 (along with some significant omissions from the earlier volume and a few 1975 publications) and adds chapters on Butler and Stevenson. The individual essays are variously subdivided but typically examine bibliographies, biographical studies, editions, collections of letters, and critical studies (with the sequel utilizing more subdivisions, giving more attention to manuscripts, and adding a discussion of film adaptations). Most include suggestions for further research (more consistently and fully in the 1978 volume). Indexed by persons. Marred only by incomplete citations, these volumes offer magisterial surveys that are essential preludes to research on any of the novelists included. Reviews: (Stevenson) Geoffrey Tillotson and Kathleen Tillotson, *Nineteenth-Century Fiction* 19 (1965): 405–10; (Ford) David J. DeLaura, *English Language Notes* 16 (1978): 178–91; Sylvère Monod, *Yearbook of English Studies* 11 (1981): 310–12.

See also

Spector, *English Gothic* (2345).

Other Bibliographies

See

Albert, *Detective and Mystery Fiction* (920).
Frank, *Guide to the Gothic* (875).
Kirby, *America's Hive of Honey* (4190).
Walker, *Twentieth-Century Short Story Explication* (1090).

Background Reading

The best general surveys of histories and specialized studies are the essays on "General Materials" by Bradford Booth (pp. 1–20) and Richard D. Altick (pp. 1–20) in the two volumes of *Victorian Fiction* (2665).

DRAMA AND THEATER

Sections L: Genres/Drama and Theater and M: English Literature/General/Drama and Theater include many works useful for research in nineteenth-century drama and theater.

Histories and Surveys

2670 Nicoll, Allardyce. *Early Nineteenth Century Drama, 1800–1850*. 2nd ed. *Late Nineteenth Century Drama, 1850–1900*. 2nd ed. Vols. 4–5 of *A His-*

tory of English Drama, 1660–1900 (1525). Cambridge: Cambridge UP, 1955–59. PR625.N52 822.09.

Emphasizing the history of the stage and dramatic forms, vol. 4 includes chapters on the theater, dramatic conditions, the illegitimate drama (e.g., melodrama, farce, burlesque), the legitimate drama, and the poetic drama not intended for production; vol. 5 has chapters on the theater, dramatic conditions, and each decade of the last half of the century. Both volumes provide an appendix listing playhouses and an author list of plays and other dramatic forms written and produced during the respective period (with details of first performance, printed editions, and manuscripts, although the last are sketchily treated). Readers should note the supplementary sections that print revisions that could not be incorporated readily into the text. Although the history of the stage requires supplementing, the volumes assemble a wealth of information, and the lists of plays produced (although not exhaustive) are the most complete available. Indexed by persons and subjects in each volume; the lists of plays are indexed, with additions and corrections, in vol. 6 (entry 1545). For further additions and corrections, see Carl J. Stratman, C.S.V., "English Tragedy: 1819–1823," *Philological Quarterly* 41 (1962): 465–74, and "Additions to Allardyce Nicoll's Hand-List of Plays: 1800–1818," *Notes and Queries* 206 (1961): 214–17.

2675 *The Revels History of Drama in English* (1530). Gen. eds. Clifford Leech and T. W. Craik. Vol. 6: *1750–1880*. London: Methuen, 1975. 304 pp. PR625.R44 822'.009.

Includes a chronology; a guide to London theaters; essays on the social and literary context, theaters and actors, and plays and playwrights; and an evaluative survey of important studies. Indexed by authors, titles, and subjects. Like other volumes of *Revels History*, this is a useful synthesis of scholarship rather than a connected history of the drama. Reviews: Jackson I. Cope, *Eighteenth-Century Studies* 9 (1976): 640–43; George Rowell, *Modern Language Review* 72 (1977): 909–11.

Guides to Primary Works

2680 Donohue, Joseph, and James Ellis, eds. *The London Stage, 1800–1900: A Documentary Record and Calendar of Performances*. In progress.

A long-term project whose goal is a detailed calendar of performances in every London theater, music hall, and other place housing dramatic entertainment. The calendar represents one project of the London Stage, 1800–1900, Research Program; others include Ellis, *English Drama of the Nineteenth Century* (2695a) and eventually "a census of archives; a checklist of pertinent newspapers and periodicals; a bibliography of the drama; a dictionary of theatrical biography; a directory of London theatres; a catalogue of iconography; . . . calendars of performances at specific theatres." As information accumulates in the London Stage, 1800–1900, Database, the editors plan to issue reference works; in the meantime, they will answer queries from researchers (Donohue, Dept. of English, U of Massachusetts, Amherst 01003; Ellis, Dept. of English, Mount Holyoke Coll., South Hadley, MA 01075). A brochure, from which the above description is taken, is available from the editors.

2685 Gänzl, Kurt. *The British Musical Theatre.* 2 vols. New York: Oxford UP, 1986. ML1731.8.L7.G36 782.81'0941.

Vol. 1: *1865–1914.* 1,196 pp.
Vol. 2: *1915–1984.* 1,258 pp.

A year-by-year account of original light musical theater produced in London's West End. Gänzl excludes operas, ballad operas, and burlesques, but otherwise encompasses a wide range of musical entertainments. Each year consists of two parts: (1) an extensive overview that combines plot summary with evaluation and comments on critical reception; (2) a list of productions, recording for each the author, librettist, producer, director, composer, theater, opening and closing dates, number of performances, original cast (along with understudies and replacements), revivals, adaptations in a different medium, some productions outside London (with cast lists for revivals and foreign productions), and touring dates. Each volume concludes with two appendixes: list of printed music; discography. Indexed separately in each volume by persons and titles of musicals. The massive and generally trustworthy accumulation of factual information makes Gänzl an indispensable source for the theater historian and should encourage a general critical history of the London musical theater as well as a host of specialized studies.

See also

Dramatic Compositions Copyrighted in the United States, 1870 to 1916 (4195).
Wearing, *London Stage, 1890–1899* (2865).

Guides to Scholarship and Criticism

2690 Conolly, L. W., and J. P. Wearing. *English Drama and Theatre, 1800–1900: A Guide to Information Sources.* American Literature, English Literature, and World Literatures in English: An Information Guide Series 12. Detroit: Gale, 1978. 508 pp. Z2014.D7.C72 [PR721] 016.822'7'08.

A selective bibliography of English-language scholarship (including dissertations) and editions through 1973. The 3,324 entries are arranged chronologically in 10 classified divisions: contemporary history and criticism; modern history and criticism; individual authors; reference works; anthologies; theaters; acting and management; critics; stage design, scenic art, and costume; and periodicals. The 110 authors have sections, when required, for collected works, major acted plays, unacted plays (listing editions and manuscripts largely from *English and American Drama of the Nineteenth Century* [2695]), bibliographies, biographies, critical studies, and author journals and newsletters. Annotations generally consist of brief descriptive comments. Since there are few cross-references, users must be certain to check the person, anonymous title, and selected subject index. Although lacking a clear statement of criteria governing selection, *English Drama and Theatre* is a convenient starting place, but coverage must be supplemented by Arnott, *English Theatrical Literature* (1560), general bibliographies on the period (entries 2480–510), "Nineteenth-Century Theatre Research" (2700), and the serial bibliographies and indexes in section G. Reviews: James Ellis, *Victorian Periodicals Review* 12 (1979): 146–49; Jan McDonald, *Theatre Notebook* 34 (1980): 42–44.

See also

International Bibliography of Theatre (1160).
"Nineteenth-Century Theatre Research" (2700).

Microform Collections

2695 *English and American Drama of the Nineteenth Century*. Ed. Allardyce Nicoll et al. New Canaan: Readex Microprint, 1965- . Microprint and microfiche.

Eventually this source will make available some 28,000 dramatic works produced, written, or translated in nineteenth-century England and America. Beside legitimate drama, the collection includes burlesques, melodramas, pantomimes, minstrel dialogues, children's plays, libretti, vocal scores, and musicals. Of particular value are the reproductions of unpublished manuscripts and acting copies submitted for licensing. A published work is represented by the earliest edition as well as significant later ones. Because of the vagaries of the Readex cataloging system, the following indexes are essential to locating works in the collection:

Ellis, James, and Joseph Donohue, eds. and comps. *English Drama of the Nineteenth Century: An Index and Finding Guide*. New Canaan: Readex Books, 1985. 345 pp. Indexes works issued through 1981 by authors, titles (including variants), and subtitles. A series of appendixes lists women dramatists, pseudonyms, arrangers, composers, privately printed plays, acting editions and other series, promptbooks, manuscripts, typescripts, and English plays in the American collection. Subsequent editions will include American plays.

Hixon, Don L., and Don A. Hennessee, *Nineteenth-Century American Drama: A Finding Guide*. Metuchen: Scarecrow, 1977. 579 pp. Indexes works in the "American Plays, 1831-1900" portion by authors and titles, and, in appendixes, by series, racial or ethnic origin of cast, and subjects.

Editions reproduced in *English and American Drama of the Nineteenth Century* through early 1982 are cataloged in OCLC (225). Although use of the collection is hampered by the lack of up-to-date finding lists, the work makes the bulk of nineteenth-century drama readily available.

Periodicals

2700 *Nineteenth Century Theatre* (*NCTR*). 1973- . 2/yr. Former title: *Nineteenth Century Theatre Research* (1973-86). PN1851.N55 792'.0942.

Publishes articles, bibliographies, documents, surveys of research, review essays, and reviews on theater history, principally of the British stage, although with vol. 12 (1984) the scope expanded to include European and other English-speaking countries. Vols. 1-10 (1973-82) print "Nineteenth-Century Theatre Research: A Bibliography for [1972-81]," a highly selective subject list indexed by scholar.

POETRY

Many works in sections L: Genres/Poetry and M: English Literature/General/Genres/Poetry are important to research in nineteenth-century poetry.

Histories and Surveys

For evaluative surveys of histories and general studies, see Frank Jordan, "The Romantic Movement in England" (pp. 1–112), in Jordan, *English Romantic Poets* (2710), and Jerome H. Buckley, "General Materials" (pp. 1–31), in Faverty, *Victorian Poets* (2715).

2705 Jackson, J. R. de J. *Poetry of the Romantic Period.* Vol. 4 of *The Routledge History of English Poetry* (1580). Gen ed. R. A. Foakes. London: Routledge, 1980. 334 pp. PR502.R58 821'.009.

Places major poems "in the context of the conventions and traditions in which they" were written by examining them in relation to similar, now neglected works in chapters on a variety of literary fashions and forms (e.g., guilt, imaginary worlds, deliberate simplicity in the treatment of ordinary experience, allegory, and satire). A chronology supplies an annotated list of important or typical poems (including many works not discussed in the text) and details of significant literary events. Indexed by authors, scholars, and periodical titles. The thematic approach offers provocative readings and comparisons but little in the way of historical or cultural context. Reviews: Marilyn Butler, *English* 29 (1980): 239–45; E. B. Murray, *Review of English Studies* ns 33 (1982): 209–13; Donald H. Reiman, *Studies in Romanticism* 20 (1981): 254–60; Jack Stillinger, *JEGP: Journal of English and Germanic Philology* 80 (1981): 581–83.

Guides to Primary Works

See

Jackson, *Annals of English Verse, 1770–1835* (2420).

Guides to Scholarship and Criticism

Surveys of Research

2710 Jordan, Frank, ed. *The English Romantic Poets: A Review of Research and Criticism.* 4th ed. New York: MLA, 1985. 765 pp. PR590.E5 016.821'7'09.

An evaluative guide to important scholarship and criticism through the early 1980s, with chapters by major scholars on the Romantic movement in England, Blake, Wordsworth, Coleridge, Byron, Shelley, and Keats. The organization of each chapter varies, but all chapters except the first include sections for reference works, editions, biographical studies, general criticism, and studies of individual works; and all examine trends and prospects in criticism as well as identify topics needing attention. As in other MLA reviews of research, the failure to cite full publication information makes tracking down articles (and some books) needlessly time-consuming. Indexed by persons (with titles of works listed under the six poets). Clear organization, judicious selection and evaluation, and authoritative commentary make this the indispensable guide to important studies of English Romanticism and the six poets.

Although largely superseded, the third edition, ed. Frank Jordan (1972, 468 pp.), is still occasionally useful for its evaluation of outdated works. A complementary volume which has not been superseded but is now badly dated is Carolyn Washburn Houtchens and Lawrence Huston Houtchens, eds., *The English Romantic Poets and Essayists: A Review of Research and Criticism*, rev. ed., Revolving Fund Series 21 (New York: New York UP, for MLA; London: U of London P, 1966, 395 pp.). Essays survey bibliographies, editions, biographical studies, and criticism on Blake, Lamb, Hazlitt, Scott, Southey, Campbell, Moore, Landor, Hunt, De Quincey, and Carlyle.

2715 Faverty, Frederic E., ed. *The Victorian Poets: A Guide to Research.* 2nd ed. Cambridge: Harvard UP, 1968. 433 pp. PR593.F3 821'.8'09.

An evaluative guide to scholarship through 1966, with chapters on general works, Tennyson, R. Browning, E. B. Browning, FitzGerald, Clough, Arnold, Swinburne, Pre-Raphaelites (D. G. Rossetti, C. Rossetti, Morris, and minor poets), Hopkins, and later Victorian poets (Patmore, Meredith, Thomson, Hardy, Bridges, Henley, Stevenson, Wilde, Davidson, Thompson, Housman, Kipling, Johnson, and Dowson). The chapters vary in organization but typically include sections for bibliographies, editions, biographies, and general criticism. Unfortunately, citations do not record full publication information, and there are more than a few errors. The directness of evaluation varies with the contributor, but all suggest topics for further research. Indexed by persons. A trustworthy guide to significant research through 1966, but a new edition is needed. Review: Kenneth Allott, *Victorian Poetry* 8 (1970): 82–91.

Supplemented by "Guide to the Year's Work in Victorian Poetry" (2720).

2720 "Guide to the Year's Work in Victorian Poetry: [1962–]." *Victorian Poetry* (2730). 1 (1963)– .

An evaluative survey of important scholarship on poetry (with some attention to nonfiction prose). The surveys for 1962–71 are by R. C. Tobias; those since 1972 consist of brief essays on general studies and established writers by a variety of scholars. The surveys for 1972 through 1974 are titled "Guide to the Year's Work in Victorian Poetry and Prose" and intended to supplement DeLaura, *Victorian Prose* (2740), but those since 1975 give less attention to nonfiction prose. (The guide for 1972, which was published as a supplement to vol. 10 [1974], covers studies published between 1966 and 1972.) The most authoritative annual survey and a valuable supplement to Faverty, *Victorian Poets* (2715). Less satisfying surveys appear in *Studies in English Literature, 1500–1900* (2480) and *Year's Work in English Studies* (330).

Other Bibliographies

2725 Reiman, Donald H. *English Romantic Poetry, 1800–1835: A Guide to Information Sources.* American Literature, English Literature, and World

Literatures in English: An Information Guide Series 27. Detroit: Gale, 1979. 294 pp. Z2014.P7.R46 [PR590] 016.821'7'09.

A selective annotated bibliography, principally of English-language scholarship through the mid-1970s. Entries are organized in eight classified divisions: general and background studies, the Romantic movement, Wordsworth, Coleridge, Byron, Shelley, Keats, and secondary poets (Beddoes, Campbell, Clare, Hogg, Hood, Hunt, Landor, Moore, Peacock, Rogers, Scott, and Southey). The author divisions have sections for reference works, editions, biographical studies, and criticism. Most of the brief annotations offer pointed evaluations, and various symbols (see p. xiii) identify levels of use and audience. Three indexes: authors; titles; subjects. Judicious selection, evaluation, and subject indexing make Reiman a trustworthy starting point for research on the minor writers and one of the better volumes in this highly uneven series. Jordan, *English Romantic Poets* (2710), is a more authoritative guide to scholarship on the major writers. Reviews: James H. Averill, *Analytical and Enumerative Bibliography* 5 (1981): 180–83; E. D. Mackerness, *Notes and Queries* ns 28 (1981): 438–40.

See also

Brogan, *English Versification, 1570–1980* (1600).
Donow, *Sonnet in England and America* (1250).
Kuntz, *Poetry Explication* (1255).

Periodicals

2730 *Victorian Poetry* (*VP*). 1963– . Quarterly. PR500.V5 811.

Publishes articles, notes, a few reviews, and occasional special issues on British poetry from 1830 to 1914. For the annual "Guide to the Year's Work in Victorian Poetry," see entry 2720. Annual index; cumulative index: vols. 1–20, Beverly DeBord, comp., Victorian Poetry*: Cumulative Index, 1963–1982* (Morgantown: West Virginia U, n.d., 61 pp.).

Background Reading

Background studies are surveyed by Jerome H. Buckley, "General Materials" (pp. 1–31), in Faverty, *Victorian Poets* (2715), and Frank Jordan, "The Romantic Movement in England" (pp. 1–112), in Jordan, *English Romantic Poets* (2710).

2735 Abrams, M. H. *The Mirror and the Lamp: Romantic Theory and the Critical Tradition*. New York: Oxford UP, 1953. 406 pp. PN769.R7.A2 801.

Examines the development of English poetic theory during the early nineteenth century in its broad intellectual context (encompassing philosophy, theology, the natural sciences, and German aesthetic theory). As Jordan (entry 2710) observes, "Encyclopedic in scope and in format, [this] . . . is perhaps the work to which most Romantics scholars return most often, using it as they would a reference work" (p. 9). Reviews: Thomas M. Raysor, *Modern Philology* 51 (1954): 281–83; A. S. P. Woodhouse, *Modern Language Notes* 70 (1955): 374–77.

PROSE

Some works in sections L: Genres/Prose and M: English Literature/General/Genres/Prose are useful for research in nineteenth-century prose.

Guides to Scholarship and Criticism

2740 DeLaura, David J., ed. *Victorian Prose: A Guide to Research.* New York: MLA, 1973. 560 pp. PR785.D4 820'.9.'008.

An evaluative survey of research through 1971 (with some publications from 1972), that includes chapters on general works, Macaulay, Thomas and Jane Carlyle, Newman, Mill, Ruskin, Arnold, Pater, the Oxford Movement, the Victorian churches, critics (Lewes, Bagehot, Hutton, Dallas, Lee, Swinburne, Symonds, Moore, Saintsbury, Gosse, Wilde, and Symons), and the unbelievers (Harrison, T. Huxley, Morley, and Stephen). Individual chapters are variously subdivided (with headings listed in the table of contents), but typically cover bibliographies, editions, manuscripts, biographies, and general studies. Unfortunately, full publication details are not cited. Evaluations are fair-minded (sometimes trenchant), and all contributors point out topics needing further research. Indexed by persons. A trustworthy, essential guide to scholarship through 1971, but a new edition is needed. Supplemented in part by "Guide to the Year's Work in Victorian Poetry" (2720). Reviews: Miriam Allott, *Victorian Studies* 19 (1975): 107–11; Alan Shelston, *Critical Quarterly* 16 (1974): 91–94; Vincent L. Tollers, *Papers of the Bibliographical Society of America* 69 (1975): 284–85.

This collection and its supplements are preferable to Harris W. Wilson and Diane Long Hoeveler, *English Prose and Criticism in the Nineteenth Century: A Guide to Information Sources*, American Literature, English Literature, and World Literatures in English: An Information Guide Series 18 (Detroit: Gale, 1979, 437 pp.), which is inadequately annotated and plagued by errors, omissions, and inconsistencies (for details, see the review by David J. DeLaura, *Analytical and Enumerative Bibliography* 5 [1981]: 61–63).

Background Reading

General studies through 1971 are evaluated by David J. DeLaura, "General Materials" (pp. 1–16), in DeLaura, *Victorian Prose* (2740); for later publications, see the general section of "Guide to the Year's Work in Victorian Poetry" (2720).

Twentieth-Century Literature

Many reference works devoted to twentieth-century literature are international in scope. Multinational works that emphasize British literature and those that treat British and American literature more or less equally appear in this part. Other works important to research in twentieth-century English literature are listed in sections

G: Serial Bibliographies, Indexes, and Abstracts; M: English Literature/General; and Q: American Literature/General, and American Literature/Twentieth-Century Literature.

Histories and Surveys

See

Sec. M: English Literature/General/Histories and Surveys.

Literary Handbooks, Dictionaries, and Encyclopedias

2755 *Encyclopedia of World Literature in the 20th Century*. Ed. Leonard S. Klein. Rev. ed. 4 vols. *Index*. Comp. Paula Rumbaugh Sonntag. New York: Ungar, 1981–84. PN771.E5 803.

Offers truly international coverage of significant twentieth-century literary activity in signed entries by established scholars on literary movements, ideas, the arts, national literatures, and authors who produced important work after 1900. Each entry concludes with a brief bibliography. The author entries—which constitute the bulk of the work—give basic biographical information, offer a general critical assessment of major works, list other publications, and provide a very selective bibliography of scholarship. Indexed by persons and topics (with national literatures subdivided by topics and major writers). Entries on some national literatures have been cloned to produce the following (all of them edited by Klein):

African Literatures in the 20th Century: A Guide. New York: Ungar, 1986. 245 pp.

Far Eastern Literatures in the 20th Century: A Guide. 1986. 195 pp.

Latin American Literature in the 20th Century: A Guide. 1986. 278 pp.

The overall reliability of the entries, breadth, critical commentary superior to what usually appears in encyclopedic compilations, balance, and currency make this source the best of the numerous encyclopedias of twentieth-century literature.

The revised edition completely supersedes the first edition (gen. ed. Wolfgang Bernard Fleischmann, 3 vols., 1967–71), and its parent *Lexikon der Weltliteratur im 20. Jahrhundert*, 3rd ed., 2 vols. (Freiburg: Herder, 1960–61). Although neither as comprehensive nor as authoritative, the following are occasionally useful supplements:

Columbia Dictionary of Modern European Literature. Gen eds. Jean-Albert Bédé and William B. Edgerton. 2nd ed. New York: Columbia UP, 1980. 895 pp. Offers somewhat fuller coverage of European writers. For a thorough evaluation, see the review by Pieranna Garavaso, Bruce Kochis, Stephen Lehmann, W. G. Regier, and Sybille Rejda, *MLN* 97 (1982): 1186–205.

Seymour-Smith, Martin. *The New Guide to Modern World Literature*. New York: Bedrick, 1985. 1,396 pp. (British ed.: *Macmillan Guide to Modern World Literature*. 3rd ed. London: Macmillan, 1985.) Offers a more or less connected critical commentary, with sparse biographical and bibliographical details.

Ward, A. C. *Longman Companion to Twentieth Century Literature*. Rev. Maurice Hussey. 3rd ed. London: Longman, 1981. 598 pp. Includes entries for genres, plot summaries, fictional characters, literary terms, and authors (principally English and Scottish, with a few others who have international reputations and whose works are available in English translation).

Bibliographies of Bibliographies

2760 Mellown, Elgin W. *A Descriptive Catalogue of the Bibliographies of Twentieth Century British Poets, Novelists, and Dramatists*. 2nd ed., rev. and enl. Troy: Whitston, 1978. 414 pp. Z2011.A1.M43 [PR471] 016.01682'08'00912.

An annotated bibliography of bibliographies (including articles and parts of books) published through 1977 of works by and about (1) British authors who were born after 1840 and published the majority of their work after 1890; (2) Scottish, Welsh, and Irish authors who were born before 1920, wrote in English, and are closely associated with English literature; and (3) a few Commonwealth writers. Under each author, entries appear in one of three sections: bibliographies of primary works, bibliographies of secondary works, and bibliographies in selected general reference sources (listed on pp. ix-xiv). Most annotations offer a detailed, but telegraphic, description of scope and content, as well as an incisive evaluation. Indexed by persons. Although the national scope is fuzzy, reasonably thorough coverage and helpful annotations make Mellown the principal bibliography of bibliographies for the period, but it must be supplemented with Howard-Hill, *Index to British Literary Bibliography* (1355) and *Bibliographic Index* (145). The first edition (*A Descriptive Catalogue of the Bibliographies of 20th Century British Writers* [1972, 446 pp.]) remains useful for its inclusion of nonliterary writers omitted from the second edition. Review: Peter Davison, *Analytical and Enumerative Bibliography* 3 (1979): 135–38.

Guides to Primary Works

MANUSCRIPTS

2765 *Location Register of Twentieth-Century English Literary Manuscripts and Letters: A Union List of Papers of Modern English, Irish, Scottish, and Welsh Authors in the British Isles*. 2 vols. London: British Library, 1988. Z6611.L7.L83 [PR471] 016.82'08'0091.

A union catalog of manuscripts (including proofs, tape recordings, and computer discs) and letters by British literary figures (including immigrants and refugees) who are currently alive or who died after 31 December 1899. Only items (including photocopies and microform copies) available for public consultation in the British Isles are listed among the approximately 50,000 entries. Under each author, manuscripts are listed alphabetically by title, followed by editorial correspondence files, and then letters in chronological order (by date of the earliest one if the entry is for a collection of letters). A typical entry consists of title or description, date, physical description, location, shelfmark, and a note on access. Important recipients of letters are interfiled in the author list. When appropriate, an author section begins with a headnote on major collections (especially outside Great Britain), an author's policy on the disposition of his or her papers, or the destruction of manuscripts. Because of the descriptive titles given several items, researchers must read the entire section for an author. The data base (The Library, P.O. Box 223, U of Reading, Whiteknights, Reading, England RG6 2AE) will likely be made available for online searching. Although the descriptions vary in detail and letters are frequently undifferentiated in large collections, the *Register* is an important resource that offers the most convenient means of locating many twentieth-century literary manuscripts.

The second phase of the project, which covers 1700–1900, got underway in 1987 (see entry 1370).

PRINTED WORKS

2770 *British Books in Print* (*BBIP*). London: Whitaker, 1874– . Annual. Updated monthly as *British Books in Print Microfiche*. 1978– . (Former title: *The Reference Catalogue of Current Literature*, 1874–1961.) Z2001.R33 015.42.

An author, title, and subject list of books in print and on sale in the United Kingdom, which cumulates and updates the weekly list in *Bookseller* (1858–). An entry cites author, title, size, number of pages, edition, series, price, publisher, date of publication, and ISBN. A directory of publishers prefaces each volume. Since *BBIP* is compiled from information supplied by publishers, it is neither comprehensive nor always accurate, but is the essential source for identifying books available for purchase in the United Kingdom and is useful for locating the current address of a British publisher. Earlier volumes, which until 1932 included publishers' catalogs, remain an important source of bibliographical information and book trade history.

Entries can be searched through BLAISE-LINE (510), and Whitaker plans to publish a CD-ROM version.

For books published during a given year, see *Whitaker's Cumulative Book List* (London: Whitaker, 1924– , annual, with larger cumulations), which is also an author, title, and subject list compiled from the weekly listings in *Bookseller*.

2775 *British National Bibliography* (*BNB*). London: British Library, Bibliographic Services Division, 1950– . Weekly with four-month, annual, and larger cumulations, including ones for 1950–84 and 1981–85. The weekly author and title indexes are cumulated each month and a subject index added. Z2001.B75 015.42.

A subject list (arranged by Dewey Decimal Classification) of books and new periodicals published in Great Britain. Entries reproduce full cataloging information, but because they are prepared from books as well as Cataloging-in-Publication (CIP) information received by the Copyright Office of the British Library, there is sometimes a lag of a year or more between publication and listing and ghosts occur when books for which CIP entries were prepared are never published. The subject and author-title indexes cite classification rather than page. For British books published simultaneously in the United States, *American Book Publishing Record* (4110) is usually a more timely source of information. Listings can be searched through BLAISE-LINE (510).

See also

"Current Literature," *English Studies* (1470).
Nineteenth Century Short Title Catalogue (2475).
Vrana, *Interviews and Conversations with 20th-Century Authors Writing in English* (4235).

Guides to Scholarship and Criticism

SURVEYS OF RESEARCH

See

YWES (330): Twentieth Century chapter.

SERIAL BIBLIOGRAPHIES

2780 "Annual Review [1970–]." *Journal of Modern Literature* (entry 2820) 1 (1970)– .

An annotated bibliography of English-language books, dissertations, articles (excluding short notes and popular journalism), special issues of journals, and miscellaneous items (e.g., conference reports, library acquisitions, sales of books and manuscripts) on the modernist period and those writers who achieved recognition after 1880 and before c. 1950. Entries are organized by form (e.g., book, dissertation, article—for a definition of these forms, see the introduction to each bibliography) in two divisions: general studies (with sections for reference works and bibliographies; literary history; themes and movements; regional, national, and ethnic literatures; comparative studies of two or more authors; general studies of modern literature; fiction; poetry; drama; and film and/as literature) and individual authors who were the subject of at least one book or several articles and dissertations. The first two bibliographies include full-length reviews of some books; in later bibliographies, books receive generous annotations (most of which are admirable for their precise descriptions and evaluative comments). Indexed by names. Although it emphasizes established writers, the excellent annotations of books make the "Annual Review" an important resource for research in the modernist period.

See also

ABELL (340): English Literature/Twentieth Century section.
Annual Bibliography of Victorian Studies (2490).
"Current Bibliography," *Twentieth Century Literature* (2790a).

MLAIB (335): English Language and Literature division in the volumes for 1921–25; English XI in the volumes for 1926–56; English X in the volumes for 1957–80; and English Literature/1900–1999 (as well as any larger chronological sections encompassing the century) in later volumes. Researchers must also check the headings beginning "English Literature" in the subject index to post-1980 volumes.

OTHER BIBLIOGRAPHIES

2785 *The New Cambridge Bibliography of English Literature* (*NCBEL*). Vol. 4: *1900–1950*. Ed. I. R. Willison. Cambridge: Cambridge UP, 1972. 1,408 cols. Z2011.N45 [PR83] 016.82.

(For a full discussion of *NCBEL*, see entry 1385.) Primary and secondary works are organized in six divisions (each subdivided and classified as its subject requires): introduction (with sections for general, book production and distribution), poetry (general, individual poets), novel (general, individual novelists, children's books), drama (general, individual dramatists), prose (critics and scholars; historians, political scientists; philosophers, theologians, scientists; travel and sport), and periodicals. Users must familiarize themselves with the organization, remember that there is considerable unevenness of coverage among subdivisions, and consult the index volume (vol. 5) rather than the provisional index in vol. 4. Despite its errors and omissions, the work offers the fullest general coverage of the period. Reviews: *TLS: Times Literary Supplement* 29 Dec. 1972: 1582; T. A. Birrell, *Neophilologus* 59 (1975): 306–15.

2790 Pownall, David E. *Articles on Twentieth Century Literature: An Annotated Bibliography, 1954 to 1970: An Expanded Cumulation of "Current Bibliography" in the Journal* Twentieth Century Literature, *Volume One to Volume Sixteen, 1955 to 1970*. New York: Kraus-Thomson, 1973– . Z6519.P66 [PN771] 016.809'04.

A descriptively annotated bibliography of some 40,000 journal articles (excluding review essays, popular journalism, and pedagogical discussions) printed between 1954 and 1970 on authors (regardless of nationality) who lived and published in the twentieth century. Pownall cumulates, verifies, and expands the quarterly "Current Bibliography," *Twentieth Century Literature* (2825) 1–16 (1955–70). Vols. 1–7 are organized alphabetically by literary authors; under each author, articles are listed alphabetically by scholar within sections for general studies and individual works. Additional volumes will have two extensively classified divisions: comparative, regional, and national literatures (with sections for themes, genres, and literary forms); and general literary subjects (including criticism, theory, and movements). The work is an important compilation because it offers more extensive coverage of articles than the serial bibliographies and indexes in section G. For studies after 1970, see "Current Bibliography," *Twentieth Century Literature* (entry 2825) 17–27.2 (1971–81), a descriptively annotated bibliography of journal articles on twentieth-century literature worldwide, and the serial bibliographies and indexes in section G.

2795 Davies, Alistair. *An Annotated Critical Bibliography of Modernism*. Harvester Annotated Critical Bibliographies. Brighton, England: Harvester; Totowa: Barnes, 1982. 261 pp. Z2014.M6.D38 [PR478.M6] 016.82'09'0091.

A selective, classified guide to "major books and articles" on literary modernism (principally in England), with the bulk of the volume consisting of separate bibliographies of Yeats, Lewis, Lawrence, and Eliot. The general division on modernism includes sections for the theory, literary context, critique, and critical reception of the movement; fiction; poetry; drama; anthologies; general studies; and literary modernism and the arts. Entries (arranged chronologically within each section or division) are accompanied by evaluative annotations that clearly delineate content. Each division has two indexes: subjects; critics. There are numerous important omissions (especially of works published in the 1970s), the indexing system is poorly conceived, the chronological organization compromised by a failure to list numerous reprinted essays by their respective years of initial publication, and scholarship on the four principal authors is more adequately covered in separate author bibliographies. Still, Davies is useful as a starting point because of its evaluations and (in the general section) compilation of studies not readily identifiable in standard bibliographies such as *MLAIB* (335) and *ABELL* (340). Review: Edward Mendelson, *TLS: Times Literary Supplement* 26 Aug. 1983: 901.

2800 Somer, John, and Barbara Eck Cooper. *American and British Literature, 1945–1975: An Annotated Bibliography of Contemporary Scholarship.* Lawrence: Regents P of Kansas, 1980. 326 pp. Z1227.S65 [PS221] 016.820'9'00914.

An annotated bibliography of 1,060 English-language books published before 1975 on critical theory, trends, patterns, topics, and backgrounds of modern literature, with accompanying unannotated lists of 162 books published after 1975 and 456 bibliographies and reference works. Somer excludes books devoted to a single author. The annotated entries are divided among sections for general studies, genres, and critical theory. The list of bibliographies and reference works (which, like that of studies published after 1975, includes a number of volumes not examined by the authors) is classified by topic (e.g., minority literature, science fiction) or type (e.g., biographical guides, handbooks). The descriptive annotations are sometimes vague and depend too much on introductory matter or tables of contents, but they do cite authors or topics that receive substantial discussion. Indexed by authors and subjects (with specific headings that offer efficient access to the annotations). Although *American and British Literature* is a valuable source for locating discussions of authors and topics buried in books, users would benefit from a more refined classification of entries. Review: Martin Tucker, *Analytical and Enumerative Bibliography* 5 (1981): 127–29.

RELATED TOPICS

2805 Havighurst, Alfred F. *Modern England, 1901–1984.* 2nd ed. Conference on British Studies Bibliographical Handbooks. Cambridge: Cambridge UP, for the North American Conference on British Studies, 1987. 109 pp. Z2020.H38 [DA566.4] 016.941.

A guide to significant primary and secondary materials published through 1984 on modern British history. The 2,670 entries are listed alphabetically in divisions for bibliographies; catalogs, guides, and handbooks; general surveys; constitutional and administrative history; political history; foreign relations; social history; economic history; labor history; urban history; agriculture; science and technology;

military and naval history; religion; fine arts; and intellectual history. The organization of most divisions in sections for primary sources, surveys, monographs, biographies, and articles is not helpful. Some entries are briefly annotated, occasionally with an evaluative phrase. Indexed by persons. Although *Modern England* is poorly organized and inadequately annotated, it is a useful selective guide. For the period 1901–14, Nicholls, *Nineteenth-Century Britain* (2520a), is a necessary complement. Fuller coverage of 1914–85 will eventually be available in K. G. Robbins, *Bibliography of British History, 1914–1985* (Oxford: Oxford UP, in progress).

See also

Annual Bibliography of British and Irish History (1400).
Hanham, *Bibliography of British History, 1851–1914* (2520).

Language

STUDIES OF LANGUAGE

2810 Quirk, Randolph, et al. *A Comprehensive Grammar of the English Language.* London: Longman, 1985. 1,779 pp. PE1106.C65 428.2.

A detailed description of the constituents and categories of grammar in Modern British and American English. After a general discussion of the English language and outline of its grammar (which serves as a guide to the remainder of the work), successive chapters examine *in extenso* verbs and auxiliaries; the semantics of the verb phrase; nouns and determiners; pronouns and numerals; adjectives and adverbs; the semantics and grammar of adverbials; prepositions and prepositional phrases; the simple sentence; sentence types and discourse functions; pro-forms and ellipsis; coordination; complex sentences; the syntactic and semantic functions of subordinate clauses; complementation of verbs and adjectives; noun phrases; theme, focus, and information processing; and sentence and text. Each chapter begins with a detailed table of contents, offers a multitude of examples, and concludes with suggestions for further reading. Three appendixes: word formation; stress, rhythm, and intonation; punctuation. Indexed by lexical items, abbreviations for grammatical categories, and general concepts. A clear, thorough, nearly exhaustive description, *Comprehensive Grammar* is the essential resource for understanding the grammar of Modern English. It supersedes Quirk et al., *A Grammar of Contemporary English* (New York: Seminar-Harcourt, 1972, 1,120 pp.). Reviews: F. G. A. M. Aarts, *English Studies* 69 (1988): 163–73; Rodney Huddleston, *Language* 64 (1988): 345–54; John M. Sinclair, *TLS: Times Literary Supplement* 28 June 1985: 715–16.

Biographical Dictionaries

See

Contemporary Authors (595).
Dictionary of Literary Biography (600).

Periodicals

GUIDES TO PRIMARY WORKS

See

Sec. K: Periodicals/Little Magazines.
Bibliography of British Newspapers (1440).
Sullivan, *British Literary Magazines* (1445).

GUIDES TO SCHOLARSHIP AND CRITICISM

See

"Victorian Periodicals: A Checklist of Criticism" (2555).

SCHOLARLY JOURNALS

Most journals in sections K: Periodicals/Scholarly Journals and M: English Literature/General/Periodicals/Scholarly Journals publish articles on twentieth-century English literature.

2815 *Contemporary Literature* (*ConL*). 1960– . Quarterly. Former title: *Wisconsin Studies in Contemporary Literature* (1960–68). PN2.W55 809.04.
Publishes articles, interviews, reviews, and occasional special issues (sometimes accompanied by a bibliography) on post–World War II literature, with an emphasis on British and American topics. Indexed every second year.

2820 *Journal of Modern Literature* (*JML*). 1970– . Quarterly. PN2.J6 809'.04.
Beginning with vol. 14 (1987), articles and occasional special issues (sometimes with a bibliography or survey of research) encompass all national literatures since 1900; earlier volumes focus on the Modernist period (1885–1950), with an emphasis on British and American writers. For the annual bibliography, see entry 2780.

2825 *Twentieth Century Literature: A Scholarly and Critical Journal* (*TCL*). 1955– . Quarterly. PN2.T8 809.04.
Publishes articles, bibliographies, and numerous special issues, primarily on British and American authors. Vols. 1–27.2 (1955–81) include a "Current Bibliography" (2790a). Annual index; cumulative index: vols. 20–30, Helen Bajan, comp., 30 (1984): 485–98.

See also

English Literature in Transition, 1880–1920 (2580).

Background Reading

See

Oxford History of England (1495).

Genres

Most works in sections L: Genres and M: English Literature/General/Genres are useful for research in twentieth-century English literature.

FICTION

Most works in sections L: Genres/Fiction and M: English Literature/General/Genres/Fiction are useful for research in twentieth-century English fiction.

Histories and Surveys

2830 Allen, Walter. *Tradition and Dream: The English and American Novel from the Twenties to Our Time*. With a new afterword. London: Hogarth, 1986. 358 pp. American ed.: *The Modern Novel in Britain and the United States*. New York: Dutton, 1964. 346 pp. PR881.A42 823.912'09.

A critical survey of the British and American novel from c. 1920 to 1960. Limited to works in English and excluding first novels published after 1955 as well as most historical fiction and short stories, *Tradition and Dream* emphasizes established authors. After an introduction outlining the relationship between the American and British novel, chapters are organized chronologically, then by country. Indexed by persons, titles, and a few subjects. A sequel to Allen, *English Novel* (1505a), this work offers a basic overview of important modern British and American novels. In the afterword to the 1986 reprint, Allen reflects on changes in his perception of the novel, discusses how he might now alter the work, and comments on major novels from 1955 to the 1980s. Reviews: *Times Literary Supplement* 13 Feb. 1964: 126; Irving Malin, *American Literature* 36 (1964): 390–91; Harvey Curtis Webster, *Kenyon Review* 26 (1964): 571–76.

Guides to Primary Works

See

Grimes, *Novels in English by Women, 1891–1920* (2640).
Leclaire, *General Analytical Bibliography of the Regional Novelists of the British Isles, 1800–1950* (2650).

Guides to Scholarship and Criticism

Although studies of modern fiction (to c. 1950) are adequately covered in the following works, there is no satisfactory current bibliography of scholarship and criticism on fiction after 1950. Both Alfred F. Rosa and Paul A. Eschholz, *Contemporary Fiction in America and England, 1950–1970: A Guide to Information Sources*,

American Literature, English Literature, and World Literatures in English: An Information Guide Series 10 (Detroit: Gale, 1976, 454 pp.), and Irving Adelman and Rita Dworkin, *The Contemporary Novel: A Checklist of Critical Literature on the British and American Novel since 1945* (Metuchen: Scarecrow, 1972, 614 pp.), are too dated and narrow in scope to offer more than minimal guidance. Horst W. Drescher and Bernd Kahrmann, *The Contemporary English Novel: An Annotated Bibliography of Secondary Sources* (Frankfurt: Athenäum, 1973, 204 pp.), is also outdated but still occasionally useful for its coverage of European (especially German) criticism. Until an adequate bibliography is published, those researching contemporary fiction will need to consult the following: *MLAIB* (335), *ABELL* (340), *Year's Work in English Studies* (330), Pownall, *Articles on Twentieth Century Literature* (2790), "Current Bibliography" in *Twentieth Century Literature* (2790a), "Annual Review" in *Journal of Modern Literature* (2780), Somer, *American and British Literature, 1945–1975* (2800), serial bibliographies and indexes in section G, and the numerous author bibliographies.

2835 Cassis, A. F. *The Twentieth-Century English Novel: An Annotated Bibliography of General Criticism*. Garland Reference Library of the Humanities 56. New York: Garland, 1977. 413 pp. Z2014.F5.C35 [PR881] 016.823'9'109.

A bibliography of studies from 1900 to 1972 of more than one novelist, the theory or technique of the novel, or the genre. The 2,832 entries are listed alphabetically by author in three divisions: bibliographies, criticism (subdivided into books and articles), and dissertations and theses. The descriptive annotations give particular attention to novelists discussed (dissertations and theses are not annotated). Two indexes: novelists; selected topics and themes. Clear annotations and the full (but not comprehensive) international scope make Cassis the best available guide to discussions of novelists in general studies, but poor organization and inadequate subject indexing render the work much less accessible than it should be. Reviews: Melvin J. Friedman, *Literary Research Newsletter* 4 (1979): 95–98; J. K. Johnstone, *English Studies in Canada* 6 (1980): 257–60.

2840 Rice, Thomas Jackson, *English Fiction, 1900–1950: A Guide to Information Sources*. 2 vols. American Literature, English Literature, and World Literatures in English: An Information Guide Series 20–21. Detroit: Gale, 1979–83. Z2014.F4.R5 [PR881] 016.823'9.

A selective annotated bibliography of works by and about British novelists (including major writers, those who "made a significant contribution to modern fiction," and minor novelists who have been the subjects of a "significant amount" of scholarship, but omitting many who are listed in other guides in this series). Vol. 1 covers English-language studies published through 1976, vol. 2, through 1980; both exclude unpublished dissertations, but otherwise the criteria determining selection are unstated. Entries are organized in two divisions: general (with sections for bibliographies; literary histories; critical studies of modern English fiction; theory of fiction; short story; studies of major types; histories and memoirs; and art, film, and music) and individual authors. Under each author, primary works appear first (with a full list of fictional works and a selection of others); secondary works are divided among bibliographies, biographical studies, book-length critical works, general articles and chapters of books, and studies of individual works. Although an asterisk marks important works, the brief annotations rarely explain the significance of a study or offer an adequate description of content. Three indexes (scholars; titles; subjects) in vol. 1, but only an index of scholars in vol. 2. Insufficient explanation of the criteria determining selection of authors and scholarship, inadequate annotations, and the lack of a subject index in vol. 2 detract significantly from the work, which is primarily useful as a starting point for research. Review: Bruce E. Teets, *Conradiana* 14 (1982): 77–80.

Complementary, but less current bibliographies, include the following:

Stanton, Robert J. *A Bibliography of Modern British Novelists*. 2 vols. Troy: Whitston, 1978. Although plagued by innumerable errors and omissions and restricted to only seventeen novelists, *Bibliography of Modern British Novelists* offers much fuller coverage of studies—especially popular journalism and reviews—and primary works (through c. 1976). Although unreliable, it is useful for its inclusion of material outside the scope of the standard serial bibliographies.

Wiley, Paul L., comp. *The British Novel: Conrad to the Present*. Goldentree Bibliographies in Language and Literature. Northbrook: AHM, 1973. 137 pp. Although it is judicious in its selection, the work is current only through c. 1971.

See also

Sec. M: English Literature/General/Genres/Fiction/Guides to Scholarship and Criticism.

Biographical Dictionaries

2845 *Contemporary Novelists*. Ed. D. L. Kirkpatrick. 4th ed. Contemporary Writers of the English Language. New York: St. Martin's, 1986. 1,003 pp. PR883.C64 823'.914'09.

A dictionary of some 600 living English-language fiction writers, the majority of whom are established British, American, and Canadian authors. Each signed entry provides basic biographical details (including address), a list of primary works, and a brief critical essay; some include one or more of the following: critical studies recommended by the entrant, a personal comment by the writer, and a note on manuscript collections. Writers recently dead are relegated to an appendix. Indexed by titles of novels and short stories; entrants are also indexed in *Biography and Genealogy Master Index* (565). Like other volumes in this series, it is a standard source for basic information. For lesser known writers, see *Contemporary Authors* (595).

Similar in execution but including dead authors among its approximately three hundred entries is James Vinson and Kirkpatrick, eds., *20th-Century Fiction*, Great Writer's Library (London: Macmillan, 1983, 781 pp.).

Periodicals

2850 *Critique: Studies in Modern Fiction* (*Crit*). 1956– . Quarterly. PN3503.C7 809.3.

Publishes articles, special issues, and occasional bibliographies, primarily on living writers "without great reputation." Although international in scope, *Critique* emphasizes British and American authors. Annual index; cumulative index: vols. 1–20, in 20.3 (1979): 65–102.

DRAMA AND THEATER

Many works in sections L: Genres/Drama and Theater and M: English Literature/General/Genres/Drama and Theater are useful for research in twentieth-century English drama and theater.

Histories and Surveys

2855 Nicoll, Allardyce. *English Drama, 1900–1930: The Beginnings of the Modern Period*. Cambridge: Cambridge UP, 1973. 1,083 pp. PR721.N45 016.822'9'1209.

Like *History of English Drama, 1660–1900* (1525), which this work effectively continues, *English Drama, 1900–1930* focuses on the history of the stage and dramatic forms of legitimate and popular theater in chapters on the theatrical world; influences, patterns, and forms; popular entertainment (musicals, revues, and melodramas); minority drama (e.g., regional and social drama); and "general" drama (essentially that by major playwrights). Nicoll excludes operas, pantomimes, plays of unestablished authorship, and most revues and music hall sketches. The concluding author list of plays (based on extensive research in the Lord Chamberlain's records) provides details of performances and printed editions but must be supplemented by J. P. Wearing, "Additions and Corrections to Allardyce Nicoll's 'Hand-List of Plays 1900–1930,'" *Nineteenth Century Theatre Research* 14 (1986): 51–96. Indexed by persons and subjects. An essential source for the history of dramatic works of the period.

2860 *The Revels History of Drama in English* (1530). Gen. ed. T. W. Craik. Vol. 7: *1880 to the Present Day*. London: Methuen; New York: Barnes, 1978. 298 pp. PR625.R44 822'.009.

Includes a chronology; essays on the social and literary context, actors and theaters, and dramatists and plays; and an evaluative survey of important studies. Indexed by authors, titles, and subjects. Like other volumes of *Revels History*, this work is a useful synthesis of scholarship rather than a connected history of the drama. Reviews: L. W. Conolly, *Theatre Journal* 32 (1980): 270–71; Robert Mace, *English* 29 (1980): 77–83.

Guides to Primary Works

2865 Wearing, J. P. *The London Stage, 1890–1899: A Calendar of Plays and Players*. 2 vols. Metuchen: Scarecrow, 1976. *The London Stage, 1900–1909: A Calendar of Plays and Players*. 2 vols. 1981. *The London Stage, 1910–1919: A Calendar of Plays and Players*. 2 vols. 1982. *The London Stage, 1920–1929: A Calendar of Plays and Players*. 3 vols. 1984. (Further volumes will extend the calendar to the present.) PN2596.L6.W37 792'.09421'2.

A calendar of first-night, professional, full-length productions in selected legitimate theaters (ranging in number from about 30 during 1890–99 to 51 during 1920–29). Available information varies, of course, with a full entry giving the following information for a first-night performance: title; genre and number of acts or scenes; author, translator, or adapter; theater; date, length of run, and number of performances; male and female casts (with changes in subsequent performances listed); production staff; selected list of first-night reviews; miscellaneous notes relating to the production or discrepancies in sources. Indexed by persons, titles, and theaters (a single index for 1890–99; a separate index of titles for the later decades). Because of the nature of the sources, some information is inaccurate, since advertisements include errors, performances were cancelled, productions were withdrawn, and substitutions were made in casts. Although not exhaustive, these works are valuable compilations for the study of trends in the legitimate theater; the popularity of genres, specific plays, and playwrights; and careers of theater personnel and players. Reviews: (1890–99) Trevor R. Griffiths, *Theatre Notebook* 31.3 (1977): 43–44; (1900–09) Griffiths, *Theatre Notebook* 37.3 (1983): 141–43; (1920–29) Margaret Watson, *Notes and Queries* ns 33 (1986): 564–65.

Guides to Scholarship and Criticism

Serial Bibliographies

2870 "Modern Drama Studies: An Annual Bibliography." *Modern Drama* (entry 1190) 17 (1974)– .

The expanded successor to "Modern Drama: A Selective Bibliography of Works Published in English in [1959–67]," 3–11 (1960–68), this covers studies published since 1972 on dramatic works by authors (with the exception of Büchner and Becque) who lived past 1899; emphasizes dramatic literature rather than theatrical history; and excludes reviews, unpublished dissertations, and works printed in non-Latin alphabets. Entries are organized in divisions for general studies and national literatures (or geographical areas); within the latter are sections for general studies and individual authors. Although the work is not comprehensive, the compiler claims that 35–40% of the entries are not listed in *MLAIB* (335). The bibliographies for 1966–80 are incorporated in Carpenter, *Modern Drama Scholarship and Criticism, 1966–1980* (2875), which the annual bibliographies after 1980 correct and update.

Other Bibliographies

2875 Carpenter, Charles A. *Modern Drama Scholarship and Criticism, 1966–1980: An International Bibliography*. Toronto: U of Toronto P, 1986. 587 pp. Z5781.C37 [PN1851] 016.8092'04.

A classified bibliography of studies of the drama worldwide since Ibsen. Excludes publications in non-Latin alphabets, discussions of theater not related to a dramatic text, unpublished dissertations, most reviews of productions, and most popular journalism; the degree of selectivity in the author lists varies with an individual's commitment to the drama. The approximately 27,300 entries are classified in divisions for general studies and national literatures or language groups (with the latter including sections for individual playwrights). Each division is prefaced by an outline of its organization. Under each dramatist are separate lists of primary works (including only critical editions of plays, essays, collections of letters, and interviews), reference works, collections of essays, and critical studies (including parts of books). A few entries are accompanied by very brief descriptive annotations. Indexed by persons. Although covering only 15 years and omitting dissertations, *Modern Drama Scholarship* is clearly a major contribution to the study of modern drama. Even with the exclusions, the scope is admirably full (Carpenter claims to double the *MLAIB* [335] coverage before 1970 and add half again as many entries for 1970–80). The work must, however, be supplemented by section H: Guides to Dissertations and Theses; *MLAIB* (335) and *ABELL* (340) for scholarship in non-Latin alphabets; and "Modern Drama Studies: An Annual Bibliography" (2870), which updates and corrects Carpenter.

Although the following pale in comparison, they are still useful—in varying degrees—for pre-1966 publications:

Adelman, Irving, and Rita Dworkin. *Modern Drama: A Checklist of Critical Literature on 20th Century Plays*. Metuchen: Scarecrow, 1967. 370 pp. Occasionally useful for its indexing of parts of books, but for its deficiencies, see Carpenter's review, *Modern Drama* 12 (1969): 49–56.

Breed, Paul F., and Florence M. Sniderman, comps. and eds. *Dramatic Criticism Index: A Bibliography of Commentaries on Playwrights from Ibsen to the Avant-Garde*. Detroit: Gale, 1972. 1,022 pp. Principally useful for its indexing of parts of books.

Carpenter, Charles A., comp. *Modern British Drama*. Goldentree Bibliographies in Language and Literature. Arlington Heights: AHM, 1979. 120 pp. Although dated, this work remains the best overall of the selective bibliographies of modern British drama from c. 1860 to the 1970s, and is completely superior to the two padded, repetitive, poorly organized, and inadequately annotated bibliographies by E. H. Mikhail: *English Drama, 1900–1950: A Guide to Information Sources*, American Literature, English Literature, and World Literatures in English: An Information Guide Series 11 (Detroit: Gale, 1977, 328 pp.)—which actually covers British drama, but lists only bibliographies for authors—and *Contemporary British Drama, 1950–1976: An Annotated Critical Bibliography* (Totowa: Rowman, 1976, 147 pp.), which includes no listings for individual authors, no introduction, no index, almost nothing that is not in the preceding work, and which in no way merits "annotated critical" in the title.

Coleman, Arthur, and Gary R. Tyler. *Drama Criticism*. Vol. 1: *A Checklist of Interpretation since 1940 of English and American Plays*. Vol. 2: *A Checklist of Interpretation since 1940 of Classical and Continental Plays*. Chicago: Swallow, 1966–71.

Harris, *Modern Drama in America and England, 1950–1970* (4290).

King, Kimball. *Twenty Modern British Playwrights: A Bibliography, 1956–1976*. Garland Reference Library of the Humanities 98. New York: Garland, 1977. 289 pp.

Palmer, *European Drama Criticism* (1170).

See also

Wildbihler, *The Musical: An International Annotated Bibliography* (4295).

Biographical Dictionaries

2880 *Contemporary Dramatists*. Ed. James Vinson and D. L. Kirkpatrick. 3rd ed. Contemporary Writers of the English Language. New York: St. Martin's, 1982. 1,104 pp. PR737.C57 822'.914'09.

A dictionary of about 300 living English-language dramatists, the majority of whom are established British, American, and Canadian writers. Each signed entry provides basic biographical details (including address), lists of primary works and theatrical activities, and a brief critical essay; some include one or more of the following: a list of critical studies recommended by the entrant, a personal comment by the dramatist, and a note on manuscript collections. Following the entries are separate lists of works or performances by screen, radio, and television writers, musical librettists, and theater groups. An appendix lists entries for seven major dramatists who died since the 1950s. Indexed by titles of plays; entrants are also indexed in *Biography and Genealogy Master Index* (565). Like other volumes in this series, a standard source for basic information. For lesser known dramatists, see *Contemporary Authors* (595).

See also

Contemporary Theatre, Film, and Television (4305).

Periodicals

2885 *TDR: The Drama Review* (*TDR*). 1955– . Quarterly. Former titles: *Tulane Drama Review*, 1957–67; *Carleton Drama Review*, 1955–56. PN2000.D68 792'.09.

Originally devoted to drama and theater, classical to contemporary, but now articles, production reviews, interviews, texts, and special issues emphasize the social, economic, and political contexts of contemporary performance (encompassing music, popular entertainment, media, and ritual, as well as theater). Vols. 3–11 (1959–67) include "Books and Theatre: [1958–66]," which varies from a highly selective list of scholarship and editions to an unsuccessful attempt to note all books published in the United States that treat drama and theater. Annual index through vol. 15 (1970–71); cumulative index: vols. 1–15, in 15.4 (1971): 130–38.

Background Reading

The bibliography in the *Revels History of Drama*, vol. 7 (2860) surveys major criticism and background studies.

POETRY

Most works in sections L: Genres/Poetry and M: English Literature/General/Genres/Poetry are useful for research in twentieth-century English poetry.

Histories and Surveys

2890 Perkins, David. *A History of Modern Poetry*. 2 vols. Cambridge: Belknap-Harvard UP, 1976–87.

Vol. 1: *From the 1890s to the High Modernist Mode*. 1976. 623 pp. PR610.P4 821'.009.
Vol. 2: *Modernism and After*. 1987. 694 pp. PS323.5.P46 821'.91'09.

A history of twentieth-century English and American poetry. Although emphasizing poets and their careers, chapters also consider "opposed and evolving assumptions about poetry [,] . . . the effects on poetry of its changing audiences, . . . premises and procedures in literary criticism, . . . publishing outlets, . . . and the interrelations of poetry with developments in the other arts—the novel, painting, film, music—as well as in social, political, and intellectual life." Among contemporary poets, only those whose reputations were of significance by the 1970s are examined in detail. Indexed in each volume by persons, titles, and a few subjects. Praised as well as damned for its breadth and impartiality, these volumes remain the only reasonably full survey of twentieth-century poetry. Review: (vol. 1) James E. Breslin, *Georgia Review* 31 (1977): 978–84.

Guides to Primary Works

See

Poetry Index Annual (1240).

Guides to Scholarship and Criticism

The *New Cambridge Bibliography of English Literature* (2785) offers the single best list of studies on modern poetry (to c. 1950), but its coverage must be supplemented by the works listed below under *See also*. Of the other available bibliographies, Charles F. Altieri, comp., *Modern Poetry*, Goldentree Bibliographies in Language and Literature (Arlington Heights: AHM, 1979, 129 pp.), emphasizes established poets who are more adequately covered in author bibliographies and is too selective and dated to be of much use. Because of its omissions, incomplete indexing, inadequate annotations, and numerous errors, Emily Ann Anderson, *English Poetry, 1900–1950: A Guide to Information Sources*, American Literature, English Literature, and World Literatures in English: An Information Guide Series 33 (Detroit: Gale, 1982, 315 pp.), cannot be recommended even for preliminary work.

Those interested in contemporary poetry will have to turn to the serial bibliographies and indexes in section G, as well as the works listed below. An adequate bibliography of scholarship and criticism on twentieth-century English poetry is a major desideratum.

See also

Gingerich, *Contemporary Poetry in America and England, 1950–1975* (4335).
Kuntz, *Poetry Explication* (1255).

Biographical Dictionaries

2895 *Contemporary Poets*. Ed. James Vinson and D. L. Kirkpatrick. 4th ed. Contemporary Writers of the English Language. New York: St. Martin's, 1985. 1,071 pp. PR603.C6 821'.91'09.

A dictionary of about 800 living English-language poets, the majority of whom are established British, American, or Canadian writers. The signed entries provide basic biographical information (including address), a list of published books, and a basic critical evaluation; some include one or more of the following: critical studies recommended by the entrant, a note on manuscript locations, and comments by the poet. An appendix prints entries for major poets who have died since 1960. Indexed by titles of books of poetry listed in the publications section of each entry; entrants are also indexed in *Biography and Genealogy Master Index* (565). Like other volumes in this series, it is a standard source for basic information. Review: Jonathan Barker, *TLS: Times Literary Supplement* 15 Aug. 1986: 900.

For lesser known poets, see *Contemporary Authors* (595).

Periodicals

See

Parnassus: Poetry in Review (4340).

PROSE

Some works in sections L: Genres/Prose and M: English Literature/General/Genres/Prose are useful for research in twentieth-century English prose.

Guides to Scholarship and Criticism

2900 Brown, Christopher C., and William B. Thesing. *English Prose and Criticism, 1900–1950: A Guide to Information Sources*. American Literature,

English Literature, and World Literatures in English: An Information Guide Series 42. Detroit: Gale, 1983. 553 pp. Z2014.P795.B76 [PR801] 016.828'91208'09.

A highly selective annotated bibliography of editions and studies (published in English before June 1982) of nonfictional prose by 37 authors (selected for the quality of their work or representativeness). Entries are organized in two divisions: general and period studies, and individual authors. The first division (which omits some important works) includes brief sections for bibliographies, literary histories, biography and autobiography, the essay and prose style, literary criticism, and travel writing. Under individual authors are separate lists of primary works (limited to books), editions, bibliographies, biographies, and critical studies. The brief annotations—essentially descriptive, with evaluative adjectives—are barely adequate to convey a sense of content. Two indexes: persons; titles. Although it is highly selective and partly superseded by author bibliographies, *English Prose and Criticism* does serve as a starting point for the study of nonfiction prose. Because of the increasing interest in the topic, a more thorough bibliography would be welcomed by scholars.

N

Irish Literature

This section is limited to works devoted exclusively to Irish literature (primarily in English). Because Irish writers are frequently included in works on English or British literature, researchers must also consult section M: English Literature. In addition, many works listed in sections G: Serial Bibliographies, Indexes, and Abstracts and H: Guides to Dissertations and Theses are useful for research in Irish literature.

Histories and Surveys

2915 Hyde, Douglas. *A Literary History of Ireland: From Earliest Times to the Present Day*. 2nd impression of new ed., with introduction by Brian Ó Cuív. New York: St. Martin's, 1980. 654 pp. PB1306.H8 820'.9.

A literary history of Irish-language literature through the eighteenth century (with copious translated extracts). Indexed by persons and subjects. As Ó Cuív points out, there are linguistic and historical errors, inconsistencies, and parts that need revision in light of new discoveries; however, *Literary History of Ireland* remains a monumental, seminal work that has never been superseded. (The new edition consists of a reprint of the 1899 edition, along with a biographical introduction on Hyde and a selective bibliography; the second impression updates the bibliography through 1979.)

2920 McHugh, Roger, and Maurice Harmon. *Short History of Anglo-Irish Literature: From Its Origins to the Present Day*. Totowa: Barnes, 1982. 377 pp. PR8711.M35 820'.9'9415.

A chronological history from the eighteenth century through the 1970s that attempts to place Anglo-Irish literature in the context of Irish, English, and European literatures. Although the discussions of Irish-language literature, the sixteenth- and seventeenth-century background, and major authors are weak, this work is the fullest history of the subject, but one more useful for its treatment of background than for critical insights. Review: Vivian Mercier, *TLS: Times Literary Supplement* 18 Feb. 1983: 167.

A good complement is A. Norman Jeffares, *Anglo-Irish Literature*, History of Literature Series (New York: Schocken, 1982, 349 pp.), which covers the same period and concludes with a chronology.

Literary Handbooks, Dictionaries, and Encyclopedias

2925 Hogan, Robert, ed. *Dictionary of Irish Literature*. Westport: Greenwood, 1979. 815 pp. PR8706.D5 820'.9'9415.

A literary dictionary consisting primarily of entries (ranging from 250 to 10,000 words) on some 500 English-language writers (including historians, editors, political writers, journalists, and the like) along with a few discussions of literature-related topics and a lengthy essay on Irish-language authors. Criteria governing the selection of authors or topics are decidedly vague. The author entries emphasize critical commentary but also provide basic biographical information and lists of book-length primary works and criticism. Concludes with a basic chronology of literary and historical events and a selected general bibliography. Indexed by titles, persons, and some subjects. Although something of a hodgepodge of entries of variable quality, the *Dictionary* does provide the fullest discussions of the handbooks devoted to Irish literature. What is needed, however, is a guide along the lines of an *Oxford Companion*. Reviews: Anne Clune, *Notes and Queries* ns 29 (1982): 265–66; Arthur E. McGuinness, *Yearbook of English Studies* 12 (1982): 241–43.

Bibliographies of Bibliographies

2930 Eager, Alan R. *A Guide to Irish Bibliographical Material: A Bibliography of Irish Bibliographies and Sources of Information*. 2nd ed., rev. and enl. Westport: Greenwood, 1980. 502 pp. Z2031.E16 [DA906] 016.0169415.

A bibliography of bibliographies, including books, articles, parts of books and articles, catalogs, unpublished materials, and works in progress through 1978. Although the majority of the 9,517 entries are for bibliographies wholly or substantially devoted to Irish topics, the *Guide* includes several that are printed in but not about the country, as well as many nonbibliographical works, for the sake of "balance." Entries are organized by Dewey Decimal Classification; a few are accompanied by a brief descriptive annotation. Supplementary entries are printed on pp. 379–81. Two indexes: scholars; subjects (including literary authors). Because of the organization, users should approach the work through the subject index (especially when searching for bibliographies about a person). Although it is not comprehensive, contains numerous errors, is marred by an inadequate description of limitations and organization, and includes several works outside its focus, the work is an essential source for identifying bibliographies on all Irish topics. For recent bibliographies, consult *Bibliographic Index* (145).

Guides to Primary Works

There is no adequate bibliography of Irish literature. The *New Cambridge Bibliography of English Literature* (2965) lists primary works by some writers, as does Frank L. Kersnowski, C. W. Spinks, and Laird Loomis, *A Bibliography of Modern Irish and Anglo-Irish Literature*, Checklists in the Humanities and Education: A Series (San Antonio: Trinity UP, 1976, 157 pp.). Although the latter cites bibliographies of primary and secondary works, its lists of books by 61 writers is highly selective and plagued by numerous errors.

Guides to Collections

2935 Lester, DeeGee, comp. *Irish Research: A Guide to Collections in North America, Ireland, and Great Britain*. Bibliographies and Indexes in World History 9. New York: Greenwood, 1987. 348 pp. Z2031.L47 [DA906] 016.9415'0025.

A guide to collections for the study of Irish culture and civilization, including biography, film, folklore, literature, and theater. Although the bulk of the entries are for libraries and museums, Lester also lists organizations and periodicals. Entries are grouped by country, then alphabetically by state, province, or county, then city, and then repository or organization. A typical entry consists of address, a brief description of the repository or organization, a note on general collections of Irish materials, a description of special collections, a list of finding aids, notes on access or restrictions, and tips for researchers. Since information is taken from questionnaires or published descriptions, the entries vary in accuracy and fullness of detail. Two appendixes: dealers specializing in Irish books; Irish local newspapers. Indexed by persons, subjects, and titles. Despite the omission of several important collections, the inclusion of many libraries that "may have" Irish material or whose holdings are essentially general, and insufficient detail of many descriptions, *Irish Research* can be a useful source for identifying collections of Irish literature and related works. Researchers must also consult the guides in sections E: Libraries and Library Catalogs/Research Libraries/Guides to Collections and F: Guides to Manuscripts and Archives/Guides to Repositories and Archives.

Manuscripts

2940 Hayes, Richard J., ed. *Manuscript Sources for the History of Irish Civilisation*. 11 vols. Boston: Hall, 1965. *First Supplement, 1965–1975*. 3 vols. 1979. Z2041.D85 016.9415.

An index to manuscripts relating to Ireland held in about 678 libraries and more than 600 private collections in 30 countries. Entries are organized in four sequences: persons and institutions (vols. 1–4), subjects (5–6), places in Ireland (7–8), and dates (9–10). An entry typically provides a brief description of a manuscript, location, and (usually) shelf number or citation to printed calendar or catalog. Vol. 11 consists of lists of manuscript catalogs of manuscripts, private collections, libraries, and various lists of Gaelic manuscripts. The supplement records newly acquired manuscripts. Although many entries are taken from other catalogs or sources and some private collections have been dispersed, Hayes is a valuable, time-saving compilation that includes numerous literary manuscripts.

See also

Sec. F: Guides to Manuscripts and Archives.
Index of English Literary Manuscripts (1365).

Printed Works

2945 *Irish Publishing Record [1967–]*. Dublin: Library, U College, Dublin, 1967– . Annual. Z2034.I87 015'.415.

A national bibliography that records books, pamphlets, new periodicals, yearbooks, musical scores, and selected government publications published in Northern Ireland and the Republic of Ireland. Entries, which provide basic card catalog information, are organized by Dewey Decimal Classification; periodicals and juveniles are listed separately. The indexes of names and titles cite classification rather than page numbers. Since information is compiled from a variety of sources, details are not always accurate, but the work does offer the most thorough record of books published in the island since 1967.

For books published in Ireland and available for purchase, see the current edition of *Irish Books in Print/Leabhair Gaeilge i gCló [1984–]* (Wicklow: Cleary, 1984– , irregular). It also includes books about Ireland that are listed in *Books in Print* (4225) and *British Books in Print* (2770).

Guides to Scholarship and Criticism

Surveys of Research

2950 Finneran, Richard J., ed. *Anglo-Irish Literature: A Review of Research.* New York: MLA, 1976. 596 pp. PR8712.A5 820'.9'9415. *Recent Research on Anglo-Irish Writers: A Supplement to* Anglo-Irish Literature: A Review of Research. Modern Language Association of America Reviews of Research. 1983. 361 pp. (A new edition, *Anglo-Irish Literature: A Guide to Research,* is scheduled for publication in 1990.) PR8712.R4 820'.9'9415.

Evaluative surveys of research on genres and dead authors of Anglo-Irish background who have been the subject of a substantial amount of scholarship. Coverage extends through 1974 in the first volume, through 1980 in the supplement, with the degree of selectivity varying with the contributor. The new edition, which adds a chapter on Beckett and covers scholarship through c. 1986, will supersede the original volume and supplement. The original volume has chapters on general works; nineteenth-century writers; Wilde; Moore; Shaw; Yeats; Synge; Joyce; four Revival figures: Lady Gregory, A. E., Gogarty, Stephens; O'Casey; and modern drama. The supplement adds modern fiction and poetry. The chapters are extensively classified, with most including sections on reference works, manuscripts, editions, biography, letters, general studies, and individual works. Each survey combines, in varying degrees, description and evaluation, with suggestions for further research. Indexed by persons. Like similar MLA surveys of research, this is marred by incomplete citations, and some reviewers have objected to a definition of Anglo-Irish background that admits Shaw and Wilde but excludes other similar writers. Still, Finneran is the indispensable, authoritative guide to scholarship. Review: Ellsworth Mason, *James Joyce Quarterly* 15 (1978): 138–46.

See also

YWES (330): Anglo-Irish writers are covered in several chapters.

Serial Bibliographies

2955 "IASAIL Bibliography Bulletin for [1970–]." *Irish University Review* (entry 3015) 2 (1972)– .

An international bibliography of studies of Anglo-Irish literature (along with some original poetry and short fiction). Since the bibliography for 1974 (6 [1976]), entries are organized in two sections: general studies and individual authors. In the earlier ones, studies are listed by country of origin. Although not comprehensive, the bibliography is useful because of its international coverage.

A useful complement is the annual "Research Report" in *American Conference for Irish Studies Newsletter* (1971– , 3/yr.), a list of publications and work in press or progress on Irish history, literature, and linguistics.

2960 "The Year's Work in Irish-English Literature." *Etudes irlandaises* (entry 3010) 1 (1972)– .

An annual selective bibliography of scholarship (beginning in the late 1960s) on Anglo-Irish literature. Entries are organized alphabetically in two divisions: general works and individual authors. The coverage of Continental scholarship makes this a useful complement to "IASAIL Bibliography Bulletin" (2955) and the other standard serial bibliographies and indexes in section G. *Etudes irlandaises* also publishes an annual "Bibliographie sélective: Histoire, politique, institutions irlandaises."

See also

Secs. G: Serial Bibliographies, Indexes, and Abstracts and H: Guides to Dissertations and Theses.

ABELL (340): Entries on Anglo-Irish writers and literature are dispersed throughout.

Annual Bibliography of British and Irish History (1400).

Bibliotheca Celtica (3155).

MLAIB (335): Until the volume for 1981, Anglo-Irish literature was included in the English Literature division. Literature in Irish Gaelic was covered in the Celtic Languages and Literatures heading under the General division in the volumes for 1928–52; in General IV [later V or VI]: Celtic Languages and Literatures in the volumes for 1953–66; and in Celtic VI: Irish Gaelic in the volumes for 1967–80. Since the volume for 1981, the Irish Literature division encompasses Irish literature in any language. Researchers must also check the "Irish Literature" heading in the subject index to post-1980 volumes.

Other Bibliographies

2965 *New Cambridge Bibliography of English Literature* (*NCBEL*). Ed. George Watson and I. R. Willison. 5 vols. Cambridge: Cambridge UP, 1969–77. Z2011.N45 [PR83] 016.82.

(For a full discussion of *NCBEL*, see entry 1385.) Sections on Anglo-Irish literature are scattered throughout the four volumes:

Vol. 1: *600–1660* has sections on Irish literature in Latin (cols. 341–44, 351–56) and Irish printing and bookselling (cols. 669–70), with Irish writers listed in various sections.

Vol. 2: *1660–1800* has sections on Irish printing and bookselling (cols. 273–74) and periodicals (cols. 1377–90), with Irish writers listed in various sections.

Vol. 3: *1800–1900* has a division for Anglo-Irish literature through 1916 (cols. 1885–948), with classified sections for Gaelic sources, general studies, poets, Yeats and Synge, and dramatists.

Vol. 4: *1900–1950* has Anglo-Irish topics and writers listed throughout the various sections.

In each volume, many of the general sections list works important to the study of Anglo-Irish literature. Coverage extends through 1962–69, depending on the volume.

Users must familiarize themselves with the organization, remember that there is considerable unevenness of coverage among subdivisions, and consult the index volume (vol. 5) rather than the provisional indexes in vols. 1–4. Despite its shortcomings (see entry 1385), *NCBEL* offers the fullest single bibliography of primary works and scholarship for the study of Anglo-Irish literature.

2970 Best, R. I. *Bibliography of Irish Philology and of Printed Irish Literature.* Dublin: HMSO, 1913. 307 pp. *Bibliography of Irish Philology and Manuscript Literature: Publications, 1913–1941.* Dublin: Dublin Inst. for Advanced Studies, 1942. 253 pp. Z2037.D81 016.8916.

Baumgarten, Rolf. *Bibliography of Irish Linguistics and Literature, 1942–71.* Dublin: Dublin Inst. for Advanced Studies, 1986. 776 pp. (A volume covering 1972–86 is in preparation.) Z7012.I73.B38 [PB1213] 016.4916'2.

A bibliography of scholarship on Irish language and literature through the latter part of the nineteenth century but excluding the Irish Revival. In the volumes by Best, entries are variously organized in two divisions: philology and literature. The first has classified sections for general works, dictionaries and lexicography, etymology (combined with lexicography in the 1913–41 volume), phonology (combined with grammar in 1913–41), grammar, metrics, inscriptions, manuscripts, and Old Irish glosses; the second has sections for general studies, tales and sagas, poetry (only through the seventeenth century in the 1913–41 volume), religious works, history, legal works, and miscellaneous works. The original volume prints additions on pp. 273–74; in the volume for 1913–41 additions appear on pp. 193–94 and corrections to the earlier volume on pp. 253–54. Baumgarten organizes entries by publication date in extensively classified sections for general works, sources, linguistics, lexicology and onomastics, grammar, literature and learning, narrative literature, verse, society (a grab-bag section), Christianity, history and genealogy, and prehistory and cultural history. A few entries are accompanied by a brief descriptive annotation or list of reviews. The original volume is indexed by persons (with numerous omissions); the one for 1913–41 has indexes for words (with separate sections for personal names, place names, and other words, as well as an index to the earlier volume), first lines of poems, and persons and subjects; the most recent one has four indexes: words and proper names, first lines of verse, sources, and authors of works cited. Although confusingly organized, not comprehensive, and lacking any statement of scope and editorial policy in the 1942–71 volume, these volumes offer the fullest general coverage of scholarship on Irish language and literature.

2975 Harmon, Maurice. *Select Bibliography for the Study of Anglo-Irish Literature and Its Backgrounds: An Irish Studies Handbook.* Port Credit: Meany, 1977. 187 pp. Z2037.H32 [PR8711] 016.82.

A highly selective annotated guide, principally to reference works and important background studies published through the mid-1970s. Entries are organized in three divisions: general reference works, background materials, and literature. The background division has sections for reference works, history, biography, topography, folk culture and anthropology, theater, Anglo-Irish language, Irish language, Gaelic literature, and newspapers and periodicals. The literature division lists entries in sections for general studies, poetry, fiction, drama, bibliographies of individual authors, and literary periodicals. The brief descriptive annotations (sometimes including evaluative comments) too infrequently offer an adequate indication of contents or accurate evaluation. The chronology for 1765–1976 has numerous gaps. The lack of an index and numerous omissions make Harmon useful only insofar as it complements or updates the much fuller coverage in *New Cambridge Bibliography of English Literature* (2965). Review: William T. O'Malley, *American Notes and Queries* 17 (1978): 66.

2980 Hayes, Richard J., ed. *Sources for the History of Irish Civilisation: Articles in Irish Periodicals*. 9 vols. Boston: Hall, 1970. Z2034.H35 016.91415'03.

A bibliography of articles, original literary works, and reviews in 152 periodicals, published in Ireland from c. 1800 through 1969, that print material useful for research in Irish intellectual and cultural life. Hayes excludes popular, trade, and current news periodicals as well as those in the Irish language. Entries (which record author, title, and publication information) are organized in four divisions: persons (vols. 1–5; library catalog main entries as well as persons as subjects and authors of books reviewed); subjects (vols. 6–8); places in Ireland (vol. 9); dates (vol. 9; works dealing with a specific date or period are organized in chronological order). Although the majority of the entries relate to Ireland, a significant number of articles and reviews on other topics, especially British literature, are also indexed. An essential source for locating works by and about Irish writers, and an important complement to the serial bibliographies and indexes in section G.

2985 McKenna, Brian. *Irish Literature, 1800–1875: A Guide to Information Sources*. American Literature, English Literature, and World Literatures in English: An Information Guide Series 13. Detroit: Gale, 1978. 388 pp. Z2037.M235 [PR8750] 016.82.

A highly selective bibliography of works by and about Anglo-Irish authors. Coverage extends through 1974 and includes a few foreign-language studies. Entries are arranged chronologically in classified divisions for anthologies, periodicals, general studies, background studies, and individual authors (each with separate lists of bibliographies, biographies, criticism, and primary works). The brief annotations rarely offer an adequate indication of content or substantiate an evaluative comment. Three indexes: authors; titles; subjects. The lack of cross-references—especially to general studies—is not fully remedied by the subject index. Because of its selectivity (which results in some significant omissions) and the fuller treatment of major figures in author bibliographies, McKenna is principally useful as a starting point for work on minor writers. Review: James Kilroy, *Analytical and Enumerative Bibliography* 3 (1979): 62–67.

McKenna's volume for 1876–1950, although announced, was never published.

See also

Schwartz, *Articles on Women Writers* (6605).

Language

Guides to Scholarship

See

ABELL (340): See especially the Dialects section in the volumes for 1920–27; the English Dialects section in the volumes for 1928–72; and the Dialects of English/British Isles section in the volumes since 1973.
Best, *Bibliography of Irish Philology* (2970).
Bibliotheca Celtica (3155).
Harmon, *Select Bibliography for the Study of Anglo-Irish Literature* (2975).
MLAIB (335): See especially the Dialectology section of the English Language division. (For an outline of this division, see p. 160.) Researchers must also check the heading "Irish English Dialect" in the subject index to post-1980 volumes.

Biographical Dictionaries

There is no fully adequate, authoritative biographical dictionary for Ireland. For an overview of general and specialized biographical dictionaries through 1979, see C. J. Woods, "A Guide to Irish Biographical Dictionaries," *Maynooth Review* 6 (1980): 16–34.

2990 Boylan, Henry. *A Dictionary of Irish Biography*. New York: Barnes, 1978. 385 pp. CT862.B69 920'.0415.

A biographical dictionary of deceased individuals, principally of Irish birth (but also including some who were of Irish descent, "made a considerable contribution to Irish affairs," or had some lasting impact on Ireland). Each brief entry provides a basic chronological account of the entrant's life. Indexed in *Biography and Genealogy Master Index* (565). Based heavily on *Dictionary of National Biography* (1425) and other sources, the *Dictionary* offers reasonably broad coverage. Brady, *Biographical Dictionary of Irish Writers* (2995), includes a greater number of writers.

2995 Brady, Anne M., and Brian Cleeve. *A Biographical Dictionary of Irish Writers*. New York: St. Martin's, 1985. 387 pp. PR8727.B5 820'.9'9415.

A biographical dictionary of Irish writers, from St. Patrick to the present, that corrects many of the errors and omissions in Cleeve, *Dictionary of Irish Writers*, 3 vols. (Cork: Mercier, 1967–71). Brady and Cleeve includes numerous contemporary authors as well as scholars whose reputation extends beyond academe, but offers no statement of the criteria used to determine who qualifies as "Irish." The very brief entries—which provide basic biographical information, a list of major publications, and summary critical comments on major writers—are organized in two divisions: writers in English, and writers in Irish and Latin. Additions appear on p. 254. This work offers the widest coverage (especially of contemporary authors) but the least information of the biographical dictionaries of Irish writers.

See also

Dictionary of Literary Biography (600).
Dictionary of National Biography (1425).
Hogan, *Dictionary of Irish Literature* (2925).

Periodicals

Guides to Primary Works

3000 North, John S. *The Waterloo Directory of Irish Newspapers and Periodicals, 1800–1900, Phase II*. Phase 2, vol. 1 of Waterloo Directory Series of Newspapers and Periodicals: England, Ireland, Scotland, and Wales, 1800–1900. Waterloo: North Waterloo Academic, 1986. 838 pp. PN5144.W2 011'.35'09415.

A bibliography of 3,932 serials published in Ireland during the nineteenth century. Publications are listed alphabetically by earliest title or issuing body for nonspecific titles; cross-references cite alternate titles, issuing bodies, and many subtitles. A main entry records, when possible, title, subtitle(s), title changes, series, volume, and issue numbering, publication dates, place(s) of publication, editor(s), proprietor(s), publisher(s), printer(s), size, price, circulation, frequency of publication, illustrations, issuing body(ies), indexing, subject matter, departments, religious or political stance, mergers, miscellaneous notes, references to studies or histories, and locations (in selected British and Irish collections). Three indexes: subjects; persons (including companies and issuing bodies); places of publication. The *Waterloo Directory*, whose entries are based on the actual examination of runs, offers the most accurate, complete accumulation of information on Irish serial publications. The extensive indexing makes essential sources for the study of nearly all facets of nineteenth-century Irish life and culture readily accessible for the first time. An indispensable work that supersedes all earlier bibliographies listing nineteenth-century Irish periodicals and newspapers and stands as an example of the kind of guide needed for serials of other countries and periods.

Since locations are restricted to 50 British and Irish libraries, consult the following for additional holdings: Fulton, *Union List of Victorian Serials* (2530); Ward, *Index and Finding List* (2535); *Union List of Serials* (640a); *British Union-Catalogue of Periodicals* (645a); OCLC (225); and RLIN (230).

Scholarly Journals

3005 *Éire-Ireland: A Journal of Irish Studies* (*Éire*). 1966– . Quarterly. DA900.E37 [AP2.E53] 941.5.

Publishes articles, notes, and reviews on a wide range of topics concerning Ireland and the Irish, with some emphasis on literature.

3010 *Etudes irlandaises: Revue française d'histoire, civilisation, et littérature de l'Irelande* (*EI*). 1972– . 2/yr. (Subtitle varies.) DA925.E86 941.50824'05.

Publishes articles and reviews on Irish culture (especially literature) as well as two annual bibliographies: "The Year's Work in Irish-English Literature" (2960) and "Bibliographie sélective: Histoire, politique, institutions irlandaises."

3015 *Irish University Review: A Journal of Irish Studies* (*IUR*). 1970– . 2/yr. PR8700.I73 820'.8'09415.

Publishes articles, bibliographies, reviews, and occasional special issues on topics of Irish interest, especially modern Anglo-Irish literature. Cumulative index: vols. 1–15, in 15 (1985): 263–300. For the annual bibliography, see entry 2955.

Background Reading

The chapters on general works in Finneran, *Anglo-Irish Literature* and *Recent Research on Anglo-Irish Writers* (2950) survey important general and background studies (pp. 1–23, 1–10, respectively).

3020 *A New History of Ireland*. Ed. T. W. Moody et al. 10 vols. Oxford: Clarendon, 1976– . DA912.N48.

Vol. 1: *Prehistoric and Early Medieval Ireland.*
Vol. 2: *Medieval Ireland, 1169–1534*. Ed. Art Cosgrove. 1987. 982 pp.
Vol. 3: *Early Modern Ireland, 1534–1691*. Ed. T. W. Moody, F. X. Martin, and F. J. Byrne. Rpt. with corrections. 1978. 736 pp.
Vol. 4: *Eighteenth-Century Ireland, 1691–1800*. Ed. Moody and W. E. Vaughan. 1986. 849 pp.
Vol. 5: *Ireland under the Union, I: 1801–1870.*
Vol. 6: *Ireland under the Union, II: 1870–1921.*
Vol. 7: *Ireland, 1921–1976.*
Vol. 8: *A Chronology of Irish History to 1976: A Companion to Irish History, Part 1*. Ed. Moody, Martin, and Byrne. 1982. 591 pp.
Vol. 9: *Maps, Genealogies, Lists: A Companion to Irish History, Part 2*. Ed. Moody, Martin, and Byrne. 1984. 674 pp.
Vol. 10: *Illustrations, Statistics, Bibliography, Documents: A Companion to Irish History, Part 3.*

A collaborative work that attempts to relate aspects of Irish life to the history of the island. Most volumes include chapters on the visual arts, music, law, language and literature, religion, social life, the economy, politics, and government. Each volume concludes with a selective bibliography and an index of subjects and persons. Although the chapters vary in quality and several volumes have been plagued by delays, this work will eventually offer one of the fullest histories of Ireland.

Genres

Some works in section L: Genres are useful for research in Anglo-Irish literature.

Fiction

Some works in section L: Genres/Fiction are useful to research in Anglo-Irish fiction.

GUIDES TO PRIMARY WORKS

3025 Brown, Stephen J., S.J. *Ireland in Fiction: A Guide to Irish Novels, Tales, Romances, and Folk-Lore.* New ed. Dublin: Maunsel, 1919. 362 pp. Z2039.F4.B8 016.823.

An annotated author list of approximately 1,700 separately published fictional works that treat Ireland or the Irish. Brown includes works by Anglo-Irish as well as foreign writers, but excludes fiction written in Irish. Entries provide title, pagination, publication information (usually for the most recent edition), and a synopsis (including occasional comments on historical accuracy or representation of dialects and quotations from reviews). Most Irish authors receive a brief biographical headnote. Three appendixes are worthy of note: appendix B is a list of series; appendix C classifies works by type or subject matter (historical fiction by date of event depicted, Gaelic epic and romantic literature, legends and folktales, fairy tales for children, Catholic clerical life, and humorous books); appendix D lists Irish periodicals publishing fiction. Additions are printed on pp. 314–16. Indexed by titles and subjects. Although the synopses are not always objective (especially for anti-Irish, anti-Catholic, or "prurient" works) and coverage is incomplete, Brown provides access to a wealth of examples of the treatment of Ireland and the Irish in fiction. Leclaire, *General Analytical Bibliography of the Regional Novelists of the British Isles* (2650) is a useful supplement.

GUIDES TO SCHOLARSHIP AND CRITICISM

Diane Tolomeo, "Modern Fiction" (pp. 268–98) in Finneran, *Recent Research on Anglo-Irish Writers* (2950) surveys scholarship and criticism.

BACKGROUND READING

Diane Tolomeo, "Modern Fiction" (pp. 268–98) in Finneran, *Recent Research on Anglo-Irish Writers* (2950) surveys general and background studies.

Drama and Theater

Some works in section L: Genres/Drama and Theater are useful to research in Anglo-Irish drama and theater.

HISTORIES AND SURVEYS

3030 Hogan, Robert, et al., eds. *The Modern Irish Drama: A Documentary History*. 6 vols. Irish Theatre Series 6–8, 10, 12. Dublin: Dolmen; Atlantic Highlands: Humanities, 1975- . PR8789.H62 [PN2602.D82] 792'.09415.

Vol. 1: *The Irish Literary Theatre, 1899–1901*. By Robert Hogan and James Kilroy. 1975. 164 pp.
Vol. 2: *Laying the Foundations, 1902–1904*. By Hogan and Kilroy. 1976. 164 pp.
Vol. 3: *The Abbey Theatre: The Years of Synge, 1905–1909*. By Hogan and Kilroy. 1978. 385 pp.
Vol. 4: *The Rise of the Realists, 1910–1915*. By Hogan, Richard Burnham, and Daniel P. Poteet. 1979. 532 pp.
Vol. 5: *The Art of the Amateur, 1916–1920*. By Hogan and Burnham. 1984. 368 pp.
Vol. 6: *The Years of O'Casey, 1921–1926*. In press.

A year-by-year account of the drama and theater, with each volume attempting "to recreate the flavour of the period" through extensive quotations from contemporary documents, accounts or reviews of performances, letters, memoirs, and the like. Vols. 4 and 5, however, do offer considerable critical commentary. Each volume includes a chronological list of significant Anglo-Irish plays and the most important Irish-language ones. Organized by year of first production (or date of publication for unperformed plays), each entry records the first edition, original cast, and date and theater of the first production. Each volume is indexed by persons, titles, and a few subjects. A well-integrated re-creation of the modern Irish theatrical and dramatic milieu.

3035 Maxwell, D. E. S. *A Critical History of Modern Irish Drama, 1891–1980*. Cambridge: Cambridge UP, 1984. 250 pp. PR8789.M39 822'.91'099415.

A critical history of Anglo-Irish drama since the beginning of the Irish Literary Theatre. Organized chronologically, the 10 chapters chronicle periods and major dramatists. Concludes with a brief chronology and selected bibliography. Indexed by persons and subjects. The fullest critical history of the Irish drama, Maxwell supersedes earlier histories. Review: Ronald Ayling, *Essays in Theatre* 5 (1987): 139–44.

GUIDES TO SCHOLARSHIP AND CRITICISM

Despite the interest in Irish drama, there is no reasonably thorough bibliography of scholarship and criticism. The following do little more than provide a starting point for research.

Surveys of Research

Finneran, *Anglo-Irish Literature* and *Recent Research on Anglo-Irish Writers* (2950) have chapters on the modern drama by Robert Hogan, Bonnie K. Scott, and Gordon Henderson (pp. 518–61) and Hogan (pp. 255–67), respectively.

Other Bibliographies

3040 King, Kimball. *Ten Modern Irish Playwrights: A Comprehensive Annotated Bibliography*. Garland Reference Library of the Humanities 153. New York: Garland, 1979. 111 pp. Z2039.D7.K56 [PR8789] 016.822'9'1408.

A partially annotated bibliography of primary and secondary works through 1977 for Behan, Boyd, Douglas, Friel, Keane, Kilroy, Leonard, McKenna, Murphy, and O'Brien. The list of primary works for each author includes all genres (as well as interviews); secondary works appear under one of three headings: criticism, dissertations (unannotated), and reviews (spottily annotated). Some of the descriptive annotations are misleading, and there are numerous other errors. Indexed by scholars. The exclusion of most reviews and several articles from Irish periodicals and newspapers along with other significant omissions render this work much less than the comprehensive bibliography claimed by the subtitle. As reviewers point out, a careful revision is needed if *Ten Modern Irish Playwrights* is to offer more than minimal guidance for research on the 10 playwrights. Reviews: Charles A. Carpenter, *Modern Drama* 24 (1981): 116–19; Richard J. Finneran, *Analytical and Enumerative Bibliography* 3 (1979): 305–19 (with a lengthy list of additions and corrections).

3045 Mikhail, E. H. *An Annotated Bibliography of Modern Anglo-Irish Drama*. Troy: Whitston, 1981. 300 pp. Z2039.D7.M528 [PR8789] 016.822'91'099415.

A bibliography limited to general studies (from 1899 through 1977), organized in five divisions: bibliographies (a hodgepodge including several works of minimal importance to the subject), reference works, books, periodical articles, and dissertations. Concludes with an incomplete list of library collections. Few of the annotations are adequately descriptive. Two indexes: persons (including authors as subjects); subjects. Plagued by inadequate indexing and annotations, numerous errors and significant omissions, the inclusion of much that is trivial, and poor organization, *Bibliography of Modern Anglo-Irish Drama* is only marginally useful for identifying discussions of playwrights and a few subjects buried in general studies. This work supersedes Mikhail, *A Bibliography of Modern Irish Drama, 1899–1970* (Seattle: U of Washington P, 1972, 51 pp.) and *Dissertations on Anglo-Irish Drama: A Bibliography of Studies, 1870–1970* (Totowa: Rowman, 1973, 73 pp.).

Complemented—somewhat—by Mikhail, *A Research Guide to Modern Irish Dramatists* (Troy: Whitston, 1979, 104 pp.), a bibliography of bibliographies of primary and secondary works. The annotations describe nothing more than the kind of bibliography, and nearly 70% of the entries refer to seven general selective bibliographies (e.g., *New Cambridge Bibliography of English Literature* [1385]; Samples, *Drama Scholars' Index* [1150a]; and Coleman, *Drama Criticism* [2875a]).

BACKGROUND READING

The chapters on the modern drama in Finneran, *Anglo-Irish Literature* and *Recent Research on Anglo-Irish Writers* (2950) survey general and background works (pp. 518–61, 255–67, respectively).

Poetry

Some works in section L: Genres/Poetry are useful to research in Anglo-Irish poetry.

GUIDES TO SCHOLARSHIP AND CRITICISM

Mary M. FitzGerald, "Modern Poetry," pp. 299–334, in Finneran, *Recent Research on Anglo-Irish Writers* (2950) surveys scholarship and criticism.

BACKGROUND READING

Mary M. FitzGerald, "Modern Poetry," pp. 299–334, in Finneran, *Recent Research on Anglo-Irish Writers* (2950) surveys general and background studies.

O

Scottish Literature

This section is limited to works devoted exclusively to Scottish literature (primarily in English). Because Scottish writers are frequently included in reference works on English or British literature, researchers must also consult section M: English Literature. Many works listed in sections G: Serial Bibliographies, Indexes, and Abstracts and H: Guides to Dissertations and Theses are useful for research in Scottish literature.

Histories and Surveys

3060 *The History of Scottish Literature*. Gen. ed. Cairns Craig. 4 vols. Aberdeen: Aberdeen UP, 1987– .

Vol. 1: *Origins to 1660 (Mediaeval and Renaissance)*. Ed. R. D. S. Jack. 1988. 310 pp.
Vol. 2: *1660–1800*. Ed. Andrew Hook. 1987. 337 pp.
Vol. 3: *Nineteenth Century*. Ed. Douglas Gifford. In progress.
Vol. 4: *Twentieth Century*. Ed. Cairns Craig. 1987. 399 pp.

A collaborative history of Scottish literature in English, Scottish, and Gaelic that emphasizes its cultural, intellectual, and linguistic contexts. Each volume consists of essays by established scholars on cultural, social, and intellectual backgrounds, genres, and major writers. Most volumes conclude with a brief list of recommended readings. Indexed in each volume by persons and subjects. Although lacking the coherence and balance possible in a connected narrative, these volumes offer the most current and thorough history of Scottish literature. Review: (vols. 1, 2, and 4) Alastair Fowler, *TLS: Times Literary Supplement* 28 Oct.–3 Nov. 1988: 1198–99.

Still needed, however, is a history that will offer a thorough, coherent treatment of Scottish literature and supersede J. H. Millar, *A Literary History of Scotland*, Library of Literary History (London: Unwin, 1903, 703 pp.), whose chapters on periods, genres, and major authors exclude writers (such as Boswell and Carlyle) who belong more properly to English literature.

Literary Handbooks, Dictionaries, and Encyclopedias

3065 Royle, Trevor. *Companion to Scottish Literature*. Detroit: Gale, 1983. 322 pp. British ed.: *The Macmillan Companion to Scottish Literature*. London: Macmillan, 1983. PR8506.R69 820'.9'9411.

A handbook with entries on authors writing in English, Scots, or Gaelic and born before 1950; movements; historical events and persons; publishing; manuscripts; places; and other topics of literary interest. The majority of the entries are for writers (including historians, philosophers, divines, and scholars) and provide basic biographical information, brief critical comments, and a list of major books (including standard editions) and citations to important scholarship. Despite occasional errors, this is a valuable, lucidly written source for quick reference.

Guides to Scholarship and Criticism

Surveys of Research

3070 "The Year's Work in Scottish Literary and Linguistic Studies [1973–]." *Scottish Literary Journal: Supplement* 1 (1975)– . Annual.

Selective, essay reviews of scholarship based on *Annual Bibliography of Scottish Literature* (3075). The separately authored essays on language, folk literature, the medieval period to 1650, 1650 to 1800, 1800 to 1900, and 1900 to the present are typically judicious in selecting and evaluating the most important scholarship. More thorough in its coverage of Scottish literature than *Year's Work in English Studies* (330), this is the best annual survey of scholarship on the field.

See also

YWES (330): Scottish writers are covered in several chapters.

Serial Bibliographies

3075 *Annual Bibliography of Scottish Literature [1969–]*. Supplement to *Bibliotheck* (entry 3105). 1970– .

A bibliography of books, articles, and reviews organized in four classified divisions: general bibliographical and reference works; general literary criticism, anthologies, and collections; individual authors (subdivided by period); and ballads and folk literature. In each division or section, entries are listed alphabetically by author in three parts: books, reviews of previously listed books, and articles. Two indexes: literary authors; scholars. Although publication now lags about three years after the year covered, the *Annual Bibliography of Scottish Literature* is an important supplement to the more current serial bibliographies and indexes in section G.

3080 *Bibliography of Scotland [1976–]*. Edinburgh: National Library of Scotland, 1978– . Annual. Z2069.B52 015.411.

A bibliography of books and music published in Scotland as well as other books, articles, theses, and music of Scottish interest. Coverage is based largely on acquisitions by the National Library and thus is full but not comprehensive. Entries—which cite author, title, and publication information—appear in two sequences: topographical (by region, then district, then specific place) and subject (following Library of Congress subject headings). Indexed by persons and place names. Offers fuller but much slower coverage of Scottish imprints than *British National Bibliography* (2775). Although the coverage of literary studies is not particularly thorough, *Bibliography of Scotland* is sometimes a useful complement to *Annual Bibliography of Scottish Literature* (3075) and the serial bibliographies and indexes in section G.

For earlier books about Scotland, see the following:

Hancock, P. D., comp. *A Bibliography of Works Relating to Scotland, 1916–1950*. 2 vols. Edinburgh: Edinburgh UP, 1959–60. Of interest to literary scholars are the classified divisions for biography, folklore, books and printing, language, and literature. Coverage of literary studies is far from complete, however.

Mitchell, Arthur, and C. G. Cash. *A Contribution to the Bibliography of Scottish Topography*. 2 vols. Publications of the Scottish History Society 2nd ser. 14–15. Edinburgh: Edinburgh UP, for Scottish History Soc., 1917. Of interest to literary scholars are the divisions for bibliography, biography, folklore, place names, and theater.

See also

Secs. G: Serial Bibliographies, Indexes, and Abstracts and H: Guides to Dissertations and Theses.

ABELL (340): English Literature division.

Annual Bibliography of British and Irish History (1400).

Bibliotheca Celtica (3155).

MLAIB (335): Until the volume for 1981, Scottish literature in English was included in the English Literature division. Literature in Scottish Gaelic was covered in a Celtic Languages and Literatures heading under the General division in the volumes for 1928–52; in General IV [later V or VI]: Celtic Languages and Literatures in the volumes for 1953–66; and in Celtic VIII:

Scottish Gaelic in the volumes for 1967–80. Since the 1981 volume, the Scottish Literature division encompasses literature in whatever language. Researchers must also check the "Scottish Literature" heading in the subject index to post-1980 volumes.

Other Bibliographies

3085 *The New Cambridge Bibliography of English Literature* (*NCBEL*). Ed. George Watson and I. R. Willison. 5 vols. Cambridge: Cambridge UP, 1969–77. Z2011.N45 [PR83] 016.82.

(For a full discussion of *NCBEL*, see entry 1385.) Scottish literature is covered throughout the volumes:

Vol. 1: *600–1660* has a section on Middle Scots poets (cols. 651–64) in the Middle English division and, in the Renaissance division, a section on Scottish printing and bookselling (cols. 967–70) and a subdivision on Scottish literature (cols. 2419–76), with classified listings for general studies, poetry and drama, and prose. Scottish writers also appear in other sections.

Vol. 2: *1660–1800* has sections on Scottish printing and bookselling (cols. 271–72) and periodicals (cols. 1369–78), and a separate division for Scottish literature (cols. 1955–2082) with sections for general studies, poetry and drama, and prose.

Vols. 3: *1800–1900* and 4: *1900–1950* treat Scottish literature and writers throughout their various divisions.

In addition, many of the general sections list works important to the study of Scottish literature. Coverage extends through 1962–69, depending on the volume.

Users must familiarize themselves with the organization, remember that there is considerable unevenness of coverage among sections, and consult the index volume (vol. 5) rather than the provisional indexes in vols. 1–4.

Despite its shortcomings (see entry 1385), *NCBEL* offers the fullest overall bibliography of primary works and scholarship on Scottish literature in English. For recent scholarship, see *Annual Bibliography of Scottish Literature* (3075).

For authors omitted from *NCBEL* or scholarship published after the cutoff dates of volumes, W. R. Aitken, *Scottish Literature in English and Scots: A Guide to Information Sources*, American Literature, English Literature, and World Literatures in English: An Information Guide Series 37 (Detroit: Gale, 1982, 421 pp.)—a highly selective and only partially annotated bibliography—is sometimes useful as supplement.

Language

Guides to Scholarship

See

ABELL (340): See especially the Dialects section in the volumes for 1920–27; the English Dialects section in the volumes for 1928–72; and the Dialects of English/British Isles section in later volumes.

MLAIB (335): See especially the Dialectology section of the English Language division. (For an outline of the division, see p. 160.) Researchers must also check the heading "Scots English Dialect" in the subject index to post-1980 volumes.

"Year's Work in Scottish Literary and Linguistic Studies" (3070).

Dictionaries

3090 *A Dictionary of the Older Scottish Tongue from the Twelfth Century to the End of the Seventeenth* (*DOST*). Ed. William A. Craigie, A. J. Aitken, and James A. C. Stevenson. Aberdeen: Aberdeen UP, 1931– . (Issued in parts which are reprinted at intervals in volumes.) PE2116.C7 427'.9411.

A historical dictionary of the Scottish language based on literary works, documents, records, and other manuscript materials. Because of the nature of the sources and changes in the language, the fullest coverage is for 1375–1600 (with words after 1600 confined to those no longer current or not coinciding with English usage), and because of changes in editorial policies and procedures, entries after vol. 2 are much more thorough. A typical entry records part of speech, selected variant spellings (with a full index of these variants in each volume), etymology, definition(s), and illustrative quotations. Users should note that additions and corrections are collected at the end of each volume. Accuracy and thoroughness make this the essential source for the historical study of the language and interpretation of Scottish literature to 1700, and a necessary complement to the *Oxford English Dictionary* (1410). Continued by *Scottish National Dictionary* (3095). For a discussion of the excerpting procedures, editing, and current editorial problems, see A. J. Aitken, "*DOST*: How We Make It and What's in It," *Dictionaries* 4 (1982): 42–64. Reviews: (pt. 1) Percy W. Long, *Journal of English and Germanic Philology* 32 (1933): 235–38; (pts. 1–2) Bruch Dickins, *Modern Language Review* 28 (1933): 243–44; (pt. 17) Hans Heinrich Meier, *English Studies* 43 (1962): 444–48; (pts. 19–21) A. Fenton, *Scottish Studies* 10 (1966): 198–205.

3095 *The Scottish National Dictionary: Designed Partly on Regional Lines and Partly on Historical Principles, and Containing All the Scottish Words Known to Be in Use or to Have Been in Use since c. 1700* (*SND*). Ed. William Grant and David D. Murison. 10 vols. Edinburgh: Scottish National Dictionary Assn., 1931–76. Reduced print ed.: *The Compact Scottish National Dictionary*, 2 vols. Aberdeen: Aberdeen UP, 1986. PE2106.S4 427.9.

A historical and dialectal dictionary of the Scottish language from c. 1700 to the mid-twentieth century that includes the following:

> (1) Scottish words that do not occur in St[andard] Eng[lish] except as acknowledged loan words; (2) Scottish words the cognates of which occur in St[andard] Eng[lish]; (3) words which have the same form in Sc[ottish] and St[andard] Eng[lish] but have a different meaning in Sc[ottish] . . . ; (4) legal, theological or ecclesiastical terms which . . . have been current in Scottish speech . . . ; (5) words borrowed since *c.* 1700 (from other dialects or languages) which have become current in Gen[eral] Sc[ottish], or in any of its dialects. . . .

A typical entry records variant spellings, part(s) of speech, status (e.g., obsolete, archaic, dialectal), meaning(s), pronunciation, inflections, etymology, and illustrative quotations (for the order of these, see vol. 1, pp. xlvi-xlvii). Vol. 10 includes various appendixes (Scottish forms of personal names, place names, fairs and markets, and a table of Scottish weights and measures, pp. 299–317); a list of abbreviations used in entries (pp. 318–23); additions and corrections (pp. 325–536); a list of works quoted (pp. 537–74); and scientific terms with Scottish connections (pp. 575–91). For the history and significance of *SND*, see A. J. Aitken, R. W. Burchfield, and Hugh MacDiarmid, "*The Scottish National Dictionary*: Three Comments on the Occasion of Its Completion," *Scottish Review* 1 (1975): 17–25. Like *Dictionary of the Older Scottish Tongue* (3090), which it continues, *SND* is an essential source for the historical study of the language and interpretation of Scottish literature, and an important complement to the *Oxford English Dictionary* (1410). Review: W. F. H. Nicolaisen, *Archiv* 214 (1977): 403–05.

Complemented by J. Y. Mather and H. H. Speitel, eds., *The Linguistic Atlas of Scotland: Scots Section* (London: Croom Helm, 1975–). The best concise dictionary is Mairi Robinson, ed., *The Concise Scots Dictionary* (Aberdeen: Aberdeen UP, 1985, 819 pp.). For its potential uses, see Mairi Robinson, "*The Concise Scots Dictionary* as a Tool for Linguistic Research," *The Nuttis Schell: Essays on the Scots Language Presented to A. J. Aitken*, ed. Caroline Macafee and Iseabail Macleod (Aberdeen: Aberdeen UP, 1987) 59–72.

Biographical Dictionaries

3100 Horden, John, ed. *Dictionary of Scottish Biography*. In progress.

A multivolume biographical dictionary that will include about 30,000 entries. Projected for completion in 1990.

See also

Sec. J: Biographical Sources.
Dictionary of National Biography (1425).
Royle, *Companion to Scottish Literature* (3065).

Periodicals

3105 *The Bibliotheck: A Scottish Journal of Bibliography and Allied Topics* (*Bibliotheck*). 1956– . 3/yr. Z2054.B58 011.

Publishes articles, descriptive bibliographies, checklists, catalogs, notes, and reviews on topics (especially literary ones) of Scottish interest. For the *Annual Bibliography of Scottish Literature*, which appears as a supplement, see entry 3075. Cumulative index: vols. 1–10, James A. Tait and Heather F. C. Tait, comps., The Bibliotheck: *An Index to Volumes 1–10 (1956–1981)* (Edinburgh: Scottish Group of the University, College, and Research Section of the Library Assn., Edinburgh U Library, 1985, 41 pp.).

3110 *Scottish Literary Journal: A Review of Studies in Scottish Language and Literature* (*ScLJ*). 1974– . 2/yr., with 2 annual supplements since 1975. PR8514.S3 820'.8'09411.

Publishes articles on Scottish literature, medieval to the present. Reviews appear in the supplements, one of which includes "The Year's Work in Scottish Literary and Linguistic Studies" (3070). Cumulative indexes: vols. 1–5 and supplements 1–8, Kate Chapman, comp. (Aberdeen: Assn. for Scottish Literary Studies, Dept. of English, U of Aberdeen, 1983, 20 pp.); vols. 6–10 and supplements 9–19, Chapman, comp. (1985, 37 pp.).

3115 *Studies in Scottish Literature* (*SSL*). 1963– . Annual. PR8500.S8 820'.9'411.

Publishes articles, notes, and reviews on all aspects of Scottish literature, as well as surveys of new fiction and poetry. Annual index.

Genres

Many works in sections L: Genres and M: English Literature/General/Genres are useful for research in Scottish literature.

Fiction

Some works in sections L: Genres and M: English Literature/General/Genres/Fiction are useful for research in Scottish fiction.

HISTORIES AND SURVEYS

3120 Hart, Francis Russell. *The Scottish Novel from Smollett to Spark*. Cambridge: Harvard UP, 1978. 442 pp. British ed.: *The Scottish Novel: A Critical Survey*. London: Murray, 1978. PR8597.H37 823'.03.

A critical history of the development of the novel in Scotland from c. 1760 to the 1970s. In discussing approximately 200 works by some 50 novelists, Hart offers generally full descriptions of content and emphasizes distinctively Scottish motifs and methods, but gives only limited attention to social context and style. Chapters are organized more or less chronologically, with a separate section on the novel of the Highlands and a concluding chapter on the theory of Scottish fiction. Indexed by persons and a few subjects. Praised for its scope and command of the topic, this work is the standard history of the Scottish novel. Reviews: John Clubbe, *JEGP: Journal of English and Germanic Philology* 78 (1979): 439–42; Cairns Craig, *Studies in Scottish Literature* 15 (1980): 302–10; David Daiches, *Nineteenth-Century Fiction* 34 (1979): 75–78.

P

Welsh Literature

This section is limited to works devoted exclusively to Welsh literature (primarily in English). Because Welsh writers are frequently included in reference sources on English or British literature, researchers must consult section M: English Literature. Many works listed in sections G: Serial Bibliographies, Indexes, and Abstracts and H: Guides to Dissertations and Theses are useful for research in Welsh literature.

Histories and Surveys

3135 Jarman, A. O. H., and Gwilym Rees Hughes, eds. *A Guide to Welsh Literature.* 6 vols. Swansea: Davies, 1976– . PB2206.G8 891'.6'6'09.

A descriptive, interpretative history of Welsh literature from the sixth century to the present. (Vol. 1 covers the sixth century to c. 1300; vol. 2, c. 1300 to 1527.) Each volume is made up of essays by major scholars on important works or writers, forms, genres, and historical background; each essay concludes with a highly selective bibliography of editions and studies. Indexed by persons, titles, and subjects in each volume. The failure to identify sources of passages and references to scholarship renders the *Guide* less useful than it might be. Although frequently offering more detailed analyses than Parry but lacking his continuity and breadth, *Guide to Welsh Literature* complements rather than supersedes his *History of Welsh Literature* (3140). Reviews: (vol. 1) Patrick K. Ford, *Speculum* 54 (1979): 812–17; Margaret Charlotte Ward, *Medium Ævum* 47 (1978): 333–37.

3140 Parry, Thomas. *A History of Welsh Literature*. Trans. H. Idris Bell. Corrected rpt. Oxford: Clarendon, 1962. 534 pp. (Translation of *Hanes llenyddiaeth Gymraeg hyd 1900*. Cardiff: U of Wales P, 1944. 323 pp.) PB2206.P33 820.9.

A history of Welsh literature from the sixth century to 1900, with an appendix by the translator carrying the record forward to c. 1950. Organized chronologically, chapters treat genres, forms, major works or authors; beginning with the nineteenth century, chapters include a section on literary, linguistic, and historical scholarship. Concludes with a highly selective bibliography of English-language scholarship. Two indexes: Welsh authors; subjects (including scholars cited). Although the translation incorporates Parry's modified views on some topics, the Welsh edition is still useful for its fuller bibliography. Authoritative but not definitive, this is the standard history of Welsh literature; it is complemented, but not superseded, by Jarman, *Guide to Welsh Literature* (3135). Review: *Times Literary Supplement* 23 Dec. 1955: 778.

Literary Handbooks, Dictionaries, and Encyclopedias

3145 *The Oxford Companion to the Literature of Wales*. Comp. and ed. Meic Stephens. Oxford: Oxford UP, 1986. 682 pp. Welsh ed.: *Cydymaith i lenyddiaeth Cymru*. Cardiff: Cwasg Prifysgol Cymru, 1986. 662 pp. PB2202.O94 891.6'6'03.

Covers Welsh literary culture from the sixth century through 1984 in some 2,825 entries on authors (including hymn writers, historians, antiquaries, critics, scholars, translators, journalists, and the like, but excluding anyone born after 1950); prosody (less fully than in the Welsh edition); genres; motifs; manuscripts; periodicals; literary works; folk songs; hymns; mythical, historical, and literary figures as well as a host of other individuals (even rugby players); folklore and legend; historical events; societies; movements; English authors important to Welsh culture; music—in short, just about anything of significance to Welsh literature. Entries emphasize factual information rather than interpretation, and many cite standard scholarly works or texts. The approximately 1,200 author entries focus on biographical details and major works, but do offer occasional evaluative comments. Concludes with a chronology of Welsh history. Although some entries have no discernible connection with Welsh literature, the *Oxford Companion* is an essential work for quick reference. Reviews: James A. Davies, *Modern Language Review* 83 (1988): 713–15; Dick Davis, *TLS: Times Literary Supplement* 6 June 1986: 624.

Guides to Primary Works

3150 Jones, Brynmor. *A Bibliography of Anglo-Welsh Literature, 1900–1965*. Swansea: Wales and Monmouthshire Branch of the Library Assn., 1970. 139 pp. Z2013.3.J64 016.8209'0091.

A selective bibliography of poetry, drama, and fiction in English by Welsh writers, of some works set in Wales by foreign authors, and of studies of Anglo-Welsh literature. Since only works utilizing a Welsh locale, characters, or idiom are included, many important plays and fictional works by Welsh writers are omitted. (The requirement for Welsh content is less strictly applied to poetry.) Entries are organized in three parts. The list of primary works includes sections for anthologies and individual authors. In the latter, works are grouped by genre, with entries citing editions, translations, and excerpts, and identifying locale in fiction and plays. The highly selective list of secondary works has sections for bibliographies and indexes, general criticism, and individual authors; some entries are briefly annotated. A concluding list of children's stories is unannotated. Two indexes: settings; persons (excluding authors of studies of individual writers). Although its value as a record of twentieth-century Anglo-Welsh literature is seriously marred by the ill-considered editorial policy that excludes works lacking a Welsh background, this work remains a useful pioneering effort. It must be supplemented, however, by other sources such as *New Cambridge Bibliography of English Literature* (1385), *British Library General Catalogue of Printed Books* (250), OCLC (225), and RLIN (230). Review: *TLS: Times Literary Supplement* 4 Dec. 1970: 1428.

Guides to Scholarship and Criticism

3155 *Bibliotheca Celtica: A Register of Publications Relating to Wales and the Celtic Peoples and Languages [1909–84]*. Aberystwyth: National Library of Wales, 1910– . Irregular. Z2071.B56 016.9429.

A classified bibliography of books, dissertations, theses, and articles of Welsh interest and acquired by the National Library. Since the volume covering 1929–33 (1939), entries are organized by Library of Congress classification system. The language and literature division includes sections for biography, Celtic languages, Celtic literature, Welsh language, Welsh literature, Anglo-Welsh literature, and Arthurian literature (for many years this last section appeared at the end of the classified list). (Until the volume for 1973–76 [1981], *Bibliotheca Celtica* also includes Irish and Scottish Gaelic language and literature.) Indexed by names. Although far in arrears and not comprehensive, *Bibliotheca Celtica* offers the fullest general coverage of scholarship on Welsh literature; it must be supplemented by *ABELL* (340), *MLAIB* (335), and the other serial bibliographies and indexes in section G.

After the volume for 1981–84, the National Library plans to replace *Bibliotheca Celtica* with *Bibliography of Wales*, which will incorporate *Subject Index to Welsh Periodicals [1931–84]* (1934– , with the final volume covering 1981–84). Entries will be organized in two parts: a subject index and an author list.

See also

Secs. G: Serial Bibliographies, Indexes, and Abstracts and H: Guides to Dissertations and Theses.

ABELL (340).

Annual Bibliography of British and Irish History (1400).

MLAIB (335): Until the volume for 1981, Welsh literature in English was included in the English Literature division. Welsh-language literature was covered in the Celtic Languages and Literatures heading under the General division in the volumes for 1928–52; in General IV [later V or VI]: Celtic Languages and Literatures in the volumes for 1953–66; and in Celtic IX: Welsh in the volumes for 1967–80. Since the 1981 volume, the Welsh Literature division encompasses Welsh literature in whatever language. Researchers must also check the "Welsh Literature" heading in the subject index to post-1980 volumes.

YWES (330).

Biographical Dictionaries

3160 *The Dictionary of Welsh Biography down to 1940.* [Ed. John Edward Lloyd and R. T. Jenkins.] London: Honourable Soc. of Cymmrodorion, 1959. 1,157 pp. Welsh ed.: *Y Bywgraffiadur Cymreig hyd 1940.* Llundain: n.p., 1953. 1,110 pp. DA710.A1.B913 920.0429.

A biographical dictionary of deceased persons of Welsh birth or parentage and of foreigners important to the country's history. The 3,500 signed entries—several of which are devoted to families—offer factual accounts of some 5,000 notorious and eminent persons from all walks of life (including a considerable number of writers). Although less discursive than in *Dictionary of National Biography* (1425), the articles incorporate much important recent research and conclude with a list of sources. The English edition corrects, revises, and expands the Welsh edition. Additional entries are printed in a separate alphabetical sequence on pp. 1113–57, and corrections and additions appear on p. lviii. Although lacking an index, the *Dictionary* cites persons discussed in family entries and pseudonyms as cross-references in the alphabetical sequence of names. The supplement covering 1941–50 was apparently never published. Scholarly and authoritative, this work is the standard biographical dictionary of Wales. Review: Penry Williams, *English Historical Review* 75 (1960): 706–08.

See also

Sec. J: Biographical Sources.
Dictionary of National Biography (1425).
Oxford Companion to the Literature of Wales (3145).

Periodicals

3165 *Anglo-Welsh Review* (*AWR*). 1949– . 3/yr. Former title: *Dock Leaves* (1949–57). PR8901.A52 891.66.

Publishes articles and reviews on Anglo-Welsh literature, with the major portion of each issue devoted to original poetry and some fiction.

Q

American Literature

This division includes works devoted primarily to the literatures—in whatever language—of the United States.

General

Researchers should also consult sections Q: American Literature/Regional Literatures and American Literature/Ethnic and Minority Literatures for other general reference works.

Guides to Reference Works

LITERATURE

3180 Gohdes, Clarence, and Sanford E. Marovitz. *Bibliographical Guide to the Study of the Literature of the U.S.A.* 5th ed., rev. and enl. Durham: Duke UP, 1984. 256 pp. Z1225.G6 [PS88] 016.81.

A selective, interdisciplinary guide to reference works, histories, critical studies, and discussions of research methods (published through early 1983) important to the study of American literature and its historical background. Entries are organized in 35 divisions: general reference works, philosophy and methodology of literary and historical study, technical procedures in literary and historical research, definitions of literary and related terms, preparation of manuscripts for publication, national bibliographies, periodical indexes, American studies or civilization (including popular culture), general works on American history, specialized studies of American history, biography, periodicals, newspapers, book trade and publishing, history of ideas, psychology, philosophy (including transcendentalism), religion, women's studies, general bibliographies of American literature, histories of American literature, poetry, drama (including theater and film), fiction, criticism, humor and other special genres (including children's literature), seventeenth- and eighteenth-century literature, twentieth-century literature, themes and topics, regionalism, minorities, relations with other countries, American language, folklore, and comparative and general literature. The generally brief descriptive annotations frequently cite related works. An appendix lists the principal biographies of 135 authors. Two indexes: subjects; names. Many divisions would benefit from more refined classification or organization; some annotations have not been revised to reflect changes in scope or organization of serial publications or revised editions; and a few outdated works or superseded editions should be excised. Nevertheless, this remains a standard guide to reference works and scholarship essential to research in American literature. It is especially valuable for its interdisciplinary scope.

Less useful guides are the following:

Fenster, Valmai Kirkham. *Guide to American Literature.* Littleton: Libraries Unlimited, 1983. 243 pp. Designed for undergraduates, but untrustworthy because of numerous inaccuracies and omissions.

Kolb, Harold H., Jr. *A Field Guide to the Study of American Literature.* Charlottesville: UP of Virginia, 1976. 136 pp. A poorly organized compilation, whose annotations consist largely of quotations from prefatory matter.

Leary, Lewis. *American Literature: A Study and Research Guide.* New York: St. Martin's, 1976. 185 pp. Designed for undergraduates and plagued by numerous errors, but more evaluative than Gohdes or Kolb.

See also

American Literary Scholarship (3265): In addition to the chapter on general reference sources, most of the other chapters evaluate reference works.

Bateson, *Guide to English and American Literature* (85).

Literary History of the United States: Bibliography (3300).

Marcuse, *Reference Guide for English Studies* (90).

RELATED TOPICS

3185 Prucha, Francis Paul. *Handbook for Research in American History: A Guide to Bibliographies and Other Reference Works.* Lincoln: U of Nebraska P, 1987. 289 pp. Z1236.P78 [E178] 016.973.

A selective guide to reference sources through c. 1985 that are important to research in American history. Works are described in two divisions: general reference works and subjects. The first has chapters covering library catalogs and guides; general bibliographies of American history; catalogs of books; book review indexes; guides to periodical literature; guides to manuscripts; guides to newspapers; dissertations and theses; biographical sources; oral history materials; printed documents of the federal government; the National Archives; state and local materials; legal sources; atlases, maps, and geographical guides; encyclopedias, handbooks, and dictionaries; and data bases. Of the subjects in the second division, those of most interest to literary researchers are political history, social history, ethnic groups, women, blacks, American Indians, religion, regional material, and travel accounts. Works are described—but too rarely evaluated—in narrative fashion, a practice that makes scanning difficult. Indexed by persons, titles, and subjects. The *Handbook* is currently the best guide to reference works on American history and includes much of importance to literary scholarship, but novice researchers would benefit from more evaluation.

3190 Sears, Jean L., and Marilyn K. Moody. *Using Government Publications.* 2 vols. Phoenix: Oryx, 1985–86. Z1223.Z7.S4 [J83] 015.73'053.

Vol. 1: *Searching by Subjects and Agencies.* 1985. 216 pp.
Vol. 2: *Finding Statistics and Using Special Techniques.* 1986. 231 pp.

A guide to searching United States government publications. Along with describing how to use the basic indexes and data bases, Sears and Moody explains the Superintendent of Documents Classification system and outlines research strategies. Of particular interest to literary researchers are the sections in vol. 1 on copyright and genealogy, and in vol. 2 on the National Archives. Indexed by subjects and titles in each volume. This work is the best introduction for those needing to search government publications. Prucha, *Handbook for Research in American History* (3185) also has a useful chapter (pp. 81–100) on locating printed documents of the federal government.

Histories and Surveys

Useful lists of histories and surveys appear in Gohdes, *Bibliographical Guide to the Study of the Literature of the U.S.A.*, pp. 95–101 (entry 3180); Kolb, *Field Guide to the Study of American Literature*, pp. 25–87 (3180a); and Leary, *American Literature: A Study and Research Guide*, pp. 11–27 (3180a). For a detailed account and assessment of major histories from 1829 through 1948, see Vanderbilt, *American Literature and the Academy* (3455).

The announcements of *Columbia Literary History of the United States* (3195) and *New Cambridge History of American Literature* (3205) elicited considerable discussion of canon and approach. See, for example, the following articles in *American Literature*: Annette Kolodny, "The Integrity of Memory: Creating a New Literary History of the United States," 57 (1985): 291–307; William C. Spengemann, "American Things/Literary Things: The Problem of American Literary History," 57 (1985): 456–81; Emory Elliott, "New Literary History: Past and Present," 57 (1985): 611–21; Sacvan Bercovitch, "America as Canon and Context: Literary History in a Time of Dissensus," 58 (1986): 99–107.

3195 *Columbia Literary History of the United States* (*CLHUS*). Gen. ed. Emory Elliott. New York: Columbia UP, 1988. 1,263 pp. PS92.C64 810'.9.

A collaborative history of literature in English and other languages from twelfth-century painted cave narratives to the 1980s. Organized by traditional periods (the beginnings to 1810, 1810 to 1885, 1885 to 1910, 1910 to 1945, 1945 to the present), each section begins with a discussion of cultural and intellectual contexts and includes essays on genres, movements, major writers, regions, groups, or historical developments. Rather than attempt a consensus or an integrated narrative, the chapters (each by a distinguished scholar) employ a variety of critical approaches and reflect the diversity of the country's literary heritage by treating ethnic, minority, regional, and Native American literatures and works by women as well as established writers, and popular as well as elite literature. Since many writers are discussed in several chapters, users must be certain to consult the index of subjects, persons, and titles. Admirably fulfilling the editor's criteria for a good literary history ("that it have a good index, readable type, sensible chapter divisions, and interesting and informative essays, and that it be inexpensive, durable, and not too heavy"), this is a worthy, much-needed successor to *Literary History of the United States* (3200). Unfortunately, it includes no bibliography volume, and the essays lack documentation or a list of suggested readings. For an outline of the project, see Emory Elliott, "New Literary History: Past and Present," *American Literature* 57 (1985): 611–21.

The best brief history remains Marcus Cunliffe, *The Literature of the United States*, 4th ed. (New York: Penguin, 1986, 512 pp.), which prints useful selective bibliographies for each chapter.

3200 *Literary History of the United States: History* (*LHUS*). Ed. Robert E. Spiller et al. 4th ed. New York: Macmillan; London: Collier, 1974. 1,556 pp. PS88.L522 810'.9.

A collaborative history by leading scholars and critics of the literature of the United States through the early 1970s (but emphasizing the nineteenth and early part of the twentieth centuries) and accompanied by a separate *Bibliography* volume (3300). Organized more or less chronologically, the 11 sections include chapters on cultural and historical background, genres, major authors, regions, and movements. Except for new chapters on Emily Dickinson and literature since World War II, the fourth edition essentially preserves the text of the first (1948). The *History* and *Bibliography* are complementary volumes and must be used together (the highly selective bibliography at the end of the *History* is meant for the "general" reader). Indexed by persons and some subjects.

Criticized for its unevenness in scale and quality, the formulaic nature of many chapters, and emphasis on history at the expense of criticism, but recognized for many years as the indispensable literary history of the United States, *LHUS* has exerted a major influence on scholarship since its publication and served as a godsend for two generations of doctoral candidates studying for preliminary examinations. Although superseded by *Columbia Literary History of the United States* (3195), it remains a major document in the historiography of American literary history. For the inception, organization, composition, and editing of *LHUS*, see Robert E. Spiller, "History of a History: A Study in Cooperative Scholarship," *PMLA* 89 (1974): 602–16; and especially Vanderbilt, *American Literature and the Academy* (3455), which also examines the academic politics behind the work, traces its critical reception, and offers a detailed assessment (pp. 413–60, 499–531, passim). Reviews: (1st ed.) Daniel Aaron, Leslie A. Fiedler, and R. A. Miller, *American Quarterly* 1 (1949): 169–83; Ralph L. Rusk, *American Literature* 21 (1950): 489–92; René Wellek, *Kenyon Review* 11 (1949): 500–06; (4th ed.) Larzer Ziff, *Review of English Studies* ns 27 (1976): 363–66.

3205 *The New Cambridge History of American Literature*. Ed. Sacvan Bercovitch. 5 vols. Cambridge: Cambridge UP. (Scheduled for publication during 1989–90.)

A collaborative history of American literature from the Colonial period to the 1980s. The overall organization is chronological, the approach historical and contextual rather than biographical and canonical, with lengthy sections by major scholars who incorporate minority, popular, Native American, and ethnic literature in treating genres, themes, representative authors, and the literary marketplace. For a discussion of the broad principles underlying the *History*, see Sacvan Bercovitch, "America as Canon and Context: Literary History in a Time of Dissensus," *American Literature* 58 (1986): 99–107, and "The Problem of Ideology in American Literary History," *Critical Inquiry* 12 (1986): 631–53. Unfortunately, no bibliography volume is planned.

The *New Cambridge History* will replace the outdated *The Cambridge History of American Literature* (*CHAL*), ed. William Peterfield Trent et al., 4 vols. (New York: Putnam's; Cambridge: Cambridge UP, 1917–21). For a detailed account of the genesis, editing, publication, and reception—as well as an assessment—of *CHAL*, see Vanderbilt, *American Literature and the Academy* (3455), pp. 3–28, 153–83, 221–36, passim.

See also

History of Southern Literature (3615).
Literary History of the American West (3660).
Ruoff, *Redefining American Literary History* (3695).

Literary Handbooks, Dictionaries, and Encyclopedias

3210 Hart, James D. *The Oxford Companion to American Literature*. 5th ed. New York: Oxford UP, 1983. 896 pp. PS21.H3 810'.9.

A wide-ranging encyclopedia, with entries on authors and other persons, works, literary terms, characters, movements and groups, awards, organizations, periodicals, historical and cultural events, foreign writers, and a host of other topics related to American literature. The bulk of the entries are for authors (recording basic career information) and plot summaries of elite as well as popular works. Concludes with a chronology of literary and social history. Breadth, accuracy, judicious selection, and wealth of detail have made the *Oxford Companion* the essential source of quick reference for beginning student through accomplished scholar. Of little use to researchers is *The Concise Oxford Companion to American Literature* (New York: Oxford UP, 1986, 497 pp.), which reprints about half of its parent volume. Reviews: Eric J. Sundquist, *Virginia Quarterly Review* 60 (1984): 521–24; Joe Weixlmann, *MELUS* 11 (1984): 103–05.

A good supplement because of its inclusion of numerous minor writers is W. J. Burke and Will D. Howe, *American Authors and Books: 1640 to the Present Day*, 3rd rev. ed., rev. Irving Weiss and Anne Weiss (New York: Crown, 1972, 719 pp.). Besides writers of all kinds, it has entries for works, literary characters, periodicals, newspapers, publishers, literary terms, associations, book collectors, libraries, places, and literature-related subjects. The first edition—*American Authors and Books, 1640–1940* (New York: Gramercy, 1943, 858 pp.)—remains useful for the numerous entries omitted in later editions.

Much less extensive is *The Cambridge Handbook of American Literature*, ed. Jack Salzman (Cambridge: Cambridge UP, 1986, 286 pp.), whose approximately 750 entries emphasize major authors and works. While informative, it lacks the scope of the *Oxford Companion*.

3215 Ehrlich, Eugene, and Gorton Carruth. *The Oxford Illustrated Literary Guide to the United States*. New York: Oxford UP, 1982. 464 pp. PS141.E74 917.3'04.

An illustrated dictionary and gazetteer to 1,586 cities, towns, and villages associated with more than 1,500 writers from Colonial times to the present. The towns are organized alphabetically within region, then state; the entry for each locality describes its associations with writers or its use as setting and locates buildings, graves, and other sites of literary interest. Indexed by states and towns at the front, by authors at the back. Although the descriptions are not always based on firsthand investigation, some important sites are omitted, and the volume is too unwieldy to carry on a literary tour, this book is the most current and comprehensive guide to places in the United States that are associated with an author or literary work. Review: John Russell, *TLS: Times Literary Supplement* 10 June 1983: 608.

See also

Sec. C: Literary Handbooks, Dictionaries, and Encyclopedias.
Cambridge Guide to Literature in English (120).

Annals

3220 Ludwig, Richard M., and Clifford A. Nault, Jr., eds. *Annals of American Literature, 1602–1983*. New York: Oxford UP, 1986. 342 pp. PS94.L83 810.2'02.

A chronology of important and representative literary works. The main column cites author, date of birth, title, and genre for each work. The secondary column lists historical and cultural events, the founding of serial publications, births and deaths of authors, and major foreign publications. (Beginning in 1783, this column is in two parts: American and foreign.) Although the arts are slighted in the secondary column, breadth and judicious selection make *Annals of American Literature* the best source for placing a work in its literary and historical context. It supersedes the treatment of American literature in *Annals of English Literature* (1345).

Samuel J. Rogal, *A Chronological Outline of American Literature*, Bibliographies and Indexes in American Literature 8 (New York: Greenwood, 1987, 446 pp.), is an occasionally useful supplement. Yearly coverage for the period 1507–1986 is limited to births and deaths of authors, a few literary events, and fairly long miscellaneous lists of books.

Bibliographies of Bibliographies

Although purporting to be an evaluative history of the bibliographical control of American belles lettres, Vito Joseph Brenni, *The Bibliographic Control of American Literature, 1920–1975* (Metuchen: Scarecrow, 1979, 210 pp.), is too incomplete, poorly organized, inaccurately descriptive, uncritically evaluative, badly written, and inadequately indexed to be of much use.

3225 Nilon, Charles H. *Bibliography of Bibliographies in American Literature*. New York: Bowker, 1970. 483 pp. Z1225.A1.N5 016.01681.

A bibliography of books, parts of books, and articles (published before 1970) that lists works by and about authors, about genres, and about subjects related to literature. Entries are classified in four divisions: bibliography, authors (organized by century, then alphabetically), genres (including literary history and criticism), and ancillary subjects (including various forms, types, and topics such as children's literature, dissertations, humor, regionalism, and travels). Occasional brief annotations comment on scope or publishing information. Indexed by titles and persons. Poor design makes scanning entries difficult. Nilon must be used with caution, since there are numerous omissions and inconsistencies in organization and since many works were not examined by the compiler. A major desideratum is an up-to-date, thorough bibliography of bibliographies of American literature. Review: *TLS: Times Literary Supplement* 2 July 1971: 788.

A few additional bibliographies published in periodicals are listed in Patricia Pate Havlice, *Index to American Author Bibliographies* (Metuchen: Scarecrow, 1971, 204 pp.).

See also

Sec. D: Bibliographies of Bibliographies.
Tanselle, *Guide to the Study of United States Imprints* (5290).

Guides to Primary Works

MANUSCRIPTS

3230 *American Literary Manuscripts: A Checklist of Holdings in Academic, Historical, and Public Libraries, Museums, and Authors' Homes in the United States* (*ALM*). 2nd ed. Comp. and ed. J. Albert Robbins et al. Athens: U of Georgia P, 1977. 387 pp. Z6620.U5.M6 [PS88] 016.81.

A finding list of manuscripts—including journals, diaries, correspondence, galley and page proofs, documents, audio and video recordings, books with marginalia, and memorabilia—held in about 600 institutions in the United States. Among the approximately 2,800 Americans are all the major authors, selected minor ones, and several quasi-literary writers such as editors, publishers, theatrical performers and producers, literary critics and scholars, and a few public figures also known (sometimes remotely) as writers. Following each author, holdings are listed alphabetically by institutional symbol, with manuscripts identified only by type and item count. (Symbols for libraries and types of manuscripts are identified on pp. xxvii-liii.) A few institutional holdings are keyed to a list (on pp. 367–77) of calendars, inventories, checklists, and other finding aids. Concludes with two appendixes (pseudonyms and alternate names, and authors for whom no holdings were reported; both should have been integrated into the main list of authors) and a bibliography of catalogs and guides, including ones listing American manuscripts held abroad. The introduction is refreshingly frank about the limitations of the checklist, with the Notes on Coverage (pp. xxii-xxvi) listing institutions whose holdings are not covered or are incompletely reported. Although the dense pages of symbols and numbers are initially forbidding, researchers soon appreciate how much drudgery this checklist can save them. Even so, much work is left for users: they must write or visit institutions that have no published finding aids to determine their exact holdings, and they must consult the works listed in section F: Guides to Manuscripts and Archives to locate additional American manuscripts. Review: John C. Broderick, *Review* 1 (1979): 295–300.

3235 Cripe, Helen, and Diane Campbell, comps. and eds. *American Manuscripts, 1763–1815: An Index to Documents Described in Auction Records and Dealers' Catalogues*. Wilmington: Scholarly Resources, 1977. 704 pp. Z1237.C89 [E195] 016.973.

An index to manuscript material written between 1763 and 1815 and described in catalogs of booksellers, autograph dealers, and auction houses in the United States. *American Manuscripts* covers selected dealers' catalogs through 1970 but auction catalogs only before 1895, when publication of *American Book Prices Current* (5415) began. Organized by date of manuscript, entries identify the catalog and note what kind of description it supplies (e.g., a summary, transcription, or reproduction). Dealers' catalogs are keyed to a list in the back; auction catalogs are cited by the number used in McKay, *American Book Auction Catalogues* (5400). Indexed by names. Although the bulk of the manuscripts are historical, Cripe and Campbell does index a considerable number of items of literary interest. Coverage of dealers' catalogs is not comprehensive and the decision to omit auction catalogs after 1895 is unfortunate, since *American Book Prices Current* is far from thorough; nevertheless, *American Manuscripts* is an important work that will save researchers a few of the hours that must be spent in tracking down and poring through these scarce catalogs. Scholars need many more such indexes to manuscripts listed in catalogs.

3240 Raimo, John W., ed. *A Guide to Manuscripts Relating to America in Great Britain and Ireland*. [Rev. ed.] Westport: Meckler, for British Assn. for American Studies, 1979. 467 pp. Z1236.C74 [E178] 016.973.

A guide to manuscripts and some rare printed works relating to the American Colonies and the United States, and held by libraries, county and local record offices, organizations, and some private collectors in Great Britain. Raimo excludes the Public Record Office, British Library, Oxford and Cambridge libraries, and London Archives, since all have separate guides (identified in the introduction). Organized alphabetically by country, then county, city, and owner, the descriptions of collections identify groups of papers or individual manuscripts and cite transcriptions, catalogs, and other finding aids. The descriptions vary in detail, but most are helpfully precise. Locations are not cited for collections identified through the National Register of Archives (1360a) to encourage scholars to consult the finding aids held there. Indexed by subjects, persons, and places. Users must remember that this work is not comprehensive and that inclusion of a collection does not mean it is accessible to researchers. Although the bulk of the papers are historical or political, Raimo locates a significant number of literary manuscripts and thus is an important preliminary source for tracking down items in British collections.

3245 *Women's History Sources: A Guide to Archives and Manuscript Collections in the United States*. Ed. Andrea Hinding and Ames Sheldon Bower. 2 vols. New York: Bowker, 1979. Z7964.U49.W64 [HQ1410] 016.30141'2'0973.

A guide to 18,026 collections in 1,586 repositories holding manuscripts by or related to women in the United States since Colonial times. Organized alphabetically by state, city, repository, and then collection title, entries record types of documents, inclusive dates, size, information on access, repository, existence of finding aids, contents, and published guides. Based on printed descriptions, responses to questionnaires, or onsite inspections, the descriptions vary considerably in sophistication, specificity, and accuracy. Indexed in vol. 2 by persons (including all forms of a woman's name), subjects, occupations, and places. *Women's History Sources* is the essential guide to a wealth of little-known material, a decent portion of which is of literary interest. Review: Gerda Lerner, *Library Quarterly* 51 (1981): 102–04.

See also

Sec. F: Guides to Manuscripts and Archives.
American Book Prices Current (5415).
Book Auction Records (5420).

PRINTED WORKS

For a survey deploring the state of the bibliography of American imprints, recommending standards and procedures, and suggesting needed research, see G. Thomas Tanselle, "The Bibliography and Textual Study of American Books," *Proceedings of the American Antiquarian Society* 95 (1985): 113–51, with a commentary (pp. 152–60) by Norman Fiering.

Tanselle, *Guide to the Study of United States Imprints* (5290) is the best source for locating works that identify or locate a particular book printed or published in the United States.

3250 Blanck, Jacob, comp. *Bibliography of American Literature* (*BAL*). Completed by Michael Winship and Virginia L. Smyers. 8 vols. New Haven: Yale UP; London: Oxford UP, 1955– . (A comprehensive index is planned.) Z1225.B55 [PS88] 016.81.

A bibliography of works by 281 authors (from the Federal period to those who died before 1931) "who, in their own time at least, were known and read" and who primarily published belles lettres. Limited to separate publications (including books, broadsides, anthologies, and ephemera) and emphasizing initial appearances, *BAL* excludes altogether "periodical and newspaper publications, . . . unrevised reprints . . . , translations into other languages, [and] volumes containing isolated correspondence." First American editions (along with variant issues and states) and English-language foreign editions preceding the first American one receive a full description; briefer descriptions are accorded volumes containing the first printing of a prose work (excluding letters) or poem, textually significant reprints or revised editions, nonbelletristic works, and edited texts.

Authors are listed alphabetically, with works normally organized by date of publication in three parts: first or revised editions of books wholly or substantially by an author and books by others containing the first book publication of a work; reprints of an author's own books; and books by others containing material by an author reprinted from earlier books, followed by a selection of bibliographies, biographies, and -ana. Some authors, because of the variety or complexity of their output, require a different organization (outlined in a headnote). A full entry includes title page, imprint, pagination, type of paper, size of leaf, collation, description of binding (including variants and notes on inserted ads, end papers, binder's and fly leaves), publication notes (citing copyright deposit date when possible and early advertisements), locations of copies examined, and miscellaneous notes, especially dealing with publishing history. These parts are repeated as necessary within an entry for each state or issue. The entry numbers have become the standard references for identifying an edition, state, or issue. Indexed by initials, pseudonyms, and anonyms in each volume.

Users must study carefully the prefatory explanation of scope, limitations, organization, terminology, and parts of an entry (especially descriptive conventions); consult the headnote to an author for information on special limitations or organization; remember that *BAL* does not list everything written by an author and is not a census of copies.

Additions and corrections regularly appear in the notes section of *Papers of the Bibliographical Society of America* (5315); published additions and corrections through 1969 are listed in vol. 1, pp. 163–64, in Tanselle, *Guide to the Study of United States Imprints* (5290). On the form for reporting additions and corrections, see G. Thomas Tanselle, "A Proposal for Recording Additions to Bibliographies," *Papers of the Bibliographical Society of America* 62 (1968): 227–36; "Additions to Bibliographies: With Notes on Procedure for *BAL*," 73 (1979): 123–25. Blanck's working manuscript, which contains much fuller descriptions and notes, additions, and corrections, will be made available to scholars upon completion of *BAL*.

Although not comprehensive (especially in listing reprints), inconsistent in treating some kinds of works (such as foreign editions and reprints), and emphasizing nineteenth-century authors, *BAL* remains—for writers not the subject of a more recent, separately published descriptive bibliography—an indispensable source for identifying and locating first editions and appearances as well as important revised editions, for obtaining details of publishing and textual history, and for dating publication.

The meticulous examination of copies in public as well as private collections, extensive research in copyright records and publisher's archives, and a remarkable degree of accuracy make *BAL* one of the monumental bibliographies of this century. Reviews: (vol. 1) John D. Gordan, *Papers of the Bibliographical Society of America* 50 (1956): 201–04; James D. Hart, *American Literature* 28 (1956): 378–81; (vol. 7) Joel Myerson, *Papers of the Bibliographical Society of America* 78 (1984): 45–56 (an important evaluation of the general strengths and shortcomings of *BAL*).

Much less satisfactory is Matthew J. Bruccoli et al., eds., *First Printings of American Authors: Contributions toward Descriptive Checklists*, 5 vols. (Detroit: Gale, 1977–87), an ambitious but flawed, inadequately descriptive record of the first American and English printings of separate publications by some 336 collectible authors from the seventeenth century through the 1970s. Given the paucity of information and inconsistencies in its presentation, *First Printings* is only occasionally useful for those few authors not in *BAL* or the subject of an author bibliography. For a detailed critique of the work, see William Matheson, "American Literary Bibliography—*FPAA* Style," *Review* 1 (1979): 173–81.

3255 *Literary Writings in America: A Bibliography*. 8 vols. Millwood: KTO–Kraus-Thomson, 1977. Z1225.L8 [PS88] 016.81.

A reproduction of the card file prepared as a Works Progress Administration project whose goal was to compile a list of creative works and reviews published by Americans between 1850 and 1940. No record exists, however, of what or how many sources were actually examined. The approximately 250,000 cards are organized by author, then alphabetically by title within sections for bibliographies, collected works, separately published works, periodical publications, biographical sources, and critical studies (including reviews) about the author. Reviews are listed under both the reviewer and the author of the book reviewed. Each card usually records author, title, publication information (omitting publishers of books), and genre or type of work. Far from complete, haphazard in its coverage (especially of books), inconsistent in format, including numerous errors, and largely unedited, *Literary Writings* is only occasionally useful for identifying periodical contributions (especially of minor authors) that are not indexed elsewhere. Review: George Monteiro, *Papers of the Bibliographical Society of America* 73 (1979): 498–502.

3260 Tanselle, G. Thomas. "Copyright Records and the Bibliographer." *Studies in Bibliography* 22 (1969): 77–124.

A discussion of the value of copyright records in literary and bibliographical research. The focus is the United States, with a summary of major provisions of copyright law and description of surviving records, published and unpublished, from 1793 through the 1960s. Concludes with a brief commentary on English copyright law. A clear introduction to these underutilized records that are valuable for establishing publication dates, authorship of anonymous and pseudonymous publications, and details of nonextant works.

See also

Sec. U: Literature-Related Topics and Sources/Anonymous and Pseudonymous Works/Dictionaries.

Guides to Scholarship and Criticism

SURVEYS OF RESEARCH

3265 *American Literary Scholarship: An Annual [1963–]* (*ALS*, *AmLS*). Durham: Duke UP, 1965– . Annual. PS3.A47 810.

A selective, evaluative survey of important studies, editions, biographies, and reference works. Currently, the volumes are divided into 22 chapters, each by an established scholar: Emerson, Thoreau, and transcendentalism; Hawthorne; Poe (since 1973); Melville; Whitman and Dickinson (with the latter added in 1967); Mark Twain; James; Pound and Eliot (since 1974); Faulkner; Fitzgerald and Hemingway; literature to 1800; nineteenth century; fiction, 1900 to 1930s; fiction, 1930s to 1960s; fiction, 1960s to the present; poetry, 1900 to 1940s; poetry, 1940s to the present; drama; black literature (since 1977); themes, topics, and criticism; foreign scholarship (since 1973, with separate essays on various countries); and general reference works (since 1977). A chapter on folklore was included from 1965 through 1974. The scope of some chapters has changed over the years, and the organization varies with the subject. Two indexes: scholars; subjects.

Judicious selectivity, currency, and frank, authoritative evaluations (usually much fuller and more critical than in typical surveys of research) make *ALS* an indispensable guide to the year's important scholarship and an essential source for keeping abreast of the increasing number of publications, especially in areas outside one's immediate fields of interest. Together, the volumes offer an incomparable source for studying trends in American literary scholarship and an important complement to *MLAIB* (335) and *ABELL* (340), especially for the superior coverage of books.

Since vol. 35 (for 1954), *Year's Work in English Studies* (330) includes American literature; however, *ALS* offers much fuller, more authoritative coverage.

3270 "A Selected, Annotated List of Current Articles on American Literature." *American Literature* (entry 3425) 54 (1982)– .

A rigorously selective, fully annotated list of the most significant current articles, along with a list of contents of important special issues devoted to a writer, scholar, topic, movement, or genre in American literature. Articles are listed in two parts (general studies, individual authors); special issues, by journal title. Published in each issue, the "List" is indispensable for its currency as well as judicious guidance to the most important new articles. It succeeds "Articles on American Literature Appearing in Current Periodicals" (vols. 1–53 [1929–82]), a much fuller classified list whose entries through 1975 are incorporated in Leary, *Articles on American Literature* (3295).

3275 Duke, Maurice, Jackson R. Bryer, and M. Thomas Inge, eds. *American Women Writers: Bibliographical Essays*. Westport: Greenwood, 1983. 434 pp. Z1229.W8.A44 [PS147] 016.81'09'9287.

Evaluative surveys of scholarship published through c. 1981 on 24 writers: Bradstreet, Rowlandson, Knight, Jewett, Freeman, Murfree, Chopin, Wharton, Stein, Barnes, Nin, Glasgow, Porter, Welty, O'Connor, McCullers, Hurston, Rourke, Buck, Rawlings, Mitchell, Moore, Sexton, and Plath. Each of the 14 chapters, which treat individuals or groups of authors, devotes sections to bibliographies, editions, manuscripts and letters (noting locations as well as scholarship), biographies, and criticism (with the last variously subdivided). Indexed by persons. The individual essays vary in selectivity and rigor of evaluation, but most are authoritative guides to scholarship and suggest topics for further research. The volume as a whole, however, would benefit from a statement of scope and policies governing the selection of scholarship and writers.

3280 Harbert, Earl N., and Robert A. Rees, eds. *Fifteen American Authors before 1900: Bibliographical Essays on Research and Criticism*. Rev. ed. Madison: U of Wisconsin P, 1984. 531 pp. PS55.F53 016.81'09.

Evaluative surveys of research by established scholars on H. Adams, Bryant, Cooper, Crane, Dickinson, Edwards, Franklin, Holmes, Howells, Irving, Longfellow, Lowell, Norris, Taylor, and Whittier. The original edition (1971, 442 pp.) included two additional essays, on southern literature. The surveys vary in selectivity, coverage of foreign scholarship and dissertations, and currency (generally citing publications through 1980, with some as late as 1983), and organization. All have sections for bibliography, editions, manuscripts and letters, biographical studies, and criticism, and offer suggestions for further research. The Dickinson essay treats recent studies separately; others incorporate new scholarship in the commentary. Unfortunately, citations do not provide full bibliographical information. Indexed by persons. An authoritative guide to winnowing the important studies from the mass published on the 15 authors. Review: David Timms, *Notes and Queries* ns 33 (1986): 276–77.

For evaluative surveys of recent scholarship on these authors, see *American Literary Scholarship* (3265).

See also

Dorson, *Handbook of American Folklore* (5860).
Horner, *Present State of Scholarship in Historical and Contemporary Rhetoric* (5565).
Inge, *Handbook of American Popular Culture* (6295).

SERIAL BIBLIOGRAPHIES

3285 "Deutsche amerikakundliche Veröffentlichungen [1945–]." *Amerikastudien/American Studies* 1 (1956)– . Former title: *Jahrbuch für Amerikastudien* (1956–73).

An irregularly published list of German, Swiss, and Austrian scholarship on American culture. Entries are organized alphabetically in 11 divisions: general works and bibliographies; language and literature; history and politics; economics; law; geography; folklore; education; the arts; philosophy, psychology, and religion; and travels and miscellaneous. A useful complement to *American Literary Scholarship* (3265) and the standard serial bibliographies and indexes in section G, which typically overlook much scholarship published in the Germanys, Switzerland, and Austria.

See also

Sec. G: Serial Bibliographies, Indexes, and Abstracts.
ABELL (340): English Literature division.
"Articles in American Studies," *American Quarterly* (3430).
MLAIB (335): American Literature division in the volumes for 1922 to the present. Researchers must also check the headings beginning "American Literature" in the subject index to post-1980 volumes.

OTHER BIBLIOGRAPHIES

3287 *Bibliography of United States Literature* (*BUSL*). 16 vols. New York: Facts on File. In progress, with the first volume scheduled for 1990.

A bibliography of all separately published works by, and selected studies about, major and representative minor writers of the United States. The volumes will be grouped by genre (fiction, verse, drama, and nonfiction prose), with the first four volumes devoted to fiction. Organization within genres is chronological (e.g., fiction will be grouped as follows: before 1865, 1866–1918, 1919–88). Within chronological divisions, writers are organized alphabetically; under each writer are sections listing first and revised second editions of separately published works, standard biographies, standard bibliographies, and the most important studies. Although limited to separately published primary works and selective in covering scholarship, *BUSL* promises to fulfill the long-standing need for a general bibliography—comparable to *New Cambridge Bibliography of English Literature* (1385)—for the literature of the United States.

3290 Jones, Steven Swann. *Folklore and Literature in the United States: An Annotated Bibliography of Studies of Folklore in American Literature.* Garland Reference Library of the Humanities 392: Garland Folklore Bibliographies 5. New York: Garland, 1984. 262 pp. Z1225.J66 [PS169.F64] 016.81'09'3.

A bibliography of books, articles, master's theses, and doctoral dissertations through 1980 that explicitly examine the influence of folklore on American literature and demonstrate "clear folkloristic competence." Jones includes a few works whose titles erroneously suggest that they treat folklore, but excludes discussions of organized religions and general works on literary humor. Listed alphabetically by scholar, entries are accompanied by full descriptive annotations, a few of which point out shortcomings in folklore methodology. (Most theses are not annotated.) This introductory work summarizes basic methodologies for studying folklore in American literature. Six indexes: literary authors; folklore genres; general theoretical studies (a single list with no headings); regional and ethnic studies (with headings only for Afro-American and general regional and ethnic studies); humor (a single list with no headings); dialect, themes, and characters (again, with no headings). Although selective, *Folklore and Literature* gathers and clearly annotates studies which are not readily identifiable in the standard serial bibliographies and indexes in section G and which are frequently omitted from folklore bibliographies. Unfortunately, the utterly inadequate subject indexing means that users in search of studies of other than specific literary authors must skim all entries.

3295 Leary, Lewis. *Articles on American Literature, 1900–1950.* Durham: Duke UP, 1954. 437 pp. Leary, with Carolyn Bartholet and Catharine Roth, comps. *1950–1967.* 1970. 751 pp. Leary and John Auchard, comps. *1968–1975.* 1979. 745 pp. (Another supplement is in progress.) Z1225.L49 016.81.

A bibliography of periodical articles, significant reviews, and review articles compiled from "Articles on American Literature Appearing in Current Periodicals" (3425a), *MLAIB* (335), other bibliographies, and some journals not covered by the preceding. The 1900–50 compilation is limited primarily to English-language studies; the later volumes admit more foreign-language articles but are also more selective. Entries are listed alphabetically in divisions for individual authors; almanacs, annuals, and gift books (1900–50 only); American literature, aims and methods; serial bibliographies; other bibliographies; biography (in the 1968–75 edition, the four preceding divisions became subdivisions—along with ethnic groups—under American literature); fiction; foreign influences and estimates; frontier; humor; Indian literature (in 1968–75, a classified section under American literature); language and style (added in 1950–67); libraries and reading; criticism; literary history; literary trends and attitudes (added in 1950–67); Negro literature (in 1968–75, a classified section under American literature); newspapers and periodicals; philosophy and philosophical trends; poetry; printing, publishing, and bookselling; prose (1900–50 only); regionalism; religion; science; social and political topics; societies; theater; and women (added in 1968–75). Since each volume includes additions and corrections to the preceding one(s), all three must be used together. There are numerous errors and inconsistencies (especially in recording dates and essential issue numbers), and articles treating more than one author or topic do not always receive multiple entries. (Thaddeo K. Babiiha discusses these problems in "The Faulkner Section in Leary's *Articles on American Literature, 1968–1975,*" *Papers of the Bibliographical Society of America* 75 [1981]: 93–98, but his generalizations are not completely accurate.) Although access would be enhanced by a more refined and detailed classification system, the volumes are a time-saving compilation. Because of their limitations, however, they must be supplemented by *American Literary Scholarship* (3265) and the serial bibliographies and indexes in section G. Review: (1950–67) J. Albert Robbins, *Papers of the Bibliographical Society of America* 65 (1971): 417–19.

3300 *Literary History of the United States: Bibliography* (*LHUS*). Ed. Thomas H. Johnson and Richard M. Ludwig. 4th ed. New York: Macmillan; London: Collier, 1974. 1,466 pp. (The 4th ed. consists of corrected reprints of the 1948 bibliography and the supplements of 1959 and 1972, with a cumulative index.) PS88.L522 810'.9.

A series of selective, usually evaluative bibliographical essays organized in four extensively classified divisions: general resources and reference works, general literature (with subdivisions for periods, background studies, American language, folk literature, Indian lore and antiquities, and popular literature), movements and influences, and 239 individual authors (covering primary works, editions, biographies, criticism, bibliographies, and public collections of manuscripts). Throughout, the emphasis is on guiding readers to the best editions and studies; in addition, many essays point out topics needing study. The supplements are keyed to the original volume, and the *Bibliography* must be used in conjunction with the *History* (3200), even though the organization frequently differs. Indexed by authors, titles, and some subjects. Confusingly organized, with numerous errors, badly dated, and largely superseded by author, subject, and period bibliographies, *LHUS* is now principally useful as a guide to older scholarship. Review: R. A. Miller, *American Quarterly* 1 (1949): 180–83.

See also

Sec. U: Literature-Related Topics and Sources/Folklore/Guides to Scholarship and Criticism.
Bailey, *English Stylistics* (6080).
Flanagan, *American Folklore: A Bibliography, 1950–1974* (5870).
Gohdes, *Literature and Theater of the States and Regions of the U.S.A.* (3570).
Haywood, *Bibliography of North American Folklore and Folksong* (5875).
Horner, *Historical Rhetoric* (5600).
Huddleston, *Relationship of Painting and Literature* (5160).
Literary Writings in America (3255).
Ross, *Film as Literature, Literature as Film* (5800).
Schwartz, *Articles on Women Writers* (6605).
Tanselle, *Guide to the Study of United States Imprints* (5290).

ABSTRACTS

Literature

3305 *American Literature Abstracts: A Review of Current Scholarship in the Field of American Literature.* San Jose: San Jose State Coll., 1967–72. 2/yr. PS1.A63 016.81.

Nonevaluative summaries of articles and a book review consensus that synthesizes reviews of recent scholarly books. Abstracts are organized by period. A commendable effort, but the value of the work is severely restricted by the limited coverage of journals (106 at its demise) and inadequate subject indexing.

See also

Sec. G: Serial Bibliographies, Indexes, and Abstracts/Abstracts.
MLA Abstracts (335a).

Related Disciplines

3310 *America: History and Life*. Santa Barbara: ABC-Clio Information Services, 1964– . Z1236.A512 016.917.

The work is currently issued in four parts:

A: Article Abstracts and Citations, 3/yr.
B: Index to Book Reviews, 2/yr.
C: American History Bibliography (Books, Articles, and Dissertations), annual.
D: Annual Index, cumulated quinquennially.

Includes some studies of American, Native American, and Canadian literature and language. The best way to approach the listings in the various parts is through the excellent subject index; entries can also be searched through Dialog (520). A supplement (designated vol. 0) covers 1954–63 (1972). An important source for identifying literary and language scholarship in historical journals, few of which are covered by the standard serial bibliographies and indexes in section G.

Abstracts from *America: History and Life* are reprinted in various topical volumes, including the following:

Harrison, Cynthia E., ed. *Women in American History: A Bibliography*. 2 vols. Clio Bibliography Series 5 and 20. 1979–85.
Smith, Dwight L., ed. *Indians of the United States and Canada: A Bibliography*. 2 vols. Clio Bibliography Series 3 and 9. 1974–83.

DISSERTATIONS AND THESES

3315 Howard, Patsy C., comp. *Theses in American Literature, 1896–1971*. Ann Arbor: Pierian, 1973. 307 pp. Z1225.H67 016.8109.

A list of baccalaureate and master's theses accepted by American and some foreign institutions. Howard covers a limited number of institutions (whether completely is unclear) and apparently only theses devoted to an identifiable author. Entries are organized alphabetically under literary authors, with cross-references for studies of multiple authors. Two indexes: subjects (inadequate); thesis authors. Although marred by a completely inadequate explanation of scope and coverage, *Theses in American Literature* will save some hunting through elusive institutional lists. Theses on southern writers are more fully covered in Emerson, *Southern Literary Culture* (3630). A companion volume is devoted to *Theses in English Literature* (1395).

3320 Woodress, James. *Dissertations in American Literature, 1891–1966*. Rev. and enl. Durham: Duke UP, 1968. 185 pp. Z1225.W8 016.8109.

A bibliography of American, British, French, New Zealand, Indian, German, Austrian, and Canadian dissertations, completed or once in progress. The approximately 4,700 entries, most of which are taken from standard national dissertation bibliographies or other published lists, are organized alphabetically by author in 34 divisions: individual authors; almanacs, gift books, and annuals; American Revolution; Civil War; criticism; drama; economic studies; education and scholarship; fiction; fine arts; folklore; foreign relationships; humor and satire; Indians; language; libraries and reading; literary history; literary nationalism; lyceum; Negro literature; nonfictional prose; periodicals and journalism; philosophy and intellectual history; poetry; politics and government; printing, publishing, and censorship; psychology and literature; Puritanism; regionalism; religion; science and technology; Transcendentalism; travel; and writers and writing. Those for genres, foreign relationships, language, literary history, periodicals and journalism, and regionalism are further classified. Each division or section concludes with cross-references to related dissertations. An entry cites author, title, institution, department (if other than English), and year, and indicates when a dissertation has been published. Indexed by dissertation writers. Although not comprehensive and citing dissertations never completed, this is a time-saving compilation from standard bibliographies (especially because of the inclusion of studies accepted by departments other than English). It must be supplemented, however, by works listed in section H: Guides to Dissertations and Theses.

See also

Sec. H: Guides to Dissertations and Theses.

"American Studies in Britain: Doctoral Theses on American Topics in Progress and Completed," *Journal of American Studies* (3440).

"Doctoral Dissertations in American Studies," *American Quarterly* (3430).

RELATED TOPICS

For other bibliographies of American history, see the chapter on general bibliographies (pp. 19–27) in Prucha, *Handbook for Research in American History* (3185).

3325 Basler, Roy P., Donald H. Mugridge, and Blanche P. McCrum. *A Guide to the Study of the United States of America: Representative Books Reflecting the Development of American Life and Thought*. Washington: Library of Congress, 1960. 1,193 pp. Basler and Oliver H. Orr, Jr. *Supplement, 1956–1965*. 1976. 526 pp. Z1215.U53 016.9173.

A selective, albeit extensive, annotated bibliography of books published through 1965 that are important to the understanding of the United States. The approximately 9,400 entries—most accompanied by extensive descriptive annotations that typically cite related works—are classified in 32 chapters covering all aspects of history, culture, the humanities, arts, and social, natural, and physical sciences. The best approach to the contents is through the extensive index of persons, titles, and subjects. Although dated, this study remains the fullest general guide to works essential for investigating life and thought before 1965 in the United States. Review: *Times Literary Supplement* 8 Sept. 1961: 594.

3330 *Harvard Guide to American History*. 2 vols. Rev. ed. Ed. Frank Freidel. Cambridge: Belknap-Harvard UP, 1974. Z1236.F77 016.9173'03.

A guide to important primary and secondary works published to 30 June 1970 on the political, social, constitutional, economic, cultural, and diplomatic history of the United States. The books and articles, selected on the basis of "potential usefulness," are variously organized in divisions for research methods and materials (with sections on reference works, printed public documents, and unpublished primary sources), biographies and personal records (with sections on travels and descriptions, and biographies), comprehensive and area histories (with a section on regional, state, and local histories), and numerous subjects. The first division consists of a narrative interspersed with lists of works; the other divisions are made up of classified lists. Two indexes: authors (with titles following each author); subjects. Needing a major revision, this standard work is now useful primarily for its discussion of research methodology and as a guide to studies published before mid-1970. Review: Justus D. Doenecke, *History Teacher* 8 (1975): 317–21.

3335 Salzman, Jack, ed. *American Studies: An Annotated Bibliography*. 3 vols. Cambridge: Cambridge UP, 1986. Z1361.C6.A436 [E169.1] 016.973.

An annotated bibliography of English-language books and collections of essays through 1983 on the culture of the United States. Salzman excludes journal articles, theoretical and methodological studies, and reference works. The 7,634 entries are listed alphabetically by author in 11 variously classified divisions: anthropology and folklore (including sections on minorities, ethnic groups, and linguistics); art and architecture; history (with sections on women, ethnicity, black history, and Native Americans); literature (with sections on general surveys, historical periods, and themes); music; political science; popular culture (with sections on general studies, literature, various genres and types of popular fiction, comics, entertainment, film, media, and material culture); psychology; religion; science, technology, and medicine; and sociology. Introducing each division are a brief overview of important reference works (including some published as late as 1986) and, in too few instances, a discussion of criteria determining scope and selection. All but a few annotations are full and accurate descriptions of content. Three indexes in vol. 3: authors; titles; subjects. Although divisions vary considerably in quality and authoritativeness (with many lacking a clear focus and effective organization), the work offers the most current general guide to books on several aspects of American culture. Review: Lawrence H. Fuchs, *American Quarterly*, 39 (1987): 292–95.

Prospects: An Annual of American Cultural Studies 11 (1987)– continues coverage, but the failure to offer any statement of editorial policy and provide a subject index reduces considerably the value of the annual bibliography.

Salzman's compilation does not completely supersede its parent, Murray G. Murphey, gen. ed., *American Studies: An Annotated Bibliography of Works on the Civilization of the United States*, 4 vols. (Washington: US Information Agency, 1982), which lists articles in several divisions but which is not widely available in the United States. Basler, *Guide to the Study of the United States of America* (3325) remains useful for its breadth and inclusion of many earlier books. The same cannot be said for David W. Marcell, *American Studies: A Guide to Information Sources*, American Studies Information Guide Series, 10 (Detroit: Gale, 1982, 207 pp.), which is incomplete, poorly organized, and uninformatively annotated.

3340 *Writings on American History [1973–   ]: A Subject Bibliography of Articles*. Washington: American Historical Assn.; White Plains: Kraus, 1974–   . Annual. Z1236.L331 016.97.

Writings on American History, 1962–73: A Subject Bibliography of Articles. 4 vols. Washington: American Historical Assn.; Millwood: KTO, 1976. Z1236.W773 [E178] 016.973.

Writings on American History [1902–61]. Millwood: KTO, 1904–78.

A bibliography of scholarship on all aspects of American history. Until the volumes for 1962–73, the work annotated books, articles, and dissertations, but subsequent volumes are unannotated and limited to journal articles and dissertations. The volumes for 1904–05 and 1941–47 were never published. Beginning with the volumes for 1962–73, entries are listed by scholar in three classified divisions: periods (including a section for bibliographies), regions, and subjects (including sections for literature, theater, and popular culture). Several works receive multiple listings. Indexed by authors. Earlier volumes are variously organized, with the later ones having a tripartite division: the historical professions; national history (with literature, theater, and folklore sections in the cultural history subdivision); and regional, state, and local history. Indexed by names, places, and subjects (although not all volumes have subject indexing); cumulative index, 1902–40: *Index to the* Writings on American History, *1902–1940* (Washington: American Historical Assn., 1956, 1,115 pp.). Although the post-1961 volumes would benefit from a more refined classification system in the first two divisions as well as subject indexing, this work includes literary studies from periodicals not covered by the standard bibliographies and indexes in section G. For historical studies, it must be supplemented by the other bibliographies and abstracts in section U: Literature-Related Topics and Sources/Social Sciences and Literature/History and Literature/Guides to Scholarship.

Language

GUIDES TO SCHOLARSHIP

3345 *Needed Research in American English (1983). Publication of the American Dialect Society* 71 (1984): 76 pp.

A collection of reports on the state of research and projects needed in linguistic geography, regional speech, usage, new words, proverbs, non-English American languages, and computer research. Particularly valuable is Raven I. McDavid, Jr., "Linguistic Geography" (pp. 4–31), an overview of publications, work in progress, location of archives, and status (as of December 1983) for each of the regional linguistic atlases.

Serial Bibliographies

See

ABELL (340): English Language division, which has a section on American English since the volume for 1927; in earlier volumes, see the Dialect section.

MLAIB (335): English Language and Literature division in the volumes for 1922–25; American Literature I: Linguistics in the volumes for 1926–40; English Language and Literature I: Linguistics in the volumes for 1941–55; English Language and Literature I: Linguistics/American English in the volumes for 1956–66; Indo-European C: Germanic Linguistics IV: English/Modern English/Dialectology in the volumes for 1967–80; and Indo-European Languages/West Germanic Languages/English Language (Modern)/Dialectology in later volumes. Researchers must also check the heading "American English Dialect" in the subject index to volumes since 1981.

Other Bibliographies

See

Leary, *Articles on American Literature* (3295).
Literary History of the United States: Bibliography (3300).
McMillan, *Annotated Bibliography of Southern American English* (3635).
Salzman, *American Studies: An Annotated Bibliography* (3335).

DICTIONARIES

3350 *Dictionary of American Regional English* (*DARE*). Ed. Frederic G. Cassidy. 5 vols. Cambridge: Belknap-Harvard UP, 1985– . PE2843.D52 427'.973.

A dictionary of words and phrases of folk usage or whose form or meaning is confined to a region or regions of the United States or to a social group. Includes Black English, Gullah, Hawaiian pidgin, and the language of children's games, but excludes artificial forms, criminal argot, trade jargon, and restricted occupational vocabularies. Information is drawn from 1,002 lengthy *DARE* questionnaires, other oral sources, and written works, with the heaviest reliance on the last. A typical entry consists of headword, part of speech, pronunciation, variant spellings, etymology for words not treated in standard dictionaries, geographical distribution, usage labels (including frequency, currency, type of user, and manner of use), cross-references, definition, and illustrative quotations from printed and oral sources. Some entries are accompanied by maps that illustrate regional distribution. The admirably clear introduction in vol. 1 outlines the history of the dictionary; explains the editorial policy, maps, and regional labels; discusses language changes especially common in American folk speech; provides a guide to pronunciation; and prints the questionnaire and data about the informants. Vol. 5 will include a bibliography, series of maps illustrating social distribution, and a summary of data from the questionnaires. Justifiably praised by reviewers for its substantial scholarship, *DARE* is a major contribution to dialect studies, sociolinguistics, and areal linguistics in the United States; an essential source for the explication of regional and folk terms in American literature; and a delight to browse in. Reviews: (vol. 1) Hugh Kenner, *TLS: Times Literary Supplement* 9 May 1986: 490–91; Walt Wolfram, *American Speech* 61 (1986): 345–52.

For a survey of the status (as of 1983) of the regional linguistic atlas projects in the United States, see Raven I. McDavid, Jr., "Linguistic Geography," *Needed Research in American English* (3345).

3355 *A Dictionary of American English on Historical Principles* (*DAE*). Ed. William A. Craigie and James R. Hulbert. 4 vols. Chicago: U of Chicago P, 1938–44. PE2835.C72 427.9.

A dictionary of words originating in the United States, having greater currency in that nation than elsewhere, or "denoting something which has a real connection with the development of the country and the history of its people." Slang and dialect terms are limited to early or prominent examples. Although the cutoff date for new words is the end of the nineteenth century, illustrative quotations extend to c. 1925. A typical entry consists of headword, definitions arranged by part of speech, illustrative dated quotations from printed sources for each meaning, combined forms, and, occasionally, pronunciation and etymology. Vol. 4 concludes with a bibliography of sources. Although far from complete, this pioneering work remains an essential source for the history of American English and the explication of American literary works. It must be complemented by *Dictionary of Americanisms* (3360), which is more current and accurate, and *Dictionary of American Regional English* (3350). Some additions, corrections, and antedatings are indexed in Wall, *Words and Phrases Index* (6025).

For an account of the genesis, compilation, and editing of *DAE*, see Craigie, "Sidelights on the *Dictionary of American English*," *Essays and Studies* 30 (1944): 100–13. For a different perspective, however, see M. M. Mathews, "George Watson and the *Dictionary of American English*," *Dictionaries* 7 (1985): 214–24, with a response by Allen Walker Read, "Craigie, Mathews, and Watson: New Light on the *Dictionary of American English*," 8 (1986): 160–63.

3360 *A Dictionary of Americanisms on Historical Principles* (*DA*). Ed. Mitford M. Mathews. 2 vols. Chicago: U of Chicago P, 1951. PE2835.D5 427.9.

A dictionary of words originating in the United States, other words with a particular American meaning, and foreign terms adopted in American English through c. 1950. A typical entry consists of headword, pronunciation and etymology for words originating in the United States and foreign terms, definitions organized by part of speech, dated illustrative quotations from printed sources for each meaning, combined forms, and occasionally a line drawing. Vol. 2 concludes with a bibliography of sources. Some additions, corrections, and antedatings are indexed in Wall, *Words and Phrases Index* (6025). More restrictive than other dictionaries in defining "Americanism" (and unfortunately vague in delineating criteria governing inclusion of certain kinds of words), this work corrects several attributions of Americanisms in *Dictionary of American English* (3355), *Oxford English Dictionary* (1410), and *English Dialect Dictionary* (1415). Although *DA* is generally more current and accurate in recording Americanisms than the preceding, these dictionaries are complementary and, along with *Dictionary of American Regional English* (3350) and updates in *The Barnhart Dictionary Companion* (3365a), essential sources for the historical study of American English and explication of American literary works. Much remains to be done, however, before we have an adequate record of Americanisms. Reviews: Norman E. Eliason, *Modern Language Review* 48 (1952): 565–67; Archibald A. Hill, *Virginia Quarterly Review* 28 (1952): 131–35.

The abridgment as Mathews, *Americanisms: A Dictionary of Selected Americanisms on Historical Principles* (Chicago: U of Chicago P, 1966, 304 pp.), is of little value for scholarly research.

3365 *Webster's Third New International Dictionary of the English Language Unabridged* (*Webster's Third*). Ed. Philip Babcock Gove. Springfield: Merriam, 1961. 2,662 pp. PE1625.W36 423.

A dictionary "of the current vocabulary of standard written and spoken English," especially in the United States. The approximately 450,000 words blend entries from the second edition with new words and meanings, but unlike its predecessor the third edition omits proper names that are not generic, terms obsolete before 1775, and "comparatively useless or obscure words." A typical main entry includes selected variant spellings; pronunciation, with variants used by educated speakers; part of speech; inflectional forms; a note on capitalization practices; etymology; status label; subject label; definitions, in historical order; illustrative quotations largely from twentieth-century sources; usage notes; cross-references; synonyms; and combined forms. Those consulting the third edition for more than a quick definition must study the detailed prefatory explanation of parts of a main entry. The preliminary matter also includes a section on forms of address.

Some later printings list additions before the main alphabet. These words are incorporated into occasional supplements, the most recent of which is *12,000 Words: A Supplement to* Webster's Third New International Dictionary (Springfield: Merriam, 1986, 212 pp.). Other sources for new words and meanings include the following:

The Barnhart Dictionary of New English since 1963. Ed. Clarence L. Barnhart, Sol Steinmetz, and Robert K. Barnhart. Bronxville: Barnhart, 1973. 512 pp. Continued by: *The Second Barnhart Dictionary of New English*. 1980. 520 pp.

The Barnhart Dictionary Companion. Cold Spring: Lexik, 1982– . Quarterly. Updates a variety of standard dictionaries, including the preceding, *Dictionary of Americanisms* (3360), *New Dictionary of American Slang* (see below), *Oxford English Dictionary* and supplement (1410), and Partridge, *Dictionary of Slang* (1410a).

Webster's Third has received a decidedly mixed reception, with the popular press generally condemning the work but linguists and lexicographers considerably more positive toward many of its innovations (especially definition style) and departures from the venerable second edition. Features that have drawn the most criticism include the typographical design; the lowercasing of all proper names (except one sense of *God*) used as headwords, with some confusing notes on capitalization practices; unnecessary citations; deletion of obsolete words; flaws in etymologies; omission of usage labels (the major criticism of those who mistakenly think that a dictionary should arbitrate usage); a confusing system for recording pronunciation; and definitions that are frequently too abridged.

However one judges its lexicographical practices, *Webster's Third* is an essential, if flawed, source for the study of current vocabulary (especially in the United States). For the explication of American literary works, it must be used with the unsuperseded second edition, *Webster's New International Dictionary of the English Language* (*Webster's Second*), ed. William Allan Neilson, 2nd ed., unabridged (Springfield: Merriam, 1934, 3,210 pp.). Reviews: R. W. Burchfield, *Review of English Studies* ns 14 (1963): 319–23; Robert L. Chapman, *American Speech* 42 (1967): 202–10; Albert H. Marckwardt, "The New Webster Dictionary: A Critical Appraisal," *Readings in Applied English Linguistics*, ed. Harold B. Allen, 2nd ed. (New York: Appleton, 1964) 476–85; James Sledd, *College English* 23 (1962): 682–87. Most of the reviews in the popular press are reprinted in James Sledd and Wilma R. Ebbitt [eds.], *Dictionaries and THAT Dictionary: A Casebook on the Aims of*

Lexicographers and the Targets of Reviewers (Chicago: Scott, 1962, 274 pp.).

As an authority for spelling, most American publishers and style manuals (including Chicago [6395] and MLA [6400]) recommend the latest edition of *Webster's Collegiate Dictionary* (currently *Webster's Ninth New Collegiate Dictionary* [Springfield: Merriam, 1983, 1,563 pp.]).

Important complementary dictionaries and other works include the following:

The Random House Dictionary of the English Language. Ed. Stuart Berg Flexner. 2nd ed., unabridged. New York: Random, 1987. 2,478 pp. Has much fuller notes on usage; however, the standard general guide to usage in American English is Wilson Follett, *Modern American Usage: A Guide*, ed. Jacques Barzun (New York: Hill, 1966, 436 pp.).

New Dictionary of American Slang. Ed. Robert L. Chapman. New York: Harper, 1986. 485 pp.

See also

English Dialect Dictionary (1415).
Oxford English Dictionary (1410).

STUDIES OF LANGUAGE

3370 Mencken, H. L. *The American Language: An Inquiry into the Development of English in the United States*. 4th ed., corrected, enl., and rewritten. New York: Knopf, 1936. 769 pp. *Supplement I*. 1945. 739 pp. *Supplement II*. 1948. 890 pp. The 4th ed. and its supplements are abridged and updated by Raven I. McDavid, Jr. (New York: Knopf, 1963, 777 pp.). PE2808.M4 427.9.

A detailed account of the development of American English and its divergence from British English. The multitude of examples are loosely organized in chapters on historical developments, influences on American English, its relationship with British English, pronunciation, spelling, the common speech, proper names, slang, and the future of American English. *Supplement I* updates chapters through the relationship with British English; *Supplement II*, from pronunciation through slang. Non-English dialects are briefly discussed in an appendix to the fourth edition. Two indexes in each volume: words and phrases; persons, subjects, and titles. Stylistically entertaining but hardly impartial, full of errors, weak in organization, and emphasizing description and accumulation of examples rather than analysis, *American Language* has had a mixed reception. It remains the fullest account of American English, even if one disagrees with Mencken's argument for its status as a language. Reviews: (supplements) Raven I. McDavid, Jr., *Language* 23 (1947): 68–73; 25 (1949): 69–77.

PERIODICALS

3375 *American Speech: A Quarterly of Linguistic Usage* (*AS*). 1925– . Quarterly. PE2801.A6 420'.97.

Publishes articles, notes, and reviews on the English language in the Western

Hemisphere (and occasionally on English in other parts of the world, languages influencing or influenced by English, and general linguistic theory), with particular attention to current usage and dialectology. Various issues of vols. 1–44 (1925–69) include a highly selective bibliography of scholarship on present-day English and general and historical studies. Annual index.

Biographical Dictionaries

3380 *Dictionary of American Biography* (*DAB*). Ed. Allen Johnson and Dumas Malone. Corrected rpt. 11 vols. New York: Scribner's, 1964. (A corrected reprint of the original 20 volumes and the first 2 supplements, 1928–58.) E176.D563 920'.073.

Index: Volumes I–XX. 1937. 613 pp.
Supplement One: To December 31, 1935. Ed. Harris E. Starr. 1944. 718 pp.
Supplement Two: To December 31, 1940. Ed. Robert Livingston Schuyler and Edward T. James. 1958. 745 pp.
Supplement Three: 1941–1945. Ed. James et al. 1973. 879 pp.
Supplement Four: 1946–1950. Ed. John A. Garraty and James. 1974. 951 pp.
Supplement Five: 1951–55. Ed. Garraty. 1977. 799 pp.
Supplement Six: 1956–1960. Ed. Garraty. 1980. 769 pp.
Supplement Seven: 1961–1965. Ed. Garraty. 1981. 854 pp.
Supplement Eight: 1966–1970. Ed. Garraty and Mark C. Carnes. 1988. 759 pp.
Dictionary of American Biography: Complete Index Guide, Volumes I–X, Supplements 1–7. 1981. 214 pp.
Concise Dictionary of American Biography: Complete to 1960. 3rd ed. 1980. 1,333 pp.

A biographical dictionary of dead individuals who have resided in what is now the United States and "have made some significant contributions to American life." British officers serving in the Colonies after the Declaration of Independence are excluded. The 17,656 entries (through the seventh supplement) encompass the eminent and the notorious, although the scope is less catholic than that of its model, the *Dictionary of National Biography* (1425). Written by established authorities, the sketches range from 500 to 16,500 words in the original dictionary, but are limited to 5,000 words after the fourth supplement; combine factual information and interpretation based on extensive original research; and conclude with a short list of sources, which frequently locates unpublished materials. With *Supplement Five*, much of the extensive family and other personal data are recorded only on forms stored in the *DAB* archives in the Library of Congress. Errata to the original 20 volumes are printed in vol. 1, pp. xxii–xxxvi, of the 1964 reprint, which also makes some corrections within entries. The 1937 *Index* consists of six indexes to the original dictionary: biographees; contributors; birthplaces (by state or country); schools and colleges; occupations; subjects. The *Complete Index Guide* indexes only biographees in the corrected reprint and the first seven supplements. The history of the work is outlined in vol. 1, pp. vii-xvi, of the 1964 reprint. Although there are errors and notable omissions (especially of women, who account for only 625 of the 13,633 entries in the original 20 volumes), the *DAB* remains the most authoritative of the numerous biographical dictionaries of notable Americans. It is, however, being updated and revised as *The American National Biography*, gen. ed. John A. Garraty, 20 vols. (New York: Oxford UP; scheduled for 1996). Reviews: Arthur M. Schlesinger, *American Historical Review* 35 (1929–30): 119–26, 624–25; 36 (1931): 402–05; 37 (1932): 353–56; 38 (1933): 336–38; 39 (1934): 337–38; 40 (1935): 343–47; 41 (1936): 344–46, 761–63; 42 (1937): 769–73.

The *Concise Dictionary* prints abridged entries for all biographees through the sixth supplement; however, individuals in *Supplements Five* and *Six* are in a separate alphabetical sequence.

Although *DAB* is far more authoritative than other American biographical dictionaries, the following are important, if much less trustworthy, sources for information on persons excluded from *DAB*:

Appleton's Cyclopædia of American Biography. Ed. James Grant Wilson and John Fiske. 6 vols. and supplement. New York: Appleton, 1887–1900. *The Cyclopedia of American Biography: Supplementary Edition*. Vols. 7–10. Ed. James E. Homans, L. E. Dearborn, and Herbert M. Linen. New York: Press Assn., 1918–26. Because of numerous fictitious biographies and fabricated publications, the original six volumes must be used with caution; see Margaret Castle Schindler, "Fictitious Biography," *American Historical Review* 42 (1937): 680–90, for an account of these deliberate falsifications.

The National Cyclopedia of American Biography. 76 vols. Clifton: White, 1898–1984. Includes a considerable number of persons not in the *DAB*. Because of the nonalphabetic organization, the cumulative *Index* (1984, 576 pp.) is essential for locating entries.

The *DAB*, its supplements, *Appleton's Cyclopædia*, and *National Cyclopedia* are indexed in *Biography and Genealogy Master Index* (565).

3385 *Notable American Women, 1607–1950: A Biographical Dictionary*. Ed. Edward T. James. 3 vols. Cambridge: Belknap-Harvard UP, 1971.

Notable American Women: The Modern Period: A Biographical Dictionary. Ed. Barbara Sicherman and Carol Hurd Green. 1980. 773 pp. CT3260.N57 920.72'0973.

A biographical dictionary of American and foreign-born residents who died before 31 December 1975 and who achieved more than local eminence or notoriety. Wives of presidents are the only women included on the basis of a husband's credentials. The 1,779 entries, ranging from 400 to 7,000 words, are based on extensive research and combine factual information with interpretation. Each entry concludes with a list of sources that typically locates manuscript and archival material. A classified list of occupations, avocations, groups, and interests concludes the 1980 dictionary and vol. 3 of the 1971 edition. Entrants are indexed in *Biography and Genealogy Master Index* (565). Although there are some notable omissions, *Notable American Women* is the most authoritative biographical dictionary of American women (many of whom receive their first and only scholarly discussion here), a valuable source for literary scholars because of its inclusion of so many authors, and an essential complement to *Dictionary of American Biography* (3380), which slights females. Reviews: Ray Ginger and Victoria Ginger, *Canadian Historical Review* 55 (1974): 106–09; Helen Vendler, *New York Times Book Review* 17 Sept. 1972: 1+; Barbara Welter, *William and Mary Quarterly* 3rd ser. 30 (1973): 518–22.

For basic biographical data (including addresses) for living women, see the current edition of *Who's Who of American Women* (3395a).

3390 Mainiero, Lina, and Langdon Lynne Faust, eds. *American Women Writers: A Critical Reference Guide from Colonial Times to the Present.* 4 vols. New York: Ungar, 1979–82. Abridged ed. Ed. Faust. 2 vols. 1983. PS147.A4 810'.9'9287.

A dictionary of about 1,000 women writers of belles lettres as well as popular forms, diaries, letters, autobiographies, and children's books. Listed under the name used by the Library of Congress, the signed entries, which range from one to five pages, provide biographical information, an overview of major works, a general critical estimate, a "complete" bibliography of primary works, and a selected list of studies. (Neither bibliography cites full publication information, however.) Indexed in vol. 4 by persons and subjects (including vocations and ethnic groups). Entrants are also indexed in *Biography and Genealogy Master Index* (565). The abridgment updates some entries and adds a few new ones. Although the essays vary considerably in quality (with many full of errors and hardly penetrating in analysis) and although blacks and other minorities could be more adequately represented, the work offers the most inclusive single guide to female writers in the United States; unfortunately, it cannot be trusted for facts or opinions. Review: (abridged ed.) Nina Baym, *Tulsa Studies in Women's Literature* 2 (1983): 247–50.

3395 *Who's Who in America [1899–].* Wilmette: Marquis, 1899– . Biennial, with supplement between editions. E176.W642 920.073.

A biographical dictionary of living citizens of the United States, Canada, and Mexico who are nationally prominent for their positions or achievements. The compact entries—largely compiled from information supplied by entrants—supply basic biographical, family, and career data; a list of significant publications and awards; and home and/or office address. Two indexes: retirees whose sketches appear in earlier volumes; persons in the regional or topical directories (see below). Entrants are also indexed in the current edition of *Who's Who in America Index: Geographic Index; Professional Area Index* (1982–); entries since 1982 can be searched through Dialog (520).

Individuals of regional rather than national importance are included in one or more of the Marquis regional or topical indexes, which overlap more with the main volume than the publisher claims. For the literary researcher, the most useful of these complementary biennial indexes are the following:

Who's Who in the East. 1943– .
Who's Who in the Midwest. 1949– .
Who's Who in the South and Southwest. 1947– .
Who's Who in the West. 1949– .
Who's Who of American Women. 1958– .

The preceding are indexed by name and geographic area in the current edition of *Marquis Who's Who Publications: Index to All Books* (1974–), and most are indexed by name in *Biography and Genealogy Master Index* (565).

Although the entries offer minimal information and are not always accurate or complete, the most recent *Who's Who* volumes are among the best sources for current information and addresses of prominent Americans.

Entries for dead persons and those over 95 are transferred to *Who Was Who in America: With World Notables [1897–]* (1943–). Beginning with vol. 5, this series also includes some persons of regional or international note who were not listed in *Who's Who in America.* Important Americans who died before the inception of *Who's Who in America* are covered in *Who Was Who in America: Historical*

Volume, 1607–1896, rev. ed. (1967), 689 pp. For many entrants, *Dictionary of American Biography* (3380) offers fuller, more accurate information.

See also

Sec. J: Biographical Sources.
Allibone, *Critical Dictionary of English Literature* (1430).
Dictionary of Literary Biography (600).
Hart, *Oxford Companion to American Literature* (3210).

Periodicals

HISTORIES AND SURVEYS

3400 Mott, Frank Luther. *A History of American Magazines, [1741–1930]*. 5 vols. Cambridge: Harvard UP, 1930–68. PN4877.M63 051'.09.

Vol. 1: *1741–1850*. New York: Appleton, 1930. 848 pp.
Vol. 2: *1850–1865*. Cambridge: Harvard UP, 1938. 608 pp.
Vol. 3: *1865–1885*. 1938. 649 pp.
Vol. 4: *1885–1905*. 1957. 858 pp.
Vol. 5: *Sketches of 21 Magazines: 1905–1930*. Cambridge: Belknap-Harvard UP, 1968. 595 pp.

A history of the development of English-language periodicals in the United States to c. 1905, with individual studies of important magazines through 1930. Excludes newspapers and annuals but otherwise surveys a representative sample of magazines. Vols. 1 through 3 include a chronological list of periodicals mentioned in the text. Indexed in each volume by persons, titles, and subjects; however, the cumulative index in vol. 5 is more thorough. For a history of the project, see "Unfinished Story; or, The Man in the Carrel" (vol. 5, pp. 341–50). Justly praised for its erudition and style, Mott is the monumental history of periodicals in the country. Vols. 2 and 3 were awarded the Pulitzer Prize in History (1939). Some literary magazines are more fully described in Chielens, *American Literary Magazines* (3410).

GUIDES TO PRIMARY WORKS

Union Lists

3405 *United States Newspaper Program National Union List*. 2nd ed. Dublin, OH: Online Computer Library Center, 1987. Microfiche.

A bibliography and union list of about 56,000 newspapers derived from the data base being compiled by participants in the United States Newspaper Program, which is attempting to catalog and eventually microfilm the more than 300,000 newspapers published in the United States and its territories. (For a description of the program and its status, see Robert B. Hartiman, Jr., "Progress toward a

National Union List of Newspapers," *Serials Review* 14.1–2 [1988]: 15–20.) Listed alphabetically by title, entries include publication information and exact holdings. Four indexes: date; audience (ethnic, political, or religious); language; place of publication or printing. Entries can also be searched by title through OCLC (225), whose records are more current than the published version. The *National Union List* is especially useful for locating runs and identifying newspapers by locale or ethnic, political, or religious focus.

This work largely supersedes Winifred Gregory, ed., *American Newspapers, 1821–1936: A Union List of Files Available in the United States and Canada* (New York: Wilson, 1937, 791 pp.); for newspapers before 1820, Brigham, *History and Bibliography of American Newspapers* (4035), frequently supplies fuller information and locations.

See also

Sec. K: Periodicals/Union Lists.

Bibliographies

3410 Chielens, Edward E., ed. *American Literary Magazines: The Eighteenth and Nineteenth Centuries*. Historical Guides to the World's Periodicals and Newspapers. New York: Greenwood, 1986. 503 pp. (A volume on the twentieth century is scheduled for 1989.) Z1231.P45.A43 [PS201] 810'.9'003.

A collection of separately authored profiles of 92 of the most important magazines founded before 1900 that print a significant amount of literature (including criticism) or are otherwise important in literary history. The essays, organized by periodical title, typically discuss publishing history, audience, and significant literary content, and conclude with a list of studies, indexes, reprints, and a few locations, as well as details of publishing history (including title changes, numbering and dating of volumes and issues, frequency, publishers, and editors). Appendix A consists of an annotated list of minor literary magazines and nonliterary ones with literary contents; appendix B is a chronology of American literary magazines and literary and social events from 1774 through 1900. Indexed by persons, magazine titles, and subjects. Although the essays vary in quality, *American Literary Magazines* is a useful compendium of information on the publishing history and contents of a small group of significant literary magazines.

See also

Kelly, *Children's Periodicals of the United States* (5510).

Indexes

Although many clipping files and unpublished indexes exist for local and regional newspapers, there is no trustworthy guide to these important sources. Because Anita Cheek Milner, *Newspaper Indexes: A Location and Subject Guide for Researchers*, 3 vols. (Metuchen: Scarecrow, 1977–82) is incomplete, poorly organized, inadequately indexed, and full of errors, researchers attempting to locate a clipping file or an unpublished index cannot depend on the work as a guide. Instead, they will usually have to contact the newspaper office and area libraries and historical societies.

For other indexes, bibliographies, and union lists of newspapers, see the chapter on guides to newspapers in Prucha, *Handbook for Research in American History* (3185).

3415 The New York Times *Index*. Current Series. New York: New York Times, 1913– . 2/mo., with quarterly and annual cumulations. Prior Series [covering September 1851–1912]. 15 vols. 1967–74. AI21.N45 071'.47'1.

A subject index with abstracts of articles and features in the late city edition and regional Sunday supplements. Abstracts are listed chronologically under a heading; reviews appear under "Book Review," "Theater," and "Motion Pictures." News stories and editorial features since 1969 can be searched online through the New York Times Information Bank (which currently indexes 10 other newspapers and 39 magazines published in North America and Europe). Besides providing excellent access to the contents of the country's leading newspaper, the *Index* can be used to determine the approximate date of stories in newspapers not indexed. The *Index* is hardly complicated enough to require anyone to endure the wretched prose and belabored explanation of Grant W. Morse, *Guide to the Incomparable* New York Times Index (New York: Fleet, 1980, 72 pp.).

Three specialized indexes also provide access to the *Times*:

Falk, Byron A., Jr., and Valerie R. Falk. *Personal Name Index to* The New York Times Index, *1851–1974*. 22 vols. Verdi: Roxbury Data Interface, 1976–83. *1975–1979 Supplement*. 3 vols. 1984–85. *1975–1984 Supplement*. 1986– . The supplements also include names overlooked in the index to 1851–1974.

The New York Times *Obituaries Index, 1858–1968*. New York: New York Times, 1970. 1,136 pp. *The* New York Times *Obituaries Index, II: 1969–1978*. 1980. 131 pp.

New York Times Book Review *Index, 1896–1970*. 5 vols. New York: Arno, 1973.

The *Times* is also indexed by subject and author in *National Newspaper Index* (3420) and in the InfoTrac data base (387).

3420 *National Newspaper Index*. Belmont: Information Access, 1979– . Monthly, with running cumulation. Microform.

An author and subject index to the *New York Times* (national and late editions), *Wall Street Journal* (eastern and western editions), *Christian Science Monitor, Los Angeles Times*, and *Washington Post*. Entries can also be searched online through Dialog (520), and the most recent four years are indexed in the InfoTrac data base (387).

These—and other major newspapers—are also separately indexed:

The Christian Science Monitor *Index [1960–]*. Ann Arbor: University Microfilms International, 1960– . Monthly, with quarterly and annual cumulations. (Title varies.)

Chicago Tribune *Index [1972–]*. Ann Arbor: University Microfilms International, 1976– . Monthly, with quarterly, annual, and larger cumulations.

The Los Angeles Times *Index [1972–]*. Ann Arbor: University Microfilms International, 1973– . Monthly, with annual cumulation. (Title varies.)

Bell and Howell Newspaper Index to the San Francisco Chronicle *[1978–]*. Wooster: Indexing Center, 1979– . Monthly, with quarterly and annual cumulations.

The Official Washington Post *Index [1971–]*. Woodbridge: Research Publications, 1975– . Monthly, with annual cumulation.

See also

Literary Writings in America (3255).

SCHOLARLY JOURNALS

Most journals in section K: Periodicals/Scholarly Journals publish material on American literature.

3425 *American Literature: A Journal of Literary History, Criticism, and Bibliography* (*AL*). 1929– . Quarterly. PS1.A6 810.5.

Publishes articles, notes, and reviews on all aspects of American literature. Since 52.3 (1980), a special section called "The Extra" is devoted to announcements of projects and meetings, calls for papers, obituaries, articles on professional topics, and other news. For "A Selected, Annotated List of Current Articles on American Literature" and its predecessor, "Articles on American Literature Appearing in Current Periodicals," see entry 3270. Annual index; cumulative index: vols. 1–30, Thomas F. Marshall, *An Analytical Index to* American Literature, *Volumes I–XXX, March 1929–January 1959* (Durham: Duke UP, 1963, 253 pp.); a cumulative index beginning with vol. 31 is in progress. The founding and early history are traced in Jay B. Hubbell, "*American Literature*, 1928–1954," *South and Southwest: Literary Essays and Reminiscences* (Durham: Duke UP, 1965) 22–48; and in Vanderbilt, *American Literature and the Academy* (3455) 285–99, 400–06, passim, which also details the academic politics behind the early volumes, especially the reviews. Noted for the quality of its articles, *AL* is the foremost journal devoted to American literature.

3430 *American Quarterly* (*AQ*). 1949– . 5/yr. AP2.A3985 051.

Devoted to the culture of the United States, with an emphasis on interdisciplinary approaches in articles, surveys of research, special issues, and reviews covering history, literature, religion, art, music, politics, folklore, customs, popular culture, women's studies, and minority issues. With vol. 26 (1974), the annual "Articles in American Studies [1954–72]," vols. 7–25 (1955–73)—a selective annotated interdisciplinary list—was replaced by a yearly bibliography issue that prints surveys of research and discussions of methodology on a theme or topic. Since vol. 38 (1986), the bibliography issue also includes an annotated author list of "Doctoral Dissertations in American Studies [1985–]." The annual bibliographies for 1954–68 are reprinted with cumulative scholar and personal name indexes as Hennig Cohen, ed., *Articles in American Studies, 1954–1968: A Cumulation of the Annual Bibliographies from* American Quarterly, 2 vols., Cumulated Bibliography Series 2 (Ann Arbor: Pierian, 1972).

3435 *American Studies International* (*ASInt*). 1962– . 2 journal and 4 newsletter issues a year. Former titles: *American Studies: An International Newsletter* (1970–75); *American Studies News* (1962–70). AP2.A3985 973'.05.

Publishes commissioned bibliographical essays and surveys of research—along with articles by scholars living outside the United States—on aspects of American culture, but with a decided emphasis, especially in the bibliographies and surveys, on literature. Cumulative index: vols. 8–24, in 25.1 (1987): 74–94.

3440 *Journal of American Studies* (*JAmS*). 1967– . 3/yr. E151.J6 973'.05.

Publishes articles, reviews, and review essays on a wide range of American topics, but with a substantial number on literature. The biennial "American Studies in Britain: Doctoral Theses on American Topics in Progress and Completed" (4 [1970]–), which originally covered M.A. and B.Litt. theses, includes a section on literature. Annual index.

3445 *Resources for American Literary Study* (*RALS*). 1971– . 2/yr. Z1225.R46 016.81.

Publishes bibliographies, surveys of research, catalogs of collections, supplements to published bibliographies (especially those in G. K. Hall's Reference Guides to Literature series), edited letters and documents, and reviews and review essays on reference works and scholarly editions. Annual index. An important source for specialized bibliographies and some of the best reviews of reference works in American literature. Unfortunately, publication is far in arrears.

3450 *Sewanee Review* (*SR*). 1892– . Quarterly. AP2.S5 810.

Publishes articles and reviews (along with poetry and fiction) on a variety of national literatures, but with an emphasis on American topics, especially southern literature. Annual index; cumulative indexes: vols. 1–10, in 10 (1902): iii-xxxi; vols. 51–90, Mary Lucia Snyder Cornelius and Elizabeth Moore Engsberg, eds., *The* Sewanee Review: *A Forty-Year Index, 1943–1982* (Oxford: Learned Information, 1983, 200 pp.), with the indexes for vols. 88–90 printed separately on pp. 177–200. For the history and content of the journal through 1930, see Alice Lucille Turner, "*The Sewanee Review,*" 40 (1932): 129–38, 257–75.

Background Reading

3455 Vanderbilt, Kermit. *American Literature and the Academy: The Roots, Growth, and Maturity of a Profession*. Philadelphia: U of Pennsylvania P, 1986. 609 pp. PS62.V28 810'.7'1273.

A history of the origins and development of the study of American literature in the United States from 1829 through 1948. Organized in three periods (1829–1921, 1921–39, 1939–48), chapters examine in detail the professional lives, publications, and other contributions of major scholars; the genesis, production, critical reception, and importance of major literary histories (especially *Cambridge History of American Literature* [3205a] and *Literary History of the United States* [3200]), scholarly works, and journals (particularly *American Literature* [3425] and *PMLA* [725]); the introduction of American literature into secondary and higher education; the development of professional organizations (especially the American Literature Group of the MLA); and the academic politics that shaped the profession. An appendix lists the leaders of the American Literature Group from 1921 through 1948. Drawing extensively on unpublished materials, Vanderbilt offers a fascinating, critical (but not always impartial) account of the evolution of the academic study of American literature in the United States. Organizers of a major cooperative scholarly venture will find the accounts of *CHAL* and *LHUS* both instructive and sobering. Readers who are English literature specialists will wish for a similar history of their profession.

3460 *Dictionary of American History*. Ed. Louise Bilebof Ketz. Rev. ed. 8 vols. New York: Scribner's, 1976–78. E174.D52 973'.03.

A dictionary of places, events, terms, concepts, groups, acts of Congress, Supreme Court decisions, military and political offices, names of ships, movements, battles—in short, virtually anything (except individuals) connected with the history of the United States. The approximately 7,200 signed entries range from a few lines to several pages, and most conclude with a reference to at least one related study. Corrections to vols. 1–7 are printed in vol. 8, pp. xi-xiii. Because of the heterogeneous contents and headings, the best approach is through the detailed analytical index (vol. 8). Although this is the standard multivolume dictionary of United States history, it must be used with care because of numerous important omissions and inadequately revised entries that do not incorporate recent scholarship or cite the best sources. Review: Robert H. Ferrell, *American Historical Review* 82 (1977): 1316–18.

The best one-volume dictionary is *Concise Dictionary of American History*, ed. David William Voorhees (New York: Scribner's 1983, 1,140 pp.), an abridgment, with some additional and updated entries, of the *Dictionary of American History*.

3465 Horton, Rod W., and Herbert W. Edwards. *Backgrounds of American Literary Thought*. 3rd ed. Englewood Cliffs: Prentice, 1974. 630 pp. PS88.H6 917.3'03.

A basic account of the historical, intellectual, social, and economic backgrounds necessary to an understanding of American literature. Separate chapters treat idealism, Puritanism, the Enlightenment, political patterns in the early republic, unitarianism and transcendentalism, expansionism, the triumph of industry, evolution and pragmatism, gentility and revolt, Marxism, literary naturalism, imperialism and isolation, the 1920s, Freudianism, the southern experience, the Depression, postwar science and philosophy, cultural revolution, and the literary reaction of the 1960s and 1970s. Each chapter has a list of suggested readings. Concludes with a comparative outline of basic tenets of several -isms. Indexed by persons and titles. An elementary but useful overview of essential backgrounds of American literature.

Genres

Most works in section L: Genres are useful for research in American literature.

FICTION

Most works in section L: Genres/Fiction are important to research in American fiction.

Histories and Surveys

3470 Cowie, Alexander. *The Rise of the American Novel.* American Literature Series. New York: American Book, 1948. 877 pp. PS371.C73 813.09.

A critical history of the evolution of the American novel during the eighteenth and nineteenth centuries, with a concluding chapter on the first four decades of the present century. Organized chronologically, chapters on groups and major authors also treat representative minor writers. Indexed by titles and authors. Although now dated, this is among the fuller surveys and remains useful for its detailed consideration of several minor novelists.

Other general histories include the following:

Chase, Richard. *The American Novel and Its Tradition.* Garden City: Doubleday, 1957. 266 pp. A critical survey from Brown to Faulkner that emphasizes major writers in exploring the relationship of the romance to the development of the American novel.

Quinn, Arthur Hobson. *American Fiction: An Historical and Critical Survey.* New York: Appleton, 1936. 805 pp. A critical history of American fiction from the eighteenth century to the 1930s, excluding juvenile, dime, and detective fiction as well as works by authors who were first published after 1920. Although it is dated, offers some questionable evaluations, and is superseded in many parts by specialized surveys, Quinn remains one of the few works covering both novels and short fiction. Review: Fred Lewis Pattee, *American Literature* 8 (1937): 468–70.

Wagenknecht, Edward. *Cavalcade of the American Novel from the Birth of the Nation to the Middle of the Twentieth Century.* New York: Holt, 1952. 575 pp. A critical history through the 1940s.

A major desideratum remains an adequate history of fiction in the United States.

Guides to Scholarship and Criticism

3475 Gerstenberger, Donna, and George Hendrick. *The American Novel, 1789–1959: A Checklist of Twentieth-Century Criticism.* 2nd ed. Swallow Checklists of Criticism and Explication. Denver: Swallow, 1961. 333 pp.

———. *The American Novel: A Checklist of Twentieth Century Criticism on Novels Written since 1789.* Vol. 2: *Criticism Written 1960–1968.* Chicago: Swallow, 1970. 459 pp. Z1231.F4.G4 016.813'03.

A selective checklist of articles, parts of books, and bibliographies published between 1900 and 1968. Gerstenberger and Hendrick favor standard works and periodicals, but exclude general literary histories and almost all reviews. Entries are organized in two divisions: authors and general studies. Under each author are sections for individual novels, general studies (of two or more works but with no cross-references under specific titles), and bibliographies. The second part has sections for general studies and centuries. Entries for parts of books and essays from collections are keyed to a list at the back. The two *Checklists* are time-consuming, frustrating works to use because of the lack of cross-references and indexing, and a layout that prevents easy identification of sections. Highly selective in coverage and now dated, *The American Novel* is principally useful for the indexing of parts of books published before 1969. Superior coverage of articles is offered by Leary, *Articles on American Literature* (3295).

3480 Weixlmann, Joe. *American Short-Fiction Criticism and Scholarship, 1959–1977: A Checklist.* Chicago: Swallow-Ohio UP, 1982. 625 pp. Z1231.F4.W43 [PS374.S5] 016.813'01'09.

A classified list of English-language articles, interviews, and bibliographies from some 325 journals and of sections in about 5,000 books on the short fiction of more than 500 authors from the eighteenth through the twentieth century. Weixlmann makes an effort to include minority writers. Entries are organized in divisions for general studies and individual authors; under the latter are sections for individual works, general studies, interviews, and bibliographies. The omission of page references in entries for parts of books and the lack of an index mar this otherwise useful compilation.

Weixlmann continues the coverage of American writers in Jarvis Thurston, O. B. Emerson, Carl Hartman, and Elizabeth B. Wright, *Short Fiction Criticism: A Checklist of Interpretation since 1925 of Stories and Novelettes (American, British, Continental) 1800–1958*, Swallow Checklists of Criticism and Explication (Denver: Swallow, 1960, 265 pp.), which is only marginally useful because of its exclusion of studies "dealing with the 'environmental' circumstances of literature (biography, genesis, source, etc.)."

See also

Leary, *Articles on American Literature* (3295).

Periodicals

3485 *Studies in American Fiction* (*SAF*). 1973– . 2/yr. PS370.S87 813'.009.
Publishes articles, notes, and reviews on fiction by United States authors.

DRAMA AND THEATER

Most works in section L: Genres/Drama and Theater are important to research in American drama and theater.

Histories and Surveys

3490 Meserve, Walter J. *An Emerging Entertainment: The Drama of the American People to 1828.* Bloomington: Indiana UP, 1977. 342 pp. PS332.M39 812'.009.

———. *Heralds of Promise: The Drama of the American People during the Age of Jackson, 1829–1849.* Contributions in American Studies 86. New York: Greenwood, 1986. 269 pp. PS343.M47 812'.3'09.

The first two volumes of a projected six-volume critical history of plays written and published in America from its colonization to the present. (Future volumes will be devoted to 1850 to 1889, 1890 to 1915, 1916 to 1945, and 1946 to the present.) After a discussion of what constitutes American drama, chapters survey the plays of a period, emphasizing their "relationship . . . to the cultural and historical progress of the country," offering a brief synopsis of each work and biographical information on important authors, and tracing "the development of American drama as a literary genre and its contribution to American theatre." Each volume concludes with a selective bibliography that (depending on the volume) lists studies of the cultural and historical background, theater histories, general bibliographies and studies, works on individual dramatists, periodicals and newspapers, manuscript and theater collections, and dissertations. The second volume lists playwrights and plays of the period in appendixes. Indexed by names and plays (separately in the first volume). Although plagued by numerous factual errors, the thoroughness of coverage and attention to the social and political conditions affecting drama make Meserve's work the best general history of American drama. Reviews: (*Emerging Entertainment*) Thomas F. Marshall, *American Literature* 50 (1978): 519–21; Kenneth Silverman, *Early American Literature* 14 (1979): 125–26.

Because of its emphasis on theater, Meserve's work does not completely supersede Arthur Hobson Quinn, *A History of the American Drama from the Beginning to the Civil War*, 2nd ed. (New York: Crofts, 1943, 530 pp.) and *A History of the American Drama from the Civil War to the Present Day*, rev. ed., 2 vols. in 1 (1936, 296 and 432 pp.).

A four-volume history of American drama under the editorship of Jordan Y. Miller is scheduled for publication by Twayne beginning in 1989.

3495 *The Revels History of Drama in English* (1530). Gen. ed. T. W. Craik. Vol. 8: *American Drama*. London: Methuen; New York: Barnes, 1977. 324 pp. PR625.R44 822'.009.

Includes a chronology; essays on the contexts of American drama, actors and other theater personnel, and dramatists and their plays; and an evaluative survey of important studies. Indexed by authors, titles, and subjects. Like other volumes of *Revels History*, this offers a useful synthesis of scholarship rather than a connected history of the drama; it complements rather than supersedes Quinn, *History of the American Drama* (3490a). Review: A. F. Sponberg, *TLS: Times Literary Supplement* 4 Aug. 1978: 886.

Literary Handbooks, Dictionaries, and Encyclopedias

3500 Bordman, Gerald. *The Oxford Companion to American Theatre*. New York: Oxford UP, 1984. 734 pp. PN2220.B6 792'.0973.

Emphasizes popular Broadway theater (through mid-1983) in entries on plays, musicals, actors, actresses, producers, directors, designers, other notable theatrical people, theaters, organizations, and periodicals. In less depth, Bordman covers other entertainment, such as minstrelsy, vaudeville, circus, and wild West and tent shows, but excludes most off-Broadway and regional works as well as recent theater people. The bulk of the entries are for plays (with length of New York run the main criterion governing selection), recording place and date of original production, length of run, cast, and producer, and providing a brief synopsis and critical commentary.

Entries for people give an overview of career. There are numerous inaccuracies, and the emphasis on popular Broadway entertainment badly distorts the picture of the American theatrical scene; nevertheless, the *Oxford Companion* is the single fullest handbook designed for quick reference. It does not approach the quality and balance one expects in an *Oxford Companion*, however. Bordman, *The Concise Oxford Companion to American Theatre* (1987, 451 pp.), adds some entries and updates others. Reviews: John Simon, *TLS: Times Literary Supplement* 26 Apr. 1985: 477 (an important discussion of weaknesses); Don B. Wilmeth, *Theatre History Studies* 5 (1985): 116–19.

A useful supplement for plays is Edwin Bronner, *The Encyclopedia of the American Theatre, 1900–1975* (San Diego: Barnes, 1980, 659 pp.), which covers plays written or adapted by Anglo-American authors and produced on and off Broadway. Entries cite date and place of original production, length of run, cast, producer, director, and screen adaptations, and include a brief synopsis.

3505 Durham, Weldon B., ed. *American Theatre Companies, 1749–1887*. New York: Greenwood, 1986. 598 pp. PN2237.A43 792'.0973. *1888–1930*. 1987. 541 pp. PN2256.A44 792'.0973. (*1931–1986* in progress.)

A collection of separately authored discussions of theatrical companies that produced more than one nonmusical play while in residence in one place for a minimum of 20 consecutive weeks. Organized alphabetically by company (with cross-references for alternate names), entries consist of two parts: a discussion of the history, commercial and artistic significance, and repertory of the company; lists of personnel (including managers, designers, technicians, and performers), works produced (selective if a full list has been published), and selected scholarship and manuscript or archival material. Each volume concludes with two appendixes: a chronology of theater companies; a list by state. Indexed in each volume by persons and play titles. Although the essays vary in quality and some companies are more extensively treated in separate studies, *American Theatre Companies* is the fullest single compendium of information on American theater companies.

Annals

3510 Odell, George C. D. *Annals of the New York Stage*. 15 vols. New York: Columbia UP, 1927–49. PN2277.N5.O4 792'.097471.

A narrative calendar of theatrical entertainment (including opera, ballet, vaudeville, minstrelsy, circus, and concert) in New York City from 1699 through 1894. Organized by season, then by theater or troupe, the commentary draws on newspapers, unpublished manuscripts and archival materials, autobiographies, playbills, and other documents to record performances (along with cast lists) as well as discuss critical reception, performers, and theater architecture. Indexed in each volume by persons, titles, subjects, and theaters; the numerous illustrations are indexed in *Index to the Portraits in Odell's* Annals of the New York Stage (N.p.: American Soc. for Theatre Research, 1963, 179 pp.). Odell offers a full, if at times discursive, record of activity in the country's major theatrical center. Reviews: Arthur Hobson Quinn, *American Literature* 1 (1929): 89–92; 3 (1931): 335–39; 8 (1937): 472–74; 9 (1937): 382–84; 10 (1938): 362–64; 12 (1940): 123–24; 13 (1941): 177–78; 14 (1943): 453–55; 22 (1950): 88–89; *Modern Language Notes* 61 (1946): 138–39.

Guides to Scholarship and Criticism

Surveys of Research

For an evaluative survey of histories and general studies (mostly after 1950), see Charles A. Carpenter, "American Drama: A Bibliographical Essay," *American Studies International* 21.5 (1983): 3–52.

See also

American Literary Scholarship (3265): Chapter on drama.

Other Bibliographies

3515 Archer, Stephen M. *American Actors and Actresses: A Guide to Information Sources*. Performing Arts Information Guide Series 8. Detroit: Gale, 1983. 710 pp. Z5784.M9.A7 [PN1998.A2] 016.79143'028'0922.

A bibliography of English-language scholarship on actors and actresses who were associated with the legitimate stage, had substantial careers, and have been the subject of scholarly study. Some foreigners important to the American theatrical tradition or who had substantial careers in the country before 1900 are included; most living persons are omitted. Archer excludes dissertations, theses, newspapers, fan magazines, and reviews of specific performances. The 3,263 entries are organized alphabetically in seven divisions: general reference works; bibliographies and indexes; general histories, surveys, and regional studies; books that discuss several performers; articles that treat several performers; biographies and autobiographies of performers not among those in the next division; 226 individual performers. The lists for individual performers conclude with cross-references to the general divisions. The brief (but adequate) descriptive annotations sometimes offer evaluative comments. Three indexes: persons; titles; subjects (including performers). Although selective, *American Actors and Actresses* offers the fullest single compilation of scholarship on significant American actors and actresses.

3520 Eddleman, Floyd Eugene, comp. *American Drama Criticism: Interpretations, 1890–1977*. 2nd ed. Hamden: Shoe String, 1979. 488 pp. *Supplement I*. 1984. 255 pp. *Supplement II*. Announced for 1989. Z1231.D7.P3 [PS332] 016.812'009.

A selective bibliography of studies published between 1890 and 1982 on plays by Americans (along with a few works by Canadian and Caribbean writers whose plays were performed in the United States). Eddleman excludes interviews, biographical studies, and author bibliographies. Under each playwright, plays are organized alphabetically by title, with each play followed by a list of studies and then reviews. *Supplement I* adds a section of general studies for each author. Entries for parts of books are keyed to a list at the back. Four indexes: scholars; adapted works and their authors; titles of plays; playwrights. Excluding author bibliographies (which would lead users to fuller lists of scholarship), plagued by numerous errors, and consisting largely of unverified entries copied from other sources,

American Drama Criticism is primarily useful for its identification of parts of books that discuss a play and as an incomplete compilation of entries from several of the standard bibliographies and indexes in section G.

Fuller, more accurate coverage of scholarship published between 1966 and 1980 on twentieth-century American drama is offered by Carpenter, *Modern Drama Scholarship* (2875); of post-1980 scholarship, by "Modern Drama Studies" (2870); and of scholarship before c. 1977 on plays before 1900, by Meserve, *American Drama to 1900* (4200).

An adequate annotated bibliography of studies of twentieth-century American drama is a major desideratum.

3525 Wilmeth, Don B. *The American Stage to World War I: A Guide to Information Sources*. Performing Arts Information Guide Series 4. Detroit: Gale, 1978. 269 pp. Z1231.D7.W55 [PN2221] 016.792'0973.

A highly selective annotated guide to English-language scholarship (through c. 1974) on the legitimate professional stage to c. 1915. Wilmeth excludes newspaper articles, popular magazines, works exclusively on playwrights or plays, dissertations, theses, and general histories of the theater. The 1,480 entries are listed alphabetically by author in 13 divisions: general reference works; bibliographies; indexes; general histories, surveys, and regional studies; state and local histories (listed by state); general sources on actors and acting on the American stage; individuals in American theater (listed by person); scenery, architecture, and lighting; foreign-language theater in America; paratheatrical forms; guides to theater collections; suspended periodicals and serials; current periodicals and serials. The brief descriptive annotations are frequently accompanied by evaluative comments, but many annotations inadequately describe content or establish the significance of a work. Three indexes: authors; titles; subjects. Wilmeth is occasionally useful only as a preliminary guide, since most topics are more fully covered in other sources, including Stratman, *American Theatrical Periodicals* (3530); Gohdes, *Literature and Theater of the States and Regions of the U.S.A.* (3570); Larson, *American Regional Theatre History* (3575); Meserve, *American Drama to 1900* (4200); and Archer, *American Actors and Actresses* (3515).

For a highly selective guide to reference works and scholarship (through April 1978) on popular theater and other live entertainments established before motion pictures, see Don B. Wilmeth, *American and English Popular Entertainment: A Guide to Information Sources*, Performing Arts Information Guide Series 7 (Detroit: Gale, 1980, 465 pp.). It emphasizes American forms in covering circus and wild West exhibitions, outdoor amusements, variety forms, optical and mechanical entertainments, musical theater and review, pantomime, music hall, and popular theater. There are, however, numerous inaccuracies and omissions.

See also

Gohdes, *Literature and Theater of the States and Regions of the U.S.A.* (3570).
Larson, *American Regional Theatre History to 1900* (3575).
Leary, *Articles on American Literature* (3295).
Stratman, *Bibliography of the American Theatre Excluding New York City* (3580).

Biographical Dictionaries

See

Wearing, *American and British Theatrical Biography* (1175).

Periodicals

Guides to Primary Works

3530 Stratman, Carl J., C.S.V. *American Theatrical Periodicals, 1798–1967: A Bibliographical Guide*. Durham: Duke UP, 1970. 133 pp. Z6935.S75 016.7902.

A preliminary bibliography of some 685 periodicals and newspapers published in the United States and devoted to the theater (defined broadly to encompass most stage entertainment, including folk performance, magic, opera, puppetry, and vaudeville but excluding television, cinema, and radio). Although the focus is American theater, Stratman includes periodicals that cover other countries as well. Organized chronologically by year of first publication, entries provide (when available) original title; editor(s); publication information; number of volumes or issues; date of first and last issues; title changes; frequency; miscellaneous notes on content, bibliographical matters, or source of information for works not examined; and locations, with exact holdings of incomplete runs. Additions are printed on pp. 86–87. A tabular overview of publication spans in the appendix offers a convenient means of identifying periodicals published during a period. Indexed by titles, subtitles, cities of publication, and sponsoring organizations. Although not comprehensive, it is the fullest single list of theatrical periodicals published in the United States.

POETRY

Most works in section L: Genres/Poetry are useful for research in American poetry.

Histories and Surveys

3533 Pearce, Roy Harvey. *The Continuity of American Poetry*. 3rd printing, with corrections and revisions. Princeton: Princeton UP, 1965. 442 pp. PS303.P4 811.009.

A critical survey, from the seventeenth century through Wallace Stevens, that emphasizes cultural history in chapters on periods, forms, and major writers. Indexed by persons, anonymous titles, and subjects. Pearce rightly sees this work as a map for the full history of American poetry that remains to be written. Reviews: Richard Beale Davis, *Criticism* 4 (1962): 379–81; E. H. Eby, *Modern Language Quarterly* 23 (1962): 397–98; Charles S. Holmes, *JEGP: Journal of English and Germanic*

Philology 62 (1963): 238–40; Reed Whittemore, *Yale Review* 51 (1962): 448–53.

A useful complement is Hyatt H. Waggoner, *American Poets from the Puritans to the Present*, rev. ed. (Baton Rouge: Louisiana State UP, 1984, 735 pp.), a critical survey of representative writers, from the Puritans through the 1970s, that argues for the centrality of Emerson to the development of American poetry.

Guides to Scholarship and Criticism

See

Brogan, *English Versification, 1570–1980* (1600).

Periodicals

3534 *American Poetry* (*AmerP*). 1983– . 3/yr. PS301.A546 811'.009.

Publishes articles, notes, documents, and reviews on the poetry of all periods but with a decided emphasis on the twentieth century.

PROSE

Most works in section L: Genres/Prose are useful for research in American prose.

Biography and Autobiography

Histories and Surveys

3535 Kagle, Steven E. *American Diary Literature, 1620–1799*. Twayne's United States Authors Series 342. Boston: Twayne, 1979. 203 pp. PS409.K3 818'.103.

———. *Early Nineteenth-Century American Diary Literature*. Twayne's United States Authors Series 495. 1986. 166 pp. (In progress is a volume on the remainder of the nineteenth century.) PS409.K33 818'.203.

A study of the diary tradition in America that attempts to establish a canon of works of literary merit and a methodology for their study. The volumes are organized by type of diary (e.g., spiritual journals, travel diaries, diaries of romance and courtship, war diaries, life diaries, transcendentalist journals), with each chapter offering an extended analysis of selective examples. Each volume concludes with a selected annotated list of diaries and scholarship. Indexed by persons and a few subjects. Although it is highly selective in coverage, Kagle's work is valuable for its methodology of the literary study of diaries. Review: (1620–1799) Richard C. Davis, *Canadian Review of American Studies* 12 (1981): 301–11.

Guides to Primary Works

3540 Arksey, Laura, Nancy Pries, and Marcia Reed. *American Diaries: An Annotated Bibliography of Published American Diaries and Journals.* 2 vols. Detroit: Gale, 1983–87. Z5305.U5.A74 [CT214] 016.92'0073.

Vol. 1: *Diaries Written from 1492 to 1844.* 1983. 311 pp.
Vol. 2: *Diaries Written from 1845 to 1980.* 1987. 501 pp.

A bibliography of approximately 6,000 English-language diaries or journals (including translations) written between 1492 and 1980 (and published as late as 1986) by American citizens anywhere in the world and by foreigners while resident in what is now the United States or treating events regarded as American. Along with traditional diaries and journals, *American Diaries* includes some expedition narratives and ships' logs that record more than weather or position. Except for some Canadian diaries, this work incorporates everything in William Matthews, *American Diaries: An Annotated Bibliography of American Diaries Written Prior to the Year 1861* (Berkeley: U of California P, 1945, 383 pp.). Organized by year of initial entry, then alphabetically by author, entries provide title, publication information, and annotation, which typically notes dates of coverage, place of birth or residence, major emphases, categories of persons discussed, occupations, historic events, modes of travel, religious affiliation, people, places, ships, customs, social milieu, and type of diary or journal. Annotations taken from Matthews frequently add comments on language and the quality of the work. Three indexes in each volume: names of writers and persons mentioned in annotations; subjects; places. The thorough annotations and detailed subject indexing make *American Diaries* an invaluable source for locating diaries on a topic or associated with a specific place, event, or group. It offers the fullest coverage of published American diaries, many of which appeared in limited editions or obscure periodicals. Review: (vol. 1) Steven E. Kagle, *Early American Literature* 20 (1985): 174–77.

A few additional published diaries are listed in Patricia Pate Havlice, *And So to Bed: A Bibliography of Diaries Published in English* (Metuchen: Scarecrow, 1987, 698 pp.); however, the best feature of this work is its combined index of diarists in Matthews, *American Diaries* (see above), *British Diaries* (1615), and *Canadian Diaries* (4765).

For a list of about 5,000 unpublished diaries and journals held in libraries and other institutions, see William Matthews, *American Diaries in Manuscript, 1580–1954: A Descriptive Bibliography* (Athens: U of Georgia P, 1974, 176 pp.). The entries are organized chronologically by initial date of entry (with a separate alphabetical list of undated works) and note location along with a brief description of content; unfortunately, works are indexed only by author. Many manuscript diaries are listed in *National Union Catalog of Manuscript Collections* (295) and in other works in sections F: Guides to Manuscripts and Archives and Q: American Literature (under Guides to Primary Works/Manuscripts).

3545 Kaplan, Louis, comp. *A Bibliography of American Autobiographies.* Madison: U of Wisconsin P, 1961. 372 pp. Z1224.K3 016.920073.

Briscoe, Mary Louise, ed. *American Autobiography, 1945–1980: A Bibliography.* Madison: U of Wisconsin P, 1982. 365 pp. Z5305.U5.A47 [CT220] 016.92'0073.

Together, these two volumes provide a bibliography of more than 11,000 separately published autobiographies (through 1980) of American citizens and foreigners resident for an appreciable time in the United States. Kaplan excludes Indian captivity, travel, and slave narratives, journals, diaries, collections of letters, manuscripts, genealogical works, fiction, and general reminiscences. Briscoe, however, broadens the scope to admit published memoirs, journals, diaries, and nonfiction works that include substantial autobiographical material. Briscoe also includes reprints of autobiographies published before 1945 as well as some works omitted in Kaplan. Kaplan cites the most convenient edition; Briscoe typically refers to the first edition. Entries, organized alphabetically by author, include birth date (and death date in Briscoe), title, publication information, pagination, location of one copy (only in Kaplan), and annotation. Kaplan's annotations rarely extend beyond occupation and principal areas of residence, but Briscoe's are much fuller, typically offering an evaluative comment and citing occupation, main focus, precise geographical locations, and important persons and events. In Briscoe, an asterisk denotes a female author. Both offer valuable subject indexes that cite occupations, places, historical events, names, and ethnic and religious groups; however, Briscoe's index is more precise, detailed, and effectively organized. Together, Kaplan and Briscoe list the majority of the separately published autobiographies of American citizens and long-time foreign residents.

Guides to Scholarship and Criticism

See

Leary, *Articles on American Literature* (3295).

Regional Literature

This section includes works limited to or emphasizing a region of the United States.

Most states and some cities have bibliographies of works by native or resident authors. For such bibliographies published through 1970, see vol. 1, pp. 164–68, in Tanselle, *Guide to the Study of United States Imprints* (5290); for later ones, see *Bibliographic Index* (145).

General

GUIDES TO SCHOLARSHIP AND CRITICISM

3570 Gohdes, Clarence. *Literature and Theater of the States and Regions of the U.S.A.: An Historical Bibliography*. Durham: Duke UP, 1967. 276 pp. Z1225.G63 016.8109.

A checklist of studies through 1964 on regional belles lettres and theater in the United States and its possessions. Gohdes excludes theses and dissertations as well as most newspaper articles, foreign scholarship, and studies of individual writers or theater personnel. Within divisions for states, possessions, and geographic regions, entries are listed alphabetically in sections for literature and theater. Two appendixes: Western literature (for studies dealing with this area, as distinct from the Midwest or West); general studies of regionalism. Because there are no indexes or cross-references and few duplicate entries, users must be certain to search the regional as well as state divisions for studies of a locale. Although superseded by Larson, *American Regional Theatre History* (3575) for studies of theater before 1900, and offering less extensive coverage than Stratman, *Bibliography of the American Theatre* (3580), Gohdes remains an indispensable compilation of general studies of regional literature. It must be supplemented by works in sections G: Serial Bibliographies, Indexes, and Abstracts and H: Guides to Dissertations and Theses.

See also

"Annual Review," *Journal of Modern Literature* (2780).
Leary, *Articles on American Literature* (3295).
Woodress, *Dissertations in American Literature, 1891–1966* (3320).

PERIODICALS

Guides to Scholarship and Criticism

See

Chielens, *Literary Journal in America to 1900* (4145).

GENRES

Drama

Guides to Scholarship and Criticism

3575 Larson, Carl F. W., comp. *American Regional Theatre History to 1900: A Bibliography*. Metuchen: Scarecrow, 1979. 187 pp. Z5781.L34 [PN2221] 016.792'0973.

A bibliography of books, articles, dissertations, theses, newspaper articles, and some manuscripts (through 1976) on regional theater outside New York City. Larson emphasizes English-language theater and studies of a specific geographical area; it excludes publications before 1900 unless their focus is historical and studies of actors, actresses, and theatrical personnel unless they emphasize a specific region. The 1,481 entries are organized chronologically by date of coverage in four divisions: states (with sections for cities and general studies), regions, miscellaneous works, and bibliographies. The chronology of numerous entries is imprecise because the compiler did not examine many items or relied on secondhand information. Three indexes: foreign-language theater; subjects (limited to persons); authors.

Although no locations are provided for manuscripts, subject indexing is inadequate, the chronological placement is not reliable, and scope is insufficiently defined (especially what "theatre history" encompasses), Larson does offer the best general coverage of regional theater for the period. It corrects several errors in Stratman, *Bibliography of the American Theatre* (3580) and Gohdes, *Literature and Theater of the States and Regions* (3570) but does not completely supersede either. Review: Don B. Wilmeth, *Nineteenth Century Theatre Research* 8 (1980): 109–10.

3580 Stratman, Carl J., C.S.V. *Bibliography of the American Theatre Excluding New York City*. Chicago: Loyola UP, 1965. 397 pp. Z1231.D7.S8 016.7920973.

A bibliography of studies through c. 1964 on the stage and theater, encompassing a wide range of theatrical activity and types of entertainment such as ballet, minstrel shows, opera, and puppetry, and extending to high school and university theater. Stratman excludes general theater and stage histories, newspaper articles, manuscripts, local or state histories, and critical studies of plays. The 3,856 entries are organized by state or region, then by city, then by publication date. Each state section concludes with a list of general works. Except for theses and dissertations, each work is located in at least one library (an especially helpful feature in the case of ephemeral publications); only periodical articles are accompanied by brief descriptive annotations. Indexed by persons and subjects. Although now dated and superseded in part by Larson, *American Regional Theatre History* (3575), Stratman remains a valuable guide to studies of the theatrical activity of a city or region and offers fuller coverage than Gohdes, *Literature and Theater of the States and Regions* (3570).

Eastern Literature

Most works in section Q: American Literature/Early American Literature, and many in American Literature/Nineteenth-Century Literature emphasize Eastern writers.

HISTORIES AND SURVEYS

3583 Westbrook, Perry D. *A Literary History of New England*. Bethlehem: Lehigh UP; London: Associated U Presses, 1988. 362 pp. PS243.W42 810'.9'974.

A literary history devoted to belles lettres and other writings by natives or residents and treating "some subject, place, or persons—imaginary or not—connected with New England and its culture." The chapters on major authors, groups, movements, and genres cover 1620 to 1950, with some recent writers mentioned in an epilogue. Concludes with a highly selective bibliography. Indexed by persons and subjects. *Literary History of New England* offers a balanced overview of literature associated with the region.

PERIODICALS

3585 *American Transcendental Quarterly: A Journal of New England Writers* (*ATQ*). 1969– . Quarterly. PS243.A55 810.

Publishes articles on nineteenth-century New England writers and literary culture. Cumulative indexes: vols. 37–52, Steven R. McKenna, comp., in 54 (1982, 56 pp.); vols. 53–57, McKenna, comp., in 57 (1985): 61–79.

3590 *The New England Quarterly: A Historical Review of New England Life and Letters* (*NEQ*). 1928– . Quarterly. F1.N62 974.005.

Publishes articles, documents, review essays, and reviews on the literature, history, and culture of New England. Vols. 1–39 (1928–66) include "A Bibliography of New England [1927–65]," a highly selective classified list of periodical articles whose coverage of historical society journals sometimes makes the literature section a useful supplement to the standard bibliographies and indexes in section G. Most entries are incorporated in Leary, *Articles on American Literature* (3295). Annual index; cumulative index: vols. 1–10, Waldo Palmer, comp., *General Index to Volumes I to X, 1928–1937* (Boston: New England Quarterly, 1941, 224 pp.).

See also

ESQ: A Journal of the American Renaissance (4165).

Midwestern Literature

GUIDES TO SCHOLARSHIP AND CRITICISM

Bibliographies on a variety of midwestern writers and subjects appear in issues of *Great Lakes Review* 1–10 (1974–84); with the title change to *Michigan Historical Review* (12 [1986]), the journal narrowed its focus to that state.

Serial Bibliographies

3595 "Annual Bibliography of Midwestern Literature [1973–]." *Midamerica* (entry 3605) 2 (1975)– .

A list of primary and secondary publications relating to authors born or resident in the Midwest as well as of fiction with a midwestern setting. General studies are listed by scholar, and primary works and studies about a writer are listed by literary author in a single alphabetical list. Custom searches of the computerized files can be performed by the compilers. The bibliography is unnecessarily difficult to scan because it is printed from a much-reduced uppercase printout. Although not comprehensive (especially for major authors), the "Annual Bibliography" does assimilate a considerable amount of the year's work on midwestern literature and serves as a useful complement to the standard bibliographies and indexes in section G.

See also

MLAIB (335): See the heading "Midwestern American Literature" in the subject index to post-1980 volumes.

Other Bibliographies

3600 Nemanic, Gerald, gen. ed. *A Bibliographical Guide to Midwestern Literature*. Iowa City: U of Iowa P, 1981. 380 pp. Z1251.W5.B52 [PS273] 016.81'08'0977.

A selective bibliography of studies of the literature and culture of the midwestern states (Illinois, Indiana, Iowa, Michigan, Minnesota, Missouri, Ohio, Wisconsin, and the eastern part of Kansas, Nebraska, and the Dakotas) and of about 150 authors whose works reflect the cultural life of the region. Entries are organized in two divisions: subjects and individual authors. The first grouping consists of extensively classified subdivisions listing primarily books on literature and language, history and society, folklore, personal narratives, architecture and graphics, Chicago, black literature, Indians, and literary periodicals. Each subdivision is preceded by a helpful evaluative overview of scholarship; most entries are succinctly and clearly annotated. Each author bibliography consists of a headnote that briefly comments on the writer's stature, notes important studies, suggests topics for research, and identifies major manuscript collections; a chronological list of major primary works; and a selective, unannotated list of scholarship. Two appendixes: brief biographical notes on an additional 101 writers; a list of 101 fictional narratives on the Midwest by writers not associated with the region. Individual bibliographies are uneven in quality; the lack of cross-references in the first part and the failure to provide a subject index substantially reduce usability; articles are generally excluded from the subject lists; and major writers are more adequately treated in separate author bibliographies; even so, the usually judicious selection and evaluative comments in the headnotes make Nemanic the first source to consult in the study of midwestern literature generally and minor writers associated with the region. Reviews: Craig S. Abbott, *Analytical and Enumerative Bibliography* 6 (1982): 135–37; Michael J. Bresnahan, *Resources for American Literary Study* 12 (1982): 111–16.

PERIODICALS

3605 *Midamerica: The Yearbook of the Society for the Study of Midwestern Literature* (*Midamerica*). 1974– . Annual. PS273.M53.

Publishes articles on midwestern literature and the "Annual Bibliography of Midwestern Literature" (3595).

Southern Literature

HISTORIES AND SURVEYS

3615 *The History of Southern Literature.* Gen. ed. Louis D. Rubin, Jr. Baton Rouge: Louisiana State UP, 1985. 626 pp. PS261.H53 810'.9'975.

A collection of essays, on authors, movements, genres, and topics, that makes a concerted effort to include African American literature and emphasizes twentieth-century writers. Unfortunately the essays exclude references to scholarship, a deficiency not compensated for by M. Thomas Inge's brief appendix surveying anthologies, reference sources, surveys, bibliographies, literary histories, and general critical studies (pp. 589–99). The quality of the essays, breadth of coverage, and currency will likely make this work the standard literary history for the region, although Jay B. Hubbell's monumental *The South in American Literature, 1607–1900* (Durham: Duke UP, 1954, 987 pp.) remains valuable for its encyclopedic treatment of the literature before 1865. Review: Melvin J. Friedman, *American Literature* 58 (1986): 427–30.

GUIDES TO SCHOLARSHIP AND CRITICISM

Surveys of Research

See

Harbert, *Fifteen American Authors before 1900*, 1971 edition (3280a).

Serial Bibliographies

3620 "A Checklist of Scholarship on Southern Literature for [1968–]." *Mississippi Quarterly* (entry 3640) 22 (1969)– .

An annual annotated bibliography of books and articles, with entries organized in five divisions: colonial (1607 to 1800), antebellum (1800 to 1865), postbellum (1865 to 1920), contemporary (1920 to the present), and general. The chronological divisions have sections for individual authors and general studies; the general division lists works alphabetically by scholar. Entries are accompanied by very brief descriptive annotations. Two indexes: literary authors without a classified section; scholars. The first eight bibliographies are cumulated and supplemented in Jerry T. Williams, ed., *Southern Literature, 1968–1975: A Checklist of Scholarship*, Reference Publication in Literature (Boston: Hall, 1978, 271 pp.). The bibliographies through 1988 are being revised and expanded in Robert L. Phillips, Jr., and Jerry T. Williams, eds., *Twenty Years of Scholarship in Southern Literature: A Bibliographical Guide* (in progress). Although it is not comprehensive, the "Checklist" is a useful continuation of Rubin, *Bibliographical Guide to the Study of Southern Literature* (3625) and supplement to the standard serial bibliographies and indexes in section G.

See also

MLAIB (335): See the heading "Southern American Literature" and related terms in the subject index to post-1980 volumes.

Other Bibliographies

3625 Rubin, Louis D., Jr., ed. *A Bibliographical Guide to the Study of Southern Literature*. Southern Literary Studies. Baton Rouge: Louisiana State UP, 1969. 351 pp. Z1225.R8 016.81.

A collection of selective bibliographies compiled by specialists on southern literature and confined largely to English-language scholarship published through the late 1960s. The bibliographies are organized in two divisions: 23 topics (including general works, periods, themes, local color, periodicals, southern speech, drama, folklore, manuscript collections, and bibliographies) and 135 individual authors. An appendix covers 68 writers of the Colonial South. Each bibliography is in two parts: an evaluative summary of scholarship (ranging from a few lines to several pages and sometimes commenting on the stature of the writer) and a selective list of studies (variously classified in the topics division). The appendix has no summaries. An asterisk denotes works including a useful bibliography. The lack of an index significantly reduces usability, there is considerable overlapping among the bibliographies, and the coverage (originally too selective for major writers) is now dated, but this remains a useful guide to the best scholarship before c. 1968 on southern literature generally and on minor writers. Review: Hensley C. Woodbridge, *Papers of the Bibliographical Society of America* 63 (1969): 332–36.

Coverage must be supplemented with "Checklist of Scholarship on Southern Literature" (3620), *American Literary Scholarship* (3265), and Jack D. Wages, *Seventy-Four Writers of the Colonial South*, Reference Publication in Literature (Boston: Hall, 1979, 252 pp.). The last work, however, is marred by omissions, frequently uninformative annotations, and cryptic abbreviations of authors' names in the index.

Dissertations and Theses

3630 Emerson, O. B., and Marion C. Michael, comps. and eds. *Southern Literary Culture: A Bibliography of Masters' and Doctors' Theses*. Rev. and enl. ed. University: U of Alabama P, 1979. 400 pp. Z1251.S7.C3 [PS261] 016.810'9'975.

Wages, Jack D., and William L. Andrews, comps. "Southern Literary Culture: 1969–1975." *Mississippi Quarterly* (entry 3640) 32 (1978–79): 13–214.

The revised edition lists about 8,000 American and foreign theses and dissertations, accepted through winter 1969, on southern literature and writers (i.e., those who "flourished" in the South). Entries are listed alphabetically by thesis or dissertation author in three classified divisions: individual writers; cultural, historical, and social background (with sections for general studies, folklore, education, theater, libraries and lyceums, onomastics, language, and southern culture through others' eyes); and general literary studies (with sections for studies that include the South, studies restricted to southern literature, bibliographies and checklists, comparative studies, newspapers and periodicals, and original works written at southern universities). Each entry provides author, title, institution, year, degree, and department; occasionally a note identifies authors or works discussed. Since a thesis or dissertation is listed only once, the lack of cross-references and index seriously mars the usability of the work. Although not comprehensive—especially in its coverage of foreign theses and dissertations on Twain—*Southern Literary Culture* is valuable for its extensive coverage, especially of studies written in a variety of departments other than English.

The supplement is more closely restricted to literary studies and omits foreign theses and dissertations. Its approximately 3,000 entries are listed alphabetically by author in 13 divisions: individual authors, multiple author studies, general culture, education, folklore, history, journalism, libraries, linguistics, music, politics, religion, and speech and theater. Only the first division is classified and includes cross-references for multiple-author studies. Except for the omission of department, entries include the same information as in the revised edition. Indexed by dissertation or thesis writers. Although lacking the breadth of coverage of its predecessor, Wages and Andrews's work remains a useful compilation but must be supplemented by section H: Guides to Dissertations and Theses.

LANGUAGE

Guides to Scholarship

3635 McMillan, James B. *Annotated Bibliography of Southern American English*. Coral Gables: U of Miami P, 1971. 173 pp. Z1234.D5.M32 016.427'9'75.

A bibliography of studies (through 1969) of English used south of the Mason-Dixon Line and Ohio River, and west to Arkansas and East Texas. McMillan includes theses, dissertations, and scholarly reviews of books, but excludes popular journalism, general works on American English, and studies of folklore and literature unless of interest to students of dialect. Entries are listed alphabetically by author in 10 divisions: general studies; historical studies; lexicon; phonology and phonetics; morphology and syntax; place names; personal and miscellaneous names; figurative language, exaggerations, and word play; literary dialect; and serial bibliographies. Only about half of the works are annotated, and many too briefly to convey an adequate sense of content; entries for books cite reviews. Two indexes: scholars; reviewers. Although there are cross-references, the lack of a subject index seriously impedes access to what is otherwise a useful compilation, especially for those interested in scholarship on the use of southern dialects in literary works.

See also

Emerson, *Southern Literary Culture* (3630).
Rubin, *Bibliographical Guide to the Study of Southern Literature* (3625).

PERIODICALS

3640 *Mississippi Quarterly: The Journal of Southern Culture* (*MissQ*). 1948– Quarterly. AS30.M58 051.

Publishes articles, notes, surveys of research, bibliographies, special issues, reviews, and review essays on the humanities and social sciences in the South (with a decided emphasis on literature). Includes two annual bibliographies: "Faulkner [1977–]: A Survey of Research and Criticism" (31 [1978]–) and "A Checklist of Scholarship on Southern Literature for [1968–]" (3620). Annual index.

3645 *The Southern Literary Journal* (*SLJ*). 1968– . 2/yr. PS261.S527 810.9'975.

Publishes essays and reviews on all aspects of southern literature. Cumulative indexes: vols. 1–12, in 12.2 (1980): n.pag.; vols. 13–17, in 17.2 (1985): n.pag.; vols. 18–22, scheduled for 22.2 (1990).

3650 *The Southern Review* (*SoR*). 1935–42, 1965– . Quarterly. AP2.S8555 051.

Emphasizes southern culture and history in articles, reviews, interviews, fiction, poetry, and special issues (including a recurring issue on "Writing in the South"). Annual index. For the history of the journal, see Lewis P. Simpson, "The *Southern Review* and a Post-Southern American Letters" (pp. 79–99), in Anderson, *Little Magazine in America* (770a).

See also

Sewanee Review (3450).

Western Literature

HISTORIES AND SURVEYS

3660 *A Literary History of the American West.* Ed. in chief J. Golden Taylor. Fort Worth: Texas Christian UP, 1987. 1,353 pp. PS271.L58 810'.9'978.

A collaborative critical history whose 75 chapters employ a variety of approaches to encompass major writers, regions, historical periods, genres, types of characters, ethnic and non-English literatures, folklore, nature writing, and movies, television, and radio. Most chapters conclude with a selective bibliography (several of which are evaluatively annotated). The volume also includes chronologies of historical (1507–1980) and literary (1510–1984) events; an appendix that surveys the development of criticism of western literature; and an incomplete and sometimes inaccurate list of major reference sources. Indexed by persons and subjects. Although uneven in execution, the impressive scope and quality of the contributors make this collection the essential starting point for research on western literature.

GUIDES TO SCHOLARSHIP AND CRITICISM

Serial Bibliographies

3665 "Annual Bibliography of Studies in Western American Literature [1965–]." *Western American Literature* (entry 3675) 1 (1966)– .

An alphabetical subject list of books and articles on western literature. More refined subject headings and cross-references would benefit users. Even so, the "Annual Bibliography" is a helpful compilation of the year's work on western writers, a continuation of Etulain, *Bibliographical Guide* (3670), and an essential complement to the bibliographies and indexes in section G. Dissertations and theses are listed in the annual "Research in Western American Literature" (which formerly included work in progress).

See also

MLAIB (335): See the heading "Western American Literature" in the subject index to post-1980 volumes.

Other Bibliographies

3670 Etulain, Richard W. *A Bibliographical Guide to the Study of Western American Literature.* Lincoln: U of Nebraska P, 1982. 317 pp. Z1251.W5.E8 [PS271] 016.81'09'978.

A selective bibliography of studies on trans-Mississippi western literature and authors (including a few major nonfiction writers), as well as outsiders who have written on the area or influenced its literature. It is limited to important scholarship (largely in English through 1981) and emphasizes recent studies. Coverage is especially selective for major authors such as Cooper, Cather, Clemens, and Steinbeck. The 5,030 entries are listed alphabetically in five divisions: bibliographies, anthologies, general works (unhelpfully divided into books, dissertations, theses, and articles), special topics (local color and regionalism, dime novels and the western, film, Indian literature and Indians in western literature, Mexican American literature and Chicanos in western literature, the Beats, and Canadian western literature), and individual authors. A very few entries are briefly annotated. Indexed by scholars. The lack of cross-references and subject indexing means that researchers looking for studies on a writer must skim the general works and special topics divisions. Although several authors are more fully covered in separate author bibliographies, this remains the standard guide to research in western literature. Reviews: Sanford E. Marovitz, *Bulletin of Bibliography* 41 (1984): 42–45; Stephen Tatum, *Western American Literature* 19 (1984): 48–49.

Coverage must be supplemented with Fred Erisman and Richard W. Etulain, eds., *Fifty Western Writers: A Bio-Bibliographical Sourcebook* (Westport: Greenwood, 1982, 562 pp.), "Annual Bibliography of Studies in Western American Literature" (3665), and the serial bibliographies and indexes in section G. Occasionally useful for writers from Arizona, New Mexico, Oklahoma, and Texas is John Q. Anderson, Edwin W. Gaston, Jr., and James W. Lee, eds., *Southwestern American Literature: A Bibliography* (Chicago: Swallow, 1980, 445 pp.). Although this lists books published before c. 1974 by authors, its coverage of scholarship on general topics, genres, and individuals is too uneven and dated (rarely extending beyond 1970) to be of much value except for the minor figures not included in Etulain.

PERIODICALS

3675 *Western American Literature* (*WAL*). 1966– . Quarterly. PS271.W46 810.9'978.

Publishes articles, occasional bibliographies, notes, interviews, essay reviews, and reviews (of both primary and secondary works) relating to western literature. For the "Annual Bibliography of Studies in Western American Literature" and "Research in Western American Literature" see entry 3665. Annual index.

Ethnic and Minority Literatures

Many works in sections G: Serial Bibliographies, Indexes, and Abstracts; H: Guides to Dissertations and Theses; L: Genres; and, especially, Q: American Literature/General are important for research in minority and ethnic literatures of the United States.

General

HISTORIES AND SURVEYS

3690 Di Pietro, Robert J., and Edward Ifkovic, eds. *Ethnic Perspectives in American Literature: Selected Essays on the European Contribution*. New York: MLA, 1983. 333 pp. PN843.E8 810'.9.

Surveys of Franco-American New England writers and the literatures of Americans of German, Greek, Hungarian, Italian, Jewish, Polish, Portuguese, Romanian, Russian, Scandinavian, and South Slavic ancestry. Organized chronologically, thematically, or by genre, the essays typically offer a basic historical overview of the development of a literature and of its major authors; some essays briefly comment on important scholarship and suggest topics for research. Indexed by persons and titles. Although the surveys vary in breadth and quality, the collection overall serves as a handy introduction to some ethnic literatures of the United States.

3695 Ruoff, A. LaVonne Brown, and Jerry Ward, eds. *Redefining American Literary History*. New York: MLA. In progress.

A collection of essays that seeks to redefine American literary history by "expanding the canon, forging new critical perspectives, and scrutinizing underlying cultural and ideological assumptions" through a focus on African American, American Indian, Asian American, Chicano, and Puerto Rican literature. The essays are organized in five divisions: discussions of "the relationship between oral and written literatures of minorities and white women and the traditional canon of

American literature"; the oral dimensions of American literature; new critical perspectives; the combination of traditional American literary conventions with ethnic values and traditions; a rethinking of the canon of American literature. Following the essays are selected bibliographies—with sections for bibliographies, anthologies, general criticism, and major authors—of multiethnic, African American, American Indian, Asian American, Chicano, and Puerto Rican literatures. Concluding the work is a list of selected presses and journals. This work promises to be an important contribution to the continuing evaluation of the canon of the literature of the United States.

See also

Columbia Literary History of the United States (3195).
Literary History of the American West (3660).
New Cambridge History of American Literature (3205).

GUIDES TO SCHOLARSHIP AND CRITICISM

3700 *Minorities in America: The Annual Bibliography [1976–]*. University Park: Pennsylvania State UP, 1985– . Annual. Z1361.E4.M57 [E184.A1] 016.973'04.

Miller, Wayne Charles. *A Comprehensive Bibliography for the Study of American Minorities*. 2 vols. New York: New York UP, 1976. Z1361.E4.M529 [E184.A1] 016.973'04.

A bibliography of English-language materials on minority groups in America. The *Comprehensive Bibliography* covers studies through c. 1973; the *Annual Bibliography* begins with 1976. Entries are organized by area of origin (Africa and Middle East, Europe, Eastern Europe and Balkans, Asia, Puerto Rico and Cuba, and America [including Indians and Mexican Americans]), then by minority group, and then by subject. Most groups include sections for language, general literary criticism, fiction, poetry, drama, folklore, and some individual writers. Entries in the annual bibliographies are accompanied by descriptive annotations; although only a few are annotated in the *Comprehensive Bibliography*, each minority group is preceded by an introduction that identifies important studies and reference works. Two indexes: authors; titles. Although the *Comprehensive Bibliography* is hardly comprehensive and the *Annual Bibliography* appears several years after the studies covered, these two works offer the fullest single record of scholarship on minority groups in the United States.

See also

"Annual Review," *Journal of Modern Literature* (2780).
Inge, *Handbook of American Popular Culture* (6295).
Leary, *Articles on American Literature* (3295).
Salzman, *American Studies: An Annotated Bibliography* (3335).

PERIODICALS

3705 *MELUS: Journal of the Society for the Study of the Multi-Ethnic Literature of the United States* (*MELUS*). 1974– . Quarterly. PN843.M18 808.8'9973.

Publishes articles, interviews, reviews, and special issues on ethnic literature and ethnicity in music, film, and television. Annual index.

African American Literature

Many works in the other sections on American literature are important to research in African American literature.

Because the Library of Congress subject headings—used in many card catalogs, data bases, and printed bibliographies—were until recently inadequate for analyzing African American resources, scholars doing extensive subject searching will find Doris H. Clack, *Black Literature Resources: Analysis and Organization*, Books in Library and Information Science 16 (New York: Dekker, 1975, 207 pp.), a valuable guide to Library of Congress subject headings and classification numbers in this field.

GUIDES TO REFERENCE WORKS

3710 Davis, Nathaniel, comp. and ed. *Afro-American Reference: An Annotated Bibliography of Selected Sources*. Bibliographies and Indexes in Afro-American and African Studies 9. Westport: Greenwood, 1985. 288 pp. Z1361.N39.D37 [E185] 016.973'0496.

An annotated guide to 642 reference sources (some published as recently as 1985) that are important to research in all aspects of African American life. Entries are listed alphabetically in 17 classified divisions: general reference works; journal abstracts, bibliographies, and guides; newspapers indexes, bibliographies, and guides; genealogy; history; slavery (with a section on slave narratives); social sciences (including linguistics); humanities; literature; mass media; education and multimedia; family and related studies; psychology; medicine; sports; armed forces; and Latin America and the Caribbean. An appendix incongruously lists works on African Americans in Los Angeles and the rest of California. The descriptive annotations typically describe scope, content, and organization. Because of some significant omissions, inclusion of several superseded works, and errors of fact and judgment in annotations, this work cannot always be trusted; yet it represents the single best guide to reference sources on African American topics.

For an exacting (but now dated) survey of reference sources devoted to African American literature and the inadequate treatment of African American writers in some standard reference works in American literature, see Richard C. Tobias, "A Matter of Difference: An Interim Guide to the Study of Black American Writing," *Literary Research Newsletter* 1 (1976): 129–46. Still valuable because of its broad topical coverage of scholarship through 1970 on African American culture and history is James M. McPherson et al., *Blacks in America: Bibliographical Essays* (Garden City: Doubleday, 1971, 430 pp.).

See also

Prucha, *Handbook for Research in American History* (3185).

HISTORIES AND SURVEYS

See

History of Southern Literature (3615).

BIBLIOGRAPHIES OF BIBLIOGRAPHIES

3715 Newman, Richard, comp. *Black Access: A Bibliography of Afro-American Bibliographies*. Westport: Greenwood, 1984. 249 pp. Z1361.N39.N578 [E185] 016.016973'0496073.

A bibliography of bibliographies through c. 1982 on all aspects of African American history, culture, and life in the United States and Canada. The approximately 3,000 works include books, pamphlets, articles, chapters in books, exhibition catalogs, calendars and guides to manuscripts, works on library collections and book collecting, and discographies; they exclude book dealers' catalogs, bibliographies appended to monographs, and works on the Civil War, the Caribbean, Latin America, and Africa. Organized in a single alphabetical list by author or title of anonymous work, entries generally provide basic publication information but no annotations. Several citations seem to be taken unverified from other sources. In the introduction, Dorothy Parker reflects on her development of the Afro-American collection at Howard University. Two indexes: chronological (by date of coverage); subjects. Although users would be better served by a classified organization—a deficiency not remedied by the subject index, which is insufficiently thorough and precise—its international scope and inclusion of numerous little known works make *Black Access* the best source for identifying bibliographies on all African American topics. For recent bibliographies, see *Bibliographic Index* (145).

GUIDES TO PRIMARY WORKS

3720 *Dictionary Catalog of the Schomburg Collection of Negro Literature and History*. 9 vols. Boston: Hall, 1962. *First Supplement*. 2 vols. 1967. *Second Supplement*. 4 vols. 1972. *Supplement 1974*. 1976. 580 pp. Continued by *Bibliographic Guide to Black Studies [1975–]*. 1976– . Annual. Z881.N592.S35.

A reproduction of the card catalog of the most important and extensive collection of material by and about people of African descent. Along with printed material, the collection includes art objects, recordings, sheet music, photographs, and manuscripts. Manuscripts are listed only in the supplements; photographs and vertical file materials are excluded in all volumes. Since the supplements and *Bibliographic Guide to Black Studies* record material newly acquired—not just recently published—users must search the supplements and the *Bibliographic Guide* as well as the original *Catalog*. An indispensable, but frequently overlooked, source for identifying authors and titles, the *Dictionary Catalog* is especially valuable for the detailed subject access it offers to works relating to all aspects of African American culture.

Other published catalogs of important collections include the following:

Afro-Americana, 1553–1906: Author Catalog of the Library Company of Philadelphia and the Historical Society of Pennsylvania. Boston: Hall, 1973. 714 pp.

Dictionary Catalog of the Arthur B. Spingarn Collection of Negro Authors, Howard University Library, Washington, DC. 2 vols. Boston: Hall, 1970.

Dictionary Catalog of the George Foster Peabody Collection of Negro Literature and History, Collis P. Huntington Memorial Library, Hampton Institute, Hampton, Virginia. 2 vols. Westport: Greenwood, 1972.

Dictionary Catalog of the Jesse E. Moorland Collection of Negro Life and History, Howard University Library, Washington, D.C. 9 vols. Boston: Hall, 1970. *First Supplement*. 3 vols. 1976.

Dictionary Catalog of the Negro Collection of the Fisk University Library, Nashville, Tennessee. 6 vols. Boston: Hall, 1974.

Dictionary Catalog of the Vivian G. Harsh Collection of Afro-American History and Literature, the Chicago Public Library. 4 vols. Boston: Hall, 1978.

The holdings of 65 southern libraries are the basis for Geraldine O. Matthews, comp., *Black American Writers, 1773–1949: A Bibliography and Union List* (Boston: Hall, 1975, 221 pp.). Although entries are frequently incomplete and only about 60% cite locations, Matthews is occasionally useful for tracking down an elusive work.

To identify other catalogs and collections, see section E: Libraries and Library Catalogs/Library Catalogs.

3725 Kallenbach, Jessamine S., comp. *Index to Black American Literary Anthologies*. Boston: Hall, 1979. 219 pp. Z1229.N39.K34 [PS153.N5] 016.8108'0896.

An author list of African American poetry, fiction, essays, and plays in some 140 literary anthologies designed for adults, primarily by African American authors, and published through c. 1975. Under each author, works are organized by genre, then alphabetically by titles. Indexed by titles. The *Index* is frequently useful for locating texts, although it is limited in scope.

Chapman, *Index to Poetry by Black American Women* (3840) and *Index to Black Poetry* (3840a) index, by subject, poems in collections.

3730 Schatz, Walter, ed. *Directory of Afro-American Resources*. New York: Bowker, 1970. 485 pp. Z1361.N39.R3 917.3'06'96073.

A guide to about 5,365 collections of books, manuscripts, documents, and other materials held by 2,108 organizations, libraries, institutions, and private and government agencies. Entries are organized alphabetically by state, then city, then institution. Entries typically include organization or institution, address and telephone, name of contact person (now outdated), services provided for researchers, purpose of organization, publications (especially guides and indexes to collections), description of individual collections (identifying subject, size, inclusive dates, scope, and content), and restrictions on use. Since entries are based on responses to questionnaires and on printed sources, they vary in accuracy and sophistication; the most complete are taken from *National Union Catalog of Manuscript Collections* (295) through 1968 or submitted by libraries, and the skimpiest are from local organizations and agencies. Two indexes: persons, subjects, institutions, and places; supervisors and administrators of organizations and collections. Although the *Directory* is now dated and omits several important institutions and organizations, its focus and extensive coverage make it still useful for identifying subject collections and locating manuscripts. The work must, however, be supplemented by *Directory of Archives and Manuscript Repositories in the United States* (280), *National Union Catalog of Manuscript Collections* (295), and works in section E: Libraries and Library Catalogs/Library Catalogs.

GUIDES TO SCHOLARSHIP AND CRITICISM

Surveys of Research

3735 Inge, M. Thomas, Maurice Duke, and Jackson R. Bryer, eds. *Black American Writers: Bibliographical Essays.* 2 vols. New York: St. Martin's, 1978. PS153.N5.B55 016.810'9'896073.

Selective surveys of research through mid-1970, with chapters devoted to major eighteenth-century writers, slave narratives, nineteenth-century polemicists, early modern authors, the Harlem Renaissance, Hughes, Wright, Ellison, Baldwin, and Baraka. The chapters are variously organized, but each has sections for bibliographies, editions, manuscripts and letters, biographical studies, and criticism; a few offer suggestions for further research. Indexed by persons in each volume. Although the essays vary in selectiveness and rigor of evaluation, most provide authoritative assessments of scholarship before mid-1970. What is needed is a revised edition that would evaluate recent scholarship and devote chapters to general reference works and studies. Review: R. Baxter Miller, *Black American Literature Forum* 13 (1979): 119–20.

See also

American Literary Scholarship (3265): Chapter on black literature.

Serial Bibliographies

3740 *Index to Periodical Articles by and about Blacks: [1950–].* Boston: Hall, 1950– . Annual, with cumulations for 1950–59 and 1960–70. Former titles: *Index to Periodical Articles by and about Negroes* (1966–72); *Index to Selected Periodicals* (1954–65); *Index to Selected Negro Periodicals* (1950–54). AI3.O4 974'.0496073.

An author and subject index to the contents of general and scholarly periodicals (currently 37) devoted to African American topics. Literary works are listed by title under genre headings; reviews are indexed by author, reviewer, and title (the last only under headings such as "Book Reviews" and "Drama Reviews"). Because of its highly selective coverage and the three-year lag between date of coverage and publication, the work is primarily useful for its indexing of a few periodicals excluded from the serial bibliographies and indexes in section G. For earlier publications, some coverage is offered by *A Guide to Negro Periodical Literature*, 4 vols. (Winston-Salem: n.p., 1941–46).

3745 "Studies in Afro-American Literature: An Annual Annotated Bibliography [1983–]." *Callaloo* (entry 3790) 7 (1984)– .

A selective, annotated bibliography of English-language scholarship (including dissertations). Entries are organized alphabetically by author in eight divisions: bibliographies, interviews, general studies, fiction, poetry, drama, autobiographies and slave narratives, and individual authors. The accompanying descriptive annotations are thorough. Two indexes: authors not listed separately in the individual authors section; scholars. Although it lacks an adequate statement of scope and explanation of criteria governing selection, it is the only current serial bibliography devoted to African American literature.

In vol. 9 (1986), *Callaloo* established two related bibliographies on black writers: "Studies in African Literatures and Oratures: An Annual Annotated Bibliography [1985–]" and "Studies in Caribbean and South American Literature: An Annual Annotated Bibliography [1985–]."

See also

Secs. G: Serial Bibliographies, Indexes, and Abstracts and H: Guides to Dissertations and Theses.

"Annual Bibliography of Afro-American Literature," *CLA Journal* (3795).

MLAIB (335): American Literature division through the volume for 1969; Afro-American heading in American Literature sections in the volumes for 1970–80; in later volumes, researchers must consult the headings beginning "Afro-American" in the subject index.

Other Bibliographies

3750 Perry, Margaret. *The Harlem Renaissance: An Annotated Bibliography and Commentary*. Garland Reference Library of the Humanities 278: Critical Studies on Black Life and Culture 2. New York: Garland, 1982. 272 pp. Z5956.A47.P47 [NX511.N4] 016.81'09'97471.

A bibliography of works (published through 1980) by and about writers associated with the Harlem Renaissance. Perry includes authors who identified themselves with the movement as well as those who lived during the 1920s through early 1930s, and covers published works as well as dissertations, theses, manuscripts, and films in English or French. The 913 entries are organized alphabetically by author in eight divisions: bibliographies and reference works (including author bibliographies), histories of African American literature that include significant discussion of the Harlem Renaissance, general studies (with sections for works on the period, and for reviews of books and plays), 19 major authors (with selected primary works listed by genre, followed by criticism), miscellaneous materials (a hodgepodge), anthologies, library and special collections (organized by institution, with descriptions of individual collections), and an unannotated list of theses and dissertations. The reasonably full annotations are largely descriptive, although some include evaluative comments. Two indexes: persons (regrettably not indexing references to writers in divisions other than that for individual authors); titles of works cited. Poor and inconsistent organization, incomplete cross-references, and inadequate indexing mean that users searching for single-author studies must skim all entries. These shortcomings coupled with the lack of clarity about criteria governing the selection of both primary and secondary works, and the exclusion of most foreign scholarship, render *Harlem Renaissance* much less useful and accessible than it should be. Review: Hensley C. Woodbridge, *American Notes and Queries* 20 (1982): 159–60.

3755 Turner, Darwin T., comp. *Afro-American Writers*. Goldentree Bibliographies in Language and Literature. New York: Appleton, 1970. 117 pp. Z1361.N39.T78 016.8108'091'7496.

A selective bibliography of primary and secondary works (chiefly in English and published through 1969) that are important to the study of African American literature. Theses, dissertations, book reviews, and general literary histories are excluded. Entries are organized in four classified divisions: aids to research (with sections for bibliographies, guides to library collections, other reference works, and periodicals); background studies (with highly selective lists of autobiographies and collections of essays; slave narratives; studies of historical, social, and intellectual backgrounds; and works on art, journalism, music, and theater); literary history and criticism (with sections for anthologies, general studies, drama, fiction, poetry, and folklore); and individual writers who have been the subject of critical or popular attention, or are otherwise important (with lists of primary works, bibliographies, and biographical studies and criticism for most authors). Additional entries appear in a supplement on pp. 105–17. Studies of African Americans as characters appear in an appendix. Important works are marked with an asterisk. Indexed by persons. Although now dated, *Afro-American Writers* remains the best selective guide to scholarship before 1970.

Theressa Gunnels Rush, Carol Fairbanks Myers, and Esther Spring Arata, *Black American Writers Past and Present: A Biographical and Bibliographical Dictionary*, 2 vols. (Metuchen: Scarecrow, 1975) offers a fuller—but much less accurate—list of works by and about some 2,000 writers. Although it is incomplete, lacks any indexes, and frequently is based on other sources, the work is useful for its inclusion of parts of books and a host of minor authors.

Modern African American culture through c. 1974 is the subject of Charles D. Peavy, *Afro-American Literature and Culture since World War II: A Guide to Information Sources*, American Studies Information Guide Series 6 (Detroit: Gale, 1979, 302 pp.), but the poor organization, inadequate definitions of scope and criteria determining selection, frequent errors, and omission of numerous significant works make it virtually useless as a selective guide. (For the numerous inadequacies, see the review by Jill Warren, *Analytical and Enumerative Bibliography* 4 [1980]: 78–85.)

A major desideratum is an authoritative and current selective bibliography of scholarship on African American literature.

See also

Leary, *Articles on American Literature* (3295).
Nemanic, *Bibliographical Guide to Midwestern Literature* (3600).
Szwed, *Afro-American Folk Culture* (5880).
Woodress, *Dissertations in American Literature, 1891–1966* (3320).

LANGUAGE

Guides to Scholarship

3760 Brasch, Ila Wales, and Walter Milton Brasch. *A Comprehensive Annotated Bibliography of American Black English*. Baton Rouge: Louisiana State UP, 1974. 289 pp. Z1234.D5.B7 016.427'973.

An author list of publications, dissertations, theses, and unpublished papers (through c. 1973 and primarily in English) on black English, as well as a few literary and folklore works that use black speech. About 80% of the approximately 2,300 entries are accompanied by brief descriptive annotations. The work is marred by an inadequate explanation of scope (especially regarding the selection of works illustrating black English), lacks an index and cross-references (thus one must skim all entries to locate studies of a particular topic), and falls far short of the comprehensiveness claimed in the title; nevertheless, Brasch offers the fullest single list of scholarship through c. 1973. It must be supplemented—even for studies before 1973—by *MLAIB* (335), *ABELL* (340), *Bibliographie linguistique* (6010), *LLBA: Linguistics and Language Behavior Abstracts* (6015), and most works in sections G: Serial Bibliographies, Indexes, and Abstracts and H: Guides to Dissertations and Theses. A major desideratum is a current, thorough, adequately indexed bibliography of scholarship on black English. Review: J[ohn] A[lgeo], *American Speech* 49 (1974): 142–46.

See also

ABELL (340): English Language division, which, since the volume for 1927, has a section on American English. In earlier volumes, see the Dialect section.

MLAIB (335): English Language and Literature division in the volumes for 1922–25; American Literature I: Linguistics in the volumes for 1926–40; English Language and Literature I: Linguistics in the volumes for 1941–55; English Language and Literature I: Linguistics/American English in the volumes for 1956–66; Indo-European C: Germanic Linguistics IV: English/Modern English/Dialectology in the volumes for 1967–80; and Indo-European Languages/West Germanic Languages/English Language (Modern)/Dialectology in the volumes since 1981. Researchers must also check the heading "Black English Dialect" in the subject index to post-1980 volumes.

BIOGRAPHICAL DICTIONARIES

Indexes

3765 Campbell, Dorothy W. *Index to Black American Writers in Collective Biographies*. Littleton: Libraries Unlimited, 1983. 162 pp. Z1229.N39.C35 [PS153.N5] 016.81'09'896073.

A name index to biographical sketches of about 1,900 black writers in 267 collective biographies that focus on African Americans and were published between 1837 and 1982. Under each writer, biographies are keyed to a list of sources. A time-saving compilation for quick identification of basic biographical information, Campbell's volume indexes a number of works not covered by *Biography and Genealogy Master Index* (565). The latter should also be checked, since it offers broader, more current coverage.

See also

Sec. J: Biographical Sources/Biographical Dictionaries/Indexes.

Dictionaries

3770 Logan, Rayford W., and Michael R. Winston, eds. *Dictionary of American Negro Biography*. New York: Norton, 1982. 680 pp. E185.96.D53 920'.009296073.

A biographical dictionary of 636 African Americans who died before 1970. Entrants, chosen on the basis of historical significance, represent a variety of walks of life. The separately authored entries provide essential details of an entrant's life and career, a brief estimate of the person's significance, and references to biographical sources and collections of papers. Although occupational and geographic indexes would increase its utility, this work is the most authoritative general biographical dictionary of African Americans, offering coverage far superior to that in *Dictionary of American Biography* (3380) and *Notable American Women* (3385). Review: Henry Louis Gates, Jr., *New York Times Book Review* 1 May 1983: 13, 29.

For basic biographical information about living African Americans, see the most recent edition of *Who's Who among Black Americans* (Lake Forest: Educational Communications, 1975–). The fullest biographical coverage of writers is offered by *Dictionary of Literary Biography* (600).

See also

Contemporary Authors (595).
Rush, *Black American Writers Past and Present* (3755a).

PERIODICALS

Some journals in section K: Periodicals/Scholarly Journals and most in section Q: American Literature/General/Periodicals/Scholarly Journals publish material on African American literature.

Guides to Primary Works

Bibliographies

3775 Daniel, Walter C. *Black Journals of the United States*. Historical Guides to the World's Periodicals and Newspapers. Westport: Greenwood, 1982. 432 pp. PN4882.5.D36 051.

A collection of profiles of about 100 magazines published between 1827 and the early 1980s. Organized alphabetically by title, each entry consists of an essay on the history and editorial policy of the periodical; highly selective lists of scholarship, indexing sources, and locations; and details of publishing history (including title changes, volumes and issue data, editor[s], and circulation). Two appendixes: a chronology of events related to African American journals; a list by geographical area. Indexed by persons, titles, and subjects. The criteria determining selection are unclear and the profiles vary considerably in thoroughness, but Daniel's work does provide an introduction to some of the important literary, scholarly, and other African American journals in the United States.

Indexes

3780 Black Periodical Fiction Project. Henry Louis Gates, director. 472 Caldwell Hall, Cornell U, Ithaca, NY 14853.

A project that is identifying fiction, poetry, book reviews, and literary criticism in some 900 newspapers and magazines published by African Americans between 1827 and 1940. The works are being reproduced in microfiche, with an index of authors and periodicals, and may also be published in CD-ROM. At the conclusion of the project, a compilation of the best works will be issued in hard copy.

Scholarly Journals

3785 *Black American Literature Forum* (*BALF*). 1967– . Quarterly. Former title: *Negro American Literature Forum* (1967–75). E185.5.N35 810'.9'896073.

Publishes articles, bibliographies, interviews, occasional special issues, and reviews on African American literature, as well as original poetry and fiction by African Americans. Beginning in vol. 22 (1988), a "Current Bibliography [October 1987–]" lists books about African Americans from unnamed trade bibliographies. Annual index. For the history of the journal, see Joe Weixlmann, "The Way We Were, the Way We Are, the Way We Hope to Be," 20 (1986): 3–7.

3790 *Callaloo: A Journal of Afro-American and African Arts and Letters* (*Callaloo*). 1976– . Quarterly. NX506.C34 700'.8996075.

Publishes creative works by and criticism, reviews, and bibliographies of African American and African writers. Of particular importance are the three selective, annotated annual bibliographies: "Studies in Afro-American Literature: An Annual Annotated Bibliography [1983–]" (3745); "Studies in Caribbean and South American Literature: An Annual Annotated Bibliography [1985–]," 9 (1986)– ;

and "Studies in African Literatures and Oratures: An Annual Annotated Bibliography [1985–]," 9 (1986)– . Cumulative index: vols. 1–11, comp. Joseph Lyle, in 11 (1988): 903–33.

3795 *CLA Journal* (*CLAJ*). 1957– . Quarterly. P1.A1.C22 400.

Since the late 1960s, articles, bibliographies, reviews, and occasional special issues emphasize African American literature. Unfortunately, "An Annual Bibliography of Afro-American Literature, [1975–76], with Selected Bibliographies of African and Caribbean Literature," 20–21 (1976–77) lasted only two issues. Annual index.

3800 *Obsidian II: Black Literature in Review* (*Obsidian*). Raleigh: Dept. of English, North Carolina State U, 1975– . 3/yr. Former title: *Obsidian: Black Literature in Review* (1975–82). PR1110.B5.O3 820'.8'0896.

Publishes articles, bibliographies, and reviews on black literatures, as well as original poetry and fiction by blacks. Indexed in every second volume.

GENRES

Some works in sections L: Genres and Q: American Literature/General/Genres are useful for research in African American literature.

Fiction

Some works in sections L: Genres/Fiction and Q: American Literature/General/Genres/Fiction are useful for research in African American fiction.

Histories and Surveys

3805 Bell, Bernard W. *The Afro-American Novel and Its Tradition*. Amherst: U of Massachusetts P, 1987. 421 pp. PS153.N5.B43 813'.009'896.

A "sociopsychological, sociocultural" history of extended prose narratives from 1853 through 1983. Organized chronologically, chapters emphasize the place of about 150 works in their respective historical, cultural, and literary contexts, with particular attention given to the relationship to oral and literary, European and African traditions. Indexed by persons, titles, and subjects. The most thorough, balanced, and sympathetic history of the African American novel, Bell supersedes earlier histories (especially Robert Bone, *The Negro Novel in America*, rev. ed. [New Haven: Yale UP, 1965], 289 pp.).

Short fiction awaits comparable treatment. Robert Bone, *Down Home: A History of Afro-American Short Fiction from Its Beginnings to the End of the Harlem Renaissance*, New Perspectives on Black America (New York: Capricorn-Putnam's, 1975, 328 pp.)—a critical survey of African American short fiction (primarily the short story) from 1885 to 1935 that emphasizes its debts to oral tradition as well as to mainstream Western literary forms, the Protestant tradition, the rural South, and the anxiety about the role of the African American writer in American society—is too restrictive in coverage and controversial in its underlying critical assumptions to serve as an adequate history of African American short fiction. For an important disagreement with these assumptions, see the review by Darwin T. Turner, *American Literature* 48 (1976): 416–18.

Guides to Primary Works

3810 Afro-American Novel Project. Maryemma Graham, director. Dept. of English, U of Mississippi, University, MS 38677.

A data base that will eventually encompass all novels published between 1853 and 1986 by African American authors. The record for each novel includes publishing history, biographical information on the author, references to selected studies, and details of content and structure. The data base is accessible by author, sex, title, publisher, genre or form, place of publication, and date of publication. Until the data base is publicly available, the project will perform searches for scholars. *The Afro-American Novel: A Checklist*, a bibliography developed from the data base, is scheduled for publication by Greenwood.

3815 Margolies, Edward, and David Bakish. *Afro-American Fiction, 1853–1976: A Guide to Information Sources*. American Literature, English Literature, and World Literatures in English: An Information Guide Series 25. Detroit: Gale, 1979. 161 pp. Z1229.N39.M37 [PS374.N4] 016.813'008'0352.

A highly selective list of novels, short story collections, and scholarship through c. 1976. Entries are organized in four divisions: novels for adults (listed alphabetically by author, then chronologically by publication date), short story collections (with separate lists of single-author collections and anthologies), 15 major novelists chosen for their historical or literary importance (authors are listed chronologically by publication date of their first novel, with separate lists of bibliographies and critical studies), and bibliographies and general studies. Only entries in the third and fourth divisions are annotated, with many works inadequately described. The appendix lists fictional works by publication date. Three indexes: authors; titles; and subjects. Because it is highly selective in all but the first division, inefficiently organized, and marred by an inadequate explanation of scope and criteria governing selection, *Afro-American Fiction* is primarily useful for its list of novels. Review: Jill Warren, *Analytical and Enumerative Bibliography* 4 (1980): 78–85.

Somewhat better—although also selective—coverage of novels published between 1965 and 1975 is offered by Helen Ruth Houston, *The Afro-American Novel, 1965–1975: A Descriptive Bibliography of Primary and Secondary Materials* (Troy: Whitston, 1977, 214 pp.), which is an annotated list—not a "descriptive" bibliography—of novels, studies, and reviews.

More than 850 short stories published between 1950 and 1982 in collections, anthologies, and periodicals are indexed by author, title, collection, and year of publication in Preston M. Yancy, comp., *The Afro-American Short Story: A Comprehensive, Annotated Index with Selected Commentaries*, Bibliographies and Indexes in Afro-American and African Studies 10 (Westport: Greenwood, 1986, 171 pp.). Coverage is far short of "comprehensive," and the work is confusingly organized and repetitive.

See also

Fairbanks, *Black American Fiction: A Bibliography* (3820).

Guides to Scholarship and Criticism

3820 Fairbanks, Carol, and Eugene A. Engeldinger. *Black American Fiction: A Bibliography*. Metuchen: Scarecrow, 1978. 351 pp. Z1229.N39.F34 [PS153.N5] 016.813.

A selective list of novels, short fiction, and English-language studies (including dissertations) through c. 1976. Under each fiction writer are sections, when appropriate, listing novels, short fiction, collections, biographical studies and criticism, and reviews (by work reviewed). General studies of African American fiction appear in a concluding list. There is no explanation of criteria governing selection and no index; many entries are copied from unidentified sources; significant omissions and incomplete citations occur; and relevant pages of parts of books are not cited. In spite of these serious deficiencies, *Black American Fiction* provides the single fullest list of works by and about African American fiction writers. The work must, though, be supplemented by Margolies, *Afro-American Fiction* (3815) as well as the serial bibliographies and indexes in section G.

See also

Margolies, *Afro-American Fiction, 1853–1976* (3815).
Weixlmann, *American Short-Fiction Criticism and Scholarship, 1959–1977* (3480).

Drama and Theater

Some works in sections L: Genres/Drama and Theater and Q: American Literature/General/Genres/Drama and Theater are useful for research in African American drama.

Guides to Primary Works

3825 Hatch, James V., and OMANii Abdullah, comps. and eds. *Black Playwrights, 1823–1977: An Annotated Bibliography*. New York: Bowker, 1977. 319 pp. Z1231.D7.H37 [PS338.N4] 016.812'009'352.

An author bibliography of about 2,700 plays by approximately 900 African Americans, along with some foreigners whose plays have been produced in the United States. Although a majority of the works are published and unpublished stage plays, some film, television, and radio dramas are also included. Each entry provides (when available) title, date of composition and/or copyright, genre, a brief summary (sometimes based on reviews or written by the playwright or an agent), cast (by race and sex), location of at least one copy, and permission information.

Concludes with selected bibliographies of books, anthologies, and dissertations and theses, and three appendixes: a list of taped interviews on the African American theater and held in Hatch-Billops archives; awards; addresses of playwrights, agents, and agencies (although more current addresses are usually available in *Contemporary Authors* [595]). Indexed by titles. Superior in coverage to the drama part of French, *Afro-American Poetry and Drama* (3845), *Black Playwrights* is the fullest record of plays by African Americans and an invaluable source for locating copies of obscure works.

It must, however, be supplemented by Bernard L. Peterson, Jr., *Contemporary Black American Playwrights: A Biographical Directory and Dramatic Index* (New York: Greenwood, 1988, 625 pp.), with entries on about 700 "black American and U.S. resident dramatists, screenwriters, radio and television scriptwriters, musical theatre collaborators, and other originators of theatrical and dramatic works, written, produced, and/or published between 1950 and" 1985. Each entry provides biographical information, address, and a list of dramatic works (noting genre, production or publication information, and source; providing a brief synopsis and production history; and locating scripts or recordings). Although not the "comprehensive" work claimed in the preface and necessarily incomplete in many entries, Peterson is an essential source for identifying and locating frequently unpublished recent dramatic works by African American writers.

For additional theatrical works (by blacks and whites) with black characters, see James V. Hatch, *Black Image on the American Stage: A Bibliography of Plays and Musicals, 1770–1970* (New York: DBS, 1970, 162 pp.), with additions by Joseph N. Weixlmann, "Black Portraiture on the Eighteenth-Century American Stage: Addenda," *Analytical and Enumerative Bibliography* 1 (1977): 203–06.

Guides to Scholarship and Criticism

There is no adequate bibliography devoted to studies of African American drama. Esther Spring Arata and Nicholas John Rotoli, *Black American Playwrights, 1800 to the Present: A Bibliography* (Metuchen: Scarecrow, 1976, 295 pp.), and Arata, *More Black American Playwrights: A Bibliography* (1978, 321 pp.), are too error-ridden, poorly organized, incomplete, and inconsistent to recommend to researchers. French, *Afro-American Poetry and Drama* (3845) is so selective that it is barely a place to begin research.

Poetry

Some works in section L: Genres/Poetry are useful for research in African American poetry.

Histories and Surveys

3830 Sherman, Joan R. *Invisible Poets: Afro-Americans of the Nineteenth Century*. Urbana: U of Illinois P, 1974. 270 pp. PS153.N5.S48 811'.009.

A series of essays on 26 poets born between 1796 and 1883 and representative of nineteenth-century African American poets, who are virtually ignored in literary histories and anthologies. The individual essays, organized by birthdate of authors, consist of a biography, critical appraisal, and selective list of sources (including manuscripts). The essays are complemented by a series of bibliographies and appendixes: a bibliography of primary works that includes manuscripts and locations of printed copies; a bibliographical essay that evaluates the bibliographies, periodical guides and indexes, biographical and critical works, anthologies, and manuscript collections important to research in nineteenth-century African American literature; a list of 35 writers who published a significant amount of poetry and who need further research; a list of other, less prolific poets who need further research; anonymous and pseudonymous poets; turn-of-the-century writers who did not publish before 1900; poets erroneously identified as African American; Creole poets of *Les Cenelles*; and selected bibliographies of Wheatley and Harmon. Indexed by persons, subjects, and anonymous titles. Besides providing the fullest history of nineteenth-century African American poets, *Invisible Poets* is an essential guide to research on the topic and a valuable source for identifying writers who need further attention. Review: Duncan MacLeod, *TLS: Times Literary Supplement* 13 June 1975: 675.

3835 Wagner, Jean. *Black Poets of the United States: From Paul Laurence Dunbar to Langston Hughes*. Trans. Kenneth Douglas. Urbana: U of Illinois P, 1973. 561 pp. (Originally published as *Les poètes nègres des Etats-Unis: Le sentiment racial et religieux dans la poésie de P. L. Dunbar à L. Hughes [1890–1940]*. Paris: Istra, 1963. 637 pp.) PS153.N5.W313 811'.009.

A detailed critical history of African American poetry that emphasizes "the interdependence of racial and religious feeling" in the works of major poets from 1890 to 1940. The chapters on early nineteenth-century African American poets, Dunbar, his contemporaries, the African American renaissance, McKay, Toomer, Cullen, Johnson, Hughes, and Brown consider biography, cultural and social contexts, and themes. The selective bibliography, extended to c. 1972 by Keneth Kinnamon, is now outdated. Indexed by persons, subjects, and titles. An encyclopedic work noteworthy for its scrupulous scholarship, it remains the standard history. Review: Robert Penn Warren, *Etudes anglaises* 28 (1975): 241–42.

Guides to Primary Works

3840 Chapman, Dorothy Hilton, comp. *Index to Poetry by Black American Women*. Bibliographies and Indexes in Afro-American and African Studies 15. New York: Greenwood, 1986. 424 pp. Z1229.N39.C45 [PS153.N5] 016.811'008'09287.

A title, first-line, and subject index to about 4,000 poems in 120 single-author collections and 83 anthologies (through c. 1984) by more than 400 African American women. Also included are about 185 anonymous poems, several of which may be by males. The title and first-line index is keyed to a list of collections. The subject index extends beyond title keywords. Although lacking an adequate explanation of the criteria governing the choice of collections and omitting some significant anthologies, the *Index* is a useful source for locating texts and identifying poems on topics. Until the companion volume on African American male poets is published, Chapman's *Index to Black Poetry* (Boston: Hall, 1974, 541 pp.) remains useful. Additional anthologies are indexed by title and author in Kallenbach, *Index to Black American Literary Anthologies* (3725). Some poems by African Americans are indexed in *Granger's Index to Poetry* (1235), *Poetry Index Annual* (1240), and *Index of American Periodical Verse* (4325).

3845 French, William P., et al. *Afro-American Poetry and Drama, 1760–1975: A Guide to Information Sources*. American Literature, English Literature, and World Literatures in English: An Information Guide Series 17. Detroit: Gale, 1979. 493 pp. Z1229.N39.A37 [PS153.N5] 016.810'9'896073.

A bibliography of primary works and selected studies in two parts: poetry from 1760 through 1975, compiled by French, Michael J. Fabre, and Amritjit Singh; and drama from 1850 through 1975, by Geneviève E. Fabre.

Poetry. This part attempts comprehensive coverage of separately published volumes of more than four pages by African Americans born in the United States as well as a few foreign-born residents. Although emphasizing written works, the part includes some folk and oral poetry. Coverage of scholarship is highly selective, especially for major writers. Entries are organized in two divisions: general studies (with sections for bibliographies and reference works, general studies, and anthologies) and individual authors (organized in three periods—1760–1900, 1901–45, 1946–75—with separate lists of primary works, bibliographies, and biographical studies and criticism for each poet). Few entries are annotated. Although coverage of scholarship is highly selective, *Afro-American Poetry and Drama* offers the fullest list of separately published volumes of poetry by African Americans and is especially valuable for its identification of numerous privately printed and ephemeral publications.

Drama. This part attempts comprehensive coverage of published plays by African Americans born or resident in the United States, includes some unpublished works, and lists selected scholarship. Entries are organized in two divisions: general studies (with sections for library collections, periodicals, bibliographies, collections of plays, and criticism) and individual authors (organized in three periods—1850–1900, 1901–50, 1951–75—with separate lists of published plays, unpublished ones, collections, and biographical studies and criticism for each playwright). Published plays are accompanied by summaries and details of first production; otherwise, few entries are annotated. Because Hatch, *Black Playwrights* (3825) offers more extensive and informative coverage of published and unpublished plays, this section is only marginally useful as a preliminary guide to scholarship.

A single index of persons, titles, and subjects encompasses both parts. Left unexplained are the justification for publishing the two parts as a single volume and the criteria governing the selection of studies. Review: Joe Weixlmann, *Black American Literature Forum* 14 (1980): 44–46.

Prose

Some works in sections L: Genres/Prose and Q: American Literature/General/Genres/Prose are useful for research in African American prose.

Guides to Primary Works

3850 Brignano, Russell C. *Black Americans in Autobiography: An Annotated Bibliography of Autobiographies and Autobiographical Books Written since the Civil War.* Rev. and expanded ed. Durham: Duke UP, 1984. 193 pp. Z1361.N39.B67 [E185.96] 016.973'0496073022.

An annotated bibliography of book-length autobiographical works by African Americans through 1982. The 710 entries are listed in four divisions: autobiographies (i.e., "volumes describing appreciable spans of the authors' lives"); autobiographical books that address a phase of the author's life; works that the compiler could not locate or read; autobiographical works published before 1865 and reprinted since 1945. Entries provide publication information, details of reprints, locations in up to 10 libraries, and in the first two parts, a descriptive annotation. Five indexes: activities, experiences, occupations, and professions; organizations; geographical locations and educational institutions; chronological listing of works by date of first publication; titles. Except for the rare volumes that have not been reprinted, citing library locations is unnecessary (especially since there is no logic to the choice of locations for commonly available books). Although the value of including post-1945 reprints of pre-1865 publications and the reasons for separating post-1865 works into three lists are unclear, Brignano offers valuable subject access to an important body of African American writing.

For earlier works, see "Annotated Bibliography of Afro-American Autobiography, 1760–1865" in William L. Andrews, *To Tell a Free Story: The First Century of Afro-American Autobiography, 1760–1865* (Urbana: U of Illinois P, 1986) 333–42, a selective list of separately published autobiographies; the annotations, however, consist of pagination and publication details for a few translations or later editions. In the same volume is "Annotated Bibliography of Afro-American Biography, 1760–1865" (343–47), which is drawn from Andrews, "Annotated Bibliography of Afro-American Biography, Beginnings to 1930," *Resources for American Literary Study* 12 (1982): 119–33; the annotations are minimal in both lists.

American Indian Literatures

Some works in section Q: American Literature/General are useful for research in American Indian literatures.

GUIDES TO REFERENCE WORKS

3860 Hirschfelder, Arlene B., Mary Gloyne Byler, and Michael A. Dorris. *Guide to Research on North American Indians.* Chicago: American Library Assn., 1983. 330 pp. Z1209.2.N67.H57 [E77] 016.970004'97.

A highly selective annotated bibliography of important reference works and studies of Indians of the United States and Alaska, along with a few major works on the rest of the Americas. The approximately 1,100 entries encompass English-language books, articles, and government documents published through 1979 (with a few as late 1982), but exclude ethnographies. Entries are organized in four divisions: general works (with sections for general bibliographies and general studies); history (including sections for descriptive narratives and autobiographies and biographies); economic and social topics (including a section for language); and religion, arts, and literature (with sections for religion and philosophy, music and dance, education, the arts, science, law, and literature). Each section begins with an essay overview of sources, followed by a list of general studies, then works devoted to a specific region, and then bibliographies. The full annotations offer detailed descriptions of contents. Two indexes: authors and titles; subjects. Superficial and inconsistent in its coverage of specialized studies (especially in the literature and literature-related sections) and now dated, it is primarily useful as a guide to important reference works before 1980.

It is far superior, however, to Marilyn L. Haas, *Indians of North America: Methods and Sources for Library Research* (Hamden: Library Professional-Shoe String, 1983, 163 pp.), an elementary guide that is frequently inaccurate and misleading. Review: (Hirschfelder and Haas) G. Edward Evans, *American Indian Culture and Research Journal* 8.4 (1984): 66–70.

See also

Prucha, *Handbook for Research in American History* (3185).

HISTORIES AND SURVEYS

3865 Wiget, Andrew. *Native American Literature.* Twayne's United States Authors Series 467. Boston: Twayne, 1985. 147 pp. PM155.W54 810'.9'897.

A critical history of the oral and narrative literatures of Native Americans of North America and Mesoamerica. The six chapters—organized variously by genre, group, or author—offer basic surveys of oral narrative (especially creation myths), oratory and oral poetry, the beginnings of a written literature, modern fiction, contemporary poetry, and recent nonfiction, autobiography, and drama. Concludes with a selected bibliography of primary and secondary works (the latter are accompanied by terse evaluative comments). Indexed by persons, works, and subjects. Although it is an introductory survey that emphasizes representative works and major authors, Wiget is currently the fullest history of Native American literatures. Given the level of interest, the time is ripe for a more comprehensive history.

See also

Columbia Literary History of the United States (3195).
New Cambridge History of American Literature (3205).

GUIDES TO PRIMARY WORKS

3870 Littlefield, Daniel F., Jr., and James W. Parins. *A Biobibliography of Native American Writers, 1772–1924.* Native American Bibliography Series 2. Metuchen: Scarecrow, 1981. 343 pp. *Supplement.* Native American Bibliography Series 5. 1985. 339 pp. Z1209.2.U5.L57 [E77] 016.973'0497.

An author list of works published between 1772 and 1924 and written in English by Native Americans of the United States (including Alaska). Except for writers known only by pseudonyms, coverage is limited to individuals definitely identified as Native Americans and to writings composed by the authors themselves. Each volume is made up of three parts: writers of established identity, writers known only by pseudonyms, and biographical notices. Under an author, entries are listed by publication date (a practice that needlessly separates later editions, reprints, and revisions from an original edition or version). A code system identifies the genre of each work, and in the *Supplement* brief descriptive annotations explain unclear titles. The biographical notices offer basic factual details; only in the *Supplement* do these cite sources. Two indexes in each volume: writers by tribal affiliation; subjects. Although not comprehensive, Littlefield is an indispensable guide to these early writings, the majority of which are indexed nowhere else. Review: A. LaVonne Brown Ruoff, *Arizona Quarterly* 38 (1982): 272–74.

GUIDES TO SCHOLARSHIP AND CRITICISM

Other Bibliographies

3875 Marken, Jack W., comp. *The American Indian: Language and Literature.* Goldentree Bibliographies in Language and Literature. Arlington Heights: AHM, 1978. 205 pp. Z7118.M27 [PM181] 016.497.

A selective bibliography of scholarship and some primary works (through c. 1976) for the study of the languages and literatures of Indians (other than the Eskimo) in the United States and Canada. The 3,695 entries are organized alphabetically by author in 16 divisions. The first four are devoted to general topics: bibliography, autobiography (both primary and secondary works), general literature (with sections for collections and anthologies, general studies of Indian authors, types of Indian literature, and general studies of Indian literature), and language (with sections for general studies; lexicography, grammar, and morphology; language classification; glottochronology and lexicostatistics; language and culture; linguists, collecting, recording, and transcribing; interrelationships of Indian languages and their relationships to other languages; sign language). The remaining divisions are devoted to regions, each with sections for literature, language, and tribal groups; under the last heading are separate alphabetical lists for literature and language. An asterisk denotes an important work. Because of the overlapping of regions and tribal groups, users should check the index to locate studies of a particular tribe. Indexed by authors, tribal groups, and subjects, but because of the organization, the subject indexing does not provide adequate access to the entries. Although selective, dated, and emphasizing written literature, this work remains the best general guide to research on Indian languages and literatures. Review: Dennis R. Hoilman, *Old Northwest* 4 (1978): 180–82.

3880 Ruoff, A. LaVonne Brown. *American Indian Literatures: An Introduction and Selected Bibliography*. New York: MLA. Scheduled for 1990.

A selective bibliography of primary works and scholarship important to the study of American Indian literatures. Following an evaluative overview of anthologies, texts, and studies are lists of special issues of periodicals and works by and about authors. Indexed by persons, genres, subjects, and tribes.

Until this work appears, a useful descriptive survey of primary sources, scholarship, and reference works is Ruoff, "American Indian Literatures: Introduction and Bibliography," *American Studies International* 24.2 (1986): 2–52.

See also

MLAIB (335): American Literature division through the volume for 1973; American Indian heading in American Literature sections in the volumes for 1974–80; in later volumes, researchers must consult the headings beginning "Native American" and related terms in the subject index.
Etulain, *Bibliographical Guide to the Study of Western American Literature* (3670).
Leary, *Articles on American Literature* (3295).
Literary History of the United States: Bibliography (3300).
Woodress, *Dissertations in American Literature* (3320).

Related Topics

3885 Clements, William M., and Frances M. Malpezzi, comps. *Native American Folklore, 1879–1979: An Annotated Bibliography*. Athens: Swallow, 1984. 247 pp. Z1209.C57 [E98.F6] 016.398'08997073.

An annotated bibliography of about 5,500 English-language books and articles (mostly published between 1879 and 1979) on the "oral narratives, songs, chants, prayers, formulas, orations, proverbs, riddles, word play, music, dances, games, and ceremonials" of Native Americans living north of Mexico. Clements and Malpezzi exclude newspaper articles, works for children, and reviews. Entries are listed alphabetically in 12 classified divisions. The first covers general studies in sections for bibliographies and reference works, collections of essays, collections of primary works in various genres, and general studies of genres. Each of the remaining divisions is devoted to a cultural area, with sections for general studies and individual tribal groups. The descriptive annotations (sometimes accompanied by evaluative comments) are succinct yet admirably clear. Two indexes: subjects; scholars. The indispensable guide to scholarship on the folklore of the Native Americans of North America. For recent studies, see section U: Literature-Related Topics and Sources/Folklore/Guides to Scholarship and Criticism.

3890 Murdock, George Peter, and Timothy J. O'Leary. *Ethnographic Bibliography of North America*. 4th ed. 5 vols. New Haven: Human Relations Area Files, 1975. Z1209.2.N67.M87 [E77] 016.97'0004'97.

A bibliography of important published scholarship and dissertations (through 1972) in Western languages on the ethnography of Native peoples of North America. Except for a few departments, Murdock and O'Leary do not attempt systematic coverage of government publications. The approximately 40,000 entries are organized alphabetically in divisions for general studies (with sections for broad geographic areas) and regions (with sections for tribes); many works appear in more than one section. The general introduction includes a detailed guide to supplementary reference works. An ethnonymy index in each volume serves as a guide to the classification of ethnic groups and tribes. The most comprehensive bibliography of scholarship on the ethnography of Native North Americans, *Ethnographic Bibliography* is useful to literature and language scholars for its extensive coverage of folklore and languages.

More selective, but also more current, are the volumes in Newberry Library Center for the History of the American Indian Bibliographical Series, gen. ed. Francis Jennings (Bloomington: Indiana UP, for Newberry Library, 1976–). Each volume evaluates important sources for the study of Indians of a region. Although variously organized, most of the essays include a brief section on language. More thorough coverage of some tribes and subjects can be found in the annotated bibliographies published thus far in Native American Bibliography Series, ed. Jack W. Marken (Metuchen: Scarecrow, 1980–).

See also

America: History and Life (3310).
Haywood, *Bibliography of North American Folklore and Folksong* (5875).
Historical Abstracts (6500).
Miller, *Folk Music in America* (5910).
Salzman, *American Studies: An Annotated Bibliography* (3335).

PERIODICALS

Guides to Primary Works

3895 Littlefield, Daniel F., Jr., and James W. Parins, eds. *American Indian and Alaska Native Newspapers and Periodicals, [1826–1985]*. 3 vols. Historical Guides to the World's Periodicals and Newspapers. Westport: Greenwood, 1984–86. PN4883.L57 051.

Vol. 1: *1826–1924*. 1984. 482 pp.
Vol. 2: *1925–1970*. 1986. 553 pp.
Vol. 3: *1971–1985*. 1986. 609 pp.

A collection of profiles of "newspapers and periodicals edited or published by American Indians or Alaska Natives and those whose primary purpose was to publish information about *contemporary* Indians or Alaska Natives." Excludes ethnological, archaeological, historical, Mexican, and Canadian publications. Organized alphabetically by most recent title (or title used when under the control of Indians or Alaska Natives), entries provide a publishing history and overview of content, and cite scholarship, indexing sources, location sources (noting a few actual locations and availability in microform collections), publication information, and editors. Alternate and earlier titles are cross-referenced to main entries. Three appendixes list titles by date of original publication, place of publication, and tribal affiliation. Indexed by persons and subjects.

Complemented by James P. Danky, ed., and Maureen E. Hady, comp., *Native American Periodicals and Newspapers, 1828–1982: Bibliography, Publishing Record, and Holdings* (Westport: Greenwood, 1984, 532 pp.), which is more exhaustive in its coverage and precise in recording holdings, but lacks the useful overviews of publishing history and is less thorough and precise in its subject indexing.

Together, these works on Native American periodicals are the essential guides to extensive but underutilized sources, many of which are omitted from standard union lists.

See also

Sec. K: Periodicals/Directories, and Periodicals/Union Lists.
United States Newspaper Program National Union List (3405).

Scholarly Journals

Some journals in sections K: Periodicals/Scholarly Journals and Q: American Literature/General/Periodicals/Scholarly Journals occasionally publish articles on American Indian literatures.

3900 *American Indian Culture and Research Journal.* 1974– . Quarterly. E75.A5124 970'.004'97.

Publishes articles, reviews, review essays, and occasional special issues on all aspects of the history and culture of American Indians. Recent issues print several articles on literature, and the reviews are among the best of any journal in this section. Annual index beginning in vol. 8; cumulative index: vols. 1–7, Velma S. Salabiye, "Index to the *American Indian Culture and Research Journal*, 1974–1983," 7.4 (1983): 109–36.

3905 *The American Indian Quarterly: Journal of American Indian Studies* (*AIQ*). 1974– . Quarterly. E75.A547 970'.004'97.

Publishes articles, reviews, and occasional special issues on the history, literature, anthropology, and arts of American Indians. Most early issues include a "Bibliography, Research, and News" section that lists selected new books and articles. Annual index.

3910 *Studies in American Indian Literatures* (*SAIL*). 1974– . Quarterly. Former title: *Newsletter of the Association for Study of American Indian Literatures* (1974–79). PM151.A87 808.

Publishes a few articles and numerous reviews on Indian literatures.

BACKGROUND READING

3915 *Handbook of North American Indians.* Gen. ed. William C. Sturtevant. 20 vols. Washington: Smithsonian Institution, 1978– . E77.H25 970'.004'97.

Vol. 1: *Introduction.*
Vol. 2: *Indians in Contemporary Society.*
Vol. 3: *Environment, Origins, and Population.*
Vol. 4: *History of Indian-White Relations.*
Vol. 5: *Arctic.* Ed. David Damas. 1984. 829 pp.
Vol. 6: *Subarctic.* Ed. June Helm. 1981. 837 pp.
Vol. 7: *Northwest Coast.*
Vol. 8: *California.* Ed. Robert F. Heizer. 1978. 800 pp.
Vol. 9: *Southwest.* Ed. Alfonso Ortiz. 1979. 701 pp.
Vol. 10: *Southwest.* Ed. Ortiz. 1983. 868 pp.
Vol. 11: *Great Basin.* Ed. Warren L. d'Azevedo. 1986. 852 pp.
Vol. 12: *Plateau.*
Vol. 13: *Plains.*
Vol. 14: *Southeast.*
Vol. 15: *Northeast.* Ed. Bruce G. Trigger. 1978. 924 pp.
Vol. 16: *Technology and Visual Arts.*
Vol. 17: *Languages.*
Vols. 18–19: *Biographical Dictionary.*
Vol. 20: *Index.*

An encyclopedic treatment of the history and culture of North American Indians. The volumes devoted to geographic areas typically include essays by established scholars on ethnography, languages, archaeology, tribal groups, art, and—occasionally—literature, religion, and mythology. The extensive list of works cited in each volume constitutes a valuable bibliography of major studies. Indexed in each volume by names and subjects. Although the essays are uneven in quality and some ignore controversies about their subject matter, the *Handbook* will eventually be the most authoritative general source of information on American Indian history, ethnography, and culture. Review: (vol. 9) Bernard L. Fontana, *Arizona Quarterly* 38 (1982): 81–85.

GENRES

Fiction

Some works in sections L: Genres/Fiction and Q: American Literature/General/Genres/Fiction are useful for research on fiction by American Indians.

Guides to Scholarship and Criticism

3920 Colonnese, Tom, and Louis Owens. *American Indian Novelists: An Annotated Critical Bibliography.* Garland Reference Library of the Humanities 384. New York: Garland, 1985. 161 pp. Z1229.I52.C65 [PS153.I52] 016.813'009'897.

A selective annotated bibliography of works (published through c. 1983) by and about 21 novelists. Under each novelist are sections for book-length primary works (with separate chronological lists of novels and other books), selected shorter works (organized by genre, then alphabetically by title), and selected studies (with separate lists of criticism—organized by primary work and including reviews—and biographical sources). Novels are accompanied by plot summaries, and studies of novels are accompanied by descriptive annotations; both are wordy and wooden. Indexed by novelists and titles. Highly selective and marred by an inadequate discussion of criteria governing selection of both novelists and studies, *American Indian Novelists* does little more than offer a place to begin research. Review: Jerome Klinkowitz, *American Indian Culture and Research Journal* 8.2 (1984): 58–60.

Prose

Guides to Primary Works

3925 Brumble, H. David, III. *An Annotated Bibliography of American Indian and Eskimo Autobiographies*. Lincoln: U of Nebraska P, 1981. 177 pp. Z1209.B78 [E89] 016.970004'97.

———. "A Supplement to *An Annotated Bibliography of American Indian and Eskimo Autobiographies*." *Western American Literature* 17 (1982): 243–60.

A bibliography of some 600 first-person narratives written by North American Indians and Eskimos or transcribed and edited by other persons. Although largely confined to published autobiographies (through c. 1979), the work includes a few in manuscript or on tape. Organized alphabetically by the commonly used name of the autobiographer, entries provide collaborator, editor, or amanuensis; gender, if not apparent from the name; title; publication information or location of tape or manuscript; birthdate; date of composition; tribal affiliation; an account of how the narrative was composed; and a detailed description of content. Three indexes: editors, anthropologists, ghostwriters, and amanuenses; tribes; subjects. Although it is imprecise and insufficiently detailed in subject indexing and incomplete in cross-referencing Indian and Anglo names, Brumble's compilation offers the fullest record of these autobiographical narratives, many of which are hidden in anthropological or historical studies. Review: Ralph Maud, *Canadian Review of American Studies* 14 (1983): 71–77.

Asian American Literature

GUIDES TO SCHOLARSHIP AND CRITICISM

3940 Cheung, King-Kok, and Stan Yogi. *Asian American Literature: An Annotated Bibliography*. New York: MLA, 1988. 276 pp. Z1229.A75.C47 [PS153.A84] 016.81'08'089507.

A bibliography of works (through July 1987) by and about writers of Asian descent resident in the United States and Canada as well as those living elsewhere who have written about the experiences of Asians in North America. Includes autobiographies, essays, and popular fiction, but excludes publications by native

Pacific Islanders, works in Asian languages not translated into English, individual poems in anthologies or periodicals, manuscripts, and works in student publications. The approximately 3,400 entries are organized in seven divisions: bibliographies and reference works, anthologies, periodicals, primary works (with sections for national groups and children's literature; each national group has separate lists of prose, poetry, and drama), scholarship and criticism (with the sections for general studies and national groups divided into three parts: books, theses, and dissertations; articles; and interviews, profiles, and commentary), fiction about Asians or Asian Americans by non-Asians, and background studies. Some works have descriptive annotations that sometimes cite reviews; unfortunately, most of the annotations are too brief to convey an adequate sense of content. Four indexes: writers; scholars; reviewers; editors, translators, and illustrators. Although it is frustratingly brief in its annotations and less accessible than it should be because of the lack of a subject index, *Asian American Literature* fills a major gap in reference sources for the literatures of the United States and Canada.

Hispanic American Literature

Some works in section Q: American Literature/General are useful to research in Hispanic American literatures.

GUIDES TO REFERENCE WORKS

3970 Robinson, Barbara J., and J. Cordell Robinson, *The Mexican American: A Critical Guide to Research Aids*. Foundations in Library and Information Science 1. Greenwich: JAI, 1980. 287 pp. Z1361.M4.R63 [E184.M5] 016.973'046872.

A selective, annotated guide to reference works (in English and Spanish, and published between 1857 and 1978) on the cultural, historical, social, political, artistic, or economic milieu of Mexican Americans. The authors cover both published and unpublished works (including dissertations, theses, and mimeographed material) and emphasize the nineteenth and twentieth centuries. The 668 entries are listed alphabetically by author in two classified divisions: general works and subject bibliographies. The first has sections for general bibliographies, library guides, biographical sources, genealogical sources, statistical sources, directories, dictionaries, newspaper and periodical guides, and audiovisual sources; the second for education, folklore, history, labor, linguistics, literature, social and behavioral sciences, and women. Each section is preceded by an evaluative overview of the reference sources. The full annotations are largely descriptive and focus on scope, content, and organization. Three indexes: authors; titles; subjects. Although it is now dated, includes several ephemeral and superseded works, and lacks an adequate explanation of criteria governing selection, this work remains a useful guide to important reference sources for the study of Mexican Americans.

Less thorough but including Cuban American and continental Puerto Rican literature as well as sociolinguistics is David William Foster, ed., *Sourcebook of Hispanic Culture in the United States* (Chicago: American Library Assn., 1982, 352 pp.). Coverage is very selective and rarely extends beyond 1975.

GUIDES TO SCHOLARSHIP AND CRITICISM

3975 Eger, Ernestina N. *A Bibliography of Criticism of Contemporary Chicano Literature*. Berkeley: Chicano Library Publications, U of California, 1982. 295 pp. Z1229.M48.E36 [PS153.M4] 016.81'08'086872073.

A bibliography of books, articles, theses, dissertations, commercial audio and video tapes, reviews, newspaper articles, unpublished convention papers, and some works in progress from 1960 to mid-1979 on Chicano and Mexican American literature of the same period. The 2,181 entries are organized alphabetically in 12 divisions: collections of critical essays; bibliographies; general studies; La Chicana as writer, critic, or literary character; general criticism; linguistic studies; poetry; fiction; theater (with sections for general studies, Teatro Campesino and Luis Valdez, other *teatros*, and theater festivals); literary festivals; individual authors; and anthologies. Studies of literature before 1960 are listed in a brief appendix; another appendix serves as a directory of Chicano literary periodicals. Two indexes: scholars; titles. Although there are several omissions as well as duplicate entries for subsequently published convention papers, Eger is the fullest list of scholarship through mid-1979. Review: Hensley C. Woodbridge, *Bilingual Review/Revista Bilingüe* 10 (1983): 69–72.

Some recent general studies—but not those of individual authors—are listed in Roberto G. Trujillo and Andres Rodriguez, comps., *Literatura Chicana: Creative and Critical Writings through 1984* (Oakland: Floricanto, 1985, 95 pp.); however, numerous omissions, poor organization, and a confusing description of scope make this source an unsatisfactory guide to critical works. More useful as a supplement to Eger is Julio A. Martínez and Francisco A. Lomelí, eds., *Chicano Literature: A Reference Guide* (Westport: Greenwood, 1985, 492 pp.), a collection of essays with selective bibliographies on established authors and some literary periods, genres, and topics, along with a chronology of Chicano literature from 1539 to 1982 and a glossary of Chicano literary terms. Unfortunately, principles governing selection are not clearly stated, and many entries are poorly written.

See also

Secs. G: Serial Bibliographies, Indexes, and Abstracts and H: Guides to Dissertations and Theses.

Etulain, *Bibliographical Guide to the Study of Western American Literature* (3670).

MLAIB (335): Until the volume for 1972, see the American Literature division; in the volumes for 1972–80, see the Mexican-American heading in American Literature sections; in later volumes, see the headings beginning "Mexican American" in the subject index.

LANGUAGE

Guides to Scholarship

3980 Teschner, Richard V., gen. ed. *Spanish and English of United States Hispanos: A Critical, Annotated, Linguistic Bibliography*. Arlington:

Center for Applied Linguistics, 1975. 352 pp. Z2695.D5.T47 [PC4826] 016.467'9'73.

Bills, Garland D., Jerry R. Craddock, and Richard V. Teschner. "Current Research on the Language(s) of U.S. Hispanos." *Hispania* 60 (1977): 347–58.

A bibliography of publications, dissertations, theses, and some unpublished papers and reports (through January 1977 in the supplement) on the Spanish and English used by Hispanic citizens or residents of the mainland United States. Excludes most discussions of language teaching. In the 1975 volume, entries are organized alphabetically in divisions for general studies, Mexican Americans (subdivided by region), Puerto Ricans, Cubans, Louisiana Canary Islanders, Spaniards, and Sephardic Jews. Each division has sections, when appropriate, for bibliographies, general studies, sociolinguistics, textbooks, Spanish phonology, Spanish grammar, Spanish lexicon, onomastics, English influence on Spanish, Spanish influence on English, English as used by the group, and code-switching. Each section begins with lists of the most important works and cross-references. Annotations typically combine detailed description with trenchant evaluation, and the introduction surveys trends in research. The author index utilizes a confusing system of sigla. (The supplement is merely an unannotated author list.) The extensive evaluative annotations in the 1975 volume make it a valuable guide to scholarship on Spanish and English as used by Hispanics in the United States. For recent studies, see *MLAIB* (335), *Bibliographie linguistique* (6010), and *LLBA: Linguistics and Language Behavior Abstracts* (6015). Review: Hensley C. Woodbridge, *Modern Language Journal* 60 (1976): 316.

See also

Eger, *Bibliography of Criticism of Contemporary Chicano Literature* (3975).

Jewish American Literature

GUIDES TO SCHOLARSHIP AND CRITICISM

3990 Nadel, Ira Bruce. *Jewish Writers of North America: A Guide to Information Sources*. American Studies Information Guide Series 8. Detroit: Gale, 1981. 493 pp. Z1229.J4.N32 [PS153.J4] 016.810'8'08924.

A selective bibliography of works by and about American and Canadian Jewish writers chosen for their "literary excellence, cultural significance, and historical importance." Coverage extends through the late 1970s. The 3,291 entries are organized in four divisions: general works (with sections for bibliographies, biographical sources, indexes, library and manuscript collections, literary history, general criticism, and anthologies), poets, fiction writers, and dramatists (with sections for reference works, and criticism and theater history). Each division or section has separate lists for American and Canadian literature and writers. Under each author are lists of bibliographies, primary works (chronologically by genre), and criticism. Appendix A is devoted to Yiddish literature in English translation, appendix B to a list of other Jewish writers. The descriptive annotations are brief but generally adequate;

however, many entries are not annotated. Three indexes: authors; titles; subjects. Users should note that some writers appear under more than one genre. Although marred by an inadequate explanation of scope and the failure to index authors and topics mentioned in annotations to the first division, this work offers the fullest single guide to North American Jewish writers. Many studies of American and Canadian Jewish literature can be identified through the headings beginning "Jewish American" or "Jewish Canadian" in the subject index to post-1980 volumes of *MLAIB* (335).

Early American Literature (to 1800)

Many works in section Q: American Literature/General are important to research in early American literature.

Guides to Primary Works

4000 Alden, John, and Dennis C. Landis, eds. *European Americana: A Chronological Guide to Works Printed in Europe Relating to the Americas, 1493–1776*. 8 vols. New York: Readex, 1980– . Z1203.E87 [E18.82] 016.97.

Vol. 1: *1493–1600*. 1980. 467 pp.
Vol. 2: *1601–1650*. 1982. 954 pp.
Vol. 3: *1651–1675*. Scheduled for the early 1990s.
Vol. 4: *1676–1700*. Scheduled for the early 1990s.
Vol. 5: *1701–1725*. In press.
Vol. 6: *1726–1750*. In press.
Vols. 7–8: *1751–1776*. (Publication will depend on availability of funding.)

A chronological guide to separately published works and editions thereof printed in Europe and related to the Americas (here defined as "the area from Greenland to the Straits of Magellan, comprising the two Americas, Central America, and geographically related islands in the Caribbean and elsewhere"). Based on the holdings of the John Carter Brown Library and listings in several bibliographies, *European Americana* includes in vol. 1 many literary and other works with only incidental references to the area; in later volumes, the scope narrows to exclude most works that have only a passing mention of the New World. Organized alphabetically within each year by author, corporate author, or title of anonymous work, entries provide title, imprint, final page number, format, a note on American content if not clear from the title, references to standard bibliographies, and locations. Users must remember that much information is taken unverified from other sources and that titles and imprints are frequently edited rather than exact transcriptions. Additions are printed in vol. 1, pp. 261–66, and vol. 2, pp. 526–27. Each volume has four indexes: geographical index of printers and booksellers; alphabetical index of printers and booksellers; authors and titles; subjects. The Alden-Landis *European Americana* supersedes Henry Harrisse, *Bibliotheca Americana Vetustissima: A Description of Works Relating to America Published between the Years 1492 and 1551* (New York: Philes, 1866, 519 pp.) and *Additions* (Paris: Tross, 1872, 199 pp.), and, for the volumes published, represents a major improvement in coverage, organization, and accuracy over Sabin, *Bibliotheca Americana* (4015). Although the work is not comprehensive and perpetuates many of the errors of its sources, its coverage, organization, and indexing make the series the indispensable source for studying the impact of the Americas on Europe. Reviews: (vol. 1) David B. Quinn, *Renaissance Quarterly* 34 (1981): 570–72; (vols. 1–2) J. A. Leo Lemay, *Resources for American Literary Study* 13 (1983): 26–32; Edwin Wolf 2nd, *Papers of the Bibliographical Society of America* 78 (1984): 91–95.

4005 Evans, Charles. *American Bibliography: A Chronological Dictionary of All Books, Pamphlets, and Periodical Publications Printed in the United States of America from the Genesis of Printing in 1639 down to and Including the Year 1820 [i.e., 1800]* (Evans). 14 vols. (vols. 1–12) Chicago: Privately printed, 1903–34; (vols. 13–14) Worcester: American Antiquarian Soc., 1955–59. (Vol. 13 is by Clifford Shipton; vol. 14, by Roger Pattrell Bristol.) Z1215.E92 015.73.

A preliminary retrospective national bibliography of printed works (excluding tickets, invitations, circulars, and forms designed to be completed in manuscript). Organized by year of publication, then alphabetically by author, corporate author, or title of anonymous work, the 39,162 entries typically cite title, imprint, pagination, size or format, locations, and contemporary auction values. A few are accompanied by bibliographical, biographical, or historical notes.

Each volume has two indexes (authors and anonymous titles; subjects). However, the author and title indexes are superseded by the *Index* (vol. 14), which lists pseudonyms, corporate authors, and authors; includes titles (as well as running titles and half titles recorded by Evans); and adds names of people, ships, and Indian tribes mentioned in titles. Because of inconsistencies in the treatment of main headings for some kinds of works, erroneous dating, and incorrect attributions of authorship, the *Index* frequently offers the only convenient way to locate unsigned publications. The lists of printers and publishers in vols. 1–12 are superseded by Bristol, *Index of Printers, Publishers, and Booksellers Indicated by Charles Evans in His* American Bibliography (Charlottesville: Bibliographical Soc. of the U of Virginia, 1961, 172 pp.), which is sometimes useful for identifying a work whose title was taken from a source other than a copy. However, Bristol indexes only what Evans records, making no attempt to correct errors. Items in Evans and *Early American Imprints* (see below) containing printed musical notation are indexed in Donald L. Hixon, *Music in Early America: A Bibliography of Music in Evans* (Metuchen: Scarecrow, 1970, 607 pp.).

To make effective use of Evans, researchers must be aware of its major deficiencies:

1. Because of numerous typographical errors and because much information is copied without verification from secondary sources—including other bibliographies, advertisements, and booksellers', auction, and library catalogs—as many as 30% of the entries are inaccurate, especially in recording titles, publication information, and date. Particularly vexing is Evans's practice of supplying descriptive titles based on advertisements. Although Evans does not identify secondhand entries, Shipton encloses within brackets titles not seen or "described by a careful bibliographer" and derives entries from booksellers' or auction catalogs only when a title page is reproduced. Users should check a printed description against an actual copy or reproduction in *Early American Imprints, Series I.*

2. Anonymous works are difficult to locate because Evans frequently misattributes authorship, place, publisher, or date, or lists such works under inconsistent or peculiar corporate author headings without supplying title cross-references. Only vol. 13 identifies attributions (within brackets) and cross-references titles of anonymous works. By utilizing more accurate, consistent corporate headings and listing short titles, the *Index* (vol. 14) allows for the location of many anonymous publications.
3. Regardless of the number of copies extant, Evans typically locates only one or two and sometimes omits locations to save an additional line of type. (Vol. 13 provides more locations.) To decipher Evans's location symbols, see John C. Munger, "Evans's *American Bibliography*: Tentative Check List of the Library Location Symbols," *Bulletin of the New York Public Library* 40 (1936): 665–68.
4. Several works are listed out of chronological sequence because they were discovered after publication of the appropriate volume. And many undatable publications are grouped under "1800."

Not surprisingly, there are numerous ghosts and duplicate entries. Also, many works or editions identified in studies and catalogs as "not in Evans" are actually there but not locatable.

The following works supplement Evans:

"American Bibliographical Notes." *Proceedings of the American Antiquarian Society* 82 (1972): 45–64; 83 (1973): 261–73; 87 (1977): 409–15; 88 (1978): 90–119, 327–28; 89 (1979): 155–57; 93 (1983): 197–221. A series of variously authored notes and lists that provide numerous additions and corrections to Evans.

Bristol, Roger P. *Supplement to Charles Evans'* American Bibliography. Charlottesville: UP of Virginia, for Bibliographical Soc. of America and Bibliographical Soc. of U of Virginia, 1970. 636 pp. Collects from a variety of sources some 11,200 additions, with locations and entry numbers for those reproduced in the Readex microfilm series. Addenda appear on pp. 631–34. Separately indexed as *Index to* Supplement to Charles Evans' American Bibliography (Charlottesville: UP of Virginia, for Bibliographical Soc. of U of Virginia, 1971, 191 pp.). Review: J. A. Leo Lemay, *Early American Literature* 8 (1973): 66–77.

Early American Imprints, Series I: Evans. New Canaan: Readex. Microprint and microfiche. Reproduces about 42,000 nonserial publications listed in Evans or Bristol, *Supplement.* Although the reproductions offer a necessary means of checking the accuracy of Evans's descriptions, researchers should be aware that missing leaves are sometimes filmed from another copy. The Readex catalog cards and RLIN (230) cataloging records incorporate revisions to Evans. The American Antiquarian Society is preparing a catalog of the series.

Federal Copyright Records, 1790–1800. Ed. James Gilreath. Comp. Elizabeth Carter Wills. Washington: Library of Congress, 1987. 166 pp. A transcript of surviving records for the period.

Shipton, Clifford K., and James E. Mooney. *National Index of American Imprints through 1800: The Short-Title Evans*. 2 vols. Worcester: American Antiquarian Soc. and Barre, 1969. An index to the microform collection that makes numerous corrections to Evans and in some instances cites the sources of his errors. It is particularly useful for identifying duplicate entries. Review: J. A. Leo Lemay, *Early American Literature* 8 (1973): 66–77.

American imprints are also included in the *Short-Title Catalogues* (1990, 1995, and 2230), which are typically more thorough and accurate than Evans. Book catalogs are more thoroughly covered in Winans, *Descriptive Checklist of Book Catalogues* (5410).

Despite its manifold deficiencies and incompleteness, Evans and its supplements currently offer the fullest record of early American imprints; provide an invaluable resource for investigating the intellectual milieu of works, surveying publishing trends, identifying works and editions by standard reference number, and locating copies; and form the basis for a fuller, more sophisticated and accurate retrospective bibliography. Only because of this preliminary bibliography has it been possible to make readily available in microform a majority of works printed before 1801 in the United States. Scholars should also search the North American Imprints Program data base (4010), which will eventually supersede Evans and its supplements.

The chronological record is continued by Shaw, *American Bibliography* (4125) and Shoemaker, *Checklist of American Imprints* (4130).

4010 North American Imprints Program (NAIP). American Antiquarian Soc., 185 Salisbury St., Worcester, MA 01609.

An attempt to establish a machine-readable union catalog of all North American imprints before 1801 (and eventually before 1877), including books, pamphlets, and broadsides, but excluding periodicals, newspapers, and engraved materials. Entries for works examined by NAIP staff contain a full transcription of title page and imprint, detailed statement of pagination, collation, notes, and references to published bibliographies. Descriptions based on reports by cooperating libraries, *Early American Imprints* (4005a), or published bibliographies are less detailed. Records are being incorporated into the *ESTC* (2230) data base; those for American Antiquarian Society holdings are included in the RLIN (230) data base; and all records will eventually be available in a microfiche catalog or CD-ROM that will allow searches by author, title, subject, genre, first line of broadside verse, printer, publisher, bookseller, place of publication, and date of publication. Progress reports appear in *Factotum* (2230a). Eventually the data base will supersede Tremaine, *Bibliography of Canadian Imprints* (4615), and Evans, *American Bibliography* and its various supplements (4005) and continuations.

Under discussion is a machine-readable union catalog, 1475–1800, that would combine expanded, edited entries from *RSTC* (1990) and Wing (1995) with NAIP and ESTC (2230) records. For details, see Henry L. Snyder, "The English Short Title Catalogue," *Papers of the Bibliographical Society of America* 82 (1988): 333–36.

4015 Sabin, Joseph, Wilberforce Eames, and R. W. G. Vail, eds. *Bibliotheca Americana: A Dictionary of Books Relating to America, from Its Discovery to the Present Time* (Sabin). 29 vols. New York: Sabin, 1868–1936. (Originally issued in parts.) Z1201.S2 015.73.

A bibliography of publications related to the political, governmental, economic, social, intellectual, and religious history of the Western Hemisphere since 1492. Until vol. 21 (1929–31), Sabin includes potentially anything even remotely touching on the Americas published up to the date of publication of a part (except that post-1800 newspapers and broadsides are generally excluded); in succeeding volumes, both scope and coverage are substantially reduced. With vol. 21, the cut-off date becomes 1876; with pt. 130 (in vol. 22 [1931–32]), the cut-off date is 1860 (earlier for certain kinds of publications—e.g., 1800 for most literary works, but 1830 for those "of historical importance"); with pt. 141 (in vol. 24 [1933–34]), virtually nothing published after 1840 is included. Researchers must be certain to read the explanation in vol. 29, pp. x-xi, of the successive narrowing in scope and coverage.

Entries are listed alphabetically by author or, for anonymous works, by title, locale, or subject. An entry includes title; publication information; size or format; pagination; occasional notes on content, editions, related titles, scholarship, reviews, other works by the author, or references to booksellers' or auction catalogs; and locations (more consistently and fully in the later volumes; location symbols are listed in vol. 29, pp. 299–305). References in the notes more than double the 106,413 numbered entries.

Users must be aware of the deficiencies of Sabin: there are numerous omissions; the volumes through 13 (1881) admit many works that can hardly be classified as Americana, but with Eames's editorship (beginning in pt. 83 [1884]), standards defining coverage are tighter; many errors exist because of Sabin's reliance on unsound secondary sources and frequent use of wrappers as sources for titles (accuracy improves under Eames's editorship); entries are not standardized and there are several duplicate entries.

John Edgar Molnar, comp., *Author-Title Index to Joseph Sabin's* Dictionary of Books Relating to America, 3 vols. (Metuchen: Scarecrow, 1974), remedies many of the difficulties in locating works in Sabin by indexing authors, editors, compilers, illustrators, corporate authors, main titles, series titles, and selected subtitles and alternate titles, as well as by identifying several anonymous and pseudonymous authors.

Despite its incompleteness and manifold deficiencies, Sabin remains the single most extensive bibliography of early works related to the Western Hemisphere. For more thorough and accessible coverage of European imprints through 1650, see Alden, *European Americana* (4000); some areas are more fully treated in bibliographies devoted to a region or country (consult Besterman, *World Bibliography of Bibliographies* [155] and *Bibliographic Index* [145]).

Lawrence S. Thompson, *The New Sabin: Books Described by Joseph Sabin and His Successors, Now Described Again on the Basis of Examination of Originals, and Fully Indexed by Title, Subject, Joint Authors, and Institutions and Agencies*, 10 vols. and cumulative index (Troy: Whitston, 1974–86), is misleadingly titled. Rather than a revision of Sabin, the work is merely a set of separate lists of and indexes to large-scale microform collections (including Wright, *American Fiction* [4180]). The entries consist of information taken from catalog cards prepared for the collections (and not from the compiler's personal examination of original copies). Cumulatively indexed by subjects, titles, joint authors, and corporate bodies. Although restricted to publications available in microform collections, awkwardly organized, and lacking cross-references to Sabin, *New Sabin* adds as well as corrects numerous entries and offers useful, but limited, subject access to works about the Americas.

See also

Boswell, *Check List of Americana in* A Short-Title Catalogue (1990a).
Eighteenth-Century Short-Title Catalogue (2230).
Pollard, *Short-Title Catalogue, 1475–1640* (1990).
Wing, *Short-Title Catalogue, 1641–1700* (1995).

Guides to Scholarship and Criticism

SURVEYS OF RESEARCH

See

American Literary Scholarship (3265): chapter on literature to 1800.
Harbert, *Fifteen American Authors before 1900* (3280).

SERIAL BIBLIOGRAPHIES

See

ABELL (340): English Literature/Seventeenth Century and Eighteenth Century sections.
Eighteenth Century: A Current Bibliography (2245).
MLAIB (335): American Literature division in the volumes for 1922–25; American III: Seventeenth and Eighteenth Centuries (1607–1815) in the volumes for 1926–28; American III: Seventeenth and Eighteenth Centuries in the volumes for 1929–40; American II: Seventeenth and Eighteenth Centuries in the volumes for 1941–80; and American Literature/1600–1699 and 1700–1799 (or any larger chronological section that encompasses either century) in volumes after 1980. Researchers must also check the headings beginning "American Literature" in the subject index to post-1980 volumes.
"Some Current Publications," *Restoration* (2250).

OTHER BIBLIOGRAPHIES

See

Rubin, *Bibliographical Guide to the Study of Southern Literature* (3625).
Wages, *Seventy-Four Writers of the Colonial South* (3625a).

THESES AND DISSERTATIONS

4020 Montgomery, Michael S., comp. *American Puritan Studies: An Annotated Bibliography of Dissertations, 1882–1981.* Bibliographies and Indexes in American History 1. Westport: Greenwood, 1984. 419 pp. Z1251.E1.A54 [F7] 016.974'02.

An annotated bibliography of 940 dissertations accepted through 1981 by American, Canadian, British, and German universities on American Puritanism from c. 1620 to c. 1730. Besides literature and language, this work encompasses philosophy, psychology, politics, history, geography, religion, recreation, economics, sociology, law, education, music, art, science, medicine, and military affairs. Arranged chronologically by date of degree, entries record author, title, degree, institution, and pagination. The typically full annotations cite *Dissertation Abstracts/Dissertation Abstracts International* (465) reference; identify full, partial, or revised publication as a monograph (but not article); and note when a dissertation is not extant. Descriptions, which consist largely of quotations from introductions or abstracts and/or a list of contents, are derived (in order of preference) from published versions, printed abstracts, or the dissertations themselves, and frequently note parts not appearing in a published version. Four indexes: authors; short titles; institutions; subjects. *American Puritan Studies* is valuable for its compilation and indexing of entries in the standard national lists of dissertations, annotation of numerous works not abstracted elsewhere, and identification of published versions. For dissertations after 1981, see section H: Guides to Dissertations and Theses.

RELATED TOPICS

4025 Gephart, Ronald M., comp. *Revolutionary America, 1763–1789: A Bibliography*. 2 vols. Washington: Library of Congress, 1984. Z1238.G43 [E208] 016.9733.

A selective, yet extensive, bibliography of primary and secondary works (through December 1972) related to the Revolutionary period. Although journal articles, theses, and dissertations are included, selection is limited to holdings of the Library of Congress. The 14,810 entries are organized alphabetically by author or title of anonymous work in most of the 12 extensively classified divisions: bibliographies and reference works (with sections for subject bibliographies, catalogs of eighteenth-century imprints, and guides to manuscript collections); general studies; the British Empire and the American Revolution; the colonies on the eve of independence; the West; the war, 1775–83; loyalists; diplomacy and other international aspects of the Revolution; confederation and consolidation of the Revolution; the Constitution, 1787–89; economic, social, and intellectual life (with sections on printers, newspapers, books, and libraries; literature; and fine arts); and biographical sources. Fewer than 40% of the entries are accompanied by descriptive annotations that frequently cite related works. The work is indexed by names and some subjects, but users must study the explanation of indexing procedures on p. 1469 before searching the index. Restricting coverage to Library of Congress holdings and works published before 1973 results in the omission of some important studies, especially in the sections related to literature, and the inclusion of several works of dubious value; even so, Gephart provides an important guide to scholarship and primary materials that range well on either side of the period 1763–89.

See also

Pargellis, *Bibliography of British History: The Eighteenth Century* (2260).

Biographical Dictionaries

4030 Levernier, James A., and Douglas R. Wilmes, eds. *American Writers before 1800: A Biographical and Critical Dictionary*. 3 vols. Westport: Greenwood, 1983. PS185.A4 810'.9'001.

A collection of biographical-bibliographical-critical essays on 786 representative writers. Each essay consists of four parts: a list of major works, biography, critical estimate, and list of selected studies (to c. 1982). Concluding the work are a chronology (1492–1800) and three appendixes (lists of writers by year of birth, place of birth, and principal residence). Indexed by persons and subjects. Although the essays are uneven in quality, several incorporate recent discoveries. Overall this is a generally trustworthy compilation of information, especially for minor writers; for authors in common, the *Dictionary of Literary Biography* (600) volumes on the period are generally superior. Review: J. A. Leo Lemay, *Early American Literature* 19 (1984): 215–17.

See also

Dictionary of Literary Biography (600).
Todd, *Dictionary of British and American Women Writers* (2265).

Periodicals

GUIDES TO PRIMARY WORKS

Bibliographies

4035 Brigham, Clarence S. *History and Bibliography of American Newspapers, 1690–1820*. 2 vols. Worcester: American Antiquarian Soc., 1947. Z6951.B86 016.071.

———. "Additions and Corrections to *History and Bibliography of American Newspapers, 1690–1820*," *Proceedings of the American Antiquarian Society* 71 (1961): 15–62.

Lathem, Edward Connery, comp. *Chronological Tables of American Newspapers, 1690–1820: Being a Tabular Guide to Holdings of Newspapers Published in America through the Year 1820*. Barre: American Antiquarian Soc., 1972. 131 pp.

A bibliography of 2,120 newspapers published through 1820 in what is now the United States. Organized alphabetically by state, then by original title (with cross-references for later ones), entries include notes on the date of establishment and cessation, frequency, title changes, printer(s), and publisher(s), followed by a list of holdings; both the notes and locations are generally fuller than those in *United States Newspaper Program National Union List* (3405). Concludes with lists of libraries and private owners. Two indexes in vol. 2: titles; printers, publishers, and editors. The *Chronological Tables*, which includes Brigham's additions, is organized by state, then city, then newspaper. A monumental work, Brigham is still the best general source for information about and locations of early American newspapers, which remain understudied by literary scholars. For other holdings, see OCLC (225) and RLIN (230).

4040 Kribbs, Jayne K., comp. and ed. *An Annotated Bibliography of American Literary Periodicals, 1741–1850*. Reference Publication in Literature. Boston: Hall, 1977. 285 pp. Z1219.K75 [PS1] 016.81'05.

A bibliography of 940 periodicals of "distinctly literary interest," excluding dailies, almanacs, and gift books. Entries are organized alphabetically by original title, with cross-references for subtitles and later titles. The amount of detail varies depending on available information, but a full entry cites title, date of first and last issue, frequency, editor(s), publisher(s), and up to two locations. (For a more complete list of locations, see section K: Periodicals/Union Lists; OCLC [225]; and RLIN [230].) Most entries conclude with a summary of literary content organized by genre and noting representative poets, types of prose works, subjects of biographies, titles of fiction and plays, and miscellaneous topics. Five indexes: chronological index of periodicals; geographical list of periodicals; editors and publishers; literary authors; titles of fiction and plays. Some information is taken from *Union List of Serials* (640a) and other standard sources rather than personal examination of runs. Although Kribbs's work is not comprehensive, cites publication information incompletely, and is highly selective in recording contents, it is nevertheless an important pioneering effort that is especially valuable for the access its indexes offer. Review: Benjamin Franklin Fisher IV, *Literary Research Newsletter* 5 (1980): 149–52.

Indexes

4045 *Index to Early American Periodicals to 1850*. Ed. Nelson F. Adkins. New York: Readex, 1964. Micropaque.

A reproduction of a card index to some 340 American magazines published between 1730 and 1850. The cards are divided into six parts:

1. General prose, with separate alphabetical sequences for authors and titles of anonymous works;
2. Fiction, also with sequences for authors and anonymous works;
3. Poetry, with alphabetical lists of authors, titles, and first lines;
4. Book reviews, with sequences for authors of books reviewed and titles of anonymous books;
5. Songs, with lists for authors, composers, titles of anonymous works, and first lines;
6. Subject index to pt. 1.

A card typically records author, title, periodical, publication information, and an occasional note on content. The illegibility of many of the handwritten cards and poor quality of the reproduction, incomplete coverage of many periodicals, numerous inconsistencies in recording information, a multitude of inaccuracies, and uneven, idiosyncratic indexing render the volume an exasperating work to consult. Yet as the only index to many of the periodicals, it remains a useful source of American literary and cultural history. A major desideratum is an index similar to the *Wellesley Index* (2545).

GUIDES TO SCHOLARSHIP AND CRITICISM

See

Chielens, *Literary Journal in America to 1900* (4145).

SCHOLARLY JOURNALS

Several journals in the following sections publish on early American literature: K: Periodicals/Scholarly Journals; M: English Literature/Restoration and Eighteenth-Century Literature/Periodicals/Scholarly Journals; and Q: American Literature/General/Periodicals/Scholarly Journals.

4050 *Early American Literature* (*EAL*). 1966– . 3/yr. Former title: *Early American Literature Newsletter* (1966–67). PS501.E2 810.

Publishes articles, occasional bibliographies, reviews, review essays, and special issues on American literature through c. 1830. Cumulative index: vols. 1–10, Dante Thomas, *Index to Volumes I–X, 1966–1976:* Early American Literature (Amherst: U of Massachusetts, n.d., 39 pp.).

See also

Seventeenth-Century News (2080).

Genres

Most works in section Q: American Literature/General/Genres and some in L: Genres are important to research in early American literature.

FICTION

Most works in section Q: American Literature/General/Genres/Fiction and some in L: Genres/Fiction are useful for research in early American fiction.

Histories and Surveys

4055 Petter, Henri. *The Early American Novel.* Columbus: Ohio State UP, 1971. 500 pp. PS375.P4 813'.03.

A descriptive, critical survey of American fiction (excluding that published in magazines) from the 1780s to 1820. Organized by subject matter (didactic, satiric, or polemic fiction; love stories; novels of adventure), the discussions of individual works typically incorporate lengthy synopses. Additional summaries are printed in an appendix. Concludes with a bibliography of primary and secondary works (although the latter is superseded by Parker, *Early American Fiction* [4065]). Indexed by persons and titles. The standard survey of early American fiction, Petter is more valuable for its description of works than critical commentary. Reviews: Alexander Cowie, *American Literature* 43 (1971): 485–86; John Duffy, *New England Quarterly* 45 (1972): 133–34.

Guides to Primary Works

4060 Pitcher, E. W. *Fiction in American Magazines before 1800: An Annotated Catalogue.* In progress.

A catalog of original fiction and translations printed in American magazines before 1800. Organized alphabetically by story title, entries cite publication information and typically include detailed notes on authorship, source, reprints, related works, content, and scholarship. Concludes with a register of fiction by magazine, chronological lists of fiction by American authors and translations, and a bibliography of scholarship. Two indexes: first lines of untitled stories; authors and subjects. With its extensive research on sources and authorship, this work promises to be an important catalog that will encourage study of a neglected area of early American fiction.

See also

Wright, *American Fiction, 1774–1850* (4180).

Guides to Scholarship and Criticism

4065 Parker, Patricia L. *Early American Fiction: A Reference Guide.* Reference Guide to Literature. Boston: Hall, 1984. 197 pp. Z1231.F4.P25 [PS375] 016.813'2.

A descriptively annotated bibliography of studies (through 1980, with a few as late as 1982) on American fiction before 1800. Entries are listed by year of publication within divisions for general and thematic studies, anonymous works, and 28 individual authors (excluding Brown, who is the subject of her *Charles Brockden Brown: A Reference Guide*, Reference Publication in Literature [Boston: Hall, 1980, 132 pp.]). Reprints are needlessly given separate entries; dissertations actually read by the compiler appear under date of acceptance but others, incongruously, under the year an abstract was published in *Dissertation Abstracts/Dissertation Abstracts International* (465). Although several works receive multiple listings, users should check the name index to locate all studies treating an author. Annotations are adequately descriptive. Two indexes: names; titles and subjects. The fullest guide to scholarship on early American fiction.

See also

Holman, *American Novel through Henry James* (4185).
Kirby, *America's Hive of Honey* (4190).

DRAMA AND THEATER

Most works in section Q: American Literature/General/Genres/Drama and Theater and some in L: Genres/Drama and Theater are important to research in early American drama and theater.

Guides to Primary Works

4070 Hill, Frank Pierce, comp. *American Plays Printed, 1714–1830: A Bibliographical Record.* Stanford: Stanford UP; London: Oxford UP, 1934. 152 pp. Z1231.D7.H6 061.812.

A bibliography of original plays and translations written and published between 1714 and 1830 by American authors, either resident in the country or abroad, and foreigners living in America. Although admitting a broad range of works, Hill excludes dialogues with fewer than three characters and grand opera libretti. Entries, listed by author or title of anonymous work, include title, publication information, pagination, size, locations (restricted to the holdings of 10 United States libraries), and occasional notes (on, for example, productions, sources, authorship, and dedicatee). Works not located are listed separately on pp. 117–20. Two indexes: titles; dates of publication. Although it includes several inaccurate descriptions, much unverified information, and many works that can hardly be considered plays or are not by Americans or foreign residents, Hill remains the standard guide. It must be used with the extensive corrections and additions recorded in three articles by Roger E. Stoddard: "Some Corrigenda and Addenda to Hill's *American Plays Printed 1714–1830*," *Papers of the Bibliographical Society of America* 65 (1971): 278–95; "Further Corrigenda and Addenda to Hill's *American Plays Printed 1714–1830*," 77 (1983): 335–37; "United States Dramatic Copyrights, 1790–1830: A Provisional Catalogue," *Essays in Honor of James Edward Walsh on His Sixty-Fifth Birthday* [ed. Hugh Amory and Rodney G. Dennis] (Cambridge: Goethe Institute and Houghton Library, 1983) 231–54.

Although superseded in its listing of published plays, Oscar Wegelin, *Early American Plays, 1714–1830: Being a Compilation of the Titles of Plays by American Authors Published and Performed in America Previous to 1830*, ed. John Malone (New York: Dunlap Soc., 1900, 113 pp.), remains useful for its attempt to cover all plays, published or not.

Guides to Scholarship and Criticism

See

Meserve, *American Drama to 1900* (4200).
Wilmeth, *American Stage to World War I* (3525).

Microform Collections

See

Wells, *Three Centuries of Drama* (1180).

POETRY

Some works in section L: Genres/Poetry are useful for research in early American poetry.

Guides to Primary Works

4075 Jantz, Harold S. "The First Century of New England Verse." *Proceedings of the American Antiquarian Society* 53 (1944): 219–508. Also separately published: Worcester: American Antiquarian Soc., 1944. 292 pp.

A historical survey, anthology, and bibliography of early New England verse, including fragments and epitaphs from gravestones. The bibliography lists all known verse, printed and manuscript, by New England writers born up to the 1670s, by immigrants before their arrival in the Colonies, and written in or about New England by transients. Under each author, individual poems or collections are listed by composition or publication date; a chronological list of anonymous verse through 1700 follows the author section. An entry typically provides title, first line, or descriptive heading, number of lines, publication information, location of manuscript or a particularly rare printed work, reprints, and occasional notes on textual or bibliographical matters. Although in need of revision and updating, Jantz remains an essential guide to identifying and locating early American verse.

4080 Lemay, J. A. Leo. *A Calendar of American Poetry in the Colonial Newspapers and Magazines and in the Major English Magazines through 1765.* Worcester: American Antiquarian Soc., 1972. 353 pp. Z1231.P7.L44 016.811'1'08.

A chronological list of American poetry (that is, English-language poems of five or more lines by American residents as well as poems about the country by foreigners) published in 52 periodicals between 1705 and 1765. Because of difficulties in establishing authorship, as many as 20% of the 2,091 entries may represent poems by foreign writers. A typical entry provides date and publication information, first line, title, number of lines, author or pseudonym, and notes (including a list of reprints, biographical information, or commentary on subject matter). Four indexes: first lines; names, pseudonyms, and titles; subjects and genres; periodicals. Because of its numerous attributions of authorship and the access to subject and genre it provides, the *Calendar* is the indispensable guide to the previously uncharted body of early American poetry.

Separately published verse is recorded in Wegelin, *Early American Poetry* (4085).

4085 Wegelin, Oscar. *Early American Poetry: A Compilation of the Titles of Volumes of Verse and Broadsides by Writers Born or Residing in North America North of the Mexican Border [1650–1820].* 2nd ed., rev. and enl. 2 vols. New York: Smith, 1930. Z1231.P7.W4 016.81.

A bibliography of separately published British and American editions of verse by residents of what is now the United States. Wegelin includes broadsides, pamphlets, and verse dialogues, but excludes plays. Vol. 1 covers 1650 to 1799, vol. 2, 1800 to 1820; each volume consists of separate alphabetical lists of works of known or ascribed authorship and of anonymous publications. Under each author, works are organized chronologically by date of earliest known edition. For the earliest known edition, a description includes title, format, pagination, a limited number of locations, and occasional notes on content, other editions, and bibliographical matters; for subsequent editions, only publication information is usually given. Indexed by titles in vol. 2.

Roger E. Stoddard is preparing a revision, which will be confined to separately published books and pamphlets of more than two leaves (excluding music books, drama, and works for children). Entries will appear in a single author list and, for the earliest known edition, record author, title, imprint, collation, number of pages, height of leaf, location of one copy, description of publisher's binding, bibliographical references, and notes. Subsequent editions will have briefer descriptions. Until the revision appears, scholars must consult the following by Stoddard:

A Catalogue of Books and Pamphlets Unrecorded in Oscar Wegelin's Early American Poetry, 1650–1820. Providence: Friends of the Library of Brown U, 1969. 84 pp. (Reprinted from *Books at Brown* 23 [1969]: 1–84.) Review: J. A. Leo Lemay, *Early American Literature* 8 (1973): 66–77.

"Further Addenda to Wegelin's *Early American Poetry*." *Papers of the Bibliographical Society of America* 65 (1971): 169–72.

"More Addenda to Wegelin's *Early American Poetry*." *Proceedings of the American Antiquarian Society* 88 (1978): 83–90.

"Fourth Addenda to Wegelin's *Early American Poetry*." *Proceedings of the American Antiquarian Society* 90 (1981): 387–90.

"Lost Books: American Poetry before 1821." *Papers of the Bibliographical Society of America* 76 (1982): 11–41.

"Poet and Printer in Colonial and Federal America: Some Bibliographical Perspectives." *Proceedings of the American Antiquarian Society* 92 (1983): 265–361.

Together, these works provide the fullest guide to separately published early American verse. For poetry in periodicals, see Lemay, *Calendar of American Poetry* (4080).

Guides to Scholarship and Criticism

4090 Scheick, William J., and JoElla Doggett. *Seventeenth-Century American Poetry: A Reference Guide*. Reference Guides in Literature 14. Boston: Hall, 1977. 188 pp. Z1227.S3 [PS312] 016.811'1.

Rainwater, Catherine, and William J. Scheick. "*Seventeenth-Century American Poetry*: A Reference Guide Updated." *Resources for American Literary Study* 10 (1980): 121–45.

An annotated bibliography of scholarship through 1979 on poetry by American immigrants or transients born before 1680. Excludes bibliographies and general literary histories. Following a division for general and thematic studies, literary influences, and aesthetics are sections for individual authors and almanacs; broadsides, ballads, and anonymous verse; and elegies. Within each division, works are listed by publication date under separate headings for books, shorter writings (including parts of books), and dissertations. (As in other early Hall Reference Guides, these headings are repeated even when no book, shorter writing, or dissertation appears in a year.) Entries are accompanied by full descriptive annotations. Although many works are given multiple entries, users should consult the index to locate all studies of a writer or type of verse. An asterisk marks the few works not seen. The index of persons and selected topics is difficult to use because of the abbreviations identifying the section in which an entry appears. Despite the omission of bibliographies and general literary histories, *Seventeenth-Century American Poetry* is an essential compilation for identifying scholarship on early American verse.

See also

Donow, *Sonnet in England and America* (1250).
Kuntz, *Poetry Explication* (1255).

PROSE

Most works in section Q: American Literature/General/Genres/Prose and some in L: Genres/Prose are important to research in early American prose.

Guides to Scholarship and Criticism

4095 Yannella, Donald, and John H. Roch. *American Prose to 1820: A Guide to Information Sources*. American Literature, English Literature, and World Literatures in English: An Information Guide Series 26. Detroit: Gale, 1979. 653 pp. Z1231.P8.Y36 [PS367] 016.818'08.

A selective bibliography of studies and editions through 1975 (but with some works as late as 1978) of nonfiction prose. Yannella and Roch emphasize twentieth-century scholarship but exclude most dissertations and foreign-language studies. Entries are organized alphabetically by author in five divisions: general studies and reference works (with sections for printing and publishing, anthologies and collections, bibliographies and checklists, genres and rhetoric, studies in period criticism, studies of periodicals and newspapers, African American slave narratives, and Indian captivity narratives), Colonial period, Revolutionary and early national period (both with sections for literary and cultural studies, anthologies and collections, and bibliographies and checklists), principal authors (with separate lists of editions, bibliographies, and biographical and critical studies under each), and other authors. Indexed by persons, titles, and selected subjects. The guide is a useful starting place for research on early prose, even though it is selective, lacks a clear explanation of criteria governing selection, and is awkwardly organized (with many sections unnecessarily split into books and articles).

Nineteenth-Century Literature

Most works in section Q: American Literature/General are important to research in nineteenth-century American literature.

Guides to Primary Works

4110 *American Book Publishing Record* (*ABPR*). New York: Bowker, 1960– . Monthly, with annual, quinquennial, and retrospective cumulations for 1876–1949, 1950–77, and 1876–1981 (microfiche). Z1219.A515 015.

An augmented, corrected cumulation of the alphabetical lists in *Weekly Record* (in *Publishers Weekly* [5270] from 1876 through 26 August 1974; after that, published separately by Bowker), *ABPR* is a classified list of books published or distributed in the United States that have been cataloged by the Library of Congress or Bowker. Excluded are "federal and other governmental publications, subscription books, dissertations, new printings (as distinct from reprints, revised or new editions), quarterlies and other periodicals, [many] pamphlets under forty-nine pages, and specialized publications of a transitory nature or intended as advertising." Books are organized by Dewey Decimal Classification (with separate alphabetical lists of adult fiction, juvenile fiction, and mass market paperbacks; the cumulations omit the last list, but the one for 1950–77 has a section for non-Dewey Decimal classified works). In addition to basic card catalog information, entries usually list price and the address of an obscure publisher or distributor. Corrected entries are substituted in the various cumulations, and the ones for 1950–77 and 1876–1981 add thousands of records taken from the *NUC*s (235 and 240). Each issue and cumulation has author, title, and Library of Congress subject-tracing indexes; in addition, there are cumulative indexes covering 1876–1981 (1982, microfiche). Unfortunately the indexes cite Dewey Decimal Classification rather than page number; thus, in the cumulations users must frequently scan several columns to locate an entry. The title index offers quicker access than the author index to books by someone with a common name such as "Susan Jones" or "John Smith." Although not comprehensive and including several ghosts and errors, *ABPR* is the most convenient source for keeping abreast of new works, editions, or reprints published or distributed in the United States; and, within the limitations of the Dewey Decimal Classification, the cumulations provide a subject guide to a majority of the books published since 1876 in the country. Review: (1950–77 cumulation) Ruth P. Burnett, *College and Research Libraries* 40 (1979): 358–62.

Works for children that are listed in *ABPR* also appear in *Fiction, Folklore, Fantasy, and Poetry for Children, 1876–1985* (5475). The 1876–1950 cumulation supersedes E. Leypoldt and R. R. Bowker, eds., *American Catalogue: Author and Title Entries of Books in Print and for Sale (Including Reprints and Importations), July 1, 1876 [–December 31, 1910]*, 8 vols. in 13 pts. (New York: Publishers Weekly, 1880–1911).

4115 *Bibliotheca Americana: Catalogue of American Publications, Including Reprints and Original Works, from 1820 to 1852, Inclusive*. Comp. O. A. Roorbach. New York: Roorbach, 1852. 652 pp. Supplements: *October, 1852, to May, 1855*. 1855. 220 pp. *May, 1855, to March, 1858*. New York: Wiley; London: Trubner, 1858. 256 pp. *March, 1858, to January, 1861*. New York: Roorbach; London: Trubner, 1861. 162 pp. Z1215.A3 015.73.

An author and title list of books published in the United States. Biographies are entered under subject rather than author; legal publications and periodicals occupy separate lists in the 1820–52 collection. An entry records author, title, number of volumes, size, binding, price, and publisher. The original compilation gives publication dates for only historical and travel literature; the first and second supplements, for most works; the last supplement, for none. Although incomplete, frequently inaccurate, and inconsistent in providing both author and title entries, *Bibliotheca Americana* remains the most comprehensive general list of works published in the country during the period. It is gradually being superseded, however, by Shoemaker, *Checklist of American Imprints* (4130).

4120 Kelly, James, comp. *The American Catalogue of Books (Original and Reprints) Published in the United States from Jan., 1861, to Jan., [1871], with Date of Publication, Size, Price, and Publisher's Name.* 2 vols. New York: Wiley, 1866–71. Z1215.A5 015.73.

An author and title list that continues *Bibliotheca Americana* (4115) and includes some pre-1861 works omitted from it. Most author and title entries cite editor, illustrator, translator, edition, size, binding, price, publication information, and date. Three appendixes: (vol. 1) pamphlets, sermons, and addresses on the Civil War; other sermons and addresses (giving topic but neither title nor publication information); (both vols.) publications of learned societies. The *American Catalogue* is incomplete (especially for works published in the South during the Civil War), frequently inaccurate, and inconsistent in supplying title entries. Nevertheless, it provides the fullest general list of works published in the country during the 10 years. It will eventually be superseded by Shoemaker, *Checklist of American Imprints* (4130). Continued by *American Book Publishing Record* (4110).

4125 Shaw, Ralph R., and Richard H. Shoemaker, comps. *American Bibliography: A Preliminary Checklist for [1801–19]* (Shaw-Shoemaker). 22 vols. New York: Scarecrow, 1958–66. Z1215.S48 015.73.

A continuation of Evans, *American Bibliography* (4005), with each volume devoted to a single year. The 51,960 entries—listed alphabetically by author, corporate author, or title of anonymous work—record title, imprint, pagination, and locations. Corrections appear in vol. 22 and in the list of omitted entries in Frances P. Newton, comp., *Printers, Publishers, and Booksellers Index; Geographical Index* (Metuchen: Scarecrow, 1983, 443 pp.). Indexed by titles in vol. 21, by authors in 22. *Early American Imprints, Series II: Shaw-Shoemaker* (New Canaan: Readex) reproduces in microform a majority of the nonserial publications.

A preliminary bibliography based entirely on secondary sources (with discrepancies resolved by reliance on what the compilers determined was the "best" source), Shaw-Shoemaker is subject to many of the same deficiencies and limitations as Evans, including misattributions of authorship, publication information, or date; inaccurate titles; and duplicate entries. Like its predecessor, however, Shaw-Shoemaker offers the fullest record of printing during the period; is a useful resource for investigating the intellectual milieu of works, surveying publishing trends, identifying works or editions by standard reference number, and locating copies; and forms part of the basis for a fuller, more sophisticated and accurate retrospective bibliography. Some additions appear in "American Bibliographical Notes," *Proceedings of the American Antiquarian Society* 82 (1972): 53–64; 83 (1973): 273–76; 84 (1974): 399–402, 404–06.

The chronological record is continued by Shoemaker, *Checklist of American Imprints* (4130).

4130 Shoemaker, Richard H., Gayle Cooper, Scott Bruntjen, and Carol Rinderknecht [Bruntjen], comps. *A Checklist of American Imprints for [1820–86]* (Shoemaker). Metuchen: Scarecrow, 1964– . Z1215.S5 015.73.

A continuation of Shaw, *American Bibliography* (4125). Like its predecessor, Shoemaker devotes a volume to each year; lists entries alphabetically by author, corporate author, or title of anonymous work; and records title, imprint, pagination, and locations of copies. Unlike Evans, *American Bibliography* (4005) and Shaw-Shoemaker, it excludes serial publications. Entries for 1820 through 1829 are indexed in two volumes compiled by M. Frances Cooper: *A Checklist of American Imprints, 1820–1829: Title Index* (Metuchen: Scarecrow, 1972, 556 pp.) and *A Checklist of American Imprints, 1820–1829: Author Index, Corrections, and Sources* (1973, 172 pp.); additional indexes are planned for each decade.

Although some entries are based on examination of copies, the majority are derived from secondary sources; thus Shoemaker is subject to many of the same limitations and deficiencies as Evans and Shaw-Shoemaker, including misattributions of authorship, publication information, or date; inaccurate titles; and duplicate entries. (Corrections are printed in Cooper, *Author Index* [see above].) Like its predecessors, however, Shoemaker offers the most thorough record of printing during the period; is a useful resource for investigating the intellectual milieu of works, surveying publishing trends, identifying works or editions by standard reference number, and locating copies; forms part of the basis for a fuller, more sophisticated and accurate retrospective bibliography; and supersedes, for the volumes published, *Bibliotheca Americana* (4115) and *American Imprints Inventory*, 52 nos. (Washington: Historical Records Survey, 1937–42).

See also

Literary Writings in America (3255).
Nineteenth Century Short Title Catalogue (2475).

Guides to Scholarship and Criticism

SURVEYS OF RESEARCH

4135 Myerson, Joel, ed. *The Transcendentalists: A Review of Research and Criticism*. Modern Language Association of America Reviews of Research. New York: MLA, 1984. 534 pp. Z7128.T7.T7 [B905] 016.141'3'0973.

A collection of evaluative surveys of research (from the nineteenth century through 1981), with individual essays on general topics (the transcendentalist movement, its historical background, relationship to Unitarianism, communities, and periodicals), 28 transcendentalists, and the contemporary reaction of 11 authors. The essays on transcendentalist writers (varying from 2 to 28 pages) include sections on bibliographies, manuscripts, editions, biographical studies, and criticism (with the last variously subdivided); the essays on major authors such as Emerson and Thoreau focus on the transcendentalist period of their careers. The other essays are variously organized, with those on contemporary writers limited to their relation to the movement. Most essays offer suggestions for further research. Unlike other MLA surveys of research, this work records full publication information in a list of works cited. Indexed by persons, anonymous titles, and some subjects. Judicious evaluation, accuracy, and thoroughness make *The Transcendentalists* the indispensable guide to the movement. Review: Kenneth Walter Cameron, *Analytical and Enumerative Bibliography* ns 1 (1987): 92–97.

For evaluations of recent scholarship, see the chapters "Emerson, Thoreau, and Transcendentalism" and "19th-Century Literature" in *American Literary Scholarship* (3265).

4140 Woodress, James, ed. *Eight American Authors: A Review of Research and Criticism*. Rev. ed. New York: Norton, 1972. 392 pp. PS201.E4 810'.9'003.

Evaluative surveys of research on Poe, Emerson, Hawthorne, Thoreau, Melville, Whitman, Twain, and James, in a collection that revises the work by Floyd Stovall, ed. (New York: MLA, 1956, 418 pp.; rpt., with bibliographic supplement by J. Chesley Mathews, New York: Norton, 1963, 466 pp.). Coverage extends through 1969, is selective (especially for articles), and excludes dissertations and foreign scholarship in some chapters. The essays—by established scholars but not necessarily specialists in the respective authors—are variously organized within a general framework that encompasses bibliographies, editions, biographical studies, and criticism. The failure to provide complete bibliographical information sometimes results in delays in tracking down an article. Indexed by persons. While *Eight American Authors* is now badly dated, its thoughtful and exacting evaluations make it an indispensable guide to studies published before 1970. For evaluative surveys of later scholarship, see *American Literary Scholarship* (3265), which has chapters on each author.

See also

American Literary Scholarship (3265): Chapters on Emerson, Thoreau, and Transcendentalism; Hawthorne; Poe; Melville; Whitman and Dickinson; Mark Twain; James; and the nineteenth century.

Romantic Movement: A Selective and Critical Bibliography (2485).

SERIAL BIBLIOGRAPHIES

See

ABELL (340): English Literature/Nineteenth Century section.

MLAIB (335): American Literature division in the volumes for 1922–25; American IV: Romantic Period (1815–1890) and V: 1890 to the Present in the volume for 1926; American III: Seventeenth and Eighteenth Centuries (1607–1815) in the volumes for 1926–28; American IV: Nineteenth Century in the volumes for 1929–34; American IV: Nineteenth Century, 1800–1870 and V: Nineteenth Century, 1870–1900 in the volumes for 1935–40; American III: Nineteenth Century, 1800–1870 and IV: Nineteenth Century, 1870–1900 in the volumes for 1941–80; and American Literature/1800–1899 (as well as any larger chronological section encompassing the century) in volumes after 1980. Researchers must also check the "American Literature" heading in the subject index to post-1980 volumes.

Biographical Dictionaries

See

Dictionary of Literary Biography (600).

Periodicals

GUIDES TO PRIMARY WORKS

See

Brigham, *History and Bibliography of American Newspapers, 1690–1820* (4035).
Index to Early American Periodicals to 1850 (4045).
Kribbs, *Annotated Bibliography of American Literary Periodicals, 1741–1850* (4040).

GUIDES TO SCHOLARSHIP AND CRITICISM

4145 Chielens, Edward E. *The Literary Journal in America to 1900: A Guide to Information Sources*. American Literature, English Literature, and World Literatures in English: An Information Guide Series 3. Detroit: Gale, 1975. 197 pp. Z6951.C57 [PN4877] 016.81'05.

A selective annotated bibliography of English-language studies (through the early 1970s) of literary periodicals as well as other periodicals that were influential in the development of American literature. Chielens excludes dailies and annuals as well as any work that has not been the subject of at least one dissertation, book, chapter, or article. Entries are listed alphabetically by author in seven divisions (some of which have sections for general studies and individual periodicals): general studies, New England, Middle-Atlantic states, the South, the West, bibliographies and checklists (including sections for some of the preceding divisions), and background studies. Studies of literary materials in nonliterary periodicals and of Poe and American literary periodicals are relegated to appendixes. The work is flawed by a narrow focus, inadequate explanation of scope, and inefficient organization, but it is a serviceable compilation of studies that are sometimes difficult to locate in the standard serial bibliographies and indexes in section G. Continued by Chielens, *Literary Journal in America, 1900–1950* (4250).

INDEXES

4150 *Poole's Index to Periodical Literature*. By William Frederick Poole et al. 6 vols. Boston: Houghton, 1888–1908. AI3.P7 016.05.

1802–81. 2 pts. Rev. ed. By William Frederick Poole and William I. Fletcher. 1891.

First Supplement: 1882–87. By William Frederick Poole and Fletcher. 1888. 483 pp.
Second Supplement: 1887–92. By Fletcher. 1895. 476 pp.
Third Supplement: 1892–96. By Fletcher and Franklin O. Poole. 1897. 637 pp.
Fourth Supplement: 1897–1902. By Fletcher and Mary Poole. 1903. 646 pp.
Fifth Supplement: 1902–07. By Fletcher and Mary Poole. 1908. 714 pp.

A subject index to 479 British and (predominantly) American periodicals published between 1802 and 1 January 1907. The supplements provide current as well as retrospective coverage for periodicals newly added. Although entries cite an abbreviated title, author (with many unauthenticated attributions), periodical title, volume, and initial page number, researchers accustomed to modern subject indexes will find *Poole's* a frustrating work to consult because (1) subject headings, derived largely from title words, are capricious and inconsistent, and offer few cross-references to related headings; (2) the imposition of uniform periodical titles and volume numbers which ignore title changes and a publisher's numbering system means that Dearing (see below) must be consulted to locate many articles; (3) literary contributions are listed by title; (4) reviews of literary works appear under the author of the work reviewed, but reviews of nonfiction books appear under the subject of the work; (5) the numerous attributions of unsigned articles must be authenticated in more reliable sources. Some of these defects are remedied in the following:

Dearing, Vinton A. *Transfer Vectors for* Poole's Index to Periodical Literature: *Number One: Titles, Volumes, and Dates*. Los Angeles: Pison, 1967. 95 pp. (The projected key to subject headings was never published.) Because it expands title abbreviations, lists title changes, provides volume–year correspondences, and converts assigned volume numbers to those actually used in periodicals, this work is essential for ascertaining the actual publication details for citations. Dearing is easier to use than Marion V. Bell and Jean C. Bacon, Poole's Index *Date and Volume Key*, ACRL Monographs 19 (Chicago: Assn. of College and Reference Libraries, 1957, 61 pp.).

Wall, C. Edward, comp. and ed. *Cumulative Author Index for* Poole's Index to Periodical Literature, *1802–1906*. Ann Arbor: Pierian, 1971. 488 pp. Provides the only access to authors listed in *Poole's*, but users must search all possible variants because Wall does not regularize names.

Additions and corrections appear in Thorvald Solberg, "Authors of Anonymous Articles Indexed in *Poole*," *Bulletin of Bibliography* 1 (1898): 91–93, 105–07, and in a series of variously authored "Errata in *Poole's Index* and Supplements," 2 (1900): 24–25, 40–41, 56–58, 75–76, (1901): 107–08, 133–34; 3 (1902): 25–26; 4 (1904): 11–12, 72.

Despite its manifold deficiencies, *Poole's* offers the only available indexing of numerous periodicals and—if approached with patience, an awareness of its limitations, and inventiveness—can yield valuable access to more than 590,000 articles. For an instructive discussion of search strategies, see pp. 37–40 in Vann, *Victorian Periodicals* (2525).

More accurate indexing of a limited number of periodicals can be found in *Nineteenth Century Readers' Guide* (400a) and *Wellesley Index* (2545); however, neither approaches the breadth of *Poole's*. Reviews published between 1880 and 1900 in 13 popular American periodicals not in *Poole's* are indexed in Patricia Marks, *American Literary and Drama Reviews: An Index to Late Nineteenth Century Periodicals*, Reference Publication in Literature (Boston: Hall, 1983, 313 pp.).

4155 Wells, Daniel A. *The Literary Index to American Magazines, 1815–1865.* Metuchen: Scarecrow, 1980. 218 pp. Z6513.W44 [PN523] 051'.01'6.

An author and subject index to articles, excerpts, reviews, and regular columns of literary or cultural interest in 25 important or representative literary magazines between 1815 and 1865. Anonymous contributors are identified only for *Dial*. Titles of articles occupy a separate list. Although the layout is poor and coverage limited, the *Literary Index* is a useful preliminary source for locating works by several minor authors and for studying the American reception of writers, native and foreign, of the period.

See also

Literary Writings in America (3255).

SCHOLARLY JOURNALS

Most journals in sections K: Periodicals/Scholarly Journals and Q: American Literature/General/Periodicals/Scholarly Journals publish on nineteenth-century American literature.

4160 *American Literary Realism, 1870–1910* (*ALR*). 1967– . 3/yr. PS228.R3.A52 810.9004.

Publishes articles, bibliographies, surveys of research, supplements to author bibliographies, documents, notes, and reviews on the period. Cumulative indexes: vols. 1–10, in 10 (1977): 431–40; vol. 11 to the present, in each volume since 13 (1980). A useful source of bibliographies and checklists on authors and topics too narrow to merit separate publication; however, in recent volumes the number of bibliographies has declined.

4165 *ESQ: A Journal of the American Renaissance* (*ESQ*). 1955– . Quarterly. Former title: *Emerson Society Quarterly* (1955–69). PS1629.E6 810'.9'003.

Publishes articles and reviews on all aspects of the Romantic transcendentalist tradition. The reviews typically encompass two or more books. Cumulative index: vols. 1–39, Robert A. Rees and R. Dilworth Rust, *Index of the First Decade (1955–1965)* (Hartford: Transcendentalist Books, 1966, 82 pp.).

4170 *Studies in the American Renaissance [1977–]* (*SAR*). 1978– . Annual. PS201.S86 810'.9'003.

Publishes biographical, historical, and bibliographical articles on the literature and culture of the period 1830–60, as well as calendars of letters, bibliographies, and edited texts. The emphasis is overwhelmingly on literature. Cumulative index: volumes for 1977–86, in *1986*: 445–55.

See also

American Transcendental Quarterly (3585).
Early American Literature (4050).
Studies in Romanticism (2605).

Background Reading

4175 Matthiessen, F. O. *American Renaissance: Art and Expression in the Age of Emerson and Whitman*. London: Oxford UP, 1941. 678 pp. PS201.M3 810.903.

An analysis of the interrelationships of Emerson, Thoreau, Whitman, Hawthorne, and Melville, emphasizing their conceptions of the function and nature of literature and concern with the democratic spirit, and the intellectual contexts and cultural politics that resulted in the imaginative flowering during the period 1850–55. A seminal work in its fusion of criticism and literary history, and its influence on the legitimization of the study of American literature in academe. Reviews: Granville Hicks, *New England Quarterly* 14 (1941): 556–66; Robert E. Spiller, *American Literature* 13 (1942): 432–35.

For an analysis of the political and theoretical underpinnings of the work, see Jonathan Arac, "F. O. Matthiessen: Authorizing an American Renaissance," in *The American Renaissance Reconsidered*, ed. Walter Benn Michaels and Donald E. Pease, Selected Papers from the English Institute ns 9 (Baltimore: Johns Hopkins UP, 1985) 90–112. Vanderbilt, *American Literature and the Academy* (3455) discusses the genesis and critical reception of the work and offers a detailed assessment (pp. 469–80).

Genres

Most works in sections L: Genres and Q: American Literature/General/Genres are useful for research in nineteenth-century American literature.

FICTION

Most works in sections L: Genres/Fiction and Q: American Literature/General/Genres/Fiction are useful for research in nineteenth-century American fiction.

Histories and Surveys

See

Petter, *Early American Novel* (4055).

Guides to Primary Works

4180 Wright, Lyle H. *American Fiction, 1774–1850: A Contribution toward a Bibliography*. 2nd rev. ed. San Marino: Huntington Library, 1969. 411 pp. Z1231.F4.W9 016.812'3.

———. *American Fiction, 1851–1875: A Contribution toward a Bibliography*. Rpt., with additions and corrections. 1965. 438 pp. Z1231.F4.W92 016.8133.

———. *American Fiction, 1876–1900: A Contribution toward a Bibliography*. 1966. 683 pp. Z1231.F4.W93 016.8134.

A bibliography of American editions of separately published American fiction, including novels, romances, tall tales, allegories, and fictitious biographies and travels, but excluding juvenile fiction, jestbooks, Indian captivity narratives, periodicals, annuals, gift books, folklore, tracts published by religious societies, dime novels, and subscription series. The 1774–1850 volume attempts to include all editions; the later volumes are limited to first or earliest located editions. Organized alphabetically by author, unidentified pseudonym, or title of anonymous work, entries provide title, publication information, pagination, format, list of contents for collections of stories, copyright deposit information, occasional notes on subject matter, and locations in selected major libraries and private collections. Stories in collections are cross-referenced to the collection. Indexed by titles in all volumes and by dates in the 1774–1850 volume. Although not comprehensive, Wright offers an incomparable record of American fiction through 1900. A number of corrections appear in Edward W. Pitcher, "Some Emendations for Lyle B. Wright's *American Fiction, 1774–1850*," *Papers of the Bibliographical Society of America* 74 (1980): 143–45. Reviews: (1774–1850) John S. Van E. Kohn, *Papers of the Bibliographical Society of America* 42 (1948): 324–30; (1876–1900) Roger E. Stoddard, *New England Quarterly* 41 (1968): 600–04.

All but a few of the works in Wright have been microfilmed in *American Fiction, 1774–1910* (Woodbridge: Research Publications, 1967–84). Post-1900 editions were compiled from the Library of Congress shelflist of American adult fiction. *American Fiction, 1774–1900: Cumulative Author Index to the Microfilm Collection* (New Haven: Research Publications, 1974, 416 pp.) and *American Fiction, 1901–1910: Cumulative Author Index to the Microfilm Collection* (Woodbridge: Research Publications, 1984, 217 pp.) are essential for locating individual titles on the microfilm reels.

Coverage is being continued by "American Fiction, 1901–1925: A Contribution toward a Bibliography," a data base located at the William Charvat Collection of American Fiction (Ohio State U Libraries, 1858 Neil Ave. Mall, Columbus 43210–1286). Using Wright's criteria for selecting titles, the project is cataloging more than 14,000 titles published during the period. Current records are available through OCLC (225) and will eventually be accessible through RLIN (230); when complete the data base will be sold at cost as a machine-readable file that can be searched by subject, genre, gender and race of author, regional association, publisher, and illustrator.

See also

Grimes, *Novels in English by Women, 1891–1920* (2640).

Guides to Scholarship and Criticism

4185 Holman, C. Hugh, comp. *The American Novel through Henry James*. 2nd ed. Goldentree Bibliographies in Language and Literature. Arlington Heights: AHM, 1979. 177 pp. Z1231.F4.H64 [PS371] 016.813.

A highly selective bibliography of English-language scholarship through 1976 that emphasizes nineteenth-century novelists. Holman excludes most studies before 1900 and most general literary histories as well as dissertations and bibliographies of bibliographies. Entries are organized in divisions for the novel as form, histories of the American novel, special studies (with sections for periods, genres, and themes or subjects), major novelists (with sections for editions, bibliographies, biographical and critical books, and essays), and lesser novelists. The supplement (pp. 141–57) is similarly organized. A few entries are accompanied by brief descriptive annotations. Indexed by scholars.

A similar work is David K. Kirby, *American Fiction to 1900: A Guide to Information Sources*, American Literature, English Literature, and World Literatures in English: An Information Guide Series 4 (Detroit: Gale, 1975, 296 pp.), with highly selective coverage through c. 1975 and an inadequate explanation of scope and criteria governing both the selection of authors and scholarship.

Highly selective and dated, *The American Novel* and *American Fiction* together offer only a preliminary guide to scholarship.

For reviews of late nineteenth-century fiction, see Clayton L. Eichelberger, comp., *A Guide to Critical Reviews of United States Fiction, 1870–1910*, 2 vols. (Metuchen: Scarecrow, 1971–74). Unfortunately, because of its numerous errors and inconsistencies, omission of significant periodicals, inclusion of many nonfictional works, and inadequate editing, Eichelberger's *Guide* cannot be trusted. (For the deficiencies of this work, see the review by Blake Nevius, *Nineteenth-Century Fiction* 27 [1972]: 245–47.)

4190 Kirby, David. *America's Hive of Honey; or, Foreign Influences on American Fiction through Henry James: Essays and Bibliographies*. Metuchen: Scarecrow, 1980. 214 pp. Z1231.F4.K573 [PS374.F64] 813'.009'3.

A selective annotated bibliography of studies of 16 major influences on the fiction of Brown, Irving, Cooper, Poe, Hawthorne, Melville, Mark Twain, James, Howells, Norris, and Crane. The work is limited to studies (through 1976 and primarily in English) that identify specific sources. Within divisions for Oriental sources, classical literature, the Bible, Dante and the Middle Ages, Spenser, Cervantes, Shakespeare and the Renaissance, Milton and his age, the eighteenth century, Austen, gothic novelists, the Romantics, Scott, the Victorians, realists, and scientific thinkers and naturalists, entries are listed alphabetically by author in sections for general studies and individual American writers. Each division begins with a headnote assessing generally the influence of the author, period, group, movement, or work. Two brief appendixes list general studies of the influence of foreign cultures on American fiction and of the reading habits of individual authors. Indexed by persons and titles of primary works. The detailed annotations make *America's Hive of Honey* a useful guide to source studies, few of which are readily identifiable in standard bibliographies and indexes.

DRAMA AND THEATER

Most works in sections L: Genres/Drama and Theater and Q: American Literature/General/Genres/Drama and Theater are useful for research in nineteenth-century American drama and theater.

Guides to Primary Works

4195 *Dramatic Compositions Copyrighted in the United States, 1870 to 1916.* 2 vols. Washington: GPO, 1918. Z5781.U55 [PN1851] 016.812.

A list of the approximately 60,000 plays registered for copyright between 1870 and 1916. Works are listed alphabetically by title, with cross-references for alternate titles or subtitles. Because of changes in copyright law, entries vary in content but typically record (when appropriate) title; author; translator; copyright claimant; and date of registration, of publication, and of deposit of copy. (Users should study the explanation of the sample entries on pp. iii-iv.) Plays registered during part of 1915 and all of 1916, along with additions and corrections, appear in a supplementary list (pp. 2659–833). Indexed by persons (with titles following each name). Copies of about 20,000 works registered before 1 July 1909 were never deposited; however, *Dramatic Compositions* is an underutilized but indispensable record of plays that were copyrighted in the United States. Since deposit copies—many of which are unpublished manuscripts or printed acting copies—are held by the Library of Congress, the work also serves as a valuable source for locating otherwise unobtainable materials. For other copyright records, see Tanselle, "Copyright Records and the Bibliographer" (3260).

See also

Hill, *American Plays Printed, 1714–1830* (4070).

Guides to Scholarship and Criticism

4200 Meserve, Walter J. *American Drama to 1900: A Guide to Information Sources.* American Literature, English Literature, and World Literatures in English: An Information Guide Series 28. Detroit: Gale, 1980. 254 pp. Z1231.D7.M45 [PS345] 016.812.

A bibliography of English-language scholarship and selected editions through c. 1977. Meserve excludes studies of theater because of the presence of Wilmeth, *American Stage to World War I* (3525) in a related Gale series. Entries are listed alphabetically by author in two divisions: general studies and major authors. The first has sections for bibliographies, indexes, library and microform collections, anthologies and collections, general histories, and history and criticism (with the last organized by period and including studies of minor authors and anonymous plays). Each of the 34 important playwrights (most of whom date from the nineteenth century) has separate lists of editions, nondramatic works, bibliographies, biographical studies, and criticism. Generous cross-references guide users to related studies.

The generally brief descriptive annotations are uneven, with many failing to convey a sense of content. Three indexes: persons; titles; subjects. Although selective and lacking an adequate explanation of scope and criteria governing selection, Meserve offers the best preliminary guide to studies of American drama before 1900 and is far superior to Eddleman, *American Drama Criticism* (3520). It must be supplemented by the serial bibliographies and indexes in section G and in section Q: American Literature/General/Guides to Scholarship and Criticism.

See also

Wilmeth, *American Stage to World War I* (3525).

Microform Collections

See

Wells, *Three Centuries of Drama* (1180).

POETRY

Some works in section L: Genres/Poetry are useful for research in nineteenth-century American poetry.

PROSE

Many works in sections L: Genres/Prose and Q: American Literature/General/Genres/Prose are useful for research in nineteenth-century American prose.

Guides to Scholarship and Criticism

4205 Partridge, Elinore Hughes. *American Prose and Criticism, 1820–1900: A Guide to Information Sources*. American Literature, English Literature, and World Literatures in English: An Information Guide Series 39. Detroit: Gale, 1983. 575 pp. Z1231.P8.P37 [PS368] 016.818'08.

A highly selective list of editions and studies through c. 1981 of nonfiction prose. Entries are organized in three divisions: general studies (with sections for bibliographies and reference works; periodicals and annual bibliographies; cultural, historical, and literary studies; and anthologies), prose (with sections for literary theory and criticism; autobiographies, memoirs, and diaries; essays and sketches; works of travel and description; educational, religious, philosophical, and scientific writings; and history and politics—each with lists of primary works and studies), and 45 individual authors (with lists of principal works; letters and journals; editions, selections, and reprints; bibliographies; biographical studies and criticism;

and related general studies). The descriptive annotations sometimes include brief evaluative comments. Indexed by persons and titles. Because of the inadequate explanation of scope and criteria governing selection, poor organization of the first division, exclusion of most articles in the lists of studies, and numerous inconsistencies, Partridge offers little more than a place to begin research on prose of the period.

See also

Yannella, *American Prose to 1820* (4095).

Twentieth-Century Literature

Most works in section Q: American Literature/General and some in section M: English Literature/Twentieth-Century Literature are important to research in twentieth-century American literature.

Histories and Surveys

4220 Hoffman, Daniel, ed. *Harvard Guide to Contemporary American Writing*. Cambridge: Belknap-Harvard UP, 1979. 618 pp. PS221.H357 810'.9'0054.

A critical history of trends and movements in American literature from 1945 to c. 1978 that emphasizes established writers and literature as an exposition of culture. Separate essays consider intellectual backgrounds; literary criticism; realists, naturalists, and novelists of manners; southern fiction; Jewish writers; experimental fiction; African American literature; women's literature; drama; and poetry. Although not a connected history and not always balanced in its treatment, the *Harvard Guide* offers the fullest overview of the period. Reviews: Nina Baym, *JEGP: Journal of English and Germanic Philology* 79 (1980): 271–75; Jerome Klinkowitz, *College English* 42 (1980): 382–89.

Literary Handbooks, Dictionaries, and Encyclopedias

See

Encyclopedia of World Literature in the 20th Century (2755).

Guides to Primary Works

4225 *Books in Print* (*BIP*). New York: Bowker, 1948– . Annual, with supplement between editions. (Currently published in four parts—authors, titles, subjects, and publishers—and available, along with *Forthcoming Books*, on CD-ROM as *Books in Print Plus*.) Z1215.P972 015.73.

A list of books published or distributed in the United States and available for general purchase. *BIP* excludes sacred texts, music, microforms, and a host of ephemeral publications. Each entry records author, title, publication information, LC card and ISBN numbers, distributor, and price. Because names are not standardized, users must check all forms of an author's name. Compiled from information supplied by publishers, *BIP* is neither comprehensive nor always accurate, but it is the most convenient source for determining what books are currently available for sale from United States publishers and distributors. (For a list of the numerous subject area guides to books in print, see the prefatory matter to the most recent *BIP*.)

Books in Print Plus (the CD-ROM version) is updated every three months; it is also available in CD-ROM as *Books in Print with Book Reviews Plus*, which includes reviews from *Publishers Weekly* (5270), *Choice* (750), and three other library journals. Since it is updated every month (more frequently during peak publishing periods) and includes books declared out of print after July 1979, the BIPS data base (searchable through Dialog [520] and BRS [515]) offers the most current information. Some books published since the latest edition of *BIP* can sometimes be found in *Weekly Record* (4110a) or *American Book Publishing Record* (4110).

The following are useful related Bowker publications:

Books out of Print. 1983– . Annual, with cumulation for 1980–85. Lists books reported by publishers as no longer available. More current information is available through the BIPS data base.

Children's Books in Print (5470).

Forthcoming Books. 1966– . Bimonthly. Compiled from information supplied by publishers, these volumes are far from complete and inevitably list books that will be delayed or never appear.

Paperbound Books in Print. 1971– . 2/yr. Offers a fuller listing of paperbacks than *BIP*.

The Publisher's Trade List Annual (*PTLA*). 1873– . Annual. Now a multivolume compilation of publishers' catalogs (of four or more pages) along with a yellow-page section comprised of smaller lists. Although far from comprehensive, *PTLA* is frequently a useful supplement to *BIP*, especially for a description of a book or list of titles within a series. Since few libraries have extensive holdings of publishers' catalogs, *PTLA* is a valuable resource for studying publishing history and reconstructing a firm's list.

For author, title, publisher, and subject lists of books published by small and private presses, see *Small Press Record of Books in Print* (Paradise: Dustbooks, 1969– , annual). Coverage is international but emphasizes English-language works printed in the United States.

Reprints are conveniently listed in *Guide to Reprints: An International Bibliography of Scholarly Reprints* (Kent: Guide to Reprints, 1967– , annual).

4230 Lepper, Gary M. *A Bibliographical Introduction to Seventy-Five Modern American Authors*. Berkeley: Serendipity, 1976. 428 pp. Z1227.L46 [PS221] 016.81.

Checklists of first printings of separately published works through 1975 by 75 authors who achieved prominence after 1945. Lepper includes signed and revised editions, ephemera (such as broadsides and mimeographed or photocopied material), and some bound proofs and advance review copies; he excludes sheet music, recordings, and edited books. Authors are listed alphabetically; works, chronologically. Entries include title, publication information, type of binding or method of reproduction, format, notes on priority of issues, identifying marks of first printings, illustrator, and series. The descriptions are not bibliographically sophisticated; criteria governing selection of authors are unstated; there are some notable omissions; and coverage is sometimes inconsistent. Nonetheless, the *Bibliographical Introduction* offers a useful and reasonably accurate preliminary guide to first printings of works by writers who are not the subject of separate author bibliographies. Some other contemporary authors are treated in Bruccoli, *First Printings of American Authors* (3250a). Review: Patricia McLaren-Turner, *Book Collector* 28 (1979): 449–50, 453.

4235 Vrana, Stan A. *Interviews and Conversations with 20th-Century Authors Writing in English: An Index*. Metuchen: Scarecrow, 1982. 239 pp. *Series II*. 1986. 288 pp. (*Series III*, a supplement covering 1981–85, with additions from 1900–80, is scheduled for 1989.) Z2013.V73 [PR471] 016.82'09'0091.

A selective author index to interviews and similar works from 1900 through 1980 in periodicals, newspapers, and books (the majority of which are published in the United States and involve American authors). Entries are listed chronologically under an author and include citations to reprints. Although not at all comprehensive—since it omits recordings and numerous serials—*Interviews and Conversations* is a useful starting point for locating interviews; however, the inadequate explanation of scope and of sources consulted means that a user will frequently end up having to duplicate much of Vrana's research.

Researchers with access to *MLAIB* (335) data base can identify additional interviews.

See also

American Book Publishing Record (4110).
Literary Writings in America (3255).
Nineteenth Century Short Title Catalogue (2475).

Guides to Scholarship and Criticism

SURVEYS OF RESEARCH

4240 Bryer, Jackson R., ed. *Sixteen Modern American Authors: A Survey of Research and Criticism*. New York: Norton, 1973. 673 pp. (A supplement is in progress.) PS221.F45 810'.9'0052.

Evaluative surveys of research and criticism on Anderson, Cather, Crane, Dreiser, Eliot, Faulkner, Fitzgerald, Frost, Hemingway, O'Neill, Pound, Robinson, Steinbeck, Stevens, William Carlos Williams, and Wolfe. Revises *Fifteen Modern American Authors* (Durham: Duke UP, 1969, 493 pp.), correcting errors, extending coverage through 1971–72, and adding the essay on Williams. The supplement will continue coverage from 1972. Although each chapter consists of five parts—bibliographies, editions, manuscripts and letters, biographical studies, and criticism, with a supplementary section for each—there is considerable variation in the extent of coverage, especially of dissertations and foreign-language scholarship. A majority of the contributors are frank in their evaluations but seldom offer suggestions for further research and do not provide full publication information for articles. These authoritative surveys remain indispensable for their winnowing of pre-1972 scholarship. For evaluative surveys of recent scholarship, see *American Literary Scholarship* (3265). Review: (1st ed.) Willard Thorp, *American Literature* 42 (1970): 122–24.

See also

American Literary Scholarship (3265): Chapters on Pound and Eliot; Faulkner; Fitzgerald and Hemingway; fiction: 1900–1930s; fiction: 1930s-1960s; fiction: 1960s-present; poetry: 1900–1940s; and poetry: 1940s-present.
Contemporary Authors: Bibliographical Series (4245).

SERIAL BIBLIOGRAPHIES

See

ABELL (340): English Literature/Twentieth Century section.
"Annual Review," *Journal of Modern Literature* (2780).
"Current Bibliography," *Twentieth Century Literture* (2790a).
MLAIB (335): American Literature division in the volumes for 1922–25; American V: 1890 to the Present in the volumes for 1926–28; American V: Contemporary Literature (occasionally called Twentieth Century) in the volumes for 1929–34; American VI: Contemporary in the volumes for 1935–40; American V: Twentieth Century (also called Contemporary in 1941–56) in the volumes for 1941–80; and American Literature/1900–1999 (as well as any larger chronological section encompassing the century) in later volumes. Researchers must also check the "American Literature" heading in the subject index to post-1980 volumes.

OTHER BIBLIOGRAPHIES

4245 *Contemporary Authors: Bibliographical Series*. Detroit: Gale, 1986– . Z6519.C64 [PN771] 016.809.

Vol. 1: *American Novelists*. Ed. James J. Martine. 1986. 431 pp.
Vol. 2: *American Poets*. Ed. Ronald Baughman. 1986. 387 pp.

A collection of surveys of research and bibliographies of works by and English-language scholarship about post–World War II authors. Organized by genre within a national literature, the volumes emphasize American and British writers but will include some foreign literatures. Each separately authored bibliography is organized in three divisions: a list of primary works (with sections for books and pamphlets, and other works, including translations, edited collections, and contributions to periodicals and books); a list of important studies (with sections for bibliographies, biographies, interviews, and criticism); and an evaluative survey of major scholarship, whose organization corresponds to the preceding list of studies. Some surveys offer suggestions for further research. Two cumulative indexes in each volume: literary authors; critics. Although highly selective in coverage of scholarship and varying in quality, their typically rigorous evaluations of scholarship make these bibliographies useful starting points for research on the authors covered.

See also

Pownall, *Articles on Twentieth Century Literature* (2790).
Somer, *American and British Literature, 1945–1975* (2800).

Language

See

Quirk, *Comprehensive Grammar of the English Language* (2810).

Biographical Dictionaries

See

Contemporary Authors (595).
Dictionary of Literary Biography (600).

Periodicals

GUIDES TO PRIMARY WORKS

See

Sec. K: Periodicals/Little Magazines.

GUIDES TO SCHOLARSHIP AND CRITICISM

4250 Chielens, Edward E. *The Literary Journal in America, 1900–1950: A Guide to Information Sources.* American Literature, English Literature, and World Literatures in English: An Information Guide Series 16. Detroit: Gale, 1977. 186 pp. Z6951.C572 [PN4877] 016.051.

An annotated, selective bibliography of English-language studies (through the early 1970s) of periodicals devoted to creative works or criticism. Chielens excludes weeklies and annuals, and includes only those publications that have been the subject of at least one dissertation, book, chapter, or article. Entries are listed alphabetically by author in eight divisions (most of which have sections for general studies and individual titles): general works, general mass circulation periodicals, little magazines, regional publications, politically radical literary periodicals, academic quarterlies of scholarship and criticism, bibliographies and checklists (including sections for some of the preceding divisions), and background studies. Scholarship on literary material in nonliterary periodicals is listed in an appendix. Most annotations are helpfully descriptive. Indexed by persons and titles. While *Literary Journal in America* is not comprehensive, is inefficiently organized, and lacks an adequate explanation of scope, it is a useful compilation of studies that are sometimes difficult to locate in standard serial bibliographies and indexes. This work continues Chielens, *Literary Journal in America to 1900* (4145).

INDEXES

See

Literary Writings in America (3255).

SCHOLARLY JOURNALS

Most journals in sections K: Periodicals/Scholarly Journals; M: English Literature/Twentieth-Century Literature/Periodicals/Scholarly Journals; and Q: American Literature/General/Periodicals/Scholarly Journals publish on twentieth-century American literature.

See

American Literary Realism, 1870–1910 (4160).

Background Reading

4255 Jones, Howard Mumford, and Richard M. Ludwig. *Guide to American Literature and Its Backgrounds since 1890*. 4th ed., rev. and enl. Cambridge: Harvard UP, 1972. 264 pp. Z1225.J65 016.81.

A selective guide to the social and intellectual background of American literature from 1890 through the 1960s. The first part is a classified list of background studies arranged in sections for general works, reference sources, histories, special topics (including economic, social, and political history; science and technology; and the fine and popular arts), and literary history (including general works, reference sources, specialized histories, themes, language, genres, biography, magazines, and publishing history). A few entries are descriptively annotated. The second part arranges reading lists of primary works in chronological divisions that have sections for topics, movements, genres, and types of works. Indexed by authors. Although *Guide to American Literature* is dated, the informed selection makes it still useful for identifying important background studies for the period. A new edition would be welcomed by researchers.

For a fuller list of background works, see Basler, *Guide to the Study of the United States* (3325).

Genres

Most works in sections L: Genres and Q: American Literature/General/Genres are important to research in twentieth-century American literature.

FICTION

Most works in sections L: Genres/Fiction and Q: American Literature/General/Genres/Fiction are useful to research in twentieth-century American literature.

Histories and Surveys

4260 Karl, Frederick R. *American Fictions, 1940–1980: A Comprehensive History and Critical Evaluation*. New York: Harper, 1983. 637 pp. PS379.K24 813'.54'09.

A critical history of American fiction that emphasizes its relationship to Modernism and favors experimental works. Indexed by persons, titles, and subjects. An encyclopedic and polemic work, it is especially valuable for placing fiction in cultural contexts. Review: Sanford Pinsker, *Georgia Review* 38 (1984): 891–93.

See also

Allen, *Tradition and Dream: The English and American Novel from the Twenties to Our Time* (2830).

Bibliographies of Bibliographies

4265 McPheron, William, and Jocelyn Sheppard. *The Bibliography of Contemporary American Fiction, 1945–1988: An Annotated Checklist*. Westport: Meckler, 1989. Z1231.F4.M36 [PS379] 016.813'54'09.

An annotated bibliography of bibliographies of works by or about fiction writers who have achieved prominence since 1945. Science fiction, fantasy, and mystery as well as "serious" works are included. Indexed by persons and subjects. Like McPheron, *Bibliography of Contemporary American Poetry* (4315), this work will likely be an essential guide to locating bibliographies of contemporary writers.

Guides to Primary Works

See

Grimes, *Novels in English by Women, 1891–1920* (2640).

Guides to Scholarship and Criticism

4270 Woodress, James. *American Fiction, 1900–1950: A Guide to Information Sources*. American Literature, English Literature, and World Literatures in English: An Information Guide Series 1. Detroit: Gale, 1974. 260 pp. Z1231.F4.W64 016.813'03.

A selective guide to scholarship (mostly in English and published before c. 1972) on 44 authors who have received substantial critical attention. Entries are organized in two divisions: general works and individual authors. The first division consists of inadequately annotated lists of reference works (including general historical and critical studies), general works on the novel (with sections for history and criticism, types, themes, and regionalism), studies of the short story, and collections of interviews. Individual authors are treated in essays, with sections for bibliographies and manuscripts, primary works, editions and reprints, biographical studies, and criticism. The commentary here is much fuller and judiciously evaluative, with important works marked by an asterisk; however, the essay form prevents skimming. Indexed by persons. Although now dated, *American Fiction* is superior to Blake Nevius, comp., *The American Novel: Sinclair Lewis to the Present*, Goldentree Bibliographies in Language and Literature (New York: Meredith-Appleton, 1970, 126 pp.), and remains useful for its guidance to important scholarship before c. 1972 on authors not included in Bryer, *Sixteen Modern American Authors* (4240). For evaluative surveys of recent scholarship, see *American Literary Scholarship* (3265).

See also

American Literary Scholarship (3265): Chapters on fiction: 1900–1930s; fiction: 1930s-1960s; and fiction: 1960s-present.
Martine, *American Novelists* (4245).

Biographical Dictionaries

See

Contemporary Novelists (2845).

Periodicals

See

Critique: Studies in Modern Fiction (2850).

DRAMA AND THEATER

Most works in sections L: Genres/Drama and Theater and Q: American Literature/General/Genres/Drama and Theater are useful for research in twentieth-century American drama and theater.

Histories and Surveys

Histories and general studies are surveyed in Jackson R. Bryer and Ruth M. Alvarez, "American Drama, 1918–1940: A Survey of Research and Criticism," *American Quarterly* 30 (1978): 298–330, and C. W. E. Bigsby, "Drama as Cultural Sign: American Dramatic Criticism," 331–57.

4275 Bigsby, C. W. E. *A Critical Introduction to Twentieth-Century American Drama.* 3 vols. Cambridge: Cambridge UP, 1982–85. PS351.B483 812'.52'09.

A critical rather than historical survey of major playwrights, theater groups, and—in vol. 3—types of drama that emphasizes alienation as the central theme of modern American drama. Vol. 1 has several appendixes listing productions by important theater groups; in vol. 3, an appendix traces the growth of nonprofit professional theater. Indexed in each volume by persons, titles, and theater groups. Densely written and omitting some important writers, Bigsby nonetheless is the best survey of the topic. Reviews: Peter L. Hays, *Theatre Research International* 8 (1983): 265–67; Myron Matlaw, *Essays in Theatre* 5 (1986): 77–81.

Literary Handbooks, Dictionaries, and Encyclopedias

4280 *Notable Names in the American Theatre.* Rev. ed. [Ed. Raymond D. McGill.] Clifton: White, 1976. 1,250 pp. PN2285.N6 790.2'0973.

An accumulation of biographical and other information on the American stage through c. 1974 that revises Walter Rigdon, ed., *The Biographical Encyclopaedia and Who's Who of the American Theatre* (New York: Heineman, 1966, 1,101 pp.). *Notable Names* is organized in nine divisions:

A title list of New York productions since 1900, with entries providing theater, opening date, and number of performances;

A title list of premieres in America since 1968, with entries citing author, date of first performance, producing group, and theater, and with an author index following;

A chronological list of premieres of American plays abroad from 9 December 1948 through 8 April 1974, with entries noting date, title, author, director, producer, theater, and location;

An alphabetical list of active and defunct American theater groups, with entries giving address, major personnel, and a brief history;

An alphabetical list of active and defunct American theaters, with entries citing address and opening date;

An alphabetical list of theater awards, with a chronological list of recipients of each;

A subject bibliography of biographies and autobiographies of American and foreign theater persons;

An alphabetical necrology of American and foreign theater persons, with entries providing birth and death dates;

A biographical dictionary of notable persons in the American theater, with stylistically wooden entries providing basic biographical information, address, and lists of credits, publications, and awards.

While the work lacks an adequate statement of scope for most of the lists, fails to provide a general index, and is sometimes inaccurate, it does bring together a significant amount of useful detail about the American stage.

Guides to Primary Works

4285 Leiter, Samuel L., ed. *The Encyclopedia of the New York Stage, 1920–1930.* 2 vols. Westport: Greenwood, 1985. (*1930–1940* is scheduled for 1989; additional volumes are in progress.) PN2277.N5.L36 792.9'5'097471.

A description of Broadway and off-Broadway plays (as well as foreign-language and ethnic theater productions reviewed in the English-language press) staged from 16 June 1920 through 15 June 1930. The approximately 2,500 productions are organized alphabetically by title. For each production, a typical entry includes (where appropriate) genre, subject categories, language if other than English, author, translator or adapter, reviser, librettist, music composer, lyricist, source, director, choreographer, set and costume designers, producer, theater, opening date, length of run, plot synopsis, and notes on critical reception. Concludes with a selected bibliography and 10 appendixes: chronological calendar of productions, with length of run; classified lists by genre, subject, and language (but confusingly organized by subcategories); awards; sources of plays; institutional theaters, with a list of plays produced; foreign companies and stars; longest running shows; critics cited; seasonal statistics; theaters. Two indexes: proper names; titles. The inclusion of cast lists and the provision of clearer subject access would increase the *Encyclopedia*'s utility; it is still, however, a valuable compendium of information on the New York theater.

See also

Dramatic Compositions Copyrighted in the United States, 1870 to 1916 (4195).
Harris, *Modern Drama in America and England, 1950–1970* (4290).

Guides to Scholarship and Criticism

Other Bibliographies

4290 Harris, Richard H. *Modern Drama in America and England, 1950–1970: A Guide to Information Sources.* American Literature, English Literature, and World Literatures in English: An Information Guide Series 34. Detroit: Gale, 1982. 606 pp. Z1231.D7.H36 [PS351] 016.822'914.

A selective bibliography of editions of British and American plays published for the first time between 1950 and 1975, and of English-language scholarship through 1975 on plays published between 1950 and 1970. Excludes plays produced during the period but published after 1975, musicals, and works by African American playwrights (presumably because such works are included in French, *Afro-American Poetry and Drama* [3845], in the same Gale series). Entries are organized in three divisions: bibliographies; general criticism; and 255 authors, each with sections for editions of plays, collaborative works, bibliographies, selected nondramatic works, and criticism. Annotations typically combine description with evaluative comment, but several are inaccurate or inadequately descriptive. Three indexes: persons; titles; subjects (including playwrights). There are significant omissions and the description of scope is confusing and incomplete; thus Harris is useful only for preliminary work. Review: Albert Wertheim, *Literary Research Newsletter* 8 (1983): 38–41. Carpenter, *Modern Drama Scholarship and Criticism, 1966–1980* (2875), offers more thorough coverage of studies after 1965.

Superior coverage of works (through c. 1981) by and about Albee, Baraka, Bullins, Gelber, Kopit, Mamet, Rabe, Shepard, Simon, and Lanford Wilson can be found in Kimball King, *Ten Modern American Playwrights: An Annotated Bibliography*, Garland Reference Library of the Humanities 234 (New York: Garland, 1982, 251 pp.), which is particularly valuable for its full annotations, coverage of foreign scholarship, lists of reviews, and inclusion of translations of primary works.

4295 Wildbihler, Hubert, and Sonja Völklein. *The Musical: An International Annotated Bibliography/Eine internationale annotierte Bibliographie.* München: Saur, 1986. 320 pp. ML128.M78.W56 016.78281'09.

A bibliography of studies through 1985 on the musical (including stage and film productions, extravaganzas, vaudeville and variety shows, and operettas), primarily in North America but also in Great Britain, the Federal Republic of Germany, and a few other countries. Most reviews of individual productions are excluded. The approximately 3,600 entries are organized by publication date in five classified divisions: general reference works (with sections for encyclopedias and guides, review and song indexes, bibliographies, yearbooks, and discographies); stage musical in North America (predecessors, history and development, elements of the musical [such as music and dance], production, and public reception); stage musical in other countries (Great Britain, Federal Republic of Germany and Austria, socialist countries, and other countries); film musical (general studies, essays and short criticism, special effects, adaptations of stage musicals, and dance); and people (general biographical works; composers, lyricists, and librettists; directors, choreographers, and producers; performers). The subtitle is misleading, since only about one-fourth of the entries are accompanied by descriptive annotations, a few of which incorporate an evaluative comment; none of the entries in the people divisions is annotated. Two indexes: scholars; subjects and titles of musicals. Despite the incomplete annotation, this work provides the fullest list of scholarship on the musical and is especially valuable for its international coverage of scholarship.

See also

Carpenter, *Modern Drama Scholarship and Criticism, 1966–1980* (2875).
"Modern Drama Studies: An Annual Bibliography," *Modern Drama* (2870).
Wilmeth, *American Stage to World War I* (3525).

Review Indexes

4300 Salem, James M. *A Guide to Critical Reviews*. 4 pts. Metuchen: Scarecrow, 1971–84. Z5781.S16 [PN2266] 016.8092.

Pt. 1: *American Drama, 1909–1982*. 3rd ed. 1984. 657 pp.
Pt. 2: *The Musical, 1909–1974*. 2nd ed. 1976. 611 pp.
Pt. 3: *Foreign Drama, 1909–1977*. 2nd ed. 1979. 420 pp.
Pt. 4: *The Screenplay from* The Jazz Singer *to* Dr. Strangelove. 2 vols. 1971.
Supplement One: 1963–1980. 1982. 698 pp.

A selective checklist of reviews in general-circulation American and Canadian periodicals and the *New York Times* of productions on the New York stage and of movie and television screenplays. Salem excludes productions of plays written before the late nineteenth century (but the precise cutoff date is unclear). Plays and musicals are listed alphabetically by author; screenplays, by title. Under each work, reviews are organized alphabetically by periodical title. Each part includes a list of major awards; lists of popular or long-running plays appear in pts. 1–3. Indexes: pt. 1 (names; titles); pt. 2 (authors, composers, lyricists; directors, designers, choreographers; original works and authors); pt. 3 (authors, adapters, translators; titles). Limited in scope, the series is principally useful as a compilation of reviews indexed in the standard general indexes in section G.

Reviews from various New York City and national newspapers, weekly magazines, and radio or television stations are printed in *New York Theatre Critics' Reviews* (New York: Critics' Theatre Reviews, 1940– , irregular).

Biographical Dictionaries

4305 *Contemporary Theatre, Film, and Television: A Biographical Guide Featuring Performers, Directors, Writers, Producers, Designers, Managers, Choreographers, Technicians, Composers, Executives, Dancers, and Critics in the United States and Great Britain*. Detroit: Gale, 1984– . Annual. PN2285.C58 791'.092'2.

The expanded continuation of *Who's Who in the Theatre* (Detroit: Gale, 1912–81) that emphasizes established, active individuals but also includes some major figures who are inactive or who died after 1960. Entries, which are modeled after *Contemporary Authors* (595), provide biographical information, career data, publications, screen credits, recordings, memberships, awards, miscellaneous details, and home, office, or agent address. All but a few entries are based on information supplied or checked by the entrant or an agent. Succeeding volumes print updated or revised entries. Cumulative index in each volume; beginning with vol. 2, the cumulative index also covers all 17 editions of *Who's Who in the Theatre* and *Who Was Who in the Theatre: A Biographical Dictionary of Actors, Actresses, Directors, Playwrights, and Producers of English-Speaking Theatre*, 4 vols., Gale Composite Biographical Dictionary Series 3 (Detroit: Gale, 1978). All these volumes are also indexed in *Biography and Genealogy Master Index* (565). Although it is not the comprehensive guide claimed by the preface and although the information supplied by entrants or agents is not always accurate or complete, *Contemporary Theatre* is a useful source of biographical and career information (as well as addresses) of important persons connected with American or British theater, film, or television.

See also

Contemporary Dramatists (2880).
Notable Names in the American Theatre (4280).

Periodicals

4310 *Studies in American Drama, 1945–Present* (*SAD*). 1986– . Annual. PN2000.A3.S78 812.

Publishes articles on theater history and technique, reviews of productions, interviews, documents, and bibliographies.

POETRY

Most works in section L: Genres/Poetry are important to research in twentieth-century American poetry.

Histories and Surveys

See

Perkins, *History of Modern Poetry* (2890).

Bibliographies of Bibliographies

4315 McPheron, William. *The Bibliography of Contemporary American Poetry, 1945–1985: An Annotated Checklist.* Westport: Meckler, 1986. 72 pp. Z1231.P7.M37 [PS323.5] 016.811'54.

A bibliography of bibliographies of works by or about American poets whose reputations were established since 1945. Coverage includes separately published bibliographies, articles, dissertations, theses, and parts of books through 1984. The 267 entries are listed in two divisions: multiple-author bibliographies (organized alphabetically by compiler or editor and including bibliographies of private presses) and single-author bibliographies (listed by publication date under each author). The annotations offer a clear description of scope and (usually) a succinct evaluation of a work's utility or quality. The introduction provides an overview of the bibliography of contemporary poetry. Although the first division includes some works that hardly qualify as bibliographies and although access is hampered by the lack of a subject index or cross-references to multiple-author bibliographies, McPheron includes a number of works not indexed in the standard serial bibliographies and indexes in section G, and is the essential guide to bibliographies of contemporary poets.

Guides to Primary Works

4320 Davis, Lloyd, and Robert Irwin. *Contemporary American Poetry: A Checklist.* Metuchen: Scarecrow, 1975. 179 pp. Davis. *Second Series, 1973–1983.* 1985. 297 pp. Z1231.P7.D38 [PS323.5] 016.811'5'4.

An author list of books of poetry by Americans born after 1900 and still publishing after 1950. The original volume covers 1950 through 1972 (as well as some earlier publications by established poets); the latter, 1973 through 1983. Both exclude vanity press books, collaborations, translations, children's books, broadsides, reprints, and most publications of fewer than 10 pages, although exceptions are made for established writers. Books are listed by publication date under each poet. Indexed by titles. Because the works are far from complete, include many errors, list several non-American writers, and take many entries unverified from unidentified sources, they are useful only as a preliminary guide to volumes of poetry published after 1950 by writers who are not the subject of an author bibliography. For most others, OCLC (225) and RLIN (230) will provide a more accurate, thorough list of separate publications.

Kirby Congdon, *Contemporary Poets in American Anthologies, 1960–1977* (Metuchen: Scarecrow, 1978, 228 pp.), is virtually useless since it indexes poets but not poems.

4325 *Index of American Periodical Verse: [1971–]*. Metuchen: Scarecrow, 1973– . Annual. Z1231.P7.I47 016.811'5'4.

An author list of poems appearing in selected periodicals, primarily English-language little magazines, university reviews, and scholarly journals published in the United States and Canada (although a few Spanish-language publications from the United States and Puerto Rico have been indexed since the volume for 1981). Coverage currently encompasses about 200 periodicals and includes poets from all periods and countries, although the majority are contemporary American writers. Entries are listed alphabetically by author; cross-references cite variant forms of names. Indexed by titles. Compilations since 1982 are also available on IBM-compatible discs from the editors. Although the criteria governing selection of periodicals are unstated and although coverage is far from comprehensive, this work is a useful source for locating poems by contemporary poets in periodicals indexed nowhere else.

Some additional periodicals are covered in *Annual Index to Poetry in Periodicals [1984–]* (Great Neck: Poetry Index, 1985– , annual), an author, title, and first-line index to poems in some 160 little magazines, university reviews, and scholarly journals published in the United States. Like *Index of American Periodical Verse*, the criteria governing selection of periodicals are unstated.

For earlier publications, see the following:

Caskey, Jefferson D., comp. *Index to Poetry in Popular Periodicals, 1955–1959*. Westport: Greenwood, 1984. 269 pp. Author, title, first-line, and subject indexes to about 7,000 poems in periodicals covered by *Readers' Guide* (400), which does not index poems after 1957.

Index to Poetry in Periodicals, 1925–1929: An Index of Poets and Poems Published in American Magazines and Newspapers. Great Neck: Granger, 1984. 265 pp. Covers about 450 periodicals and newspapers.

Index to Poetry in Periodicals, 1920–1924: An Index of Poets and Poems Published in American Magazines and Newspapers. Great Neck: Granger, 1983. 178 pp. Covers 302 periodicals and newspapers.

Index to Poetry in Periodicals: American Poetic Renaissance, 1915–1919: An Index of Poets and Poems Published in American Magazines and Newspapers. Great Neck: Granger, 1981. 221 pp. An author index to 122 American magazines and newspapers.

Poems in several single-author collections are indexed by author, title, and title keywords in *American Poetry Index: An Author, Title, and Subject Index to*

Poetry by Americans in Single-Author Collections [1981–] (Great Neck: Granger, 1983– , annual).

4330 Reardon, Joan, and Kristine A. Thorsen. *Poetry by American Women, 1900–1975: A Bibliography*. Metuchen: Scarecrow, 1979. 674 pp. Z1229.W8.R4 [PS151] 016.811'008.

An author bibliography of about 9,500 separately published volumes of poetry by some 5,500 female United States citizens who published significant works between 1900 and 1975. Reardon and Thorsen exclude collaborative and mixed-genre works, foreign-language editions, reprints, and most broadsides. Entries—listed by publication date under an author—cite title, publication information, and pagination. Although the sources of entries are not identified and the authors are inconsistent in citing later editions and providing cross-references for pseudonyms and variant forms of names, this is a serviceable compilation.

See also

Baughman, *American Poets* (4245).
Poetry Index Annual (1240).

Guides to Scholarship and Criticism

4335 Gingerich, Martin E. *Contemporary Poetry in America and England, 1950–1975*. American Literature, English Literature, and World Literatures in English: An Information Guide Series 41. Detroit: Gale, 1983. 453 pp. Z1231.P7.G56 [PS303] 016.811'5.

An annotated selective bibliography of English-language studies (published through 1978, but with some additions through 1981) on contemporary British and American poetry. The approximately 100 poets (two-thirds of them American) are selected on the basis of having been the subject of a reasonable amount of criticism, although writers who appear in other volumes in the series are excluded. The studies included seem to represent what the compiler found in standard bibliographies and indexes. The descriptively annotated entries are organized alphabetically in eight divisions: bibliographies and reference works, contemporary culture and sociology, general aesthetics and poetic theory, general studies of poetry and poets, general studies of American poets and literature, general studies of British poets and literature, studies of two or more poets, and individual authors (each with sections, when needed, for books of poetry, bibliographies, biographies, books about, and articles about). Users must consult existing author bibliographies, since Gingerich supplements but does not duplicate listings in them, and use the name index to locate general studies that discuss an author, since there are no cross-references. Two indexes: names; titles of works cited. The considerable gaps in coverage and lack of a subject index leave this work far short of the sorely needed bibliography of scholarship and criticism on contemporary poetry. It is, however, far superior to Phillis Gershator, *A Bibliographic Guide to the Literature of Contemporary American Poetry, 1970–1975* (Metuchen: Scarecrow, 1976, 124 pp.), which relies extensively on other sources, is far from complete, is inadequately indexed, and includes only books published between 1970 and 1975.

See also

Sec. M: English Literature/Twentieth-Century Literature/Genres/Poetry/Guides to Scholarship and Criticism.

American Literary Scholarship (3265): Chapters on poetry: 1900–1940s and poetry: 1940s–present.

Baughman, *American Poets* (4245).

Kuntz, *Poetry Explication* (1255).

Biographical Dictionaries

See

Contemporary Poets (2895).

Periodicals

Scholarly Journals

4340 *Parnassus: Poetry in Review* (*Parnassus*). New York: Poetry in Review Foundation, 1972– . 2/yr. PN6099.6.P36 809.1.

Devoted to lengthy reviews of works by twentieth-century poets, with occasional attention to critical studies as well as new editions of nineteenth-century poets; also publishes poems and a few critical articles. International in scope, but with an emphasis on American authors.

PROSE

Some works in sections L: Genres/Prose and Q: American Literature/General/Genres/Prose are useful for research in twentieth-century American prose.

Guides to Scholarship and Criticism

4345 Brier, Peter A., and Anthony Arthur. *American Prose and Criticism, 1900–1950: A Guide to Information Sources*. American Literature, English Literature, and World Literatures in English: An Information Guide Series 35. Detroit: Gale, 1981. 242 pp. Z1231.P8.B74 [PS362] 016.81'08'0052.

A bibliography of works (though the mid-1970s) by and about prose writers "who transcend the idiom and intention of purely journalistic or academic writing." The entries are organized in two separate parts: prose and criticism. The first is composed of two divisions: general works (with sections for handbooks, bibliographies and checklists, intellectual background, rhetorical studies, anthologies, and studies of periodicals) and individual authors, who are categorized as entertainers, teachers, or reporters, and then ranked in three groups: A, who receive an annotated list of primary and secondary works; B, for whom selected primary works and studies are summarized in a few paragraphs; and C, who are given a couple of sentences each. The criticism part is composed of three divisions: general works (with sections for bibliographies, general histories of criticism, studies of schools and movements, and literary histories important to the history of criticism), collections of critical essays, and major critics (with separate lists of bibliographies and critical works, an essay discussion of representative studies, and a list of other sources). In both parts, annotations or discussions are largely descriptive. Three indexes: scholars; titles; subjects. Because of the incomplete coverage and lack of criteria governing the selection of both writers and studies, *American Prose and Criticism* is only marginally useful as a starting point for research and must be supplemented by the serial bibliographies and indexes in section G.

R

Other Literatures in English

This section includes works devoted exclusively to literatures in English outside of England, Scotland, Wales, Ireland, and the United States. Because writers in some of these literatures are included in reference works on English or British literature, researchers must consult section M: English Literature. Many works listed in sections G: Serial Bibliographies, Indexes, and Abstracts and H: Guides to Dissertations and Theses cover these literatures.

General

Literary Handbooks, Dictionaries, and Encyclopedias

See

Cambridge Guide to Literature in English (120).

Guides to Primary Works

4370 *International Books in Print [1979–]: English-Language Titles Published Outside the United States and the United Kingdom*. München: Saur, 1979– . Annual. Z2005.I57 018'.4.

An author and title list of English-language books published outside the United States and the United Kingdom and available for sale. *International Books in Print* includes microforms but excludes most publications of fewer than 50 pages, unsigned juveniles, periodicals, and ephemeral local publications. In the author and title list, entries typically cite author or editor, title, publication date, number of pages, price, ISBN, and publisher or distributor. Because entries are compiled from information supplied by publishers, many are incomplete. Nonfiction publications are indexed by Dewey Decimal Classification, except that works about a national literature are combined with a related language in the 400 class. Belles lettres (as well as nonfiction about a specific country) are indexed by country of publication. Overall, subject indexing is inexact. The directory of publishers and distributors is organized by country and accompanied by a name index. *International Books in Print* is far from comprehensive and depends completely on publishers for information, but it offers the most extensive coverage of current English-language works published outside the United States and United Kingdom and is thus an important complement to the other works in this section for identifying creative and scholarly works as well as translations.

See also

Books in English (375a).
Cumulative Book Index (375).

Guides to Scholarship and Criticism

SERIAL BIBLIOGRAPHIES

4375 "Annual Bibliography of Commonwealth Literature [1964–]." *Journal of Commonwealth Literature* (entry 4395) 1 (1965)– .

A classified bibliography of primary and secondary works with divisions in most years for general studies, East and Central Africa, Western Africa, Australia (with Papua New Guinea), Canada, India, Malaysia and Singapore, New Zealand (including the South Pacific islands), Sri Lanka, West Indies, Pakistan, and South Africa. Each division is prefaced by an overview of the year's publications and has sections for bibliographies, research aids, primary works (by genre), criticism (classified by general works and individual authors), nonfiction, and new periodicals. Even though "Annual Bibliography of Commonwealth Literature" is not comprehensive, it offers the best coverage of current studies of English-language literature in several of the countries or areas. See New, *Critical Writings on Commonwealth Literatures* (4380) for scholarship before 1964.

See also

Secs. G: Serial Bibliographies, Indexes, and Abstracts and H: Guides to Dissertations and Theses.
ABELL (340).
MLAIB (335): English Literature division (especially English III: General) through the volume for 1956; English XI: Australia, Canada, Etc. section in the volumes for 1957–66; English II: Australia, Canada, Etc. section in the volumes for 1967–80; and the British Commonwealth section in later

volumes. Researchers must also check the "British Commonwealth Literature" heading in the subject index to post-1980 volumes.

YWES (330): African, Caribbean, and Canadian Literatures in English chapter since vol. 63 (for 1982); expanded to include Australian, New Zealand, and Indian literatures in vol. 64 (for 1983).

OTHER BIBLIOGRAPHIES

4380 New, William H. *Critical Writings on Commonwealth Literatures: A Selective Bibliography to 1970, with a List of Theses and Dissertations*. University Park: Pennsylvania State UP, 1975. 333 pp. Z2000.9.N48 [PR9080] 016.82'09.

A selective bibliography of scholarship on Commonwealth literatures in English. The 6,576 entries are organized in two parts: published works, and theses and dissertations. In each part, entries are listed alphabetically by author in classified divisions for general works and countries or areas (East and West Africa, Australia, Canada, New Zealand, South Africa and Rhodesia, South Asia [India, Pakistan, and Ceylon], Southeast Asia [Malaysia, Singapore, and Philippines], and West Indies). Where appropriate, each division has sections for reference works, general studies, and individual authors. Indexed by scholars. Unfortunately, *Critical Writings on Commonwealth Literatures* separates published works from theses and dissertations—an unnecessary distinction; moreover, it is superseded in parts by recent bibliographies of a national literature or area. Still, the work remains an indispensable source that includes a significant number of studies overlooked by the standard bibliographies and indexes in section G. For scholarship since 1964, see "Annual Bibliography of Commonwealth Literature" (4375).

Periodicals

GUIDES TO PRIMARY WORKS

4385 Warwick, Ronald, comp. and ed. *Commonwealth Literature Periodicals: A Bibliography, Including Periodicals of Former Commonwealth Countries, with Locations in the United Kingdom*. London: Mansell, 1979. 146 pp. Z2000.9.W37 [PR9080] 016.805.

A bibliography and finding list of English-language scholarly and literary journals published through mid-1977 in or about current and former Commonwealth countries (excluding the United Kingdom). Journals are placed according to focus rather than country of publication, in divisions for general works, Africa, Australia, Canada, Caribbean, Hong Kong, Malaysia and Singapore, Mediterranean, New Zealand, Pacific Islands, South Asia, and former Commonwealth nations. Many are subdivided by region or genre. A typical entry cites title, frequency of publication, date of first and last issue, place of publication, publisher, editor, variant titles, and holdings in United Kingdom libraries. (North American scholars will want to consult OCLC [225], RLIN [230], *Union List of Serials* [640a], and *New Serial Titles* [640] for locations.) Although the inevitable omissions and errors appear in this first attempt at a comprehensive list of Commonwealth literary journals, it is an essential source for identifying and locating frequently elusive publications.

INDEXES

See

Index to Commonwealth Little Magazines (795).

SCHOLARLY JOURNALS

Many journals in section K: Periodicals/Scholarly Journals publish articles on other literatures in English.

4390 *Ariel: A Review of International English Literature* (*ArielE*). 1970– . Quarterly. PR1.R352 820.9.

Emphasizes literatures other than English and American in articles, reviews, special issues, and original and translated poems, with a preference for comparative studies. Annual index; cumulative index: vols. 1–12, David Oakleaf and Richard C. Davis, comps., *A Cumulative Index, 1970–1981* (Calgary: U of Calgary P, 1984, 44 pp.).

4395 *Journal of Commonwealth Literature* (*JCL*). 1965– . 2/yr. PR1.J67 820.05.

Publishes articles on the literature of present and former Commonwealth countries (except Great Britain). Most issues include a symposium section devoted to a topic and a checklist of studies of a writer. For the "Annual Bibliography of Commonwealth Literature," see entry 4375.

4400 *Kunapipi*. 1979– . 3/yr. PR9080.5.K8 800.

Publishes articles on the new literatures in English and related topics such as film and history, original fiction and poetry, reviews, interviews, and occasional special issues. The annual "The Year That Was" offers a highly selective overview, by country, of new creative works. Annual index.

4405 *World Literature Written in English* (*WLWE*). 1962– . 2/yr. Former titles: *CBCL Newsletter* (1962–66); *WLWE Newsletter* (1967–71). PR1.W65 [PN1] 820'.9.

Publishes articles, notes, interviews, bibliographies, reviews, and occasional special issues on literatures—other than British and American—in English.

African Literatures in English

Works in section R: Other Literatures in English/General are important to research in African literatures in English.

Guides to Primary Works

4420 Jahn, Janheinz, and Claus Peter Dressler. *Bibliography of Creative African Writing*. Nendeln: Kraus-Thomson, 1971. 446 pp. Z3508.L5.J28 016.8088.

A bibliography of works by and about African authors writing in English and in a variety of other European and African languages. Jahn and Dressler include all books published before 1900 but only creative works from 1910 to c. 1970 (along with some manuscripts ready for publication); except for plays, they exclude separate works in periodicals and anthologies. Coverage of scholarship (including reviews) is selective but international in scope. Entries are organized alphabetically by author within five classified divisions: general (with sections for bibliographies, journals, general studies, negritude, and general anthologies), Western Africa, Central Africa, Eastern Africa, and Austral Africa. Within each region are sections for general studies, anthologies, and individual works; general studies of an author precede the list of his or her primary works, and studies of a specific work are listed after the work. Additions appear on pp. 376–77. Forgeries are listed in an appendix. Four indexes: books by African language (classified according to the four regions); translations, organized by language of the translation; books, by country; persons. Users should study the introductory discussion of limitations and editorial practices. Impressive in its accuracy and breadth, *Bibliography of Creative African Writing* remains the best single list of creative works published before 1970. Parts have now been superseded by more recent author and regional bibliographies, however.

See also

"Annual Bibliography of Commonwealth Literature" (4375).

Guides to Scholarship and Criticism

4425 Lindfors, Bernth. *Black African Literature in English: A Guide to Information Sources*. American Literature, English Literature, and World Literatures in English: An Information Guide Series 23. Detroit: Gale, 1979. 482 pp. *Black African Literature in English, 1977–1981: Supplement*. New York: Africana, 1986. 382 pp. (A supplement covering 1982–86 is in progress.) Z3508.L5.L56 [PR9340] 016.82.

A bibliography of important scholarship and critical editions from 1936 through 1981. Lindfors excludes reviews, political biographies, and newspaper articles on nonliterary activity by authors. Entries are organized in two divisions: genres, topics, and reference sources; individual authors. The first division has sections for bibliographies, biographical sources, interviews with critics and multiple authors, general studies, fiction, drama, poetry, criticism, autobiography, children's literature, popular literature, language and style, literature and commitment, role of the writer, folklore and literature, image of the African, audience, craft of writing, periodicals, publishing, censorship, research (dissertation guides, surveys of research, and discussions of reference works), teaching, organizations and associations, conferences, and festivals; most of these sections have separate lists of bibliographies and studies. Bibliographies, biographical works, interviews, and criticism are listed separately under each author. Most sections conclude with a lengthy list of cross-references. Only a few entries are briefly annotated, principally with a list of authors discussed but sometimes with a note on content or evaluative comment. Four indexes: persons; titles of works cited; subjects; regions. Authoritative in its selection of the most important scholarship and including numerous works omitted from the standard bibliographies and indexes in section G, Lindfors is the indispensable guide to the topic; however, users will wish for more extensive annotations by one of the foremost scholars of black African literature in English.

See also

Lindfors, "Researching African Literatures" (4865).
MLAIB (335): See the English Literature division, especially English III: General, in volumes through 1956; English XI: Australia, Canada, Etc./Africa section in the volumes for 1957–66; English II: Australia, Canada, Etc./Africa section in the volumes for 1967–80; and the African Literature division in later volumes. For African literatures in other languages, see General VII: Oriental and African section in the volumes for 1965–66; Oriental and African Literatures III: Africa in the volume for 1967; and the African Literature division in later volumes. Researchers must also check the "African Literature" heading in the subject index to post-1980 volumes.
New, *Critical Writings on Commonwealth Literatures* (4380).
Schwartz, *Articles on Women Writers* (6605).
"Studies in African Literatures and Oratures" (3790a).
YWES (330): African literature has been covered in the African, Caribbean, Canadian, Australian, New Zealand, and Indian Literatures in English chapter since vol. 63 (for 1982).

Australian Literature

Works in section R: Other Literatures in English/General are important to research in Australian literature.

Guides to Reference Works

4440 Lock, Fred, and Alan Lawson. *Australian Literature: A Reference Guide.* 2nd ed. Australian Bibliographies. Melbourne: Oxford UP, 1980. 120 pp. Z4011.L6 [PR9604.3] 016.82.

A selective guide to reference sources important to research in Australian literature. The 417 entries—which comprise general works as well as those specific to Australia—are variously organized in seven classified divisions: bibliographies; other reference works (including encyclopedias, language dictionaries, guides to quotations and proverbs, biographical dictionaries, literary handbooks, and literary and cultural histories); individual authors (limited to bibliographies, textual studies, and biographies); periodicals; library resources (with informative descriptions of important collections of Australian literature in the country's libraries); general guides to literary, bibliographical, and biographical research; and professional associations.

Many sections are preceded by headnotes that compare works and offer helpful tips on research procedures. The full annotations clearly describe and frequently evaluate works. Judiciously selective and informative, this is the essential guide to research in Australian literature. Review: Laurie Hergenhan, *Australian Literary Studies* 9 (1980): 542–47.

The best general guide to reference works (through 1974) on Australia is D. H. Borchardt, *Australian Bibliography: A Guide to Printed Sources of Information* [3rd ed.] (Rushcutters Bay: Pergamon, 1976, 270 pp.). The descriptive surveys, keyed to a list of works cited and accompanied by an inadequate subject index, are difficult to scan, however.

Histories and Surveys

4445 Green, H. M. *A History of Australian Literature Pure and Applied: A Critical Review of All Forms of Literature Produced in Australia from the First Books Published after the Arrival of the First Fleet until 1950 [i.e., 1980]*. Rev. by Dorothy Green. 3 vols. Sydney: Angus, 1984– . PR9604.3.G74 820'.9'994.

A critical history of belletristic, philosophical, biographical, theological, historical, and scholarly writing by Australian residents or those influenced by their stay in the country. The history is organized in five periods (1789–1850, 1850–90, 1890–1923, 1923–50, and 1950–80), each divided in two parts—belles lettres and applied literature—with chapters on genres or types of works. Indexed in vol. 2 by persons, titles, and some subjects. Although in need of updating and superseded in parts by more specialized studies, Green remains the seminal history of Australian literature.

The best short history is Ken Goodwin, *A History of Australian Literature* (New York: St. Martin's, 1986, 322 pp.), which extends to 1984 and includes a chronology that supplements Johnston, *Annals of Australian Literature* (4460). Less satisfactory is *The Oxford History of Australian Literature*, ed. Leonie Kramer (Melbourne: Oxford UP, 1981, 509 pp.), which lacks the coherence and depth of Green. It does include a useful evaluative bibliographical survey by Joy Hooton (pp. 427–90).

Literary Handbooks, Dictionaries, and Encyclopedias

4450 Wilde, William H., Joy Hooton, and Barry Andrews. *The Oxford Companion to Australian Literature*. Melbourne: Oxford UP, 1985. 760 pp. PR9600.2.W55 820'.9'944.

Covers all aspects of Australian literary culture in about 3,000 entries on authors (including historians, critics, and journalists, but with very selective coverage of contemporary writers), major works, literary and scholarly journals, awards, societies, movements, publishers, literary characters and types, cultural and scholarly organizations, Australian life and history, places, other literature-related topics, and foreign writers who visited the continent or had an impact on its literature. Author entries (which predominate in the listings) include basic biographical information, a brief overview of important works, appreciative commentary in some instances, and (for major writers) a selective list of criticism. Judicious selection and commentary make the *Oxford Companion* a valuable source for quick reference. Review: Miriam J. Shillingsburg, *Review* 9 (1987): 231–39.

4455 *The Dictionary of Australian Quotations*. Ed. Stephen Murray-Smith. Richmond: Heinemann, 1984. 464 pp. (A second edition is in progress.) PN6081.D496 828'.02.

A dictionary of quotations ranging from aboriginal times to 1984 and encompassing "anything worth retrieving and repeating that has been said by outsiders *about* Australia, and anything worth collecting that Australians have said about *anything*." The approximately 4,000 quotations are organized alphabetically by author. Two indexes: keywords; subjects. The original edition will remain useful for quotations deleted in the second edition. The *Dictionary* is the best source for locating quotations from Australian authors or about the country.

Annals

4460 Johnston, Grahame. *Annals of Australian Literature*. Melbourne: Oxford UP, 1970. 147 pp. Z4021.J6 016.82.

A chronology from 1789 through 1968 of Australian literary works (interpreted broadly to include historical, biographical, political, anthropological, and philological works). Under each year the main column lists author, year of birth, literary work (primarily books), and genre; the secondary column notes births and deaths of writers, the founding of newspapers and periodicals, and publication of nonliterary books by Australians and of significant foreign works referring to Australia. Indexed by authors. Interpreting entries requires continual reference to the key to abbreviations and symbols (p. xi). The exclusion of political, cultural, and historical events, and limitation to books make *Annals of Australian Literature* less useful than it could be for placing a work or author in an intellectual context. Reviews: L. T. Hergenhan, *Australian Literary Studies* 4 (1970): 421–24; S. J. Routh, *Meanjin Quarterly* 29 (1970): 555–59.

The chronology in Goodwin, *History of Australian Literature* (4445a) is a useful supplement.

Guides to Primary Works

Lock, *Australian Literature* (4440) has a valuable discussion of how to identify and locate Australian books (pp. 15–17) and descriptions of Australian library collections (pp. 90–97).

4465 *Australian National Bibliography* (*ANB*). Canberra: National Library of Australia, 1961– . Monthly, with four-month, eight-month, and annual cumulations. Available since 1980 on microfiche. Z4015.A96 015.94.

A national bibliography of Australian publications deposited for copyright in the National Library, as well as of some foreign works by Australian authors or about the country. *ANB* is currently published in four parts: a subject list organized by Dewey Decimal Classification (with full cataloging information for each entry); author, title, and series index; subject index; and publishers' directory. Both indexes cite classification rather than page. *ANB* is the fullest record of current Australian publications.

ANB continues the *Annual Catalogue of Australian Publications [1936–60]*, 25 vols. (Canberra: National Library of Australia, 1937–61), a combined main entry and subject list of books deposited for copyright and foreign publications about Australia. In progress is *Retrospective National Bibliography*, which will cover Australian imprints, as well as foreign publications by Australians or about the country, published between 1901 and 1950.

Since works by ethnic writers were frequently not submitted for copyright, researchers should also consult the following:

Houbein, Lolo. *Ethnic Writings in English from Australia: A Bibliography*. 3rd ed. Adelaide A. L. S. Working Papers. Adelaide: Australian Literary Studies, 1984. 124 pp.

Lumb, Peter, and Anne Hazell, eds. *Diversity and Diversion: An Annotated Bibliography of Australian Ethnic Minority Literature*. Richmond, Victoria: Hodja, 1983. 123 pp.

4470 Ferguson, John Alexander. *Bibliography of Australia*. Facsimile ed. 7 vols. Canberra: National Library of Australia, 1975–77. *Addenda, 1784–1850 (Volumes I to IV)*. 1986. 706 pp. Z4011.F47 [DU96] 016.994.

A retrospective national bibliography covering 1784 to 1900 that attempts to record for the period 1784–1850 all Australian imprints as well as foreign publications "relating in any way" to the country; for the years 1851–1900, excludes belles lettres, periodicals, and governmental papers, as well as legal, scientific, technical, and certain ephemeral publications. Works by Australians published elsewhere and lacking a reference to the country are sometimes mentioned in notes. In vols. 1–4 (1784–1850), entries are organized by year of publication, then alphabetically by author, corporate author, or title of anonymous work; vols. 5–7 (1851–1900) consist of a single alphabetical list. Entries provide a transcription of title page; size; pagination; list of contents or description of content relating to Australia; publication information (if not on the title page); occasionally extensive notes on content, reprints and other editions, related scholarship, and bibliographical matters; and locations of copies (with a list of supplementary locations inserted in vols. 1–2 of the facsimile edition). Vol. 2 prints additions to 1; vol. 4, additions and corrections to 1–3. The *Addenda* incorporates these additions and corrections, adds new entries, revises some existing ones, and lists additional locations; if resources become available, the National Library will issue additions and corrections to vols. 5–7, along with a cumulative index. Indexed by titles, authors, and corporate authors in each of the first four volumes.

While the numerous omissions, errors, and inconsistencies make Ferguson untrustworthy as a descriptive bibliography, it remains the most complete guide to Australian literature through 1850; the record is continued, although less satisfactorily, to 1950 by Macartney, *Australian Literature* (4475a). Review: Brian McMullen, *Australian Library Journal* 25 (1976): 39–40.

4475 Miller, E. Morris. *Australian Literature from Its Beginnings to 1935: A Descriptive and Bibliographical Survey of Books by Australian Authors in*

Poetry, Drama, Fiction, Criticism, and Anthology with Subsidiary Entries to 1938. Facsimile rpt., with corrections and additions. 2 vols. Sydney: Sydney UP, 1975. Z4021.M5 016.82'08.

A bibliography of separately published works by Australian natives or residents who wrote or commenced at least one book in the country. Although the focus is belles lettres, the notes cite a substantial number of other books by philosophers, artists, historians, and scientists who published at least one literary work. Entries are organized by genre: poetry, drama, fiction, and criticism (with sections for essays and reviews; English, Australian, classical, and modern literature; anthologies and miscellanies). Within each section, authors are listed chronologically by date of first publication in the genre. A typical author entry consists of a list of separately published literary works (and some editions thereof) accompanied by bibliographical notes and, for fiction, a one- or two-sentence summary; references to scholarship, bibliographies, and manuscripts; reprints and excerpts in anthologies, and some periodical contributions; and major nonliterary works. (The amount and organization of information vary from author to author, however.) Each genre division is prefaced by a lengthy historical introduction composed largely of biographical and critical discussions of authors. In the facsimile reprint, the separately issued additions and corrections appear on pp. 1075–78. An appendix lists novels associated with Australia by foreign authors. Three indexes: subjects of fiction; subjects of Australian literature and persons not in the general index of Australian authors; Australian authors.

Australian Literature: A Bibliography to 1938, extended to 1950 and ed. Frederick T. Macartney (Sydney: Angus, 1956, 503 pp.) extends coverage to 1950, incorporates Miller's corrections and rearranges entries into a straightforward author list, but deletes nonbelletristic works, children's books, translations, critical and scholarly works except those about Australian literature, anthologized reprints, contributions to periodicals, references to scholarship and bibliographies, introductions, and indexes. A few corrections and additions to the enlarged edition are listed in Clive Hamer, " 'Not in Miller,' " *Meanjin* 15 (1956): 419, which is followed by Miller's brief description of his compilation of the original bibliography (pp. 420–21). Macartney's defense of his reworking of Miller and rejoinder to several negative reviews (such as Russel Ward, *Meanjin* 15 [1956]: 212–14) make up *An Odious Comparison: Considered in Its Relation to* Australian Literature (Black Rock: Bulldozer Booklets, 1956, 15 pp.).

Although Macartney's revision is more current and consolidates an author's separately published literary works, the original edition includes much more complete information and provides some subject access. Together, the two offer the single fullest record of separately published Australian literary works from 1850 to 1950. Before 1850, more thorough and accurate coverage is offered by Ferguson, *Bibliography of Australia* (4470). *Retrospective National Bibliography* (4465a) will offer a superior record of post-1900 Australian imprints.

See also

Andrews, *Australian Literature to 1900* (4485).
"Annual Bibliography of Commonwealth Literature" (4375).
"Annual Bibliography of Studies in Australian Literature" (4480).

Guides to Scholarship and Criticism

SERIAL BIBLIOGRAPHIES

4480 "Annual Bibliography of Studies in Australian Literature [1963-]." *Australian Literary Studies* (entry 4505) 1 (1964)- .

A selective list of "useful" books and articles, along with the "more important reviews and prefaces, studies on Australian language, and new books (with reviews of them) by contemporary writers whose work has attracted substantial discussion." Entries—drawn partly from other bibliographies—are listed in two divisions: general studies and individual authors. Although not comprehensive, the "Annual Bibliography" provides more current and thorough coverage of scholarship than the Australia division of "Annual Bibliography of Commonwealth Literature" (4375)—which offers fuller coverage of primary works, especially by new writers—and the standard serial bibliographies and indexes in section G.

See also

Secs. G: Serial Bibliographies, Indexes, and Abstracts and H: Guides to Dissertations and Theses.

ABELL (340).

"Annual Bibliography of Commonwealth Literature" (4375).

MLAIB (335): English Literature division (especially English III: General) through the volume for 1956; English XI: Australia, Canada, Etc./Australia section in the volumes for 1957–66; English II: Australia, Canada, Etc./Australia section in the volumes for 1967–80; and the Australian Literature section in later volumes. Researchers must also check the "Australian Literature" heading in the subject index to post-1980 volumes.

YWES (330): Australian literature has been covered in the chapter for African, Caribbean, Canadian, Australian, New Zealand, and Indian Literatures in English since vol. 64 (for 1983).

OTHER BIBLIOGRAPHIES

4485 Andrews, Barry G., and William H. Wilde. *Australian Literature to 1900: A Guide to Information Sources*. American Literature, English Literature, and World Literatures in English: An Information Guide Series 22. Detroit: Gale, 1980. 472 pp. Z4021.A54 [PR9604.3] 016.82.

A selective, annotated bibliography of primary and secondary works (published through 1976) on Australian literature from 1788 to 1900. Andrews and Wilde include 72 authors who had significant work published before 1900 or who clearly belong to the 1890s, but generally exclude their publications not related to the country. The 1,576 entries—augmented by numerous others cited in annotations or headnotes—are organized in three divisions: general works (including sections for bibliographies, reference works, literary history and criticism, Australian English, nineteenth-century periodicals, and anthologies), individual authors (including a biographical headnote and sections for bibliographies, primary works—by genre, with a note on manuscript collections—and studies), and selected nonfiction (with sections for exploration, transportation, travel, history and biography, and literary and theatrical autobiographies). Although a work is entered only once, cross-references are provided in headnotes to sections. The typically full annotations are generally informative and frequently evaluative. Two indexes: persons; titles. Judicious selection, accuracy, and helpful annotations make this a valuable guide to the study of Australian literature before 1900. Reviews: L. T. Hergenhan, *Australian Literary Studies* 10 (1981): 137–39; Alan Lawson, *Modern Language Review* 78 (1983): 692–94.

See also

Boos, *Bibliography of Women and Literature* (6600).
New, *Critical Writings on Commonwealth Literatures* (4380).
Oxford History of Australian Literature (4445a).
Schwartz, *Articles on Women Writers* (6605).

Language

GUIDES TO SCHOLARSHIP

See

ABELL (340): See the Language/English Dialects section through the volume for 1972, then the English Language/Varieties of English/Dialects/Australia and New Zealand section in later volumes.
Andrews, *Australian Literature to 1900* (4485).
"Annual Bibliography of Studies in Australian Literature" (4480).
Day, *Modern Australian Prose, 1901–1975* (4530).
MLAIB (335): See the English I: Linguistics section through the volume for 1966; the Indo-European C: Germanic Linguistics IV: English/Modern English/Dialectology section in the volumes for 1967–80; and the English Language (Modern)/Dialectology section in later volumes. Researchers must also check the "Australian English Dialect" heading in the subject index to post-1980 volumes.

DICTIONARIES

4490 *The Australian National Dictionary: A Dictionary of Australianisms on Historical Principles* (*AND*). Ed. W. S. Ramson. Melbourne: Oxford UP, 1988. 814 pp. PE3601.Z5.A97.

A historical dictionary of terms distinctly or prominently Australian. The approximately 6,000 main entries provide pronunciation; part(s) of speech; variant spellings; a note on history and derivation, with a cross-reference, where appropriate, to the *Oxford English Dictionary* (1410); definition(s) organized by part of speech; and illustrative quotations, arranged chronologically, for each definition. The editor plans to make the text available in computer-readable form. *AND* is an essential complement to the *Oxford English Dictionary* and the indispensable source for the historical study of Australian English and explication of literary works by Australian writers.

The best treatment of colloquial language is G. A. Wilkes, *A Dictionary of Australian Colloquialisms*, 2nd ed. (Sydney: Sydney UP, 1985, 470 pp.), with dated quotations accompanying definitions. Also useful is *The Macquarie Dictionary*, ed. A. Delbridge et al., rev. ed. (St. Leonards: Macquarie Library, 1985), 2,009 pp.

Biographical Dictionaries

4495 *Australian Dictionary of Biography* (*ADB*). Gen. eds. Douglas Pike, Bede Nairn, and Geoffrey Serle. 12 vols. Carlton: Melbourne UP; London: Cambridge UP, 1966– . DU82.A9 920.094.

Vols. 1–2: *1788–1850.*
Vols. 3–6: *1851–90.*
Vols. 7–12: *1891–1939.*

A biographical dictionary that includes some 6,000 entries on important and representative Australians whose significant contributions occurred before 1939. (Other than vetting by various committees, selection criteria are undefined.) Placement in the three chronological divisions is determined by the period of the individual's most important work. A typical entry summarizes basic biographical and career information and concludes with a brief list of important scholarship and unpublished papers. Separate lists of corrections are tipped in vols. 1–4; later volumes are accompanied by a cumulative list of corrections. Vols. 1–5 are indexed by occupation in Julie G. Marshall and Richard C. S. Trahair, *Occupational Index to the* Australian Dictionary of Biography *(1788–1890), Volumes I–VI*, Paper 43 (Bundoora: Dept. of Sociology, La Trobe U, 1979, 139 pp.), and *Occupational Index to the* Australian Dictionary of Biography *(1891–1939), Volumes VII–IX, A-Las*, Paper 71 (1985, 100 pp.). Although it lacks the indexes and fuller bibliographies of the other major national biographical dictionaries, *ADB* is the standard general source for biographical information on Australians.

For persons not in *ADB*, consult Percival Serle, *Dictionary of Australian Biography*, 2 vols. (Sydney: Angus, 1949), and the current edition of *Who's Who in Australia* (Melbourne: Herald and Weekly Times, 1922–).

Periodicals

GUIDES TO PRIMARY WORKS

4500 Stuart, Lurline. *Nineteenth Century Australian Periodicals: An Annotated Bibliography*. Sydney: Hale, 1979. 200 pp. Z6962.A8.S78 [PN5517.P4] 011'.34.

A bibliography of periodicals (excluding newspapers) of some literary interest published in Australia during the nineteenth century. The 449 entries, arranged alphabetically by original title, include (when possible) title, subtitle, motto or epigraph, editor(s), frequency, dates of publication and title changes, size, average number of pages, price, presence of illustrations, locations in Australian collections, description of content, and important writers and articles published. Concludes with a selected bibliography. Indexed by persons and titles. Although a subject index would greatly increase its usefulness, Stuart is the essential guide to identifying and locating these frequently scarce and ephemeral nineteenth-century periodicals.

SCHOLARLY JOURNALS

Many journals in section K: Periodicals/Scholarly Journals publish articles on Australian literature. Lock, *Australian Literature* (4440) has a useful annotated list of Australian scholarly and literary periodicals (pp. 80–89).

4505 *Australian Literary Studies* (*ALS*). 1963– . 2/yr. PR9400.A86 820'.9'994.

Publishes articles, bibliographies, notes, documents, reviews, a list of work in progress, and occasional special issues on all aspects of Australian literature. For the "Annual Bibliography of Studies in Australian Literature," see entry 4480. Annual index.

4510 *Meanjin*. 1940– . Quarterly. (Title varies.) AP7.M4 820.

Publishes articles, interviews, reviews, and special issues on a variety of aspects of Australian life and culture, as well as original fiction and poetry. One of the most influential Australian literary periodicals. For a fully documented, but contentious, history of the journal, see Lynne Strahan, *Just City and the Mirrors:* Meanjin Quarterly *and the Intellectual Front, 1940–1965* (Melbourne: Oxford UP, 1984, 314 pp.). Annual index; cumulative index: Marjorie Tipping, comp., Meanjin Quarterly *Index, 1940–1965* (Melbourne: Meanjin, 1969, 140 pp.), but this is unreliable.

4515 *Southerly: A Review of Australian Literature* (*Southerly*). 1939– . Quarterly. (Former title: *Southerly: A Literary Magazine*, 1939–56.) AP7.S6 820'.5.

Publishes articles, interviews, and reviews on Australian literature, along with some poems and short stories. The origin and history are outlined in S. E. Lee, "The First Fifty Years, II: *Southerly*, 1939–1974," 34 (1974): 112–41.

Background Reading

See *Oxford History of Australian Literature* (4445a) for a useful evaluative survey of background studies (pp. 437–41).

4520 *The Australian Encyclopedia*. 4th ed. 12 vols. Sydney: Grolier Soc. of Australia, 1983. DU90.A82 994'.003.

A general encyclopedia of all aspects of Australian life, past and present. Statistics that change frequently are relegated to an appendix in vol. 12, which also includes a subject index. Earlier editions remain useful for the historical perspective they offer. This is the best general encyclopedia devoted to Australia.

Genres

Some works in section L: Genres are useful for research in Australian literature.

FICTION

Some works in section L: Genres/Fiction are useful for research in Australian fiction.

Guides to Primary Works

4525 Torre, Stephen. *The Australian Short Story, 1940–1980: A Bibliography.* Sydney: Hale and Iremonger, 1984. 367 pp. Z4024.S5.T67 [PR9612.5] 016.823'01'08994.

An index to English-language short fiction (along with selected criticism) by writers born, resident in, or otherwise associated with Australia, and first published between 1940 and 1980 in anthologies, single-author collections, or 12 major Australian periodicals. Torre excludes fiction for children and transcriptions of oral narratives, but otherwise defines "short story" broadly. The entries are organized in five divisions: an author bibliography of short stories and criticism (with sections for single-author collections, including the contents of each; individual short stories, with the publishing history of each in the periodicals, collections, and anthologies selected for indexing; anthologies and miscellanies edited by the author; other publications by the author that are of some importance to his or her short fiction; and critical studies, including reviews); a list of periodicals that publish short fiction by Australian authors, including the 12 selected for full indexing; a title list of anthologies and miscellanies indexed; a superfluous list of single-author collections indexed; and general studies of short stories and reference works, the bulk of which are on Australian short fiction. An appendix provides a chronological list of the journals that hosted *Tabloid Story*. Although the work is not comprehensive, especially for periodical fiction, and although much information is taken secondhand, Torre is the single best source for identifying Australian short stories and critical studies of them.

Guides to Scholarship and Criticism

4530 Day, A. Grove. *Modern Australian Prose, 1901–1975: A Guide to Information Sources.* American Literature, English Literature, and World Literatures in English: An Information Guide Series 29. Detroit: Gale, 1980. 462 pp. Z4011.D38 [PR9604.3] 016.82.

A highly selective, annotated bibliography of primary and secondary works that also includes a brief section on drama. Limited to works (generally published between 1901 and 1975) about Australia by citizens and others resident in the country, *Modern Australian Prose* excludes some important publications by Australian authors. The general cutoff for studies is 1976 (although a few later publications are admitted). Entries are organized in four classified divisions: general works (with sections for bibliographies, reference works, literary history and criticism, Australian English, periodicals, and anthologies), fiction (organized by author, with sections under each for bibliographies, primary works, and criticism), nonfiction (a highly selective list organized by genre or topic and including a section on aborigines), and drama (with sections for bibliographies, studies, and primary works). Most of the annotations are adequately descriptive. Three indexes: scholars; book titles; subjects (including authors). Because of the degree of selectivity (recent authors are slighted) and numerous errors, Day is useful primarily as a starting point for research on prose. (The drama section, seemingly an afterthought, is completely inadequate.) Reviews: Laurie Hergenhan, *Australian Literary Studies* 10 (1982): 407–08; Alan Lawson, *Modern Language Review* 78 (1983): 692–94.

For fiction before 1901, see Andrews, *Australian Literature to 1900* (4485). Supplement coverage with Rose Marie Beston and John B. Beston, "Critical Writings on Modern New Zealand and Australian Fiction: A Selected Checklist," *Modern Fiction Studies* 27 (1981): 189–204; New, *Critical Writings on Commonwealth Literatures* (4380); and "Annual Bibliography of Commonwealth Literature" (4375).

DRAMA AND THEATER

Some works in section L: Genres/Drama and Theater are useful for research in Australian drama and theater.

Histories and Surveys

4535 Love, Harold, ed. *The Australian Stage: A Documentary History*. Kensington: New South Wales UP with Australian Theatre Studies Centre School of Drama, U of New South Wales, 1984. 383 pp. PN3011.A97 792'.0994.

A collection of extracts from documents (including reviews, articles, autobiographies, manuscripts, illustrations, and photographs) that depict the history of the Australian stage to 1980. The emphasis is on Australian drama professionally produced in Sydney and Melbourne, with less attention to foreign-language, amateur, and educational theater, and excluding opera, film, and television. The heart of the work is the extensive extracts, which describe productions of both Australian and foreign plays. The extracts are organized chronologically in four periods (1788–1853, 1854–1900, 1901–50, and 1950–80), followed by a section reproducing pictorial documents depicting productions, theaters, sets, and performers. Each period begins with a summary of theatrical activity and includes one or two essays on aspects of the theater of the time (e.g., theater of the convict era, dramatic criticism from 1850 to 1890, Australian plays on Australian topics, vaudeville, state theater companies, and alternative theater). Most essays conclude with an evaluative guide to further reading, and the last section of the book is an extensive bibliography of studies of Australian theater. Indexed by persons, titles, and subjects. Valuable for its extensive documentation, this is the most trustworthy source of information on the Australian stage. More extensive but less factually reliable coverage of Australian drama is offered by Rees, *History of Australian Drama* (4540).

4540 Rees, Leslie. *A History of Australian Drama.* 2 vols. Sydney: Angus, 1978. PR9611.2.R43 822'.009.

Vol. 1: *The Making of Australian Drama from the 1830s to the Late 1960s.* Rev. ed. 435 pp. (A reprint of *The Making of Australian Drama: A Historical and Critical Survey from the 1830s to the 1970s.* 1973. 510 pp.)
Vol. 2: *Australian Drama in the 1970s.* 270 pp.

A critical history of the development of Australian drama from the colonial period through 1976. Encompasses stage as well as radio and television plays by Australians, resident or not, and—in early chapters—about the country by foreign authors. The overall organization is chronological, with chapters devoted to types of plays, major authors, periods, movements, and topics. Among the various appendixes are, in vol. 1, a history of the Playwrights Advisory Board; in vol. 2, a chronology of selected plays published since 1936; chronological lists (by decade) of radio (since 1935) and television plays (since 1955) produced by the Australian Broadcasting Commission; and a discussion of Australian noncommercial theaters. Vol. 2 concludes with a selective bibliography. Each volume is indexed by persons, titles, and topics. Although frequently unreliable in factual matters and impressionistic in judgment, Rees's work represents the fullest history of the country's drama.

More accurate but less thorough in covering Australian drama is Love, *Australian Stage* (4535).

Guides to Scholarship and Criticism

See

Day, *Modern Australian Prose, 1901–1975* (4530).

POETRY

Guides to Primary Works

4545 Webby, Elizabeth. *Early Australian Poetry: An Annotated Bibliography of Original Poems Published in Australian Newspapers, Magazines, and Almanacks before 1850.* Sydney: Hale, 1982. 332 pp. Z4008.P63.W42 [PR9610.4] 016.821.

A bibliography of original periodical verse. Entries are organized by Australian state, medium of publication, city, periodical, and then date of publication. A typical entry consists of title, author (if known) or pseudonym, date of publication, page, and a brief note on content. Indexed by poets and titles of newspapers, magazines, and almanacs. Webby is the essential source for identifying Australian periodical verse before 1850.

Guides to Scholarship and Criticism

There is no adequate guide to studies of Australian poetry. Herbert C. Jaffa, *Modern Australian Poetry, 1920–1970: A Guide to Information Sources*, American

Literature, English Literature, and World Literatures in English: An Information Guide Series 24 (Detroit: Gale, 1979, 241 pp.)—which is not actually a guide to information sources—has too many omissions to serve even as a starting point. (For the multiple deficiencies of this work, see the review by Alan Lawson, *Analytical and Enumerative Bibliography* 5 [1981]: 130–34.)

Canadian Literature

This section includes works devoted exclusively to Canadian literature (in whatever language). Many works in sections Q: American Literature and R: Other Literatures in English/General are also important to research in Canadian literature.

Guides to Reference Works

4555 Ryder, Dorothy E. *Canadian Reference Sources: A Selective Guide*. 2nd ed. Ottawa: Canadian Library Assn., 1981. 311 pp. Z1365.R8 [F1008] 011'.02'0971.

A selective, annotated guide to reference sources for Canadian topics. Entries are organized alphabetically by author, editor, or title of anonymous work in five extensively classified divisions: general reference works, history and allied subjects, humanities, sciences, and social sciences. The literature subdivision includes sections for general works; bibliographies of primary works and criticism; biographical sources; dictionaries, guides, and handbooks; literary histories; periodical indexes; dictionaries of pseudonymous and anonymous works; and genres. The linguistics subdivision includes sections for general works, Canadian English, and French, Indian, and Inuit languages. The brief annotations are largely descriptive. Four appendixes outline the history and scope of major reference works, including *Canadiana* (4595) and *Canadian Periodical Index* (4635). Indexed by persons, titles, and selected subjects. Although researchers would benefit from an explanation of scope, organization, and selection criteria (the omission of which is inexplicable in a guide such as this) and fuller, more critical annotations, Ryder is the essential general guide to reference sources on Canadian topics.

Sheehy, *Guide to Reference Books* (60) and Walford, *Walford's Guide to Reference Material* (65) list numerous Canadian reference sources.

See also

Beugnot, *Manuel bibliographique des études littéraires* (4905).

Histories and Surveys

4560 Grandpré, Pierre de, ed. *Histoire de la littérature française du Québec*. Corrected rpt. 4 vols. Montréal: Beauchemin, 1971–73. PQ3917.G7 840.

A collaborative history of French-language literature from 1534 to the 1960s, with three of the volumes devoted to the twentieth century. Organized chronologically, with chapters on intellectual and social life, genres, history, journalism, the essay, and literary criticism, the volumes emphasize historical and intellectual contexts. Two indexes in each volume: persons; titles. Vol. 4 concludes with a selective bibliography of studies on French-Canadian literature. Despite poor organization and inconsistency in the quality of chapters, Grandpré offers the fullest history of French-Canadian literature. Reviews: (vol. 1) David M. Hayne, *Canadian Historical Review* 49 (1968): 415–16; (vols. 2–4) Hayne, *Canadian Historical Review* 51 (1970): 459–61.

4565 *Literary History of Canada: Canadian Literature in English*. Gen. ed. Carl F. Klinck. Corrected rpt. of 2nd ed. 3 vols. Toronto: U of Toronto P, 1976–77. (An additional volume, covering 1972 to 1984 and edited by W. H. New, is scheduled for 1990.) PR9184.3.K5 810'.9'005.

A critical history, from the seventeenth century to the early 1970s, of English-Canadian literature. Chapters, usually by major scholars, treat philosophy, history, the social and natural sciences, religion, literary criticism and scholarship, travel writing, and children's literature, as well as fiction, poetry, and drama. Some include a highly selective bibliography. Each volume concludes with a very brief general bibliography and an index of names, anonymous works, and subjects. The volumes comprise the most comprehensive history of English-Canadian literature, although belles lettres are frequently overshadowed by the extensive treatment accorded non-literary topics (especially in vol. 3). Reviews: John Ferns, *Modern Language Review* 74 (1979): 186–88; W. J. Keith, *University of Toronto Quarterly* 46 (1977): 461–66.

Good complements are W. J. Keith, *Canadian Literature in English*, Longman Literature in English Series (London: Longman, 1985, 287 pp.), which emphasizes major writers and concludes with a useful chronology and selective bibliography; and W. H. New, *A History of Canadian Literature* (Basingstoke: Macmillan, 1988, 272 pp.).

See also

Wiget, *Native American Literature* (3865).

Literary Handbooks, Dictionaries, and Encyclopedias

4570 *Dictionnaire des oeuvres littéraires du Québec*. Ed. Maurice Lemire. 5 vols. Montréal: Fides, 1980–87. PQ3901.D5.

Vol. 1: *Des Origines à 1900*. 2nd ed., rev. and corrected. 1980. 927 pp.
Vol. 2: *1900–1939*. 1980. 1,363 pp.
Vol. 3: *1940–1959*. 1982. 1,252 pp.
Vol. 4: *1960–1969*. 1984. 1,123 pp.
Vol. 5: *1970–1975*. 1987. 1,133 pp.

A dictionary of literary works by Québec authors or related to the province. Organized by title, the signed entries, which range from 250 to 3,000 words, typically provide a summary, discussion of the work's place in its author's canon, critical commentary, and (sometimes lengthy) lists of editions and studies. A brief biographical notice precedes the entry for an author's first work. Each volume includes a chronology; selective bibliographies of literary works, reference works, and critical studies; and an index of persons. The entries vary in quality, of course, but the *Dictionnaire* offers impressively thorough coverage of the bulk of French-Canadian literature through 1969. Review: B.-Z. Shek, *University of Toronto Quarterly* 54 (1985): 471–74.

4575 Hamilton, Robert M., and Dorothy Shields. *The Dictionary of Canadian Quotations and Phrases*. Rev. and enl. ed. Toronto: McClelland, 1979. 1,063 pp. PN6081.H24 818'.02.

A dictionary of about 10,300 quotations and phrases from Canadian sources (and some British, French, and American ones) on distinctly Canadian topics, as well as by Canadians about other subjects. Organized by subject, then chronologically under a heading, an entry consists of quotation and citation to a printed source. Indexed by authors. To locate cross-references, users must consult the prefatory list of subject headings. This is the best source for locating and identifying Canadian quotations.

4580 *The Oxford Companion to Canadian Literature*. Gen. ed. William Toye. Toronto: Oxford UP, 1983. 843 pp. PR9180.2.O94 809'.8971.

A guide to Canadian literature, primarily in English and French, with entries on authors, genres, important works, literary magazines, publishers, and ethnic and regional literatures. The signed entries primarily treat authors and genres, emphasize modern literature, and are more extensive, evaluative, and exclusively literary than in the typical *Oxford Companion*. Author entries combine biographical and bibliographical information with critical commentary. Reviewers have pointed out biases, inconsistencies, omissions, and errors, but this work is, overall, a reliable desktop companion. Reviews: Sherrill E. Grace, *Canadian Literature* 104 (1985): 113–15; Linda Hutcheon, *University of Toronto Quarterly* 53 (1984): 440–42; Robert Lecker, *Queen's Quarterly* 92 (1985): 402–05; Eli Mandel, *Canadian Poetry* 16 (1985): 83–86; Robin Mathews, *Canadian Poetry* 16 (1985): 74–82.

Although superseded in their treatment of literature, Norah Story, *The Oxford Companion to Canadian History and Literature* (Toronto: Oxford UP, 1967, 935 pp.) and *Supplement*, gen. ed. William Toye (1973, 318 pp.), are still useful for their coverage of literature-related topics that are dropped in the 1983 edition.

The most current source for information on a variety of aspects of Canadian life is *The Canadian Encyclopedia*, ed. James H. Marsh, 3 vols. (Edmonton: Hurtig, 1985), whose approximately 8,000 signed entries include some on authors and literary works.

Bibliographies of Bibliographies

4585 Lochhead, Douglas, comp. *Bibliography of Canadian Bibliographies/ Bibliographie des bibliographies canadiennes*. 2nd ed. Toronto: U of Toronto P, in association with Bibliographical Soc. of Canada, 1972. 312 pp. Z1365.A1.L6 016.01571.

A bibliography of bibliographies (through c. 1970) of works primarily on Canadian topics but also a few volumes published in Canada or by Canadians on other subjects. Lochhead excludes bibliographies that appear as parts of books, dissertations, or articles. The 2,325 entries—many of them taken from other sources—are listed alphabetically by author, corporate author, or title (for anonymous works). Indexed by subjects and authors. Although not comprehensive, it is the best single source for bibliographies on Canadian topics. For recent bibliographies, see *Bibliographic Index* (145).

See also

Sec. D: Bibliographies of Bibliographies.
Kempton, *French Literature: An Annotated Guide to Selected Bibliographies* (4905a).
Newman, *Black Access: A Bibliography of Afro-American Bibliographies* (3715).

Guides to Primary Works

MANUSCRIPTS

4590 *Union List of Manuscripts in Canadian Repositories/Catalogue collectif des manuscrits des archives canadiennes.* Ed. E. Grace Maurice. Rev. ed. 2 vols. Ottawa: Public Archives, 1975. Supplements (with French title as *Catalogue collectif des manuscrits conservés dans les dépôts d'archives canadiennes*): *1976.* 1976. 322 pp. *1977–1978.* 1979. 236 pp. *1979–1980.* Ed. Grace Maurice Hyam. 1982. 243 pp. *1981–1982.* Ed. Peter Yurkiw. 1985. 616 pp. CD3622.A2.U54 016.971.

A union list of significant collections of manuscripts and records held by Canadian institutions. Entries are listed alphabetically by the author or corporate body who created or accumulated the collection. A typical entry includes location, a brief description of content, size, dates covered, and, when necessary, restrictions on use and finding lists or other aids. Two indexes: repositories; names, corporate bodies, places, and selected subjects mentioned in annotations. As is usual in other national union lists of manuscripts, the sophistication and accuracy of descriptions vary depending on the reporting institution, and in large collections individual writers, especially of letters, go unmentioned in the annotations (and thus in the index). Since this work is a list of collections (with only a few entries for individual manuscripts), users searching for writings by an author should begin with the name, place, and subject index. Not comprehensive, but the best single source for locating manuscripts by Canadian writers. Lecker, *Annotated Bibliography of Canada's Major Authors* (4605), also notes locations of manuscript collections.

See also

Sec. F: Guides to Manuscripts and Archives.

PRINTED WORKS

4595 *Canadiana: Canada's National Bibliography/La bibliographie nationale du Canada.* Ottawa: National Library of Canada, 1951– . Monthly, with annual and larger cumulations. The parts for 1950 and 1951 are cumulated and revised as *Canadiana 1950 and 1951* (1962, 346 pp.). Z1365.C214 015'.71.

A bibliography of Canadian imprints and foreign publications since 1950 that were written by Canadian citizens and residents or that are of Canadian interest. Coverage depends heavily on copyright deposits and acquisitions by the National Library: films and some ephemeral material are excluded. (For a full discussion of changes in scope, see Ryder, *Canadian Reference Sources* [4555], pp. 235–39.) Entries, which provide full cataloging information, are organized by Dewey Decimal Classification in two parts: Canadian imprints; foreign imprints with Canadian association. Covering both are five indexes: authors, titles, series; English subject headings; French subject headings; ISBN numbers; ISSN numbers. Index entries cite classification rather than page. Although not exhaustive (especially for foreign imprints relating to the country), *Canadiana* offers the fullest coverage of recent Canadian imprints and is a useful source of books about Canadian topics.

Less thorough and accurate is *Canadian Books in Print* (Toronto: U of Toronto P, 1967– , annual), which excludes most French-language titles. Earlier, less thorough coverage is offered by *The Canadian Catalogue of Books Published in Canada, about Canada, as Well as Those Written by Canadians [1921–49]*, 28 nos. (Toronto: Toronto Public Library, 1923–50). A cumulation of listings for English-language titles was published as *The Canadian Catalogue of Books Published in Canada, about Canada, as Well as Those Written by Canadians, with Imprint 1921–1949*, 2 vols. (Toronto: Toronto Public Libraries, 1959).

Retrospective coverage is offered by *Canadiana, 1867–1900: Monographs/Monographies* (Ottawa: National Library of Canada, 1980– , microfiche), which is published in six parts: a register (with full cataloging information) and five cumulative indexes: authors and titles; year of publication; publishers and printers; places of publication and printing; subjects. For additional retrospective bibliographies, see Ryder, *Canadian Reference Sources* (4555), pp. 2–4.

4605 Lecker, Robert, and Jack David, eds. *The Annotated Bibliography of Canada's Major Authors* (*ABCMA*). 8 vols. Toronto: ECW, 1979– . Z1375.A56 [PR9184.3] 016.81.

A collection of author bibliographies of works by and about important English- and French-Canadian writers, with half of the volumes devoted to poets and half to prose writers. Each volume attempts comprehensive coverage (up to one to three years before publication) of primary works (all editions, reprints, translations, excerpts, audiovisual materials, manuscripts, but only selected contributions to anthologies) and secondary materials. The overall organization is chronological. Under primary works, separate publications—classified by genre, form, or medium—appear first (with later editions and translations listed under the first edition), followed by manuscripts (by collection, with a description of contents), then other publications (by type or form). Secondary works—accompanied by descriptive annotations—are classified by form: books, articles and parts of books, theses and dissertations, interviews, awards and honors, and selected reviews. Through vol. 3 an introduction to each author offers a cursory survey of criticism and a necessary discussion of limitations in coverage. Each author section is separately indexed by persons. Numerous reviewers have objected to the choice of major authors and to the poetry and prose division. The individual bibliographies vary widely in accuracy, and many are far short of the comprehensive coverage (especially for secondary works) the editors claim for the work; moreover, there is rarely any logic to groupings in volumes, and inconsistencies abound. However, *ABCMA* is an important contribution to Canadian literary scholarship and an essential starting point for research on many of the authors. Reviews: (vol. 1) David Jackel, *Canadian Literature* 88 (1981): 147–50; Donald Stephens, *English Studies in Canada* 8 (1982): 96–100; (vol. 2) R. G. Moyles, *Analytical and Enumerative Bibliography* 6 (1982): 49–51; (vols. 1–2) D. G. Lochhead, *Canadian Poetry* 9 (1981): 100–03, with a reply by Lecker and David, 10 (1982): 132–36, and a response by Lochhead, pp. 136–37; (vol. 3) Terry Goldie, *Canadian Literature* 96 (1983): 153–55; (vols. 5–6) David Staines, *Literary Research* 11 (1986): 188–91.

4610 "Letters in Canada [1935–]." *University of Toronto Quarterly* (entry 735) 5 (1936)– .

An annual selective review of English- and French-Canadian literary, critical, and scholarly works. Beginning with vols. 56 (1986–87), the fall issue is devoted entirely to the survey. Separate signed essays examine fiction, poetry, drama, translations, social history, and religion; the humanities section now consists of individual signed reviews of critical and scholarly books by Canadian authors on a wide range of topics and national literatures. The early surveys include selective checklists of titles. Indexed by books reviewed. For the history of "Letters in Canada," see W. J. Keith and B.-Z. Shek, "A Half-Century of *UTQ*," *University of Toronto Quarterly* 50 (1980): 146–54. Although selective in coverage, "Letters in Canada" is the best annual evaluative survey of books by Canadians.

4615 Tremaine, Marie. *A Bibliography of Canadian Imprints, 1751–1800*. Toronto: U of Toronto P, 1952. 705 pp. Z1365.T7 015.71.

A retrospective national bibliography of Canadian imprints (including newspapers and magazines) from 1751 through 1800. The 1,240 entries are divided in two parts. The first is devoted to books, pamphlets, broadsides, handbills, and other separately printed matter. Organized by year of printing, then alphabetically by author, corporate author, or title of anonymous work, the detailed entries consist of a quasi-facsimile transcription of the title page; collation; list of contents; extensive notes on the printer, author, subject matter, advertisements, printing or publishing records, related scholarship, and post-1800 editions; and locations in public and private collections. The second part lists newspapers by province and then magazines. Each entry provides thorough notes on printing and publishing history, and a list of locations with exact holdings. Concludes with descriptions of Canadian printing offices. Thoroughly indexed by authors, titles, subjects, and types of printed matter. The detailed, careful descriptions make Tremaine the essential record of Canadian imprints and publishing history for the latter half of the eighteenth century. Researchers must also consult the North American Imprints Program data base (4010), which will eventually offer a more complete record of Canadian imprints through 1800.

Coverage is continued by Patricia Lockhart Fleming, *Upper Canadian Imprints, 1801–1841: A Bibliography* (Toronto: U of Toronto P, with the National Library of Canada and the Canadian Government Publishing Centre, 1988, 555 pp.).

4620 Watters, Reginald Eyre. *A Checklist of Canadian Literature and Background Materials, 1628–1960*. 2nd ed., rev. and enl. Toronto: U of Toronto P, 1972. 1,085 pp. Z1375.W3 013'.971.

A bibliography of separately published English-Canadian literary and related works by some 7,000 Canadian authors (with "Canadian" broadly inclusive). The approximately 16,000 titles are organized alphabetically by author in two parts. Pt. 1 is meant to be a comprehensive list of literary works, with entries divided among sections for poetry, poetry and prose mixed, fiction, and drama. Pt. 2 is a selective list of books important as backgrounds to Canadian literature, with entries grouped by topics: biography, essays and speeches, local history and description, religion and morality, social history, scholarship and criticism on literature and the humanities, and travel and description. In both parts, works published before 1951 are located in up to five libraries (primarily in Canada). Two indexes: titles of anonymous works; authors, initials, and pseudonyms. Users must remember that (1) this is a list of works, not an exhaustive bibliography of editions; (2) there are numerous errors and inconsistencies, since the majority of entries were compiled from library catalogs and other sources rather than personal examination of copies; (3) pt. 2 includes several works only marginally related to Canadian literature; (4) the reliance on library call numbers to identify genre or subject matter means there will be classification errors. Although unsophisticated as a bibliography, Watters offers the fullest record of English-Canadian literature. Reviews: (1st ed.) H. P. Gundy, *Queen's Quarterly* 66 (1959): 326–28; (2nd ed.) Robert L. McDougall, *Queen's Quarterly* 81 (1974): 120–22; Peter C. Noel-Bentley, *Humanities Association Review* 24 (1973): 340–41.

For literary works, Watters supersedes Vernon Blair Rhodenizer, *Canadian Literature in English* (Montreal: Privately printed, 1965, 1,055 pp.), a poorly organized compilation of miscellaneous information on books by Canadian citizens and residents which must be used with Lois Mary Thierman, comp., *Index to Vernon Blair Rhodenizer's* Canadian Literature in English (Edmonton: La Survivance, [1968], 469 pp.). For post-1960 works, see *Canadiana* (4595). Wagner, *Brock Bibliography of Published Canadian Plays* (4725), provides fuller coverage of drama but does not list locations.

See also

"Annual Bibliography of Commonwealth Literature" (4375).
Canadian Literature Index (4630).
Canadian Periodical Index (4635).
Cheung, *Asian American Literature* (3940).
Eighteenth-Century Short-Title Catalogue (2230).
Lecker, *Canadian Writers and Their Works* (4645).
Moyles, *English-Canadian Literature to 1900* (4650).
Nineteenth Century Short Title Catalogue (2475).
North American Imprints Program (4010).
Sabin, *Bibliotheca Americana* (4015).

Guides to Scholarship and Criticism

SERIAL BIBLIOGRAPHIES

4625 "Bibliographie de la critique [1974–]." *Revue d'histoire littéraire du Québec et du Canada français* (entry 4695) 1 (1979)– .

A bibliography of books and articles—almost all published in Canada—on québécoise and French-Canadian literature. Entries are listed by publication date in two divisions: books and articles. The first division has sections for reference works; anthologies, histories, and guides; and essays and monographs. The second has classified sections for general studies, genres, and individual authors. Indexed by scholars. Although largely restricted to French-language works published in Canada, awkwardly organized (especially in the separation of books and articles), and inadequately cross-referenced, the "Bibliographie" offers the fullest current guide to scholarship and criticism on French-Canadian literature. Its coverage must be supplemented by the other serial bibliographies in this section and in section G: Serial Bibliographies, Indexes, and Abstracts. For articles published before 1974, see Pierre Cantin, Normand Harrington, and Jean-Paul Hudon, *Bibliographie de la critique de la littérature québécoise dans les revues des XIXe et XXe siècles*, 5 vols., Documents de travail du Centre de recherche en civilisation canadienne-française 12–16 (Ottawa: Centre de recherche en civilisation canadienne-française, U d'Ottawa, 1979).

4630 *Canadian Literature Index: A Guide to Periodicals and Newspapers [1985–]*. Canadian Index Series. Toronto: ECW, 1987– . Quarterly, with annual cumulation. Z1375.C3.

An index of creative works by Canadian authors, studies of Canadian literary works, and reviews of books by Canadians and about the country's literature—all published in some 100 periodicals and newspapers, the majority of which originate in Canada. The entries are organized in two parts: an author list of publications indexed, and a subject list, with headings for writers, literary works, and some topics (with subject heads in English only). Vague titles are usually accompanied by a phrase indicating content. Despite *Canadian Literature Index*'s drawbacks—it lacks an explanation of the criteria used to determine "Canadian," is limited in coverage, needlessly separates literary works from their respective authors in the subject division (a practice that occasions unnecessary duplicate entries), and employs subject headings that are usually too broad—it is a welcome addition to Canadian reference sources.

An important source for earlier scholarship is "Canadian Literature/Littérature canadienne [1959–74]: An Annotated Bibliography/Une bibliographie avec commentaire," [for 1959–70] *Canadian Literature* (entry 4685) 3–48 (1960–71); [for 1971] *Essays on Canadian Writing* (entry 4690) 9 (1977–78): 190–326; [for 1972–74] *Journal of Canadian Fiction* (entry 4715) 2–23 (1973–79), a bibliography of primary and secondary works (including dissertations, theses, and reviews) related to English- and French-Canadian literature. The bibliographies for 1959–63 are cumulated and slightly expanded in Inglis F. Bell and Susan W. Port, eds., *Canadian Literature, 1959–1963: A Checklist of Creative and Critical Writings/Littérature canadienne, 1959–1963: Bibliographie de la critique et des œuvres d'imagination* (Vancouver: U of British Columbia, 1966, 140 pp.)

4635 *Canadian Periodical Index: An Author and Subject Index/Index de périodiques canadiens: Auteurs et sujets*. Ottawa: Canadian Library Assn., 1928–1932, 1938– . Monthly, with annual and larger cumulations. Former titles: *Canadian Periodical Index* (1928–47); *Canadian Index to Periodicals and Documentary Films: An Author and Subject Index/Index de périodiques et de films documentaires canadiens: Auteurs et sujets* (1948–63). AI3.C242 051.

An author and subject index to reviews, original literary works, and articles "of real substance and . . . of genuine value" in some 140 (currently) scholarly and popular periodicals published in Canada. Subject headings are in English (with French-language cross-references for articles in French). Articles are usually indexed under only one subject heading; book reviews are grouped under "Book Reviews"; poems appear under "Poems"; short stories, under "Short Stories"; and art works, under the name of the artist. Like *Readers' Guide* (400), which it resembles, this series is useful for its coverage of periodicals not indexed in the bibliographies and indexes in this section and in section G.

4640 "Preliminary Bibliography of Comparative Canadian Literature (English-Canadian and French-Canadian)." *Canadian Review of Comparative Literature/Revue canadienne de littérature comparée* (entry 5015) 3 (1976)– .

An annual bibliography of comparative studies of English- and French-Canadian literature. Entries are organized alphabetically by author in 12 classified divisions: bibliographies; reference works; bilingual anthologies; current periodicals publishing studies of both English- and French-Canadian literature; literary histories; general studies; comparative studies of authors, works, genres, themes, and language and style; literary translation. The "Preliminary Bibliography" is particularly useful as a complement to the bibliographies in this section and in G: Serial Bibliographies, Indexes, and Abstracts that sometimes overlook or inadequately index comparative studies.

See also

Sec. G: Serial Bibliographies, Indexes, Abstracts.
ABELL (340).
"Annual Bibliography of Commonwealth Literature" (4375).
"Letters in Canada" (4610).
MLAIB (335): For English-Canadian literature see the English Literature division, especially English III: General, in volumes through 1956; English XI: Australia, Canada, Etc./Canada section in the volumes for 1957–66; English II: Australia, Canada, Etc./Canada section in the volumes for 1967–80; and the Canadian Literature division in later volumes. For French-Canadian literature, see the French division (especially French II) in the pre-1981 volumes and the French-Canadian division in the later ones. Researchers must also check the "Canadian Literature" and "French Canadian Literature" headings in the subject index to post-1980 volumes.
YWES (330): Canadian literature has been covered in the African, Caribbean, Canadian, Australian, New Zealand, and Indian Literature in English chapter since vol. 63 (for 1982).

OTHER BIBLIOGRAPHIES

4645 Lecker, Robert, Jack David, and Ellen Quigley, eds. *Canadian Writers and Their Works* (*CWTW*). 20 vols. Toronto: ECW, 1983– . PR9180.C36 810'.9'971.

A collection of chapters on major writers of the last 200 years, with 10 volumes devoted to fiction and 10 to poetry. Each volume treats five authors or related groups in essays that include a biography, discussion of milieu, survey of major studies, critical commentary on important works, and selected bibliographies of primary works and scholarship. Indexed by persons and titles of primary works in each volume. Although there is considerable unevenness in the quality of individual essays, *CWTW* is a useful introduction to the work of and scholarship on major Canadian writers.

4650 Moyles, R. G. *English-Canadian Literature to 1900: A Guide to Information Sources*. American Literature, English Literature, and World Literatures in English: An Information Guide Series 6. Detroit: Gale, 1976. 346 pp. Z1375.M68 [PR9184.3] 016.81'08.

A selective bibliography of primary and secondary works (published through the early 1970s) important to the study of nineteenth-century English-Canadian literature. Entries are listed in seven divisions: reference works (including sections for bibliographies, biographical sources, indexes to serials, theses, and microforms, and library catalogs), general literary history and criticism, anthologies, 12 major authors, 36 minor authors, travel writing, and nineteenth-century literary periodicals. Under each author are sections for bibliographies and manuscripts, collected works, biographical materials, primary works (by genre), and criticism. Less than half of the entries are descriptively annotated. Two indexes: persons; titles (incomplete). Although marred by an inadequate explanation of scope and criteria governing selection, Moyles is an essential supplement to Watters, *On Canadian Literature* (4655), and Watters, *Checklist of Canadian Literature* (4620); as a selective bibliography, it is superior to Michael Gnarowski, *A Concise Bibliography of English-Canadian Literature*, rev. ed. (Toronto: McClelland, 1978, 145 pp.), which is restricted to major authors and too dated to be of much use.

4655 Watters, Reginald Eyre, and Inglis Freeman Bell, comps. *On Canadian Literature, 1806–1960: A Check List of Articles, Books, and Theses on English-Canadian Literature, Its Authors, and Language*. Rpt., with corrections and additions. Toronto: U of Toronto P, 1973. 165 pp. Z1375.W33 016.8109.

A classified list of biographical, critical, and scholarly studies, published between 1806 and 1960, on English-Canadian literature and language. Entries are organized alphabetically in two divisions: general and topical studies, and individual authors. The first has sections for general bibliographies; Canadian culture and background; language and linguistics; general studies on Canadian literature; drama and theater; fiction; poetry; general criticism; literary history; regionalism; songs, folksongs, and folklore; journalism, publishing, and periodicals; libraries and reading; and censorship and copyright. The work's flaws—it lacks an index, is not comprehensive, includes several unverified entries taken from other sources, and is superseded in parts—do not outweigh its usefulness as a starting point for identifying studies published before 1961. Review: Gordon Roper, *University of Toronto Quarterly* 36 (1967): 411–13.

For scholarship on theater, see Ball, *Bibliography of Canadian Theatre History* (4735).

See also

Boos, *Bibliography of Women and Literature* (6600).
Cheung, *Asian American Literature* (3940).
Etulain, *Bibliographical Guide to the Study of Western American Literature* (3670).

Lecker, *Annotated Bibliography of Canada's Major Authors* (4605).
Marken, *American Indian: Language and Literature* (3875).
Nadel, *Jewish Writers of North America* (3990).
New, *Critical Writings on Commonwealth Literatures* (4380).
Pownall, *Articles on Twentieth Century Literature* (2790).
Schwartz, *Articles on Women Writers* (6605).
Watters, *Checklist of Canadian Literature and Background Materials, 1628–1960* (4620).

DISSERTATIONS AND THESES

4660 Gabel, Gernot U. *Canadian Literature: An Index to Theses Accepted by Canadian Universities, 1925–1980*. Köln: Gemini, 1984. 157 pp. Z1375.G32 [PR9184.3] 016.81'09'005.

A classified bibliography of baccalaureate, master's, and doctoral theses accepted by Canadian institutions and treating English- or French-Canadian literature. The 1,531 entries are organized by degree candidate in two divisions: general literary history (with sections for general studies, poetry, fiction, drama and theater, and periodicals), and individual literary authors. An entry cites title, degree, university, and date. Two indexes: authors of theses; subjects. The fullest single list of Canadian theses on the country's literature, Gabel supersedes Michael Gnarowski, *Theses and Dissertations in Canadian Literature (English): A Preliminary Check List* (Ottawa: Golden Dog, 1975, 41 pp.), and saves users from having to search Namaan, *Répertoire des thèses littéraires canadiennes* (470a), *Canadian Graduate Theses* (470a), and *Canadian Theses* (470). For post-1980 theses accepted by Canadian universities, see *Canadian Theses*; for dissertations on Canadian literature from non-Canadian institutions, see section H: Guides to Dissertations and Theses.

RELATED TOPICS

4665 Fowke, Edith, and Carole Henderson Carpenter, comps. *A Bibliography of Canadian Folklore in English*. Toronto: U of Toronto P, 1981. 272 pp. Z5984.C33.F68 [GR113] 016.39'000971.

A selective bibliography of English-language studies (along with a very few in French) published through 1979. The 3,877 entries are listed by author in variously classified divisions for reference works, periodicals, general studies, genres (folktale, music and dance, folk speech and names, minor genres, superstition and popular belief, folklife and customs, and art and material culture), biographies and appreciations of folklorists, records, films, and theses and dissertations. The genre divisions include sections for general studies and ethnic groups. An elaborate, rather confusing code (see p. xx) identifies audience, quality, content, or type of work in most entries. Users must study the discussion of classification and limitations in the introduction, which also surveys broadly the scholarship and identifies topics needing attention. Indexed by scholars. It is selective (with several unverified entries from other sources) and lacks a subject index; nevertheless, the *Bibliography of Canadian Folklore* is the most complete list of English-language studies of Canadian folklore. Review: Gerald Thomas, *Canadian Literature* 95 (1982): 161–65.

See also

Sec. U: Literature-Related Topics and Sources/Folklore.
America: History and Life (3310).
Clements, *Native American Folklore, 1879–1979* (3885).
Murdock, *Ethnographic Bibliography of North America* (3890).

Language

GUIDES TO SCHOLARSHIP

4670 Avis, Walter S., and A. M. Kinloch. *Writings on Canadian English, 1792–1975: An Annotated Bibliography*. Toronto: Fitzhenry, [1978]. 153 pp. Z1379.A88 [PE3208] 016.427'9'71.

Lougheed, W. C. *Writings on Canadian English, 1976–1987: A Selective, Annotated Bibliography*. Strathy Language Unit Occasional Papers 2. Kingston: Strathy Language Unit, Queen's U, 1988. 66 pp.

Bibliographies of popular and scholarly studies (including dissertations, theses, and reviews) published through 1987. The two volumes exclude works concerned solely with onomastics, the influence of Canadian English on other languages, or pedagogy. In both works, entries are organized in a single alphabetical sequence; in *1792–1975*, this material is followed by a section listing additions, including selected publications through 1977. The annotations clearly describe the scope and contents of works. Indexed in *1792–1975* by co-authors and co-editors, and in *1976–1987* by persons and subjects. The lack of a classified organization, cross-references, or subject index in the original volume means that users interested in a specific topic must skim all entries; however, *Writings on Canadian English* represents the most complete single list of studies through 1987. For later scholarship, see *MLAIB* (335) and *ABELL* (340).

See also

ABELL (340): English Language division, which has a section on American English since the volume for 1927; in earlier volumes, see the Dialect section.
MLAIB (335): English Language and Literature division in the volumes for 1922–25; English Language and Literature I: Linguistics section in the volumes for 1926–66; the Indo-European C: Germanic Linguistics IV: English/Modern English/Dialectology section in the volumes for 1967–80; and the Indo-European Languages/West Germanic Languages/English Language (Modern)/Dialectology section in the later volumes. Researchers must also check the headings "Canada" and "Canadian English Dialect" in the subject index to post-1980 volumes.
Watters, *On Canadian Literature, 1806–1960* (4655).

DICTIONARIES

4675 *A Dictionary of Canadianisms on Historical Principles*. Ed. Walter S. Avis et al. Toronto: Gage, 1967. 927 pp. PE3243.D5 427'.9'71.

A dictionary of words, expressions, and meanings "native to Canada or . . . distinctively characteristic of Canadian usage." A typical entry includes headword, pronunciation, part of speech, etymology, usage labels (for vocation, locale, or currency), definition, dated illustrative quotations from printed works, and, occasionally, a line drawing. Concludes with a bibliography of sources. The essential dictionary for the historical study of Canadian English and for the explication of Canadianisms in literary works. Canadian English is also included in *Dictionary of American English* (3355), *Dictionary of Americanisms* (3360), and *Oxford English Dictionary* (1410). For contemporary Canadian English, see *Gage Canadian Dictionary*, ed. Walter S. Avis et al., Dictionary of Canadian English Series (Toronto: Gage, 1983, 1,313 pp.).

Biographical Dictionaries

4680 *Dictionary of Canadian Biography* (*DCB*). Gen. eds. George W. Brown, David M. Hayne, and Francess G. Halpenny. 12 vols. Toronto: U of Toronto P, 1966– . French ed.: *Dictionnaire biographique du Canada* (*DBC*). Gen. eds. Marcel Trudel, André Vachon, and Jean Hamelin. Québec: P de l'U Laval, 1966– . F1005.D49 [FC25] 920'.071.

Vol. 1: *1000 to 1700*. 1966. 755 pp.
Vol. 2: *1701 to 1740*. 1969. 759 pp.
Vol. 3: *1741 to 1770*. 1974. 782 pp.
Vol. 4: *1771 to 1800*. 1979. 913 pp.
Index: Volumes I to IV, 1000 to 1800. 1981. 254 pp.
Vol. 5: *1801 to 1820*. 1983. 1,044 pp.
Vol. 6: *1821 to 1835*. 1987. 960 pp.
Vol. 7: *1836 to 1850*. In progress.
Vol. 8: *1851 to 1860*. 1985. 1,129 pp.
Vol. 9: *1861 to 1870*. 1976. 967 pp.
Vol. 10: *1871 to 1880*. 1972. 823 pp.
Vol. 11: *1881 to 1890*. 1982. 1,092 pp.
Vol. 12: *1891 to 1900*. Scheduled for 1990.

A biographical dictionary encompassing a broad range of Canadians and others who at least set foot in the country. Entries are listed alphabetically, with placement in a volume determined by the date of an entrant's death. The biographies, ranging from two hundred to ten thousand words, combine facts with interpretation and conclude with a bibliography of works by and about the individual (frequently citing unpublished material). Each volume prints introductory essays on aspects of its period, a general bibliography, and index of names; volumes published or reprinted since 1979 include occupation/vocation and geographical indexes. The cumulative index to vols. 1–4 has four indexes: subjects of biographies; occupations/vocations; geographical area; names. Cumulative indexes are planned for vols. 5–8 and 9–12. *DCB* is a well-edited, authoritative, scholarly source that fully deserves the praise accorded it by reviewers and its rank among the great biographical dictionaries such as *Dictionary of National Biography* (1425) and *Dictionary of American Biography* (3380); it is especially useful to the literary researcher for its biographies of Canadian writers and historical figures depicted in Canadian literature as well as for the numerous citations to unpublished materials. Reviews: (vol. 1) H. P. Gundy, *Dalhousie Review* 46 (1966): 405–11; (vol. 4) Carl F. Klinck, *English Studies in Canada* 7 (1981): 496–500; (vol. 9) Clara Thomas, *English Studies in Canada* 5 (1979): 227–31; (vol. 11) Shirley Neuman, *Canadian Literature* 101 (1984): 82–83.

A useful basic biographical dictionary is W. Stewart Wallace, ed., *The Macmillan Dictionary of Canadian Biography*, rev. W. A. McKay, 4th ed. (Toronto: Macmillan, 1978, 914 pp.). For living persons, see the current edition of *Canadian Who's Who* (Toronto: U of Toronto P, 1910–); *Who's Who in America* (3395) also includes Canadians.

See also

Sec. J: Biographical Sources.
Dictionary of Literary Biography (600).
Oxford Companion to Canadian Literature (4580).

Periodicals

GUIDES TO PRIMARY WORKS

See

Sec. K: Periodicals/Directories and Periodicals/Union Lists.
Warwick, *Commonwealth Literature Periodicals* (4385).

INDEXES

See

Goode, *Index to Commonwealth Little Magazines* (795).

SCHOLARLY JOURNALS

Many journals in section K: Periodicals/Scholarly Journals publish essays on Canadian literature.

4685 *Canadian Literature/Littérature canadienne* (*CanL*). 1959– . Quarterly. PS8061 819.

Publishes articles, notes, reviews, and occasional special issues on English- and French-Canadian literature, as well as original poetry and reviews of Canadian literary works. The annual bibliography "Canadian Literature [1959–70]" (4630a) appears in vols. 3–48 (1960–71). Cumulative index: vols. 1–102, Glenn Clever, comp., *An Index to the Contents of the Periodical* Canadian Literature, *Nos. 1–102* (Ottawa: Tecumseh, 1984, 218 pp.). Supplements covering vols. 103–07, 108–11, and 112–15 are in progress.

4690 *Essays on Canadian Writing* (*ECW*). 1974– . 2/yr. PR9180.E8 [PS8043] 810'.9.

Publishes articles, bibliographies, interviews, and reviews, typically in special issues devoted to authors or topics. Vol. 9 (1977–78) hosts the annual bibliography "Canadian Literature [1971]" (4630a). Cumulative index: vols. 1–12, David H. Jorgensen, comp., Essays on Canadian Writing: *An Index: Numbers 1–12, Winter 1974–Fall 1978* (Downsview: ECW, 1979, 48 pp.).

4695 *Revue d'histoire littéraire du Québec et du Canada français* (*RHLQCF*). 1979– . Irregular. PQ3900.H58 840'.9'9714.

Publishes articles, notes, edited manuscripts, summaries of master's theses and doctoral dissertations, and reviews on québécoise and French-Canadian literature and film. For "Bibliographie de la critique," see entry 4625.

4700 *Studies in Canadian Literature* (*SCL*). 1976– . 2/yr. PR9180.S88 [PS8071] 810'.9'971.

Publishes articles, notes, reviews, and occasional special issues on all periods of English-Canadian and French-Canadian literature, with an emphasis on the former.

See also

Sec. R: Other Literatures in English/General/Periodicals/Scholarly Journals. *University of Toronto Quarterly* (735).

Genres

Some works in section L: Genres are useful for research in Canadian literature.

FICTION

Some works in section L: Genres/Fiction are useful for research in Canadian fiction.

Guides to Primary Works

There is no adequate bibliography devoted solely to English-Canadian fiction. Margery Fee and Ruth Cawker, *Canadian Fiction: An Annotated Bibliography*

(Toronto: Martin, 1976, 170 pp.), a selection aid for teachers, is too incomplete to be of much use. Until an adequate bibliography appears, researchers will have to make do with Watters, *Checklist of Canadian Literature* (4620).

4705 Hayne, David M., and Marcel Tirol. *Bibliographie critique du roman canadien-français, 1837–1900.* Toronto: U of Toronto P, 1968. 144 pp. Z1377.F8.H3 016.843.

A bibliography of French-language novels published separately before 1901 by Canadian citizens or permanent residents, and of selected scholarship and criticism through 1966. Entries are organized in three divisions: bibliographies, general biographical and critical works, and individual novelists. Under each author, novels are listed alphabetically, with editions, translations, and extracts in periodicals following in chronological order (with locations in Canadian libraries and the Library of Congress). Concluding each author section is a selective list of studies. Although its record of secondary works is far from complete, this remains an essential source for the study of the early French-Canadian novel. Unfortunately, there is no comparable bibliography of twentieth-century French-Canadian novels.

See also

Wright, *Author [Chronological; Title] Bibliography of English Language Fiction* (1060).

Guides to Scholarship and Criticism

4710 Hoy, Helen. *Modern English-Canadian Prose: A Guide to Information Sources.* American Literature, English Literature, and World Literatures in English: An Information Guide Series 38. Detroit: Gale, 1983. 605 pp. Z1377.F4.H69 [PR9192.5] 016.818'508.

A selective bibliography of primary and secondary works through 1980 that emphasizes fiction writers but also includes essayists, nature writers, critics, and biographers. Of the 78 authors, 10 are nonfiction writers and all were born before 1942; those in Moyles, *English-Canadian Literature to 1900* (4650) are excluded. The approximately 5,250 entries are organized in three divisions: reference works (with sections for bibliographies and general reference works, biographical dictionaries, periodical and dissertation indexes, and guides to manuscripts and special collections), general studies (divided into books and articles), and individual authors (with separate sections for fiction and nonfiction). Under each author, primary works are divided into books and shorter pieces (each classified by genre) and include a list of manuscript collections; secondary works are listed in three sections: bibliographies, criticism, and book reviews (from major periodicals). Only reference works and a few general studies are annotated (the majority inadequately so). Three indexes: persons; book titles; subjects. Although the criteria governing inclusion of authors are vague, the bases for selection of secondary works are unstated, and many entries appear to be copied without verification from other sources, Hoy is at least a starting point for research on established fiction writers. Review: W. J. Keith, *Essays on Canadian Writing* 30 (1984–85): 136–39.

Biographical Dictionaries

See

Contemporary Novelists (2845).

Periodicals

4715 *The Journal of Canadian Fiction* (*JCF*). 1972– . Quarterly. PR9195.7.J68 813'.54'080971.

Publishes articles, interviews, reviews, and special issues on English- and French-Canadian fiction, as well as original short fiction. The annual bibliography "Canadian Literature [1972–74]" (4630a) appears in 2–23 (1973–79).

DRAMA AND THEATER

Some works in section L: Genres are useful for research in Canadian drama and theater.

Guides to Primary Works

4720 Rinfret, Édouard G. *Le Théâtre canadien d'expression française: Répertoire analytique des origines à nos jours*. 4 vols. Collection Documents. Ottawa: Leméac, 1975–78. PQ3911.R5 792'.09714.

An annotated author bibliography of published and unpublished French-Canadian plays (including radio and television drama) written through the early 1970s. A typical entry gives title, type of play, number of acts or scenes or playing time, cast, setting, synopsis (usually lengthy), first production, and (for published works) publication information and locations of copies in Canadian libraries. Television dramas are listed separately in vol. 4. Indexed by titles in vol. 4. A valuable compendium of information on French-Canadian drama, much of which is unpublished.

4725 Wagner, Anton, ed. *The Brock Bibliography of Published Canadian Plays in English, 1766–1978*. Toronto: Playwrights, 1980. 375 pp. Z1377.D7.B75 [PR9191.2] 016.812.

A bibliography of plays (including some radio and television dramas) written by Canadians—native, naturalized, or landed immigrants—primarily while resident in the country. Wagner includes only extant dramatic works published separately or in periodicals or newspapers. Entries are organized by century of composition, then alphabetically by author, and then by title. Each entry provides publication information (but not a list of all editions), number of acts, number of male and female characters, genre, plot summary, and date and place of first production. Indexed by short titles. The organization by century (which is too gross to indicate trends) results in the placement of several authors in two places, and the lack of author, subject, and genre indexes make the bibliography much less accessible than it should be. There are several omissions and errors (especially in bibliographical details), but the *Brock Bibliography* is the fullest single source of information on published English-Canadian plays. Review: Ron Davies, *Canadian Theatre Review* 31 (1981): 144–45.

An essential complement because of its broader definition of what constitutes Canadian drama and its inclusion of unpublished works is Patrick B. O'Neill, "A Checklist of Canadian Dramatic Materials to 1967," *Canadian Drama* 8 (1982): 173–303; 9 (1983): 369–506. Although offering a less complete list of dramatic works, Watters, *Checklist of Canadian Literature* (4620), is still useful, since it provides locations of copies. For plays published after 1978, see *Canadiana* (4595).

Guides to Scholarship and Criticism

Surveys of Research

4730 Wagner, Anton. "From Art to Theory: Canada's Critical Tools." *Canadian Theatre Review* 34 (1982): 59–83.

A survey of the state of research that evaluates bibliographies and reference works, discusses problems facing researchers in Canadian drama, identifies needed reference works, and concludes with a selective list of bibliographies and guides.

Other Bibliographies

4735 Ball, John, and Richard Plant. *A Bibliography of Canadian Theatre History, 1583–1975*. Toronto: Playwrights Co-op, 1976. 160 pp. *The Bibliography of Canadian Theatre History: Supplement, 1975–1976*. 1979. 75 pp. Z1377.D7.B33 [PN2301] 016.792'0971.

A bibliography of studies through 1976 on Canadian theater history, with much fuller coverage of English- than French-Canadian theater. Excludes almost all newspaper articles as well as discussions of ballet, opera, and music. Entries are organized by publication date in most of the classified divisions: general surveys; theater history to 1900; twentieth-century English-Canadian theater; twentieth-century French-Canadian theater (Quebec theater in the supplement); little theater movement (with community theater added in the supplement); Dominion Drama Festival (Theatre Canada in the supplement); Stratford Festival; theater education; theater architecture, facilities, stage design, and lighting; biographies and criticism of actors, actresses, and playwrights; theses and dissertations; periodicals; bibliographies of bibliographies; and, in the supplement, stagecraft. Additions and corrections to the first volume appear in the supplement (pp. 73–74). The principles of selection are not clear, the chronological organization is unsuitable for many divisions, and there are omissions, but *Bibliography of Canadian Theatre History* is an important preliminary attempt at organizing the scholarship on Canadian theater. Reviews: Ann P. Messenger, *Canadian Literature* 74 (1977): 90–95; Patrick B. O'Neill, *Dalhousie Review* 56 (1976): 596–98.

See also

Carpenter, *Modern Drama Scholarship and Criticism, 1966–1980* (2875).
Eddleman, *American Drama Criticism* (3520).
International Bibliography of Theatre (1160).
"Modern Drama Studies" (2870).
Wildbihler, *Musical: An International Annotated Bibliography* (4295).

Biographical Dictionaries

See

Contemporary Dramatists (2880).

Periodicals

4740 *Canadian Drama/L'Art dramatique canadien*. 1975– . 2/yr. PS8177 812'.009.

Publishes articles, reviews, and occasional special issues on English- and French-Canadian drama, as well as texts of plays.

4745 *Theatre History in Canada/Histoire du théâtre au Canada*. 1980– . 2/yr. PN2009.T473 792'.0971.

Publishes articles and reviews on the history of English- and French-Canadian drama, including that for television and radio.

POETRY

Some works in section L: Genres/Poetry are useful for research in Canadian poetry.

Guides to Primary Works

4750 McQuarrie, Jane, Anne Mercer, and Gordon Ripley, comps. and eds. *Index to Canadian Poetry in English*. Toronto: Reference, 1984. 367 pp. Z1377.P7.M35 [PR9190.2] 016.811'008'0971.

Title and first-line, author, and subject indexes to about 7,000 poems (including some translations of French-Canadian works) from 51 collections. The title and first-line index is keyed to a list of anthologies; the author and subject indexes are keyed to the title and first-line index. Although highly selective, this is a convenient source for locating the text of a poem or for identifying works about a topic or theme. *Granger's Index to Poetry* (1235), *Index of American Periodical Verse* (4325), and *Poetry Index Annual* (1240) also index some English-Canadian poems.

Guides to Scholarship and Criticism

4755 Stevens, Peter. *Modern English-Canadian Poetry: A Guide to Information Sources*. American Literature, English Literature, and World Literatures in English: An Information Guide Series 15. Detroit: Gale, 1978. 216 pp. Z1377.P7.S79 [PR9184.3] 016.811'5.

A highly selective bibliography of primary and secondary works (published almost exclusively in English through the early 1970s) for the study of English-Canadian poetry. Entries are organized in classified divisions for reference sources (with sections for bibliographies; biographical sources; indexes to serials, theses, and microforms; and manuscript and special collections), literary histories and general studies, anthologies, periodicals, and 60 poets. The poets are grouped by period (1900–40, 1940–60, and 1960–70s), and each has separate lists of primary works and criticism. Several annotations are inadequately or imprecisely descriptive; few entries in the author division are annotated. Three indexes: persons; book titles; subjects. Because of its inadequate explanation of scope and criteria governing selection of both poets and secondary works, significant omissions, and numerous unverified entries, Stevens is only marginally useful as a guide to modern English-Canadian poetry. Review: R. G. Moyles, *Essays on Canadian Writing* 16 (1979–80): 229–33.

See also

"Year's Work in Canadian Poetry Studies" (4760a).

Biographical Dictionaries

See

Contemporary Poets (2895).

Periodicals

4760 *Canadian Poetry* (*CanPo*). 1977– . 2/yr. PR9190.2.C35 811'.009'971.

Focuses on English-Canadian poetry in articles, documents, reviews, and "The Year's Work in Canadian Poetry Studies [1976–86]," 2–20 (1978–87), a selective, partly annotated bibliography of studies on English-Canadian poetry.

PROSE

Some works in section L: Genres/Prose are useful for research in Canadian prose.

Guides to Primary Works

4765 Matthews, William, comp. *Canadian Diaries and Autobiographies*. Berkeley: U of California P, 1950. 130 pp. Z5305.C3.M3 016.920071.

An author list of 1,276 published and manuscript diaries, journals, travel accounts, reminiscences, autobiographies, and the like by Canadians or relating to Canada. Users should note the list in the preface of kinds of material excluded (e.g., French works before the French and Indian Wars, journals by world explorers, and writings by American travelers—for the last, see Arksey, *American Diaries* [3540]). A typical entry includes birth and death dates, occupation, title of published work and publication information or type of manuscript, and time span; a brief description of content; and location and number of pages for a manuscript. Additions appear on pp. 129–30. Indexed by subjects (but inadequately so, since only major or broad topics are included). While far from comprehensive, emphasizing the better known published works and manuscripts in major libraries, and including several errors, Matthews is still a useful place to begin a search for autobiographical material of Canadian interest. It must be supplemented, however, by *Union List of Manuscripts in Canadian Repositories* (4590) and the works in section F: Guides to Manuscripts and Archives. Review: Marie Tremaine, *Canadian Historical Review* 33 (1952): 78–79.

Some additional published Canadian diaries are listed in Patricia Pate Havlice, *And So to Bed: A Bibliography of Diaries Published in English* (Metuchen: Scarecrow, 1987, 698 pp.); however, its chief feature is a combined index of diarists in Matthews, *Canadian Diaries*; *British Diaries* (1615); and *American Diaries* (3540a).

See also

Brumble, *Annotated Bibliography of American Indian and Eskimo Autobiographies* (3925).
Hoy, *Modern English-Canadian Prose* (4710).

Guides to Scholarship and Criticism

See

Hoy, *Modern English-Canadian Prose* (4710).

Caribbean-Area Literatures in English

Works in section R: Other Literatures in English/General are important to research in Caribbean-area literatures.

Literary Handbooks, Dictionaries, and Encyclopedias

4780 Herdeck, Donald E., ed. *Caribbean Writers: A Bio-Bibliographical-Critical Encyclopedia.* Washington: Three Continents, 1979. 943 pp. PN849.C3.C3 809'.89729.

A biographical and bibliographical guide to Caribbean literature in four parts: Anglophone literature, Francophone literature, Netherlands Antilles and Surinam, and Spanish-language literature. Each part begins with an overview of the social, linguistic, and literary history of the area, and a list of writers by country or region; each concludes with various bibliographies of primary works and studies. The bulk of the work consists of author entries that provide basic biographical and career information, occasional critical comments, and an incomplete list of primary works and a highly selective list of studies. Because of the organization and incomplete cross-referencing of pseudonyms and variant forms of names, an author index would make entries much easier to locate. The work is inconsistent in places and stylistically wooden but is packed with information; it offers the fullest general guide to Caribbean writers and their work. Review: Marian Goslinga, *Revista interamericana de bibliografía* 30 (1980): 183–84.

More current information on the writers included can be found in Daryl Cumber Dance, ed., *Fifty Caribbean Writers: A Bio-Bibliographical Critical Sourcebook* (New York: Greenwood, 1986, 530 pp.). Each essay provides a biography, discussion of major works, survey of important scholarship, and selected bibliography of primary and secondary sources.

Bibliographies of Bibliographies

4785 Jordan, Alma, and Barbara Comissiong. *The English-Speaking Caribbean: A Bibliography of Bibliographies.* Reference Publication in Latin American Studies. Boston: Hall, 1984. 411 pp. Z1595.J67 [F2161] 016.0169729.

A bibliography of published and unpublished national, regional, and topical bibliographies available through April 1981 on British Caribbean territories. Works are listed alphabetically by author, editor, or sponsoring organization under variously classified divisions, with the following of most interest to language and literature researchers: library catalogs; regional, national, and general bibliographies; biography (including several literary authors); folklore; history; language and linguistics; and literature. The literature division includes sections for general works, criticism, drama, fiction, indexes, periodicals, poetry, and countries or areas. Entries are accompanied by full descriptions of content and locations of copies (principally in Caribbean libraries). Two indexes: names; subjects. Although some classifications could be more refined and the coverage of parts of books is weak, *English-Speaking Caribbean* is an essential source for the identification and location of bibliographies treating the Caribbean (many of which are mimeographed works of severely limited distribution). A quick perusal will reveal how much basic bibliographical work remains to be done on Caribbean literatures.

Guides to Scholarship and Criticism

4790 Allis, Jeannette B. *West Indian Literature: An Index to Criticism, 1930–1975*. Reference Publication in Latin American Studies. Boston: Hall, 1981. 353 pp. Z1502.B5.A38 [PR9210] 016.820'9'9729.

A highly selective bibliography of English-language books, a very few collections of essays, and articles from 77 journals and newspapers (with some coverage extending beyond 1975). Entries are organized in three divisions: the first includes studies of specific writers (with sections for general criticism and individual works); the last lists general studies by date of publication. The middle division repeats the entries in the other two as a scholar/critic list; a simple name index would accomplish the same in one-tenth of the 120 pages. General books on West Indian literature are relegated to an appendix. Only the entries in the third division are descriptively annotated, but the lack of an index means one must search through the entire list to find works that treat a particular writer or topic. The high degree of selectivity, lack of an adequate statement of criteria governing selection, poor organization, and lack of indexing make *West Indian Literature* useful only as an occasional supplement to New, *Critical Writings on Commonwealth Literatures* (4380) and "Annual Bibliography of Commonwealth Literature" (4375).

Some additional studies can be found in Lambros Comitas, *The Complete Caribbeana, 1800–1975: A Bibliographic Guide to the Scholarly Literature*, 4 vols. (Millwood: KTO-Kraus-Thomson, 1977). In particular, see the following chapters in vol. 2: 22, "Creative Arts and Recreation" (including literature); 24, "Folklore"; and 25, "Language and Linguistics." Theses and dissertations are listed in Samuel B. Bandara, "A Checklist of Theses and Dissertations in English on Caribbean Literature," *World Literature Written in English* 20 (1981): 319–34.

See also

Secs. G: Serial Bibliographies, Indexes, and Abstracts and H: Guides to Dissertations and Theses.

ABELL (340).

"Annual Bibliography of Commonwealth Literature" (4375).

MLAIB (335): English Literature division (especially English III: General) through the volume for 1956; English XI: Australia, Canada, Etc. section in the volumes for 1957–66; English II: Australia, Canada, Etc. section in the volumes for 1967–80; and the English Caribbean Literature section in later volumes. Researchers must also check the headings beginning "English Caribbean" in the subject index to post-1980 volumes.

New, *Critical Writings on Commonwealth Literatures* (4380).

"Studies in Caribbean and South American Literature" (3790a).

Szwed, *Afro-American Folk Culture* (5880).

YWES (330): Caribbean-area literatures have been covered in the chapter African, Caribbean, Canadian, Australian, New Zealand, and Indian Literature in English since vol. 63 (for 1982).

Indian Literature in English

Most works in section R: Other Literatures in English/General are important to research in Indian literature in English.

Guides to Primary Works

4800 Singh, Amritjit, Rajiva Verma, and Irene M. Joshi. *Indian Literature in English, 1827–1979: A Guide to Information Sources*. American Literature, English Literature, and World Literatures in English: An Information Guide Series 36. Detroit: Gale, 1981. 631 pp. Z3208.L5.S56 [PR9484.3] 016.82.

A bibliography of English-language creative works and translations by Indian writers and of selected studies of these works. Except for some plays, coverage of primary works is limited to separate publications (attempting but not achieving comprehensiveness). Entries are organized in two divisions: general studies (with sections for philosophy, religion, and the arts; history, society, and politics; reference works; criticism and literary history; and anthologies) and individual writers (organized by genre, then by author, with primary works followed by studies). Selected lists of Indian periodicals and publishers appear as appendixes. Many entries are copied from other sources; a very few works are annotated (inadequately) in the first division. Three indexes: literary authors listed in the second division (with a separate alphabet for each genre); other persons; titles. The work is hard to use because of the poor organization of the individual writers part and its corresponding index (which requires checking four alphabets for some writers) and because of a design and typography that make sections difficult to distinguish. Still, it is the fullest bibliography of primary and secondary works representing Indian writing in English, and is especially valuable for its coverage of ephemeral and limited-circulation publications. Review: Prabhu S. Guptara, *Yearbook of English Studies* 16 (1986): 311–13.

Guides to Scholarship and Criticism

See

Secs. G: Serial Bibliographies, Indexes, and Abstracts and H: Guides to Dissertations and Theses.

ABELL (340).

"Annual Bibliography of Commonwealth Literature" (4375).

MLAIB (335): English Literature division (especially English III: General) through the volume for 1956; English XI: Australia, Canada, Etc./Indian section in the volumes for 1957–66; English II: Australia, Canada, Etc./Indian section in the volumes for 1967–80; and the Indian Literature section in later volumes. Researchers must also check the headings beginning "Indian Literature" in the subject index to post-1980 volumes.

New, *Critical Writings on Commonwealth Literatures* (4380).

YWES (330): Indian literature has been covered in the chapter African, Caribbean, Canadian, Australian, New Zealand, and Indian Literature in English since vol. 64 (for 1983).

New Zealand Literature in English

Works in section R: Other Literatures in English/General are important to research in New Zealand literature.

Guides to Reference Works

For an evaluative survey of some basic general reference sources, see J. E. Traue, "Bibliographic Sources for New Zealand Studies," *Australian and New Zealand Studies*, ed. Patricia McLaren-Turner, British Library Occasional Papers 4 (London: British Library, 1985) 137–53.

Guides to Primary Works

4810 Bagnall, A. G., ed. and comp. *New Zealand National Bibliography to the Year 1960*. 5 vols. Wellington: Government Printer, 1969–85. Z4101.B28 015.931.

A retrospective national bibliography of books and pamphlets published in New Zealand or containing "significant references" to the country. (For a full discussion of kinds of publications excluded, see vol. 1, pt. 1, p. vii, and vol. 2, pp. viii-ix). Vol. 1 covers 1663–1889; vols. 2–4, 1890–1960. Listed alphabetically by author, corporate author, or title of anonymous work, entries supply title, imprint, pagination, size, and an occasional note on content. A double asterisk denotes a work not seen by the compiler; a title set in italic identifies a work outside the bibliography's scope but which researchers might expect to find listed. Vol. 1, pt. 2 prints additions (pp. 1159–70) and two indexes: chronological; subjects, titles, joint authors. Vol. 5 includes additions and corrections to vol. 1 (pp. 619–37) and vols. 2–4 (pp. 1–279), as well as a subject, title, and joint author index to entries for 1890–1960. Bagnall offers the fullest guide to works published in and about the country.

Although largely superseded by Bagnall, T. M. Hocken, *A Bibliography of the Literature Relating to New Zealand* (Wellington: Mackay, 1909, 619 pp.), is still useful because of its inclusion of articles and newspapers, classified organization (with sections for language and literature), and extensive notes. See also A. H. Johnstone, comp., *Supplement to Hocken's Bibliography of New Zealand Literature* (Auckland: Whitcombe, 1927, 73 pp.), and L. J. B. Chapple, *A Bibliographical Brochure Containing Addenda and Corrigenda to Extant Bibliographies of N. Z. Literature* (Dunedin: Reed, 1938, 47 pp.).

4815 *New Zealand National Bibliography [1966–]*. Wellington: National Library of New Zealand, 1968– . Monthly, with annual cumulations. Microfiche only since 1983.

A national bibliography of publications deposited since 1966 under the country's copyright act. After the bibliography for 1985, nonbook publications are omitted. A single author, title, and subject list through the volume for 1982, it is currently published in four parts: register (with entries listed by National Library card number), subject list, author and title list, and publishers' addresses. Each of the first three parts provides full cataloging information. *New Zealand National Bibliography* offers the most complete record of current New Zealand publications. Works published before 1966 are listed in *Index to New Zealand Periodicals and Current National Bibliography of New Zealand Books and Pamphlets Published in [1950–65]* (Wellington: National Library of New Zealand, 1951–66) and before 1960 in Bagnall, *New Zealand National Bibliography* (4810).

See also

"Annual Bibliography of Commonwealth Literature" (4375).

Guides to Scholarship and Criticism

4820 Thomson, John. *New Zealand Literature to 1977: A Guide to Information Sources.* American Literature, English Literature, and World Literatures in English: An Information Guide Series 30. Detroit: Gale, 1980. 272 pp. Z4111.T45 [PR9624.3] 016.82.

A bibliography of primary and secondary works (including theses, dissertations, popular journalism, and numerous unpublished checklists and ephemeral items) covering literature in English and Maori. Entries are organized in seven classified divisions: bibliographies and reference works (with sections for general works, biographical dictionaries, indexes to serial publications, guides to special collections, and New Zealand English), literary history and criticism, anthologies, individual authors (with sections for bibliographies, collected works, biographical materials, primary works, and criticism), other writers (listing works by minor or unestablished authors), periodicals, and nonfiction prose (by New Zealanders as well as foreigners) about the country. A headnote outlines the scope and organization of each division. Most annotations are full, with many offering evaluative comments; however, several entries are left unannotated. Two indexes: persons; titles. Although the coverage of nineteenth-century literature is weak, Thomson is the most complete single guide to scholarship on New Zealand literature. Review: Shaun F. D. Hughes, *Modern Fiction Studies* 27 (1981): 173–88.

Some additional studies of prose fiction are recorded in Rose Marie Beston and John B. Beston, "Critical Writings on Modern New Zealand and Australian Fiction: A Selected Checklist," *Modern Fiction Studies* 27 (1981): 189–204.

See also

Secs. G: Serial Bibliographies, Indexes, and Abstracts and H: Guides to Dissertations and Theses.
ABELL (340).
"Annual Bibliography of Commonwealth Literature" (4375).

Boos, *Bibliography of Women and Literature* (6600).
MLAIB (335): English Literature division (especially English III: General) through the volume for 1956; English XI: Australia, Canada, Etc./New Zealand section in the volumes for 1957–66; English II: Australia, Canada, Etc./New Zealand section in the volumes for 1967–80; and the New Zealand Literature division in later volumes. Researchers must also check the headings beginning "New Zealand" in the subject index to post-1980 volumes.
New, *Critical Writings on Commonwealth Literatures* (4380).
Schwartz, *Articles on Women Writers* (6605).
YWES (330): New Zealand literature has been covered in the chapter African, Caribbean, Canadian, Australian, New Zealand, and Indian Literature in English since vol. 64 (for 1983).

Language

GUIDES TO SCHOLARSHIP

See

ABELL (340): See the Language/English Dialects section through the volume for 1972, then the English Language/Varieties of English/Dialects/Australia and New Zealand section in later volumes.
MLAIB (335): See the English I: Linguistics section through the volume for 1966; the Indo-European C: Germanic Linguistics IV: English/Modern English/Dialectology section in the volumes for 1967–80; and the English Language (Modern)/Dialectology section in later volumes. Researchers must also check the heading "New Zealand English Dialect" in the subject index to post-1980 volumes.
Thomson, *New Zealand Literature to 1977* (4820).

Biographical Dictionaries

4825 *A Dictionary of New Zealand Biography*. Ed. G. H. Scholefield. 2 vols. Wellington: Department of Internal Affairs, 1940. CT2886.S35 920.0931.

A biographical dictionary of whites and Maoris of some significance in New Zealand history since the beginning of the European migration. The entries provide basic biographical and career information; most conclude with selected references to biographical sources. Additional entries are printed in vol. 2, pp. 538–47. Indexed by entrants mentioned in other entries. Although dated, not broadly representative, and largely written by Scholefield, the work is the fullest biographical dictionary of New Zealanders.

In progress is a new *Dictionary of New Zealand Biography* that will be more representative, especially in its inclusion of women, ethnic minorities, and Maoris. On the scope of the new work, see W. H. Oliver, "The *Dictionary of New Zealand*

Biography and the State of New Zealand Historical Studies," *Australian and New Zealand Studies*, ed. Patricia McLaren-Turner, British Library Occasional Papers 4 (London: British Library, 1985) 30–40.

For living New Zealanders, see the latest edition of *Who's Who in New Zealand* (Wellington: Reed, 1908–).

Periodicals

Journals in Section R: Other Literatures in English/General/Periodicals/Scholarly Journals publish on New Zealand literature.

4830 *Landfall*. 1947– . Quarterly. AP7.L35 052.

Publishes creative works, criticism, notes, and reviews by New Zealanders and about New Zealand literature. Indexed in every fifth volume.

Genres

FICTION

Guides to Primary Works

4835 Burns, James. *New Zealand Novels and Novelists, 1861–1979: An Annotated Bibliography*. Auckland: Heinemann, 1981. 71 pp. Z4114.F4.B83 [PR9632.2] 016.823'008'09931.

A chronological list of novels by New Zealanders, including those resident abroad, and some by foreigners that are set in New Zealand; Burns excludes works for children. Listed by date of first publication, the approximately 1,000 entries cite author, title, publication information, number of pages or volumes, translations, and appearances in periodicals. The very brief (and frequently inadequate) annotations describe content. Two indexes: titles; authors. *New Zealand Novels and Novelists* offers the fullest list of New Zealand novels, but a subject index would enhance its usefulness.

S

Foreign-Language Literatures

This section is limited to guides to reference works that will direct researchers to essential sources, along with a very few important bibliographies of bibliographies or major serial bibliographies. For a basic list of specialized bibliographies, literary dictionaries and encyclopedias, and other reference works on a particular literature, consult Thompson, *Key Sources in Comparative and World Literature* (4850), Sheehy, *Guide to Reference Books* (60), or Walford, *Walford's Guide to Reference Material* (65).

Users should also remember that studies of all literatures (except classical Greek and Latin) are covered by *MLAIB* (335).

General

Guides to Reference Works

4850 Thompson, George A., Jr. *Key Sources in Comparative and World Literature*. New York: Ungar, 1982. 383 pp. Z6511.T47 [PN523] 016.809.

A highly selective, annotated guide to reference works on a variety of literatures, but emphasizing those in English and Western European languages. Entries are organized in 11 extensively classified divisions: comparative, general, and international literatures; classical; Romance; French; Italian; Hispanic; German; literatures in English; other European literatures; Oriental literatures; and related fields. Many sections list bibliographies and concordances for major authors. The annotations are typically descriptive, noting scope, organization, related works, and (sometimes) reviews. While some are full, many of the annotations inadequately detail the content or significance of a work. Poor layout makes skimming difficult. Three indexes: names; selected titles and institutions; subjects. Although it does not really emphasize comparative literature, omits several essential works, and is frequently uncritical in selection or annotation, Thompson is the best general guide to essential bibliographies, handbooks, histories, and other reference works for foreign literatures.

Guides to Scholarship and Criticism

4855 *Year's Work in Modern Language Studies* (*YWMLS*). London: Modern Humanities Research Assn., 1931– . Annual. PB1.Y45 405.8.

A selective, evaluative review of research on Romance, Celtic, Germanic, and Slavonic languages and literatures. Currently organized by language or geographic area within six divisions (general linguistics, Latin, Romance languages, Celtic languages, Germanic languages, and Slavonic studies), with essays on language and literary periods as required by the extent of the scholarship. For example, in vol. 45 (for 1983) French Studies takes 10 essays while Swedish Studies needs only two.

The necessarily selective coverage depends on availability of material, individual contributors, the extent of coverage in other bibliographies, and—since vol. 45 (for 1983)—the number of pages allocated by the editors to a chapter. As in *Year's Work in English Studies* (330), the quality and objectivity of individual essays vary depending on the contributor(s), but most attempt judicious evaluations of the significant scholarship. Citations are fuller than in *Year's Work in English Studies*, and recent volumes have been published in the year following that of the scholarship covered. Two indexes: subjects; persons.

Although some topics are covered more exhaustively in other sources, *YWMLS* is the single most comprehensive evaluative survey of scholarship on European and Latin American languages and literatures. Taken together, the annual volumes offer an incomparable record of scholarly and critical trends as well as of the fluctuations of academic reputations of literary works and authors.

African Literatures

4865 Lindfors, Bernth. "Researching African Literatures." *Literary Research Newsletter* 4 (1979): 171–80.

An evaluative overview of bibliographies, biographical sources, and other reference works (through early 1979) important for the study of African literatures. Although now dated, it remains a useful guide, since many of the works have not been superseded. Additional bibliographies are listed in Yvette Scheven,

"Bibliographies on African Literature since 1970," *Research in African Literatures* 15 (1984): 405–19.

Scholars should regularly scan *Research in African Literatures* (1979– , quarterly), which prints descriptions of research centers, lists of dissertations, and frequent bibliographies. A useful introduction to important scholarship on selected literatures is B. W. Andrzejewski, S. Piłaszewicz, and W. Tyloch, eds., *Literatures in African Languages: Theoretical Issues and Sample Surveys* (Cambridge: Cambridge UP; Warszawa: Wiedza Powszechna, 1985, 672 pp.).

See also

Sec. R: Other Literatures in English/African Literatures in English.

Asian Literatures

4875 Anderson, G. L. *Asian Literature in English: A Guide to Information Sources.* American Literature, English Literature, and World Literatures in English: An Information Guide Series 31. Detroit: Gale, 1981. 336 pp. Z3001.A655 [PR9410] 016.895.

A bibliography of English-language translations and important studies (published through c. 1978) of East Asian literature. Indian literature, which is the subject of Singh, *Indian Literature in English* (4800), is excluded. The 2,224 entries are organized in 16 divisions: Far East, China, Japan, Korea, Southeast Asia, Burma, Cambodia, Indonesia, Laos, Malaya and Singapore, Thailand, Vietnam, Mongolia, Tibet, Turkic and other literatures, and periodicals about Central Asian literature. The divisions are variously classified, but most have sections for bibliographies, reference works, anthologies, general literary history and criticism, periodicals, genres, earlier literature, and modern literature, as well as individual authors and anonymous works. About half of the very brief annotations are descriptive, with the remainder offering an evaluative comment; however, few adequately describe the content or significance of a work. Indexed by persons and English-language titles of literary works. Users should be sure to note the explanation on p. xiv of conventions governing names (however, the use of brackets around variant pen names and parentheses around real names is not consistently followed). Although marred by an insufficient explanation of scope and criteria governing selection, omitting several important studies, and inadequately annotated, Anderson is useful as a preliminary compilation of English-language translations and studies of East Asian literature.

Classical Literatures

Guides to Reference Works

4885 Halton, Thomas P., and Stella O'Leary. *Classical Scholarship: An Annotated Bibliography.* White Plains: Kraus, 1986. 396 pp. Z6207.C65.H34 [DE59] 016.938.

A guide to important reference works and scholarship (through c. 1980) for the study of classical Greek and Roman civilization. Entries are organized alphabetically by author in 15 classified divisions: bibliographies and reference works; literary history and criticism; history and influence of the classical tradition; transmission of the classics (including sections on books and libraries, palaeography, and textual criticism); language and style; metrics, song, and music; epigraphy; political and cultural history; numismatics; art and archaeology; religion, mythology, and magic; philosophy; science and technology; teaching aids; and collections. Most entries include a list of reviews and an annotation that describes scope and contents, identifies the work's importance to classical scholarship, and evaluates its quality. Two indexes: subjects; scholars. *Classical Scholarship* is marred by an inadequate explanation of scope and criteria governing selection and by several annotations that are less precisely descriptive and evaluative than one expects in a critical bibliography; nevertheless, it is the best available selective guide in English to reference works and scholarship on classical civilization.

Guides to Scholarship and Criticism

4890 *L'année philologique: Bibliographie critique et analytique de l'antiquité gréco-latine [1924–]*. Collection de bibliographie classique. Paris: Belles Lettres, 1928– . Annual. Z7016.M35A.

An international bibliography of scholarship on all aspects of the Greco-Latin world to c. AD 800. Entries are organized in two parts: authors and anonymous works, and subjects. Under each author or anonymous work are separate lists of bibliographies, collections of essays, editions, and studies. The second part consists of 10 variously classified divisions: literary history (with sections for genres, folklore and mythology, and Judeo-Christian, Byzantine, and medieval literature); linguistics and philology (with sections for grammar; metrics, rhythm, and prosody; and chants, music, and choreography); history of texts (including palaeography, papyrology, and textual criticism); antiquities; history; law; philosophy and history of ideas; science, technology, and work; the study of the classics; and collections of essays. Entries are accompanied by descriptive annotations (predominantly in French but also in English and German) and citations to reviews. The type and number of indexes vary, with recent volumes providing four: subject headings; names from antiquity; places; scholars. The international scope and impressive degree of coverage make this the indispensable guide to scholarship on Greek and Latin language and literature to c. AD 800. Complemented by *MLAIB* (335) for studies of Greek and Latin language of all ages and for studies of literature after c. 800.

Scholarship before 1924 is covered in the following:

Engelmann, Wilhelm, ed. *Bibliotheca Scriptorum Classicorum*. Rev. E. Preuss. 8th ed. 2 vols. Leipzig: Engelmann, 1880–82. (Covers 1700–1878.)

Klussman, Rudolf, ed. *Bibliotheca Scriptorum Classicorum et Graecorum et Latinorum*. 4 pts. in 2 vols. Leipzig: Reisland, 1909–13. (Covers 1878–96.)

Lambrino, Scarlat. *Bibliographie de l'antiquité classique, 1896–1914*. Collection de bibliographie classique. Paris: Belles Lettres, 1951. 761 pp. (The second volume, which was to cover subjects, will not be published.)

Marouzeau, J. *Dix années de bibliographie classique: Bibliographie critique et analytique de l'antiquité gréco-latine pour la période 1914–1924*. 2 vols. Paris: Belles Lettres, 1927–28.

Researchers will find a useful key to acronyms and abbreviations of book, series, and journal titles in Jean Susorney Wellington, *Dictionary of Bibliographic Abbreviations Found in the Scholarship of Classical Studies and Related Disciplines* (Westport: Greenwood, 1983, 393 pp.)

4893 Carlsen, Hanne. *A Bibliography to the Classical Tradition in English Literature.* Anglica et Americana 21. Copenhagen: [Dept. of English, U of Copenhagen], 1985. 164 pp. Z2014.C55.C37 [PR127] 016.82'09'3.

A classified bibliography of scholarship, published between 1900 and 1983, on the relationship of English literature to the Greek and Latin classical tradition. The 1,692 entries include studies published in English (for the most part), French, German, Italian, and the Scandinavian languages, but exclude dissertations. Entries are listed alphabetically by author in 16 sections: general studies, Middle Ages, Chaucer, sixteenth century excluding Shakespeare, Shakespeare, seventeenth century excluding Milton, eighteenth century, nineteenth century, twentieth century, Greek authors, Latin authors, myths and themes, literary genres, translation, philology, and art. The lack of cross-references means that users must consult the index to locate all listed works on a literary author or anonymous work. A few entries are annotated with a phrase that is seldom adequate to describe the content of a study. Indexed by literary authors, anonymous titles, and some subjects. Although broader in scope than Kallendorf, *Latin Influences on English Literature* (4895) and claiming to include all entries therein, Carlsen is less helpfully annotated, less thoroughly indexed, and overlooks a considerable number of studies. It is, though, a time-saving compilation that, for post-1900 scholarship, supersedes Huntington Brown, "The Classical Tradition in English Literature: A Bibliography," *Harvard Studies and Notes in Philology and Literature* 18 (1935): 7–46; and the brief bibliography and notes (pp. 550–705) in Gilbert Highet, *The Classical Tradition: Greek and Roman Influences on Western Literature* (New York: Oxford UP, 1949, 763 pp.).

4895 Kallendorf, Craig. *Latin Influences on English Literature from the Middle Ages to the Eighteenth Century: An Annotated Bibliography of Scholarship, 1945–1979.* Garland Reference Library of the Humanities 345. New York: Garland, 1982. 141 pp. Z2012.K34 [PR127] 016.82'09.

A selective bibliography of books and articles (in English, French, German, Italian, and Dutch) that clearly focus on the influence of classical Latin authors on English literature. Thus, discussions of medieval and Neo-Latin authors, technical studies of translation, and purely linguistic scholarship are excluded. Entries are organized in seven variously classified divisions: basic works on the classical tradition; rhetoric and English prose style; medieval literature; Renaissance literature; English Literature, 1600–60; Elizabethan, Jacobean, and Caroline drama; and Restoration and eighteenth-century literature. The descriptive annotations are sometimes too brief to convey an adequate sense of content, but they are more informative than those in Carlsen, *Bibliography to the Classical Tradition in English Literature* (4893). Indexed by authors and subjects. Although there are notable omissions, Kallendorf is a time-saving compilation that brings together widely scattered studies. Review: Fram Dinshaw, *Notes and Queries* ns 31 (1984): 265–66.

French-Language Literatures

4905 Beugnot, B., and J.-M. Moureaux. *Manuel bibliographique des études littéraires: Les bases de l'histoire littéraire, les voies nouvelles de l'analyse critique*. Nathan-Université. Paris: Nathan, 1982. 478 pp. Z6511.B48 [PN544] 016.809.

A guide to reference works (through c. 1980) important to the study of French-language literature. The approximately 3,400 entries are listed by publication date within extensively classified divisions: general reference works (with sections for general works, bibliographies, periodicals, surveys of research, and textual criticism and major editions), literary history and criticism (history of criticism, literary history, literature and other arts, ideas and themes, genres, poetic theory, imagery and myth, literature and psychoanalysis, and literature and sociology), and new areas of study (French-language literature outside France, and children's and popular literature). Few entries are annotated, but each division, section, and subsection is preceded by a brief overview of reference works. Two indexes: scholars (at the end of the book); subjects (at the beginning). This is the fullest guide to reference works on French literature, but users would benefit from more annotations.

A judiciously selective, evaluative guide to bibliographies is Richard Kempton, *French Literature: An Annotated Guide to Selected Bibliographies*, Selected Bibliographies in Language and Literature 2 (New York: MLA, 1981, 42 pp.), which includes brief sections on French-Canadian and other French-language literatures. Although now dated, Fernande Bassan, Paul F. Breed, and Donald C. Spinelli, *An Annotated Bibliography of French Language and Literature*, 2nd rev. printing, Garland Reference Library of the Humanities 26 (New York: Garland, 1977, 306 pp.), remains useful for its annotations.

For the beginning researcher, a simpler guide with fuller annotations is Robert K. Baker, *Introduction to Library Research in French Literature* (Boulder: Westview, 1978, 137 pp.).

German Literature

4915 Hansel, Johannes. *Bücherkunde für Germanisten: Studienausgabe*. 8th ed. Rev. Lydia Tschakert. Berlin: Schmidt, 1983. 209 pp. Z2235.A2.H3 [PT84] 016.43.

An annotated guide to reference works (primarily in German) important to the study of German language and literature. The approximately 1,250 entries are organized in five classified divisions: general reference works on linguistics and literary history and scholarship (with sections for general literary and linguistic studies, German language and literature, and general reference works), closed bibliographies (general bibliographies of scholarship on language and literature, German language and literature, general topics), serial bibliographies of scholarship (general bibliographies of scholarship on language and literature, German language and literature, bibliographies of bibliographies), other serial bibliographies (national bibliographies, dissertation bibliographies, bibliographies of periodical articles), and periodicals. Each section is preceded by a comparative overview of works, but the annotations tend to be very brief descriptions of scope and content. Two indexes: persons and titles; subjects.

Although less current, Uwe Faulhaber and Penrith B. Goff, *German Literature: An Annotated Reference Guide*, Garland Reference Library of the Humanities 108 (New York: Garland, 1979, 398 pp.), offers broader coverage (especially of English-language reference works) and fuller, evaluative annotations. More current than Hansel, addressed to the beginning researcher, and focusing on "German studies" is Larry L. Richardson, *Introduction to Library Research in German Studies: Language, Literature, and Civilization*, Westview Guides to Library Research (Boulder: Westview, 1984, 227 pp.), but in emphasizing works generally available in United States or Canadian libraries, it omits several important reference sources. The annotations are full but lack the evaluative guidance of those in Faulhaber.

Italian Literature

4925 Puppo, Mario. *Manuale critico-bibliografico per lo studio della letteratura italiana*. 13th ed. Torino: Internazionale, 1980. 432 pp. PQ4037.P8.

A guide to reference works (through 1979) that are important to the study of Italian language and literature. The first division lists general guides to Italian literature, bibliographies, journals, collections and anthologies, and encyclopedias and dictionaries. The remaining divisions consist of essay overviews accompanied by selective bibliographies on literary criticism and philology (with discussions of textual criticism, criticism, and literary history); linguistics and stylistics (language, grammar, and vocabulary; the Italian language; the history of language in Italy; and stylistics); literary periods or movements; and 21 major authors. An appendix describes poetic forms and metrical terminology. Although more descriptive than evaluative, with access hampered by the lack of an index, Puppo is the standard guide to Italian literary scholarship.

Latin-Language Literatures (Medieval and Neo-Latin)

4935 IJsewijn, Jozef. *Companion to Neo-Latin Studies*. Amsterdam: North-Holland, 1977. 370 pp. PA8020.I37 870'.9'003.

A survey and bibliography of Latin-language works written since 1300 in Europe (principally), Asia, Africa, and North and South America. Chapters are devoted to bibliographies, literature (organized by country or continent), texts and editions, language and style, prosody and metrics, forms and genres, scholarly and scientific works, and general studies. Each chapter or section thereof begins with a survey and concludes with a bibliography of primary works and scholarship. The essential guide to the subject, important for its historical surveys as well as its compilation of widely dispersed scholarship and editions.

Useful brief surveys are Fred J. Nichols, "Latin Literature," *The Present State of Scholarship in Fourteenth-Century Literature*, ed. Thomas D. Cooke (Columbia: U of Missouri P, 1982) 195–257; and Lawrence V. Ryan, "Neo-Latin Literature," *The Present State of Scholarship in Sixteenth-Century Literature*, ed. William M. Jones (Columbia: U of Missouri P, 1978) 197–257.

4940 Strecker, Karl. *Introduction to Medieval Latin*. Trans. and rev. Robert B. Palmer. 4th ed. Dublin: Weidmann, 1967. 174 pp. PA2816.S87.

A survey of reference sources, editions, and scholarship (principally through 1955, with some additions through 1961) that describes and occasionally evaluates general reference works, dictionaries, literary histories, periodicals, libraries, palaeographical guides, and studies of language, poetry, and prose. Additions and corrections appear on pp. 161–74. Two indexes: subjects; scholars. Although poorly organized in places and now dated, the *Introduction* remains a standard guide. Supplement coverage with IJsewijn, *Companion to Neo-Latin Studies* (4935) and Albert C. Friend, "Medieval Latin Literature," pp. 1–33 in Fisher, *Medieval Literature of Western Europe* (1830).

Portuguese-Language Literatures

4950 Chamberlain, Bobby J. *Portuguese Language and Luso-Brazilian Literature: An Annotated Guide to Selected Reference Works*. New York: MLA, 1989. 95 pp. Z2725.A2.C45 [PC5041] 016.869.

A selective guide to reference works for the study of the Portuguese language and Luso-Brazilian literature. The approximately 550 entries are organized in extensively classified divisions for Portuguese language, Portuguese literature, and Brazilian literature. The annotations are largely descriptive, although some offer evaluations. Indexed by authors.

Russian Literature

4960 Zalewski, Wojciech. *Fundamentals of Russian Reference Work in the Humanities and Social Sciences*. Russica Bibliography Series 5. New York: Russica, 1985. 170 pp. Z2491.A1.Z3 016.016947.

A guide to important reference works for the study of the humanities and social sciences in Russia. The essay overviews (interspersed with lists of works) are organized in two divisions: general works (with sections for publishing; theory and history of bibliography; libraries, archives, and museums; general bibliographies; other reference sources) and subject bibliographies (with sections for bibliographic institutions, history, literature, linguistics and languages, social sciences, law, and the humanities). Particularly helpful are the evaluations and comparisons of works, descriptions of Russian bibliographical networks, and suggestions for search strategies. Concludes with a list of numbered monographic series published in the West. Indexed by persons. An indispensable guide to the identification and effective use of reference sources for research in the humanities and social sciences in Russia.

Spanish-Language Literatures

4970 Woodbridge, Hensley C. *Guide to Reference Works for the Study of the Spanish Language and Literature and Spanish American Literature*. Selected Bibliographies in Language and Literature 5. New York: MLA, 1987. 183 pp. Z2695.A2.W66 [PC4071] 016.86.

A selective, annotated bibliography of reference works essential in the study of Spanish language and literature in Europe and the Western Hemisphere. Woodbridge emphasizes works published between 1950 and c. 1985, gives preference to annotated bibliographies, and includes works devoted to a single author. The 908 entries are organized in five extensively classified (and variously organized) divisions: general bibliographies, Spanish of Spain, American Spanish, Spanish literature of Europe, and Spanish literature of the Western Hemisphere. The brief annotations are largely descriptive, although some offer evaluative comments. Two indexes: authors, editors, and compilers; literary authors. Judicious selection and clear annotations make Woodbridge a valuable guide to the major reference works in its field.

A useful but dated supplement is David William Foster and Virginia Ramos Foster, comps., *Manual of Hispanic Bibliography*, 2nd ed., rev. and expanded, Garland Reference Library of the Humanities 85 (New York: Garland, 1977, 329 pp.). Broader in scope, but less trustworthy in its selection and accuracy, is Donald W. Bleznick, *A Sourcebook for Hispanic Literature and Language: A Selected, Annotated Guide to Spanish, Spanish-American, and Chicano Bibliography, Literature, Linguistics, Journals, and Other Source Material*, 2nd ed. (Metuchen: Scarecrow, 1983, 304 pp.).

T

Comparative Literature

This section is highly selective and emphasizes those works likely to be of most value to researchers whose primary interest is literatures in English. For additional reference works in comparative literature, consult Thompson, *Key Sources in Comparative and World Literature* (4850).

General Introductions

4990 Weisstein, Ulrich. *Comparative Literature and Literary Theory*. Trans. William Riggan. Bloomington: Indiana UP, 1973. 339 pp. (Translation and partial revision of *Einführung in die Vergleichende Literaturwissenschaft* [Stuttgart: Kohlhammer, 1968], 256 pp.) *Vergleichende Literaturwissenschaft: Erster Bericht, 1968–1977*. Jahrbuch für Internationale Germanistik, Reihe C: Forschungsberichte 2. Bern: Lang, 1981. 218 pp. (Another supplement is in progress.) PN874.W4 809.

An introduction to the history and theory of comparative literature, with chapters on the definition of the discipline and its study of influence and imitation; reception and survival; epoch, period, generation, and movement; genre; thematology; and relations of literature to the other arts. Concluding the study are two appendixes (a history of comparative literature and an evaluation of the major bibliographies) and a selected bibliography (through June 1973). Indexed by persons and anonymous works. The supplement updates the chapters and selective bibliography, and adds discussions of publications and projects of the Association Internationale de Littérature Comparée, new periodicals and festschriften, and national images. The volumes remain a useful general introduction to the theory and methodology of comparative literature. Review: (German ed.) Richard Bjornson, *Monatshefte* 62 (1970): 186–88.

Covering much the same ground—but less authoritatively—is S. S. Prawer, *Comparative Literary Studies: An Introduction* (London: Duckworth, 1973, 180 pp.).

See also

Barricelli, *Interrelations of Literature* (5955).

Guides to Scholarship and Criticism

Serial Bibliographies

4995 "Revue des revues." *Canadian Review of Comparative Literature/Revue canadienne de littérature comparée* (entry 5015) 1 (1974)– .

An annual collection of abstracts of general comparative studies published in a wide range of journals. Entries are listed alphabetically by author in three divisions: literary history and relations, literary theory, and literature and the other arts. Two indexes: persons; subjects. Not comprehensive but useful for its full abstracts.

Studies by British and Irish scholars and foreigners at British universities are listed in "Bibliography of Comparative Literature in Britain and Ireland [1975–]," *Comparative Criticism: A Yearbook* 1 (1979)– .

See also

ABELL (340): Comparative Literature division in the volumes for 1923–60.
"Bibliography on the Relations of Literature and the Other Arts" (5965).
MLAIB (335): General VII: Literature, General and Comparative/Other General and Comparative section in the volumes for 1953–55; General II: Literature, General and Comparative/Other General and Comparative section in the volume for 1956; General III: Literature, General and Comparative/Comparative Literature section in the volumes for 1957–80; and Professional Topics/Comparative Literature section in later volumes. Researchers must also check the "Comparative Literature" heading in the subject index to post-1980 volumes.

Other Bibliographies

5000 Baldensperger, Fernand, and Werner P. Friederich. *Bibliography of Comparative Literature*. U of North Carolina Studies in Comparative Literature 1. Chapel Hill: U of North Carolina Studies in Comparative Literature, 1950. 701 pp. Z6514.C7.B3 016.809.

A selective bibliography of publications and "significant" American dissertations through 1949 on comparative and world literature (principally of the Western Hemisphere). Although international in scope, *Bibliography of Comparative Lit-*

erature emphasizes scholarship from Western Europe and North America. The approximately 33,000 entries are organized in four extensively classified divisions:

general topics (with sections for comparative, world, and European literatures; literature and politics; literature and arts and sciences; intermediaries; comparisons, sources, and imitations; themes; collective motifs; and genres and forms);
Orient, classical antiquity, Judaism, early Christianity, and Mohammedanism (with sections for the Orient, classical antiquity, Greek literature, Latin literature, and Hebraism and Christianity);
aspects of Western culture (with sections for modern Christianity, various literary movements, and international literary relations);
the modern world (with sections for Celtic and Arthurian, Provençal, Italian, Spanish, Portuguese, Dutch and Belgian, French, English, Swiss, German, North and South American, Scandinavian, and East European literatures).

Most sections are extensively subdivided. Entries for books usually omit subtitles; those for articles, page numbers. Users must remember that (1) coverage varies considerably from section to section (e.g., the treatment of genres, literary theory, and Oriental and East European literatures are especially weak; in many sections, selection seems arbitrary); (2) because the classification is heavily dependent on titles, works are frequently inappropriately classified; (3) influence studies are listed under the influencer; (4) effective use requires close familiarity with the classification system outlined on pp. v-x. The lack of any index or sufficient cross-references, the classification practices, and inconsistencies mean that users must exercise considerable ingenuity to track down studies (and will usually end up searching entry by entry through several sections). Although it lacks an adequate explanation of scope, limitations, and principles of organization and selection, omits many important works, and is frustrating to use because of its classification practices and lack of indexing, the work remains the most complete bibliography of comparative scholarship before 1950. (Scholars would thank the selfless person who compiles a subject index to this bibliography.) Reviews: B. Munteano, *Revue de littérature comparée* 26 (1952): 273–83; Sigmund Skard, *Journal of English and Germanic Philology* 52 (1953): 229–42.

Although the supplement planned for 1955 was never published, the "Annual Bibliography [1949–69]," *YCGL: Yearbook of Comparative and General Literature* (entry 5035) 1–19 (1952–70), continued coverage through 1969. Until the bibliography for 1960 (10 [1961]), the organization followed Baldensperger. Then, until the bibliography's unfortunate demise, entries were organized in eight classified divisions: comparative, world, and general literature; translations, translators, correspondents, travelers, and other intermediaries; themes, motifs, and topoi; genres, types, forms, and techniques; epochs, currents, periods, and movements; Bible and classical antiquity, and larger geographic and linguistic groups; individual countries; individual authors.

Some additional coverage is offered by *Bibliographie générale de littérature comparée [1949–58]* (Paris: Didier, 1950–59), with sections for bibliographies, theory, stylistics, genres, themes and types, general studies, intermediaries, movements and periods, and individual countries. (This work is essentially a cumulation of the bibliographies for 1949 through 1958 in *Revue de littérature comparée* [entry 5030].)

5005 Dyserinck, Hugo, and Manfred S. Fischer, eds. *Internationale Bibliographie zu Geschichte und Theorie der Komparatistik*. Hiersemanns Bibliographische Handbücher 5. Stuttgart: Hiersemann, 1985. 314 pp. Z6514.C7.I6 [PN870.5.].

A bibliography of studies (from 1800 through autumn 1982) on the history, theory, and teaching of comparative literature. The entries are placed by publication date in one of two divisions: 1800–99 and 1900–82. In the first division, entries are organized alphabetically by author in three sections: general works on the theory of comparative literature; bibliographies and studies of special topics, terminology, and the relationship to other disciplines; and works on the history of comparative literature. The 1900–82 division is organized chronologically, with each year divided into the same three sections as in the 1800–99 division. Two indexes: proper names and subjects (with headings in German); scholars. The *Bibliographie* is confusing and inconsistent in organization and omits some important works, but is still the most complete guide to scholarship on the history and theory of comparative literature. Reviews: Adrian Marino, *Archiv für das Studium der Neueren Sprachen und Literaturen* 224 (1987): 124–28; Ulrich Weisstein, *YCGL: Yearbook of Comparative and General Literature* 34 (1985): 161–63.

Periodicals

5010 *Arcadia: Zeitschrift für Vergleichende Literaturwissenschaft* (*Arcadia*). 1966– . 3/yr. PN851.A7 809.

Publishes articles, notes, and reviews on comparative literature and literary history.

5015 *Canadian Review of Comparative Literature/Revue canadienne de littérature comparée* (*CRCL*). 1974– . Quarterly. PN851.C35 800.

Publishes articles, notes, bibliographies, documents, reviews, review essays, and frequent special issues, with an emphasis on comparative studies of literary history and theory. Includes two annual bibliographies: "Revue des revues" (4995) and "Preliminary Bibliography of Comparative Canadian Literature (English-Canadian and French-Canadian)" (4640). Annual index.

5020 *Comparative Literature* (*CL*). 1949– . Quarterly. PN851.C595 805.

Along with reviews, publishes articles not confined to a single national literature on literary theory and history, with a decided emphasis on the Western Hemisphere (especially Europe). Cumulative index: George N. Belknap, *Cumulative Index, Volumes 1–15, 1949–1963* (n.d., 37 pp.).

5025 *Comparative Literature Studies* (*CLS*). 1963– . Quarterly. PN851.C63 809.

Publishes articles not confined to a single literature on literary history and the history of ideas, a few book reviews, and an occasional review essay. Since vol. 18 (1981), every second volume prints a special issue on East-West literary relations. Cumulative index: vols. 1–20, in 21 (1984): 115–59.

5030 *Revue de littérature comparée* (*RLC*). 1921– . Quarterly. PN851.R4 809.

Publishes articles, notes, documents, and reviews involving two or more literatures or the theory, history, and methodology of comparative literature. Most issues include a section listing the contents of recent periodicals received. A selective bibliography of books and articles on comparative literature was discontinued after vol. 34 (1960); those for 1949 through 1958 are gathered in *Bibliographie générale de littérature comparée* (5000a). Annual index; cumulative index after every tenth volume.

5035 *YCGL: Yearbook of Comparative and General Literature* (*YCGL*). 1952– . Annual. PN851.Y4.

Publishes interdisciplinary and intercultural studies on genres, modes, motifs, themes, periods, and movements, as well as the theory, study, and history of comparative literature, comparative study of the arts, and translation theory and practice; reviews of research; occasional bibliographies; reviews; and "Bibliography on the Relations of Literature and the Other Arts" (5965). Earlier volumes include two other useful bibliographies:

"Annual Bibliography [of Comparative, General, and World Literature: 1949–69]," 1–19 (1952–70). See entry 5000a.

"List of Translations: [1960–78/79]," 10–29 (1961–80). A list of English-language translations—for the most part separately published in the United States—organized by language of the original work.

For an evaluative survey of the first 25 volumes, see Erwin Koppen, "Twenty-Five Volumes of the *YCGL*: An Evaluation," 27 (1978): 63–71. Cumulative index: vols. 1–30, in 33 (1984): 111–28.

U

Literature-Related Topics and Sources

Acronyms

5045 *Acronyms, Initialisms, and Abbreviations Dictionary: A Guide to More Than [number] Acronyms, Initialisms, Abbreviations, Contractions, Alphabetic Symbols, and Similar Condensed Appellations.* Detroit: Gale, 1960– . Biennial. (Title varies.) P365.A28 423'.1.

The work is currently published in three volumes:

Vol. 1: *Acronyms, Initialisms, and Abbreviations Dictionary.* 3 pts.

Vol. 2: *New Acronyms, Initialisms, and Abbreviations.* 2 pts. (An inter-edition supplement.)

Vol. 3: *Reverse Acronyms, Initialisms, and Abbreviations Dictionary.* 3 pts.

A guide to acronyms and the like—derived from English-language terms and foreign ones in international use—from a variety of fields, including academic degrees, associations, books of the Bible, brand names, American and British government and military terms, colleges and universities, Library of Congress library symbols, OCLC (225) symbols, personal names, religious orders, titles and forms of address, television and radio call letters, brand names, and online data bases. Vol. 1 is an acronym list; vol. 3, a list by source or phrase; vol. 2 includes both. Although not comprehensive, the work is the fullest guide to these frequently indecipherable coinages.

For foreign acronyms not in common international use, see *International Acronyms, Initialisms, and Abbreviations Dictionary: A Guide to over [number] Foreign and International Acronyms, Initialisms, Abbreviations, Alphabetic Symbols, Contractions, and Similar Condensed Appellations in All Fields*, 3 vols. (Detroit: Gale, 1985– , biennial).

Addresses

Individuals

5060 Directory. *PMLA* (entry 725). Published annually as the Sept. issue.

An annual directory of names and addresses of members of the Modern Language Association; department administrators (by institution) of literature and language departments of four-year colleges and universities, junior and community colleges, ethnic studies programs, language and area studies programs, and women's studies programs; organizations of independent scholars; and selected publishers and learned and professional societies. In addition, it identifies members of the MLA staff, delegate assembly, and committees, as well as executive committees of divisions and discussion groups; describes selected fellowships and grants available to language and literature scholars; lists, by date, forthcoming meetings and conferences (this information also appears in each issue of *PMLA*); and outlines the procedure for organizing meetings at the annual MLA convention. Although the directory is a useful general source of information and addresses, the following are more comprehensive: *National Faculty Directory* (5070) for addresses of faculty; *Grants Register* (5940) for grants; and *Publishers' International Directory* (5090) for addresses of publishers.

5065 *A Directory of American Poets and Fiction Writers: Names and Addresses of [number] Contemporary Poets and Fiction Writers Whose Work Has Been Published in the United States*. New York: Poets and Writers, 1980– . Biennial. (Title varies.) PS129.D55 810'.25'73.

A directory of published fiction writers and poets who are citizens or permanent residents of the United States. The *Directory* also includes a few writers who perform their works rather than rely on print, but excludes children's authors, playwrights, and nonfiction writers. Entries are organized by state or foreign country of residence (with countries grouped after the state lists), then alphabetically by name. An entry includes address; occasionally a phone number; identification as a poet, fiction writer, or performer; and a few recent publications. The publisher will also answer written or telephone inquiries for addresses of writers who have moved or are not listed in the current editions (201 W. 54 St., New York, NY 10019; 212–757–1766). Indexed by writer. This is the most current source for addresses of American writers published by legitimate (rather than vanity) presses.

5070 *The National Faculty Directory: An Alphabetical List, with Addresses of Approximately [number] Members of Teaching Faculties at Junior Colleges, Colleges, and Universities in the United States and at Selected Canadian Institutions*. Detroit: Gale, 1970– . Annual, with a supplement between editions. (Title varies.) L901.N34 378.1'2'02573.

A list of teaching faculty at United States and Canadian institutions "using instructional materials primarily in English." Based on institutional catalogs and course lists and compiled from a data base designed to generate mailing lists for textbook and academic publishers, the *Directory* excludes faculty members who do not have teaching responsibilities or who cannot be identified with a specific subject area. Entries provide name, department, and institutional address. Although incomplete, this work is the most comprehensive source for addresses of faculty at United States and several Canadian institutions.

Another source of addresses is *Directory of American Scholars*, 8th ed., 4 vols. (New York: Bowker, 1982). It is less current and comprehensive, but includes compact biographical entries that allow for differentiation between persons of the same name. A new edition is planned, but no publication date has been set.

For addresses of faculty at British and Commonwealth universities, see the current edition of *Commonwealth Universities Yearbook: A Directory to the Universities of the Commonwealth and the Handbook of Their Association* (London: Assn. of Commonwealth Universities, 1914– , annual). The use of initials rather than first names makes identifying common last names maddening.

5075 *The Writers Directory*. Chicago: St. James, 1973– . Biennial. PS1.W73 808.

An international directory of some 16,000 poets, dramatists, and fiction and nonfiction authors who have written at least one book in English. Entries, composed largely from information supplied by the entrant, consist of name, pseudonym, citizenship, year of birth, type of writing, current and past positions and appointments, a selected list of books, and address. A "yellow pages" section indexes entrants by genre or general subject matter of their writing. Lacking any statement of criteria determining selection, the work is essentially a grab bag that emphasizes established creative writers and university and college faculty, and is useful primarily for its international scope.

See also

Sec. U: Literature-Related Topics and Sources/Book Collecting/Directories of Book Dealers.
Arts and Humanities Citation Index (365).
Contemporary Authors (595).
Contemporary Dramatists (2880).
Contemporary Novelists (2845).
Contemporary Poets (2895).
Contemporary Theatre, Film, and Television (4305).
Current Biography (585).
International Authors and Writers Who's Who (595a).
International Who's Who (590).
International Who's Who in Poetry (595a).
Twentieth-Century Children's Writers (5505).
Who's Who (1435).
Who's Who in America (3395).

Institutions

5080 *World of Learning*. London: Europa, 1947– . Annual. AS2.W6 060.25.
A guide to learned organizations and institutions throughout the world. Following a list of international organizations, entries are organized by country, then classified as academies (alphabetically), learned societies (by subject), research institutes (by subject), libraries and archives (including government, public, and university ones, organized by type, then city), museums (by city), or universities and colleges (by type, then alphabetically). An entry typically includes a brief description of the organization or institution, address, officers, and list of serial publications; entries for academies usually list members, and those for universities and colleges, major administrators and sometimes faculty. Indexed by organizations and institutions. The lists are selective and entries vary considerably in detail (with no explanation of the criteria governing selection or reasons for variation); however, *World of Learning* is a handy source of addresses of and basic information about a variety of learned organizations and institutions throughout the world.

Organizations

5085 *Encyclopedia of Associations: A Guide to Over [number] National and International Organizations Including Trade, Business, and Commercial; Agricultural and Commodity; Legal, Governmental, Public Administration, and Military; Scientific, Engineering, and Technical; Educational; Cultural; Social Welfare; Health and Medical; Public Affairs; Fraternal, Foreign Interest, Nationality, and Ethnic; Religious; Veterans, Hereditary, and Patriotic; Hobby and Avocational; Athletic and Sports; Labor Unions, Associations, and Federations; Chambers of Commerce, Trade, and Tourism; and Greek Letter and Related Organizations*. Detroit: Gale, 1956– . Annual. (Title varies.) Also available on CD-ROM. AS22.E5 060.

The work is currently published in four volumes:

Vol. 1: *National Organizations of the U.S.* 3 pts. (Updated twice in *Updating Service* between editions.)

Vol. 2: *Geographic and Executive Indexes.*

Vol. 3: *New Associations and Projects.* 2 pts. (Interedition supplements to vol. 1.)

Vol. 4: *International Organizations.* (With two interedition supplements.)

A directory primarily of nonprofit organizations of more than regional or local interest. Entries are compiled from questionnaires as well as from other sources for organizations that could not be contacted directly.

Vol. 1, pts. 1–2 consist of descriptions of United States associations organized alphabetically by title or (added) keyword within the subject areas listed in the subtitle. Entries provide organization name, acronym, address of permanent national headquarters or chief official, telephone number, chief official and title, founding date, number of members, annual budget, a brief description of purpose and activities, computerized and telecommunications services, official publications, affiliated organizations, name changes, and details of upcoming conventions and meetings. (Changes are reported in the *Updating Service.*) Entries from these two parts and from vol. 4—along with organizations that are inactive or defunct and additional groups that might qualify as nonprofit and are listed in 14 other standard directories—are indexed by name and keyword in vol. 1, pt. 3.

Vol. 2 indexes entries in vol. 1 by geographic area and by chief executive; entries in vol. 1 can also be searched online through Dialog (520).

Vol. 3 lists new organizations (accompanied by a keyword and title index), but does not update information in vol. 1.

Vol. 4, a directory of nonprofit organizations that are international in scope and headquartered outside the United States, follows the same format as vol. 1 and has keyword and title, geographic, and chief executive indexes.

The best way to locate entries is through the keyword and title indexes because of the organization by keywords (many of which are added to accord with Gale's system of classification) and because of the inclusion in this index of entries for organizations that are defunct, inactive, or described in other standard directories but not accorded entries in vols. 1, 3, or 4. *Encyclopedia of Associations* is the most comprehensive source of information on nonprofit organizations.

For organizations of regional or local interest, see *Encyclopedia of Associations: Regional, State, and Local Organizations*, 7 vols. (1987– , biennial).

For associations in the British Isles, see *Directory of British Associations and Associations in Ireland*, 8th ed., ed. G. P. Henderson and S. P. A. Henderson (Beckenham: CBD Research, 1986, 506 pp.). Organized alphabetically by title, entries provide address and other basic information. Indexed by subjects.

Publishers

5090 *Publishers' International Directory with ISBN Index/Internationales Verlagsadressbuch mit ISBN-Register.* Handbook of International Documentation and Information/Handbuch der Internationalen Dokumentation und Information 7. München: Saur, 1964– . Annual. Z282.P8 070.5'025.

A directory of periodical and book publishers, including small presses, alternative presses, institutions, organizations, and even some individuals. Publishers are organized by country, then alphabetically by official name. An entry includes address, telephone, and ISBN; some list a few subject specializations. Indexed by ISBN prefix (a useful feature when one knows a publisher's ISBN but not official name). The *Directory*, although insufficiently cross-referenced, is the most comprehensive source for addresses of publishers (especially outside the United States).

The following works are less thorough but offer fuller information about United States and Canadian publishers:

Books in Print (4225).

Canadian Books in Print (4595a).

Literary Market Place: The Directory of American Book Publishing. New York: Bowker, 1940– . Annual. Although it is a trade publication, some parts are of interest to literary researchers: a highly selective alphabetical list of United States and Canadian publishers (recording address, telephone number, major editorial personnel, and subject interests), with the United States section indexed by states, kinds of publishers or types of books, and subjects; literary agents (with submission instructions); literary and writers' associations; literary awards, contests, and grants; and book review and index journals. Criteria determining inclusion are unstated, and all lists are seriously incomplete. Publishers are indexed in *Publishers Directory* (see below).

Publishers Directory: A Guide to Approximately [number] New and Established, Commercial and Nonprofit, Private and Alternative, Corporate and Association, Government and Institution Publishing Programs and Their Distributors. Detroit: Gale, 1977– . Annual, with *Supplement* between editions. Organized alphabetically by official name, entries list address, telephone number, major editorial personnel, subject interests, and up to six representative titles. Three indexes: publishers, imprints, and distributors; subjects; geographical location (by state or province, then city). Excludes publishers listed in *Literary Market Place* (above) but includes them in the index. The subject index can sometimes be helpful in identifying places to submit a manuscript.

For British publishers, see *British Books in Print* (2770).

Anonymous and Pseudonymous Works

General Introductions

5105 Taylor, Archer, and Fredric J. Mosher. *The Bibliographical History of Anonyma and Pseudonyma*. Chicago: U of Chicago P, for Newberry Library, 1951. 289 pp. Z1041.T3.

A history of the study from the early Christian era to the mid-twentieth century of anonymous and pseudonymous writings. Especially valuable is the selective, annotated bibliography of dictionaries and lists of anonyma and pseudonyma. The list concludes with a guide classified by language or geographical area and subject. The text, but not the bibliography, is indexed by persons and anonymous works. *Bibliographical History* is now dated, but it remains a valuable guide to extensive early scholarship, much of which has not been superseded.

Dictionaries

5110 Halkett, Samuel, and John Laing. *A Dictionary of Anonymous and Pseudonymous Publications in the English Language* (Halkett and Laing). Vol. 1: *1475–1640*. 3rd rev. and enl. ed. Ed. John Horden. London: Longman, 1980. 271 pp. (Vol. 1 will eventually be revised to form part of *Dictionary of Concealed Authorship: Publications in English, 1475–1700*, ed. John Horden, 3 vols.) Z1065.H18 014'.2.

———. *Dictionary of Anonymous and Pseudonymous English Literature* (Halkett and Laing). New and enl. ed. Ed. James Kennedy et al. 9 vols. Edinburgh: Oliver, 1926–62. Z1065.H17 014'.2.

Vols. 1–6: A-Z and Supplement. Ed. James Kennedy, W. A. Smith, and A. F. Johnson. 1926–32.

Vol. 7: *Index and Second Supplement*. Ed. Kennedy, Smith, and Johnson. 1934. 588 pp.

Vol. 8: *1900–1950*. Ed. Dennis E. Rhodes and Anna E. C. Simoni. 1956. 397 pp.

Vol. 9: Addenda to Volumes I–VIII. Ed. Rhodes and Simoni. 1962. 477 pp.

A title list of English-language works (including translations, and bilingual or multilingual publications with a significant portion in English) that were published anonymously or pseudonymously and whose authorship has been ascribed.

Second edition (1926–62). The second edition lists about 75,000 titles from 1475 through 1949, and includes some works of unattributed authorship. Entries, listed alphabetically by title, cite attributed author, format, pagination, source of the entry, and place and date of publication. Two indexes in vols. 7–9: authors; initials and pseudonyms. Since the indexes cite volume and page, locating an entry is usually time-consuming, since researchers must hunt through a title entry to find a name or initials. Users should keep several points in mind: (1) because many entries are taken from other sources—especially the British Museum *General Catalogue of Printed Books* (250a) and *Dictionary of National Biography* (1425), both notoriously inaccurate in attributing authorship—there are numerous errors in transcription of titles (thus making impossible the location of some works), identification of authorship, and inclusion of works not truly anonymous; (2) although the source of an entry is usually recorded, evidence for attribution is not; thus, there is no immediate way of assessing the accuracy of an ascription; (3) because of the organization, books published between 1475 and 1900 are included in vols. 1–6 as well as the supplements in vols. 6, 7, and 9, and books published between 1900 and 1949 are in vols. 8 and 9. Although incomplete, inaccurate, and time-consuming to use, Halkett and Laing remains an essential, if untrustworthy, source for identifying the author of an anonymous or pseudonymous publication. It is being superseded by the much improved third edition. For a history of the first and second editions, see the preface to vol. 1 of the third edition.

Third edition. The third edition is limited to separately published English-language works (including translations, and bilingual or multilingual publications with a substantial portion in English) that appeared anonymously or pseudonymously between 1475 and 1800 and for which authorship has been established or ascribed. It excludes works falsely attributed or unattributed, although exceptions are made for any works listed in the second edition. With the publication of vols.

2 and 3 (*1641–1700*), the title will change to *Dictionary of Concealed Authorship: Publications in English, 1475–1700* to reflect the inclusion of publications whose authorship is hidden (e.g., under initials or abbreviated forms on a title page, or by the appearance of the author's name or initials somewhere else in the work) along with truly anonymous works. Vol. 1 will eventually be expanded to conform with the other volumes. Whether the *Dictionary* proceeds beyond 1700 will depend on the treatment of anonymous and pseudonymous publications in *Eighteenth-Century Short-Title Catalogue* (2230) and *Nineteenth Century Short Title Catalogue* (2475). While the former offers sophisticated treatment of these publications, it is unlikely that the latter will ever do so.

The new edition is a major improvement over its predecessor: along with defining scope more precisely, adding numerous works, correcting many errors, and basing descriptions on the actual examination of copies, the third edition records the evidence and its source for attributions, along with title, place and date of publication, and references to standard bibliographies. Editorial practices are clearly and fully explained in the introduction (pp. xxii-xliv) to vol. 1. Additions and corrections to vol. 1 appear on p. 221. Indexed by writers' names, with a list of pseudonyms keyed to the index; in addition, vol. 1 prints useful concordances for entry numbers in Greg, *Bibliography of the English Printed Drama to the Restoration* (2135); *Short-Title Catalogue* (1990; although references are not based on the final version of vol. 1); and A. F. Allison and D. M. Rogers, *A Catalogue of Catholic Books in English Printed Abroad or Secretly in England, 1558–1640*, 2 pts., Bibliographical Studies 3.3–4 (Bognor Regis: Arundel, 1956). Vols. 2 and 3 will have a concordance for Wing, *Short-Title Catalogue* (1995).

The careful assimilation and evaluation of widely scattered evidence for attributions and many new ascriptions make this new edition of Halkett and Laing the indispensable starting point for identifying the authors of anonymously and pseudonymously published works (before 1700), and the worthy successor to a venerable but flawed reference work.

The *National Union Catalogs* (235, 240, and 245) and *British National Bibliography* (2775) are also useful sources for identifying the author of an anonymous or pseudonymous work.

5115 *Pseudonyms and Nicknames Dictionary: A Guide to 80,000 Aliases, Appellations, Assumed Names, Code Names, Cognomens, Cover Names, Epithets, Initialisms, Nicknames, Noms de Guerre, Noms de Plume, Pen Names, Pseudonyms, Sobriquets, and Stage Names of 55,000 Contemporary and Historical Persons, Including the Subjects' Real Names, Basic Biographical Information, and Citations for the Sources from Which the Entries Were Compiled.* Ed. Jennifer Mossman. 3rd ed. 2 vols. Detroit: Gale, 1987. (A periodic supplement appears under the title *New Pseudonyms and Nicknames.*) CT120.P8 920'.02.

A dictionary of pseudonyms and the like of prominent individuals from all ages and walks of life, with the bulk of the entries for authors, entertainers, and athletes. Names are listed in a single alphabetical sequence, with the main entry (giving birth and death dates, sources for further information, nationality, occupation, and assumed names) under the real name and cross-references for other names. Although this is the fullest single international source for identifying assumed names, the following works include additional literary ones:

Atkinson, Frank. *Dictionary of Literary Pseudonyms: A Selection of Popular Modern Writers in English.* 3rd ed. London: Bingley, 1982. 305 pp.

Marshall, Alice Kahler. *Pen Names of Women Writers from 1600 to the Present: A Compendium of the Literary Identities of 2,650 Women Novelists, Playwrights, Poets, Diarists, Journalists, and Miscellaneous Writers*. Camp Hill: Alice Marshall Collection, 1985. 181 pp.

Sharp, Harold S., comp. *Handbook of Pseudonyms and Personal Nicknames*. 2 vols. Metuchen: Scarecrow, 1972. *First Supplement*. 2 vols. 1975. *Second Supplement*. 1982. 289 pp.

Art and Literature

For an introduction to the interdisciplinary study of literature and art, see Ulrich Weisstein, "Literature and the Visual Arts" (pp. 251–77) in Barricelli, *Interrelations of Literature* (5955). Several works in section U: Literature-Related Topics and Sources/Interdisciplinary and Multidisciplinary Studies treat the relationship of art and literature.

Guides to Reference Works

5130 Arntzen, Etta, and Robert Rainwater. *Guide to the Literature of Art History*. Chicago: American Library Assn.; London: Art Book, 1980. 616 pp. Z5931.A67 [N380] 016.709.

A guide to reference works, general studies, and exhibition catalogs (through 1977) important in the study of art history, especially architecture, sculpture, drawing, painting, prints, photography, and decorative and applied arts. Although international in coverage, *Guide to the Literature of Art History* emphasizes works in Western languages (especially in English and published in the United States) and excludes studies of individual artists. The 4,150 entries are organized alphabetically by author in four divisions: general reference sources (including sections for bibliographies, visual resources, dictionaries and encyclopedias, and iconography); general primary and secondary sources (with a section on histories and handbooks); the individual arts; and serials. Most sections are extensively classified by period and country. The annotations fully describe content, and most include helpful evaluative comments. Two indexes: authors and titles; subjects (however, the subject indexing is incomplete and frequently vague). Arntzen is now dated and less international in scope than it should be, but it remains the best general guide to reference works and important studies. Reviews: Margaret Girvan, *Art Libraries Journal* 6.3 (1981): 73–79; Alex Ross, *Art Bulletin* 65 (1983): 169–72.

More current but also more elementary and lacking the breadth of Arntzen are Lois Swan Jones, *Art Research Methods and Resources: A Guide to Finding Art Information*, 2nd ed., rev. and enl. (Dubuque: Kendall/Hunt, 1984, 332 pp.), and Elizabeth B. Pollard, *Visual Arts Research: A Handbook* (New York: Greenwood, 1986, 165 pp.). Both offer helpful discussions of research methods, but in each the organization leads to difficulty in locating specific reference works. Pollard gives more attention to interdisciplinary research.

More specialized guides that complement the preceding are a series by Donald L. Ehresmann:

Applied and Decorative Arts: A Bibliographic Guide to Basic Reference Works, Histories, and Handbooks. Littleton: Libraries Unlimited, 1977. 232 pp. Includes works published between 1875 and 1975 in Western languages.

Architecture: A Bibliographic Guide to Basic Reference Works, Histories, and Handbooks. Littleton: Libraries Unlimited, 1984. 338 pp. Covers books published between 1875 and 1980 that are available in the United States.

Fine Arts: A Bibliographic Guide to Basic Reference Works, Histories, and Handbooks. 2nd ed. Littleton: Libraries Unlimited, 1979. 349 pp. Limited to works published between 1833 and 1 Sept. 1978 and devoted to at least two of the major media (architecture, sculpture, and painting), this volume is particularly useful for its frequent evaluative comments.

Future volumes are planned for sculpture, painting, and graphic arts.

Handbooks, Dictionaries, and Encyclopedias

5135 *Encyclopedia of World Art*. 16 vols. New York: McGraw, 1959–83. Published simultaneously in Italy as *Enciclopedia universale dell'arte*, 15 vols., corrected rpt. (Firenze: Sansoni, 1971–76). N31.E4833 703.

An extensively illustrated encyclopedia that encompasses the representational arts of all eras and countries. The entries—all by internationally recognized scholars, and many extending to several thousand words—cover cultures, nations, schools, periods, artists, theories, methodologies, iconographic themes, techniques, artistic genres, and related topics. Many of the lengthy entries consist of separately authored parts; all entries conclude with a bibliography. The English-language edition has a more extensive article on American art, some 300 additional biographical entries, and English-language titles added to many bibliographies. Vol. 16 is a supplement that incorporates recent scholarship in 18 essays on cultures or periods. Because of the organization of topical entries and the grouping of plates at the end of each volume, readers searching for a specific topic should begin with the detailed analytical index (vol. 15) of terminology, names, and subjects. The accompanying *Guide to the* Encyclopedia of World Art, comp. Donald Goddard (1968, 38 pp.), describes the organization, discusses how to use the work, and lists articles by historical periods, concepts, and geographical areas. The *Encyclopedia of World Art* is the most authoritative and comprehensive of the numerous general encyclopedias of art, with many entries remaining the standard discussion of their respective topics.

The most comprehensive dictionaries of artists are Ulrich Thieme and Felix Becker, eds., *Allgemeines Lexikon der bildenden Künstler von der Antike bis zur Gegenwart* (Thieme-Becker), 37 vols. (Leipzig: Seeman, 1907–50), and Hans Vollmer, ed. *Allgemeines Lexikon der bildenden Künstler der XX. Jahrhunderts*, 6 vols. (Leipzig: Seeman, 1953–62).

Useful general dictionaries include the following:

McGraw-Hill Dictionary of Art. Ed. Bernard S. Myers. 5 vols. New York: McGraw, 1969. The approximately 15,000 entries emphasize biographies of artists.

The Oxford Companion to Art. Ed. Harold Osborne. Oxford: Clarendon, 1970. 1,277 pp. The best concise general dictionary in English.

Guides to Scholarship and Criticism

SERIAL BIBLIOGRAPHIES

Although there is considerable overlap among the following, each has its particular strengths and all are ultimately complementary. However, *RILA* (5155) and *RAA* (5150) plan to merge into a single bibliography (as yet untitled) covering scholarship on Western art from late antiquity to 1945 and contemporary art worldwide. Organized in classified divisions for general works, general art history, and historical periods, entries will be accompanied by abstracts in French or English, indexed by subject in both languages, and accessible through Dialog (520).

5140 *ARTbibliographies Modern [1969–].* Oxford: Clio, 1969– . 2/yr. Former title: *LOMA (Literature on Modern Art: An Annual Bibliography)* (1969–71). Z5935.L64 016.709'04.

A bibliography of dissertations, exhibition catalogs, and other scholarship on art and related topics since the late nineteenth century. Since vol. 4 (1973), entries—accompanied by brief nonevaluative abstracts—are organized in a single subject list, which incorporates generous cross-references. (The earlier volumes are organized by artist, have little other subject access, and are limited to twentieth-century art.) Two indexes in each issue: authors; museums and galleries. Cumulative index (with expanded coverage of artists): vols. 6–10, *Five Year Index, Volumes 6–10, 1975–1979* (1982, 264 pp.); cumulations are planned for vols. 1–5 and 11–15. Although *ARTbibliographies* offers the best coverage of modern and contemporary art, the lack of thorough subject indexing—especially of the abstracts—means that researchers looking for studies involving literary works or authors should perform an online search of the Dialog (520) file, which includes entries since 1974 and allows for keyword searches of abstracts.

5145 *Art Index [1929–].* New York: Wilson, 1930– . Quarterly, with annual and larger cumulations. Z5937.A78 016.7.

An author and subject index to articles in (currently) about 190 art periodicals, yearbooks, and museum bulletins, with coverage now extending to archaeology, architecture, art history, city planning, crafts, films, graphic arts, industrial design, interior design, landscape architecture, museology, photography, and related fields. The serials indexed are determined by subscriber vote, but coverage is reasonably international. Articles are indexed by author and subject; exhibitions and reproductions by artist. Since vol. 22 (1973–74), book reviews are listed separately at the end. Entries since October 1984 can be searched through WILSONLINE (525) and on CD-ROM through WILSONDISC. Although the work is the most selective in coverage and limited to articles, it is also the broadest, most current, and easiest to use of the art indexes and is particularly useful for locating a reproduction of an art work.

5150 *Répertoire d'art et d'archéologie (de l'époque paléochrétienne à 1939)* (*RAA*). Paris: Centre de Documentation Sciences Humaines, 1910– . Quarterly, with annual cumulative index. Z5937.R4 016.7.

A bibliography of books, articles, and exhibition and auction catalogs on the history of art from the early Christian era through 1939. The scope and organization have altered considerably since 1910. Books are excluded until vol. 24 (1920); coverage of primitive and popular art is discontinued with the combined vols. 49–51 (1945–47), and Oriental, Islamic, and classical art since ns 1 (1965). *RAA* was originally composed of a list of contents of journals organized by country of publication; since ns 9 (1973), entries are organized in five extensively classified divisions: general works (including sections for reference works, theory of art, and iconography); general art history; Middle Ages; Renaissance and seventeenth and eighteenth centuries; and nineteenth and twentieth centuries. The period divisions have sections for general studies, architecture, sculpture, painting and graphic arts, and decorative arts, with each subdivided by country. Two indexes in each issue since ns 9 (1973): artists and subjects (cumulated annually); earlier volumes are variously indexed by authors, artists, and/or places. Many entries in recent volumes are accompanied by brief descriptive annotations in French. Entries since 1973 can be searched through the FRANCIS data base (available in the United States through Questel, Inc.). Of the major art bibliographies, *RAA* currently offers the fullest coverage. (For the merger of *RILA* [5155] and *RAA*, see the headnote to this section.)

5155 *RILA: International Repertory of the Literature of Art/Répertoire international de la littérature de l'art* (*RILA*). Williamstown: Getty Art History Information Program, 1975– . 2/yr. Z5937.R16 [N7510] 016.7.

An abstracting service for publications (including dissertations and reviews of books and exhibitions) on the history of Western art from the fourth century to the present. Entries are now organized in seven classified divisions: reference works; general studies; medieval; Renaissance, baroque, and rococo; neoclassicism and modern (to 1945); modern (1945 to the present); collections and exhibitions. Where appropriate, each division has sections for general studies; architecture; sculpture; pictorial arts; decorative arts; and artists, architects, and photographers. The abstracts are descriptive, with several by document authors. Two indexes in each issue: authors; subjects; cumulative indexes: *1975–1979* (1982, 837 pp.); *1980–1984* (in progress). Entries can be searched online through Dialog (520). Although *RILA* is generally the least current of the major art bibliographies, the abstracts and extensive subject indexing make it an essential source. (For the merger of *RILA* and *RAA* [5150], see the headnote to this section.)

See also

Humm, *Annotated Critical Bibliography of Feminist Criticism* (6170).

ART AND LITERATURE

5160 Huddleston, Eugene L., and Douglas A. Noverr. *The Relationship of Painting and Literature: A Guide to Information Sources*. American Studies Information Guide Series 4. Detroit: Gale, 1978. 184 pp. Z5069.H84 [N66] 016.75913.

A checklist of paintings and analogous works of American literature and of English language studies, through c. 1976, of the relationship between the two. Entries are organized in six divisions: analogous American paintings and American poems (organized by artist in six chronological periods, with a numbering system defining the closeness of the analogy); American poems on paintings (organized by poet); American poems on painters; American poems on unspecified paintings, painters, and related subjects; studies of the relationship between poetry and painting; studies of the relationship between fiction and painting. Additions to the last two divisions appear on pp. 147–49. A very few entries are annotated, and those are done inadequately. Three indexes: authors; painters; paintings, books, and poems. Highly selective and misleadingly titled, *Relationship of Painting and Literature* is only marginally useful as a starting point for research.

See also

"Bibliography on the Relations of Literature and the Other Arts" (5965).
MLAIB (335): See the headings beginning "Art" in the subject index to post-1980 volumes.
Rice, *English Fiction, 1900–1950* (2840).

Author Bibliographies

All major and numerous minor authors are the subject of at least one author bibliography. Because of their number, wide variation in quality, and ease of identification (in library catalogs, bibliographies of bibliographies, and serials bibliographies and indexes), individual author bibliographies are not listed in this *Guide*.

Although it is generally the best place to begin extensive research on an author or specific work, an author bibliography, like any other reference work, must be used with due regard for its scope, limitations, and accuracy. As I point out in *On Compiling an Annotated Bibliography* (30):

> Several of these bibliographies are models of their kind: intelligent, accurate, thorough, efficiently organized works that foster scholarship by guiding readers through accumulated studies as well as implicitly or explicitly isolating dominant scholarly concerns, identifying topics that have been overworked, and suggesting needed research. Unfortunately, many are flawed in either conception or execution, and some are downright shoddy.

Before searching out entries, users must study the prefatory explanation of scope and organization, become familiar with the index(es), and assess the accuracy of the work. A good bibliography will begin with a precise statement of what it includes and excludes, its chronological span, organization and content of entries, and relationship to other bibliographies. (Because many bibliographies are inexcusably vague about some or all of these matters, researchers will have no immediate way of determining how complete a work is.) An efficient, effective search of an author bibliography requires an understanding of the organization of entries and the nature of the index(es). For example, when searching for scholarship on a specific work in an author bibliography with sections for individual literary works, it is essential to know whether general studies are cross-referenced, accorded multiple listings, or accessible only through an index. Because judging accuracy is best accomplished through repeated use, researchers consulting a bibliography for the first time should search out reviews; unfortunately, too few author bibliographies are subjected to rigorous reviewing.

Because no bibliography is comprehensive and every one is outdated even before the last sheet of paper is cranked out of the typewriter or computer printer, researchers will also have to consult appropriate serial bibliographies and indexes listed throughout this *Guide*.

Awards and Prizes

5175 *Literary and Library Prizes*. Ed. and rev. Olga S. Weber and Stephen J. Calvert. 10th ed. New York: Bowker, 1980. 651 pp. PN171.P75.L5 807.9.

A selective guide to 454 currently awarded international, American, British, and Canadian literary and library prizes of more than local interest. Weber and Calvert exclude journalism awards and include only a few for periodical articles and short stories. Awards are organized alphabetically by sponsor in four divisions: international, American, British, and Canadian. The American division, which constitutes the bulk of the work, has sections for general, publishers', juvenile, poetry, drama, short story, and library awards. Following the description of purpose, criteria, and submission or nomination procedure for each award is a chronological list of recipients and works. Indexed by sponsoring organizations, winners, and names of awards (including discontinued ones listed in earlier editions). Earlier editions remain useful for descriptions and winners of discontinued awards. Although not as comprehensive as *Awards, Honors, and Prizes* (see below), *Literary and Library Prizes* is the best source for identifying recipients and works awarded important international, American, British, and Canadian literary awards. For foreign awards and recipients, see *Foreign Literary Prizes: Romance and Germanic Languages*, ed. E. C. Bufkin (New York: Bowker, 1980, 300 pp.), a highly selective list of current and defunct awards (as of 1978), with a list of recipients of each.

Additional awards and prizes—but not recipients—are listed in the following:

Awards, Honors, and Prizes: An International Directory of Awards and Their Donors Recognizing Achievement in Advertising, Architecture, Arts and Humanities, Business and Finance, Communications, Consumer Affairs, Ecology, Education, Engineering, Fashion, Films, Journalism, Law, Librarianship, Literature, Medicine, Music, Performing Arts, Photography, Public Affairs, Publishing, Radio and Television, Religion, Science, Sports, and Transportation. Detroit: Gale, 1969– . Irregular. (Title varies.)

Grants and Awards Available to American Writers. New York: PEN American Center, 1969– . Biennial. Describes both creative and scholarly awards, principally those worth more than $500 or ensuring the publication or production of a work.

See also

Grants Register (5940).

Bibliography and Textual Criticism

This section is devoted to analytical bibliography and the Anglo-American tradition of textual criticism. Several closely allied works appear in the immediately following section, Book Collecting.

Handbooks, Dictionaries, and Encyclopedias

5190 Glaister, Geoffrey Ashall. *Glaister's Glossary of the Book: Terms Used in Papermaking, Printing, Bookbinding, and Publishing, with Notes on Illuminated Manuscripts and Private Presses*. 2nd ed. rev. London: Allen, 1979. 551 pp. Z118.G55 686.2'03.

A dictionary of technical terms, presses, binderies, organizations, awards, periodicals, printers, publishers, binders, calligraphers, booksellers, and other persons associated with the book, paper, printing, and publishing trades. The 3,932 entries, which range from a few lines to several pages, offer clear definitions or biographies, cite important scholarship, and provide extensive cross-references to related entries. Several are accompanied by illustrations; unfortunately, many of the black and white ones are unclear. Four appendixes: selected type specimens; Latin place names in imprints of early books; British proof correction symbols; a selected bibliography. Generally authoritative and accurate, Glaister is the essential glossary of terminology related to the history and production of books and manuscripts. The first edition—*An Encyclopedia of the Book* (Cleveland: World, 1960, 484 pp.); *Glossary of the Book* (London: Allen, 1960, 484 pp.)—remains useful for entries and illustrations subsequently dropped. Reviews: (1st ed.) *Times Literary Supplement* 3 Feb. 1961: 78; (2nd ed.) Paul S. Koda, *Papers of the Bibliographical Society of America* 75 (1981): 219–21; G. Thomas Tanselle, *Printing History* 4 (1982): 78–79.

Occasionally useful complements are the following:

Feather, John. *A Dictionary of Book History*. New York: Oxford UP, 1986. 278 pp. Entries cover the book trade, printers, publishers, booksellers, bibliographers, presses, libraries, collectors, printing, paper, binding, periodicals, reference books, organizations, and bibliographical terminology. The selection is miscellaneous and the explanations less thorough and far less reliable than in Glaister, but the entries typically cite related sources or studies.

Peters, Jean. *The Bookman's Glossary*. 6th ed., rev. and enl. New York: Bowker, 1983. 223 pp. The entries for terms used in publishing, book manufacturing, bookselling, and the antiquarian trade are much briefer than those in Glaister or Feather.

See also

Carter, *ABC for Book Collectors* (5340).

General Introductions

5195 Gaskell, Philip. *A New Introduction to Bibliography*. Rpt. with corrections. Oxford: Clarendon, 1985. 438 pp. (Readers should avoid the uncorrected second printing of the American edition [New York: Oxford UP, 1975], since it omits several passages and duplicates others. The corrected second printing begins with "were" rather than "for" on p. 11.) Z116.A2.G27 686.2'09.

An introduction to the technical processes of book production from 1500 to 1950 in Great Britain and America. The bulk of the work consists of a history of book production organized in two extensively illustrated divisions: the handpress period (1500–1800) and the machine press period (1800–1950). The first discusses the technical details of printing type, composition, paper, imposition, presswork, the warehouse, binding, decoration and illustration, patterns of production, and the English book trade; the second, plates, type from 1800 to 1875, paper, edition binding, printing machines, processes of reproduction, mechanical composition and type from 1875 to 1950, printing practices, and the book trade in Britain and America. Following the history is a too-brief section on bibliographical applications: the identification of edition, impression, issue, and state; bibliographical description (with sample descriptions printed as an appendix); and textual bibliography (with two analyses of transmission of texts in an appendix). Another appendix reprints McKerrow's discussion of Elizabethan handwriting (see below). Concludes with a useful, but now dated, selective bibliography that evaluates important scholarship through the early 1970s. Thoroughly indexed by persons and subjects. Although it is better in its treatment of the machine press era and the eighteenth century than the earlier period, inadequate in its attention to analytical bibliography and demonstration of the applications of physical bibliography to the transmission of texts, and densely written in many places, this work provides the best basic introduction to the technical aspects of book production and a necessary prelude to Bowers, *Principles of Bibliographical Description* (5205) and Gaskell, *From Writer to Reader* (5220). Reviews: Fredson Bowers, *Papers of the Bibliographical Society of America* 67 (1973): 109–24; Albert H. Smith, *Library* 5th ser. 28 (1973): 341–44; G. Thomas Tanselle, *Costerus* ns 1 (1974): 129–50.

(Researchers who must use the uncorrected second printing should obtain *Corrections to the 1975 "Second Printing" American Edition of Gaskell's* New Introduction to Bibliography, Occasional Publication 4 [New York: Book Arts P, School of Library Science, Columbia U, 1975, 3 pp.].)

Although now dated in some respects, Ronald B. McKerrow, *An Introduction to Bibliography for Literary Students*, 2nd impression with corrections (Oxford: Clarendon, 1928, 359 pp.), has not been superseded in its integration of the history of book production, bibliographical theory, and application to textual matters in handpress books of the period 1560–1660. McKerrow and Gaskell must be read together.

5200 Williams, William Proctor, and Craig S. Abbott. *An Introduction to Bibliographical and Textual Studies*. 2nd ed. New York: MLA, 1989. 114 pp. Z1001.W58 010'.42.

An introduction to the methods and applications of twentieth-century Anglo-American textual and bibliographical scholarship. Chapters discuss analytical bibliography, descriptive bibliography, transmission of texts, and textual criticism; a selective bibliography concludes the work. Particularly informative are the description of the process of preparing a critical edition and the appendix on textual notation, a convenient guide for readers puzzled by the symbols and lists in the editorial apparatus of a critical edition. Although not a substitute for Gaskell, *New Introduction to Bibliography* (5195) and McKerrow, *Introduction to Bibliography* (5195a), this is a serviceable introduction for the reader who needs a basic understanding of bibliography and textual criticism. Reviews: Hugh Amory, *Papers of the Bibliographical Society of America* 80 (1986): 243–53; John Feather, *Library* 6th ser. 9 (1987): 196–97.

See also

Tanselle, "Copyright Records and the Bibliographer" (3260).

Descriptive Bibliography

5205 Bowers, Fredson. *Principles of Bibliographical Description*. Princeton: Princeton UP, 1949. 505 pp. Z1001.B78 010.1.

A detailed guide to the principles and methods of descriptive bibliography that consolidates scattered scholarship, offers a rationale for the field, and establishes norms for bibliographical description. The 12 chapters provide exacting, detailed treatment of the nature of descriptive bibliography; edition, issue, and state, and ideal copy in the handpress period; the bibliographical description of books of the sixteenth through eighteenth centuries; the transcription of title pages and other features; format and collation formula; reference notation; statement of signing, pagination and foliation, and other elements of a description; special considerations for the description of eighteenth-century books; incunabula; the bibliography of nineteenth- and twentieth-century books; the determination of publication, edition, impression, issue, and state in the machine press period; and the description of nineteenth- and twentieth-century books. Three important appendixes conclude the work: a digest of the collation and pagination or foliation formulas; sample descriptions of books of different periods; collation formulas for incunabula. Indexed by persons, subjects, and titles. *Principles of Bibliographical Description* is more thorough in its treatment of books published before 1700 and has been modified and extended in some areas by recent scholarship; nevertheless, it remains the indispensable guide to the theory and practice of descriptive bibliography.

Essential complements are G. Thomas Tanselle, "A Sample Bibliographical Description, with Commentary," *Studies in Bibliography* 40 (1987): 1–23, which consolidates and illustrates modifications made to Bowers's principles; and David L. Vander Meulen, "The History and Future of Bowers's *Principles*," *Papers of the Bibliographical Society of America* 79 (1985): 197–219, which surveys modifications and extensions, as well as summarizes the reception and impact of this magisterial work.

Because *Principles of Bibliographical Description* requires a sound knowledge of printing practices and bibliographical techniques, readers should first master Gaskell, *New Introduction to Bibliography* (5195) and McKerrow, *Introduction to Bibliography* (5195a). Those daunted by Bowers's detailed instructions for transcribing title pages and other parts of a book, determining format, and recording collation and pagination will find M. J. Pearce, *A Workbook of Analytical and Descriptive Bibliography* (London: Bingley, 1970, 110 pp.), a helpful beginning guide. (Gaskell's section on bibliographical description is also helpful, but it adopts several modifications to Bowers that have not gained wide acceptance.)

Textual Criticism

G. Thomas Tanselle, "Textual Scholarship" (pp. 29–52) in Gibaldi, *Introduction to Scholarship* (25) offers a succinct, balanced overview of textual criticism.

5210 Greg, W. W. "The Rationale of Copy-Text." *Studies in Bibliography* 3 (1950–51): 19–36. Reprinted with minor changes in Greg, *Collected Papers*, ed. J. C. Maxwell (Oxford: Clarendon, 1966) 374–91.

The classic formulation of the theory of copy-text (a text chosen as an expedient guide in formal matters for a critical edition) and the distinction between substantive readings (those "that affect the author's meaning or the essence of his expression") and accidental readings (those that affect mainly the formal presentation of the text). Although sometimes misunderstood and misapplied, Greg's theory, its subsequent modifications, and the debates engendered by the theory are central to modern Anglo-American textual editing. For a history and critique of the responses and modifications to Greg's theory, see G. Thomas Tanselle, "Greg's Theory of Copy-Text and the Editing of American Literature," *Studies in Bibliography* 28 (1975): 167–229; "Recent Editorial Discussion and the Central Questions of Editing," *Studies in Bibliography* 34 (1981): 23–65; and "Historicism and Critical Editing," *Studies in Bibliography* 39 (1986): 1–46. (These articles are reprinted as *Textual Criticism since Greg: A Chronicle, 1950–1983* [Charlottesville: UP of Virginia, for Bibliographical Soc. of the U of Virginia, 1987, 154 pp.].)

5215 Committee on [formerly, Center for] Scholarly Editions (CSE). MLA, 10 Astor Pl., New York, NY 10003.

The Committee on Scholarly Editions was established in 1976 to encourage the highest standards in scholarly editing of all kinds of works or documents by

> serv[ing] as a clearinghouse for information about scholarly editing and editorial projects; offer[ing] advice and consultation to editors on request; honor[ing] excellence in editing by awarding emblems to qualified volumes; promot[ing] dissemination of reliable texts for classroom use and among general readers.

Prospective editors are sent a list of "Guiding Questions" that explain the standards and procedures for obtaining the CSE emblem. Although the committee does not prescribe an editorial methodology or procedure, it does insist that an edition include a textual essay and apparatus, and that it undergo formal inspection by a CSE representative.

"The Committee on Scholarly Editions: Aims and Policies," *PMLA* 103 (1988): 414–16 outlines procedures and general editorial standards. "The Center for Scholarly Editions: An Introductory Statement," *PMLA* 92 (1977): 583–97 remains useful for its valuable bibliography of works on editorial theory and practice.

The CSE is the successor to the Center for Editions of American Authors (CEAA), which was established to oversee the preparation of critical editions of American literature (primarily of the nineteenth century). Standards and procedures governing CEAA-approved editions are explained in *Statement of Editorial Principles and Procedures* (5235). A list of editions approved by the CSE and CEAA is available from the Modern Language Association.

5220 Gaskell, Philip. *From Writer to Reader: Studies in Editorial Method*. Oxford: Clarendon, 1978. 268 pp. PN162.G3 808'.02.

A collection of case studies that demonstrate how textual evidence can be used to produce editions for various kinds of audiences. The 12 examples—which range from 1591 to 1974 and encompass poetry, drama, nonfiction prose, and fiction—are effectively chosen to illustrate the kinds of problems that confront an editor and to show that each textual situation is unique. For each example, Gaskell characterizes the surviving forms and their relationship, discusses the choice of copy-text, proposes emendations, and suggests an appropriate kind of edition or examines an existing one. The introduction briefly discusses authorial intention, copy-text, techniques of presentation and annotation, regularization, and works not intended for publication as a printed book. Indexed by persons and subjects. Designed to complement *New Introduction to Bibliography* (5195), *From Writer to Reader* presumes a knowledge of the history of printing and the basic concepts and theories underlying textual criticism. Although reviewers have raised serious objections to several of Gaskell's assertions, this work is a valuable illustration of the range of problems facing editors. Reviews: Vinton A. Dearing, *Analytical and Enumerative Bibliography* 3 (1979): 105–16; D. F. Foxon, *Review of English Studies* ns 30 (1979): 237–39; Daniel Karlin, *Essays in Criticism* 30 (1980): 71–78; G. Thomas Tanselle, *Library* 6th ser. 2 (1980): 337–50 (essential reading for its exposure of numerous weaknesses in the work).

5225 Kline, Mary-Jo. *A Guide to Documentary Editing*. Baltimore: Johns Hopkins UP, 1987. 228 pp. Z113.3.K55 808'.02.

A guide to the principles and practices of editing documents, especially unpublished materials such as letters, journals, diaries, speeches, and ledgers. Following an overview of American documentary and critical editing, chapters proceed more or less in order of the tasks facing an editor: organizing a project, locating, collecting, and organizing materials, and maintaining records; determining the scope and organization of an edition; evaluating and transcribing the source text; deciding on the presentation of the text, with discussions of type facsimiles, diplomatic transcriptions, and inclusive, expanded, and clear texts; using editorial symbols (for interlineations, deletions, and the like, with a helpful list on pp. 134–38 of symbols that have been employed) and writing textual notes; understanding general rules and their exceptions, emending the text, and handling variant forms of a document; dealing with the mechanics of establishing a text; preparing an edition for the printer (including writing annotations, indexing, and drafting a statement of editorial method); and handling relations with the publisher. Each chapter concludes with a helpful list of suggested readings. An appendix prints sample inquiries addressed to librarians, booksellers, and auction houses. Based on a solid command of editorial theory and extensive familiarity with related scholarship and published editions, this work combines theory and practical advice to produce the best overall guide to documentary editing. Kline is addressed primarily to those working with historical documents, but editors of all kinds will benefit from the sound advice about all aspects of the organization, preparation, and production of an edition.

Robert Halsband, "Editing the Letters of Letter-Writers," *Studies in Bibliography* 11 (1958): 25–37, remains one of the best general introductions to the editing of correspondence.

5230 Shillingsburg, Peter L. *Scholarly Editing in the Computer Age: Theory and Practice*. Athens: U of Georgia P, 1986. 178 pp. PN162.S45 808'.02.

An introduction to the use of computers in the preparation of scholarly editions. The first part surveys the principles underlying textual criticism in chapters on the concept of textual authority, the forms (or details of presentation) of a text, authorial intention, the "ontological status of literary works," authorial expectations (in relation to editing by a publisher), artistic closure, and the concept of ideal text. The second part discusses the selection of copy-text, emendation, and types and arrangement of apparatus. Using the CASE programs developed for the Thackeray edition as an example, the last part addresses the practical applications of computers to collation, manuscript preparation, and typesetting. Indexed by persons and subjects. *Scholarly Editing* is not a manual, but it does offer substantial practical advice on using a computer to prepare a critical edition.

5235 *Statement of Editorial Principles and Procedures: A Working Manual for Editing Nineteenth-Century American Texts*. Rev. ed. New York: MLA, 1972. 25 pp. PN162.M6 808.02.

A manual of principles and procedures for those preparing editions under the auspices of the Center for Editions of American Authors or who planned to seek the CEAA emblem of approval. (The CEAA was succeeded in 1976 by the Center for [now, Committee on] Scholarly Editions [5215].) The brief sections address the assembling of relevant forms of the text, sight and machine collation, choosing and emending the copy-text, recording emendations and variant readings, preparing explanatory notes, writing the historical essay, examining printer's copy and proof, the responsibility for collation and editorial choices, and the duties of the general editor. The selective overview of textual scholarship in the appendix is superseded by the list concluding "The Center for Scholarly Editions: An Introductory Statement," *PMLA* 92 (1977): 583–97. Although it is addressed to those editing nineteenth-century American literary works and although the principles underlying CEAA editions have engendered considerable debate, the manual remains a valuable source of practical advice for those editing literary texts. Prospective editors should also obtain a copy of Committee on Scholarly Editions, "Guiding Questions" (5215a), which prints a useful list of practical questions that every editor will need to ask.

See the CSE "Introductory Statement" for a list of CEAA editions (pp. 587–88) and of the responses, pro and con, to the editions and principles underlying them (pp. 591–92).

The CEAA also authorized a special seal for the textual apparatus to a work that cannot be printed because of copyright restrictions. However, few approved apparatuses have been published (as an example, see Matthew J. Bruccoli, *Apparatus for F. Scott Fitzgerald's* The Great Gatsby [Under the Red, White, and Blue], South Carolina Apparatus for Definitive Editions [Columbia: U of South Carolina P, 1974, 138 pp.]).

5240 Thorpe, James. *Principles of Textual Criticism*. San Marino: Huntington Library, 1972. 209 pp. PR65.T5 801'.959.

A discussion of the importance and imperfection of textual criticism that stresses the need for aesthetic judgment by an editor. Successive chapters draw on a wide range of examples from British and American literature to examine basic principles of textual criticism: the aesthetics of textual criticism (favoring the argument that textual criticism is a system of perfectible details rather than a science); the ideal of textual criticism ("to present the text which the author intended"); the province of textual criticism (especially its relationship to bibliography); the basic principles of textual analysis; the treatment of accidentals; and the establishment of the text. Indexed by persons and subjects. Although some of Thorpe's assertions have occasioned disagreement among textual critics, this work is essential reading for those who would edit or use critical editions.

Other important discussions are in the following:

Bowers, Fredson, *Bibliography and Textual Criticism*. The Lyell Lectures, Oxford, Trinity Term, 1959. Oxford: Clarendon, 1964. 207 pp. In his argument for the importance of analytical bibliography in textual analysis, Bowers emphasizes the assessment of textual evidence.

Dearing, Vinton A. *Principles and Practice of Textual Analysis*. Berkeley: U of California P, 1974. 243 pp. A highly technical discussion of mathematical methods for determining relationships among forms of a text.

McGann, Jerome J. *A Critique of Modern Textual Criticism*. Chicago: U of Chicago P, 1983. 146 pp. McGann argues that many principles of modern textual criticism—especially the emphasis on an author's final intentions—ignore the complex social nature of literary production. An important critique of McGann is David J. Nordloh, "Socialization, Authority, and Evidence: Reflections on McGann's *A Critique of Modern Textual Criticism*," *Analytical and Enumerative Bibliography* ns 1 (1987): 3–12, with a response by Craig S. Abbott (13–16).

See also

Sec. U: Literature-Related Topics and Sources/Computers and the Humanities/General Introductions.

Moorman, *Editing the Middle English Manuscript* (1760).

Book Trade and Publishing History

Suggestions for research are offered in "Research Opportunities in the Early English Book Trade," *Analytical and Enumerative Bibliography* 3 (1979): 165–200, a special section consisting of three articles on the sixteenth through eighteenth centuries, and in David D. Hall and John B. Hench, eds., *Needs and Opportunities in the History of the Book: America, 1639–1876* (Worcester: American Antiquarian Soc., 1987, 280 pp.), which reprints surveys of research on printing, publishing, distribution, books and popular culture, and bibliography and textual study from *Proceedings of the American Antiquarian Society* 94.2–96.1 (1984–86).

INDEXES

5245 British Book Trade Index. University of Newcastle upon Tyne Library, Newcastle upon Tyne, England NE1 7RU.

A machine-readable index to individuals active in the book trade in the British Isles to 1851. The record for each person includes address(es), biographical and trading dates, trade, and the source(s) of information. The data base can be searched by name, town, county, dates, and trades. This work will eventually incorporate most of the standard published indexes as well as information from archival materials and private files.

SURVEYS OF RESEARCH

5255 Tanselle, G. Thomas. "The Historiography of American Literary Publishing." *Studies in Bibliography* 18 (1965): 3–39.

An evaluative survey of scholarship about and sources for the history of literary publishing in the United States. In emphasizing how to reconstruct a list of works by a publisher, Tanselle treats national, regional, and other bibliographies; unpublished papers; reminiscences of publishers; and histories of firms. Authoritative evaluations, practical advice, and numerous suggestions for research make "The Historiography of American Literary Publishing" an essential introduction to a neglected area of scholarship.

HISTORIES

5258 Feather, John. *A History of British Publishing*. London: Croom Helm, 1988. 292 pp. Z325.F414 070.5'0941.

A history from 1476 to the 1980s of the development of publishing in Great Britain that stresses the organizational role of the publisher, the importance of copyright laws, the marketing of books, and censorship. Indexed by subjects. Rather cursory in its treatment of several aspects of publishing, Feather is principally useful as an overview. A full history remains to be written.

5260 Tebbel, John. *A History of Book Publishing in the United States*. 4 vols. New York: Bowker, 1972–81. Z473.T42 070.5'0973.

Vol. 1: *The Creation of an Industry, 1630–1865*. 1972. 646 pp.
Vol. 2: *The Expansion of an Industry, 1865–1919*. 1975. 813 pp.
Vol. 3: *The Golden Age between Two Wars, 1920–1940*. 1978. 774 pp.
Vol. 4: *The Great Change, 1940–1980*. 1981. 830 pp.

An extensive history of book publishing from 1630 to 1980, with discussions of printing, bookselling, economics of the trade, publishers, copyright, bestsellers, illustration, production, censorship, and specialized types of publishing (especially religious, children's, music, private press, book club, and university press). In some volumes, these topics are broken down by geographical area. Five appendixes: (in vol. 2) a year-by-year breakdown by category of American publishing from 1880–1918, tables depicting book publication, and directory of publishers for 1888, 1900, and 1919; (in vol. 3) an economic overview, and a list of bestsellers. Indexed in each volume by persons, places, titles, subjects, and publishers. More valuable for its accumulation of information than its interpretation, the *History* presents the fullest account of book publishing in the United States. It must be used cautiously, however, because of uncritical reliance on sources and numerous errors. Reviews: (vol. 3) Gordon B. Neavill, *Publishing History* 6 (1979): 107–11; Susan O. Thompson, *Papers of the Bibliographical Society of America* 75 (1981): 230–33.

A less extensive but more scholarly history is Hellmut Lehmann-Haupt, *The Book in America: A History of the Making and Selling of Books in the United States*, 2nd ed. (New York: Bowker, 1951, 493 pp.). The first edition—*The Book in America: A History of the Making, the Selling, and the Collecting of Books in the United States* (1939, 453 pp.)—remains useful for its additional material, especially a history of book collecting and libraries, by Ruth Shepard Granniss.

PERIODICALS

Scholarly Journals

5265 *Publishing History: The Social, Economic, and Literary History of Book, Newspaper, and Magazine Publishing*. 1977– . 2/yr. Z280.P8 658.8'09'0705730941.

Publishes articles and occasional reviews on the history of publishing, primarily in the English-speaking world and especially in Great Britain since 1700. Cumulative index: vols. 1–10, in 10 (1981): 95–98.

Trade Journals

5270 *Publishers Weekly: The Journal of the Book Industry* (*PW*) 1872– . Weekly. Former title: *The Publishers' and Stationers' Weekly Trade Circular* (1872); various subtitles. Z1219.P98 658.8.

The American book trade periodical that emphasizes popular rather than scholarly publishing. Through vol. 206 (26 Aug. 1974) includes *Weekly Record* (4110a). *PW* is useful to literary researchers for charting trends in publishing, information on merchandising and sales figures, interviews with writers, features on publishers, occasional historical articles, and prepublication notices of books.

Guides to Scholarship

G. Thomas Tanselle, "The Periodical Literature of English and American Bibliography," *Studies in Bibliography* 26 (1973): 167–91, identifies where English-language bibliographical journals are indexed. Tanselle's survey is complemented by B. J. McMullin, "Indexing the Periodical Literature of Anglo-American Bibliography," *Studies in Bibliography* 33 (1980): 1–17, an evaluation of the indexing of bibliographical scholarship in the 1974 volumes of *ABHB: Annual Bibliography of the History of the Printed Book* (5275), *Bibliographic Index* (145), *British Humanities Index* (370), *Essay and General Literature Index* (380), *Humanities Index* (385), *Internationale Bibliographie der Zeitschriftenliteratur* (390), *Library Literature*, *ABELL* (340), and *MLAIB* (335). McMullin's conclusion that *ABELL* is "the most satisfactory index to Anglo-American bibliography" must be modified because of the introduction of subject indexing with the *MLAIB* for 1981. However, there is still no serial bibliography that thoroughly covers bibliographical scholarship.

SERIAL BIBLIOGRAPHIES

5275 *ABHB: Annual Bibliography of the History of the Printed Book and Libraries: [1970–]* (*ABHB*). Dordrecht: Nijhoff, 1973– . Annual. Z117.A55 016.00155'2.

A bibliography of scholarship (including dissertations and reviews) on the history of the printed book since the fifteenth century and the arts, crafts, and techniques involved in its production, distribution, and description throughout the world. *ABHB* excludes discussions of manuscripts and modern technical processes, as well as most textual studies. Entries are organized in 12 divisions: general; paper, inks, printing materials; calligraphy, type design, type founding; layout, composition, printing, presses; illustration; binding; book trade and publishing; book collecting; libraries and librarianship; legal, economic, and social aspects of book history; newspapers and journalism; other subjects. Except for the last—which is organized by Dewey Decimal Classification—each division has sections for general studies and countries, with the latter subdivided by century and then persons, places, or subjects, depending on the topic of the division. Two indexes: scholars and anonymous titles; geographical and personal names discussed. *ABHB* is sometimes far behind in coverage (with volumes typically including several retrospective entries), inconsistent in indexing journals ostensibly scanned on a regular basis, and frequently inaccurate in transcription and classification. Still, *ABHB* and *Bibliographie der Buch- und Bibliotheksgeschichte* (5280) are the only reasonably complete and current bibliographies of international scholarship on the history of the printed book. Neither, however, adequately fills the need for a thorough, trustworthy bibliography of the topic. For a detailed evaluation of *ABHB*, see B. J. McMullin, "Indexing the Periodical Literature of Anglo-American Bibliography," *Studies in Bibliography* 33 (1980): 1–17.

Selected studies before 1970 are listed in these works:

Myers, Robin. *The British Book Trade from Caxton to the Present Day: A Bibliographical Guide Based on the Libraries of the National Book League and St. Bride Institute*. London: Deutsch, 1973. 405 pp. Although this work is a highly selective and sometimes idiosyncratic list of English-language books, it is far superior to Paul A. Winckler, *History of Books and Printing: A Guide to Information Sources*, Books, Publishing, and Libraries Information Guide Series 2 (Detroit: Gale, 1979, 209 pp.), which omits too many significant works and is replete with errors.

"A Selective Check List of Bibliographical Scholarship for [1949–72]." *Studies in Bibliography* (entry 5320) 3–27 (1950–74). A list of works on printing and publishing history, bibliography, and textual criticism, with an emphasis on Western literature, especially English and American. Although selective, it is the best general bibliography of pre-1970 scholarship. The bibliographies for 1949 through 1955 are reprinted with corrections and a cumulative index as vol. 10 (1957); those for 1956 through 1962 are reprinted with a cumulative index as *Selective Check Lists of Bibliographical Scholarship, Series B, 1956–1962*, ed. Howell J. Heaney and Rudolf Hirsch (Charlottesville: UP of Virginia, for Bibliographical Soc. of the U of Virginia, 1966, 247 pp.).

5280 *Bibliographie der Buch- und Bibliotheksgeschichte [1980–]* (*BBB*). Bad Iburg: Meyer, 1982– . Annual. Z4.B54 016.002.

A bibliography of books, articles, and reviews on bibliography and the history of the book and libraries. It was originally limited to scholarship on German-speaking countries, but coverage is now international. Entries are organized in eight variously classified divisions: general studies (including sections for bibliographies of bibliographies, national bibliographies, and analytical and descriptive bibliography); individual authors; textual criticism; book production (including sections for handwriting and typography, composition, printing, paper, illustration, and binding); types of printed works (including children's books, periodicals, newspapers, and ephemera); bookselling, publishing, book collecting, and libraries (including a section on bookplates); curiosa; and reviews. Five indexes: scholars; reviewers; persons as subjects; places; subjects. Although it now overlaps considerably with *ABHB: Annual Bibliography of the History of the Printed Book* (5275), *BBB* is somewhat more current and accurate (however, like *ABHB*, it contains numerous errors, misclassifications, and omissions). The two should be used together. Reviews: B. J. McMullin, *Papers of the Bibliographical Society of America* 79 (1985): 260–62; 80 (1986): 263–65; 81 (1987): 81–82.

See also

Secs. G: Serial Bibliographies, Indexes, and Abstracts and H: Guides to Dissertations and Theses.

ABELL (340): Bibliography division.

MLAIB (335): See the Bibliographical heading in the General division in volumes for 1935–52; General III: Bibliographical in the volumes for 1953–55; General IX: Bibliographical in the volumes for 1956–66; General VI: Bibliographical in the volumes for 1967–69; General V: Bibliographical in the volumes for 1970–80; and the Bibliographical division in pt. 4 of the later volumes. Researchers must also consult the headings beginning "Bibliographical," "Textual," "Printing," and "Publishing" in the subject index to post-1980 volumes.

OTHER BIBLIOGRAPHIES

5285 *Index to Selected Bibliographical Journals, 1933–1970.* London: Bibliographical Soc., 1982. 316 pp. Z1002.I573 016.002.

Barr, Bernard. "The Bibliographical Society: *Index to Selected Bibliographical Journals* (Addenda)." *Library* 6th ser. 9 (1987): 44–52.

An author and subject index to signed articles, notes, and some letters—but not reviews—published for the most part from 1933 through 1969 in 11 major bibliographical journals. Under each author or subject, entries are listed alphabetically by journal, then chronologically by publication date. Because the *Index* is derived from a Bodleian Library card index that was compiled over several years by various persons, there are numerous errors in transcriptions, oversights (e.g., an entire volume of *Library* was omitted, although it is indexed in Barr's addenda), and inconsistencies in subject headings. Subject indexing is frequently superficial or inaccurate because of the reliance on title keywords. While the work is not trustworthy, it is the single best index to an important body of bibliographical scholarship. Review: B. J. McMullin, *Papers of the Bibliographical Society of America* 78 (1984): 57–67.

A major desideratum remains a full and accurate index to bibliographical publications.

5290 Tanselle, G. Thomas. *Guide to the Study of United States Imprints.* 2 vols. Cambridge: Belknap-Harvard UP, 1971. Z1215.A2.T35 016.015'73.

A bibliography of published research through 1969 on printing and publishing in the United States. Entries are organized geographically and then chronologically by date of coverage or publication in most of the nine divisions: regional lists; genre lists (by type, form, or subject); author lists (limited essentially to descriptive bibliographies or lists of editions); published copyright records; important or representative auction, booksellers', exhibition, and library catalogs; retrospective book trade directories; studies of individual printers and publishers; general studies; checklists of secondary material. Some entries cite selected reviews. An appendix lists 250 essential works on printing and publishing in the United States. Indexed by persons, publishers, and subjects. Users must be certain to read the introduction, which clearly outlines the scope and organization of each division, cites additional sources, and offers valuable advice on the uses of each type of work listed and research procedures. Tanselle, while not comprehensive, nonetheless offers the fullest list of published research through 1969 on printing and publishing in the country and is an important source for locating reference works that will identify a particular printed book. For studies published after 1969, consult *ABHB: Annual Bibliography of the History of the Printed Book* (5275). Review: Hensley C. Woodbridge, *Papers of the Bibliographical Society of America* 67 (1973): 351–56.

See also

Howard-Hill, *Index to British Literary Bibliography* (1355).
Leary, *Articles on American Literature* (3295).
New Cambridge Bibliography of English Literature (1385).
Woodress, *Dissertations in American Literature, 1891–1966* (3320).

REVIEW INDEXES

5295 *Index to Reviews of Bibliographical Publications: An International Annual [1976–]*. Troy: Whitston, 1977– . Annual. Vol. 1 was also published as *Analytical and Enumerative Bibliography* 1.4 (1977). Z1002.I57 028.1.

An index of reviews (published in 300–400 journals) of general bibliographical books and articles, studies of the book trade and printing history, and bibliographies, editions, concordances, and manuscript studies of English and American literature. Since vol. 7 (for 1982), reviews are organized by author or editor in seven divisions: general studies; textual criticism (including individual editions); facsimiles; concordances and indexes; enumerative and descriptive bibliography (including individual bibliographies); collections and exhibitions; production, trade, and impact of books and manuscripts. Three indexes: subjects; titles; scholars (including reviewers). Organization, indexing, and coverage have improved markedly during the course of publication: through vol. 6 (for 1981), reviews appear in a single author/editor list, with editions entered under author or "anon." rather than editor. Until vol. 4 (for 1979), the subject indexing was too imprecise to be of much use; with vol. 3 (for 1978), foreign-language journals were covered and title, editor, and reviewer indexes added. Although it still faces major gaps in coverage and cites its share of insignificant mentions, the *Index* offers the fullest guide to reviews of bibliographical and textual scholarship on English and American literature.

Unfortunately, publication is far in arrears. Review: (vol. 4) James E. Tierney, *Eighteenth Century: A Current Bibliography* ns 8 (1982): I: 21–23.

Periodicals

Peter M. VanWingen, "Periodicals for Collectors, Dealers, and Librarians," *Rare Books 1983–84: Trends, Collections, Sources*, ed. Alice D. Schreyer (New York: Bowker, 1984) 93–106, offers an overview and classified list of journals and newsletters of interest to bibliographers and book collectors.

5300 *AEB: Analytical and Enumerative Bibliography* (*AEB*). 1977– . Quarterly. Z1007.A115 016.05.

Publishes articles, notes, reviews, and occasional review essays on analytical and enumerative bibliography, textual criticism, and publishing history; some enumerative bibliographies; and editions of English political dialogues, 1641–51. Vol. 1 of *Index to Reviews of Bibliographical Publications* (5295) appeared as 1.4 (1977). *AEB* is one of the best sources for reviews of descriptive and enumerative bibliographies; unfortunately, recent volumes are running far behind schedule.

5305 *Gutenberg-Jahrbuch* (*GJ*). 1926– . Annual. Z1008.G98 655.1.

Publishes articles and reviews on the history of the printed book, illustration, paper, typography, binding, and significant collections, ranging from the fifteenth century to the present, with an emphasis on the Continental book trade. Cumulative index: 1926–75, Annemarie Kordecki-Widmann, comp., *Register zum* Gutenberg-Jahrbuch, *1926–1975* (Mainz: Gutenberg-Gesellschaft, 1981, 326 pp.).

5310 *The Library* (*Library*). 1889– . Quarterly. Merged with *Transactions of the Bibliographical Society* (1893–1920) in 4th ser. 1 (1920). Z671.L69 010.5.

Publishes articles, notes, and reviews on analytical and historical bibliography, textual criticism, printing, publishing, and the book trade, with a decided emphasis on Great Britain. The annotated lists of "Recent Books" and "Recent Periodicals" are particularly valuable for the coverage of East European scholarship. Since 5th ser. 27 (1972), a "Projects and Information" section keeps readers apprised of current bibliographical endeavors. Of the journals in this section, *Library* is the most exacting in its reviews. Annual index; cumulative index: George Watson Cole, *An Index to Bibliographical Papers Published by the Bibliographical Society and the Library Association, London, 1877–1932* (Chicago: U of Chicago P, for Bibliographical Soc. of America, 1933, 262 pp.).

5315 *The Papers of the Bibliographical Society of America* (*PBSA*). 1906– . Quarterly. Z1008.B51 010.6.

Publishes articles, notes, reviews, and review essays on analytical, enumerative, and historical bibliography, textual criticism, and publishing and printing history, with an emphasis on British and American books and manuscripts; as well as occasional analytical and enumerative bibliographies on a variety of topics. Many of the notes supply additions and corrections to published bibliographies, especially Blanck, *Bibliography of American Literature* (3250). Annual index; cumulative indexes: vols. 1–25, *Index to the Publications of the Bibliographical Society of America and of the Bibliographical Society of Chicago, 1899–1931* (Chicago: U of Chicago P, 1931, 43 pp.); vols. 26–45, *Index to the* Papers of the Bibliographical Society of America, *Volumes 26–45, 1932–1951* (New York: Bibliographical Soc. of America, 1954, 84 pp.).

5320 *Studies in Bibliography* (*SB*). 1948– . Annual. Z1008.V55 010.6275549.
Publishes articles on analytical bibliography, textual criticism, manuscript study, the history of printing and publishing, and related topics, with more emphasis on theory and methodology than the other journals in this section. Vols. 3–27 (1950–74) include "A Selective Check List of Bibliographical Scholarship for [1949–72]" (5275a).

5325 *TEXT: Transactions of the Society for Textual Scholarship*. 1984– . Annual. P47.T39 801'.959'05.
Encourages articles on the theory and methodology of textual and bibliographical scholarship in a variety of disciplines and media, but the bulk of the articles are on literary topics.

See also

Sec. U: Literature-Related Topics and Sources/Book Collecting/Periodicals.

Book Collecting

The preceding section, Bibliography and Textual Criticism, includes many works closely allied to book collecting.

Handbooks, Dictionaries, and Encyclopedias

5340 Carter, John. *ABC for Book Collectors*. 6th ed., with corrections and additions by Nicolas Barker. London: Granada, 1980. 218 pp. Z1006.C37 002'.075'03.
A dictionary of terms used by book collectors and the antiquarian book trade in Great Britain and the United States. Carter excludes foreign-language terms except for those in common use or without an English equivalent. The sometimes detailed entries, based on Carter's years of experience as collector and member of the trade, offer clear definitions (frequently leavened with wit) and make effective use of the book itself for illustrating some terms. Instructive and entertaining, *ABC for Book Collectors* is the essential companion for collectors or occasional readers of auction and booksellers' catalogs.
For foreign-language terms, see Menno Hertzberger, ed. *Dictionnaire à l'usage de la librairie ancienne pour les langues française, anglaise, allemande, suédoise, danoise, italienne, espagnole, hollandaise, japonaise/Dictionary for the Antiquarian Booktrade in French, English, German, Swedish, Danish, Italian, Spanish, Dutch, and Japanese* ([Paris?]: International League of Antiquarian Booksellers, 1978, 202 pp.).

5345 Zempel, Edward N., and Linda A. Verkler, eds. *First Editions: A Guide to Identification: Statements of Selected North American, British Commonwealth, and Irish Publishers on Their Methods of Designating First Editions*. Peoria: Spoon River, 1984. 231 pp. Z1033.F53.F57 016.094'4.

A guide to the phrases, devices, symbols, and other marks used by about 1,000 American, British, and Irish publishers to designate a first printing or impression. Organized alphabetically by firm, entries consist of publishers' statements outlining practices through 1982. Although incomplete and not always accurate, Zempel is the best guide to identifying a first printing or impression.

Henry S. Boutell, *First Editions of Today and How to Tell Them: American, British, and Irish*, 4th ed., rev. and enl. by Wanda Underhill (Berkeley: Peacock, 1965, 227 pp.), remains an important complement for practices between 1947 and 1964. Statements from earlier editions no longer protected by copyright are reprinted in Zempel.

Some additional—but not always accurate—information on the practices of American publishers can be found in Jack Tannen, *How to Identify and Collect American First Editions: A Guide Book*, 2nd ed., rev. and enl. (New York: Arco, 1985, 142 pp.).

See also

Glaister, *Glaister's Glossary of the Book* (5190).

General Introductions

5350 Carter, John. *Taste and Technique in Book Collecting*. Rpt. with additions. London: Private Libraries Assn., 1970. 242 pp. Z987.C35 020'.75'08.

A study of the relationship between taste and technique in book collecting. Following a prefatory definition of *book collector*, chapters (replete with examples) are divided between two parts: the evolution of book collecting from 1812 to the early 1900s in Great Britain and the United States; a discussion of method, including the education of a collector, tools and terminology, bookstores and auction rooms, the concept of rarity, and the importance of condition. The 1970 reprint has corrections and notes on pp. 203–05, and an epilogue covering 1928–69 (pp. 209–42). Because *Taste and Technique* presumes a familiarity with the terminology of bibliography and book collecting, the beginning collector should have a copy of Carter, *ABC for Book Collectors* (5340) in hand. Although not a manual, *Taste and Technique* remains the classic introduction to book collecting.

Among the numerous manuals, the best complements to Carter are the following:

Peters, Jean, ed. *Book Collecting: A Modern Guide*. New York: Bowker, 1977. 288 pp. A collection of essays on buying from dealers and auctions; the antiquarian book market; manuscript collecting; descriptive bibliography; fakes, forgeries, and facsimiles; the physical care of books and manuscripts; organizing a collection; appraisal; the book collector and the world of scholarship; and the literature of book collecting (for the last, see entry 5355).

———, ed. *Collectible Books: Some New Paths*. New York: Bowker, 1979. 294 pp. A series of essays that describe unexplored and nontraditional areas for collecting.

Rees-Mogg, William. *How to Buy Rare Books: A Practical Guide to the Antiquarian Book Market*. Christie's Collectors Guides. Oxford: Phaidon, 1985. 159 pp. A practical guide for the beginning collector; topics include catalogs, relations with dealers, tastes and trends in collecting (with emphasis on the traditional subjects and expensive books), the physical makeup of a book, and care and conservation.

Winterich, John T., and David A. Randall. *A Primer of Book Collecting*. 3rd rev. ed. New York: Crown, 1966. 228 pp. Emphasizes the fundamentals of collecting, with discussions of kinds of collectible books, rarity, condition, the mechanics of collecting, bibliographical points, and reference works.

Beginning collectors should be especially wary of the numerous recent publications that stress book collecting as an investment. None of these works is adequate as a guide to either collecting or investing.

The best introduction to the related field of manuscript collecting remains Charles Hamilton, *Collecting Autographs and Manuscripts* (Norman: U of Oklahoma P, 1961, 269 pp.). Among the extensively illustrated chapters are discussions of building a collection, making finds, detecting forgeries, and collecting various kinds of materials, including literary manuscripts. Although it is addressed to the beginning collector and emphasizes American manuscripts, Hamilton is an entertaining and instructive introduction by one of the foremost dealers. Also useful is Mary A. Benjamin, *Autographs: A Key to Collecting*, corrected and rev. ed. (New York: Benjamin, 1963, 313 pp.).

Guides to Scholarship

5355 Tanselle, G. Thomas. "The Literature of Book Collecting." *Book Collecting: A Modern Guide* (entry 5350a). Ed. Jean Peters. New York: Bowker, 1977. 209–71. Z987.B68 020'.75.

An evaluative survey of general introductions and manuals; glossaries; histories of printing and allied trades; histories of collecting and bookselling; guides to and studies of collectors; periodicals; bibliographies; auction, booksellers', exhibition, and library catalogs; guides to prices; directories of dealers and collectors; works on conservation, bookplates, and manuscripts; and guides to further reading. Unfortunately, many of the authors and works cited are excluded from the index to the volume. Judicious selection and authoritative evaluation make Tanselle's survey the best guide to works about or essential in book collecting. An important complement is Tanselle's essay review of six recent manuals in *Papers of the Bibliographical Society of America* 72 (1978): 265–81.

See also

ABELL (340): Bibliography division in volumes for 1920–33; Bibliography/Book Production, Selling, Collecting, Librarianship, the Newspaper (with variations in the title) in the volumes for 1934–72; and Bibliography/Booksellers', Exhibition, and Sale Catalogues, and Bibliography/Collecting and the Library in later volumes.

ABHB: Annual Bibliography of the History of the Printed Book (5275).
Bibliographie der Buch- und Bibliotheksgeschichte (5280).
MLAIB (335): In volumes before 1981, studies of collecting and collectors are sometimes listed with bibliographical scholarship (see p. 562 for an outline of that section). In volumes after 1980, researchers must consult the "Book Collecting" and "Collection Study" headings in the subject index.

Directories of Book Dealers

For early dealers in the United States, see Madeleine B. Stern, *Antiquarian Bookselling in the United States: A History from the Origins to the 1940s* (Westport: Greenwood, 1985, 246 pp.), which concludes with a brief survey of primary sources and scholarship.

5360 *American Book Trade Directory*. New York: Bowker, 1915– . Triennial. Updated between editions by *Updating Service*. Z475.A5 655.473.

A directory of the retail and wholesale book trade in the United States and Canada. Of most interest to literary scholars is the division listing retail and antiquarian booksellers. Organized alphabetically by state (with Canadian provinces following the list of states), city, then store or bookseller, entries note kind of store, address, telephone number, name of owner, number of volumes in stock, subject specializations, and services (such as searching for specific titles). A separate division classifies booksellers by subject specializations; another lists auctioneers, appraisers, and dealers in foreign-language books. Indexed by names of stores and dealers. The fullest list of United States and Canadian antiquarian booksellers, *American Book Trade Directory* is the best source for identifying those specializing in an author, period, or subject.

Other useful but less thorough guides to North American antiquarian booksellers are the following:

AB: Bookman's Yearbook. 2 pts. Clifton: Bookman's Weekly, 1954– . Annual. With subject and geographical directories of dealers as well as lists of appraisers and auction houses.

ABAA Membership Directory. New York: Antiquarian Booksellers Assn. of America. The current directory, with geographic and subject indexes, is available free from the association office (50 Rockefeller Plaza, New York, NY 10020).

5365 *Sheppard's Book Dealers in the British Isles: A Directory of Antiquarian and Secondhand Book Dealers in the United Kingdom, the Channel Islands, the Isle of Man, and the Republic of Ireland*. London: Europa, 1952– . Annual. Z327.D57 070.5'025'41.

Sheppard's Book Dealers in North America: A Directory of Antiquarian and Secondhand Book Dealers in the U.S.A. and Canada. London: Europa, 1954– . Irregular. Z475.B63.

Geographical directories of bookstores and private dealers. A typical entry includes address, hours, a very general indication of size and nature of stock, specializations, and number of catalogs issued each year. Two indexes: names of persons and shops; subject specializations. Although the subject specialization headings are too broad, these are important guides to British or North American book dealers, especially the smaller shops and private dealers.

Biographical Dictionaries of Collectors

5370 Dickinson, Donald C. *Dictionary of American Book Collectors*. New York: Greenwood, 1986. 383 pp. Z989.A1.D53 002'.075'0922.

A biographical dictionary of 359 American book collectors who died before 31 December 1984 and whose collections were "distinguished by the quality, unity, . . . superior physical condition," and intrinsic importance of the books. An entry notes the disposition of the collection by auction or by sale or gift to an institution; provides basic biographical information; comments on the collector's major interests, the development and influence of the collection, and noteworthy items; and concludes with a selective bibliography of catalogs and studies of the collection as well as works by or about the collector. Two appendixes: a list of collectors by areas of specialization; a chronological list of important American book auctions from 1860 through 1984. Indexed by persons, titles, and subjects. As the most complete biographical dictionary of important American collectors, Dickinson is a valuable source for tracing the disposition of a collection and thus locating individual copies.

Carl L. Cannon, *American Book Collectors and Collecting from Colonial Times to the Present* (New York: Wilson, 1941, 391 pp.), treats additional collectors, but the topical organization and essay format make it difficult to locate information on minor collectors.

5375 Quaritch, Bernard, ed. *Contributions towards a Dictionary of English Book-Collectors: As Also of Some Foreign Collectors Whose Libraries Were Incorporated in English Collections or Whose Books Are Chiefly Met with in England*. 14 pts. London: Quaritch, 1892–1921. Z989.Q1 020'.75.

A collection of separately authored profiles of 78 collectors from the thirteenth through nineteenth centuries. The individual entries, which appear in no particular order, typically consist of two parts: (1) a biography of the collector and discussion of the nature, highlights, and dispersal of the collection; (2) a list of important manuscripts and printed works, a few of which record current owners. Many of the entries, which vary considerably in informativeness and length, were written by dealers involved in the formation of the collection or individuals acquainted with the collector. Part 12 is a preliminary list of several hundred collectors from 1316 to 1898. Quaritch remains the most comprehensive guide to English book collectors and is still valuable for tracing the provenance of important items. Additional collectors are treated in Seymour de Ricci, *English Collectors of Books and Manuscripts (1530–1930) and Their Marks of Ownership* (New York: Macmillan; Cambridge: Cambridge UP, 1930, 203 pp.). The time is ripe, however, for a dictionary of British book collectors similar to Dickinson, *Dictionary of American Book Collectors* (5370).

See also

Lehmann-Haupt, *Book in America* (5260a).
Tanselle, "The Literature of Book Collecting" (5355) lists additional directories (pp. 266–67).

Periodicals

5380 *American Book Collector* (*ABC*). 1950– . Monthly. Former titles: *The Amateur Book Collector* (1950–55); *Book Collector's Market* (1976–79). Z990.A52 002'.075'05.

Publishes articles on book collecting (emphasizing modern first editions and private press books), bibliographies of authors and presses (primarily of the twentieth century), reports on exhibitions and book fairs, notes on auctions, lists of new dealers' catalogs (with brief notes on content), and reviews of books (especially author bibliographies). Cumulative indexes: vols. 1–5 (Chicago: n.p., 1955, n.pag.); vols. 6–10, Joan Willer, 11.1 (1960), 8 pp.; vols. 11–15, Willer (1965, 8 pp.); vols. 16–20, by Barbara Kirk (1970, 8 pp.); vols. 21–25 (1975, 7 pp.). While not as scholarly as *Book Collector* (5390), *American Book Collector* is more current in its coverage of the book collecting world and a good source for information on current dealers' catalogs.

5385 *Antiquarian Book Monthly Review*. 1974– . Monthly. Z990.A57 002'.075.

Publishes articles on authors, collectors, members of the trade, and subject collections (all with an emphasis on English-language books of the past two centuries); book reviews; and reports on auctions and new catalogs (with a list of the latter). Like *American Book Collector* (5380), *Antiquarian Book Monthly Review* is less scholarly and international in scope than *Book Collector* (5390), but it does offer good current coverage of the book collecting world and dealers' catalogs.

5390 *The Book Collector* (*BC*). 1952– . Quarterly. Z990.B6 020'.75.

A continuation of *Book Handbook* (1947–52), *Book Collector* publishes articles, notes, queries, reviews, review essays, and occasional special issues on book collecting, bibliography, and bookbinding. Each issue prints a lengthy "News and Comments" section, with reports on major auctions, important dealers' catalogs, and exhibitions, as well as news of prominent collectors and dealers. The most scholarly of the book collecting periodicals. Annual index; cumulative index: vols. 1–10, Enid D. Nixon, comp., The Book Collector*: Index, 1952–1961, Volume I, no. 1 to Volume X, No. 4* (n.d., 59 pp.).

See also

Sec. U: Literature-Related Topics and Sources/Bibliography and Textual Criticism/Periodicals.

Booksellers' and Auction Catalogs

Booksellers' and auction catalogs are among the most underutilized scholarly resources. Although they are frequently difficult to locate (even in libraries that hold major collections) and (in the case of booksellers' catalogs) are rarely indexed, these catalogs are valuable for identifying hitherto unrecorded printed works, editions, or manuscripts; finding descriptions (and sometimes reproductions or transcriptions) of unique items no longer locatable; tracing the provenance of a copy (and thus possibly locating it); and reconstructing an individual's library.

For a discussion of the importance of auction catalogs and the pitfalls involved in using them, see Michael Hunter, "Auction Catalogues and Eminent Libraries," *Book Collector* 21 (1972): 471–88. On the use of catalogs and other resources for tracing provenance, see Robert Nikirk, "Looking into Provenance," *A Miscellany for Bibliophiles*, ed. H. George Fletcher (New York: Grastorf, 1979) 15–45. Of major value would be a series of indexes to manuscript material and association copies in catalogs issued by at least the major booksellers.

HISTORIES AND SURVEYS

5395 Taylor, Archer. *Book Catalogues: Their Varieties and Uses*. 2nd ed. Rev. by Wm. P. Barlow, Jr. New York: Beil, 1987. 284 pp. Z1001.T34 011'.3.

An examination of the types, history, and uses of catalogs of booksellers, auction houses, private collections, institutions, and publishers. Taylor emphasizes catalogs published before 1900 of printed books, and for the most part excludes unpublished catalogs and those of manuscripts. The revised edition reprints the first edition (Chicago: Newberry Library, 1957, 284 pp.), with a prefatory list of corrections and additions that unfortunately does not incorporate scholarship since the mid-1950s. The first chapter describes the kinds of catalogs—especially their varieties and historical development—and surveys bibliographies based on them; the second details the uses of catalogs in scholarly research; the third surveys bibliographies of catalogs, emphasizing their uses and historical development; the last chapter prints an annotated list of important private library catalogs published before 1824. Four indexes: dealers, institutions, owners, and publishers; kinds of books and subjects listed in catalogs; subjects treated in catalogs and compilations based on them; compilers, editors, collectors, and bibliographers of catalogs. Although now dated, Taylor remains important as a general history of early catalogs, an account of individual ones, and a guide to their uses in research.

GUIDES TO PRIMARY WORKS

Bibliographies

5400 McKay, George L., comp. *American Book Auction Catalogues, 1713–1934: A Union List*. Rpt. with supplements. Detroit: Gale, 1967. 560 pp. Z999.M15 018.3.

A chronological list of about 10,000 book auction catalogs (including some miscellaneous catalogs having more than five pages of books) issued in the United States from 1713 through 1934. Organized chronologically by opening date of sale, entries cite (when known) date, owner(s), auction firm, number of pages and/or lots, and locations of copies (noting priced or marked ones) or source of information for those unlocated. Many entries for eighteenth-century catalogs are based on newspaper advertisements or other sources, and a sizable number probably are for manuscript inventories. A separate grouping of auctions listed in newspaper advertisements that do not specify issuance of a catalog appears on pp. 461–91; additions and corrections to the main list are printed on pp. 493–95; the two supplements from *Bulletin of the New York Public Library* (50 [1946]: 177–84; 52 [1948]: 401–12) are reprinted after the index. An introduction, by Clarence S. Bingham, is entitled "History of Book Auctions in America" (pp. 1–37). Indexed by owners. Despite flaws—the work is incomplete, records a limited number of locations, and offers no indication of contents—it does provide the fullest list of United States auction catalogs from 1801 through 1934. Earlier catalogs are more thoroughly and accurately described by Winans, *Descriptive Checklist of Book Catalogues Separately Printed in America* (5410).

5405 Munby, A. N. L., and Lenore Coral, comps. and eds. *British Book Sale Catalogues, 1676–1800: A Union List*. London: Mansell, 1977. 146 pp. Z999.5.M86 011.

A union list of extant auction catalogs and some retail lists with prices fixed by a dealer. Munby excludes catalogs of sales open to only members of the book trade. Catalogs are listed chronologically by date of commencement of the sale; those not datable by at least the month are grouped alphabetically by consignor or title at the end of a year. A typical entry provides consignor, short title, details of the conduct of the sale if not an auction, auctioneer or bookseller, location of the sale, locations of copies (including some shelf numbers) in about ninety public and private collections in the United States and Great Britain, references to other bibliographies, and information about reprints. Two indexes: consignors; auctioneers and booksellers. The most thorough list of extant auction catalogs of the period, Munby is invaluable for identifying a catalog of the library of an individual and for locating copies (which are not only scarce but also difficult to identify in most library catalogs). Review: R. J. Roberts, *Library* 5th ser. 33 (1978): 336–38 (with additions and corrections).

Until the volume for 1801–1900 of *British Book Sale Catalogues* appears, *List of Catalogues of English Book Sales, 1676–1900, Now in the British Museum* (London: British Museum, 1915, 523 pp.) offers the most complete list of nineteenth-century auction catalogs. Because cataloging practices make these publications difficult to identify in the *British Library General Catalogue of Printed Books* (250), *List of Catalogues* remains an important source of shelf numbers for the extensive collection, which includes several auctioneers' priced sets. Also, Coral will answer queries about the existence and location of nineteenth-century British catalogs (Music Library, 225 Lincoln Hall, Cornell U Libraries, Cornell U, Ithaca, NY 14853).

Sale catalogs of the libraries of several British writers are reproduced in *Sale Catalogues of Libraries of Eminent Persons*, gen. ed. A. N. L. Munby, 12 vols. (London: Mansell, 1971–75).

5410 Winans, Robert B. *A Descriptive Checklist of Book Catalogues Separately Printed in America, 1693–1800*. Worcester: American Antiquarian Soc., 1981. 207 pp. Z1029.W56 018.

A chronological list of 689 separately published booksellers', publishers', auction, and circulating, private, social, and college library catalogs. (Lists of manuscript catalogs and ones printed in periodicals, newspapers, and books are in progress.) The catalogs are listed by year of publication, then alphabetically by author, auctioneer, bookseller, or title of anonymous work. The 278 located catalogs have full entries that include author; title; publication information; collation; pagination; list of contents; notes on the type of catalog, number and kind of entries, organization, and other matters, including the presence of prices and the basis for dating undated publications; references to other bibliographies and scholarship; reprints; and locations of copies (primarily in East Coast libraries). Entries for unlocated items are, of course, much briefer, and cite references in other sources; entries for what are probably manuscript inventories listed in McKay, *American Book Auction Catalogues* (5400), merely cite McKay. Thoroughly indexed by authors, owners, printers, cities, and subjects. Complemented by Winans, "The Beginnings of Systematic Bibliography in America up to 1800: Further Explorations," *Papers of the Bibliographical Society of America* 72 (1978): 15–35. Admirably thorough and accurate in its bibliographical descriptions but insufficiently informative in notes on contents, Winans supersedes McKay, *American Book Auction Catalogues* for auction catalogs before 1801 and is an invaluable source for identifying and locating catalogs essential in bibliographical research, book trade history, and cultural studies. Review: Stephen Botein, *Papers of the Bibliographical Society of America* 76 (1982): 223–26.

See also

American Book Collector (5380).
Antiquarian Book Monthly Review (5385).
Taylor, *Book Catalogues* (5395).

Indexes

5415 *American Book Prices Current [1894–]* (*ABPC*). Washington: Bancroft-Parkman, 1895– . Annual. Z1000.A51 018'.3.

A list of books and manuscripts sold in the principal European and North American auction houses. Until vol. 64 (1958), *ABPC* covers only auctions in the United States; after vol. 73 (1971), it gradually becomes more international, but is still selective in reporting Dutch and German sales. Recent volumes exclude items which bring less than $50 (those from vols. 76–85 [1970–79], less than $20; and earlier volumes, less than $10), works in non-Western languages that sell for less than $100, books in lots, and incomplete sets and runs of periodicals. Entries are currently organized in two parts: autographs and manuscripts (including original illustrations for books, documents, letters, corrected proofs, and signed photographs) and books (including single sheets, broadsides, and uncorrected proofs). Works are listed alphabetically by author, title of anonymous work, or (when it is the main interest) private press, publisher, or printer. Entries record title, place and date of publication, edition, size, binding, condition, important features (such as provenance, bibliographical points, inscriptions, or marginalia), auction house, date of sale and lot number, price, and (since vol. 66 [1960]) purchaser (when reported on a price list). The publisher claims that entries for books have been independently verified, but the nature of this verification is not made clear. The fastest access to entries is through the cumulative indexes: 1916–22, comp. Philip Sanford Goulding and Helen Plummer Goulding (1925, 1,397 pp.); 1923–32, comp. Eugenia Wallace and Lucie E. Wallace (1936, 1,007 pp.); 1933–40, comp. and ed. Edward Lazare (1941, 765 pp.); 1941–45, comp. and ed. Colton Storm (1946, 1,126 pp.); 1945–50, comp. and ed. Lazare (1951, 1,404 pp.); 1950–55, ed. Lazare (1956,

1,709 pp.); 1955–60, ed. Lazare (1961, 1,533 pp.); 1960–65, ed. Lazare (1968, 2,085 pp.); 1965–70, 2 pts. (1974, 2,545 pp.); 1970–75, 2 pts. (1976, 2,061 pp.); 1975–79, 2 pts. (1980, 2,325 pp.).

Although *ABPC* is more scholarly, current, comprehensive, and trustworthy than *Book Auction Records* (5420), the two are ultimately complementary works and invaluable as indexes to auction catalogs and as aids for identifying and tracing unique items (especially manuscripts and association copies). Those using *ABPC* or *Book Auction Records* to evaluate books must remember that prices now reflect buyers' premiums (denominated for each auction house in the explanatory notes to individual volumes of *ABPC*) and fluctuating exchange rates, and depend on condition and other factors.

Some additional British and American sales (with coverage of the latter beginning in vol. 30 [1916]) are indexed in *Book-Prices Current: A Record of the Prices at Which Books Have Been Sold at Auction, from [December, 1886 to August, 1956]*, 64 vols. (London: Witherby, 1888–1957, with cumulative indexes for vols. 1–10, 11–20, and 21–30). Beginning in vol. 35 (1921), *Book-Prices Current* includes some manuscripts. The early volumes are organized by auction house, then sale, with entries providing minimal information. Later volumes consist of a single alphabetical list, with entries citing author, title, publisher, condition, important features, auction house, date of sale, lot number, price, and sometimes buyer. If more than one copy was sold during the season, those copies with noteworthy features have full entries; for others, only auction house, date, and price are recorded. Because so many copies receive truncated entries, *American Book Prices Current* and *Book Auction Records* are superior indexes to sales covered in common.

5420 *Book Auction Records: A Priced and Annotated Annual Record of International Book Auctions [1902–]* (*BAR*). Folkestone: Dawson, 1903– . Annual. Z1000.B65 017.3.

An index to books, other printed materials, and some manuscripts sold at auction, originally in London, then Great Britain, the United States (vols. 12–18 [1915–21], 37 [1940]–), and, since vol. 64 (1968), other countries. Only items selling for more than £50, $100, or the equivalent in foreign currencies are currently included. Since vol. 77 (1981), entries are listed alphabetically by author, title of anonymous work, press, or subject heading in two parts: printed books and atlases; printed maps, charts, and plans. Previous volumes list printed material in a single alphabetical list, with the earliest ones organized by sale; those from vol. 43 (1945–46) through vol. 50 (1952–53) place important early manuscripts in a separate section. A typical entry records author, title, date of publication, press, important features such as provenance or binding, auction house, date of sale, lot number, price, and (sometimes) buyer. Early volumes provide significantly less information. The most convenient access is through the cumulative indexes: vols. 1–9, William Jaggard (1924, 1,142 pp.); vols. 10–20, ed. Kathleen L. Stevens (1928, 1,467 pp.); vols. 21–30, ed. Stevens (1935, 1,314 pp.); vols. 31–40, ed. Henry Stevens and Henry R. Peter Stevens (1948, 1,022 pp.); vols. 41–45, ed. Patricia B. Sargent (1951, 955 pp.); vols. 46–55, ed. Henry Stevens and J. G. Garratt (1962, 1,536 pp.); vols. 56–60, ed. Virginia Clarke and Garratt (1966, 1,146 pp.); vols. 61–65 (1971, 1,739 pp.); vols. 66–69, ed. D. Batho (1977, 1,129 pp.); vols. 77–81, ed. Dorothy C. Batho (1985, 1,008 pp.); no index is planned for vols. 70–76.

Although *BAR* is less accurate and current than *American Book Prices Current* (5415), the two must be used together, since *Book Auction Records* covers more European and provincial English sales.

5425 *Bookman's Price Index: A Guide to the Values of Rare and Other Out-of-Print Books* (*BPI*). Ed. Daniel F. McGrath. Detroit: Gale, 1964– . 2/yr. Z1000.B74 018'.4.

Bookman's Price Index: Subject Series. Ed. McGrath. 1987– . Z1000.B743 018'.4.

A list of selected rare and antiquarian books offered for sale in recent catalogs of a small group of established dealers, almost exclusively in Great Britain and the United States. Each volume selectively indexes the catalogs of 40 to 180 dealers, which change over the course of the volumes. The *Subject Series* combines new entries with those from earlier volumes of *BPI*, e.g., *Modern First Editions* (vol. 1 of the *Subject Series*) draws from the 1984–86 volumes of *BPI*. Books are listed alphabetically by author or title of anonymous work, with editions following in chronological order. Each entry provides author, title, place and date of publication, a brief description of the copy offered (noting, for example, provenance, binding, condition, and important bibliographical points), dealer's name, catalog and item number, and selling price. Since vol. 32 (1986), there are separate lists of association copies, bindings, and fore-edge paintings. A directory of dealers prefaces each volume. *BPI* covers only a small number of the thousands of dealers (and omits many of the more important ones), lacks any statement of principles governing the selection of dealers or books listed, and is full of misprints; still, it is the only index of frequently valuable but ephemeral sources of information and is an essential source for tracking down inscribed or annotated copies, books owned by authors or important collectors, and other unique items. Researchers using *BPI* as a source for evaluating the worth of a book must remember that the retail prices quoted vary widely among dealers and are based on a variety of factors such as condition, provenance, and edition. Reviews: (vol. 1) Walter Goldwater, *Papers of the Bibliographical Society of America* 60 (1966): 110–14; (vols. 1–12) Paul S. Koda, *Analytical and Enumerative Bibliography* 2 (1978): 76–80.

Michael Cole, *International Rare Book Prices* (London: Butterworth; New York: Bowker, 1987– , annual) indexes selected catalogs in five volumes: modern first editions since 1900; science and medicine; arts and architecture; voyages, travels, and exploration; and printed books before 1800.

See also

Cripe, *American Manuscripts, 1763–1815: An Index to Documents Described in Auction Records and Dealers' Catalogues* (3235).

Tanselle, "The Literature of Book Collecting" (5355) lists additional indexes and price guides (pp. 259–64).

Children's Literature

Guides to Reference Works

5440 Haviland, Virginia. *Children's Literature: A Guide to Reference Sources*. Washington: Library of Congress, 1966. 341 pp. Haviland and Margaret N. Coughlan. *First Supplement*. 1972. 316 pp. *Second Supplement*. 1977. 413 pp. Z1037.A1.H35 016.8098'928'2.

A guide to reference works and general studies (including dissertations) through 1974 that are important to the study of children's literature. Although the work is international in scope, Haviland emphasizes British and North American literature. Entries are listed alphabetically by author, editor, or title in eight classified divisions: history and criticism, authorship (including sections on writing for children, individual authors, and biographical dictionaries), illustration (including studies of illustrators), bibliographies, books and children (including storytelling, folklore, nursery rhymes, poetry, and magazines; a section on pedagogy was added in the first supplement), libraries and children's books, international studies, and national studies (with sections on Western Europe, Eastern Europe, Latin America, South Africa, and Asia; ones for the Near East and Africa were added in the first supplement, and for French Canada in the second supplement). Concludes with a directory of associations and agencies. The full annotations are largely descriptive, although some offer evaluative comments. Indexed by persons and some titles. Haviland is now dated but remains the best guide to reference works and international scholarship through 1974. For recent publications, see Rahn, *Children's Literature* (5485), Hendrickson, *Children's Literature* (5480), and the serial bibliographies and indexes in section G.

See also

Beugnot, *Manuel bibliographique des études littéraires* (4905).
Gohdes, *Bibliographical Guide to the Study of the Literature of the U.S.A.* (3180).

Histories and Surveys

5445 Darton, F. J. Harvey. *Children's Books in England: Five Centuries of Social Life.* 3rd ed. Rev. Brian Alderson. Cambridge: Cambridge UP, 1982. 398 pp. PR990.D3 011'.62.

A social history of literature written to entertain children. Ranging from the Middle Ages to c. 1901, the chapters on periods, major types of children's literature, topics, publishers, and authors emphasize social, historical, literary, and commercial contexts. Each chapter concludes with an annotated list for further reading. While retaining Darton's text as much as possible, the third edition makes numerous factual corrections and provides fuller documentation, additional illustrations, and supplementary appendixes, including one devoted to late nineteenth-century works. Concludes with a selected, annotated bibliography. Fully indexed by persons, subjects, and titles. The classic history of children's literature in England before 1900, this is especially strong in its treatment of the eighteenth century. Review: Julia Briggs, *TLS: Times Literary Supplement* 26 Mar. 1982: 341–42.

See also

Literary History of Canada (4565).
Tebbel, *History of Book Publishing in the United States* (5260).

Literary Handbooks, Dictionaries, and Encyclopedias

5450 Carpenter, Humphrey, and Mari Prichard. *The Oxford Companion to Children's Literature.* Oxford: Oxford UP, 1984. 587 pp. PN1008.5.C37 809'.89282.

A dictionary of British and North American children's literature, as well as foreign works important to the English-language tradition, through May 1983 (although coverage is less thorough for post-1945 publications and persons). The approximately 2,000 entries encompass works, authors, genres, critics, scholars, publishers, illustrators, organizations, characters, magazines, awards, fairy tales, folklore, and children's literature in various foreign languages and countries. Entries for persons combine biographical and career information with critical commentary; those for works, plot summary and publication history with a critical estimate. Although entries are sometimes uneven, inaccurate, or conservative in their criticism, and although there are notable omissions (especially for North American writers and works), Carpenter is the best desktop companion for the study of children's literature in English. Reviews: Brian Alderson, *Library* 6th ser. 8 (1986): 187–89; Hugh Brogan, *TLS: Times Literary Supplement* 4 May 1984: 505–06; Irving P. Cummings, *Children's Literature* 14 (1986): 187–93.

Annals

5455 Bingham, Jane, and Grayce Scholt. *Fifteen Centuries of Children's Literature: An Annotated Chronology of British and American Works in Historical Context.* Westport: Greenwood, 1980. 540 pp. Z1037.A1.B582 [PN1009.A1] 028.52.

An annotated chronology of important or representative books written for or appropriated by children in Great Britain and the United States from 523 to 1945. The entries are organized in six periods, each of which is prefaced by a superficial and frequently inaccurate discussion of historical background, the development of books, and attitudes toward and treatment of children. English-language books are listed by date of publication; a foreign work is listed by the year it was introduced into Great Britain or the United States; works by a prolific or popular author are grouped under the year of his or her first important or popular publication (a practice that results in some lengthy, incomplete, and generally useless lists). A typical entry includes author, illustrator, translator, or editor; title; publisher or printer; annotation (with a brief description of content and list of other books by the person); and locations of copies in a limited number of collections. Three appendixes: a chronological list of American periodicals for children, 1789–1941; a chronological list of British periodicals for children, 1757–1941; an incomplete list of facsimiles and reprints of works cited in the chronology (which should have been incorporated into the individual entries). A selective bibliography of scholarship concludes the work. Two indexes: persons; titles. Marred by the uncritical inclusion of numerous works that hardly qualify as children's literature, uneven annotations, incomplete publication information for several works, numerous factual errors, and the unfortunate practice of grouping works by an author under one year, *Fifteen Centuries of Children's Literature* is useful for isolating only very broad trends (especially after 1800). Scholars still need an adequate chronology of children's literature. Reviews: Brian Alderson, *Phaedrus* 8 (1981): 87–88; Irving P. Cummings, *Children's Literature* 14 (1986): 187–93.

Bibliographies of Bibliographies

See

Nilon, *Bibliography of Bibliographies in American Literature* (3225).

Guides to Primary Works

GUIDES TO COLLECTIONS

5460 Field, Carolyn W., ed. *Special Collections in Children's Literature*. Chicago: American Library Assn., 1982. 257 pp. Z688.C47.S63 026.0285'0973.

A subject guide to collections of children's literature in various media held by public institutions in the United States and Canada. Field excludes private collections as well as general ones in academic libraries. Under subject headings, collections are listed alphabetically by state, then institution. A typical entry includes name of institution; a brief description of size, general content, and scope of holdings; and an indication of whether the collection is cataloged. Since entries are based on responses to questionnaires and published sources, descriptions vary in accuracy and fullness. Concludes with a directory of institutions and two appendixes: a list of publications on collections; authors and illustrators in major collections but not cited in the subject list. Although the descriptions tend to be too brief, Field offers the fullest guide to specialized collections of children's literature in North America. To identify other collections, see section E: Libraries and Library Catalogs/Library Catalogs/Guides to Collections.

MANUSCRIPTS

5465 Fraser, James H., comp. *Children's Authors and Illustrators: A Guide to Manuscript Collections in United States Research Libraries*. Phaedrus Bibliographic Series 1. New York: Saur, 1980. 119 pp. Z6611.L76.F73 [PN1009.A1] 028.52.

A guide to collections of manuscripts and original illustrations held in United States libraries and other institutions. Organized alphabetically by author or artist, the descriptions typically indicate the general kind and amount of manuscript material and describe the content of a collection. (Additions appear on p. 83.) There is a separate list of authors represented in the Kerlan Collection, University of Minnesota. Since they are based on reports from institutions, published descriptions, or entries in *National Union Catalog of Manuscript Collections* (295), the entries vary considerably in detail and sophistication. (To understand the descriptions, users must become familiar with the explanation of terminology on p. x.) Concludes with a directory of institutions. Indexed by titles. Although Fraser is incomplete, cites collections of adult material for some writers, is based almost solely on reports or secondary sources, and emphasizes American writers, it at least offers an initial guide to the location of manuscripts and illustrations by children's authors. It must be supplemented with *National Union Catalog of Manuscript Collections* and other works listed under the heading "Manuscripts" in the various sections of this *Guide*.

For the Kerlan Collection, see Karen Nelson Hoyle, comp., *The Kerlan Collection: Manuscripts and Illustrations for Children's Books: A Checklist* (Minneapolis: Kerlan Collection, U of Minnesota Libraries, 1985, 432 pp.).

See also

Sec. F: Guides to Manuscripts and Archives.

PRINTED WORKS

5470 *Children's Books in Print*. New York: Bowker, 1969- . Annual. Z1037.A1.C482 028.52.

Author, title, illustrator, and subject indexes to currently available children's books published or distributed in the United States. *Children's Books in Print* excludes textbooks, toybooks, and workbooks, but otherwise leaves the definition of "children's book" to the publishers who supply information. The author, illustrator, and title indexes—along with a directory of publishers and distributors—occupy one volume; the other volume is devoted to the subject guide. Entries typically cite author, editor, illustrator, translator, title, number of volumes, language (when other than English), LC card number, grade range, year of publication, price, ISBN, and publisher or distributor. Since entries are based on information supplied by publishers, some are incomplete or inaccurate, and names and titles are not standardized. The subject index, while utilizing some broad or inexact headings, is useful for identifying works about a topic. Although not exhaustive, this work is the standard guide to children's books currently for sale in the United States. Most entries for imaginative works through 1985 are incorporated into *Fiction, Folklore, Fantasy, and Poetry* (5475).

5475 *Fiction, Folklore, Fantasy, and Poetry for Children, 1876–1985*. 2 vols. New York: Bowker, 1986. Z1037.A2.F53 [PN1009.A1] 016.80806'8.

Author, title, and illustrator lists of editions and reprints of imaginative books for children published or distributed in the United States between 1876 and 1985. Incorporates records in the *American Book Publishing Record* (4110) and *Children's Books in Print* (5470) data bases—as well as from other sources—with selection largely determined by Library of Congress classifications and subject tracings. The author and title indexes provide full entries which, when the information is available, cite author, editor, illustrator, title, series, pagination, size, publication date, grade level, edition, LC card number, ISBN, publisher, and selected list of awards. Details vary with changes in Library of Congress cataloging rules and are frequently incomplete for early works. Entries in the illustrator index cite title, author, publisher, date, and selected awards. A separate list of winners of twenty children's books awards is also included. Although incomplete in its coverage and sometimes inaccurate (and subject to many of the same shortcomings as the cumulative *American Book Publishing Record*), *Fiction, Folklore, Fantasy, and Poetry* is the fullest single list of imaginative works for children published in the United States between 1876 and 1985.

Although limited to the "best" books (as determined by panels of librarians), the following are useful for their descriptive annotations and subject indexing of books for children as well as about children's literature, all but a few of which are in print:

Children's Catalog. 15th ed. Ed. Richard H. Isaacson, Ferne E. Hillegas, and Juliette Yaakov. Standard Catalog Series. New York: Wilson, 1986. 1,298 pp. (Annual supplements between editions.)

Junior High School Library Catalog. 5th ed. Ed. Isaacson. Standard Catalog Series. New York: Wilson, 1985. 835 pp. (Annual supplements between editions.)

Senior High School Library Catalog. 12th ed. Ed. Gary L. Bogart and Isaacson. Standard Catalog Series. New York: Wilson, 1982. 1,299 pp. (Annual supplements between editions.)

Each work organizes nonfiction by Dewey Decimal Classification, followed by an author list of fiction, and then short story collections. An entry is accompanied by a description of contents or quotations from reviews. Earlier editions remain useful for their subject access to works subsequently dropped.

See also

Cheung, *Asian American Literature* (3940).
New Cambridge Bibliography of English Literature, vols. 2–4 (1385).

Guides to Scholarship and Criticism

SERIAL BIBLIOGRAPHIES

See

Secs. G: Serial Bibliographies, Indexes, and Abstracts and H: Guides to Dissertations and Theses.
ABELL (340): English Literature/General/Literature for Children in volumes since that for 1975.
Annual Bibliography of Victorian Studies (2490).
Bibliographie der Buch- und Bibliotheksgeschichte (5280).
MLAIB (335): General IV/Children's Literature in the volumes for 1976–80. In later volumes, researchers must consult the "Children—as Audience" heading in the subject index.

OTHER BIBLIOGRAPHIES

5480 Hendrickson, Linnea. *Children's Literature: A Guide to the Criticism*. Reference Publication in Literature. Boston: Hall, 1987. 664 pp. Z2014.5.H46 [PR990] 011'.62.

An annotated bibliography of significant English-language books, articles, and dissertations (through the mid-1980s) on imaginative works written for or read by children. Although the work is international in scope and covers some classics published before 1900, Hendrickson emphasizes twentieth-century works in English. The entries are organized alphabetically in two divisions: individual authors (with highly selective lists for those who are not principally children's authors), and subjects, themes, genres, and national literatures (along with a substantial section on critical theory). The brief descriptive annotations frequently do not offer clear outlines of content. Two indexes: critics; authors, subjects, and titles of children's books. Hendrickson is wider in scope, fuller in coverage (especially of twentieth-century literature), and more current than Rahn, *Children's Literature* (5485). However, the principles governing the selection of both primary authors and scholarship are unclear; subject headings and the classification of entries are frequently imprecise; and there are numerous significant omissions. Hendrickson and Rahn should be used together (especially because of the latter's superior annotations and coverage of older scholarship).

Although dated, Anne Pellowski, *The World of Children's Literature* (New York: Bowker, 1968, 538 pp.) remains a useful complement to Hendrickson and Rahn, *Children's Literature* because of its annotations of foreign scholarship.

5485 Rahn, Suzanne. *Children's Literature: An Annotated Bibliography of the History and Criticism*. Garland Reference Library of the Humanities 263. New York: Garland, 1981. 451 pp. Z1037.R15 [PR990] 011'.62.

A selective bibliography of important English-language scholarship published through c. 1979 on imaginative works written expressly for children. Rahn excludes dissertations and theses, as well as studies of educational works and adult literature appropriated by children. The 1,328 entries are organized alphabetically in four divisions: discussions of the definition and aims of children's literature, historical studies and annotated catalogs of collections (inadequately organized in sections for general histories and specialized ones), genres (extensively classified by type and including magazines), and important authors (with sections for individuals and for multiple-author studies and collections of essays). An appendix describes important scholarly journals. The full descriptive annotations usually include comments on the quality or importance of a work. Indexed by persons. The cross-references that conclude each section do not compensate for the lack of subject indexing and the imprecise classification system. Although selective and insufficiently precise and detailed in its classification of entries, Rahn is nevertheless valuable for its judicious annotations. It must be supplemented by Haviland, *Children's Literature* (5440), Hendrickson, *Children's Literature* (5480), and the serial bibliographies and indexes in section G. Review: Selma K. Richardson, *Children's Literature Association Quarterly* 9 (1984): 44–45.

See also

Boos, *Bibliography of Women and Literature* (6600).
Haviland, *Children's Literature* (5440).
Inge, *Handbook of American Popular Culture* (6295).
Lindfors, *Black African Literature in English* (4425).
New Cambridge Bibliography of English Literature, vols. 2–4 (1385).

ABSTRACTS

5490 *Children's Literature Abstracts*. Llanbrynmair: Children's Libraries Section, International Federation of Library Assns., 1973- . Quarterly, with two supplements. Z1037.C5446 [PN1009.A1] 028.52.

An abstract service for scholarship on children's literature. The international coverage extends to a wide range of journals and a few newspapers (mostly British); beginning in late 1984, books and pamphlets are abstracted in two supplements each year. Entries are currently organized in classified divisions for children's books and reading responses; audiovisual materials; handicapped children; history of children's books; children's fiction; adolescent fiction; nonfiction; poetry; drama; psychological, educational, and social criteria; illustration; book selection and reading guidance; awards and prizes; major exhibitions; organizations and societies; publishing; translation; authors; and illustrators. The English-language abstracts, prepared by a team of international contributors, tend to be brief but adequately descriptive. Cumulative author and subject indexes are issued irregularly. Although it is not comprehensive—especially in its coverage of books—currency and international scope make this work an important source for identifying studies of children's literature. It should be used with the surveys in *Phaedrus* (5535), which are less current but sometimes more comprehensive for individual countries.

REVIEW INDEXES

5495 *Children's Book Review Index*. Detroit: Gale, 1975- . Annual, with cumulation for 1965-84. Z1037.A1.C475 028.52.

An author or editor list of reviews of children's books that is cloned from *Book Review Index* (415), which offers more current information on recent titles. Although it is restricted in its coverage of periodicals and does not distinguish between substantive reviews and brief descriptive notices, *Children's Book Review Index* does index the important serials that regularly review books for children.

Biographical Dictionaries

INDEXES

5500 *Children's Authors and Illustrators: An Index to Biographical Dictionaries*. Ed. Joyce Nakamura. 4th ed. Gale Biographical Index Series 2. Detroit: Gale, 1987. 799 pp. Z1037.A1.N18 016.809.

An index to some 145,000 biographies of about 25,000 writers and illustrators of English-language children's books (including translations) in approximately 450 standard biographical dictionaries, including several not confined to children's literature. Each entrant is followed by a coded list of dictionaries that include entries about him or her. Cloned from *Biography and Genealogy Master Index* (565) and suffering from many of the same editorial shortcomings, *Children's Authors and Illustrators* provides some additional entries and attempts to standardize variant forms of names, differentiate those of the same name, and cross-reference pseudonyms (but without eliminating duplicate entries). Although lacking an explanation of the criteria governing the selection of works indexed and not discriminating between substantial biographical discussions and brief entries, this work is a time-saving source for determining what dictionaries to consult for biographical information about children's authors and illustrators.

Complemented by *Writers for Young Adults: Biographies Master Index: An Index to Sources of Biographical Information about Novelists, Poets, Playwrights, Nonfiction Writers, Songwriters and Lyricists, Television and Screenwriters Who Are of Interest to High School Students and to Teachers, Librarians, and Researchers Interested in High School Reading Materials*, 2nd ed., ed. Adele Sarkissian, Gale Biographical Index Series 6 (Detroit: Gale, 1984, 354 pp.). It indexes some 15,000 entries from about 500 dictionaries but suffers from a lack of clear focus and criteria governing selection of entrants.

Entries in these two indexes that also appear in *Biography and Genealogy Master Index* can be searched through Dialog (520).

See also

Sec. J: Biographical Sources/Biographical Dictionaries/Indexes.

BIOGRAPHICAL DICTIONARIES

5505 *Twentieth-Century Children's Writers*. Ed. D. L. Kirkpatrick. 2nd ed. Great Writers of the English Language. New York: St. Martin's, 1983. 1,024 pp. PN1009.A1.T9 809'.89282.

A biographical, bibliographical, and critical dictionary of about 700 established twentieth-century writers and illustrators of English-language literature for children. A typical entry consists of three parts: biographical information, including address or agent; a list of separately published works (including those for adults); a signed critical essay. Some entries also note the location of manuscript collections and print a comment by the entrant. Important nineteenth-century writers are grouped in an appendix. Concludes with a very selective list of foreign authors whose works have been translated into English. Indexed by titles of books for children; entrants in this edition and earlier ones are indexed in *Children's Authors and Illustrators* (5500) and *Biography and Genealogy Master Index* (565). The brief critical commentaries vary considerably in quality, but *Twentieth-Century Children's Writers* is a useful source of basic biographical and bibliographical information about established children's authors. The *Dictionary of Literary Biography* (600) volumes on children's literature are superior sources of information for those writers and illustrators in common.

See also

Sec. J: Biographical Sources/Biographical Dictionaries/General Biographical Dictionaries.
Dictionary of Literary Biography (600).

Periodicals

GUIDES TO PRIMARY WORKS

5510 Kelly, R. Gordon, ed. *Children's Periodicals of the United States*. Historical Guides to the World's Periodicals and Newspapers. Westport: Greenwood, 1984. 591 pp. PN4878.C48 051'.088054.

A collection of separately authored profiles of about 100 representative American children's periodicals from 1789 to 1980. Entries, listed alphabetically by title, typically provide an overview of contents and publishing history; a selected list of scholarship, indexing sources, and locations; and a record of title changes, frequency, publisher(s), place(s) of publication, and editor(s). The preface surveys the state of general scholarship on children's periodicals. Three appendixes: title, chronological, and geographic lists of 423 American children's periodicals. Indexed by persons, titles, and subjects. While the work is flawed—it lacks an adequate statement of criteria governing selection, is admittedly weak in coverage of religious publications, excludes foreign-language periodicals, and is uneven in the quality of individual essays—it still offers some of the fullest discussions of children's periodicals published in the United States.

SCHOLARLY JOURNALS

For an evaluative survey of major British and North American scholarly journals, see Jim Silverman, "A Rack of Journals: Research in Children's Literature," *Children's Literature* 8 (1980): 193–204.

5515 *Children's Literature: Annual of the Modern Language Association Division on Children's Literature and the Children's Literature Association* (*ChildL*). 1972– . Annual. (Subtitle varies.) PN1009.A1.C514 809'.89282.

Publishes articles and reviews on children's literature, primarily British and American. Since vol. 4 (1975), *Children's Literature* prints an annotated list of selected North American dissertations. Cumulative indexes: vols. 1–5, comp. Constance Gremore, in 6 (1977): 272–94; vols. 6–10, comp. Lance Tatro, in 11 (1983): 221–33.

5520 *Children's Literature Association Quarterly* (*CLAQ*). 1976– . Quarterly. Former title: *Children's Literature Association Newsletter* (1976–79). PN1008.2.C48 809'.89282.

Publishes articles on children's literature and related topics, reviews, and an extensive news section. Recent issues focus on a specific topic. Cumulative index: vols. 8–12, in 12 (1987): 201–06.

5525 *Children's Literature in Education: An International Quarterly*. 1970– . Quarterly. Z1037.A1.C5 028.52.

Publishes articles on literature for children and young adults. Recent volumes emphasize scholarship and criticism rather than pedagogy. Annual index.

5530 *The Lion and the Unicorn: A Critical Journal of Children's Literature* (*L&U*). 1977– . 2/yr. PN1009.A1.L54 809'.89282.

Publishes articles, interviews, and occasional reviews on children's literature worldwide. Each issue focuses on a theme or genre.

5535 *Phaedrus: An International Annual of Children's Literature Research* (*Phaedrus*). 1973– . Annual. Z1037.A1.P5 [PN1009] 028.52.

Publishes only solicited essays (with recent volumes focusing on a topic) and surveys of research. The surveys (organized by countries, which vary from year to year) range from mere checklists to combinations of full reviews and annotated lists of books, articles, theses, and dissertations. The surveys vary considerably in completeness and organization. Of the periodicals devoted to children's literature, *Phaedrus* is the most international in scope and rigorous in its reviews.

Genres

POETRY

Guides to Primary Works

5540 *Index to Children's Poetry: A Title, Subject, Author, and First Line Index to Poetry in Collections for Children and Youth.* Comp. John E. Brewton and Sara W. Brewton. New York: Wilson, 1942. 965 pp. *First Supplement.* 1957. 405 pp. *Second Supplement.* 1965. 451 pp. *Index to Poetry for Children and Young People, 1964–1969.* Comp. Brewton, Brewton, and G. Meredith Blackburn III. 1972. 574 pp. *1970–1975.* Comp. John E. Brewton, Blackburn, and Lorraine A. Blackburn. 1978. 472 pp. *1976–1981.* 1984. 317 pp. PN1023.B7 821.0016.

An author, title, subject, and first-line index to English-language poems and translations for readers through grade 12 and printed in single-author collections and anthologies published from the early twentieth century through 1981. Selection is by vote of a committee of consulting librarians and teachers. The title entries cite author or translator, variant titles, and first line when needed to differentiate poems with the same title; other entries are more abbreviated; all refer by code to a prefatory list of collections indexed. Although limited in scope, the *Index* is a convenient source for identifying children's poems on a subject and locating texts.

Subject access to some additional poems is offered by *Subject Index to Poetry for Children and Young People*, comp. Violet Sell et al. (Chicago: American Library Assn., 1957, 582 pp.); supplement, *1957–1975*, comp. Dorothy B. Frizzell Smith and Eva L. Andrews (1977, 1,035 pp.).

Composition and Rhetoric

This section is limited to works that emphasize composition at the postsecondary level and to reference sources in historical rhetoric of value in composition research or literary criticism.

Guides to Reference Works

5555 Scott, Patrick, and Bruce Castner. "Reference Sources for Composition Research: A Practical Survey." *College English* 45 (1983): 756–68.

An annotated, evaluative survey of reference sources essential to research in historical rhetoric and composition. The full annotations are interspersed with useful hints on research procedures. Until someone produces the much-needed detailed guide to research methods and reference sources in composition, Scott is the best introduction.

In describing the obstacles hindering bibliographic control of composition research and the need for systematic coverage, Scott, "Bibliographical Problems in Research on Composition," *College Composition and Communication* 37 (1986): 167–77, provides valuable, if implicit, guidance on techniques for identifying scholarship.

Handbooks, Dictionaries, and Encyclopedias

5560 Lanham, Richard A. *A Handlist of Rhetorical Terms: A Guide for Students of English Literature.* Berkeley: U of California P, 1968. 148 pp. PE1445.A2.L3 423.1.

A handlist of basic rhetorical terms, most of them classical but extending through the mid-seventeenth century, that students of literature will confront. In the alphabetical list, a typical entry indicates pronunciation, offers a brief definition or cross-reference to a synonymous term, summarizes differing interpretations when necessary, and sometimes cites an example. Following the alphabetical list are sections classifying terms according to the divisions of rhetoric, by type, and as ornaments; a concluding section lists terms useful in literary criticism. Clear, brief explanations make Lanham a useful desktop companion for the interpretation of rhetorical terminology.

For recent terms, consult Linda Woodson, *A Handbook of Modern Rhetorical Terms* (Urbana: National Council of Teachers of English, 1979, 78 pp.).

Guides to Scholarship

SURVEYS OF RESEARCH

5565 Horner, Winifred Bryan, ed. *The Present State of Scholarship in Historical and Contemporary Rhetoric.* Columbia: U of Missouri P, 1983. 230 pp. PN183.P7 808'.0072.

Surveys of scholarship accompanied by selective bibliographies on rhetoric, classical to contemporary. Essays focus on periods—classical, Middle Ages, Renaissance, eighteenth century, nineteenth century, and the twentieth century—with all but the first two emphasizing British and American traditions. Although varying in organization, essays typically survey primary works (noting editions and translations), bibliographies, and important scholarship; provide an overview of major concerns in the period; suggest areas for research; and conclude with a selective bibliography. Indexed by persons, anonymous works, and a few subjects. Addressed specifically to the literature scholar, Horner is a valuable introductory survey of the most important primary works and scholarship. It should, however, be supplemented with Horner, *Historical Rhetoric* (5600). Review: Donald F. Reid, *Rhetoric Society Quarterly* 14 (1984): 145–51.

5570 McClelland, Ben W., and Timothy R. Donovan, eds. *Perspectives on Research and Scholarship in Composition*. New York: MLA, 1985. 266 pp. PE1404.P45 808'.042'072.

A collection of essays that survey the state of research and assess important scholarship (through c. 1984) in composition theory and practice. The individual essays address the relationship of literary and rhetorical theory to composition theory, linguistics and writing, collaborative learning, empirical research, cognitive studies and the teaching of writing, research on error and correction, young writers, technical communication, and the potential importance of artificial intelligence research to composition studies. Indexed by persons and subjects. A clear introduction to the major philosophical issues, kinds of research, and new areas of study in composition research.

George Hillocks, Jr., *Research on Written Composition: New Directions for Teaching* (Urbana: National Conference on Research in English, 1986, 369 pp.), surveys empirical studies from 1963 through c. 1982 and concludes with an extensive bibliography. Earlier studies are surveyed or listed in Richard Braddock, Richard Lloyd-Jones, and Lowell Schoer, *Research in Written Composition* (Champaign: National Council of Teachers of English, 1963, 142 pp.).

5575 Moran, Michael G., and Ronald F. Lunsford, eds. *Research in Composition and Rhetoric: A Bibliographic Sourcebook*. Westport: Greenwood, 1984. 506 pp. Z5818.E5.R47 [PE1404] 016.808'042'07.

Selective surveys of scholarship (through c. 1982) designed to complement the first edition of Tate, *Teaching Composition* (5580). The 16 essays cover the writing process; psychology of composition; writing blocks, anxiety, and apprehension; philosophy and rhetoric; literature, literary theory, and the teaching of composition; reading and writing; research methods; grading and evaluation; preparing assignments; basic writing; the sentence; the role of spelling in composition for older students; vocabulary development; punctuation; usage; and the paragraph. The chapters vary in organization, depth, and rigor of evaluation; some suggest topics for further research. Appendixes evaluate textbooks and usage manuals. Two indexes: authors; subjects. Along with Tate (which is less thorough and accessible), this is an essential starting place for research in rhetoric and composition. Reviews: Kenneth Dowst, *Rhetoric Review* 4 (1986): 239–43; Richard Fulkerson, *Teaching English in the Two-Year College* 13.1 (1986): 51–57; Nancy Shapiro, *Literary Research* 11 (1986): 71–73.

5580 Tate, Gary, ed. *Teaching Composition: Twelve Bibliographical Essays*. Rev. and enl. ed. Fort Worth: Texas Christian UP, 1987. 434 pp. PE1404.T39 808'.042'07.

A collection of selective surveys of scholarship (through c. 1985) on rhetoric and composition that revises *Teaching Composition: Ten Bibliographical Essays* (1976, 304 pp.). Chapters by leading scholars examine rhetorical invention; structure and form in nonnarrative prose; approaches to the study of style; aims, modes, and forms of discourse; tests of writing ability; basic writing; language varieties and composition; literacy, linguistics, and rhetoric; literary theory and composition; the study of rhetoric and literature; writing across the curriculum; and computers and composition. The essays vary considerably in organization, rigor of assessment, and scope, with some authors merely updating rather than revising their original contributions. Three indexes: persons; subjects; titles. Because of the difficulty in determining which essay treats a particular topic, users should generally approach the work through the subject index. As Tate points out in his preface, both this work and Moran, *Research in Composition* (5575) "are unsystematic and incomplete," yet both are essential starting points for research in rhetoric and composition. In general, Moran is more effectively organized and thorough than Tate. Review: Chris Anderson, *Rhetoric Review* 6 (1988): 220–24.

SERIAL BIBLIOGRAPHIES

5585 "Annotated Bibliography of Research in the Teaching of English [1966–]." *Research in the Teaching of English* (entry 5615) 1 (1967)– .

A selective bibliography of articles, dissertations, and ERIC (5590) documents on all aspects of the teaching of English. Since vol. 18 (1984), entries are organized alphabetically by author in four divisions: writing (with sections for contexts, status surveys, instruction, processes, text analysis, assessment, rhetoric, and writing and learning), language (with sections for processing, development, interrelationships, and language and schooling), literature, and teacher education. Many of the descriptive annotations are too brief to offer an adequate sense of content. Although it is highly selective, this was, for many years, the only serial bibliography that systematically covered research in composition.

5590 ERIC [Education Resources Information Center]. Office of Educational Research and Improvement, U.S. Dept. of Education, Washington, DC 20208.

An information network established in 1966 to index, abstract, and disseminate research in education, including journal articles and reviews, books, dissertations, and unpublished material such as conference papers, curriculum guides, and research reports. A central office in Washington coordinates the work of 16 clearinghouses, each of which is responsible for abstracting research in a particular subject area. The citations and abstracts make up the ERIC data base, which is available in printed form as the following:

CIJE: Current Index to Journals in Education (*CIJE*). Phoenix: Oryx, 1969– . Monthly, with semiannual cumulations. An index to education and related journals (currently 780). Organized by clearinghouse, then in order of processing, entries consist of clearinghouse and ERIC document numbers, bibliographical citation, a list of descriptors (based on the current edition of *Thesaurus of ERIC Descriptors*) and identifiers (terms not in the *Thesaurus*) used to create the subject index, and an abstract prepared by clearinghouse staff. Three indexes in each issue and cumulation: subjects, authors, journal contents; cumulative index: *CIJE: Current Index to Journals in Education: Cumulated Author Index, 1969–1984* (1985, 2,218 pp.). Copies of many articles are available through UMI Article Clearinghouse; see the most recent issue of *CIJE* for ordering information.

Resources in Education (*RIE*). Washington: GPO, 1967– . Monthly, with annual cumulation. (Former title: *Office of Education Research Reports [1956–65]*, 1967.) An index to books, dissertations, theses, audiovisual materials, computer programs, and a variety of unpublished materials such as conference papers, research reports, and curriculum guides—in short, material on education not indexed in *CIJE*. Organized like *CIJE*, entries include clearinghouse and ERIC document numbers, bibliographical information, type of document, subject descriptors and identifiers, and abstract. Indexes—by subject, author, institution, and document type—are cumulated semiannually. Because clearinghouses abstract virtually all of the unpublished materials submitted to them, *RIE* includes far too many substandard papers, reports, guides, and the like. Many of the works included in *RIE* are available through the ERIC Document Reproduction Service. For information on ordering, see the most recent issue of *RIE*. Several libraries maintain a collection of all ERIC documents reproduced in microfiche.

Because of their lack of organization, *CIJE* and *RIE* must be approached through their thorough subject indexes, which should be consulted with the current edition of *Thesaurus of ERIC Descriptors* in hand.

The most effective and efficient way to search the ERIC data base is through BRS (515) or Dialog (520), or the CD-ROM version available in some libraries. The BRS and Dialog files are updated monthly; the CD-ROM, quarterly. The data base can be searched by subject descriptors and identifiers, keywords in titles or abstracts, authors, journals, year of publication, language, document type, and clearinghouse code; these fields can be combined in various ways to limit or expand a search.

The ERIC data base is of interest to language and literature scholars for its indexing of works on composition and rhetoric—and occasionally on literature in journals not covered by the standard serial bibliographies and indexes in section G.

Although less extensive in coverage, *Education Index* (New York: Wilson, 1929– , 10/yr., with annual and larger cumulations) offers author and subject indexing of publications before 1966 and is usually more accessible than *CIJE* and *RIE* for post-1966 works. Entries since December 1983 can be searched through WILSONLINE (525) and on CD-ROM through WILSONDISC.

5595 *Longman Bibliography of Composition and Rhetoric [1984–]*. New York: Longman, 1987– . Annual. Z5818.E5.L55 [PE1404] 016.808'042'07.

A selective annotated bibliography of English-language books, essays, textbooks, dissertations abstracted in *Dissertation Abstracts International* (465), documents in *Resources in Education* (5590a), computer software, videotapes, and sound recordings on English-language composition and its teaching. Entries are organized in six variously classified divisions: bibliographies; theory and research; teacher education, administration, and social roles; curriculum (including teaching methods); textbooks and instructional materials; testing, measurement, and evaluation. Entries are accompanied by very brief descriptive annotations; however, several in the original volume are based on information supplied by publishers rather than personal examination by a contributor. Indexed by authors. Although each section concludes with a list of cross-references, users would be much better served by a subject index. The *Longman Bibliography* fills a major gap in the reference tools needed in rhetoric and composition, and will likely become the standard source in the field.

5598 "Selected Bibliography of Scholarship on Composition and Rhetoric [1973–78, 1986–]." *College Composition and Communication* (entry 5610) 26–30, 38 (1975–79, 1987)– .

A highly selective annotated bibliography of current scholarship on composition and rhetoric at the post-secondary level. Excluded are book reviews, textbooks, descriptions of teaching activities, and most historical studies. Currently listed alphabetically by author within 12 categories, entries are accompanied by full descriptive annotations. Although far more selective than the other composition and rhetoric serial bibliographies, it is a convenient source for keeping abreast of important scholarship.

Most of the entries from the 1973 through 1978 installments will be incorporated into a selective bibliography of important studies from 1973 through 1985. Compiled by Richard L. Larson and scheduled for 1989 by the Conference on College Composition and Communication, the work will exclude dissertations, theses, ERIC documents, and textbooks.

See also

"Current Bibliography from the *Weekly Record*," *Rhetoric Society Quarterly* (5630).

MLAIB (335): Literary Forms/Rhetoric in the General part, and Stylistics/Rhetoric (as well as the Stylistics/Rhetoric section in individual language divisions) in the Linguistics part since 1981. Researchers must also check the headings beginning "Rhetoric" in the subject index to post-1980 volumes.

OTHER BIBLIOGRAPHIES

Although the Conference on College Composition and Communication planned a bibliography that would cover 1900 through 1973, the project has been abandoned. However, the result of the search of one decade is available as Nancy Jones, ed., *Bibliography of Composition, 1940–1949*, Rhetoric Society Quarterly Bibliographies in the Teaching of Composition 1, *Rhetoric Society Quarterly* (5630), special issue 2 (1987), 75 pp., an author list and subject classification of 612 works in the theory, practice, and teaching of composition. Scholarship from 1973 through 1985 is selectively covered in a bibliography being compiled by Richard L. Larson (5598a).

5600 Horner, Winifred Bryan, ed. *Historical Rhetoric: An Annotated Bibliography of Selected Sources in English*. Reference Publication in Literature. Boston: Hall, 1980. 294 pp. Z7004.R5.H57 [PN187] 016.808.

A highly selective bibliography of primary works and scholarship (through c. 1978) important to the study of rhetoric through the nineteenth century. Although encompassing some classical and European writers, Horner emphasizes English-language works on English and American literature. The entries are listed in five separately compiled divisions (classical, Middle Ages, Renaissance, eighteenth century, and nineteenth century), each with separate lists of primary and secondary works preceded by an introductory overview and statement of scope and limitations. The divisions vary considerably in their coverage (especially of foreign-language scholarship) and in the quality of their descriptive annotations. Indexed by persons, primary works, and subjects (but there are omissions and inaccuracies). Addressed to the novice, *Historical Rhetoric* is a convenient source for identifying the major primary works and studies, but it must be supplemented with Horner, *Present State of Scholarship* (5565). Review: Victor J. Vitanza, *Analytical and Enumerative Bibliography* 6 (1982): 25–28.

Periodicals

GUIDES TO PRIMARY WORKS

5605 Anson, Chris M., and Hildy Miller. "Journals in Composition: An Update." *College Composition and Communication* 39 (1988): 198–216.

A title list of some 100 journals devoted to the study and teaching of composition. A typical entry includes title, auspices or organization responsible for publication, frequency, audience and circulation, areas of emphasis, subscription price, address for submissions, subscription address. For information on editorial policies and submission requirements, researchers should check a recent issue. The inclusion of major as well as regional periodicals makes this useful to those wanting to identify journals specializing in a particular area or searching for an appropriate place to submit an article.

For an evaluative survey of major periodicals, see Robert J. Connors, "Journals in Composition Studies," *College English* 46 (1986): 348–65.

SCHOLARLY JOURNALS

5610 *College Composition and Communication* (*CCC*). 1950– . Quarterly. PE1001.C6 808'.042'0711.

Focuses on "theory, practice, history, and politics of composition and its teaching at all college levels; research into the processes and teaching of writing; the preparation of writing teachers; and the relationships of literature, language studies, rhetoric, communications theory, and other fields to composition and its teaching." See entry 5598 for the annual bibliography in some volumes. Indexed in every third volume.

5615 *Research in the Teaching of English*. 1967– . Quarterly. PE1066.R47 420.07.

Publishes articles and reviews on a variety of topics related to the teaching of English—especially composition—and language arts at all levels. See entry 5585 for the annual "Annotated Bibliography of Research in the Teaching of English."

5620 *Rhetorica: A Journal of the History of Rhetoric* (*Rhetorica*). 1983– . Quarterly. PN183.R45 808'.009.

Publishes articles, occasional bibliographies, and a few reviews on the theory and practice of rhetoric, classical to modern.

5625 *Rhetoric Review: A Journal of Rhetoric and Composition.* 1982– . 2/yr. PN171.4.R44 808'.005.

Publishes articles and reviews on the theory and method of composition and rhetoric, and on pedagogy in the field. Cumulative index: vols. 1–5, in 6 (1987): 125–28.

5630 *Rhetoric Society Quarterly* (*RSQ*). 1968– . Quarterly. Former title: *Newsletter: Rhetoric Society of America* (1968–75). PN171.4.R46 808'.005.

Publishes articles, reviews, and bibliographies on rhetorical theory and criticism, the history of rhetoric, and pedagogy. Most issues since vol. 3.3 (1973) print a "Current Bibliography from the *Weekly Record*," a minimally classified list of books copied from *Weekly Record* (4110a). For a bibliography of the bibliographies in the journal, see Charles W. Seefeldt, "Fifteen Years of the *Rhetoric Society Quarterly*: A Bibliography of Bibliographies" 16 (1986): 99–105. Cumulative index: vols. 1–8, in 8 (1978): 180–91.

Computers and the Humanities

This section presumes a basic knowledge of computers and especially of word processing. Books addressed to the humanities scholar interested in learning to program include John R. Abercrombie, *Computer Programs for Literary Analysis* (Philadelphia: U of Pennsylvania P, 1984, 203 pp., with selected programs available on diskettes); Susan Hockey, *SNOBOL Programming for the Humanities* (Oxford: Clarendon, 1985, 178 pp.); Nancy M. Ide, *Pascal for the Humanities* (Philadelphia: U of Pennsylvania P, 1987, 375 pp.); and Christopher Butler, *Computers in Linguistics* (Oxford: Blackwell, 1985, 266 pp.). Of the four, Hockey is the most generally useful because of its clear organization and explanations of both programming and applications; Ide is more restricted in its discussion of applications but has the advantage of teaching a programming language more widely available than SNOBOL in the United States; Butler is essentially a primer on SNOBOL 4, which is now little used by linguists; and the shortcomings of Abercrombie as a programming guide and source of adaptable programs are outlined in a review by Nancy M. Ide, *Computers and the Humanities* 20 (1986): 108–10.

General Introductions

5645 Feldman, Paula R., and Buford Norman. *The Wordworthy Computer: Classroom and Research Applications in Language and Literature.* New York: Random, 1987. 228 pp. PN73.F44 808'.02'0285.

An introduction to the use of a computer in the classroom and literary research. Following an introductory discussion of word processing (with tips on what to look for in hardware and software), the first part briefly addresses classroom applications. The second part offers an overview of uses in research in language and literature, with chapters on data bases, concordances, the interpretation of statistical data, stylistic analysis, and scholarly publishing (with an inadequate section on textual criticism). Four appendixes: (1) sources of information, including networks, bibliographical data bases, repositories of machine-readable texts, and professional organizations; (2) selected journals and periodicals; (3) selected bibliography, with a prefatory subject index; (4) glossary. Indexed by titles, subjects, and persons. In its emphasis on using available software rather than original programming, *Wordworthy Computer* is a valuable—but occasionally superficial—introduction for the neophyte. Its currency and first three appendixes make it a useful complement to Hockey, *Guide to Computer Applications in the Humanities* (5650) and Oakman, *Computer Methods for Literary Research* (5655), both of which offer more detailed considerations of research applications.

5650 Hockey, Susan. *A Guide to Computer Applications in the Humanities.* Baltimore: Johns Hopkins UP, 1980. 248 pp. AZ105.H63 001.3028'54.

An introduction to the use of computers in language and literary research. Following a brief overview of computers, extensively illustrated chapters discuss input and output; word indexes, concordances, and dictionaries; vocabulary studies, collocations, and dialectology; morphological and syntactic analysis, and machine translation; stylistic analysis and authorship studies; textual criticism (a weak discussion); sound pattern analysis; indexing, cataloging, and information retrieval; and a guide to starting a computer project. Most chapters end with a list of suggested readings. Concludes with a very selective general bibliography and a glossary of computer terms. Indexed by persons and subjects. Hockey covers many of the same topics as Oakman, *Computer Methods for Literary Research* (5655), but gives more attention to linguistic applications, is more technical, emphasizes British technology and software, and is more of a manual. The novice should begin with Oakman for its more general, less technical overview and Feldman, *Wordworthy Computer* (5645) for its discussion of software, then proceed to Hockey for its fuller treatment of applications. Hockey and Oakman, however, need updating in light of advances in hardware and software. Reviews: L. D. Burnard, *TLS: Times Literary Supplement* 9 May 1980: 533; T. H. Howard-Hill, *Analytical and Enumerative Bibliography* 4 (1980): 279–84; Louis T. Milic, *Modern Philology* 79 (1981): 233–39; Michael J. Preston, *English Language Notes* 18 (1980): 153–56.

5655 Oakman, Robert L. *Computer Methods for Literary Research.* Rev. ed. Athens: U of Georgia P, 1984. 235 pp. PN73.O24 802'.8'5.

An introduction to the use of computers in literary research. The first part consists of a nontechnical overview of the fundamentals of literary computing (including discussions of information processing, input and output, and flowcharting and programming); the second part examines applications (with chapters on concordances, dictionaries and bibliographies, textual editing, stylistic analysis, and data bases). Each chapter ends with an annotated list of works for further reading. Concludes with a selected bibliography (through 1977). The revised edition adds an introductory survey of trends through 1983 and sometimes updates the lists for further reading, but unfortunately leaves the text and selected bibliography unchanged. Although now dated in many of its discussions of hardware and software and largely restricted to IBM products, Oakman nevertheless remains the best nontechnical introduction to the uses and limitations of computers in literary research. Reviews: L. D. Burnard, *TLS: Times Literary Supplement* 9 May 1980: 533; Louis T. Milic, *Modern Philology* 79 (1981): 233–39; Philip H. Smith, Jr., *Review* 3 (1981): 209–17.

Hockey, *Guide to Computer Applications in the Humanities* (5650) covers many of the same topics but gives more attention to linguistic applications and is more of a manual. The novice should begin with Oakman for its more general, less technical overview and Feldman, *Wordworthy Computer* (5645) for its discussion of software, then proceed to Hockey for fuller explanations of applications.

See also

Howard-Hill, *Literary Concordances* (5680).
Shillingsburg, *Scholarly Editing in the Computer Age* (5230).

Word Processing

For those who have avoided word processing because of fear of or disdain for computer technology, the most reassuring introduction is William Zinsser, *Writing with a Word Processor* (New York: Harper, 1983, 117 pp.). Less entertaining but addressed to the needs of the humanities scholar is Alan T. McKenzie, ed., *A Grin on the Interface: Word Processing for the Academic Humanist*, Technology and the Humanities 1 (New York: MLA, 1984, 82 pp.).

The choice of a word-processing program necessarily depends on the kind of writing one does, the computer one uses, recommendations of colleagues, and, not least, price. Although there are several programs (such as *Applewriter*, *WordPerfect*, and *Microsoft Word*) suitable for most writing done by literary researchers, the best is *Nota Bene* 3.0 (New York: Dragonfly; also available through Modern Language Association and Oxford Electronic Publishing), a word-processing, text retrieval, and indexing program designed specifically for the humanist. Among *Nota Bene*'s important features are these:

- text retrieval that allows a writer to search files of notes and incorporate them into a document;
- built-in style sheets (including MLA [6400], Chicago [6395], and American Psychological Association);
- Western European keyboards (with Greek, Russian, and Hebrew versions also available);
- three indexing levels, each with three sublevels;
- nine windows that allow for editing nine files at one time;
- automatic generation of bibliographies, footnotes, and tables of contents;
- on-screen formatting;
- spelling checker and thesaurus;
- redlining and blue-penciling (for recording additions and deletions);
- mail merge.

Nota Bene requires a DOS 2.0 or higher operating system, two double-sided disk drives or a hard disk, a minimum of 256K of memory (although more is preferable), and, for the use of the foreign-language keyboards, a printer capable of supporting foreign characters. Although it is expensive and not easy to learn (however, the manuals are clearly written and organized), reviewers agree that *Nota Bene* is the best word-processing program for scholars in the humanities. For detailed reviews (including comparisons with other programs) see: (version 1.0) Willard McCarty, *Computers and the Humanities* 20 (1986): 62–71; Edward Mendelson, *Yale Review* 74 (1985): 615–40; (version 2.0) Gavan Daws, *TLS: Times Literary Supplement* 13 Feb. 1987: 167–68.

For thorough reviews and comparative assessments of 55 word-processing programs for the IBM PC, see *PC Magazine* 7.4 (1988): 92–345.

Guides to Scholarship

A current serial bibliography of scholarship on computer and the humanities is a major desideratum.

See

Sec. G: Serial Bibliographies, Indexes, and Abstracts.
ABELL (340): Language, Literature, and the Computer division since the volume for 1971.
"Annual Bibliography," *Computers and the Humanities* (5660).
MLAIB (335): General IV: Themes and Types/Computer-Assisted [Literary] Research in the volumes for 1966–80; and Professional Topics/Computer-Assisted Research in pt. 4 of the later volumes. Researchers must also check the headings beginning "Computer" in the subject index to post-1980 volumes.

Periodicals

Because of rapid changes in technology and improvements in software, scholars interested in computer applications in the humanities should scan current issues of the following journals. Also, the HUMANIST computer discussion group (accessible through Bitnet) is an important source of current information.

5660 *Computers and the Humanities* (*CHum*). 1966– . Quarterly. Z699.5.H8.C65.

Publishes articles on the theory and practice of computer applications in the humanities, and reviews of books (especially concordances), hardware, and software. Recent volumes include several special issues. Unfortunately, the "Annual Bibliography for [1966–77]," which devoted a section to language and literature, and the "Directory of Scholars Active," with descriptions of work in progress, were discontinued after vol. 13 (1979). The "Abstracts and Brief Notices" section, which printed summaries of articles and reports, appears in most issues through 18.1 (1984). Annual index in some volumes; cumulative index: 1–5, *Author-Subject Index to* Computers and the Humanities, *Volumes 1–5 (1966–1971)* (New York: Pergamon, 1976, 86 pp.).

5665 *Literary and Linguistic Computing: Journal of the Association for Literary and Linguistic Computing*. Oxford: Oxford UP, 1986– . Quarterly. (A merger of *ALLC Bulletin* 1–13 [1973–85] and *ALLC Journal* 1–6 [1980–85].) P98.L568 410'.28'5.

Publishes articles, notes, bibliographies, and reviews of books and software on computer applications in language and literature, word processing for the humanities, pedagogy, and computer-assisted language learning.

Concordances

Although it is an essential tool for analyzing imagery, themes, and style as well as for locating specific passages, a concordance must be used with due regard for its editor's choice and handling of the base text(s). Specifically, researchers must evaluate the following:

which edition(s) are used as base text(s), since a corrupt base text will result in a worthless concordance;
which words or forms, if any, have been excluded;
how variant spellings are recorded;
how variant readings and cancelled passages are handled;
whether homographs are differentiated;
what the bases for the frequency counts are (e.g., if homographs are undifferentiated, a frequency count is of no value).

Those using a concordance for extensive analysis of an author or work will do well to spend an hour with Howard-Hill, *Literary Concordances* (5680).

Some concordances are listed in Brewer, *Dictionaries, Encyclopedias, and Other Word-Related Books* (6020).

General Introductions

5680 Howard-Hill, T. H. *Literary Concordances: A Guide to the Preparation of Manual and Computer Concordances*. Oxford: Pergamon, 1979. 97 pp. Z695.92.H68 802'.8'5.

An examination of the principles and practices of editing a concordance, with discussions of selection and pre-editing of a base text, arrangement of entries, organization of entries under headwords, selection of entries, statistical information, preliminary and subsidiary matter (such as statistical tables), and special forms of concordances. Concludes with an appendix by Robert L. Oakman on the now outdated COCOA program, a selective bibliography, and a glossary. Indexed by persons and subjects. Although now dated in its treatment of computer hardware and software, Howard-Hill remains the best introduction to the principles and techniques of editing a concordance and is essential reading for both prospective editors and those evaluating published concordances. Reviews: Serge Lusignan, *Computers and the Humanities* 14 (1980): 129–30; Michael J. Preston, *English Language Notes* 18 (1981): 321–24.

See also

Sec. U: Literature-Related Topics and Sources/Computers and the Humanities/General Introductions.

Computer Programs

5685 Hockey, Susan, and Ian Marriot. *Oxford Concordance Program* (OCP). Version 2.0. Oxford: Oxford U Computing Service, 1987.

Hockey, Susan. *Micro-OCP (Oxford Concordance Program)*. Oxford: Oxford UP, 1987.

A natural language program designed for the production of concordances, word-lists, and frequency counts for use in analyzing style, vocabulary, grammatical forms, and rhyme schemes. The program has the advantages of being flexible, inexpensive, machine-independent, and accompanied by an intelligible user's manual (a rarity in this genre). And version 2.0 runs more quickly and economically than the original. Although OCP is superior to COCOA or CLOC, two other widely used concordance programs, some computer centers that had problems installing version 1.0 (1980) report that Oxford U Computing Service offered virtually no technical support. For a description of OCP 2.0, see S. Hockey and J. Martin, "The Oxford Concordance Program Version 2," *Literary and Linguistic Computing* 2 (1987): 125–31. Review: (version 1.0) Frank O'Brien, *Computers and the Humanities* 20 (1986): 138–41 (with comments and evaluations by a variety of users).

Another useful package is *WordCruncher* (Provo: Electronic Text, 1987). Users should watch *Computers and the Humanities* (566) and *Literary and Linguistic Computing* (5665) for notices of new concordance programs.

Copyright

Whether writing for publication or hire, quoting from or editing published or manuscript works, engaging in desktop publishing, or reproducing printed material for classroom use, scholars must be aware of the basic provisions (as well as subsequent administrative guidelines or regulations) in appropriate national copyright acts that govern literary property rights.

Researchers needing to identify the holder of a copyright in the United States will find helpful basic advice in "How to Investigate the Copyright Status of a Work," circular R-22 (available free from the Copyright Office, Library of Congress, Washington, DC 20559).

General Introductions

5700 Johnston, Donald F. *Copyright Handbook*. 2nd ed., 2nd printing with revisions. New York: Bowker, 1983. 381 pp. KF2994.J63 346.7304'82.

An explanation of United States copyright law, with chapters devoted to the kind of material that can be copyrighted; duration of copyright; rights conferred by copyright; ownership, transfer, and licensing of copyright; copyright notices; copyright deposit in the Library of Congress; copyright registration; transnational aspects of copyright law; remedies for copyright infringement; the "fair use" provision of the 1976 copyright act; copyright and teaching activities; copyright and library reproduction; limits on rights of performance and display; and compulsory licenses. Five appendixes: text of the 1976 copyright act; selected Copyright Office regulations; application forms for registration of copyright; text of the fair use guidelines developed under various auspices; text of the Copyright Act of 1909. The clear organization and explanations make this work essential reading for owners of copyrights and those producing copyrightable material. For recent developments in copyright law, see *Journal of the Copyright Society of the USA* (5705).

For a clear, concise explanation of provisions affecting literature scholars, see Achtert, *MLA Style Manual* (6400) 32–42.

Periodicals

5705 *Journal of the Copyright Society of the USA*. 1953– . Quarterly. Former title: *Bulletin of the Copyright Society of the USA* (1953–80). KF2987.C66 346.7304'82'05.

Each issue consists of up to five parts: articles on the history and interpretation of United States, international, and foreign copyright law; summaries of legislative and administrative developments; summaries of copyright conventions, treaties, and proclamations; summaries of judicial developments affecting literary and artistic property; and an annotated bibliography of publications on copyright. Annual index; cumulative index: vols. 1–20, *Cumulated Index, Volumes 1–20, 1953–1973*, comp. Meira G. Pimsleur (South Hackensack: Rothman, 1975, 229 pp.). The *Journal* is the best general source for keeping abreast of changes in the copyright law that affect those who write or reproduce copyrighted material.

Encyclopedias

Guides to Primary Works

5720 Kister, Kenneth F. *Best Encyclopedias: A Guide to General and Specialized Encyclopedias*. Phoenix: Oryx, 1986. 356 pp. AE1.K57 028.1'2.

An evaluative guide to encyclopedias published through 1985. The heart of the work is the section devoted to 52 general English-language encyclopedias. Organized alphabetically by title, these entries are typically in four parts: a description of scope and publishing history; an evaluation of content, organization, accuracy, scholarship, indexing, and illustrations, along with a comparison to similar works; information on purchasing a copy; and a selected bibliography of studies and reviews. Usually several pages long, entries typically offer helpful descriptions and evaluations; especially useful are the comparisons. Five appendixes: charts comparing features of related groups of the 52 encyclopedias; a subject list of 450 specialized encyclopedias, with brief descriptions and evaluative comments drawn chiefly and sometimes uncritically from reviews in library journals; an annotated list of general encyclopedias in Dutch, French, German, Italian, Japanese, Russian, and Spanish; an evaluatively annotated selective bibliography of publications about encyclopedias; a directory of North American encyclopedia publishers and distributors. The best approach is through the index of titles and subjects. The full descriptions and pointed evaluations make Kister the most trustworthy guide to the host of competing general encyclopedias. Because of the much briefer descriptions and generally derivative evaluations, the same cannot be said about the treatment of specialized encyclopedias. Review: Ann H. Paulsen, *American Reference Books Annual* 18 (1987): 24–25.

A sometimes useful supplement for identifying specialized encyclopedic works is Bohdan S. Wynar, ed., *ARBA Guide to Subject Encyclopedias and Dictionaries* (Littleton: Libraries Unlimited, 1986, 570 pp.). It collects reviews (sometimes revised) from *American Reference Books Annual* (745) of works published since c. 1970; however, both selection and evaluation are frequently untrustworthy.

S. Padraig Walsh, *Anglo-American General Encyclopedias: A Historical Bibliography, 1703–1967* (New York: Bowker, 1968, 270 pp.), describes and usually evaluates older general encyclopedic works in English.

See also

Brewer, *Dictionaries, Encyclopedias, and Other Word-Related Books* (6020).

General Encyclopedias

5725 *The New Columbia Encyclopedia.* Ed. William H. Harris and Judith S. Levey. New York: Columbia UP, 1975. 3,052 pp. AG5.C725 031.

A general encyclopedia that encompasses literature, the arts, geography, and the physical, social, and life sciences of all periods and countries. The compact entries on persons, places, concepts, terms, theories, movements, events, and the like are liberally cross-referenced and frequently conclude with suggestions for further reading (many of which fail to cite precise titles or publication information). An invaluable source for quick, reliable factual information on an impressive range of topics, *New Columbia Encyclopedia* is the best single-volume general encyclopedia in English and a reference source that belongs in every researcher's personal library.

5730 *The New Encyclopædia Britannica.* Ed. Philip W. Goetz. 15th ed., 1985 printing. 32 vols. Chicago: Encyclopædia Britannica, 1985. Annual supplement: *Britannica Book of the Year.* AE5.E363 031.

The general encyclopedia is organized in three extensively illustrated parts:

Propædia (1 vol.): a topical outline of and subject guide to the articles in the other parts;
Micropædia (12 vols.): approximately 61,000 short articles on places, persons, things, and ideas; several are distillations of lengthier discussions (or parts thereof) in the *Macropædia*;
Macropædia (17 vols.): 681 lengthy signed articles by eminent authorities, accompanied by selective bibliographies.

Because of the organization, users must approach the contents through the analytical index. The annual *Britannica Book of the Year* includes revisions and additions to the articles and accompanying bibliographies in the *Macropædia*, an overview of the year's major events, and an extensive section on statistical data for the world.

Because of its separation of long and short articles (a radical departure from earlier editions and from the traditional organization of general encyclopedias), inadequate cross-referencing, and inexplicable lack of an index, the fifteenth edition was universally criticized for its inaccessibility. In response to the adverse reception, the 1985 printing was completely reset, many of the articles were revised, several *Macropædia* articles were condensed and shifted to the *Micropædia*, thousands of cross-references were introduced, and a two-volume analytical index added. Still lacking, however, is a general table of contents and an adequate guide to using the work. Despite these revisions, the organization still mystifies many users: the *Propædia* remains useless for those needing quick information; cross-references are typically hidden within an article; and the analytical index, while extensive, is not sufficiently thorough. Although the *New Britannica* remains the most authoritative and scholarly of the English-language general encyclopedias, it is also the most inaccessible and is not without serious errors and deficiencies. (See, for example, Samuel McCracken, "The Scandal of *Britannica 3*," *Commentary* 61.2 [1976]: 63–68, an important discussion of the numerous shortcomings of the original printing of the 15th edition.) The contents are searchable through the NEXIS data base services. Earlier editions remain useful for the historical perspective they offer, especially in their articles on the arts and humanities.

Of the other English-language general encyclopedias, these are the best:

Collier's Encyclopedia. Ed. William D. Halsey and Emanuel Friedman. 24 vols. New York: Macmillan; London: Collier, 1985.

Encyclopedia Americana. International ed. 30 vols. Danbury: Grolier, 1829– . Now revised annually, it emphasizes North American topics.

For major encyclopedias in other languages, see Sheehy, *Guide to Reference Books* (60), pp. 138–45, and Walford, *Walford's Guide to Reference Material* (65) vol. 3, pp. 122–31.

Film and Literature

This section is limited to reference works of particular value to the study of the relationship between English-language film and literature. Because of the nature of the film industry and its documentation, factual information about individual films and persons is sometimes contradictory or unavailable; thus researchers must exercise more than usual care when consulting film reference sources.

Many drama and theater reference works include film (e.g., see section K: Genres/Drama and Theater) as do some in section U: Literature-Related Topics and Sources/Interdisciplinary and Multidisciplinary Studies.

For an introduction to the interdisciplinary study of literature and film, see Gerald Mast, "Literature and Film" (pp. 278–306) in Barricelli, *Interrelations of Literature* (5955).

Guides to Reference Works

5745 Fisher, Kim N. *On the Screen: A Film, Television, and Video Research Guide*. Reference Sources in the Humanities Series. Littleton: Libraries Unlimited, 1986. 209 pp. Z5784.M9.F535 [PN1994] 016.7914.

A guide to English-language reference sources, for the most part published in the United States between 1960 and 1985. Entries are organized in 14 classified divisions, most of which have separate sections for film and television: bibliographic guides; dictionaries and encyclopedias; indexes, abstracts, and data bases; biographical sources; credits; film reviews and television programming; catalogs; directories and yearbooks; filmographies and videographies; bibliographies; handbooks and miscellaneous sources; periodicals; research centers and archives; societies and associations. The full annotations are accompanied by generally rigorous evaluations. Two indexes: authors and titles; subjects. Although the classification system is not as refined as it could be, judicious selection and evaluation make *On the Screen* the best guide to reference sources for the study of film in the United States. What is still needed is a similar guide that is international in scope.

See also

Neil Barron, "Science Fiction on Film and Television" (pp. 672–86) in Barron, *Anatomy of Wonder* (1015).

Handbooks, Dictionaries, and Encyclopedias

There is no satisfactory general encyclopedia of film. Of those available, the least objectionable is Ephraim Katz, *The Film Encyclopedia* (New York: Crowell, 1979, 1,266 pp.), but the bulk of its entries are biographies. *The International Encyclopedia of Film*, gen. ed. Roger Manvell (New York: Crown, 1972, 574 pp.) is commendably broad in coverage but outdated. Although they are often found in reference sections of libraries, Leslie Halliwell, *Halliwell's Filmgoer's Companion*, 8th ed. (New York: Scribner's, 1984, 704 pp.), and, especially, *The Oxford Companion to Film*, ed. Liz-Anne Bawden (New York: Oxford UP, 1976, 767 pp.) are too inaccurate and biased to recommend.

5750 Beaver, Frank E. *Dictionary of Film Terms*. New York: McGraw, 1983. 392 pp. TR847.B43 791.43'03'21.

A dictionary of genres, styles, techniques, and concepts associated with film. The full definitions are accompanied by specific examples and sometimes by illustrations. Concludes with a chronological outline of film history from the eleventh century through 1981. Two indexes: terms and film titles; general topics (such as camera operation, criticism, editing). Clear and concise, Beaver is a useful reference for those writing as well as reading film studies.

See also

Enciclopedia dello spettacolo (1130).

Bibliographies of Bibliographies

5755 Wulff, Hans Jürgen, comp. and ed. *Bibliography of Film Bibliographies/Bibliographie der Filmbibliographien*. München: Saur, 1987. 326 pp. Z1002.W85.

A bibliography of bibliographies, including those appended to books and articles as well as booksellers' and library catalogs. The approximately 1,200 entries are in two parts (works in Germanic and Romance languages; those in Slavic languages, compiled by Andrzej Gwóźdź and Anna Wastkowska). Each part is organized in nine extensively classified divisions: formal bibliographies (including filmographies and discographies), general bibliographies of film literature, film theory and research, special topics, history of the cinema, genre studies, national cinemas, persons, and related fields (including communications research and television). Most entries are accompanied by brief descriptive annotations. Two indexes: authors and editors; subjects. Impressive in its international coverage, Wulff is the essential source for identifying film bibliographies.

Guides to Primary Works

FILMOGRAPHIES

5760 *The American Film Institute Catalog of Motion Pictures Produced in the United States*. Berkeley: U of California P, 1971– . PN1998.A57 016.7'9143'0973.

Vol. A: *Film Beginnings, 1893–1910*. In progress.
Vol. F1: *Feature Films, 1911–1920*. 2 pts. Scheduled for 1989.
Vol. F2: *Feature Films, 1921–1930*. 2 pts. Ed. Kenneth W. Munden. 1971.
Vol. F3: *Feature Films, 1931–1940*.
Vol. F4: *Feature Films, 1941–1950*.
Vol. F5: *Feature Films, 1951–1960*.
Vol. F6: *Feature Films, 1961–1970*. 2 pts. Ed. Richard P. Krafsur. 1976.
Vol. S1: *Short Films, 1911–1920*.
Vol. S2: *Short Films, 1921–1930*.
Vol. S3: *Short Films, 1931–1940*.
Vol. S4: *Short Films, 1941–1950*.
Vol. S5: *Short Films, 1951–1960*.
Vol. S6: *Short Films, 1961–1970*.
Vol. N1: *Newsreels, 1908–1920*.
Vol. N2: *Newsreels, 1921–1930*.
Vol. N3: *Newsreels, 1931–1940*.
Vol. N4: *Newsreels, 1941–1950*.
Vol. N5: *Newsreels, 1951–1960*.
Vol. N6: *Newsreels, 1961–1970*.

A catalog of films produced for public showing in the United States. Although the criteria governing inclusion vary from volume to volume, each utilizes a combination of length, audience, and country of origin. Assignment to a volume is based on release date (or, lacking that information, date of copyright, initial showing, or licensing by a state commission). Within a volume, films are listed alphabetically by original title (with cross-references to alternate and variant titles). A typical entry consists of four parts, with the components of each depending on the period and kind of film: identification and physical description (citing title, country of origin, producer or production company, original distributor, date of release, copyright date, audio information, color, gauge and length, and MPAA rating); production credits (including persons, groups, companies, and organizations); cast (both performers and their roles); and description of contents (including genre, source, lengthy synopsis, and subject indexing terms). Notes explain any conflicts in sources. Because many films are not extant or available for screening and sources vary considerably in completeness and accuracy, several entries are necessarily incomplete or inaccurate in some details. Each volume is accompanied by two indexes: credits (including all personal and corporate names, with a separate alphabetic list for literary source credits); subjects (including headings for genres, character types, themes, dates and seasons, historical events and persons, places, institutions, physical objects, cinematic devices, animals, and literary works enacted). Inevitably there are errors, but the thoroughness of coverage, assimilation of widely scattered factual information, detailed synopses, and excellent indexes make the published volumes indispensable sources that supersede other catalogs for the respective periods.

Unfortunately, work on the remaining volumes proceeds slowly. Review: (vol. F2) Herman G. Weinberg, *Film Quarterly* 25.2 (1971–72): 59–65.

5765 Gifford, Denis. *The British Film Catalogue, 1895–1985: A Reference Guide.* New York: Facts on File, 1986. n.pag. PN1998.G543 016.79143'0941.

A catalog of films produced for public entertainment and made in the British Isles or by British subjects elsewhere in the world between 1895 and 1985. Gifford includes both feature length and short films, but excludes amateur productions, films made for and shown exclusively on television, animations, documentaries, and travelogues. The 15,289 films are listed chronologically by month of initial exhibition. A typical entry identifies original title (and title changes), length, censor's rating, sound, color system, screen ratio, production company, distributor, reissues (with date and any title changes), producer, director, author and source of story, author and source of screenplay, narrator, important members of the cast (with roles), type of film (see pp. 12–13 for an explanation of categories), and awards; each entry concludes with a one-sentence synopsis and, if appropriate, notes on the work's importance in the history of film. Entries after 1970 identify additional technical and artistic personnel. Since entries covering 1971–85 are grafted to a corrected reprint of Gifford, *The British Film Catalogue, 1895–1970: A Reference Guide* (New York: McGraw, 1973, n.pag.), users must contend with two introductions (the second, which is hidden after the 1970 listings, identifies additional abbreviations and notes some important modifications of scope and parts of an entry) and two title indexes (with that for 1895–1970 having a separate alphabetic sequence at the end for additions). Although not exhaustive (especially in the case of shorts and pre-1927 releases), Gifford is a monumental accumulation of information, but one whose value is considerably diminished by the lack of subject indexing.

5770 Nash, Jay Robert, and Stanley Ralph Ross. *The Motion Picture Guide.* 12 vols. Chicago: Cinebooks, 1985–87. PN1995.N346.

Vols. 1–8: *1927–1983.*
Vol. 9: *1927–1983; 1984.*
Vol. 10: *Silent Film, 1910–1936.* By Robert Connelly.
Vols. 11–12: *Index.*
Annual supplement: *The Motion Picture Guide Annual.* 1987– .

A filmography of English-language feature films (along with important foreign-language ones) since 1927 and silent films from 1910 through 1936. *Motion Picture Guide* includes films released only on videocassettes, but excludes X-rated productions (and comparable ones before the initiation of MPAA ratings), documentaries, made-for-television films, shorts, serials, and newsreels (although the publisher plans volumes on some of the preceding). Entries are organized alphabetically by title, with cross-references for variant and alternate titles; foreign-language titles beginning with articles are alphabetized by the articles. An entry consists of title; a subjective rating of quality; year of release in the United States; country of origin if not the United States; running time; production and distribution companies; color; complete cast with roles; synopsis with evaluative comments; producer, director, and other technical and artistic personnel; remakes and sequels; information on dubbing and subtitles; genre or subject; and MPAA rating. Four indexes: alternate titles; series; awards (by award, then year, then category); names. Although not fulfilling the foreword's hyperbolic, italicized claim of being "the only definitive and all-encompassing film encyclopedia in the world," Nash is currently the most extensive filmography of English-language feature films and a valuable, if not always trustworthy, compilation of information.

In progress are a 16-volume guide to foreign films and a 12-volume biographical dictionary of performers and others associated with film.

GUIDES TO LITERARY SOURCES

5775 Dimmitt, Richard Bertrand. *A Title Guide to the Talkies: A Comprehensive Listing of 16,000 Feature-Length Films from October, 1927, until December, 1963*. 2 vols. New York: Scarecrow, 1965. Andrew A. Aros. *A Title Guide to the Talkies, 1964 through 1974*. 1977. 336 pp. *1975 through 1984*. 1986. 347 pp. PN1998.D55 791.438.

A guide to plays, short stories, novels, poems, screen stories, story ideas, and other sources of feature films since 1927. Although the original compilation is limited to American films, the continuations include foreign ones exhibited in the United States and extend coverage to novelizations. Organized by film title, each entry consists of a brief note on the source of the script, screenplay, or idea. Indexed by authors. Although many entries fail to record exact publication details or are frustratingly vague in identifying a source merely as "a story by" someone, no other work covers so many kinds of sources or as many movies.

While not as thorough in coverage, the following list additional films or sometimes identify sources more precisely:

Daisne, Johan. *Dictionnaire filmographique de la littérature mondiale/Filmographic Dictionary of World Literature/Filmographisches Lexikon der Weltliteratur/Filmografisch Lexicon der Wereldliteratuur.* 2 vols. Gand: Story-Scientia, 1971–75. *Supplement.* 1978. 638 pp. The only guide offering decent coverage of sources of foreign films (through 1977).

Emmens, Carol A. *Short Stories on Film and Video.* 2nd ed. Littleton: Libraries Unlimited, 1985. 337 pp. Unlike Dimmitt and Aros, Emmens cites titles of short stories.

Enser, A. G. S. *Filmed Books and Plays: A List of Books and Plays from Which Films Have Been Made, 1928–86*. Aldershot: Gower, 1987. 770 pp. Limited to English-language films, but includes made-for-television movies.

Langman, Larry. *Writers on the American Screen: A Guide to Film Adaptations of American and Foreign Literary Works.* Garland Reference Library of the Humanities 658. New York: Garland, 1986. 329 pp. Limited to American film adaptations of printed works and marred by an inadequate explanation of scope; includes some films not in Enser (and vice versa).

See also

American Film Institute Catalog of Motion Pictures Produced in the United States (5760).

Hubin, *Crime Fiction, 1981–1985* (915).

Guides to Scholarship and Criticism

SERIAL BIBLIOGRAPHIES

5780 *Film Literature Index [1973–]: A Quarterly Author-Subject Index to the International Periodical Literature of Film and Television/Video.* Albany: Film and Television Documentation Center, SU of New York at Albany, 1973– . Quarterly, with annual cumulation. (Subtitle varies.) Z5784.M9.F45 791.43'01'6.

An author and subject index to material on film, television, and video published in some 300 periodicals worldwide. Excludes fan magazines and technical journals. Expanded coverage of television begins in vol. 5 (1977), of video in vol. 14 (1986). Since vol. 14, entries are organized in two parts: film; television and video. Each part consists of a single author and subject index, with liberal cross-references and with subject headings including titles of films or television programs, persons, geographical areas, and corporate bodies. With its inclusion of television and broader coverage of periodicals that print only occasional material on film or television, this is an important complement to *International Index to Film Periodicals* (5785). Since each work indexes journals omitted by the other, the two together offer the best coverage of periodicals since 1972 and are essential sources for identifying articles on film and television adaptations of literary works as well as reviews of films, programs, and related books.

The indexing of periodicals before the advent of *Film Literature Index* and *International Index to Film Periodicals* is unsatisfactory. Although there is considerable overlap among the following, each must be checked either because of its scope or its organization:

Batty, Linda. *Retrospective Index to Film Periodicals, 1930–1971.* New York: Bowker, 1975. 425 pp. An index to articles and reviews in only 14 English-language film periodicals (each of which is indexed in both Gerlach and MacCann—see below) and the *Village Voice.* The dates in the title are misleading, since only two of the journals were being published before 1950. The best that can be said for this work is that it includes reviews and that its subject indexing is better than in MacCann.

Bowles, Stephen E., comp. and ed. *Index to Critical Film Reviews in British and American Periodicals, Together with Index to Critical Reviews of Books about Film.* 3 vols. in 2. New York: Franklin, 1974–75. A title index to reviews of films (vols. 1–2) and books (vol. 3) in 31 major British and American film periodicals through 1971. Entries indicate the approximate number of words. Unfortunately, not all issues of some journals are indexed and few of those covered were published before 1950. Since the other retrospective indexes seldom include reviews (especially of books), this is an essential, if limited, source.

The Film Index: A Bibliography. 3 vols. White Plains: Kraus, 1941–85. A subject guide to English-language materials published through 1935 (with occasional later entries). *Film Index* includes fan and trade magazines, reviews of films and books, but excludes newspaper articles. In vol. 1, *The Film as Art* (1941, 723 pp.), the approximately 8,600 entries are organized in two extensively classified divisions: history and technique; types of films (including a section on adaptations). Vols. 2 and 3—*The Film as Industry* (1985, 587 pp.) and *The Film in Society* (1985,

507 pp.)—include, respectively, sections on the history of the industry and censorship. Indexed by persons, titles, and a few subjects. The fullest guide to pre-1936 publications, *Film Index* is particularly useful for its descriptive annotations.

Gerlach, John C., and Lana Gerlach. *The Critical Index: A Bibliography of Articles on Film in English, 1946–1973, Arranged by Names and Topics*. New Humanistic Research Series. New York: Teachers College P, 1974. 726 pp. An annotated list of articles from 22 British, American, and Canadian film journals and about 60 general periodicals. The approximately 5,000 entries are organized in two parts: works about persons; subjects. Although overlapping considerably with MacCann and difficult to use, Gerlach does index some additional articles.

MacCann, Richard Dyer, and Edward S. Perry. *The New Film Index: A Bibliography of Magazine Articles in English, 1930–1970*. New York: Dutton, 1975. 522 pp. An annotated bibliography of articles from both film and general-interest periodicals. The approximately 12,000 entries are organized chronologically within classified subject divisions. Although the work is incomplete and less than accessible because of its poor subject organization, MacCann offers the broadest coverage of the retrospective indexes.

5785 *International Index to Film Periodicals [1972–]: An Annotated Guide*. London: International Federation of Film Archives, 1973– . Annual. Z5784.M9.I49 016.79143.

A subject index that currently covers 86 periodicals published worldwide. Since the volume for 1983, entries are organized in three divisions: general subjects (organized by country, then alphabetically by author under subject headings, including one for "adaptations"), individual films (organized alphabetically by original title), and biographical discussions (organized by biographee). Each entry is accompanied by a brief descriptive annotation. Two indexes: authors; directors. Although it covers fewer journals than *Film Literature Index* (5780), the *International Index* does annotate entries. Since each work indexes journals omitted by the other, the two together offer the best coverage of film periodicals since 1972 and are essential sources for identifying articles on film adaptations of literary works and reviews of films.

See also

Sec. F: Serial Bibliographies, Indexes, and Abstracts.
"Annual Review," *Journal of Modern Literature* (2780).
Art Index (5145).
"Bibliography on the Relations of Literature and the Other Arts" (5965).
MLAIB (335): General IV/Cinema in the volumes for 1975–80, and the Film division in pt. 4 of later volumes. In the post-1980 volumes, several national literature divisions have a Film heading in the 1900–1999 section, and there are listings for individual directors. Researchers must also consult the headings beginning "Film" in the subject index to post-1980 volumes.
RILM Abstracts (6240).
"Year's Scholarship in Fantastic Literature" (1010).

OTHER BIBLIOGRAPHIES

5790 Rehrauer, George. *The Macmillan Film Bibliography*. 2 vols. New York: Macmillan, 1982. Z5784.M9.R423 [PN1993.5.A1] 016.79143'09.

An annotated selective bibliography of English-language books published through c. 1980 on all aspects of film. Rehrauer includes reference works, biographies, and published filmscripts, but excludes novelizations and fictional works about the film industry. Listed alphabetically by title, most of the 6,762 entries are accompanied by full descriptions of content and brief evaluative commentary. Because of the organization, users should generally approach the work through the subject, author, and filmscript indexes; however, they are sometimes inconsistent and lack sufficient cross-references. The criteria governing selection are insufficiently explained; the evaluations are frequently bland or too generous; and there are numerous typographical errors. Still, Rehrauer is the most complete bibliography of English-language books about the subject and an especially valuable resource for identifying discussions of a film, performer, or film-related subjects. Review: Raoul Kulberg, *Journal of Popular Film and Television* 10 (1983): 183–84.

This work supersedes Rehrauer, *Cinema Booklist* (Metuchen: Scarecrow, 1972, 473 pp.), *Supplement One* (1974, 405 pp.), and *Supplement Two* (1977, 470 pp.).

Although less complete than Rehrauer, the following works list a few additional books:

Armour, Robert A. *Film: A Reference Guide*. American Popular Culture. Westport: Greenwood, 1980. 251 pp. A selective guide to some 1,500 English-language books published through c. 1979 and principally concerned with American film.

Dyment, Alan R. *The Literature of the Film: A Bibliographical Guide to the Film as Art and Entertainment, 1936–1970*. London: White Lion, 1975. 398 pp. An annotated, highly selective subject list of English-language books.

Ellis, Jack C., Charles Derry, and Sharon Kern. *The Film Book Bibliography, 1940–1975*. Metuchen: Scarecrow, 1979. 752 pp. An annotated list of English-language books and dissertations organized by subject.

DISSERTATIONS AND THESES

5795 Fielding, Raymond, comp. *A Bibliography of Theses and Dissertations on the Subject of Film, 1916–1979*. University Film Association Monograph 3. Houston: University Film Assn., 1979. 70 pp. Z5784.M9.

A list of theses and dissertations accepted by academic institutions in the United States between 1916 and 1979, although coverage after 1976 is incomplete. The 1,420 entries are listed alphabetically by author, with each entry recording title, degree, institution, and date of graduation. Indexed by subject at the beginning. Although the subject headings are usually too broad to be of much use, Fielding does bring together dissertations and theses accepted in a variety of departments. Researchers should also consult the works in section H: Guides to Dissertations and Theses.

LITERATURE AND FILM

5800 Ross, Harris. *Film as Literature, Literature as Film: An Introduction to and Bibliography of Film's Relationship to Literature*. Bibliographies and Indexes in World Literature 10. New York: Greenwood, 1987. 346 pp. Z5784.M9.R66 [PN1995.3] 016.79143'01'5.

A bibliography of about 2,500 English-language books and articles published between 1908 and 1985. Most reviews and newspaper articles are excluded. Entries are organized alphabetically by author in divisions for general studies of literature and film, language and film (including linguistic approaches), prose fiction and film, drama and film, poetry and film, general studies of adaptation, writers and the film industry, American writers, writers of the United Kingdom, Shakespeare and film, classical writers, European writers, Latin American writers, published scripts by literary figures and scripts of adaptations, pedagogy, and bibliographies and filmographies. The divisions treating writers have sections for individual authors; that for Shakespeare has sections for individual plays. Entries are accompanied by a list of writers or films discussed only when a title needs clarification. Although the introductory survey of basic issues involving the relationship between literature and film comments on numerous works, it is no substitute for annotations. Two indexes: scholars; subjects. *Film as Literature* is marred by the failure to annotate all entries and is restricted to English-language works; nevertheless, it is the best guide to scholarship on literature and film.

Jeffrey Egan Welch, *Literature and Film: An Annotated Bibliography, 1909–1977*, Garland Reference Library of the Humanities 241 (New York: Garland, 1981, 315 pp.), remains useful for its brief annotations of English-language scholarship on film adaptations of literary works, the relationship of film and literary genres, and the teaching of literature and film.

See also

Etulain, *Bibliographical Guide to the Study of Western American Literature* (3670).
Fishburn, *Women in Popular Culture* (6590).
Frank, *Guide to the Gothic* (875).
Gilbert, *Women's Studies: A Bibliography of Dissertations, 1870–1982* (6615).
Humm, *Annotated Critical Bibliography of Feminist Criticism* (6170).
Rice, *English Fiction, 1900–1950* (2840).
Salem, *Guide to Critical Reviews* (4300).
Salzman, *American Studies: An Annotated Bibliography* (3335).
Wildbihler, *The Musical: An International Annotated Bibliography* (4295).

Biographical Dictionaries

See

Sec. J: Biographical Sources/Biographical Dictionaries.
Contemporary Theatre, Film, and Television (4305).

Periodicals

GUIDES TO PRIMARY WORKS

5805 Slide, Anthony, ed. *International Film, Radio, and Television Journals.* Historical Guides to the World's Periodicals and Newspapers. Westport: Greenwood, 1985. 428 pp. Z5784.M9.I485 [PN1993] 016.79143'05.

A collection of signed profiles of about 190 important or representative scholarly and popular film periodicals from throughout the world, but emphasizing those published in the United States and Great Britain. Organized alphabetically by periodical title, each profile consists of two parts: a discussion of the history, general contents, and quality of the work; and a list of indexing sources, reprints, selected locations, title changes, volume and issue data, publisher(s) and place(s) of publication, and editor(s). Six appendixes: fan club journals; fan magazines (mostly American, since some British ones are given regular profiles); in-house journals; national film journals; a list of journals by country; a list by subject. Indexed by persons, journal titles, and some subjects. Although the profiles vary in quality, Slide is a convenient source of descriptions and evaluations of major film periodicals.

SCHOLARLY JOURNALS

5810 *Literature/Film Quarterly* (*LFQ*). 1973– . Quarterly. PN1995.3.L57 791.43'05.

Publishes articles on film adaptations of literary works, individual movies, cinematic qualities of an author or work, and other aspects of the relationship between film and literature; interviews; a few bibliographies; occasional special issues; and reviews of books and film adaptations.

See also

Critical Inquiry (6145).
Diacritics (6150).
Eighteenth-Century Life (2300).
MELUS: Journal of the Society for the Study of Multi-Ethnic Literature of the United States (3705).

Folklore and Literature

This section is limited to reference works of particular importance to the investigation of the relationship between literatures in English and folklore; consequently, special attention is accorded works on narrative folklore genres in Great Britain and North America. Works devoted to the relationship between folklore and a specific literature are listed with the appropriate national literature.

For an introduction to the interdisciplinary study of literature and folklore, see Bruce A. Rosenberg, "Literature and Folklore" (pp. 90–106) in Barricelli, *Interrelations of Literature* (5955).

Guides to Reference Works

5825 Brunvand, Jan Harold. *Folklore: A Study and Research Guide*. New York: St. Martin's, 1976. 144 pp. Z5981.B78.GR66 016.398.

An introduction to folklore research for undergraduates. The first chapter surveys theories and scholars, past and present. The second describes and briefly evaluates important studies and reference works (published through the mid-1970s and largely in English) in sections on bibliographies and dictionaries, journals, histories and surveys, theories of folklore, genres, and folk groups. The last chapter explains how to prepare a research paper. Indexed by authors. Although it is now dated, emphasizes American folkloristics, is addressed to the undergraduate, and is flawed by the lack of subject and title indexing and the failure to provide sufficient and precise bibliographical information for many works, Brunvand remains the only general introduction to folklore scholarship. Review: Bert Feintuch, *Journal of American Folklore* 91 (1978): 872–74.

A useful, although highly selective, complement is Richard M. Dorson, "American Folklore Bibliography," *American Studies International* 16.1 (1977): 23–37, an evaluative overview by one of the foremost American folklorists.

A major desideratum is a current, international guide to reference works.

See also

Gohdes, *Bibliographical Guide to the Study of the Literature of the U.S.A.* (3180).

Webb, *Sources of Information in the Social Sciences* (6460), whose section on anthropology (pp. 332–402) encompasses folklore.

Handbooks, Dictionaries, and Encyclopedias

5830 *Enzyklopädie des Märchens: Handwörterbuch zur historischen und vergleichenden Erzählforschung*. Ed. Kurt Ranke et al. 12 vols. and supplement. Berlin: de Gruyter, 1977– . (Issued in fascicles; publication will not be complete before the year 2000.) GR72.E58.

A comparative, historical dictionary that ranges beyond folktales to include animal stories, jests, fairy tales, novelle, and legends. The signed articles by major scholars emphasize the religious, social, psychological, and historical backgrounds of European, Mediterranean, and Asian oral and written narratives, with those of the rest of the world treated in regional or national surveys. The approximately 3,600 planned entries include extensive articles on theories, methods, genres, major tale-types and motifs, figures, themes, scholars, nations, and regions. Each entry concludes with a selected bibliography. (Articles scheduled for future parts are listed in a periodic *Sprichwortliste*.) An extensive, authoritative compilation, *Enzyklopädie des Märchens* is especially valuable for its attention to literary works.

Hans-Jörg Uther, "The Encyclopedia of the Folktale," *Fairy Tales and Society: Illusion, Allusion, and Paradigm*, ed. Ruth B. Bottigheimer (Philadelphia: U of Pennsylvania P, 1986) 187–93, outlines the history and scope of the work.

5835 *Funk and Wagnalls Standard Dictionary of Folklore, Mythology, and Legend*. Ed. Maria Leach. [Corrected rpt.] New York: Funk, 1972. 1,236 pp. GR35.F82 398'.042.

A dictionary of mythological and folk figures, dances, festivals, rituals, food, games, customs, riddles, rhymes, witchcraft, magic, folk beliefs, folktales, regions, scholars, motifs, material culture, and a host of other topics related to folklore, especially of the Americas. Entries range from a sentence to several pages; some are signed, and a few conclude with a selective bibliography. The brief index of countries, regions, cultures, tribes, and groups added in the 1972 reprint does not offer adequate access to topics and persons not accorded separate entries. (A full analytical index and bibliography was promised but never published.) Although the work is seriously flawed because of numerous errors, inadequate cross-referencing and indexing, many uneven and unrepresentative entries, and generally slipshod editing, it remains the fullest English-language general dictionary of folklore. Superior coverage of classical mythology is offered by *Oxford Classical Dictionary* (115); for scholars and topics related to narrative folklore, *Enzyklopädie des Märchens* (5830) is the essential source. Reviews: (original printing) Wayland D. Hand, *Midwest Folklore* 1 (1951): 267–72; Stanley Edgar Hyman, *Journal of American Folklore* 64 (1951): 325–28; Hyman, *Kenyon Review* 12 (1950): 721–30; Branford P. Millar, *Southern Folklore Quarterly* 14 (1950): 123–28, 15 (1951): 171–72.

Gertrude Jobes, *Dictionary of Mythology, Folklore, and Symbols*, 3 vols. (New York: Scarecrow, 1961–62), covers a number of additional topics but the brief entries typically read like undigested notes.

Guides to Primary Works

TYPE- AND MOTIF-INDEXES

Bibliographies

5840 Azzolina, David S. *Tale Type- and Motif-Indexes: An Annotated Bibliography*. Garland Reference Library of the Humanities 565: Garland Folklore Bibliographies 12. New York: Garland, 1987. 105 pp. Z5983.L5.A98 [GR74.6] 016.3982.

An annotated bibliography of type- and motif-indexes published worldwide through 1985. Azzolina cites dissertations and theses as well as books and articles, but excludes indexes of proverbs and most ballad indexes. The 186 entries are listed alphabetically by author or editor. Each is accompanied by a descriptive annotation that frequently cites reviews or related scholarship as well. Three indexes: subjects; geographic areas; additional authors. Admirably broad in coverage, Azzolina is the essential guide to type- and motif-indexes.

Indexes

5845 Thompson, Stith. *Motif-Index of Folk-Literature: A Classification of Narrative Elements in Folktales, Ballads, Myths, Fables, Mediaeval Romances,*

Exempla, Fabliaux, Jest-Books, and Local Legends. 6 vols. Rev. and enl. ed. Bloomington: Indiana UP, 1955–58. GR67.T52 398.012.

A systematic classification of motifs occurring in traditional oral and written narratives throughout the world. Thompson excludes "superstitions, customs, religious beliefs, riddles, or proverbs except as they happen to form an organic part of a narrative"; and it silently ignores nearly everything sexual or scatological. The motifs are organized in 23 broad subject divisions (e.g., animals, ogres, mythological motifs, captives and fugitives, the dead) that are extensively subdivided (with each division prefaced by a detailed outline). Where possible, individual motifs are accompanied by references to locations, collections, lists of variants, scholarship, related motifs, and Aarne-Thompson tale-types (5850). Thompson's citations are more fully and accurately identified in Polly Grimshaw, ed., Motif-Index of Folk-Literature: *Bibliography and Abbreviations* (N.p.: n.p., [1976?], 38 pp.). Indexed by subjects. To locate specific motifs, users should begin with the outline prefacing each division or the thorough analytical subject index. A monumental compilation that is underutilized by literature scholars, Thompson is the indispensable source for identifying, locating, cataloging, and referring (by Thompson numbers) to motifs in oral and written literatures worldwide. Review: Kurt Ranke, *Journal of American Folklore* 71 (1958): 81–83.

An important complementary source for identifying motifs and tale-types in English-language literature in Great Britain and North America is Ernest W. Baughman, *Type and Motif-Index of the Folktales of England and North America*, Indiana U Folklore Series 20 (The Hague: Mouton, 1966, 606 pp.). The organization of the tale-type index is modeled on Aarne-Thompson (5850) and the motif-index on Thompson, with entries similar to the latter's in content. Although Baughman lacks its own subject index, users can locate individual types and motifs by consulting the one in Thompson.

5850 Aarne, Antti. *The Types of the Folktale: A Classification and Bibliography* (Aarne-Thompson). Trans. and enl. Stith Thompson. 2nd revision. FF Communications 184. Helsinki: Suomalainen Tiedeakatemia, 1961. 588 pp. GR1.F55 016.3982.

A classification by tale-type of oral folktales from Europe, Western Asia, and areas settled by peoples from these regions. *Types of the Folktale* excludes local legends and literary tales outside the oral tradition. Unlike a motif-index, which focuses on elements within tales, Aarne-Thompson classifies entire works. Organized within divisions for animal tales, ordinary folktales, jokes and anecdotes, formula tales, and unclassified tales, entries provide a brief summary, list of motifs, citations to texts, and the number of recorded instances in each country. Because these tales lack formal titles and exist in numerous variants, the best approach to the contents is through the subject index. An index to motifs would improve access. A model for tale-type classifications of other regions, *Types of the Folktale* is the standard source for locating texts of traditional oral narratives of Europe and Western Asia and for identifying tale-types (Aarne-Thompson numbers are the standard for citing tale-types). Review: Haim Schwarzbaum, *Fabula* 6 (1963): 182–94 (with numerous additions and corrections).

OTHER GUIDES

5855 Briggs, Katharine M. *A Dictionary of British Folk-Tales in the English Language: Incorporating the F. J. Norton Collection*. 4 vols. Bloomington: Indiana UP, 1970–71. GR141.B69 398.2'0942.

Pt. A: *Folk Narratives*. 2 vols. 1970.
Pt. B: *Folk Legends*. 2 vols. 1971.

A dictionary of English-language folk narratives and legends of the British Isles. Pt. A has divisions for fables and exempla, fairy tales, jocular tales, novelle, and nursery tales; Pt. B, for black dogs, bogies, devils, dragons, fairies, ghosts, and giants. In each division, tales are organized by title, with the full text or extensive summary followed by source(s); Aarne-Thompson (5850) tale-type number; Thompson (5845), Baughman (5845a), or other motif-index numbers; cross-references; and commentary. Each part is prefaced by two indexes: tale-types; titles. Although an index of motifs would be welcome, *Dictionary of British Folk-Tales* is an important compilation that saves researchers from hunting out widely scattered texts.

Guides to Scholarship and Criticism

SURVEYS OF RESEARCH

5860 Dorson, Richard M., ed. *Handbook of American Folklore*. Bloomington: Indiana UP, 1983. 584 pp. GR105.H36 398'.0973.

A collection of essays that describe the state of research (as of c. 1978) in various areas of American folklore. Organized in divisions for topics of research (with sections on ethnic groups and movements, cultural myths, settings, entertainments, and forms and performers), interpretation of research, research methods (including an essay on folklore and American literature and an inadequate overview of bibliographies and indexes), and the presentation of research. The essays variously outline a topic, comment on important scholarship, discuss methodology, and suggest topics for further research. Indexed by persons, titles, and subjects. The brief essays vary considerably in quality, but together they offer a useful, if flawed, introduction to the study of American folklore. Review: Bruce Jackson, *New York Folklore* 10.1–2 (1984): 99–112.

For a history of folklore studies in the United States, see Simon J. Bronner, *American Folklore Studies: An Intellectual History* (Lawrence: UP of Kansas, 1986, 213 pp.); for European folkloristics, see Giuseppe Cocchiara, *The History of Folklore in Europe*, trans. John N. McDaniel, Translations in Folklore Studies (Philadelphia: Inst. for the Study of Human Issues, 1981, 703 pp.).

See also

"Year's Work in Scottish Literary and Linguistic Studies" (3070).

SERIAL BIBLIOGRAPHIES

5865 *Internationale volkskundliche Bibliographie/International Folklore Bibliography/Bibliographie internationale d'ethnologie [1917–]* (*IVB*). Bonn: Habelt, 1919– . Irregular, with recent volumes covering two years. (Title varies.) Z5982.I523 016.398.

A selective bibliography of important or representative scholarship on the folklore of Europe, North and South America, and South Africa. Although the scope has broadened over the years (with the early volumes emphasizing Europe), the organization has remained fairly consistent. Entries are now listed alphabetically by author in 21 extensively classified divisions: general works; settlements; buildings; objects; signs; technology, arts and crafts, and industries; characteristics and types of peoples; costume and adornment; food; manners and customs, festivals, and pastimes; social traditions and common law; popular beliefs; folk medicine; popular science; general studies of folk literature; popular poetry; music and dance; märchen, folktales, myths, and legends; folk drama; other folk literature; and popular speech. (The division for names was dropped with the volume for 1975–76.) Two indexes: authors; subjects (in German, but with separate ones in English, beginning with the 1979–80 volume, and in French, beginning with the 1981–82 volume). The editors are planning a more sophisticated subject indexing system and exploring the possibility of online access. For the history of the work, see Rolf Wilhelm Brednich, "*The International Folklore Bibliography*," *International Folklore Review* 1 (1981): 17–21.

Although *IVB* now offers the most extensive coverage of any serial bibliography of folklore scholarship on the four continents, it must be supplemented by the Folklore division of *MLAIB* (335), which is more timely and truly international but less thorough in covering the regions the works have in common. For a discussion of *MLAIB*'s coverage of folklore, see entry 335 and Michael Taft, "The Folklore Section of the *MLA International Bibliography*," *International Folklore Review* 2 (1982): 61–64.

For earlier scholarship, the following defunct serial bibliographies and abstracts remain important:

Abstracts of Folklore Studies. 13 vols. Austin: U of Texas P, for American Folklore Soc., 1963–75. Coverage is selective—more precisely, inconsistent—with the descriptive abstracts varying considerably in detail and quality. Because entries are organized by journal, the annual index of authors, subjects, and titles is essential for locating specific articles.

"Annual Bibliography of Folklore [c. 1948–62]." *Journal of American Folklore* (entry 5895) 62–76 (1949–63). (The earlier bibliographies are called "Folklore in Periodical Literature" and are scattered throughout issues; the bibliographies in later years appear in a supplement to the journal.) Continued by: "Annual Bibliography [1963–64]." *Abstracts of Folklore Studies* 2–3 (1964–65). Coverage is selective, with works organized in divisions for general studies; material culture; customs, beliefs, and superstitions; linguistic folklore; prose narratives; folksong and folk poetry; music; dance; games; drama; folklore and literature; and peripheral materials.

"Folklore Bibliography for [1937–72]." *Southern Folklore Quarterly* 2–37 (1938–73). Continued by: *Folklore Bibliography for [1973–76]*. Comp. Merle E. Simmons. Indiana U Folklore Institute Monograph Series

[28–29, 31, 33]. Philadelphia: Inst. for the Study of Human Issues, 1975–81. The scope has varied considerably over the years, but with the bibliography for 1967 (32 [1968]), it narrows to works about the Americas, Spain, Portugal, and other Spanish- or Portuguese-speaking areas, as well as studies by folklorists in those regions. The descriptively annotated entries are listed in 10 divisions: general folklore; prose narrative; song, game, and dance; drama; ritual and festival; belief and practice; material culture; speech; proverbs; and riddles. Indexed by authors.

See also

Sec. G: Serial Bibliographies, Indexes, and Abstracts.
ABELL (340): Ancillary Studies/Mythology, Legend, and Folklore section in the volumes for 1934–72; Folklife division in the volume for 1973; and Folklore and Folklife division in later volumes.
L'année philologique (4890).
Annual Bibliography of Scottish Literature (3075).
"Deutsche amerikakundliche Veröffentlichungen," *Amerikastudien* (3285).
International Medieval Bibliography (1835).
Minorities in America (3700).
MLAIB (335): Through the volume for 1980, many national literature divisions have a Folklore heading or section. See also the Folklore heading in the General division in the volume for 1928, General VII [or V]: Folklore and Folklore Motifs in Literature section in the volumes for 1929–32; the Folklore heading in the General division in the volumes for 1933–54; General V [or VIII]: Folklore in the volumes for 1955–68; and the Folklore division in later volumes. Researchers must also check the headings beginning "Folk" and "Folklore" in the subject index to post-1980 volumes.

OTHER BIBLIOGRAPHIES

5870 Flanagan, Cathleen C., and John T. Flanagan. *American Folklore: A Bibliography, 1950–1974*. Metuchen: Scarecrow, 1977. 406 pp. Z5984.U6.F55 [GR105] 016.398'0973.

A bibliography of publications on the verbal folklore of the United States. Flanagan excludes notes, newspaper articles, and most reviews. The 3,639 or so entries are listed alphabetically by author in 15 divisions (only a few of which are minimally classified): collections of essays; reference works; study and teaching of folklore; general studies; ballads and songs; tales and narrative material; legends; myth; beliefs, customs, superstitions, and cures; folk heroes; folklore in literature; proverbs, riddles, Wellerisms, and limericks; speech, names, and cries; minor genres; and obituaries of folklorists. Many entries are accompanied by brief descriptive annotations, a few of which include evaluative comments. Indexed by authors. There are numerous errors in citations, inconsistencies in classification, and significant omissions, and the insufficiently classified divisions, lack of cross-references, and inexcusable failure to provide a subject index make *American Folklore* a time-consuming work to consult. Yet this and Haywood, *Bibliography of North American Folklore* (5875) remain essential sources principally because they offer the most thorough coverage of scholarship before 1975 on most genres of American folklore;

fortunately, parts are gradually being superseded by bibliographies of individual genres. Reviews: Jan Harold Brunvand, *Western Folklore* 38 (1979): 66–70; Robert W. Halli, Jr., *Tennessee Folklore Society Bulletin* 44 (1978): 45–47.

5875 Haywood, Charles. *A Bibliography of North American Folklore and Folksong*. 2nd rev. ed. 2 vols. New York: Dover, 1961. Z5984.U5.H32 016.398.

Vol. 1: *The American People North of Mexico, Including Canada.*
Vol. 2: *The American Indians North of Mexico, Including the Eskimos.*

A bibliography of primary and secondary works (including some fiction) through mid-1948 related to the folklore of North America (along with a few works on the British Isles). The second edition is actually an uncorrected reprint of the original one (New York: Greenberg, 1951, 1,291 pp.) with a new index of composers, arrangers, and performers. The approximately 40,000 entries are organized in seven variously classified divisions: (vol. 1) general studies, regions, ethnic groups, occupations, and miscellaneous; (vol. 2) general studies and cultural areas. Each of the various subdivisions typically includes sections for folklore and folksong. A few entries are accompanied by brief descriptive or evaluative annotations. Two indexes: authors, subjects, and titles of folk works; composers, arrangers, and performers. A conglomeration of entries that is confusingly organized, admits much that is inconsequential or outside the realm of folklore, includes numerous errors, and has major gaps in coverage, Haywood is, however, an essential source for identifying studies before mid-1948 on North American folklore. Fortunately, it is now being superseded in many areas by bibliographies on individual genres. Reviews: (1951 ed.) Richard M. Dorson, *Southern Folklore Quarterly* 15 (1951): 263–66; MacEdward Leach, *Journal of American Folklore* 65 (1952): 98–101; (2nd ed.) Dorson, *Southern Folklore Quarterly* 27 (1963): 346.

5880 Szwed, John F., and Roger D. Abrahams. *Afro-American Folk Culture: An Annotated Bibliography of Materials from North, Central and South America, and the West Indies*. 2 vols. Publications of the American Folklore Society: Bibliographical and Special Series 31–32. Philadelphia: Inst. for the Study of Human Issues, 1978. Z5984.A44.S95 [GR103] 016.909'04'96.

A bibliography of published scholarship, some literary works, and record notes (through 1973) on Afro-American folk culture. The entries are listed alphabetically in six divisions: bibliographies, general studies, North America, Caribbean, Central America, and South America (with the last three subdivided by region or country). Many of the very brief annotations are inadequately descriptive, and several works are unannotated. Two cumulated indexes in each volume: subjects; places. Annotations are frequently uninformative; there are significant omissions; and studies about a particular topic are difficult to locate because of the unrefined organization and inadequate, incomplete subject indexing. Even so, *Afro-American Folk Culture* is useful because of its breadth of coverage.

See also

Baer, *Folklore and Literature of the British Isles* (1390).
Clements, *Native American Folklore, 1879–1979* (3885).
Comitas, *Complete Caribbeana, 1800–1975* (4790).
Fowke, *Bibliography of Canadian Folklore in English* (4665).

Jones, *Folklore and Literature in the United States* (3290).
Jordan, *English-Speaking Caribbean* (4785).
Kiell, *Psychoanalysis, Psychology, and Literature* (6540).
Lindfors, *Black African Literature in English* (4425).
Literary History of the United States: Bibliography (3300).
Miller, *Comprehensive Bibliography for the Study of American Minorities* (3700).
Murdock, *Ethnographic Bibliography of North America* (3890).
Nemanic, *Bibliographical Guide to Midwestern Literature* (3600).
Rubin, *Bibliographical Guide to the Study of Southern Literature* (3625).
Salzman, *American Studies: An Annotated Bibliography* (3335).
Watters, *On Canadian Literature, 1806–1960* (4655).

DISSERTATIONS AND THESES

5885 Dundes, Alan, comp. *Folklore Theses and Dissertations in the United States*. Publications of the American Folklore Society: Bibliographical and Special Series 27. Austin: U of Texas P, for American Folklore Soc., 1976. 610 pp. Z5981.D85 [GR65] 016.398.

A bibliography of master's theses and doctoral dissertations on folklore accepted between 1860 and 1968 by institutions in the United States. Organized chronologically by year of acceptance, then alphabetically by author, entries cite title, degree, department, institution, and number of pages. Three indexes: subjects; authors; institutions. Because of the chronological organization, the best approach to contents is through the detailed analytical subject index (which, however, is based on titles). The introduction discusses the importance of folklore theses and dissertations. Coverage is less complete after 1964, and the nature of the sources means that there are inevitably omissions, errors, and incomplete entries; however, Dundes is a time-saving compilation of theses and dissertations from a variety of sources.

See also

Sec. H: Guides to Dissertations and Theses.
Emerson, *Southern Literary Culture: A Bibliography of Masters' and Doctors' Theses* (3630).
Woodress, *Dissertations in American Literature, 1891–1966* (3320).

Periodicals

5890 *Folklore*. 1890– . 2/yr. GR1.F5 398'.05.

Publishes articles and brief reviews on folklore throughout the world, but with an emphasis on British topics and a considerable number of articles on literary works. Annual index; cumulative indexes: vols. 1–68, Wilfrid Bonser, *A Bibliography of Folklore as Contained in the First Eighty Years of the Publications of the Folklore Society*, Publications of the Folklore Society 121 (London: Glaisher, for the Folk-Lore Soc., 1961, 126 pp.); vols. 69–78, Bonser, comp., *A Bibliography of Folklore for 1958–1967, Being a Subject Index, Vols. 69–78, of the Journal* Folklore, Publications of the Folklore Society 130 (1969, 54 pp.).

5895 *Journal of American Folklore* (*JAF*). 1888– . Quarterly. GR1.J8 398.

Publishes articles, notes, and reviews of books, exhibitions, records, and films on folklore worldwide. Its reviews are among the most rigorous of any journal in the field. Vols. 62–76 (1949–63) print the "Annual Bibliography of Folklore [c. 1948–62]" (entry 5865a); the earlier bibliographies are titled "Folklore in Periodical Literature" and are scattered through issues, while the later ones appear in a supplement to the journal. Annual index in some volumes; cumulative indexes: vols. 1–70, Tristram P. Coffin, *An Analytical Index to the* Journal of American Folklore, *Vols. 1–67, 68, 69, 70* (Philadelphia: American Folklore Soc., 1958, 384 pp.), with each of the last three volumes indexed separately; vols. 1–100, *The Centennial Index: One Hundred Years of the* Journal of American Folklore, ed. and comp. Bruce Jackson, Michael Taft, and Harvey S. Axlerod, 101.402 (1988): 502 pp.

5900 *Journal of Folklore Research* (*JFR*). 1964– . 3/yr. Former title: *Journal of the Folklore Institute* (1964–82). GR1.I5 398'.05.

Since vol. 20 (1983), *Journal of Folklore Research* emphasizes articles on current theories and methodologies; it also publishes brief notes on new books and occasional special issues. The most emphatically theoretical of journals in the field.

Genres

Coverage here is limited to genres that have reference sources of interest to literary researchers.

FABLE

5905 Carnes, Pack. *Fable Scholarship: An Annotated Bibliography*. Garland Reference Library of the Humanities 367: Garland Folklore Bibliographies 8. New York: Garland, 1985. 382 pp. Z5896.C37 [PN980] 016.3982.

An international bibliography of books, articles, and dissertations, for the most part published between 1880 and 1981 (with some works from 1982). Listed alphabetically by scholar, the 1,457 entries are accompanied by full descriptive annotations which frequently include evaluative comments and cite Aarne-Thompson (5850), Thompson (5845), and Perry numbers. Three indexes: names and subjects; fables (by Perry number); tale-types (by Aarne-Thompson number). Although *Fable Scholarship* is selective, the full annotations, international coverage, and thorough indexing make it the essential starting point for research on the fable.

MUSIC

Guides to Scholarship

5910 Miller, Terry E. *Folk Music in America: A Reference Guide*. Garland Reference Library of the Humanities 496. New York: Garland, 1986. 424 pp. ML128.F74.M5 016.781773.

An annotated bibliography of books, articles, and dissertations through 1984 on folk music in the United States. Miller emphasizes recent ethnomusicological publications; it excludes articles in newspapers and popular magazines, record notes, and reviews, as well as most master's theses, articles of fewer than nine pages, and works published before 1900. The 1,927 entries are organized in nine variously classified divisions: general works (including bibliographies, discographies, reference works, and general studies), music of the American Indians and Eskimos, Anglo-American folksongs and ballads, later developments in Anglo-American folk music (especially bluegrass, country and western, folksong revival, and protest music), traditional instruments and instrumental music; American psalmody and hymnody, singing school and shape-note traditions, Afro-American music, and music of various ethnic traditions. Several of the descriptive annotations, which sometimes include an evaluative comment, inadequately summarize contents. Two indexes: scholars; subjects. Confusing in its explanation of criteria governing inclusion and omitting numerous studies, *Folk Music in America* is only a starting point for research on folk music in the United States.

See also

"Current Bibliography, Discography, and Filmography," *Ethnomusicology* (5913).

Periodicals

5913 *Ethnomusicology: Journal of the Society for Ethnomusicology* (*Ethnomusicology*). 1953– . 3/yr. ML1.E77 781.7'2'005.

Publishes articles and reviews of books, recordings, and films on ethnomusicology worldwide. Of particular note in each issue is the unannotated "Current Bibliography, Discography, and Filmography," with sections for general studies, areas of the world, and dissertations and theses. Annual index; cumulative indexes: vols. 1–10 (Middletown: Wesleyan UP, 1967, 42 pp.); vols. 11–20, comp. Gerard Béhague, Marie Labonville, and Carol Morgan (1977, 78 pp.); and vols. 21–30 (1986, 68 pp.).

PROVERB

Dictionaries

5915 *The Oxford Dictionary of English Proverbs*. Rev. F. P. Wilson. 3rd ed. Oxford: Clarendon, 1970. 930 pp. PN6421.O9 398.9'2'03.

A dictionary of selected proverbs used in written works in England since the fourteenth century. Listed alphabetically by the first significant word, with cross-references for other words, each proverb is followed by a chronological list of dated examples and variants. For some additions and corrections, see Robert D. Dunn, "Corrections to *The Oxford Dictionary of English Proverbs*," *American Notes and Queries* 24 (1985): 52–54. Although this is the best overall dictionary for identifying proverbs in English, it must be supplemented by the following:

Stevenson, Burton. *The Home Book of Proverbs, Maxims, and Familiar Phrases*. New York: Macmillan, 1948. 2,957 pp. (Reprinted as *The Macmillan Book of Proverbs, Maxims, and Famous Phrases*, 1965.)

Taylor, Archer, and Bartlett Jere Whiting. *A Dictionary of American Proverbs and Proverbial Phrases, 1820–1880*. Cambridge: Belknap-Harvard UP, 1958. 418 pp.

Tilley, Morris Palmer. *A Dictionary of the Proverbs in England in the Sixteenth and Seventeenth Centuries: A Collection of the Proverbs Found in English Literature and the Dictionaries of the Period*. Ann Arbor: U of Michigan P, 1950. 854 pp. Much of this material is incorporated in *Oxford Dictionary*.

Whiting, Bartlett Jere. *Early American Proverbs and Proverbial Phrases*. Cambridge: Belknap-Harvard UP, 1977. 555 pp.

Whiting, Bartlett Jere, and Helen Wescott Whiting. *Proverbs, Sentences, and Proverbial Phrases from English Writings Mainly before 1500*. Cambridge: Belknap-Harvard UP, 1968. 733 pp.

Both Sheehy, *Guide to Reference Books* (60), p. 423, and Walford, *Walford's Guide to Reference Material* (65), vol. 2, pp. 361–64, list additional dictionaries.

See also

Bartlett, *Familiar Quotations* (6315).

Guides to Scholarship

5920 Mieder, Wolfgang. *International Proverb Scholarship: An Annotated Bibliography*. Garland Reference Library of the Humanities 342: Garland Folklore Bibliographies 3. New York: Garland, 1982. 613 pp. Z7191.M543 [PN6401] 016.398'9.

An international bibliography of books, articles, and dissertations from 1800 through c. 1981 on proverbs. Mieder excludes collections of proverbs, literary studies that are lists unaccompanied by critical analysis, and most brief notes. Listed alphabetically by scholar, the 2,142 entries are accompanied by full descriptive (and sometimes evaluative) annotations. Three indexes: names; subjects; specific proverbs. Thoroughly indexed and clearly annotated, *International Proverb Scholarship* is the essential guide to international paremiological scholarship (including numerous studies of proverbs in literary works), but it must be supplemented by *MLAIB* (335). Continued in "International Proverb Scholarship: An Updated Bibliography through [1981–]" and "Recent International Proverb Scholarship: An Annotated Bibliography for [1982–]," both in *Proverbium* (5925).

Periodicals

5925 *Proverbium: Yearbook of International Proverb Scholarship [1984–]*. 1984– . Annual. PN6401.P77 398'.9'05.

Publishes articles, reviews, and bibliographies on proverbs throughout the world. Of particular note are three annual bibliographies: "International Proverb Scholarship: An Updated Bibliography through [1981–]," "Recent International Proverb Scholarship: An Annotated Bibliography for [1982–]" (both of which continue Mieder, *International Proverb Scholarship* [5920]), and "International Bibliography of New and Reprinted Proverb Collections [1975–]."

Grants

5940 *The Grants Register.* New York: St. Martin's, 1969– . Biennial. LB2338.G7 378.34.

A guide to grants, fellowships, exchange programs, awards, and honoraria sponsored by foundations, institutions, and government agencies in the United States, Canada, United Kingdom, Ireland, Australia, New Zealand, South Africa, and several developing countries. Listed alphabetically by sponsor, entries consist of name of the grant, purpose, subjects, number offered, value, eligibility requirements, deadline, tenability, notes on selection process, and address for further information. Indexed at the front by subjects, at the back by grants and organizations. The fullest international guide, *Grants Register* describes several grants of interest to literature and language scholars.

Other sources for locating grants of interest to literary scholars include these works:

Annual Register of Grant Support: A Directory of Funding Sources. Wilmette: National Register, 1969– . Annual. Restricted to sources that fund applicants from the United States or Canada or otherwise benefit either country. The literature division lists numerous prizes and awards that are not grants.

The Foundation Directory. New York: Foundation Center, 1960– . Irregular. A directory of private, nonprofit foundations in the United States that have assets of at least $1,000,000 and made at least $100,000 in grants during the past year.

Grants and Awards Available to American Writers (5175a).

PMLA, Directory issue (5060).

Interdisciplinary and Multidisciplinary Studies

This section is limited to reference works that treat the relationship of literature to several other arts, disciplines, or fields of knowledge. Works devoted to a single art, discipline, or field appear in one of the following divisions of section U: Art and Literature, Film and Literature, Medicine and Literature, Music and Literature, Philosophy and Literature, Religion and Literature, Science and Literature, and Social Sciences and Literature.

General Introductions

5955 Barricelli, Jean-Pierre, and Joseph Gibaldi, eds. *Interrelations of Literature*. New York: MLA, 1982. 329 pp. PN45.8.I56 809.

A collection of introductions to the interdisciplinary study of literature and linguistics, philosophy, religion, myth, folklore, sociology, politics, law, science, psychology, music, visual arts, and film. Although the emphasis varies from essay to essay, each essay typically outlines the nature of the relationship, provides a historical overview, comments on important studies, describes major theories and approaches, suggests areas for research, and concludes with a selective, briefly annotated bibliography. A glossary covers all essays. Indexed by persons and anonymous titles. Written by distinguished scholars, the essays provide the nonspecialist with informed introductions to the study of literature in relationship to other fields.

James Thorpe, ed., *Relations of Literary Study: Essays on Interdisciplinary Contributions* (New York: MLA, 1967, 151 pp.), with essays on history, myth, biography, psychology, sociology, religion, and music, remains useful for its historical perspective.

Handbooks, Dictionaries, and Encyclopedias

5960 *Dictionary of the History of Ideas: Studies of Selected Pivotal Ideas*. Ed. Philip P. Wiener. 5 vols. New York: Scribner's, 1973–74. CB5.D52 909.

Interdisciplinary, cross-cultural, and transnational examinations of seminal concepts and topics in intellectual history. Written by major scholars, the approximately 300 articles include several on literary forms, techniques, movements, themes, and aesthetics. Each article concludes with a selected bibliography and cross-references to related articles. (For an overview by discipline, see the analytical table of contents in vol. 1, pp. ix-xv.) The best approach to contents is through the detailed index of persons and subjects (vol. 5). A monumental work, *Dictionary of the History of Ideas* is especially valuable to literary researchers for its interdisciplinary coverage. Review: F. E. L. Priestley, *Journal of the History of Ideas* 35 (1974): 527–37.

Guides to Scholarship and Criticism

5965 "Bibliography on the Relations of Literature and the Other Arts [1952–]." *YCGL: Yearbook of Comparative and General Literature* (entry 5035) 34 (1985)– .

1959–84: *A Bibliography on the Relations of Literature and the Other Arts*. Hanover: Dartmouth Coll., Dept. of German, 1959–[85?]. Annual.

1973–75: "Bibliography on the Relations of Literature and the Other Arts." *Hartford Studies in Literature* 6–8 (1974–76).

1952–67: *A Bibliography on the Relations of Literature and the Other Arts, 1952–1967*. New York: AMS, 1968. (A reprint of the issues covering 1952–67.)

1952–58: Neumann, Alfred E., comp. David V. Erdman, ed. *Literature and the Other Arts: A Select Bibliography, 1952–1958*. New York: New York Public Library, 1959. 37 pp.

An annual bibliography of studies involving literature and music, the visual arts, or dance; those for 1974 through 1984 include film and literature. Entries are now organized by author in four divisions: general and theoretical studies, music and literature, visual arts and literature, and dance and literature. Except for the first, each division has sections for general studies and historical periods appropriate to the subject. A few entries are accompanied by brief descriptive annotations. Although not comprehensive, this work is the single best source for identifying those interdisciplinary studies that are frequently impossible to locate in the standard serial bibliographies and indexes in section G. Because few libraries hold complete runs of the annual volumes through 1984, an augmented cumulation—or at least a collected reprint—would be welcomed by researchers.

See also

Sec. G: Serial Bibliographies, Indexes, and Abstracts.
Baldensperger, *Bibliography of Comparative Literature* (5000).
"Revue des revues," *Canadian Review of Comparative Literature* (4995).
"Selective Current Bibliography for Aesthetics and Related Fields," *Journal of Aesthetics and Art Criticism* (5970).

Periodicals

5970 *Journal of Aesthetics and Art Criticism* (*JAAC*). 1941– . Quarterly. N1.J6 701.1.

Publishes articles and reviews involving the study of the visual arts, literature, music, and theater arts from a philosophic, scientific, or theoretical perspective (including psychology, sociology, anthropology, cultural history, or art criticism). Vols. 1–31 (1941–73) print "Selective Current Bibliography for Aesthetics and Related Fields," a classified bibliography of studies on the philosophical, scientific, or theoretical study of the arts. Annual index; cumulative index: vols. 1–35, Lars Aagaard-Mogensen, *Cumulative Index Volumes I–XXXV, 1941–1977* (1979, 193 pp.).

5975 *Journal of the History of Ideas* (*JHI*). 1940– . Quarterly. B1.J75 105.

Publishes articles, notes, and review essays that examine the historical development of ideas in, or interrelationship of, the history of philosophy, art, literature, religion, politics, and natural and social sciences. Recent volumes tend to focus on the eighteenth and nineteenth centuries. Annual index; cumulative indexes: vols. 1–25, Esther F. Kandel and Elizabeth Rapaport (1966, 84 pp.); vols. 26–30, Kandel (1969, 64 pp.).

See also

Journal of Literary Semantics (6060).

Linguistics and Literature

This section is limited to reference works of use to researchers interested in linguistic approaches to and aspects of literature. It also includes some essential reference works on the English language.

For an introduction to the interdisciplinary study of literature and linguistics, see Jonathan Culler, "Literature and Linguistics" (pp. 1–24) in Barricelli, *Interrelations of Literature* (5955). Winfred P. Lehmann provides a succinct overview of the field in "Linguistics" (pp. 1–28) in Gibaldi, *Introduction to Scholarship in Modern Languages and Literatures* (25).

General Introductions

5990 Fowler, Roger. *Linguistic Criticism*. New York: Oxford UP, 1986. 190 pp. P123.F65 410.

An introduction to the study of literature as social discourse that "demonstrate[s] the value to criticism of an analytic method drawn from linguistics." The chapters on semantic processes, textual structure and construction, contexts of communication, dialogue, point of view, and ordering of experience employ a variety of examples from literary works. Fowler concludes with a selective list of works on linguistics and linguistic criticism and stylistics; most entries are accompanied by a brief evaluative comment. Indexed by subjects, persons, and literary works. The work, which presumes a basic knowledge of linguistics on the reader's part, is a handy introduction to the linguistic criticism of literature by one its leading theorists.

For a more detailed introduction to stylistic criticism, see Anne Cluysenaar, *Aspects of Literary Stylistics: A Discussion of Dominant Structures in Verse and Prose* (New York: St. Martin's, 1975, 160 pp.).

5995 Traugott, Elizabeth Closs, and Mary Louise Pratt. *Linguistics for Students of Literature*. New York: Harcourt, 1980. 444 pp. P123.T67 410.

An introductory guide to the application of linguistics in literary study, with chapters on linguistics and literary analysis, phonetics and phonology, morphemes and words, syntax, semantics, speech acts and speech genres (actually a conglomeration of topics), discourse, varieties of English, and English in contact with other languages. Using a generative model, each chapter describes an aspect of language, demonstrates its applications in literary study, and concludes with a list of suggested readings. Three indexes: literary authors; authors of linguistic and critical works; subjects. Although Traugott emphasizes linguistics more than literature and is not always successful in demonstrating applications in literary study, the work is useful as an introductory overview. Reviews: Peter C. Collins, *General Linguistics* 22 (1982): 65–70; Herbert Penzl, *Language* 57 (1981): 782–83.

See also

Sec. U: Literature-Related Topics and Sources/Computers and the Humanities/General Introductions.

Histories of the English Language

6000 Baugh, Albert C., and Thomas Cable. *A History of the English Language*. 3rd ed. Englewood Cliffs: Prentice, 1978. 438 pp. PE1075.B3 420.'9.

A history of the development of the language from Anglo-Saxon to Modern

English. After an initial discussion of present-day English and its future, chapters proceed chronologically to examine the internal and external factors that shaped the language from its Indo-European origins to the present. Each chapter concludes with a selected bibliography. Two appendixes: specimens of Middle English dialects; examples of early orthography. Indexed by persons, subjects, and anonymous works. Although it ignores recent developments in linguistic theory and trends in scholarship, Baugh remains one of the best general introductions to the history of English in Great Britain and the United States. Review: R. A. Peters, *Journal of English Linguistics* 13 (1979): 94–95.

A good complement is Thomas Pyles and John Algeo, *The Origins and Development of the English Language*, 3rd ed. (New York: Harcourt, 1982, 383 pp.), a descriptive traditional approach to the internal history of the English language since the Anglo-Saxon period.

Handbooks, Linguistic Dictionaries, and Encyclopedias

6005 Crystal, David. *A Dictionary of Linguistics and Phonetics*. [2nd ed.] Language Library. Oxford: Blackwell, 1985. 339 pp. P29.C65 410'.3'21.

A dictionary of terminology used in twentieth-century linguistic and phonetic scholarship. Crystal excludes terms restricted to applied linguistics and comparative philology, as well as those not current after 1900. A typical entry consists of a definition, discussion of historical context, examples, generous cross-references to related terms, and citations to fuller explanations in selected basic studies. It is an introductory work, but the clear, objective definitions make the *Dictionary* an essential guide to the terminology of twentieth-century linguistics and phonetics.

Although dated and less full in its definitions, R. R. K. Hartmann and F. C. Stork, *Dictionary of Language and Linguistics* (London: Applied Science, 1972, 302 pp.), remains a good complement because of its breadth and inclusion of terms before 1900. For applied linguistics, consult Jack Richards, John Platt, and Heidi Weber, *Longman Dictionary of Applied Linguistics* (Harlow: Longman, 1985, 323 pp.).

As Crystal points out in his introduction, a comprehensive dictionary of linguistics is a major desideratum.

General Linguistics

GUIDES TO SCHOLARSHIP

A major need is a judiciously selective, current bibliography of scholarship on linguistics and the English language. Among available ones, Harold B. Allen, comp., *Linguistics and English Linguistics*, 2nd ed., Goldentree Bibliographies in Language and Literature (Arlington Heights: AHM, 1977, 175 pp.), is outdated; and Minoru Yasui, comp., *Current Bibliography on Linguistics and English Linguistics, 1960–1978* (Tokyo: Kaitakusha, 1979, 269 pp.) and *1978–82* (1983, 887 pp.), are based on no clear principles governing selection, omit numerous essential works, and are either imprecise (*1960–1978*) or uncontrolled (*1978–1982*) in subject organization.

Surveys of Research

See

Sec. U: Literature-Related Topics and Sources/Composition and Rhetoric/Guides to Scholarship/Surveys of Research.
YWES (330): Chapter on English language.
Year's Work in Modern Language Studies (4855): General Linguistics division.

Serial Bibliographies

6010 *Bibliographie linguistique/Linguistic Bibliography [1939–]*. Dordrecht: Nijhoff, 1949– . Annual. Z7001.P4 [P121] 016.41.

An international bibliography of scholarship (including book reviews and dissertations) on linguistics and languages worldwide. Entries are organized alphabetically by author in classified divisions for general works (including bibliographies), general linguistics, and major language families or areas. The General Linguistics division and individual languages with sufficient scholarship now have sections for bibliographies and general studies, phonetics and phonology, grammar, lexis, semantics and pragmatics, stylistics, metrics and versification, translation, script and orthography, psycholinguistics and neurolinguistics, historical and comparative linguistics, mathematical and computational linguistics, and onomastics. Under languages not needing subdivision, bibliographies appear first, followed by other studies in alphabetical order. Indexed by scholars (excluding reviewers). The lack of cross-references and subject indexing hinders access to many works, especially those treating more than one concept, topic, or language. Although the number of entries in each volume is swollen by the inclusion of works listed earlier and subsequently reviewed, *Bibliographie linguistique* offers generally fuller coverage of linguistic scholarship—especially that published outside North America—than *MLAIB* (335) and *LLBA* (6015), the other major linguistics serial bibliographies. However, both *MLAIB* and *LLBA* offer superior access because of their subject indexing and are more current by about a year.

Although not as accessible as it should be, *Bibliographie linguistique* is an essential source for identifying current linguistic scholarship; for the literature researcher, it is valuable for its inclusion of numerous studies—especially of stylistics and metrics—that are omitted from the standard serial bibliographies and indexes in section G.

6015 *LLBA: Linguistics and Language Behavior Abstracts* (*LLBA*). San Diego: Sociological Abstracts, 1967– . Quarterly. Former title: *LLBA: Language and Language Behavior Abstracts* (1967–84). Z7004.P4.L106 016.

Nonevaluative abstracts of books, articles, and dissertations since 1966 on language behavior, linguistics, and related topics. Except for dissertations, which are generally limited to those in *Dissertation Abstracts International* (465), coverage is international and, especially for journals, encompasses several disciplines. The scope has expanded somewhat since the initial volume, and the organization has become more refined. Since vol. 11 (1977) entries are listed alphabetically by author in 30 classified divisions: psycholinguistics, applied linguistics, phonology, syntax, semantics, morphology, discourse analysis and text linguistics, theory of linguistics, history of linguistics, anthropological linguistics, structural linguistics, descriptive linguistics, lexicography, orthography and writing systems, typology, interpersonal behavior and communication, sociolinguistics, poetics and stylistics (with sections for poetics and stylistics, literary criticism, and literary theory), nonverbal communication, semiotics, philosophy of language, phonetics, hearing and speech physiology, pathological and normal hearing, pathological and normal language, learning disabilities, mental retardation, psychopathology, special education, and psychometrics. A typical entry consists of author(s), address of primary author, title and publication information, LC and ISBN numbers for books, and a detailed abstract. Three indexes in each issue: authors; journals and issues indexed; subjects. (The last is a detailed analytic index based on a controlled thesaurus, with each entry providing essentially an abstract of the abstract.) The indexes are cumulated annually; there is also a cumulative index for vols. 1–5 (2 pts., 1971). Entries since 1974 can be searched through Dialog (520) and BRS (515). The multidisciplinary coverage and full subject indexing make *LLBA* a useful source for identifying studies of stylistics, literary theory, and literary criticism, especially in journals not covered (or accessibly indexed) in the standard serial bibliographies and indexes in section G.

See also

ABELL (340): English Language division.
L'année philologique (4890).
Bullock, *Guide to Marxist Literary Criticism* (6175).
MLAIB (335): See the national literature divisions in the volumes for 1921–32; General/Linguistics and the linguistics section in national literature divisions in the volume for 1933; General/Linguistics, General/Experimental Phonetics, and linguistics sections in national literature divisions in the volumes for 1934–45; General/General Linguistics, General/Experimental Phonetics, and linguistic sections in national literature divisions in the volumes for 1946–50; General/Linguistics, General/Semantics, and linguistics sections in national literature divisions in the volumes for 1951–52; General VI: Language and linguistics sections in national literature divisions in the volumes for 1953–55; General III: General Language and Linguistics and linguistics sections in national literature divisions in the volume for 1956; General I: General Language and Linguistics and linguistics sections in national literature divisions in the volumes for 1957–66; and the Linguistics division in later volumes (especially General Linguistics IV: Stylistics/Linguistics and Literature in the volumes for 1968–80). Researchers must also check the headings beginning "English Language" and "Linguistics" in the subject index to post-1980 volumes.
Psychological Abstracts (6530).
RILM Abstracts (6240).

Special Topics

LEXICOGRAPHY

Guides to Primary Works

Bibliographies

6020 Brewer, Annie M., ed. *Dictionaries, Encyclopedias, and Other Word-Related Books: A Classified Guide to Dictionaries, Encyclopedias, and Similar Works, Based on Library of Congress Catalog Cards, and Arranged According to the Library of Congress Classification System*. 3 vols. 3rd ed. Detroit: Gale, 1982. Z5848.B73 [AE5] 016'.03.

Vol. 1: *English Books*. 519 pp.
Vol. 2: *Multiple Languages (with English as One Language)*. 462 pp.
Vol. 3: *Non-English Books*. 695 pp.

A subject list of dictionaries, encyclopedias, concordances, glossaries, lexicons, thesauri, vocabularies, and similar works. Since the approximately 28,000 entries consist of reproductions of Library of Congress catalog cards issued between 1966 and October 1981, the three volumes potentially include any "word-related" book published or reprinted during that period as well as numerous pre-1966 publications for which LC cards were prepared. In each volume, the cards are organized by LC classification (an inadequate keyword index is printed at the front of each volume). Additions are printed at the end of vols. 1 and 3. The uncritical reliance on LC cards leads to considerable duplication of entries (especially of unrevised reprints), serious gaps in coverage (especially of books published before 1966), and inconsistencies in the classification of works; and the lack of a subject index is a major impediment. Although seriously flawed, Brewer is the most extensive single list of "word-related books." What would be welcome is a thorough, carefully organized, effectively indexed annotated bibliography based on personal examination of these kinds of publications.

For an evaluative survey of important dictionaries through the late 1960s, see Robert L. Collison, *Dictionaries of English and Foreign Languages: A Bibliographical Guide to Both General and Technical Dictionaries with Historical and Explanatory Notes and References*, 2nd ed. (New York: Hafner, 1971, 303 pp.). Organized by language or geographical area, chapters typically comment on the history and use of general, etymological, slang, dialect, specialist, and bilingual dictionaries. Technical dictionaries are listed by field in an appendix. Collison remains useful for its evaluations of dictionaries published before 1970.

More current (but not rigorous in selection or evaluation) are the sections on dictionaries in Walford, *Walford's Guide to Reference Material* (65) vol. 3, pp. 223–307, and Sheehy, *Guide to Reference Books* (60), pp. 146–208.

Indexes

6025 Wall, C. Edward, and Edward Przebienda, comps. *Words and Phrases Index: A Guide to Antedatings, New Words, New Compounds, New Mean-*

ings, and Other Published Scholarship Supplementing the Oxford English Dictionary, Dictionary of Americanisms, Dictionary of American English, *and Other Major Dictionaries of the English Language.* 4 vols. Ann Arbor: Pierian, 1969–70. PE1689.W3 016.423.

An index to additions, antedatings, and corrections published in *American Notes and Queries* 1–8 (1941–49) and 1–5 (1962–67); *American Speech* 1–41 (1925–66); *Britannica Book of the Year* (1945–67); *California Folklore Quarterly* 1–6 (1942–47); *College English* 1–29 (1939–68); *Dialect Notes* 1–6 (1890–1939); *Notes and Queries* 148–211 (1925–66); *Publication of the American Dialect Society* 1–47 (1944–67); and *Western Folklore* 7–26 (1948–67). Vols. 1 and 3 are word indexes; vols. 2 and 4, keyword-out-of-context indexes to phrases. Wall is a useful source for identifying scholarship on individual words and phrases, since few of the standard serial bibliographies and indexes in section G provide this kind of information.

Periodicals

6030 *Dictionaries: Journal of the Dictionary Society of North America* (*Dictionaries*). 1979– . Annual. P327.D53 413'.028.

Publishes articles and reviews on lexicography and specific dictionaries, including ones in progress.

METAPHOR

Guides to Scholarship

6035 Noppen, J. P. van, S. de Knop, and R. Jongen, comps. *Metaphor: A Bibliography of Post-1970 Publications.* Amsterdam Studies in the Theory and History of Linguistic Science, Series 5: Library and Information Sources in Linguistics 17. Amsterdam: Benjamins, 1985. 497 pp. Z7004.M4.N66 [P301.5.M48] 016.808.

Shibles, Warren A. *Metaphor: An Annotated Bibliography and History.* Whitewater: Language P, 1971. 414 pp. Z7004.M4.S5 011.

International bibliographies of books, articles, dissertations, and theses on metaphor in a variety of disciplines and periods. Organized alphabetically by author (then by title in Shibles, by date in Noppen), some entries are accompanied by descriptive annotations: in Shibles, the annotations vary considerably in quality, and most foreign-language works are not annotated; Noppen offers few annotations, but they tend to be fuller. Both appear to take many entries unverified from other sources. Noppen concludes with a list of recommended works for beginners. Shibles has three indexes: extensive works on metaphor; general subjects; aspects of metaphor. However, the indexing is uncontrolled, inconsistent, and imprecise. Noppen also has three indexes: general subjects; uses and theory of metaphor; tenors, vehicles, and their semantic fields (which is useful for locating studies of types of imagery or specific images). Although Noppen's indexing is superior, the combination of entry number and date is extremely confusing and the additions (pp. 486–97) are excluded. Both works suffer from an inadequate statement of scope and coverage. Although they are plagued by errors, inconsistent in annotations, include much that seems only vaguely related to metaphor, omit significant works, and are inadequately indexed in the case of Shibles, the two volumes together encompass an impressive range of international scholarship. For additions to Shibles, see the anonymous, untitled contribution in *Newsletter: Rhetoric Society of America* 4.3 (1974): 5–13. Reviews: Rosemarie Gläser, *Zeitschrift für Anglistik und Amerikanistik* 23 (1975): 170–71; (Shibles) Winfried Schleiner, *Comparative Literature Studies* 10 (1973): 394–95.

ONOMASTICS

Guides to Scholarship

6040 Rajec, Elizabeth M. *The Study of Names in Literature: A Bibliography.* New York: Saur, 1978. 261 pp. *Supplement.* 1981. 298 pp. Z6514.N35.R34 [PN56.N16] 016.809'92.

An international bibliography of selected reference sources on onomastics in general and of studies (including dissertations and reviews through 1979) of the use of names in literature. The 3,023 entries are listed alphabetically by author, but their number is swollen by separate listings of book reviews. Few of the brief annotations adequately convey a sense of contents. Except for literary authors and titles of anonymous works, the headings in the subject index are generally too broad (especially in the 1978 volume). The inadequate explanation of criteria governing selection, uninformative annotations, numerous errors, omissions, and ineffective subject indexing in the original volume make Rajec little more than a place to begin research on literary onomastics.

Periodicals

6045 *Names: Journal of the American Name Society* (*Names*). 1953– . Quarterly. P769.N3 929.405.

Publishes articles, reviews, and notes, a significant number of which treat names in literary works. For several years *Names* included two selective bibliographies: "Bibliography of Personal Names, [1952–75]," 1–24 (1953–76), and "Place-Name Literature, [1946–79]," irregularly in 3–27 (1955–79). Annual index; cumulative indexes: vols. 1–15, Clarence L. Barnhart, 15 (1967): 245–340; vols. 16–30, Kelsie B. Harder, 30 (1982): 235–329.

PRAGMATICS

Guides to Scholarship

6050 Nuyts, Jan, and Jef Verschueren, comps. *A Comprehensive Bibliography of Pragmatics.* 4 vols. Amsterdam: Benjamins, 1987. Z7004.P73.N89 [P99.4.P72] 016.4'01'9.

A bibliography of publications (including reviews) through 1984 on pragmatics, including speech act theory, implicature, frame analysis, and presupposition. Entries are generally limited to studies of natural language, linguistic communication, or verbal behavior; coverage is most complete for works written in English, French, German, or Dutch. Organized in a single author list, most of the entries are accompanied by full, informative descriptive annotations. Four indexes (in vol. 1): persons; languages discussed; words; subjects. The compilers plan regular updates and eventually a computer-readable version. Although not comprehensive, Nuyts is the fullest guide to scholarship on the subject and supersedes Verschueren, *Pragmatics: An Annotated Bibliography*, Amsterdam Studies in the Theory and History of Linguistic Science, Series 5: Library and Information Sources in Linguistics 4 (Amsterdam: Benjamins, 1978, 270 pp.), and the supplements in *Journal of Pragmatics* 2–6 (1978–82).

SEMANTICS

Guides to Scholarship

6055 Gordon, W. Terrence. *Semantics: A Bibliography, 1965–1978*. Metuchen: Scarecrow, 1980. 307 pp. *1979–1985*. 1987. 292 pp. Z7004.S4.G67 [P325] 016.415.

A bibliography of scholarship (including dissertations) in English, French, German, Italian, Spanish, and Portuguese on semantics. Although Gordon's work encompasses studies from linguistics, philosophy, psychology, and anthropology, it excludes several topics of particular interest to literary researchers: general semantics, history of semantics, semiotics, meaning and style, discourse analysis, lexicology, and logical semantics. The approximately 6,000 entries are listed alphabetically by author in divisions for books; general surveys; definitions and models of meaning; reference and pragmatics; ambiguity, indeterminacy, and generic meaning; synonymy; antonymy; polysemy; homonymy; morphosemantics; associative senses in the lexicon; semantic fields and componential analysis; kinship terminology; color terms; semantics of parts of speech; syntax; negation; idioms; case grammar; child language; comparative semantics; and semantic universals. A very few entries are accompanied by brief descriptive (occasionally evaluative) annotations. Although each division concludes with cross-references, the unrefined classification system and lack of subject indexing make locating works difficult. Two indexes: lexical terms; authors. The exclusion of so many areas of study and numerous omissions of works falling within its scope make Gordon little more than a starting point for identifying studies of semantics.

Periodicals

6060 *Journal of Literary Semantics: An International Review* (*JLS*). 1972– . 3/yr. PN54.J68 809.

Publishes articles and reviews dealing with the application of theoretical linguistics to literary texts and the philosophical discussion of the relationships between literature and other disciplines. Cumulative index: vols. 1–10 (N.p.: n.d., 12 pp.).

SEMIOTICS

Handbooks, Dictionaries, and Encyclopedias

6065 *Encyclopedic Dictionary of Semiotics*. Gen. ed. Thomas A. Sebeok. 3 vols. Approaches to Semiotics 73. Berlin: Mouton, 1986. P99.E65 001.51'03.

An encyclopedia of terms (treating both historical background and current uses), dead semioticians and others important in the development of the field, and the relationship of semiotics to other areas (including a 15-page article titled "Literature"). The 426 signed entries, ranging from 1 to 32 pages, refer extensively to the combined bibliography in vol. 3. The essential work for clarifying—and codifying—the sometimes abstruse terminology used in semiotics.

Guides to Scholarship

6070 Eschbach, Achim, and Viktória Eschbach-Szabó, comps. *Bibliography of Semiotics, 1975–1985*. 2 vols. Amsterdam Studies in the Theory and History of Linguistic Science, Series 5: Library and Information Sources in Linguistics 16. Amsterdam: Benjamins, 1986. Z7004.S43.E76 [P99] 016.00151.

Eschbach, Achim, and Wendelin Rader. *Semiotik-Bibliographie I*. Frankfurt: Syndikat, 1976. 221 pp. Z7004.S43.E77 [P99].

Eschbach, Achim. *Zeichen-Text-Bedeutung: Bibliographie zu Theorie und Praxis der Semiotik*. Kritische Information 32. München: Fink, 1974. 508 pp. Z7004.S43.E78.

International bibliographies of publications with some connection to semiotics. *Bibliography of Semiotics* includes book reviews but excludes works published in the Soviet Union. The 10,839 entries are listed alphabetically by author. Two indexes: book reviews; subjects. *Semiotik-Bibliographie* organizes about 4,000 works (published between 1965 and June 1976) in 12 unclassified divisions: architecture, film, semiotic theory and terminology, history of semiotics, art, literature, music, nonverbal communication, pragmatics, semantics, sociosemantics, and miscellaneous works. Two indexes: scholars; subjects. *Zeichen-Text-Bedeutung* includes dissertations. Entries are listed alphabetically by author in six classified divisions: general studies, systematic studies (syntax, semantics, and pragmatics), communication theory and text analysis, background studies, interdisciplinary studies, and works by and about individual semioticians. Indexed by scholars. Although all include a considerable number of studies of literary works, locating these studies is frequently impossible except in *Semiotik-Bibliographie*: *Zeichen-Text-Bedeutung* lacks a subject index, and the one in *Bibliography of Semiotics* is nothing more than an uncritical alphabetic list of title keywords (with no attempt to reconcile equivalent terms in various languages). In all three compilations, the heavy reliance on other bibliographies leads to the inclusion of numerous works only remotely related to semiotics. The lack of any stated criteria governing what constitutes semiotic scholarship results in a hotchpotch that would benefit from judicious organization and indexing.

STYLISTICS

Guides to Scholarship

Serial Bibliographies

6075 "Stylistics Annual Bibliography [1966–86]." *Style* (entry 6095) 1–21 (1967–87).

A bibliography of books, dissertations in *Dissertation Abstracts International* (465), and articles from a core list of about 175 journals. Since the bibliography for 1979 (vol. 15 [1981]), entries are listed alphabetically by author in six divisions: bibliographies; general theory; culture, history, and style—period, nation, and genre; the author; the text; and the reader. The last four have subdivisions for theoretical and applied studies, with the latter classified by elements of style. Entries are accompanied by descriptive annotations. Two indexes: subject terms (since the bibliography for 1980, in vol. 16 [1982]); persons as subjects (since that for 1981, in vol. 17 [1983]). Although not comprehensive, the bibliography is the best source for identifying stylistic scholarship published between 1967 and 1986.

Other Bibliographies

6080 Bailey, Richard W., and Dolores M. Burton, S.N.D. *English Stylistics: A Bibliography*. Cambridge: MIT P, 1968. 198 pp. Z2015.S7.B2 016.808.

A bibliography of primary works and scholarship (including dissertations) through c. 1966 on the stylistic study of English and American literary texts since 1500. Bailey also includes highly selective coverage of classical and medieval literature. The approximately 2,000 entries are organized in three divisions: bibliographies, language and style before 1900 (with each period subdivision including sections for primary works and related scholarship, and general studies), and the twentieth century (with sections on creativity and style, modes of stylistic investigation, statistical approaches, translation, prose stylistics, and poetry). A few entries are accompanied by brief descriptive annotations. Two indexes: literary authors as subjects; scholars. The rather confusing organization, the lack of cross-references, and the failure to provide a subject index seriously impede locating studies on topics, stylistic features, or methodologies. Despite this drawback and the incomplete coverage, Bailey is useful because it represents the fullest list of stylistic studies before 1966 of English and American literature. Review: Louis T. Milic, *Style* 2 (1968): 239–43.

More comprehensive coverage of statistical studies is offered by Richard W. Bailey and Lubomír Doležel, comps. and eds., *An Annotated Bibliography of Statistical Stylistics* (Ann Arbor: Department of Slavic Languages and Literatures, U of Michigan, 1968, 97 pp.). For some additions, see the review by Robert S. Wachal, *Style* 6 (1972): 66–70.

Louis T. Milic, *Style and Stylistics: An Analytical Bibliography* (New York: Free P; London: Collier, 1967, 199 pp.), whose approximately 800 entries are mostly English-language studies of literatures in English, is much less thorough than Bailey but it does cite some works omitted in Bailey and is more accessible, thanks to a subject index. Review: Richard W. Bailey, *Style* 2 (1968): 233–38.

Because stylistic studies are virtually impossible to locate readily in most of the standard serial bibliographies and indexes in section G, these three bibliographies and Bennett, *Bibliography of Stylistics* (6085), are indispensable guides to scholarship.

6085 Bennett, James R. *A Bibliography of Stylistics and Related Criticism, 1967–83*. New York: MLA, 1986. 405 pp. Z6514.S8.B46 [PN203] 016.809.

A selective bibliography of works on the stylistic criticism of literature. Bennett covers studies published between 1967 and 1983 (along with a few from 1984), but excludes dissertations, theoretical studies that do not involve literary application, most psychoanalytic works as well as those about film and literature, and all articles (except for bibliographies and a few in collections of essays). The approximately 1,500 entries are organized by publication date in six classified divisions: bibliographies and reference works (with sections for annual bibliographies and journals, and other bibliographies and reference works); general studies and concepts of style; works on period, national, and genre style (with sections for theoretical studies; diction, imagery, and tropes; syntax and schemes; prosody and sound patterns in prose; and studies involving several linguistic levels); single-author studies (with the same sections as the preceding division); studies of individual texts (again, with the same sections as the preceding division); and the phenomenology of readers (with sections for theoretical and practical studies). A majority of the entries are descriptively annotated (although the annotations too often rely on quotations from the works) and accompanied by citations to reviews (with frequent quotations from reviews). Three appendixes: a chronology of important works and events in stylistics from 1878 to early 1985; a classification of critics by theoretical or methodological approach; a suggested reading list on aspects of stylistic criticism. Four indexes: terms; literary authors and anonymous works; critics and theorists; authors of works cited. Although Bennett is limited by its exclusion of articles and dissertations, unevenly and incompletely annotated (especially for foreign-language works), and incomplete in its coverage of studies of individual authors and works, its international coverage and clear indexing make the *Bibliography* an essential preliminary guide to book-length theoretical studies and practical applications of stylistic criticism and theory. Users will have to supplement coverage with "Stylistics Annual Bibliography" (6075), Bailey, *English Stylistics* (6080), *MLAIB* (335), *Arts and Humanities Citation Index* (365), the bibliographies and indexes in section G, and works in section H: Guides to Dissertations and Theses.

Periodicals

6090 *Language and Style: An International Journal* (*Lang&S*). 1968– . Quarterly. PN203.L35 808'.005.

Publishes articles, a few reviews, and occasional special issues on all aspects of style in the arts, but with a decided emphasis on literature (especially British and American) and with considerable attention to metrics. Annual index.

6095 *Style*. 1967– . Quarterly. PE1.S89.

Publishes articles, annotated bibliographies, reviews, review essays, and occasional special issues on stylistic features of literary works, on the theory and methodology of stylistics, and on literary theory in general. Special features are "Stylistics

Annual Bibliography [1966–86]" (6075) and James R. Bennett, "A Stylistics Checklist [a glossary]," 10 (1976): 350–401, 11 (1977): 425–45, 15 (1981): 326–62, and 17 (1983): 429–53. Annual index; cumulative indexes:

Vols. 1–5: Hardin, John O. "A Methodological Guide to Books Reviewed in *Style*, Volumes I–V." 6 (1972): 317–30.

Vols. 1–6: Bennett, James R. "A Methodological Guide to Articles in *Style*, Volumes I–VI." 6 (1972): 331–43.

Vols. 6–10: Packert-Hall, Beth, and Michael Packert-Hall. "A Guide to *Style*: Reviews, Volumes VI–X; Essays and Bibliographies, Volumes VII–X." 10 (1976): 519–44.

Vols. 11–14: Orr, Sarah Roden. "A Guide to *Style*: Essays and Bibliographies, Volumes XI–XIV; Reviews, Volumes XI–XIV." 15 (1981): 102–24.

SYNTAX

General Introductions

6100 Visser, F. Th. *An Historical Syntax of the English Language*. 4 vols. Leiden: Brill, 1963–73. PE1361.V5.

A diachronic study of the development, in written language, of syntactic constructions with a verb form as a nucleus. Organized according to the number of verbs in a phrase, then by syntactic unit, the detailed analysis and history of each structural pattern is accompanied by numerous illustrations from Old English to the present century. Indexed by word in vols. 1 and 2, with a cumulative index in 4. The organization is confusing at times, and there are numerous typographical errors. Although reviewers have disagreed with some interpretations, all admit that this is a monumental contribution to the study of English syntax. Literary researchers will find it particularly useful in interpreting syntactic structures in literary works. Reviews: Norman Davis, *Review of English Studies* ns 17 (1966): 73–75, 20 (1969): 196–200, 22 (1971): 64–66, 26 (1975): 454–58.

Guides to Scholarship

6105 Scheurweghs, G., et al. *Analytical Bibliography of Writings on Modern English Morphology and Syntax, 1877–1960*. 5 vols. Louvain: Nauwelaerts, 1963–79. Z2015.A1.S33.

Vol. 1: Scheurweghs. *Periodical Literature and Miscellanies of the United States of America and Western and Northern Europe*. 1963. 293 pp. (With an appendix by Hideo Yamaguchi on Japanese publications.)

Vol. 2: Scheurweghs. *Studies in Bookform, Including Dissertations and Programmabhandlungen, Published in the United States of America and Western and Northern Europe*. 1965. 232 pp. (With appendixes on Japanese and Czechoslovak publications by Yamaguchi and Ján Šimko, respectively.)

Vol. 3: Scheurweghs. *Soviet Research on English Morphology and Syntax*. Ed. G. C. Pocheptsov; M. Mincoff et al. *English Studies in Bulgaria, Poland, Rumania, and Yugoslavia*. 1968. 267 pp.

Vol. 4: Scheurweghs and E. Vorlat. *Addenda and General Indexes.* 1968. 123 pp.
Vol. 5: Vorlat, ed. *Articles in Periodicals, 1961–1970.* 1979. 416 pp.

Bibliographies of publications and dissertations from several countries on English morphology and syntax since c. 1500. Pedagogical studies and popular journalism are excluded. Vols. 1–4 are organized by country, then by type of publication (journal articles, books, dissertations), then alphabetically by author; vol. 5 is organized by periodical, with articles following in order of publication. The individual volumes vary considerably in the thoroughness of their coverage. Some entries in vols. 1–4 are accompanied by descriptive annotations; vol. 5 offers extensive descriptions of each article. Vol. 4 prints additions to vols. 1 and 2. Two indexes (scholars and subjects) in each volume; the appendixes and the five countries in vol. 3 are separately indexed, and vol. 5 has an additional index of literary authors and works referred to. Vols. 1–3 are cumulatively indexed in five indexes in vol. 4: scholars; authors discussed; dissertations (by country, then institution); subjects of articles and books; subjects of dissertations. Although the *Analytical Bibliography* is valuable for its extensive (but not complete) coverage of foreign-language scholarship and inclusion of several studies of literary works, the lack of effective organization and insufficiently thorough indexing make locating works sometimes difficult.

Literary Criticism and Theory

This section is limited to important reference works, basic surveys or introductions, and journals. For a succinct overview of contemporary criticism and theory, see the essays by Lawrence Lipking (pp. 79–97) and Paul Hernadi (pp. 98–115) in Gibaldi, *Introduction to Scholarship in Modern Languages and Literatures* (25).

Histories and Surveys

6120 Wellek, René. *A History of Modern Criticism, 1750–1950.* 7 vols. New Haven: Yale UP, 1955– . PN86.W4 801.95'09.

Vol. 1: *The Later Eighteenth Century.* 1955. 358 pp.
Vol. 2: *The Romantic Age.* 1955. 459 pp.
Vol. 3: *The Age of Transition.* 1965. 389 pp.
Vol. 4: *The Later Nineteenth Century.* 1965. 671 pp.
Vol. 5: *English Criticism, 1900–1950.* 1986. 343 pp.
Vol. 6: *American Criticism, 1900–1950.* 1986. 345 pp.
Vol. 7: *Criticism on the Continent of Europe, 1900–1950.*

A history of Western literary theory and criticism, with excursions into aesthetics, literary history, and practical criticism. Initially restricted to England, Scotland, France, Germany, and Italy, coverage expands to the United States and Russia in vol. 3. Volumes are organized around chapters devoted to major critics, groups, movements, or countries, with each chapter providing summaries of works and theories along with considerations of their place in Western critical thought. Each volume concludes with a chronology, by country, of critical works. Two indexes in each volume: persons; topics and terms. Although some reviewers have objected to Wellek's definition of criticism, most agree that this is a masterful, balanced, indispensable exposition of modern critical thought. Reviews: (vols. 1–2) Erich Auerbach, *Romanische Forschungen* 67 (1956): 387–97; George Watson, *Essays in Criticism* 7 (1957): 81–84; (vols. 3–4) Roger Sale, *Hudson Review* 19 (1966): 324–29; (vols. 5–6) Jonathan Culler, *Journal of the History of Ideas* 49 (1988): 347–51.

American criticism is also surveyed in John W. Rathbun, Harry H. Clark, and Arnold L. Goldsmith, *American Literary Criticism [1800–1965]*, 3 vols., Twayne's United States Authors Series 339–41 (Boston: Twayne, 1979).

6125 Jefferson, Ann, and David Robey, eds. *Modern Literary Theory: A Comparative Introduction*. 2nd ed. Totowa: Barnes, 1986. 240 pp. PN94.M6 801.

A collection of separately authored introductions to the principles of Russian formalism, linguistic literary theory, new criticism, structuralism and post-structuralism, reader response theories (including hermeneutics, phenomenology, and reception theory), psychoanalytic criticism, Marxist literary theory, and feminist literary theory. An essay typically traces the historical development of a theory, surveys writings of the chief theorists and schools, explores relationships with other theories, and concludes with a list of selected readings. Two indexes: concepts; theorists. A readable introduction to recent major theories.

Covering some of the same ground are the following:

Eagleton, Terry. *Literary Theory: An Introduction*. Minneapolis: U of Minnesota P, 1983. 244 pp. A Marxist examination of the development of English as a subject; phenomenology, hermeneutics, and reception theory; structuralism and semiotics; post-structuralism; psychoanalytic theory; and politics and theory.

Natoli, Joseph, ed. *Tracing Literary Theory*. Urbana: U of Illinois P, 1987. 371 pp. Essays trace the historical development of modern schools of theory.

Selden, Raman. *A Reader's Guide to Contemporary Literary Theory*. Lexington: UP of Kentucky, 1985. 153 pp. A lucid, informative introduction to Russian formalism and to Marxist, structuralist, post-structuralist, reader-oriented, and feminist theories.

More detailed consideration of some of these schools can be found in these works:

Bennett, Tony. *Formalism and Marxism*. New Accents. New York: Methuen, 1979. 200 pp.

Fowler, *Linguistic Criticism* (5990).

Holub, Robert C. *Reception Theory: A Critical Introduction*. New Accents. London: Methuen, 1984. 189 pp.

Norris, Christopher. *Deconstruction: Theory and Practice*. New Accents. London: Methuen, 1982. 157 pp.

Handbooks, Dictionaries, and Encyclopedias

6130 Fowler, Roger, ed. *A Dictionary of Modern Critical Terms*. Rev. and enl. ed. London: Routledge, 1987. 262 pp. PN41.D4794 801.95.

A dictionary of separately authored entries, ranging from one to three pages, on critical and rhetorical terminology, critical theories, and genres. Although contributors were asked to explore "potentialities for literary inquiry" rather than merely define terms, most tend to do the latter in succinct, informative discussions, the majority of which cite examples and conclude with a list of related works or scholarship. Unfortunately, many of the entries or lists are not updated in the revised edition. Although it is not as provocative as the editor envisions, the work is a welcome alternative to the brief treatment usually accorded critical terms in standard literary dictionaries and handbooks. Much needed, however, is a thorough dictionary of critical terminology.

Guides to Scholarship and Criticism

There is no adequate selective bibliography of criticism and theory. Vernon Hall, comp., *Literary Criticism: Plato through Johnson*, Goldentree Bibliographies in Language and Literature (New York: Appleton, 1970, 119 pp.), is too dated (and usually too selective anyway) to be of much use.

SERIAL BIBLIOGRAPHIES

6133 New Literary History *International Bibliography of Literary Theory and Criticism [1984–]*. Baltimore: Johns Hopkins UP, 1988–. Annual. Z6514.C97.C65 [PN500.5] 016.801'95.

An international bibliography of works about literary theory and criticism. Each of the linguistic or geographical divisions is organized as contributors deem appropriate to the particular critical tradition, for example, that for English (United States, Canada, and Great Britain) has subdivisions for aesthetics, cultural criticism and sociological theory, deconstruction and poststructuralism, the discipline and profession of literary study, discourse analysis, feminism, figure, general, genre and narrative theory, hermeneutics and theory of interpretation, history, language and linguistic theory, Marxism, philosophy, poetics, psychoanalysis, reading theory, rhetoric, semiotics, and structuralism, while that for French has subdivisions for aesthetic theory; feminism; history and historiography; institution of literary study, criticism, and scholarship; language and stylistics, communication theory, and language philosophy; literature and society, social and cultural theory, and Marxism; narrative and genre theory; philosophy, anthropology, ethnology, sociology, and psychoanalytical theory; and semiotics. Some subdivisions are further classified by historical periods or major figures; entries are listed alphabetically by author. Placement of a work is determined by the national tradition it addresses (although there is a separate division for French theory in the Anglo-American context). Many entries are accompanied by descriptive annotations, which vary considerably in their length and informativeness. Indexed by authors. As with any group compilation, the thoroughness and consistency of coverage varies from division to division. Although an admirable attempt at international coverage, the work would benefit from a clearer statement of scope and editorial principles (especially regarding the classification of entries, exclusion of certain kinds of works, and sources consulted), from more consistency across divisions in organization, and from a subject index (a particular necessity because of the difficulty of classifying many entries, inconsistencies in terminology, and the lack of cross-references). Despite its failure to address fully the organizational and terminological difficulties posed by a bibliography of theory and criticism, this compilation will, if it continues to attract a willing group of contributors, become the essential source for identifying works about theory and criticism.

With the inauguration of this annual, bibliographers can now turn to preparing an adequate international bibliography of critical and theoretical studies published before 1984.

OTHER BIBLIOGRAPHIES

6135 Marshall, Donald G. *Contemporary Critical Theory: A Selective Bibliography*. New York: MLA. Scheduled for 1990.

A selective bibliography of books (primarily in English) important to the understanding of critical theory and major theorists since c. 1965. Although he emphasizes contemporary theory in the United States, Marshall also includes works by important foreign theorists and about earlier theory. Following a brief section on the history of criticism, entries are organized by schools or approaches: formalism, structuralism, post-structuralism, and deconstruction; hermeneutics and phenomenology; psychological and psychoanalytic criticism; cultural criticism, Marxism, orality and literacy, myth and anthropology; and feminist theory. Each division or subdivision has three parts: collections and anthologies; books about the school or approach; and works by major theorists of the field. A headnote briefly surveys the development and major figures of each school or movement, or—for theorists—summarizes his or her leading ideas and career. Some entries are briefly annotated with notes on content and an occasional evaluative comment. *Contemporary Critical Theory* will provide a welcome, trustworthy guide to those unfamiliar with the cross-currents of recent theory.

See also

Secs. G: Serial Bibliographies, Indexes, and Abstracts; H: Guides to Dissertations and Theses; and U: Literature-Related Topics and Sources/Composition and Rhetoric/Guides to Scholarship/Surveys of Research.

ABELL (340): Literature, General/Literary Criticism in the volumes for 1922–67; Literature, General/Literary Criticism/General in the volumes for 1968–72; Literary History and Criticism/General in the volume for 1973; and English Literature/General/Literary History and Criticism in later volumes.

Brier, *American Prose and Criticism, 1900–1950* (4345).

Brown, *English Prose and Criticism, 1900–1950* (2900).

LLBA: Linguistics and Language Behavior Abstracts (6015).

MLAIB (335): General/Aesthetics and Literary Criticism in the volumes for 1933–50; General/Aesthetics, and General/Literary Criticism in the volumes for 1951–53; General I: Aesthetics and Literary Criticism in the volumes for 1954–56; General II: Aesthetics, Literary Criticism, and Literary Theory [or Aesthetics and Literary Criticism] in the volumes for 1957–66;

General I: Aesthetics, and General II: Literary Criticism and Theory in the volumes for 1967–80; and Criticism and Literary Theory divisions in pt. 4 of the later volumes. Researchers must also consult the "Criticism" and "Literary Theory" headings in the subject index to post-1980 volumes.

Partridge, *American Prose and Criticism, 1820–1900* (4205).

Somer, *American and British Literature, 1945–1975* (2800).

YWES (330): Chapters on literary history and criticism and (since vol. 62 [1981]) on literary theory.

Periodicals

6145 *Critical Inquiry* (*CritI*). 1974– . Quarterly. NX1.C64 700'.9.

Encourages pluralism and lively debate in articles and in a "Critical Response" section on critical theory and method in literature, film, art, and music. Occasional special issues.

6150 *Diacritics: A Review of Contemporary Criticism* (*Diacritics*). 1971– . Quarterly. PN80.D5 805.

The bulk of each issue consists of lengthy review essays on contemporary criticism of and critical approaches to literature, the arts, cinema, and miscellaneous topics. *Diacritics* also publishes occasional articles on the methodology and ideology of criticism, as well as interviews with writers and theorists.

6155 *New Literary History: A Journal of Theory and Interpretation* (*NLH*). 1969– . 3/yr. PR1.N44 820.1.

Publishes "theoretical articles on literature that deal with such subjects as the nature of literary theory, the aims of literature, the idea of literary history, the reading process, hermeneutics, the relation of linguistics to literature, literary change, literary value, the definitions of periods and their uses in interpretation, the evolution of styles, conventions, and genres, and articles from other disciplines that help interpret or define the problems of literary history or literary study." Many articles include responses, and most issues focus on a topic. Cumulative index: Libby O. Cohen, New Literary History*: 10 Year Index: Volumes I–X, 1969–1979* (Charlottesville: New Literary History, U of Virginia, 1982, 92 pp.). Ralph Cohen, "On a Decade of *New Literary History*," *Bulletin of the Midwest Modern Language Association* 12.1 (1979): 3–10, discusses the founding and editing of the journal; see also Cohen, "The Aims and Roles of *New Literary History*," *Yearbook of English Studies* 16 (1986): 177–87.

6160 *Poetics: International Review for the Theory of Literature* (*Poetics*). 1971– 6/yr. PN45.P58 801.

Publishes articles and occasional special issues devoted to theoretical explorations of the foundations of literary studies, text structures, discourse, literary history and theory, the history of literary theory, the relationship of literature to other disciplines, and the methodology of empirical research.

6165 *Poetics Today: International Journal for Theory and Analysis of Literature and Communication* (*PoT*). 1979– . Quarterly. Former title: *Poetics Today: Theory and Analysis of Literature and Communication* (1979–83). PN1039.P74 821.

Publishes articles and reviews on contemporary literary theory, literature in relationship to other fields, and language and literature. Issues are organized around a topic or genre.

See also

Style (6095).

Types, Schools, and Movements

FEMINIST CRITICISM

6170 Humm, Maggie. *An Annotated Critical Bibliography of Feminist Criticism*. Harvester Annotated Critical Bibliographies. Boston: Hall, 1987. 240 pp. Z7963.F44.H85 [HQ1206] 016.3054'2.

A selective bibliography of books and articles, through 1985, representing feminist criticism in England and the United States. Although Humm includes numerous fugitive and limited circulation items, the criteria determining selection are unclear. Entries are organized by publication date in divisions for theory and sexual politics; literary criticism; sociology, politics, and economics; arts, film, theater, media, and music; psychology; history; anthropology and myth; and education and women's studies. Unfortunately, many of the descriptive annotations do not convey an adequate sense of content. Two indexes: subjects; scholars. Although the work is valuable for its breadth, the high degree of selectivity means that Humm is only a place to begin research.

Additional English-language articles utilizing a feminist approach are listed in Wendy Frost and Michele Valiquette, *Feminist Literary Criticism: A Bibliography of Journal Articles, 1975–1981*, Garland Reference Library of the Humanities 784 (New York: Garland, 1988, 867 pp.). The approximately 1,950 entries, culled from 450 scholarly and popular periodicals, are accompanied by lists of indexing terms that are the bases for the indexes of subjects, literary authors, and scholars. Although far from complete even within its seven-year period of coverage, with the choice of many journals depending more on availability than on other criteria, this work does isolate a considerable number of studies using a feminist approach.

See also

Gilbert, *Women's Studies: A Bibliography of Dissertations, 1870–1982* (6615).

MARXIST CRITICISM

6175 Bullock, Chris, and David Peck, comps. *Guide to Marxist Literary Criticism*. Bloomington: Indiana UP, 1980. 176 pp. Z2014.C8.B84 [PR77] 801'.95.

An annotated bibliography of English-language studies (published through mid-1979) of English, English-Canadian, and American literature and culture. Bullock also includes non-Marxist criticism (identified by the acronym NM) on Marxist works or writers as well as studies important in the development of Marxist criticism. The unevenly and inconsistently annotated entries are classified in sections for bibliographies; collections; journals; general Marxist criticism; national literatures (genre and period studies); individual authors; teaching English; language, linguistics, and literacy; literature and society (sociology and literature); and mass culture. Most unfortunate, however, is the failure to include studies already listed in published bibliographies of Marxist criticism on an author or critic. Users must study the introduction to understand the organization, the confusing numbering system, and the cross-listings practices. Not explained in the introduction is that journal acronyms are identified only in the section listing journals (pp. 6–7). The two indexes are inexplicably restricted to critics "who have at least three separate items in different sections" and to topics "that are treated in at least three items." Despite these shortcomings and several significant omissions, *Guide to Marxist Literary Criticism* is a useful compilation of studies not easily identified in standard bibliographies. Reviews: James Steele, *English Studies in Canada* 9 (1983): 527–32 (with numerous additions); Michael Wilding, *Modern Language Review* 73 (1983): 632–34.

PSYCHOLOGICAL CRITICISM

See

Kiell, *Psychoanalysis, Psychology, and Literature* (6540).

Medicine and Literature

For an introduction to the interdisciplinary study of medicine and literature, see G. S. Rousseau, "Literature and Medicine: The State of the Field," *Isis* 72 (1981): 406–24.

Guides to Primary Works

6190 Trautmann, Joanne, and Carol Pollard. *Literature and Medicine: An Annotated Bibliography*. Rev. ed. Contemporary Community Health Series. Pittsburgh: U of Pittsburgh P, 1982. 228 pp. Z6514.M43.T7 [PN56.M38] 016.8088'356.

A selective bibliography of important or representative literary works that treat medical topics. The works range from classical to contemporary and include some from Western Europe, but the majority are published after 1800 in Great Britain and the United States. Organized alphabetically by author within period divisions, the 1,396 entries include publication information for an accessible text, a list of medical topics treated, and a lengthy critical synopsis focusing on medical themes.

Works added in the revised edition are grouped in an author list after the twentieth-century division. Indexed by 39 topics. Because *Literature and Medicine* includes some works only remotely treating medical themes, omits some important titles, provides much dubious critical commentary, and is vague in some of the topics indexed, it is principally useful as a starting point for thematic investigations of the treatment of medicine in literature.

See also

"Relations of Literature and Science" (6440).
Schatzberg, *Relations of Literature and Science* (6445).

Periodicals

6195 *Literature and Medicine* (*L&M*). 1982– . Annual. PN56.M38.L7 809'.93356.

Publishes articles, reviews, and creative works on literature and medicine (including psychiatry). Most volumes focus on a theme.

Microforms

Although despised by researchers who must hunch over a poorly designed, ill-lit reader, microforms are essential components of any research library. Once essentially a medium for reproducing a document, rare book, thesis, or dissertation needed by a distant scholar, microform now provides a means for preserving deteriorating materials, for making organized collections of research materials widely available at a fraction of the cost in hard copy, and for conserving space in overcrowded libraries.

6210 *Guide to Microforms in Print: Incorporating* International Microforms in Print. Westport: Meckler, 1978– . Annual. Z1033.M5 016.099.

Separate subject and author/title lists of books, serials, collections, and other materials (except theses and dissertations) available in microform from publishers worldwide. Books are listed by author, editor, compiler, or corporate author; serials, collections, and anonymous works, by title. In the subject list, the broad headings derived from the Library of Congress subject classifications are too general to be of much use. A typical entry cites author, title, number of volumes, date, price, publisher, and type of microform. Because microform publications are not included in the national books in print volumes, the *Guide* is the essential source for locating works currently available. Entries can also be searched through BRS (515). For fuller descriptions of collections, see *Microform Research Collections* (6215).

To locate microform masters from which other copies can be reproduced, see *National Register of Microform Masters*, Library of Congress Catalogs (Washington: Library of Congress, 1965–84; with a cumulation for 1965–75); after 1983, masters are listed in *NUC: Books* (245) and *New Serial Titles* (640). Newspapers, manuscripts, and United States dissertations and theses are excluded from these lists.

6215 *Microform Research Collections: A Guide*. Ed. Suzanne Cates Dodson. 2nd ed. Meckler Publishing Series in Library Micrographics Management 9. Westport: Meckler, 1984. 670 pp. Z1033.M5.D64 011.36.

A selective guide to microform *collections*, not reproductions of individual works (for those, see *Guide to Microforms in Print* [6210]). Organized alphabetically by collection title, descriptions typically include publisher, format, technical specifications, size, review citations, arrangement, finding aids, and a description of scope and content. Because many do not have official or fixed titles, the best way to locate collections is through the index of authors, editors, titles of finding aids, subjects, and collection titles and variants. Although based almost exclusively on publishers' descriptions (which are notoriously unreliable for microform collections), reviews, questionnaires, and printed guides, Dodson's compilation is currently the best general guide to collections.

For recently published collections, see *Guide to Microforms in Print*. For evaluations of collections, the best source is *Microform Review* (1972– , quarterly). Author and title indexes to the contents of 26 collections make up Ann Niles, ed., *An Index to Microform Collections*, 2 vols., Meckler's Series in Library Micrographics Management 11 and 13 (Westport: Meckler, 1984–88.). Only a few of the collections are of marginal literary interest.

Music and Literature

For an introduction to the interdisciplinary study of literature and music, see Steven Paul Scher, "Literature and Music" (pp. 225–50) in Barricelli, *Interrelations of Literature* (5955). Researchers should note that many reference works on drama and theater cover musical theater and opera (see, e.g., section K: Genres/Drama and Theater) as do several in section U: Literature-Related Topics and Sources/Interdisciplinary and Multidisciplinary Studies.

Guides to Reference Works

6230 Duckles, Vincent, and Michael A. Keller, comps. *Music Reference and Research Materials: An Annotated Bibliography*. 4th ed. New York: Schirmer; London: Collier, 1988. ML113.D83 016.78.

A selective international guide to reference sources important in the study of music worldwide. The approximately 3,000 entries are organized alphabetically by author, editor, or title in variously classified divisions for dictionaries and encyclopedias, histories and chronologies, guides to systematic and historical musicology, bibliographies of music literature, bibliographies of music, catalogs of music libraries and collections, catalogs of musical instrument collections, histories and bibliographies of music printing and publishing, discographies, yearbooks and directories, miscellaneous works, and women and music. Most entries are accompanied by succinct but informative annotations that cite important reviews and are frequently trenchant in evaluating works. In addition, many sections begin with a brief evaluative overview. Three indexes: authors, editors, and reviewers; subjects; titles. Duckles is the indispensable guide to reference sources for the study of music.

Researchers interested in American music will find valuable guidance in

D. W. Krummel, *Bibliographical Handbook of American Music*, Music in American Life (Urbana: U of Illinois P, 1987, 269 pp.).

Handbooks, Dictionaries, and Encyclopedias

6235 *The New Grove Dictionary of Music and Musicians* (*New Grove*). 20 vols. Ed. Stanley Sadie. London: Macmillan, 1980. ML100.N48 780'.3.

An encyclopedia of music and musicians from all periods and countries. Although encompassing non-Western and folk music, *New Grove* emphasizes the European art tradition in Western music, with more than half of the approximately 22,500 entries devoted to composers and the rest to performers of international achievement, writers about music, other persons of importance in musical history, terminology, genres and forms, instruments, places with a significant musical tradition, institutions and organizations, concepts, and countries. Written by major scholars, the articles range from a paragraph to more than 160 pages; most conclude with a selective bibliography. Those on major composers provide a complete list of compositions (including locations of manuscripts); those on lesser figures, a selected list. Although vol. 20 has an index of terms used in articles on non-Western music, folk music, and related entries, the lack of a detailed general subject index is a major hindrance because many terms, concepts, and topics are buried in general entries and not identified by cross-references.

Although reviewers have argued with some interpretations, identified at least one spurious composer, noted omissions, and corrected numerous factual errors, *New Grove* is, overall, an authoritative guide that is noteworthy for its scholarship, breadth, and general impartiality. Reviews: J[ohn] B[oulton] and T[homas] A. F. L[eighton], *Music Review* 42 (1981): 268–88; D. W. Krummel, *Choice* 18 (1981): 762–66; Charles Rosen, *New York Review of Books* 28 May 1981: 26–38; and two omnibus reviews by several hands, *19th Century Music* 5 (1981): 155–69, 253–67; *Ethnomusicology* 29 (1985): 138–76, 314–51.

The inadequate treatment of music in the United States is redressed by *The New Grove Dictionary of American Music*, ed. H. Wiley Hitchcock and Stanley Sadie, 4 vols. (London: Macmillan, 1986), which incorporates some revised articles from *New Grove* with many new articles on music made in the country by citizens and foreign residents. Musical instruments—especially those used in folk and non-Western music—are more fully treated in *The New Grove Dictionary of Musical Instruments*, 3 vols., ed. Stanley Sadie (1984).

Die Musik in Geschichte und Gegenwart: Allgemeine Enzyklopädie der Musik (*MGG*), 14 vols., ed. Friedrich Blume (Kassel: Bärenreiter, 1949–68) and *Supplement*, 2 vols. (1973–79)—the other major general dictionary of music—is less current in its scholarship but remains an important complement to *New Grove*.

Because of its lack of a general index and the length of many articles, *New Grove* is frequently unsuitable for quick reference. On those occasions, one of the following will offer better service:

Baker's Biographical Dictionary of Musicians. Rev. Nicolas Slonimsky. 7th ed. New York: Schirmer-Macmillan; London: Collier, 1984. 2,577 pp. Entrants, from classical, rock, and other forms, include the famous and obscure among composers, performers, musicologists, critics, scholars, conductors, patrons—in short, nearly anyone (even bibliographers) connected with music. The typically succinct entries offer essential as well as merely interesting biographical details, a list of important works, and a selected bibliography of scholarship. At times irreverent, opinionated, and witty—but also accurate and reliable in factual matters—Baker's is one of the most entertaining biographical dictionaries of any field.

The New Harvard Dictionary of Music. Ed. Don Michael Randel. Cambridge: Belknap-Harvard, 1986. 942 pp. Although it includes both non-Western and popular music, *New Harvard Dictionary* emphasizes Western art music in entries on terms, concepts, instruments, genres, national and ethnic traditions, styles, major works, and movements. It excludes separate entries on composers and musicians. Many of the longer articles are signed and conclude with a selective bibliography.

The New Oxford Companion to Music. 2 vols. Ed. Denis Arnold. Oxford: Oxford UP, 1983. International in scope but emphasizing the Western tradition, the work treats a wide range of topics (with composers predominating). A few entries are signed and conclude with a brief list of selected readings. The broadest in coverage of the compact music dictionaries.

See also

Piper's Enzyklopädie des Musiktheaters (1145).

Guides to Scholarship

6240 *RILM Abstracts [1967–].* New York: RILM, 1967– . Quarterly, with annual cumulative index. ML1.I83 780'.5.

Abstracts of significant books, articles, reviews, dissertations, and other materials produced since 1967. Entries are organized alphabetically by author within classified divisions; of most interest to literature researchers are those for reference materials, music and other arts (including sections for drama and film, and poetry and other literature), and music and related disciplines (including linguistics and semiotics, and printing and publishing). The descriptive abstracts tend to be brief but adequate. Indexed by authors in each issue; the fourth issue is an author and subject index to the volume. Cumulative indexes: vols. 1–5 (n.d., 302 pp.); vols. 6–10 (n.d., 529 pp.). The subject indexes should be consulted with a copy of the most recent *RILM Thesaurus* in hand. Entries since 1972 can be searched online through Dialog (520). Although the criteria governing selection are unclear, its breadth of coverage and thorough subject indexing make *RILM* the best source for identifying music scholarship that treats literary works or authors. Unfortunately, coverage is about five years in arrears.

Although it is more current than *RILM* and offers better coverage of popular music, *The Music Index: A Subject-Author Guide to Current Music Periodical Literature [1949–]* (Detroit: Information Coordinators, 1949– , monthly with annual cumulation) is marred by unrefined, inconsistent, and incomplete subject indexing (and thus is nearly useless to those hunting studies treating a literary author or work). Since cross-references appear only in the annual cumulation (which is now six years in arrears), users must approach each issue with the annual *Subject Heading List* in hand.

See also

"Bibliography on the Relations of Literature and the Other Arts" (5965).
Brogan, *English Versification, 1570–1980* (1600).
"Current Bibliography, Discography, and Filmography," *Ethnomusicology* (5913).
Haywood, *Bibliography of North American Folklore and Folksong* (5875).
Humm, *Annotated Critical Bibliography of Feminist Criticism* (6170).
Miller, *Folk Music in America* (5910).
MLAIB (335): See the headings beginning "Music" in the subject index to post-1980 volumes.
Rice, *English Fiction, 1900–1950* (2840).
Salzman, *American Studies: An Annotated Bibliography* (3335).
Wildbihler, *The Musical: An International Annotated Bibliography* (4295).

Periodicals

6245 *Music and Letters* (*M&L*). 1920– . Quarterly. ML5.M64 780.5.

Publishes frequent articles and reviews on the relationship between musical and literary works. Cumulative index: vols. 1–40 (1962, 140 pp.).

See also

Critical Inquiry (6145).
Journal of Aesthetics and Art Criticism (5970).

Philosophy and Literature

For an introduction to the interdisciplinary study of literature and philosophy, see Thomas McFarland, "Literature and Philosophy" (pp. 25–46) in Barricelli, *Interrelations of Literature* (5955). Some works in section U: Literature-Related Topics and Sources/Interdisciplinary and Multidisciplinary Studies treat literature and philosophy.

Guides to Reference Works

6260 De George, Richard T. *The Philosopher's Guide to Sources, Research Tools, Professional Life, and Related Fields*. Lawrence: Regents P of Kansas. 1980. 261 pp. Z7125.D445 [B53] 016.1.

A selective guide to reference sources and other publications through the late 1970s important to the study of philosophy. International in scope, the *Philosopher's Guide* cites works in several European languages but emphasizes those in English. Entries are organized alphabetically in three classified divisions: philosophy, general research works, and related fields. The philosophy division, which is the heart of the book, has sections for general histories and reference works; history of philosophy (subdivided by period, with each having lists of works by and about individual philosophers); systematic philosophy, including branches, schools and movements, and nations and regions; and serials and publishing. Although the other two divisions are adequate, users will find better guidance in Sheehy, *Guide to Reference Books* (60) or Walford, *Walford's Guide to Reference Material* (65), and specialized guides. A headnote explaining principles of selection prefaces many sections; the generally brief annotations are mostly descriptive, with evaluations offered only when there is consensus among scholars about the quality of a work. Indexed by scholars, subjects, and some titles. Users would benefit from fuller, more evaluative annotations, but De George is the best guide to reference sources in the field through the late 1970s.

More current in coverage and offering fuller, occasionally evaluative annotations is Hans E. Bynagle, *Philosophy: A Guide to the Reference Literature*, Reference Sources in the Humanities Series (Littleton: Libraries Unlimited, 1986, 170 pp.); however, it includes many works of dubious value, neglects many important older sources, and is less effectively organized.

Handbooks, Dictionaries, and Encyclopedias

6265 *The Encyclopedia of Philosophy*. Ed. Paul Edwards. 8 vols. New York: Macmillan; London: Collier, 1967. B41.E5 103.

A dictionary of philosophy, ancient through modern, and its relationships to other fields, with analytical and historical discussions of persons, branches of the discipline, concepts, theories, historical topics, schools, and movements. About three-fifths of the 1,500 entries are devoted to individuals, with an overview of the person's contributions to philosophy and important theories. Written by major scholars, the articles are frequently lengthy and conclude with (now dated) selective bibliographies of primary works and scholarship. Since many persons, concepts, theories, and terms are treated in general articles, the index of persons and subjects in vol. 8 is frequently the best place to begin. (See especially the entries under "Language," "Linguistic," "Literary," and "Literature.") A generally authoritative compilation, this work is the best encyclopedia of the subject. Reviews: *Australasian Journal of Philosophy* 46 (1968): 1–27; *Philosophical Quarterly* 18 (1968): 68–81; Elmer H. Duncan, *Journal of Aesthetics and Art Criticism* 27 (1969): 463–65.

More compact dictionaries are listed on pp. 12–17 in De George, *Philosopher's Guide to Sources* (6260). Among the trustworthy ones are these:

[Flew, Antony, ed.] *A Dictionary of Philosophy*. Rev. 2nd ed. New York: St. Martin's, 1984. 380 pp.

Reese, William L. *Dictionary of Philosophy and Religion, Eastern and Western Thought*. Hassocks: Harvester; Atlantic Highlands: Humanities, 1980. 644 pp.

Bibliographies of Bibliographies

6270 Guerry, Herbert, comp. and ed. *A Bibliography of Philosophical Bibliographies*. Westport: Greenwood, 1977. 332 pp. Z7125.A1.G83 [B53] 016.0161.

A bibliography of bibliographies through 1974, the majority published separately or in a journal. The 2,353 entries are listed alphabetically by author or editor in two divisions: philosophers and subjects. About half of the works are accompanied by brief descriptive annotations, a few of which include evaluative comments. Indexed by authors. There are significant omissions, and using the subject division demands ingenuity; still, this is the fullest list of philosophical bibliographies through 1974.

Guides to Scholarship

For other bibliographies, see pp. 9–12 in De George, *Philosopher's Guide to Sources* (6260).

6275 *The Philosopher's Index: An International Index to Philosophical Periodicals and Books*. Bowling Green: Philosophy Documentation Center, Bowling Green State U, 1969– . Quarterly, with annual cumulation. Former title: *The Philosopher's Index: An International Index to Periodicals* (1969–82). Z7127.P47 016.105.

The Philosopher's Index: A Retrospective Index to U.S. Publications from 1940. 3 vols. 1978.
The Philosopher's Index: A Retrospective Index to Non-U.S. English Language Publications from 1940. 3 vols. 1980.

An index to major philosophical journals (currently about 420) in English, French, German, Spanish, Italian, and selected other languages, some interdisciplinary journals, English-language books (since the volume for 1980), and selected foreign-language ones (beginning in the volume for 1984). Entries are now organized in three parts: (1) a subject index, with headings for persons, historical periods, major fields of philosophy and their branches, and topics; (2) an author index, with descriptive abstracts of several works (beginning with the volume for 1969); (3) a book review index (since the volume for 1970). The organization, subject indexing, and design have improved markedly over the years; unfortunately, more than half of the works—especially in foreign languages—in an annual volume are not abstracted. Entries are searchable through Dialog (520). The *Retrospective Index to Non-U.S. English Language Publications* covers books published between 1940 and 1978 and articles between 1940 and 1966; *U.S. Publications* includes books from 1940 through 1976 and articles from 1940 through 1966. Both have separate subject and author indexes, but the majority of the works in each lack abstracts. Although not comprehensive, *Philosopher's Index* series offers the most complete coverage of current philosophical scholarship and cites numerous literary studies omitted from the standard serial bibliographies and indexes in section G.

See also

MLAIB (335): See the headings beginning "Philosophical" or "Philosophy" in the subject index to post-1980 volumes.

Periodicals

6280 *Philosophy and Literature* (*P&L*). 1976– . 2/yr. PN2.P5 809.

Publishes articles, notes, reviews, and review essays on "philosophical interpretations of literature, literary investigations of classic works of philosophy, . . . the aesthetics of literature, philosophy of language relevant to literature, and the theory of criticism." What was to have been an annual bibliography appeared only once (1 [1977]: 366–85). Annual index in vol. 1; thereafter, a biennial index.

Popular Culture

Although "popular culture" embraces multifarious aspects of culture, this section is limited to reference sources that focus on written works.

Guides to Scholarship and Criticism

There is no satisfactory general guide to scholarship and criticism in popular culture, and, given the breadth and eclecticism of the field, there likely never will be. Researchers interested in a particular kind of popular literature will do better to consult reference works devoted to genres or periods.

6295 Inge, M. Thomas, ed. *Handbook of American Popular Culture*. 3 vols. Westport: Greenwood, 1978–81. E169.1.H2643 301.2'1.

Surveys of research devoted to selected aspects of mass culture in the United States. Among the topics are a considerable number that are of literary interest: children's literature, detective and mystery novels, film, gothic novels, pulps, science fiction, stage entertainments, the western, best-sellers, historical fiction, romantic fiction, popular poetry, women in popular culture, minorities in popular culture, and magazines. Each essay provides a historical outline of its subject; surveys important reference sources, research collections, and scholarship; and concludes with a selected bibliography (through c. 1977) and list of periodicals. (The historical outlines and bibliographies are reprinted—sometimes with revisions—in *Concise Histories of American Popular Culture*, ed. M. Thomas Inge, Contributions to the Study of Popular Culture 4 [Greenwood: Westport, 1982, 504 pp.].) Indexed in each volume by persons. Although the surveys vary considerably in completeness, rigor of evaluation, and overall quality, many offer the best introductions to research in their respective topics. Collectively, they form the most trustworthy and systematic guide to reference sources and studies in the major areas of popular culture. The following works are also useful, within limits:

Landrum, Larry N. *American Popular Culture: A Guide to Information Sources*. American Studies Information Guide Series 12. Detroit: Gale, 1982. 435 pp. The 2,173 descriptively annotated works—few of them published after 1979 and some inaccurately described—are organized in divisions for general bibliographies, indexes, and abstracts; general studies; anthologies and collections; aspects of everyday life; ideology; heroes and celebrities; material culture; games; sports; music; dance;

public art; advertising; theater; entertainments; literature (classified by types of popular literature); and media. The lack of clear principles of selection and organization turns *American Popular Culture* into a conglomeration that omits numerous important works and indiscriminately mixes reference works, histories, critical studies, anthologies, and miscellaneous publications in most divisions.

Wertheim, Arthur Frank, ed. *American Popular Culture: A Historical Bibliography*. Clio Bibliography Series 14. Santa Barbara: ABC-Clio, 1984. 246 pp. The 2,719 abstracts are listed alphabetically by author in seven divisions: popular culture in historical perspective; popular arts (including sections on literature and theater); mass media and communications; folk culture; customs, behavior, and attitudes; science and religion; and theory, research, and pedagogy. A miscellaneous, poorly organized hotchpotch that is completely dependent on the *America: History and Life* (3310) data base for 1973–80, Wertheim is useless for any systematic guidance to popular culture scholarship and doesn't even come near to being the "comprehensive research tool" that the preface claims. Similarly miscellaneous is the short-lived *Abstracts of Popular Culture: A Biannual Publication of International Popular Phenomena*, 7 nos. (Bowling Green: Bowling Green U Popular P, 1976–82).

See also

Fishburn, *Women in Popular Culture* (6590).
MLAIB (335): See the "Popular Culture" heading in the subject index to post-1980 volumes.
Salzman, *American Studies: An Annotated Bibliography* (3335).
Writings on American History (3340).

Periodicals

6300 *Journal of Popular Culture* (*JPC*). 1967– . Quarterly. AP2.J8325 800.

Publishes articles and frequent special issues encompassing all aspects of popular culture, including, for example, literature, television, video games, comics, baseball, music, religion, and science fiction. Although *JPC* is international in scope, North America predominates in the articles. Cumulative index: vols. 1–10, Ray B. Browne and Christopher D. Geist, eds., *Popular Abstracts:* Journal of Popular Culture, *1967–1977;* Journal of Popular Film, *1972–1977;* Popular Music and Society, *1971–1975* [Bowling Green: Bowling Green U Popular P, 1978?], 255 pp.

Quotations

6315 Bartlett, John. *Familiar Quotations: A Collection of Passages, Phrases, and Proverbs Traced to Their Sources in Ancient and Modern Literature*. Ed. Emily Morison Beck. 15th ed., rev. and enl. Boston: Little, Brown, 1980. 1,540 pp. PN6081.B27 808.88'2.

A collection of some 22,500 quotations chosen for their "familiarity and worth" (or sometimes "literary power") from literary works, sacred writings, and other sources throughout the world. The approximately 2,500 authors are listed by date of birth (ranging from c. 2650–2600 BC, for the author of "Song of the Harper," to 1950, for Stevie Wonder); anonymous works follow the author list. Under each author, passages are organized by publication date; sources are identified by act, scene, line, stanza, or chapter whenever possible. Indexed by authors at the front, by keywords (with context) at the back. Long a standard source, this is the fullest, most accurate, representative, and thoroughly indexed dictionary of quotations. Because passages are dropped, earlier editions remain useful. (For an overview of editions and changes in editorial policy, see Historical Notes, pp. xi-xiii).

An essential complement to Bartlett, which retains an American emphasis, is *The Oxford Dictionary of Quotations*, 3rd ed. (Oxford: Oxford UP, 1979, 907 pp.), which is more thorough in covering literary works, especially by English authors. Because of extensive revisions in the third edition, the second (1953, 1,003 pp.) remains an important source.

Most reference collections stock an array of other general and specialized dictionaries of quotations. For convenient lists, see Sheehy, *Guide to Reference Books* (60), pp. 417–22, and Walford, *Walford's Guide to Reference Material* (65), vol. 3, pp. 532–36. If none of these yields the source, consult one or more of the following:

1. a concordance to the Bible (King James version) or Shakespeare, the two most frequently quoted sources;
2. historical dictionaries—such as *Oxford English Dictionary* (1410), *Dictionary of American English* (3355), *Dictionary of Americanisms* (3360), or *Webster's Third* (3365)—which cite illustrative quotations;
3. first-line indexes to poems such as *Granger's Index to Poetry* (1235);
4. dictionaries of proverbs (see section U: Literature-Related Topics and Sources/Folklore/Proverbs/Dictionaries).

If these fail, send a query to *Notes and Queries* (1475).

See also

Dictionary of Australian Quotations (4455).
Hamilton, *Dictionary of Canadian Quotations and Phrases* (4575).

Religion and Literature

This section is limited to reference works of use to researchers seeking information on the relationships between religion (especially Christianity) and literature. Other reference works on religion are listed in Gorman, *Theological and Religious Reference Materials* (6330), Sheehy, *Guide to Reference Books* (60), pp. 340–91, and Walford, *Walford's Guide to Reference Material* (65), vol. 2, pp. 31–79. Some works in section U: Literature-Related Topics and Sources/Interdisciplinary and Multidisciplinary Studies treat religion and literature.

For an introduction to the interdisciplinary study of literature and religion, see Giles Gunn, "Literature and Religion" (pp. 47–66) in Barricelli, *Interrelations of Literature* (5955).

Guides to Reference Works

6330 Gorman, G. E., and Lyn Gorman. *Theological and Religious Reference Materials.* 4 vols. Bibliographies and Indexes in Religious Studies 1–2, 7. Westport: Greenwood, 1984– . Z7770.G66 [BS511.2] 016.2.

Vol. 1: *General Resources and Biblical Studies.* 1984. 526 pp.
Vol. 2: *Systematic Theology and Church History.* 1985. 401 pp.
Vol. 3: *Practical Theology.* 1986. 388 pp.
Vol. 4: *Judaism and Islam.* Scheduled for 1991.

An international, interdenominational guide to reference works in Western languages for the study of theology and religion, but with a decided emphasis on English-language works treating Christianity. The entries are listed alphabetically by author, editor, or title in divisions for general reference works, biblical studies, systematic theology and ethics, church history, missions and ecumenicism, religious orders, practical theology, liturgy and worship, homiletics, education, counseling, and sociology; each division is subdivided by type of reference works (usually bibliographies, dictionaries, and handbooks), a system that does not allow for a sufficiently refined organization of many sections. The annotations are uneven: at their best they provide hints on uses, pointed evaluations, and cross-references to related works; many, however, are too brief to offer either an adequate description of contents or guidance on use. The lack of judicious selectivity leads to extensive lists that indiscriminately mix the scholarly and the popular, the authoritative and the untrustworthy. Moreover, several superseded works and editions are cited. Three indexes in each volume: authors; titles; subjects. Vol. 1 prints an introduction on the study and use of theological literature. Despite its faults, however, Gorman is the best guide to the extensive body of reference material on theology and religion.

Handbooks, Dictionaries, and Encyclopedias

For a much fuller list of general dictionaries, see Gorman, *Theological and Religious Reference Materials* (6330), vol. 1, pp. 123–53.

6335 *Encyclopaedia Judaica.* 16 vols. Jerusalem: Encyclopaedia Judaica; New York: Macmillan, 1971–72. *Decennial Book, 1973–1982* (n.d.); *Yearbook, 1983/5* (1985). DS102.8.E496 909'.04924.

An encyclopedia of persons, places, concepts, doctrines, sects, beliefs, practices, rituals, and terminology associated with Judaism. The approximately 25,000 signed entries range from a few sentences to nearly a volume, and most conclude with a selected bibliography. Although it contains numerous biographies of decidedly minor individuals and abounds in typographical errors, this work is the standard English-language encyclopedia of Judaism. Review: *TLS: Times Literary Supplement* 23 Mar. 1973: 309–11.

6340 *The Encyclopedia of Religion.* Ed. Mircea Eliade. 16 vols. New York: Macmillan; London: Collier, 1987. BL31.E46 200'.3'21.

An encyclopedia of the theoretical, practical, and sociological dimensions of popular, primitive, and traditional religions throughout the world from Paleolithic times to the present. The approximately 3,000 signed articles by major scholars emphasize the history of religion in covering beliefs, archaeological finds, myths, systems, practices, rituals, symbols, traditions, deities, cults, areas of the world, and relationships with other fields (including, e.g., an entry for "Literature"). Each article concludes with cross-references and a selected bibliography. Besides an analytic subject index, vol. 16 prints a synoptic outline of contents by religion and religious phenomena. Impressive in scope and scholarship, this is a worthy successor to *Encyclopedia of Religion and Ethics*, ed. James Hastings, 13 vols. (New York: Scribner's, 1908–26).

6345 *New Catholic Encyclopedia*. 17 vols. New York: McGraw, 1967–79. BX841.N44 282'.03.

An encyclopedia of the institutions, important dead individuals, history, places, terminology, religious orders, symbolism, canon law, theology, teachings, doctrines, and rituals associated with the Catholic church, as well as philosophies, religions, movements, and scientific and intellectual developments that have affected Catholicism. Although international in scope, *New Catholic Encyclopedia* emphasizes English-speaking countries, especially the United States. The approximately 17,000 signed articles are by major scholars, many of whom are not Catholic; most entries conclude with cross-references and a selected bibliography. Indexed by subject in vol. 15. Two supplements: vol. 16 covers 1967 to 1974; vol. 17 incorporates changes brought about by Vatican Council II. The articles, while Catholic in perspective, are rarely partisan. An authoritative guide to Catholicism and related topics (including entries on some 850 writers and literary subjects). Reviews: *Booklist* 68 (1971): 161–65; *Times Literary Supplement* 28 Sept. 1967: 899.

The Catholic Encyclopedia: An International Work of Reference on the Constitution, Doctrine, Discipline, and History of the Catholic Church, ed. Charles G. Herbermann et al., 16 vols. and 2 supplements (New York: Gilmary Soc., 1907–51), remains occasionally useful for topics omitted in the new edition.

The most authoritative and balanced compact dictionary is *The Oxford Dictionary of the Christian Church*, ed. F. L. Cross and E. A. Livingstone, 2nd ed., rpt. with corrections and revisions (London: Oxford UP, 1983, 1,520 pp.), which emphasizes Christianity in Europe.

Guides to Scholarship

SERIAL BIBLIOGRAPHIES

6350 *Religion Index One: Periodicals* (*RIO*). Chicago: American Theological Library Assn., 1952– . 2/yr., including annual cumulation. (Vols. 1–4, rev. and expanded ed., 1985.) Former title: *Index to Religious Periodical Literature* (1952–77). Z7753.A5 [BL1] 016.2.

Religion Index Two: Multi-Author Works (*RIT*). 1976– . Annual. Z7751.R35 [BL48] 016.2.

Religion Index Two: Festschriften, 1960–1969. Ed. Betty A. O'Brien and Elmer J. O'Brien. 1980. 741 pp.

Religion Index Two: Multi-Author Works, 1970–1975. Ed. G. Fay Dickerson. 2 vols. 1982.

Subject indexes to articles in periodicals (currently about 400) and collections of essays on religion, especially in the West. Entries are interspersed with liberal cross-references. Indexed by authors and editors (with the indexes in vols. 12–18 [for 1975–85] including abstracts). With vol. 18 (for 1986), abstracts are discontinued and book reviews relegated to *Index to Book Reviews in Religion* (*IBRR*) (1986– , bimonthly). Although far from comprehensive, this is generally accounted the best serial bibliography devoted to articles on religion. The thorough subject indexing makes it an important source for identifying numerous literary studies in journals not covered by the standard serial bibliographies and indexes in section G. (See particularly the "Literary," "Literature," "Language," and "Linguistic" heads.) Entries can also be searched through BRS (515). For other serial bibliographies, see Gorman, *Theological and Religious Reference Materials* (6330), vol. 1, pp. 60–123.

LITERATURE AND RELIGION

6355 "Bibliography [1957–]." *Christianity and Literature* (entry 6360) 9.2 (1958)– . In each issue.

A bibliography of books and articles, all but a few in English and on American and British literature. Entries are listed alphabetically by scholar in eight unclassified divisions: general studies, ancient and medieval biblical literature to 1500, ancient and medieval nonbiblical literature to 1500, and then by century. The accompanying descriptive annotations vary in fullness, and several are based on other abstracts rather than the works themselves. Highly incomplete and inconsistent, coverage seems dictated by what the compilers discover rather than by any clear principles of selection. Although the "Bibliography" is sometimes useful for isolating studies treating aspects of Christianity in literature, the inconsistency in coverage and lack of indexing mean that users are in for an issue-by-issue search for discussions of authors or topics.

See also

MLAIB (335): See the headings beginning "Religion" or "Religious" in the subject index to post-1980 volumes.

Woodress, *Dissertations in American Literature, 1891–1966* (3320).

Periodicals

6360 *Christianity and Literature: An Interdisciplinary Journal* (*C&L*). 1950– . Quarterly. Former title: *Newsletter of the Conference on Christianity and Literature* (1950–73). PN49.C49 810'8'0054.

Publishes articles and reviews on the relationship between Christianity and literature (almost exclusively British and American). For the bibliography in each issue, see entry 6355.

6365 *Religion and Literature* (*R&L*). 1960– . 3/yr. Former titles: *Notre Dame English Journal: A Journal of Religion in Literature* (1978–83); *Notre Dame English Journal* (with variations, 1960–78). PR1.N6 809.

Publishes articles and reviews on all aspects of literature and religion, especially Christianity. Cumulative index: 1960–80, comp. Lisa Mary McCartney, 11 (1980): 175–206.

Scholarly Writing and Publishing

This section is limited to works related to scholarly writing and publishing in literature and language. Those interested in freelancing should consult the current edition of *Writer's Market: Where to Sell What You Write [1922–]* (Cincinnati: Writer's Digest, 1922– , annual). Besides lists of book publishers and magazines (with information on subject interests, submission instructions, and details of payment) and literary agents, it offers helpful advice on the business. Information is updated between editions in *Writer's Digest* (1920– , monthly.).

Handbooks and Guides to Publishing

6375 McKerrow, R. B. "Form and Matter in the Publication of Research." *Review of English Studies* 16 (1940): 116–21.

A plea, largely unheeded, for "precision and intelligibility" in organizing and presenting research. Full of sensible advice (e.g., provide a title that describes what the article or book is about; avoid ambiguity) and pithy asides (" 'pedant' is merely the name which one gives to anyone whose standard of accuracy happens to be a little higher than one's own"), this should be read or reread before submitting the next article or book. Frequently reprinted, e.g., *PMLA* 65.3 (1950): 3–8; Beaurline, *Mirror for Modern Scholars* (20), pp. 383–89.

6380 Luey, Beth. *Handbook for Academic Authors*. Cambridge: Cambridge UP, 1987. 226 pp. PN146.L84 808'.02.

A guide to general scholarly publishing practices in the United States (and not an official handbook for Cambridge authors). Addressed to the publish-or-perish American academic, chapters offer practical advice on publishing journal articles (including the selection of a journal and book reviewing), revising a dissertation as articles or a book, finding a publisher (with discussions of kinds of publishers, letters of inquiry, and the refereeing process), working with a publisher (with sections on basic contract provisions, working with an editor, and publicity), editing collections of essays and anthologies, finding and working with a publisher for a textbook, the mechanics of authorship (preparing a manuscript, obtaining permissions, proofreading, indexing, and using a computer), and the economics of publishing (a basic overview of costs and prices). Concludes with a selective annotated bibliography. Indexed by subjects. Although the *Handbook* is burdened by an insistently jaundiced attitude toward evaluation by a dean or tenure and promotion committee, it is packed with sound practical advice for academic authors, especially those writing a first book, in all fields and will repay the time needed for skimming by those preparing a first book. For a more succinct discussion of many of the same points, see Achtert, *MLA Style Manual* (6400).

Weldon A. Kefauver, ed., *Scholars and Their Publishers* (New York: MLA, 1977, 59 pp.), addresses the sometimes "vexed" relations between academic authors and scholarly publishers, in discussions of economic and scholarly factors that affect a decision to publish, the questions most frequently asked by authors, the role of the publisher's manuscript readers, the contract, and the impact of reprographic technology (now outdated).

Guidelines for Journal Editors and Contributors (New York: MLA, 1984, 19 pp.) succinctly outlines the general practices and responsibilities of authors and journal editors. The Conference of Editors of Learned Journals (c/o MLA) offers to mediate misunderstandings and differences of opinion.

See also

Sec. U: Literature-Related Topics and Sources/Copyright.
Hartman, *Women in Print* (6595).

Guides to Writing

6385 Strunk, William, Jr. *The Elements of Style* (Strunk and White). With revisions and additions by E. B. White. 3rd ed. New York: Macmillan; London: Collier, 1979. 85 pp. PE1408.S772 808.

A guide to the fundamentals of usage and basic principles of composition. The rules and guidelines are concisely presented in five sections: elementary rules of usage, elementary principles of composition, matters of form, words and expressions commonly misused, and matters of style. Each rule or entry on usage is clearly explained and accompanied by illustrative examples. A model of the clarity, accuracy, and brevity it expounds, Strunk and White is the classic guide to style and a work that repays frequent rereading.

6390 Frank, Francine Wattman, and Paula A. Treichler. *Language, Gender, and Professional Writing: Theoretical Approaches and Guidelines for Nonsexist Usage*. New York: Commission on the Status of Women in the Profession, MLA, 1989. 341 pp. PE1460.F64 428'.008804.

A collection of essays that address the theoretical and historical contexts of sexist language and a set of guidelines for nonsexist usage in scholarly and professional discourse. Among the topics addressed in the guidelines are the generic *he*; *man*, its compounds, and other false generic terms; gender marking; notes and citations; and indexes. Concludes with a bibliography of other guidelines and works about sexist language. Indexed by persons and terms. Full of helpful examples of alternatives to sexist usage but not a guidebook per se, *Language, Gender, and Professional Writing* is helpful reading for writers who wish to produce nondiscriminatory prose (an expectation of significantly more publishers each year).

Style Manuals

The following are the major style manuals used by North American and British publishers of literary scholarship and criticism. For manuals in other fields, see John Bruce Howell, *Style Manuals of the English-Speaking World: A Guide* (Phoenix: Oryx, 1983, 138 pp.).

GENERAL MANUALS

6395 *The Chicago Manual of Style for Authors, Editors, and Copywriters* (*Chicago*). 13th ed., rev. and expanded. Chicago: U of Chicago P, 1982. 738 pp. Z253.U69 808'.02.

A manual for authors and editors that explains all aspects of manuscript preparation, editing, and publication. The 20 chapters are organized in three divisions:

bookmaking, which covers the parts of a book, manuscript preparation and copyediting (with a section on how a copyeditor marks a manuscript), proofs (with a table of proofreaders' marks), and rights and permissions (with an excellent sample letter for requesting permission to reprint copyrighted material in a scholarly book);

style, with chapters on punctuation; spelling and distinctive treatment of words (such as foreign words, slang, and letters used as words); names and terms; numbers; foreign languages (including capitalization, word division, and special characters); quotations; illustrations, captions, and legends; tables; abbreviations; documentation (with illustrations of four styles); bibliographic forms (illustrating two styles); note forms; and

indexing (see entry 6415); production and printing, which is of interest primarily to editors.

Each chapter is preceded by a detailed outline of content and includes a wealth of examples and illustrations. Concludes with a selective bibliography. Thoroughly and admirably indexed by subjects. Thoroughness, clarity, and general good sense make this the long-time standard that both reflects and determines the practices of most American publishers. For those writing for publication, *Chicago* is an indispensable desktop companion. For a history of the work, see Catharine Seybold, "A Brief History of *The Chicago Manual of Style*," *Scholarly Publishing* 14 (1983): 163–77. Review: Gerald Trett, *Review* 6 (1984): 201–35.

Kate L. Turabian, *A Manual for Writers of Term Papers, Theses, and Dissertations*, 5th ed., rev. and expanded by Bonnie Birtwistle Honigsblum, Chicago Guides to Writing, Editing, and Publishing (Chicago: U of Chicago P, 1987, 300 pp.), is a commonly used distillation of *Chicago Manual of Style* and sometimes offers clearer explanations of basic points.

The British equivalent of *Chicago* is Judith Butcher, *Copy-Editing: The Cambridge Handbook*, 2nd ed. (Cambridge: Cambridge UP, 1981, 331 pp.), which is addressed more to copyeditors than to authors and offers far fewer examples.

One Book/Five Ways: The Publishing Practices of Five University Presses (Los Altos: Kaufmann, 1978, 337 pp.) offers an instructive comparison of how five North American university presses handled the same manuscript from submission through manufacture.

6400 Achtert, Walter S., and Joseph Gibaldi. *The MLA Style Manual*. New York: MLA, 1985. 271 pp. PN147.A28 808'.02.

An attempt to provide the language and literature scholar with "a comprehensive guide to publishing in the humanities." Besides the expected sections treating the new MLA documentation system, abbreviations, proofreading symbols, and mechanics (such as punctuation, personal names, capitalization, titles, quotations, and transliteration), *MLA Style Manual* provides a helpful overview of writing and publication (with discussions of audience, types of scholarship, plagiarism, manu-

law) and detailed advice on the preparation of manuscript (including requirements for preparing a machine-readable one). A concluding chapter on theses and dissertations offers a brief overview of common graduate-school requirements. Indexed by subject. For the scholar and graduate student, this volume replaces Gibaldi, *MLA Handbook for Writers of Research Papers* (3rd ed., 1988, 248 pp.), which is addressed to the undergraduate. Although *Chicago Manual of Style* (6395) is more wide-ranging and detailed in its treatment of matters of manuscript style, *MLA Style Manual* is required reading for those who submit manuscripts for publication, since so many literature journals and some academic presses (especially in the United States) follow it.

Writers who have trouble remembering MLA style when constructing a list of works cited will find help with Marvin Shapiro and Ted Salzman, *Bibliography Generator* (Freeport: Educational Activities, 1987), a computer program that converts bibliographical information to MLA format, inserts capitals and punctuation (but not diacritics), and alphabetizes entries.

Many British journals follow *MHRA Style Book: Notes for Authors, Editors, and Writers of Dissertations*, 3rd ed., ed. A. S. Maney and R. L. Smallwood (London: Modern Humanities Research Assn., 1981, 73 pp.).

See also

Sec. U: Literature-Related Topics and Sources/Computers and the Humanities/Word Processing.

COPYEDITING GUIDES

6405 Cook, Claire Kehrwald. *[The MLA's] Line by Line: How to Edit Your Own Writing*. Boston: Houghton, 1985. 219 pp. PE1441.C66 808'.042.

A handbook designed by the MLA's head copy editor to "show writers how to edit their own work." Chapters address major style problems (needless words, word order, parallelism, agreement, and punctuation) with clear explanations illustrated by apt examples. Two appendixes: the parts of a sentence; a glossary of questionable usage. Indexed by subjects. Replete with practical advice on detecting and correcting errors, *Line by Line* should be a constant companion for anyone who writes.

ELECTRONIC MANUSCRIPTS

Submission on disk or tape can save considerable time and money in the publishing process, but authors must be aware of the potential for errors in the final version. More than one printed text has been garbled by electronic interference, and at least one article has been deliberately altered by someone who came upon an untended screen while the author was entering copyediting changes on a disk (see *Early American Literature* 22 [1987]: 230).

6410 *Chicago Guide to Preparing Electronic Manuscripts for Authors and Publishers*. Chicago Guides to Writing, Editing, and Publishing. Chicago: U of Chicago P, 1987. 143 pp. Z286.E43.U54 070.5'028'5.

A general overview of the procedures and requirements for preparing and publishing a computer-readable manuscript. Of most interest to authors are the first two parts: (1) general instructions for authors, with discussions of hardware and software, typing (including important warnings about the disastrous effects of using "el" for the numeral 1 and instituting ill-considered global substitutions), preparing the text for a publisher, editing, proofing, and indexing; (2) generic coding (with a handy list of codes as one of the appendixes). Although each publisher will eventually develop specifications and coding systems, the *Chicago Guide* remains a useful general introduction to the advantages and pitfalls of preparing, submitting, and publishing an electronic manuscript.

INDEXING GUIDES

6415 "Indexes." Chapter 18 of *The Chicago Manual of Style* (entry 6395). 13th ed. Chicago: U of Chicago P, 1982. 511–57. Z253.U69 686.2'24.

A succinct, straightforward, practical guide to the mechanics and principles of preparing an index. Major sections explain indexing definitions, the step-by-step process of preparing an index, general principles (such as determining what to index, choosing terms for entries, and deciding between variants in names and titles), and alphabetization practices. Each point is illustrated with clear examples. Essential reading for an author required to index a book.

Another authoritative guide is G. Norman Knight, *Indexing, the Art of: A Guide to the Indexing of Books and Periodicals* (London: Allen & Unwin, 1979, 218 pp.), which includes chapters on indexing periodicals and preparing cumulative indexes (as well as a delightful survey of humor in indexes).

Book Reviewing

6420 Hoge, James O., ed. *Literary Reviewing*. Charlottesville: UP of Virginia, 1987. 139 pp. PN441.L487 808'.066028.

A collection of essays that address the need for greater rigor in the reviewing of literary scholarship. The bulk of the contributions are devoted to the theory and practice of evaluating kinds of books: works of literary theory; literary histories; literary biographies; editions of letters, journals, and diaries; enumerative bibliographies; and descriptive bibliographies. Other essays discuss factors that affect the quality of reviews. Dedicated to improving the quality and prestige of book reviewing, these essays are required reading for both the seasoned and the novice reviewer.

Klemp, "Reviewing Academic Books" (6425a), is also full of sound practical advice.

Much less useful is A. J. Walford, ed., *Reviews and Reviewing: A Guide* (Phoenix: Oryx, 1986, 248 pp.), which unsuccessfully attempts to provide guidelines for reviewing in a variety of disciplines.

Periodicals

6425 *Scholarly Publishing: A Journal for Authors and Publishers* (*SchP*). 1969– . Quarterly. Z286.S37.S33 655.4.

Publishes articles and occasional reviews on all aspects of scholarly publishing. Along with discussions of marketing, technology, copyediting, and publishing are several essays offering practical advice to the scholar:

Schoeck, R. J. "The Publication of Group Scholarship." 2 (1971): 255–64.
Halpenny, Francess G. "The Thesis and the Book." 3 (1972): 111–16.
Holmes, Olive. "Thesis to Book: What to Get Rid Of." 5 (1974): 339–49; 6 (1974): 40–50.
———. "Thesis to Book: What to Do with What Is Left." 6 (1975): 165–76.
Klemp, P. J. "Reviewing Academic Books: Some Ideas for Beginners." 12 (1981): 135–39.
Wolper, Roy S. "On Academic Reviewing: Ten Common Errors." 16 (1985): 269–75.
Meyers, Jeffrey. "On Editing Collections of Original Essays." 17 (1986): 99–108.

The articles by Holmes and Halpenny, along with several others, are reprinted as *The Thesis and the Book*, ed. Eleanor Harman and Ian Montagnes (Toronto: U of Toronto P, 1976, 88 pp.). Annual index; cumulative index to vols. 1–15, in 15 (1984): 337–84.

Science and Literature

For an introduction to the interdisciplinary study of science and literature, see George Slusser and George Guffey, "Literature and Science" (pp. 176–204) in Barricelli, *Interrelations of Literature* (5955).

Guides to Scholarship

SERIAL BIBLIOGRAPHIES

6440 "Relations of Literature and Science [1950–]." *PSLS: Publication of the Society for Literature and Science* 1 (1986)– .

1980–83: *Relations of Literature and Science: A Bibliography of Scholarship [1980–83]*. Ed. Walter Schatzberg. 4 vols. Worcester: Clark UP, 1982–84.
1972–79: *Clio* (entry 6505) 4–10 (1974–80).
1950–66: *Symposium: A Quarterly Journal in Modern Foreign Literatures* 5–21 (1951–67).

An international bibliography of scholarship (including dissertations) treating in some fashion the relationship between literature and science. Although the scope has never been defined, it apparently is the same as Schatzberg, *Relations of Literature and Science* (6445), which supersedes the annual bibliographies through

1980. Entries are listed alphabetically by author in seven divisions: general studies, antiquity, Middle Ages, Renaissance, seventeenth and eighteenth centuries, nineteenth century, and twentieth century. (Periods are combined in some volumes.) A few works are briefly annotated. There are omissions, but this is the best source for identifying current scholarship on literature and science. Researchers should also check "Science" and related headings in the subject index of post-1980 volumes of *MLAIB* (335).

OTHER BIBLIOGRAPHIES

6445 Schatzberg, Walter, Ronald A. Waite, and Jonathan K. Johnson, eds. *The Relations of Literature and Science: An Annotated Bibliography of Scholarship, 1880–1980*. New York: MLA, 1987. 458 pp. Z6511.R44 [PN55] 016.809'93356.

An annotated bibliography of scholarship (including dissertations) on the relationship between science and Western literature (primarily English, American, French, and German). International in scope, the work covers studies that treat a specific aspect of the relationship between the two areas, including the literary qualities of scientific works, scientific and literary discourse, and the representation of science or pseudoscience in literary works. Studies of medicine in literature are limited to those dealing with scientific aspects of the field, and studies of science fiction are restricted to those examining the treatment of science per se. Schatzberg excludes general works on cultural history and the history of science.

The approximately 2,500 entries are organized alphabetically by author in eight divisions: general works (with sections for the interactions of literature and science, and surveys), antiquity, Middle Ages, Renaissance, then by century. Each period division has sections for general studies and individual authors (but to locate all studies on an author, one must consult the subject index). Annotations clearly describe the focus and content of works and cite reviews of books. Two indexes: scholars; subjects. Thorough within its limits, clearly annotated, and effectively indexed, the *Annotated Bibliography* is the essential source for identifying studies of the treatment of individual scientists and scientific themes, theories, and disciplines in literature.

Schatzberg incorporates and expands the annual "Relations of Literature and Science" and Fred A. Dudley, ed., *The Relations of Literature and Science: A Selected Bibliography, 1930–1967* (Ann Arbor: University Microfilms, 1968, 137 pp.). For studies after 1980, see "Relations of Literature and Science" (6440).

See also

Woodress, *Dissertations in American Literature, 1891–1966* (3320).

Social Sciences and Literature

For introductions to the interdisciplinary study of literature and the social sciences, see Priscilla B. P. Clark, "Literature and Sociology" (pp. 107–22) and Richard Weisberg and Jean-Pierre Barricelli, "Literature and Law" (pp. 150–75) in Barricelli,

Interrelations of Literature (5955). Several works in section U: Literature-Related Topics and Sources/Interdisciplinary and Multidisciplinary Studies treat literature and the social sciences.

General

GUIDES TO REFERENCE WORKS

6460 Webb, William H., et al. *Sources of Information in the Social Sciences: A Guide to the Literature.* 3rd ed. Chicago: American Library Assn., 1986. 777 pp. Z7161.S666 [H61] 016.3.

A guide to reference sources (through c. 1984) for the social sciences generally as well as history, geography, economics and business administration, sociology, anthropology (including folklore and linguistics), psychology, education, and political science. Each subject division begins with a general survey of scholarship, then proceeds to an annotated classified list of reference works variously organized as the subject requires. In some sections, entries are interspersed with occasional commentary that compares works and mentions others. The annotations vary widely in fullness, quality, accuracy, currency, and rigor. At their best they combine evaluation with full description of scope and organization; several, though, are inadequately descriptive or inaccurate. Although the divisions are uneven in quality and selection, Webb offers the most complete overall guide to reference sources in the social sciences.

HANDBOOKS, DICTIONARIES, AND ENCYCLOPEDIAS

6465 *International Encyclopedia of the Social Sciences.* Ed. David L. Sills. 18 vols. New York: Macmillan; London: Collier, 1968–79. H40.A2.I5 300'.3'21.

An encyclopedia of concepts, processes, institutions, doctrines, persons, forms, and methodologies in anthropology, economics, geography, history, law, political science, psychiatry, psychology, sociology, and statistics. The signed articles by major scholars conclude with selective bibliographies. Although there are liberal cross-references, vol. 17, with its index and list of articles by area or discipline, offers the best access to contents. Vol. 18 is entitled *Biographical Supplement.* Besides the articles under the headings "Language," "Linguistics," and "Literature," the work is useful for background on the treatment of social science concepts in literary works. Reviews: Joshua A. Fishman and Joav Findling, *Language* 45 (1969): 458–63; composite review, *American Sociological Review* 33 (1968): 798–813.

The *Encyclopaedia of the Social Sciences*, ed. Edwin R. A. Seligman and Alvin Johnson, 15 vols. (New York: Macmillan, 1930–35) remains useful for its historical perspective.

GUIDES TO SCHOLARSHIP

Serial Bibliographies

6470 *Social Sciences Index*. New York: Wilson, 1974– . Quarterly, with annual cumulation. Preceded by *Social Sciences and Humanities Index* (entry 385). AI3.S62 016.3.

An author and subject index to about 350 (currently) English-language periodicals in a variety of fields, including anthropology, economics, geography, political science, psychology and psychiatry, sociology, and minority studies. Like other Wilson indexes, periodicals are chosen by subscriber vote. Although *Social Sciences Index* is limited in coverage, its subject indexing and extensive cross-references make it a good source for locating articles on literary topics and authors in journals not covered by the standard bibliographies and indexes in section G. Entries since April 1983 can be searched through WILSONLINE (525) and on CD-ROM through WILSONDISC.

Although it offers broader coverage, *SSCI: Social Sciences Citation Index [1966–]: An International Multidisciplinary Index to the Literature of the Social, Behavioral, and Related Sciences* (Philadelphia: ISI, 1966– , quarterly, with annual and quinquennial cumulations) suffers from the same limitations as *Arts and Humanities Citation Index* (365). Entries can be searched in the Social SciSearch data base through BRS (515) and Dialog (520).

See also

Bullock, *Guide to Marxist Literary Criticism* (6175).
MLAIB (335): See the "Social Sciences," "Sociological," and "Sociology" headings in the index to post-1980 volumes.

Abstracts

6475 *Sociological Abstracts*. San Diego: Sociological Abstracts, 1953– . 5/yr. HM1.S67 301.

Nonevaluative abstracts of articles from selected sociological and related journals. Although recent issues include the classified section Sociology of the Arts, the best approach to contents is through the annual subject index. Abstracts since 1963 can be searched online through BRS (515) and Dialog (520). A useful source for identifying articles on sociological topics in and approaches to language and literature.

History and Literature

The following is a highly selective listing of major general reference sources of particular use in literary research. Works limited to a country are listed in appropriate national literature divisions.

For an introduction to the use of historical scholarship in literature, see Barbara Kiefer Lewalski, "Historical Scholarship" (pp. 53–78) in Gibaldi, *Introduction to Scholarship in Modern Languages and Literatures* (25).

GUIDES TO REFERENCE WORKS

There is no reasonably current, adequate general guide to reference works in history. Despite its promising title, R. C. Richardson, comp., *The Study of History: A Bibliographical Guide*, History and Related Disciplines Select Bibliographies (Manchester: Manchester UP, 1988, 98 pp.) lists almost no bibliographies, historical encyclopedias, guides, data bases, or other reference sources. Both Helen J. Poulton, *The Historian's Handbook: A Descriptive Guide to Reference Works* (Norman: U of Oklahoma P, 1972, 304 pp.), and *The American Historical Association's Guide to Historical Literature*, ed. George Frederick Howe et al. (New York: Macmillan, 1961, 962 pp.) are outdated, although the latter is still useful for its annotations on works published before c. 1960. Both Sheehy, *Guide to Reference Books* (60), pp. 973–1131, and Walford, *Walford's Guide to Reference Material* (65), vol. 2, pp. 543–53, 578–701, have extensive sections on history; however, neither is sufficiently rigorous in selection or evaluation of works. Even though coverage is spotty, the best general guide is the history section in Webb, *Sources of Information in the Social Sciences* (6460), pp. 63–148. For American history, see Prucha, *Handbook for Research in American History* (3185).

HANDBOOKS, DICTIONARIES, ENCYCLOPEDIAS, AND ATLASES

6480 *An Encyclopedia of World History: Ancient, Medieval, and Modern*. Ed. William L. Langer. 5th ed. rev. and enl. Boston: Houghton, 1972. 1,569 pp. D21.L27 902'.02.

An encyclopedia of world history through 1970. Organized by era, then by country or region, and then by periods, subjects, or peoples, the brief paragraphs on individuals, events, and groups appear in chronological sequence. Because of the organization, the *Encyclopedia* emphasizes political, military, and diplomatic matters and is less thorough in its coverage of economic, cultural, and intellectual history. Throughout are numerous maps and genealogical charts of ruling dynasties. Indexed by places, persons, and subjects. Not the typical encyclopedia, it is primarily useful for placing an individual or event in its chronological context.

6485 *The Times Atlas of World History*. Ed. Geoffrey Barraclough. Rev. ed. Maplewood: Hammond, 1984. 360 pp. G1030.T54 911.

A historical atlas with maps depicting political geography, social history, migrations, invasions, empires, towns, trade routes, battles, and the spread of civilizations and religions. The numerous plates and accompanying commentary are organized in seven chronological divisions that emphasize broad movements rather than specific events from prehistory to 1975. Concludes with a glossary. Indexed by place names. This is now the most thorough and current historical atlas in

English; however, William R. Shepherd, *Shepherd's Historical Atlas*, 9th ed., rev., updated, and rpt. with revisions (Totowa: Barnes, 1980, n.pag.) remains useful for its more precise maps of some topics. Review: J. H. Elliott, *New York Review of Books* 7 Dec. 1978: 14–15.

BIBLIOGRAPHIES OF BIBLIOGRAPHIES

6490 Henige, David, comp. *Serial Bibliographies and Abstracts in History: An Annotated Guide*. Bibliographies and Indexes in World History 2. Westport: Greenwood, 1986. 220 pp. Z6201.A1.H45 [D20] 016.9.

A guide to currently published serial bibliographies and abstracts, appearing separately or in periodicals, on historical topics. Encompassing "bibliographies which address in whole or part *any* aspect of the past," Henige covers several areas tangential to history. It excludes most bibliographies that list only books. The 874 entries are ostensibly organized by library catalog main entry but are actually entered inconsistently under title, journal, or organization. A typical entry includes title; journal; notes on scope, organization, size, and currency as of the early 1980s, along with occasional evaluative or comparative commentary; ISSN and OCLC numbers; and cross-references to related works. Indexed by subjects. The inclusion of numerous works only loosely related to the study of history, failure to provide adequate publication information (especially the titles of bibliographies in periodicals) or to indicate when coverage began or important changes in scope or taxonomy, frequently inaccurate evaluations, poor organization, and barely adequate subject indexing mean that this work must be used with care to identify serial bibliographies in history.

GUIDES TO SCHOLARSHIP

Serial Bibliographies

6495 *International Bibliography of Historical Sciences/Internationale Bibliographie der Geschichtswissenschaften/Bibliografía internacional de ciencias históricas/Bibliographie internationale des sciences historiques/Bibliografia internazionale delle scienze storiche [1926–]*. München: Saur, 1930– . Annual. Z6205.I61 016.9.

A selective bibliography of books and articles of more than local interest on all aspects of world history. (Vol. 15 [for 1940] was never published.) Entries are listed alphabetically by author in classified divisions for auxiliary sciences (including palaeography, history of the book, and linguistics); manuals and general works (including folklore and literary history); prehistory; ancient Near East; Greek history; Rome, ancient Italy, and the Roman Empire; the church to Gregory the Great; Byzantine history since Justinian; Middle Ages; general works on modern history; religious history; modern culture (including literature, music, theater, and cinema); economic and social history; legal and constitutional history; international relations; Asia; Africa; America; and Oceania. Two indexes: names; places. Coverage is erratic and inconsistent. Because the vague criteria governing selection make this something of a hotchpotch (with the literature and theater sections, in particular, decidedly idiosyncratic and unrepresentative), it is useful primarily as an occasional complement to the serial bibliographies and abstracts limited to a country or region.

See also

MLAIB (335): See the headings beginning "Historical" or "History" in the subject index to post-1980 volumes.

Abstracts

6500 *Historical Abstracts.* Santa Barbara: ABC-Clio Information Services, 1955– . Currently issued in two parts. A: Modern History Abstracts, 1450–1914; B: Twentieth Century Abstracts, 1914–[current year]. Quarterly, including cumulative index. D299.H5 909.8082.

Nonevaluative abstracts of scholarship on history and related topics. Originally restricted to articles on the period 1775–1945, *Historical Abstracts* now covers books and dissertations, and has undergone several changes in scope: with vol. 16 (1970), coverage of the United States and Canada was transferred to *America: History and Life* (3310); in vol. 17 (1971), chronological coverage was extended from 1775 to the present; in vol. 19 (1973), chronological coverage was extended back to 1450. The subject index offers the most efficient access to literature- and language-related entries. Entries since 1973 are searchable online through Dialog (520).

PERIODICALS

6505 *Clio: A Journal of Literature, History, and the Philosophy of History* (*ClioI*). 1971– . Quarterly. Former title: *Clio: An Interdisciplinary Journal of Literature, History, and the Philosophy of History* (1971–79). D1.C5 901.

Publishes articles, reviews, and occasional special issues on the relationship of history or the philosophy of history to literature and on historical works as literature. Vols. 4–10 (1974–80) include the annual "Relations of Literature and Science: A Bibliography of Scholarship [1972–79]" (6440). Indexed in every second volume.

6510 *Literature and History* (*L&H*). 1975– . 2/yr. AS122.T45.A25 052.

Publishes articles, reviews, and review articles on the relations between literature, history, and ideology, especially during the last two centuries in Great Britain. For a discussion of the history, editorial policy, and contents of the journal, see R. C. Richardson, "*Literature and History*: The Identity and Purpose of the Journal" 11 (1985): 3–11.

Political Science and Literature

For an introduction to the interdisciplinary study of literature and political science, see Matei Calinescu, "Literature and Politics" (pp. 123–49) in Barricelli, *Interrelations of Literature* (5955).

GUIDES TO REFERENCE WORKS

6515 Holler, Frederick L. *Information Sources of Political Science.* 4th ed. Santa Barbara: ABC-Clio, 1986. 417 pp. Z7161.H64 [JA71] 016.32.

A guide to reference sources (to December 1983) useful for the study of political topics. The 2,423 entries are organized by type of work within classified divisions for general reference sources; social sciences (with sections for anthropology, economics, education, geography, history, political science, psychology, and sociology); American government, politics, and public law; international relations and organizations; comparative and area studies of politics and government; and—of most immediate literary interest—political theory. Many entries are accompanied by full annotations that provide helpful descriptive comments but too few evaluative ones. In addition to a preliminary outline of general research procedures, headnotes to many sections offer advice on processes and techniques. Four indexes: authors; titles; subjects; types of reference works. Although users would benefit from more evaluative comments, the full descriptions and advice on research procedures make Holler the essential guide to reference sources for the study of political science.

See also

Webb, *Sources of Information in the Social Sciences* (6460).

GUIDES TO SCHOLARSHIP

6520 *International Political Science Abstracts/Documentation politique internationale [1950–].* Paris: International Political Science Assn., 1951– . 6/yr. JA36.I5 320.82.

Nonevaluative abstracts, in English or French, of articles in journals and yearbooks. Coverage is selective, emphasizing scholarly and "scientific" studies in major political science journals and omitting popular or "redundant" articles. Indexed by subjects in each issue; cumulative author and subject indexes in each volume. The subject index offers the best way to locate discussions of literary topics and authors. Although coverage is far from complete, the abstracts and subject indexing make *International Political Science Abstracts* the best source for identifying articles on literary topics published in political science journals and rarely included in the standard serial bibliographies and indexes in section G.

An occasionally useful supplement is *International Bibliography of the Social Sciences/Bibliographie international des sciences sociales: International Bibliography of Political Science/Bibliographie internationale de science politique [1952–]* (London: Tavistock, 1954, annual). Also highly selective, it covers books, dissertations, and theses as well as articles, but it is much less current. Because subject indexing is limited generally to title keywords, the *International Bibliography* is generally of little value to literary researchers. Of almost no value because of its lack of effective organization and indexing is *CRIS: Combined Retrospective Index Set to Journals in Political Science, 1886–1974*, ed. Annadel N. Wile, 8 vols. (Washington: Carrollton, 1977–78).

See also

Baldensperger, *Bibliography of Comparative Literature* (5000).
MLAIB (335): See the headings beginning "Political" or "Politics" in the subject index to post-1980 volumes.

Psychology and Literature

For an introduction to the interdisciplinary study of literature and psychology, see Murray M. Schwartz and David Willbern, "Literature and Psychology" (pp. 205–24) in Barricelli, *Interrelations of Literature* (5955).

GUIDES TO REFERENCE WORKS

See

Webb, *Sources of Information in the Social Sciences* (6460).

HANDBOOKS, DICTIONARIES, AND ENCYCLOPEDIAS

6525 *Encyclopedia of Psychology*. Ed. Raymond J. Corsini. 4 vols. New York: Wiley, 1984. BF31.E52 150'.3'21.

An encyclopedia of concepts, terms, theories, persons, and other topics related to psychology. The majority of the approximately 2,100 entries, which range from 200 to 9,000 words, are by major scholars. Articles typically cite important scholarship and conclude with cross-references to related entries. Vol. 4 has a cumulative bibliography and two indexes: names; subjects. The most authoritative encyclopedia in its field, it is useful to literature researchers for its summaries of concepts and theories.

More compact sources are the following:

Encyclopedia of Psychology. Ed. H. J. Eysenck, W. Arnold, and R. Meili. 3 vols. New York: Herder, 1972.

The Encyclopedic Dictionary of Psychology. Ed. Rom Harré and Roger Lamb. Cambridge: MIT P, 1983. 718 pp. Offers somewhat better coverage of psycholinguistics and fringe topics.

GUIDES TO SCHOLARSHIP

Abstracts

6530 *Psychological Abstracts: Nonevaluative Summaries of the World's Literature in Psychology and Related Disciplines* (*Psych Abstracts*). Arlington:

American Psychological Assn., 1927– . Monthly, with annual, triennial, and larger expanded cumulated author and subject indexes. BF1.P65 150'.5.

Nonevaluative abstracts of research in psychology. Although recent issues have a Language and Speech section and a Literature and Art section, the excellent subject indexing offers the best approach to contents. For the most efficient use of the subject index, consult the current edition of *Thesaurus of Psychological Index Terms*. Abstracts since 1967 can be searched in the PsycINFO data base through BRS (515) and Dialog (520). Researchers unfamiliar with *Psych Abstracts* will benefit from Barbara Allen and Barry Strickland-Hodge, *How to Use* Psychological Abstracts *and* Biological Abstracts, Information Sources in the Medical Sciences Series (Aldershot: Gower, 1987, 76 pp.). A valuable source for identifying studies of psychological topics in and approaches to literary works and language.

Literature and Psychology

6535 *IPSA Abstracts and Bibliography in Literature and Psychology*. Gainesville: Inst. for Psychological Study of the Arts, Dept. of English, U of Florida, 1986– . Annual. Z6513.I34.

Publishes abstracts of forthcoming books and articles along with an author list of published studies and dissertations. Coverage begins with 1 February 1986 for abstracts and 1985 for the bibliography, and principally includes English-language publications. Now highly selective, it could become a valuable resource if coverage is expanded.

6540 Kiell, Norman, ed. *Psychoanalysis, Psychology, and Literature: A Bibliography*. 2nd ed. 2 vols. Metuchen: Scarecrow, 1982. (A supplement covering 1981–87 is scheduled for 1989.) Z6514.P78.K53 [PN56.P93] 016.801'92.

An international bibliography of scholarship (including some dissertations) treating an aspect of psychology or psychoanalysis and literature. Although Kiell covers studies from 1790 through 1980, the bulk of the works date from the twentieth century. The 19,674 entries are organized alphabetically by author in 14 unclassified divisions: autobiographies, biographies, diaries, and letters; literary, psychoanalytical, and psychological criticism; drama; fairy tales and fables; fiction; film; folklore and folktales; myths and legends; poetry; Scriptures; technical studies; therapy; wit, humor, and jokes; ancillary topics. Three indexes in vol. 2: literary authors as subjects; titles of literary works; general subjects. Because of the imprecise and unrefined classification system, the subject indexes offer the best access to contents. Although several entries appear to be taken without verification from other sources, *Psychoanalysis, Psychology, and Literature* is the most thorough guide to studies of psychology and literature and is particularly valuable for its coverage of journals in psychology and psychoanalysis. It does, however, admit numerous studies only remotely connected with psychology.

Joseph Natoli and Frederik L. Rusch, comps., *Psychocriticism: An Annotated Bibliography*, Bibliographies and Indexes in World Literature 1 (Westport: Greenwood, 1984, 267 pp.), focuses more clearly on the relationship between formal psychology and literature, covers a wide range of literatures, ancient to modern, offers annotated entries, and provides a good subject index. However, coverage is incomplete and limited to English-language books and articles published between 1969 and 1982.

See also

MLAIB (335): See the headings beginning "Psychoanalysis," "Psychoanalytic," "Psychological," and "Psychology" in the subject index to post-1980 volumes.
Woodress, *Dissertations in American Literature, 1891–1966* (3320).

PERIODICALS

6545 *American Imago: A Psychoanalytic Journal for Culture, Science, and the Arts* (*AI*). 1939– . Quarterly. BF173.A2.A55.

Publishes articles and occasional special issues involving the application of psychoanalysis to the humanities, especially literature. Annual index; cumulative index: vols. 1–10, in 10 (1953): 379–402.

6550 *Literature and Psychology (L&P)*. 1951–81, 1986– . Quarterly. PN49.L5.

Publishes articles and reviews on "literary criticism as informed by depth psychology (psychoanalysis)." An untitled annual annotated bibliography on literature and psychology for the years 1968–70 appears in vols. 20–23 (1970–73). Cumulative indexes: vols. 1–10 (n.d., n.pag.); vols. 11–15 (n.d., n.pag.).

See also

Literature and Medicine (6195).

Translations

Guides to Primary Works

6565 *Index Translationum [1932–40, 1948–]: Répertoire international des traductions/International Bibliography of Translations/Repertorio internacional de traducciones*. Paris: UNESCO, 1932–40, 1949– . Annual. Z6514.T7.I42 011'.7.

A bibliography of translated books published for the most part in UNESCO member countries. Coverage varies, ranging from a low of six to more than 70 countries. Organized alphabetically by country of publication (using the French form of name), then by Universal Decimal Classification main category, then alphabetically by author or editor, entries cite title of translation, translator, publication information, and—if known—language of the source and original title. Indexed by original authors; some early volumes have indexes of translators and publishers (both classified by country). Although it is compiled from a variety of sources that vary widely in accuracy, is necessarily incomplete, and is far behind in publication, *Index Translationum* does provide the fullest list of translations published each year. Organization by original author would be more convenient for most literature researchers.

The *Cumulative Index to English Translations, 1948–1968*, 2 vols. (Boston: Hall, 1973) reproduces, by author, entries for all translations listed from Australia, Canada,

New Zealand, Ireland, South Africa, United Kingdom, and United States in vols. 1–21 of the new series of the UNESCO *Index*. It is, though, frustrating to use because of the numerous errors, inconsistencies, and lack of cross-references.

See also

"List of Translations," *YCGL: Yearbook of Comparative and General Literature* (5035).

Women and Literature

This section includes works encompassing women writers in several national literatures, as well as interdisciplinary women's studies sources that have a substantial literature component. Numerous works on women writers appear in appropriate national literature and other divisions.

Guides to Reference Works

For a survey of the bibliographical resources for the study of English and American women writers, see the appendix to Deborah S. Rosenfelt, "The Politics of Bibliography: Women's Studies and the Literary Canon" (vol. 1, pp. 11–35), in Hartman, *Women in Print* (6595).

6580 Searing, Susan E. *Introduction to Library Research in Women's Studies.* Westview Guides to Library Research. Boulder: Westview, 1985. 257 pp. Z7961.S42 [HQ1206] 016.3054.

A selective guide to research and reference sources. Addressed to the undergraduate, the work begins with a basic introduction to using a library. The second part, an annotated guide to commonly available English-language reference sources, is organized by type of work: guides to bibliographies and reference sources, general bibliographies, multidisciplinary bibliographies and indexes, bibliographies and indexes in individual fields (including sections on film, theater, history, popular culture, linguistics, literature, and minority studies), library catalogs and guides to special collections of books and archives, biographical sources, directories of organizations and services, microform sources, online sources, periodicals, and miscellaneous guides and handbooks. The descriptive annotations are sometimes helpfully evaluative; those accompanying general works focus on their value to women's studies. One appendix consists of a superfluous list of review essays in *Signs* (6620). Three indexes: authors; titles; subjects. Although Searing provides the fullest, most current guide to the subject, numerous errors in citations and annotations render the work an untrustworthy source. The field is overdue for a rigorous guide to reference sources and research techniques.

See also

Gohdes, *Bibliographical Guide to the Study of the Literature of the U.S.A.* (3180).

Prucha, *Handbook for Research in American History* (3185).

Bibliographies of Bibliographies

6585 Ballou, Patricia K. *Women: A Bibliography of Bibliographies*. 2nd ed. Women's Studies Publications. Boston: Hall, 1986. 268 pp. Z7961.B32 [HQ1121] 016.0163054.

A bibliography of bibliographies, surveys of research, library catalogs, and guides to archives or manuscript repositories published as books, parts of books, articles, or data bases from 1970 through June 1985. Although international in scope, it emphasizes works about the United States and Canada, and includes a very few publications not in English. Basing selection on "scope, availability, organization, and commentary," Ballou excludes bibliographies of individuals and small groups, nonprint media, auction and booksellers' catalogs, and most out-of-print publications. The 906 entries are organized in four divisions: general and interdisciplinary works, bibliographies devoted to a type of publication or format (including library catalogs, biographical sources, and guides to archives and manuscript collections), geographical areas, and subjects (including sections for history, literature, mass media and popular culture, performance art, and anthropology, which encompasses folklore). The literature section includes subdivisions for general works; American, Canadian, English, French, Spanish and Latin American, and other literatures; feminist criticism; and children's literature. Except for studies involving the United States or Canada, a geographical focus takes precedence over a topical one in organizing works; hence, users should generally begin with the subject index. Entries are accompanied by full descriptive annotations, but only a few offer an evaluative comment. Three indexes: persons; titles; subjects. Although the work is limited in its coverage, it is the fullest bibliography of bibliographies devoted to women's studies.

Jane Williamson, *New Feminist Scholarship: A Guide to Bibliographies* (Old Westbury: Feminist P, 1979, 139 pp.), remains an important complement, since it cites works before 1970 and others omitted in Ballou.

Guides to Primary Works

See

Grimes, *Novels in English by Women, 1891–1920* (2640).
Marshall, *Pen Names of Women Writers from 1660 to the Present* (5115).
Reardon, *Poetry by American Women, 1900–1975* (4330).
Women's History Sources (3245).

Guides to Scholarship and Criticism

SURVEYS OF RESEARCH

6590 Fishburn, Katherine. *Women in Popular Culture*. American Popular Culture. Westport: Greenwood, 1982. 267 pp. HQ1426.F685 305.4'0973.

A survey of scholarship through c. 1980 on the role and image of women in popular culture. Although Fishburn does not provide any explanation of scope or criteria governing selection, she emphasizes recent studies in chapters on histories of women in popular culture; women in popular literature; women in magazines and magazine fiction; women in film; women in television; women in advertising, fashion, sports, and comics; and theories of women in popular culture. The essays vary in organization and breadth, but most conclude with a brief commentary on important reference works and a selective bibliography. Five appendixes: selected periodicals; special issues of periodicals; selected reference works; a chronology; a list of research centers and institutions. Indexed by persons, subjects, and titles. In spite of the lack of a statement of editorial policy, *Women in Popular Culture* is valuable for its detailed descriptions and sometimes trenchant evaluations of studies.

6595 Hartman, Joan E., and Ellen Messer-Davidow, eds. *Women in Print.* 2 vols. New York: MLA, 1982. PN481.W656 809'.89287.

Vol. 1: *Opportunities for Women's Studies Research in Language and Literature.* 198 pp.
Vol. 2: *Opportunities for Women's Studies Publication in Language and Literature.* 173 pp.

A collection of surveys of areas needing research and publishing outlets. In vol. 1 the essays on bibliography, archival research, and language and on lesbian, black, working-class, and national literatures selectively survey scholarship as well as define topics for further research. Vol. 2 focuses on how and where to publish, including scholarly, textbook, alternative, and trade publishers. At their best, the essays are full of solid practical advice about what and where to publish.

See also

Duke, *American Women Writers: Bibliographical Essays* (3275).
Inge, *Handbook of American Popular Culture* (6295).

OTHER BIBLIOGRAPHIES

6600 Boos, Florence, ed. *Bibliography of Women and Literature: Articles and Books [1974–81] by and about Women from 600 to 1975.* 2 vols. New York: Holmes, 1988.

A bibliography of English-language books, articles, dissertations, and reviews (from 1974 through 1981) on literature by and about women. Vol. 1 (1974–78) is a revised, enlarged cumulation of the annual bibliographies published in 1976 through 1978 as supplements to *Women and Literature*; vol. 2 (1979–81) extracts entries from *MLAIB* (335) and *ABELL* (340). Although emphasizing British and American writers, Boos includes some of the other literatures in English (especially Canadian, Australian, and New Zealand). The approximately 10,000 entries are organized in divisions for general works, British literature (before 1660, 1660–1800, 1800–1900, and 1900–75), American literature (before 1800, 1800–1900, 1900–75), Canadian literature, other literatures in English, and (in vol. 1) foreign-language writers; each is subdivided by genre (including children's literature and one subdivision for the treatment of women by male writers), then by literary author. Some entries in vol. 1 are accompanied by brief descriptive annotations. Three indexes: scholars; literary authors; genres. Although covering only eight years and a restricted number of journals, Boos is a time-saving compilation that demonstrates the need for both retrospective and current serial bibliographies of scholarship and criticism on women and literature.

6605 Schwartz, Narda Lacey. *Articles on Women Writers: A Bibliography [1960–84]*. 2 vols. Santa Barbara: ABC-Clio, 1977–86. Z2013.5.W6.S37 [PR111] 016.82'09'9287.

A checklist of English-language articles and dissertations listed in *Dissertation Abstracts International* (465) on women since the Middle Ages writing in English in the United States, Great Britain, Ireland, Australia, Canada, New Zealand, and Africa. Vol. 1 covers studies appearing between 1960 and 1975; vol. 2, between 1976 and mid-1984. Writers are listed alphabetically by the most commonly used name (but without cross-references for other forms); under each, studies are organized in up to three sections: bibliographies, general studies, and individual works. Indexed by scholars. Limited in scope, omitting numerous studies, and taking most entries from other bibliographies rather than the journals themselves, *Articles on Women Writers* is principally useful as a starting place, and one that must be supplemented by the serial bibliographies and indexes in section G.

Including works about women in literature as well as about female writers, two books by Carol Fairbanks Myers—*Women in Literature: Criticism of the Seventies* (Metuchen: Scarecrow, 1976, 256 pp.) and *More Women in Literature: Criticism of the Seventies* (1979, 457 pp.)—cover only 1970 through 1976, are riddled with errors, omit numerous studies, and are generally useless because of a lack of subject indexing. Some additional publications are listed in Linda K. Lewis, "Women in Literature: A Selected Bibliography," *Bulletin of Bibliography* 35 (1978): 116–22, 131.

See also

Humm, *Annotated Critical Bibliography of Feminist Criticism* (6170).
International Medieval Bibliography (1835).
MLAIB (335): See the headings beginning "Woman" or "Women" in the subject index to post-1980 volumes.
Salzman, *American Studies: An Annotated Bibliography* (3335).

ABSTRACTS

6610 *Women's Studies Abstracts*. Rush: Rush, 1972– . Quarterly, with annual cumulated index. Z7962.W65 016.30141'2'05.

Nonevaluative abstracts and lists of studies on a wide range of topics relating to women. Literature studies are listed in the section Literature and Art (formerly Women in History and Literature; History, Literature, and Art). Although subject indexing has improved over the years, the indexes are not reliable for locating literary authors or works mentioned in abstracts or titles. Many articles are listed without abstracts. Although inconsistent in coverage and annotations, *Women's Studies Abstracts* is useful for its inclusion of numerous works overlooked by the standard bibliographies and indexes in section G.

DISSERTATIONS AND THESES

6615 Gilbert, V. F., and D. S. Tatla. *Women's Studies: A Bibliography of Dissertations, 1870–1982*. Oxford: Blackwell, 1985. 496 pp. Z7961.G55 [HQ1180] 016.3054.

A classified list of dissertations and some theses accepted through 1982 by British, Irish, Canadian, and United States institutions. Gilbert excludes North American master's theses as well as most studies of gender difference, marriage, and motherhood. The works are organized in 23 variously classified divisions, among which are ones for the arts (including film), language, and literature (with subdivisions for comparative and general studies, feminist criticism, and then national literatures, some of which are broken down by period and individual authors). An entry cites author, title, degree, institution, and date. Indexed by subjects. Because of a classification based on titles, a lack of cross-references, and an insufficiently thorough subject index (which has more than its share of errors), researchers are generally better served by the keyword indexing of *Comprehensive Dissertation Index* (460) for North American dissertations. Despite its faults, however, *Women's Studies* is a convenient compilation.

See also

Sec. H: Guides to Dissertations and Theses.

Biographical Dictionaries

See

Mainiero, *American Women Writers* (3390).
Notable American Women (3385).
Todd, *Dictionary of British and American Women Writers, 1660–1800* (2265).
Who's Who of American Women (3395a).

Periodicals

6620 *Signs: Journal of Women in Culture and Society* (*Signs*). 1975– . Quarterly. HQ1101.S5 301.41'2'05.

Publishes articles, reviews, review essays, documents, frequent special issues, and notes on meetings and new publications on various topics dealing with women.

6625 *Tulsa Studies in Women's Literature* (*TSWL*). 1982– . 2/yr. PN471.T84 809'.89287.

Publishes articles, notes, reviews, review essays, and occasional special issues on women writers and feminist theory and criticism. Although international in scope, *TSWL* emphasizes American and British literature. Cumulative index: vols. 1–5, [Suzanne Ward, comp.], 6 (1987): 161–73, 369.

6630 *Women's Studies: An Interdisciplinary Journal* (*WS*). 1972– . Quarterly. HQ1101.W77 301.41'2'05.

Publishes articles, film and book reviews, poetry, fiction, and occasional special issues about women in all fields, but with a decided emphasis on literature.

See also

American Quarterly (3430).

Index of Names

The index of names includes all authors, editors, compilers, translators, revisers, and other persons responsible for any of the works in citations or annotations. It excludes reviewers, compilers of indexes to scholarly journals, literary authors, and other names mentioned in passing in annotations. Entries are alphabetized letter by letter. Numbers generally refer to entry numbers; *a* following a number means that the name will be found in the annotation rather than the citation; *p.* or *pp.* preceding a number indicates a page reference.

Index of Titles

This index includes the current, former, and variant titles of all books, essays, and periodicals (cited as a separate work) in the citations and annotations. Titles used as cross-references, nondistinctive titles (such as "Bibliography" or "History and Criticism"), and indexes to journals are not indexed. To conserve space, shortened titles are listed when possible.

As in the other indexes, entries are alphabetized letter by letter; numbers are entry numbers (a number followed by the letter *a* means that the title will be found in the annotation; a number preceded by *p.* or *pp.* is a page number).

Subject Index

Along with subjects treated in a substantial way by the works cited, this index includes types of reference works. Numbers generally refer to entry numbers; page references are preceded by *p.* or *pp.* Users should also note that there are extensive cross-references in most sections.